THE PRO WRESTLING HALL OF FAME
HEROES & ICONS

ALSO IN THIS SERIES

HEROES & ICONS

STEVEN JOHNSON and GREG OLIVER

with **MIKE MOONEYHAM**

foreword by **J.J. DILLON**

THE PRO WRESTLING HALL OF FAME

Published by ECW Press
2120 Queen Street East, Suite 200, Toronto, Ontario, Canada M4E 1E2
416-694-3348 / info@ecwpress.com

Library and Archives Canada Cataloguing in Publication

Johnson, Steven, 1957–
The Pro Wrestling Hall of Fame : heroes & icons / Steven
Johnson and Greg Oliver, with Mike Mooneyham.

ISBN 978-1-77041-037-4
Also issued as: 978-1-77090-268-8 (PDF); 978-1-77090-269-5 (ePub)

1. Wrestlers—Biography.   2. Wrestling. I. Oliver, Greg
II. Mooneyham, Mike   III. Title.

GV1196.A1J65 2012   796.812092'2   C2012-902741-3

Editor for the press: Michael Holmes
Cover design: Tania Craan
Cover images: (Front cover) © Mike Mastrandrea,(Back cover) Steve Austin © Devin Chen,
Jim Londos courtesy of Scott Teal/Crowbar Press; (spine) Hulk Hogan © Andrea Kellaway
Printing: United Graphics   5   4   3   2   1

We acknowledge the financial support of the Government of Canada through the Canada
Book Fund for our publishing activities. The marketing of this book was made possible with
the support of the Ontario Media Development Corporation.

Printed and bound in the United States

This book is dedicated to J Michael Kenyon, of whom was once written, "he was often more interesting than the stories he was covering," and the other historians who pore through old newspapers, microfilm, and historical data, gather interviews and anecdotes, organize results from arenas big and small, and, when asked, share what they have learned with others.

WAYNE MCCARTY

J Michael Kenyon delivers his speech after receiving the James C. Melby Award for his contributions to professional wrestling journalism at the George Tragos/Lou Thesz Professional Wrestling Hall of Fame in Waterloo, Iowa, in July 2010.

Cowboy Bob Ellis gets his boots ready, as Mighty Igor and Tex McKenzie (back to camera) listen to Ben Justice in the babyface dressing room in Toronto's Maple Leaf Gardens.

ROGER BAKER

TABLE OF CONTENTS

PRE—WORLD WAR II

AFRICAN-AMERICANS

POST-WAR TERRITORIAL ERA

ETHNIC HEROES

HOMETOWN HEROES

COWBOYS & INDIANS

NATIONAL ERA

ANTI-HEROES

Bruno Sammartino, Luis Martinez, and Dominic Denucci are all smiles, just the way babyfaces should be.

FOREWORD

The concept of professional wrestling is very simple. It comes down to *mano e mano* usually portrayed as good against evil. The fans may be subjected to disappointments along a series of confrontations because villains have been known to cheat, bend the rules, and do whatever is necessary to get a win. However, in the end the loyal wrestling fan can feel confident that the babyface will ultimately prevail. The "final confrontation" usually unfolds in a classic battle that could go either way until that final moment when the babyface triumphs. This last battle is seldom quick and decisive so the fan usually gets everything anticipated and then some. Professional wrestling traditionally has delivered more than advertised. The heel, though beaten and battered, survives to fight again another day.

Though the faces change and the level of intensity may vary, the basic story is retold over and over again in some form. The individual personas of the various characters involved give the ongoing telling of "the story" a sense of freshness. It only works with both parts of the equation involved. The hottest of heels must eventually meet a hero worthy of meeting the challenge. To achieve the maximum results you need the very best babyface to challenge the red hot heel.

In *The Pro Wrestling Hall of Fame: The Heels* we saw wrestling's greatest villains showcased. Now with *Heroes and Icons* the authors are putting wrestling's greatest babyfaces in the spotlight.

I spent most of my career being hated by the fans. The great run of The Four Horsemen had longevity because when the bell rang, across the ring were "The American Dream" Dusty Rhodes and his friends. In truth, we needed Dusty to have financial success. It wasn't always smooth sailing. How many times has a man said, "Women . . . you can't live with them, and you can't live without them." Well, every successful heel will tell you, "Babyfaces . . . they can be frustrating to deal with, but you can't achieve success without them."

— J.J. Dillon, December 2011

A bloody Dusty Rhodes battles J.J. Dillon in a bullrope match in Florida in 1972.

INTRODUCTION

Wrestling hero worship takes many forms, in many places. Jules Strongbow, the long-time California-based booker and promoter, was touring Africa when he came across two native children locked in a free-for-all. Local residents pulled them apart, and a guide explained the source of their discontent to Strongbow and the members of his traveling party: "They were getting ready to wrestle and they were fighting over who would be Jimmy Londos."

In the great valley of East Tennessee, a boyish Les Thatcher joined with a lean, soft-spoken, glass factory worker named Whitey Caldwell to form a heroic duo that took the region by storm in 1969 and 1970. One day, they received mail at Channel 26 in Knoxville, the local TV wrestling outlet, and opened a Christmas card signed by all the members of a University of Tennessee sorority. "It amazes me to think, 'My God, you made that kind of impact and left that kind of impression,'" Thatcher said, "because at the time it doesn't even cross your mind that you're doing something that will move people to do something like that."

And a hero moved schoolchildren in an elementary school in Mobile, Alabama, in March 1972. Popular "Cowboy" Bob Kelly had earned a suspension for mistakenly slugging a National Wrestling Alliance representative — actually a rep from another Southern promotion — who climbed into the ring to halt an out-of-control battle with Don Fargo. With no master guidance, thousands of petitions suddenly started appearing at the Gulf Coast wrestling office in support of Kelly. Future pro Michael Norris was in sixth grade and he remembers Kelly's impact on his fans. "All the kids at my school signed one. Kelly told me later that they got something like 2,000 signatures, plus letters from fans that they kept for years in the office," Norris said.

Heroes are an important part of every sport, but nowhere more so than in professional wrestling, which is based primarily on a good guy/bad guy

Masters at work: Jack Brisco sells Dory Funk Jr.'s abdominal stretch.

dynamic, or was until recent years. Dr. David M. Reiss, a California-based psychiatrist who studies wrestling, calls it the most psychologically intriguing, complex, and exciting brand of athletic competition around, and believes the hero is an essential part of that mix. In football or baseball, fans usually root more for teams than for individuals, since the allegiances of today's players can change on a dime because of free agency or other factors. Even competitors in individual sports like boxing or mixed martial arts, the genres closest to wrestling, don't involve the audience, tell a story, or cultivate a deep emotional attachment like Londos or Kelly or hundreds of other wrestlers, Reiss said. "What you're offering to fans is an alliance with invulnerable heroes," according to Reiss, a contributor at Cauliflower Alley Club seminars, who relates the way fans think: "'I may not be able to overcome everything. But he or she is, and if I can connect with them, I share some of that' . . . It's a sense of connecting with an invulnerable hero."

This book is about the heroes and icons of pro wrestling, though you'll often encounter the insider term "babyface," which generally means the chap who is wrestling as the fan favorite. We prefer broader terms like heroes and icons because somehow the word "babyface" doesn't fit quite right under an 8x10 of a nail-spitting Dick "The Bruiser" or a middle-finger-flipping "Stone Cold" Steve Austin, both of whom nonetheless wrestled on the side of right for sizable chunks of their careers. Of course, it takes two to tango, and any discussion of crowd pleasers, however they are defined, owes a hat tip to the heels that make their success possible. "Leaping" Lanny Poffo explained exactly how he learned how every hero needs a great protagonist. Poffo's second match ever in Madison Square Garden was against Terry Funk in July 1985. "I walked down the aisle to what I would call polite applause. I wasn't exactly The Beatles of 1964. I mean, they weren't unhappy to see me but they weren't going crazy. So Terry Funk comes down the aisle and he takes two steps and he gets in an argument with a fan. And then he takes two more steps and he wants to kill somebody. And then they want to kill him. I think it took him five minutes to get to the ring, and he's torn the house down, and I'm thinking to myself, 'I've got to be the luckiest guy in the world. All I have to do is stand here.' Losing to Terry Funk made me more important in the eyes of the fans and to the office than if I had beaten three guys." As Dr. Tom Prichard, a long-time star and later a trainer in Florida Championship Wrestling, put it, "Superman had to have Lex Luthor. Batman had the Joker, the Penguin. I believe Hulk Hogan and The Iron Sheik were made for each other. Hulk Hogan and Macho Man were made for each other. Hulk Hogan was Superman, but without that foe to conquer, what do you have?"

Experts say there's no single "best" type of hero — they come in many different flavors and they all can be effective box office attractions, depending on such variables as marketing, fan preferences, or booking patterns. Traditionally, New York, Texas, and southern California were strongholds for Latino or ethnic attractions. Midwest cities such as St. Louis and Minneapolis were more associated with an athletic, amateur-based style, while Tennessee was synonymous with smaller wrestlers and a Southern style of brawling. The annals of wrestling are full of matinee idols like Billy Darnell, who made female fans swoon; gimmick guys like The Mighty Igor, who practiced a blend of childlike innocence and superhuman strength; and technical greats like Sonny Myers, who adapted his silky-smooth style to coax a great match out of even the least skilled adversary. That kind of variety was essential, said star Johnny Powers, who owned part of the Cleveland office, because promoting the right hero was a hit-and-miss proposition. "Part of it was the push you gave to the individual, which we did, myself included, in our area, and then the other part was what I called the natural inclination of the natives, the local fans, to accept or not accept you," he said. "Sometimes a guy would draw in Cleveland and Akron for some reason, so-so in Buffalo, but then he wouldn't do much in Rochester or Syracuse or Utica or Binghamton. It would be the same angle off the same TV with the same guys. That's why you absolutely needed some variety in your promotion."

The hero's job

"Superfly" Jimmy Snuka once described the role of the hero or babyface in twelve words. "Go out, get your heat, one big babyface comeback, and go home." That's about as simplistic as it gets, and in many respects it's not far from the truth. The good guy suffers an unconscionable beating, comes back against insurmountable odds to regain control of the match, and either wins or loses, depending on the plans for that particular contest or program. But that belies the dozens of little nuances that successful heroes must master as part of their job description. It's not enough, Florida Championship Wrestling President Steve Keirn said, to brush your teeth, comb your hair, and smile for the fans. "When you're a babyface in this industry, it's pretty difficult to just get over. To me, you can walk out, flip everybody off, and you're automatically a heel. But if you walk out and wave at everybody, that doesn't make you a babyface. You've got to learn to entertain that audience, earn their hearts doing good spots."

Foremost among budding wrestlers' homework is learning the difference between registering, selling, and dying, the three degrees of beatdowns virtually every hero must undergo. Each elicits much-desired sympathy from the audience, but there is a subtle and important distinction between them. George South, who's been wrestling and training in the Mid-Atlantic for three decades, calls it one of the most misunderstood aspects of the profession. "People don't sell when they should sell. People die when they should sell. It's an art form and it's very difficult to teach." Think of registering, he said, as a flinch from a punch or a hold that momentarily shakes up a babyface. Selling is the next step on the agony scale, and it takes pain to a higher level. "Old-timers relate it to a fish. They're just flopping along like a fish out of water. But you can still throw a punch. You still have some life left in you," South said.

What the hero can't do in all but the most exceptional circumstances is "die" — lie motionless on the mat or the floor — because then all hope is lost and fans' confidence in the character's resiliency is shaken to the core. Fans have to have some belief that their hero is down, but not out. "Rip Hawk and Swede Hanson taught me that at an early age — don't die out there," said Jerry Brisco. "Don't go out and just flop around and die. Your body is always moving, you always have some tightness to your body, and you're always fighting back . . . It made their job easier. You fight them, let them get you down, you fight 'em, get 'em down, build it up, you build that comeback up. After the third or fourth time, you start fighting and you pop them with a full-blown comeback. It's a big difference between fighting and coming back."

Ah, the comeback. Nothing brings the crowd to its feet like a great comeback, but even that is an art form, not a wild series of untimed punches. Thatcher, who's wrestled, trained, announced, and done just about everything else in his career, compares it to a slow burn with a big explosion at the end, like a Fourth of July sparkler. The hero might be on his knees, shaking the cobwebs from the beating — not dying, mind you — when he reaches back for a shot to the gut just as the heel comes in to finish him off. "Just enough to slow him," Thatcher cautioned. "The heel comes back in. This time the babyface gets a shot in; it's a little stronger, it's got a little more juice in it. And then finally the heel gets rocked a little bit, and when that happens, it should be hell-bent for action. The people should be ready for it and the babyface, that's when he should be shaking his fists, the heel's backing off and begging for forgiveness and that's when the babyface gets to him and starts bumping him."

Since the babyface, by definition, abides by the rules of fair play — or is supposed to — he is more confined in the tactics he can employ and thus at a definite disadvantage against a no-holds-barred monster. Though the onslaught of kick-ass babyfaces since the 1990s has changed that equation, for most of wrestling history, heroes lost credence with their followers if they stooped to the gutter level of their foes. WWE star Al Snow said that should influence the way the hero approaches his match. "As a heel I can put my hand up, I can put my hand down. I can back up. I can duck out of the ring. I can get on my knees and beg. He can't do any of those things. I can cheat. I can do absolutely anything I want. Babyfaces have to be more aggressive than the heel. They have to take the fight to the heel because the more the babyface takes the fight to the heel, more than ever, the heel has a reason to do anything he can do to beat the guy."

The life of a good guy

It was, Bobby Fulton thought in retrospect, kind of like the paparazzi chasing Princess Diana, though on a different scale. Fulton and tag team partner Tommy Rogers were the heartthrob Fantastics tag team in the Mid-Atlantic when they set out from Charlotte, North Carolina, to Greensboro. Somehow, a pack of fans found them and started trailing them along Interstate 85, waving, cheering, and blowing their horns. Fearful that they were about to be run into a ditch, the Fantastics tried to outrace their admirers, with no luck. Finally, as a last resort, Fulton and Rogers chased away their devotees, telling them to stay away or suffer the consequences.

And the fans told on them. They called the office, and Fulton and Rogers found themselves reamed out for being rude. "That was [Jim] Crockett and they called us in and said, 'Hey, we have a complaint, some of the fans said you were not nice to them.' But we were babyfaces, and as babyfaces we had people following us and sometimes jeopardizing our safety. And sometimes we didn't want them to know where we lived and they would beat us home, beat us to our place. Hey, I like the wrestling fans and everything but sometimes it's just tough."

Being a hero is not always what it's cracked up to be. Just about every babyface has a story about being interrupted in a restaurant or a restroom by overzealous fans, and it can be draining. "The people expect more of you, and especially back then, they expected you to be what you were selling, the clean-cut, Mom's apple pie and Chevrolet," Thatcher said. "I did enjoy the fans but there were times when you wanted to say leave me alone." More significantly, there is general agreement that a babyface in the ring should possess at least some of the attributes of a babyface outside of it, lest the dissonance between the personalities confuse fans. There might be no better example of that than the late Gino Hernandez, who, with his long black hair and considerable sex appeal, was the embodiment of a wrestling pinup model. Only one problem. "With all due respect, Gino Hernandez was not a babyface," Prichard said. "Even though they tried to portray him as a young, good-looking babyface, Gino was an asshole and he came across that way. There was no denying that. Gino Hernandez was a heel ever since he was a kid. I say kid; I'd known him since he was eighteen years old. There has to be some connection between the person and the wrestler, or else the audience is going to sense that and turn their backs on him."

It's not true that every babyface is an out-of-control narcissist in love with himself. Having a big ego, in fact, is probably a requirement for a top hero — if you don't believe in yourself, how can you expect the paying fan to? "The babyfaces are prima donnas, or they wouldn't be babyfaces," opined Gil Hayes. "I've known guys that were babyfaces, making less money, because they wanted to be babyfaces. If they were working as heels, they would have made more money, but they gave up the opportunity of making more money because they felt they were happier just being a babyface."

The problem comes when the heroes start listening too much to their adoring public, effectively blurring the line between wrestling and reality.

"Nightmare" Ken Wayne worked a long program with tag team partner Danny Davis all over the South with Tommy and Johnny Rich, and saw how the mind of a hero can take something out of context. "We were doing stuff to where we'd put them over, but we'd still kick the shit out of them afterward so we'd get our heat back. I think the world of Tommy, don't get me wrong, but he'd sit out there amongst the fans signing autographs, and hear, 'Aw man, them Nightmares kicked y'all's ass last week.' He'd come in the dressing room and go, 'Hey man, we need to go over because they say y'all are kicking our ass.' Now, Tommy was at one time probably the best babyface in the country, but that's an example of getting totally wrapped up the wrong way."

Little wonder then that many wrestlers prefer to have people hate their guts. When Rick O'Toole (Brogdon) broke into wrestling in Detroit in the 1970s, he had a fan's perception of a wrestling hero — the guy who gets all the wine, women, and song — so he walked up and down Allen Road near trainer Lou Klein's gymnasium, wearing tie-dyed pants and muscle shirts. "I thought it would be something else to be a worker, get put over, and get women and girls," he said. "Then, as I kept walking so many miles to draw attention, I began to get hungry. I didn't have a penny, but I looked good. It didn't take me long to figure out this is all about money and making a living . . . You never have to worry about what the fan is thinking, because as a heel you do not worry so much about the fans' thoughts, just the fact that what you do gets those fans thinking and reacting."

Wrestling enthusiasts have gotten closer than ever to the sport through developments like social media and fan fest–style events, so they quickly can develop a jaundiced view of a hero who walks around with his nose in the air, too self-absorbed to deal with the masses. At the same time, though, some wrestlers see the changing relationship between fan and star as a way to reestablish an emotional connection unmoored when the business became less shielded from the outside world. They can show that they care about their fans, and their fans can show that they care about them. "I'm not going to lie to you; after three hours of doing a meet and greet, physically I'm tired — because I stand. When I do my appearances, I don't sit in a chair and have my eyes staring at the table, not making eye contact with the people," said Sean Waltman, who worked as the 1-2-3 Kid, X-Pac, and Sixx. "I stand up the whole time, whether it's two, three, or however many hours it is. I don't sit behind the table. I interact with the people, I stand with them, and I talk with them, we have conversations. It takes a little bit longer to do it that way. I enjoy it, and the people enjoy it."

Heroes in history

Where would wrestling's good guys be without Mother Russia? During the Cold War, many a grappler was gainfully employed by administering patriotic whippings to Soviet sympathizers like Ivan Koloff, Nikolai Volkoff, and Nikita Mulkovich. Even in 1908, nearly a decade before the Bolsheviks stormed the Winter Palace, Frank Gotch beat Georg Hackenschmidt, the Russian Lion — actually an Estonian — for the world championship, popularizing wrestling in North America. When Gotch won a celebrated and controversial rematch in 1911, he cemented his status as one of the most admired athletes of the day. "Never will there rise a champion who will 'toe hold' his way deeper than Frank Gotch into the hearts of the followers of the game," said C.E. McBride, sports editor of the *Kansas City Star*. Though his career is outside of the time frame of this book, Gotch was the prototype of heroes for years to come — a strapping, clean-living Iowa farm boy, stout of heart and skill. He died at just thirty-nine, but his legacy lived on in champions like Joe Stecher and Earl Caddock, and it's not an exaggeration to say that stars such as Lou Thesz and Verne Gagne fit neatly into the Gotch lineage.

And where would wrestling's good guys be without the support of the common folk? After Gotch left the scene, promoters turned to footballers Gus Sonnenberg and Wayne Munn to attract crossover sports fans, but business waned until Jim Londos took over as champion in 1930 and set attendance records everywhere he went. Londos was a break from the past, a Greek immigrant considered too small and too foreign to be the sport's brand name until promoters gave him a shot. Though Londos did not invent the babyface character who overcomes great odds — that goes back to David, Goliath, and biblical times — he perfected it as a template for generations to use. Inventiveness and resourcefulness were his stock cards, and his appeal to blue-collar workers, women, and ethnic fans kept the turnstiles clicking, without the aid of TV or the internet. "With the possible exception of Frank Gotch, there never was a more colorful champion in American wrestling history than Jim Londos," *Ring* magazine editor Nat Fleischer wrote in his famous wresting study, *From Milo to Londos*. "The Greek Adonis had what is commonly known as 'It,' with a capital 'T.' He was dramatic and knew the meaning of the word showmanship."

Finally, where would wrestling's good guys be without TV? The advent of nationally televised wrestling in the late 1940s strengthened babyfaces' hands; it was easier to depict good versus evil on a video screen than it was in a newspaper headline, while engaging styles and physiques became more important than ever. "Celebrities like Sheik Lawrence of Arabia, Argentine Rocca, and the famous wrestling team of Garibaldi, father and son, are destroying the prominence of names like Gable and Turner," wrote Bob Cooke of the *New York Herald-Tribune*. Vincent J. McMahon, father of the current WWE chieftain, once quipped that Rocca sold more TVs in the industry's infancy than comedian Milton Berle. That was wrestling hyperbole, but Rocca was the precursor of acrobatic artists that soon could be found in every promotion in the country.

Starting in the late 1950s, and extending through the 1970s, though, a sea change swept over the industry, affecting the fates of babyfaces, whether they were All-American boys or overseas imports. Many of the old-line territorial promotions were acquired by active wrestlers who installed themselves as the face of the franchise. A sample and by no means inclusive: Ray Gunkel took a majority of the Atlanta office from Paul Jones and Don McIntyre in 1958. Lee Fields bought the Gulf Coast territory in 1959, just before "Cowboy" Clarence Luttrall asked Eddie Graham to join him in the Florida booking office, which Graham ran for twenty-five years. Gagne purchased the Minneapolis office and was proclaimed champion of the nascent American Wrestling Association in 1960. Fred Kohler, the forward-thinking Chicago promoter who brought wrestling into living rooms across the country, sold his territory in 1965 to Dick the Bruiser (Afflis) and Wilbur Snyder. The Sheik (Edward Farhat) acquired Detroit from non-wrestlers Jim Barnett and Johnny Doyle. Bill Watts acquired the Tri-State promotion from Leroy McGuirk, and added Oklahoma to the fold when McGuirk left the business in 1982.

In virtually every case, the new boss was on top. Gagne held the AWA world title nine times in the 1960s and 1970s, once for more than seven years. Bruiser's World Wrestling Association was centered in Indianapolis and on Bruiser, the federation's top titleholder fifteen times in twenty years. Fifteen also was the magic number for The Sheik in Detroit, as he held the U.S. championship at least that many times. And you'd need an abacus and a mainframe to tally up Jerry Lawler's reigns as Southern heavyweight after he and Jerry Jarrett took control of Memphis from Nick Gulas in 1977; the most reasonable estimate appears to be forty-one.

Wrestling is a fickle business, so owners-wrestlers knew they could rely on themselves, if no one else. "In those days, most of the wrestlers had a share of the office, to be sure that we could count on their backing, loyalty," said Yvon Robert Jr., who founded Grand Prix Wrestling in Montreal with his father, Edouard Carpentier, Maurice and Paul Vachon, and other partners. Even as late as the 1990s, Vincent K. McMahon had good reason to move from behind

Edouard Carpentier battles Blackjack Lanza in a test of strength.

the play-by-play microphone to the most visible figure in his company. World Championship Wrestling was on the ascendancy until McMahon became the lead heel in WWE following the infamous 1997 double-cross of Bret Hart in Montreal. "When the promoter makes himself the champion, everybody says that's bad. I say that's good," Poffo said. "When you trust somebody, do you know what they might do with the belt? They might go to another territory with your belt. After all the people took the money and defected to the WCW, Vince McMahon knew that he was going to be loyal to himself."

It makes sense to trust yourself if your money is on the line, but it's also fair to say the owner-wrestler phenomenon created a glass ceiling for other heroes and babyfaces, even unintentionally. "You couldn't surpass the guy who owned the shop," said Powers, who switched from a hero to a heel when he entered the AWA. "You had no choice. The structure of the industry was such that you had to adjust a character to make sure you were going where the money was." Frankie Cain has been observing wrestling his whole life and believes McMahon had easy pickings when WWE started going national in the 1980s. "Eddie Graham sure as the world didn't look like no babyface. How'd you like to digest Dick the Bruiser for years and years as a top babyface? Dick the Bruiser, Fritz von

Erich, the list goes on and on of promoters that shoved themselves down the fans' throats, which consequently led to the demise of the business. I mean, you may like Tony Bennett as a singer, but my God, you don't want to see him every week after week," Cain said. "Eighty percent of it was the promoters' fault. Out of jealousy, whatever, they just wouldn't give anyone else a push. Vince McMahon didn't kill the business. The damn business was dead." McMahon's choice of a new top hero, Hulk Hogan, was as invincible as Londos or Bruno Sammartino, who both went undefeated for years as world champions. Hogan also was marketed unlike any of his predecessors, the first of the champions whose likeness was as common to ice cream bars and vitamins as wrestling posters. "The post office needs a separate truck just to deliver my mail," Hogan declared in 1985. "There's never been anything like Hulkamania." At least not until "Hell, yeah!" replaced "Eat your vitamins" as a wrestling catchphrase.

Babyfaces jump the shark

The sound of shattered glass resonates through the arena's audio system, and an intense, shaved-headed wrestler stomps to the ring, flipping the bird at everyone in sight. The entrance of Stone Cold Steve Austin? Perhaps, but it's just as likely that it's one of the Austin wannabes on the independent wrestling circuit. No wrestler since Hogan has had a greater impact on the way fans perceive heroes than the Texas Rattlesnake. "In this day and age, the bad guy has almost become the good guy in a lot of respects," said Ken "Mister" Anderson. "Steve Austin was a heel by nature, he was a bad guy by nature. He just never broke the rules, he never cheated. He would just look a guy straight in the eye and kick him down low. That's just the way he was. I think, in some respects, that kind of Attitude Era changed the business."

But Wayne, who sees Stone Cold imitators at his training facility outside of Memphis, says they're taking the wrong lesson from the anti-authority hero. "They think selling is being a wimp or something," he said. "What you have to tell them is there were times when Steve Austin did get beat down, so when he did kick that ass, it meant something. But that's become one of the big changes in the business, the loss of selling." In fact, it's an everyday occurrence to watch a wrestler kick out of a move that once would have been considered a deadly finishing hold. Boris Zhukov, known to Mid-Atlantic fans as Private Jim Nelson, said that undermines the hero's opportunity to draw sympathy and tell a story in the ring. Case in point: Mick Foley finished the match at the 1998 King of the Ring after The Undertaker chokeslammed him off the top of a sixteen-foot-high cage and through the mat. "Sure, it made him super heroic. But if he had laid dead there, juicing like he was, the people would have thought Undertaker tried to kill him. If you get up from that, then what the heck is left?" Zhukov asked. "That's the psychology I'm talking about. Guys will take suplexes, big dangerous moves, and they just get up and do something else. Sell that dadgum thing. You're not Superman."

At the same time, wrestling fans have been changing, showing less of an affinity for fair play and rejecting the conventional designations of good guy and bad guy. Kevin Nash has seen the transition and thinks it is part of a larger societal trend. "Everybody loves the underdog, but as soon as you get the strap, the fans are like, 'Ugh, he's the champ.' I remember when [Bill] Goldberg was the champion and we wrestled at Starrcade. The people were chanting 'Goldberg sucks' and chanting my name. I stuck him in the middle one-two-three, and the people exploded," Nash told Bob Kapur of SLAM! Wrestling. Then, just as quickly, the audience uttered a collective groan. "'Wait a minute. We didn't want him to get beaten.' We're so jaded as a society that if a person becomes too successful, we want to see that person fail. . . . People just want to see other people fail. It's a hard place to be as a champion."

Can a true babyface exist in today's world? More opportunities to test the hypothesis might help to provide the answer. In the territorial days, wrestlers learned night after night what worked and what didn't, refining their craft in front of live audiences. While WWE and TNA have developmental territories, their rosters are just a fraction of the size of the rosters of the 1970s and 1980s. "Each territory was like going to a new school," Thatcher said. "You need three, four different territories. Everyone is not suited to the way I train. They are guys who flourish with me, but there are guys who might have made it but couldn't take what I dished out."

Let's give the final word to Greg Gagne, a good-guy wrestler and son of one of the legendary heroes in the business. He thinks some re-education of fans and a redefinition of ring styles is in order. But he also is convinced that the bond between wrestler and fan still lies there, waiting to be tapped. "It can be done. But the way it's geared for TV, you've got five to seven minutes before the break, so these guys go out and try to get in every single move they can. They think that's what gets them over. But actually, if you do a few things that mean a lot and grab the people, you're going to get over quicker. People still want to believe. Make

"Stone Cold" Steve Austin is the ultimate anti-hero.

'em believe. If you can do that, it doesn't matter how big you are, or how mean you are. If you can get them to believe what you're doing, you can make money."

About the wrestlers in this book

In this volume, we've tried to offer a representative cross-section of heroes and icons, with more or less equal weight given to different time periods. As professional wrestling has undergone a nationalization process since the 1980s, the hometown or territorial hero has become a thing of the past, but he was an important part of the business for generations of fans. So we've also tried to add geographic balance by telling the stories of wrestlers who might not have made much of an impression outside of their home territories, but who were every bit as cheered and loved as Hulk Hogan, Andre the Giant, and the mega-stars who became household names. As always, our page count is limited; one way to rectify oversights is through the use of cyberspace. On the SLAM! Wrestling website at www.canoe.ca/Slam/Wrestling, we'll be presenting the stories of other wrestlers, as well as tidbits and overflow from our notebooks.

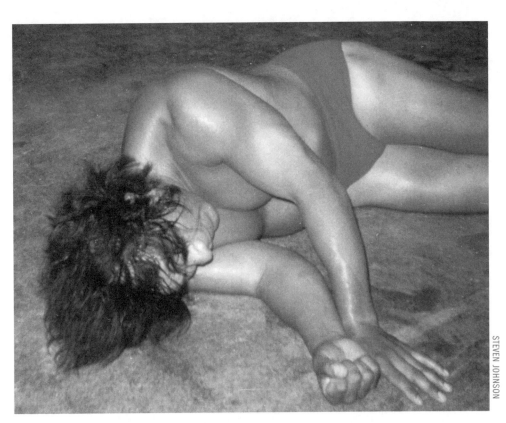

STEVEN JOHNSON

Luis Martinez demonstrates the art of dying.

As a rule, we've avoided ranking wrestlers who are more or less active, recognizing that a lot of wrestlers never truly retire. With input from many journalists and historians, we have tried to rank them based on a few key factors, such as drawing power, longevity as a hero, originality, and historical significance. We also know that fans don't want mathematical models to calculate the length of the stride in Jackie Fargo's strut or the height of Jack Brisco's arm drags. That it's all about emotion and excitement, not to be distilled into cold or dispassionate numbers, so we urge readers to approach our work with that caveat. In the end, the best wrestler is the one who makes you drop to your knees when he's down and out and leap to the heavens when he makes his comeback. So . . . on with the leaping.

THE TOP TWENTY

1. JIM LONDOS

CHRIS SWISHER COLLECTION

Jim Londos, the tanned Greek god.

Everything in moderation. Jim Londos wrestled the way he lived life: methodically and deliberately, no rash impulses and nothing to excess, at his own pace and on his own terms. Growing up in Columbus, Ohio, Frankie Cain watched films of Londos in action in promoter Al Haft's barn nearly seventy years ago and thought he looked like a basketball point guard at the top of the key, probing the defense for weaknesses until the right opportunity came along. "Al had a little old screen and he'd put all those old tapes for us little kids. Londos always stood out in my mind. He was always retreating, not going to lock up right away, he's like a point guard, he's looking around to see where he's going to pass the ball," said Cain, who later got to know him. "I thought, 'My God, this man has psychology.'"

Everything in moderation. Londos was no prude, but his classic Greek approach to health, life, and well-being was built on a foundation of self-restraint, not one of self-indulgence. Veteran Johnny Heidemann, who broke

1

into the business in New York before World War II, learned that riding around with him as a young wrestler. "In them days, cigars were about ten or fifteen cents," Heidemann told historian Scott Teal in a 2000 interview. "I lit one up once and Londos says, 'Johnny, what did you pay for that cigar?' I'd say, 'Fifteen cents.'" Londos responded quietly, "I'll give you a quarter to throw it out the window."

Londos stood only five-foot-six to five-foot-eight, depending upon who was doing the measuring, but nearly a century after his first pro match, no one can claim to have cast a bigger influence on wrestling. He walked with kings and queens, with presidents and mayors. More than anyone, he was responsible for keeping wrestling alive during the Depression and representing achievement to immigrants, underdogs, and women, all of whom he attracted in record numbers. He was the first wrestler to draw crowds of more than 10,000 fans to dusky arenas in five different decades, culminating in a record crowd of 14,000 in Sydney, Australia, in January 1959, when he was sixty-five. His reserved, understated approach added an air of respectability to wrestling and even when he was well into retirement, sportswriters who ridiculed the sport — if they paid any attention to it at all — invoked his name in almost reverential tones. "I shook Jimmie's hand and said his people can be proud of him," David Condon of the *Chicago Tribune* wrote in 1974, a year before Londos died. "Shucks, I shivered to be with the great Golden Greek. He is a page from history."

If Horatio Alger had been Greek, "Jeemy" might have been the subject of one of his inspirational tomes about how a youngster can overcome modest beginnings through pluck and hard work. Londos, born Chris Theophelos, was as coy as any Hollywood starlet about his age, but most documentation points to his birth date as January 2, 1894, in Koutsopodi, Greece. As he later related, his mother wanted her son, one of thirteen children, to be a minister, while his father wanted him to be a soldier. Theophelos wanted neither and sailed to New York in October 1909 when he was about fifteen, part of a historic wave of emigration that saw more than 350,000 Greeks, mostly young males, land in the U.S. between 1900 and 1920.

Working his way westward around 1911, Theophelos got a job on a Southern Pacific railroad crew in Ogden, Utah, where promoter Charles Reveliotis, a fellow Greek better known as Charles Revell, took a liking to the teenager and helped him get some wrestling matches. Their tight bond endured until Revell died in 1960, though Theophelos had to leave Ogden after being fired for accidentally stripping the gears on a handcar. Settling in San Francisco, he worked odd jobs as a bus boy and on a milk wagon, and crashed at a volunteer firehouse when he couldn't afford a place to stay. Ernest Berger, the chief instructor for the San Francisco YMCA and a former German army wrestling champ, saw promise in him and coached Theophelos to the 168-pound class title in the 1912 Pacific Association wrestling championships. He won another tournament, the well-regarded Portola championships, the following year in both the 175-pound and unlimited classes. His official debut as a pro came on February 24, 1914, when he beat Tony Ajax in Oakland.

Wrestling was hardly a full-time job in the World War I years, and Theophelos made a living in traveling troupes, wearing a moth-eaten leopard skin to show off his physique — "the most wonderfully developed man of the age," according to the excited billing of Sullivan & Considine promotions. He swapped Chris Theophelos for Jim Londos, announcing November 29, 1915, in a Portland, Oregon, newspaper that fans were cracking their jaws pronouncing his real name. Jim Londos — he said he cribbed the moniker from writer Jack London — was "a perfectly good name and one that does not sound anything out of the ordinary." For a couple of years, Londos barnstormed from town to town, sometimes working under different identities as part of a practice known as "ringing in." In February 1917, Cy Sherman, the dean of Nebraska sportswriters, found out he was wrestling in the state simultaneously as "Young Samson" and "Polk," and called him on it. "The 'Polk' business excites suspicion," Sherman wrote. "By this method the 'alias' wrestlers are able to hide their identity and to 'ring in' on unsuspecting opponents of only local fame." Left unstated was that the ruse was a common part of betting schemes, and Londos' critics hurled allegations of shady business dealings at him for years.

Before Londos, wrestling champions came in two flavors — strapping farm boys who came from the heartland of America, like Frank Gotch, Ed "Strangler" Lewis, and Joe Stecher, or jocks-turned-wrestlers, like footballers Gus Sonnenberg and Wayne Munn. An undersized, thickly accented Greek immigrant who lacked the requisite business and political connections was left on the outside looking in. Londos' popularity grew through the Roaring Twenties, though, and he developed a style that was borderline revolutionary. He perfected the role of the hero in peril, and played "rope-a-dope" with his opponents like a master strategist. Case in point: against good buddy Ray Steele in Philadelphia in February 1927, Londos let his rival dominate him for the first seventy minutes, and then made his comeback in the final ten, as always, through the intelligent application of counterholds like his Japanese wristlock, not fire-in-the-belly kicks and punches. "The tiger cannot change his stripes and so the Hellenic mat marvel cannot vary his tactics," the *Philadelphia Inquirer* reported. One of his favorite tricks, little used today: he'd let his opponent secure a headlock, but then act like he was glued to the canvas, denying his foe the satisfaction of pulling him to his feet. Asked about his ring work, Londos contrasted it with his friend, boxing great Jack Dempsey, and attributed it to the calculating moderation that was the centerpiece of his life. "I try to be colorful, as Dempsey is when he fights, but I just can't change my tactics," he said in 1928. "An athlete has just so much strength in him. If he uses it up in attacking — is aggressive from the bell — he may be too tired to break a punishing hold that is clamped on him later. . . . I must keep my wits about me and be alert on the defensive."

Thanks in part to an alliance with Chicago-based manager Ed White and Philadelphia promoter Ray Fabiani — they'd eventually own a skating rink together — Londos got a brief run with one version of the world title in 1929. He reprised that on June 6, 1930, when he threw Dick Shikat on a rain-soaked mat at an outdoor show in Philly and changed wrestling forever. Madison Square Garden had done well to draw 4,000 fans for cards topped by Lewis and Stecher; Londos' next four appearances there averaged more than 20,000 each. In Philadelphia, Londos sold out the downtown arena with Tiny Roebuck, leaving an estimated 5,000 standing outdoors in the rain. Historian Matt Farmer, who has compiled wrestling attendance records, credits Londos with thirty-one gates of 10,000-plus fans in 1931 alone. Attendance numbers are notoriously rigged, but no wrestler before had ever registered even ten houses of 10,000-plus in a single year. Writing in the *New Yorker*, Joel Sayre said: "It is doubtful if fifteen thousand dollars' worth of fans could be persuaded into Madison Square Garden to watch Strangler Lewis wrestle the best two out of three falls with Herbert Clark Hoover. But put Jimmie Londos in there any night

COURTESY OF SCOTT TEAL/CROWBAR PRESS

The conductor and his star: Philadelphia promoter Ray Fabiani and the great Jim Londos.

with Jake the Plumber, and it's bound to be a five-alarm. What a man! What an artist!" Houston promoter Morris Sigel repeated an oft-quoted figure that Londos brought in $5 million through the turnstiles from 1930 to 1935, often commanding one-third of the gate. By any measure, he was one of the highest-paid and most well-known athletes in the world.

Although he became an American citizen in 1927, Londos was still a national hero in Greece, equal parts Adonis and Hercules. In December 1928, as part of a months-long European tour, he whipped Karol Zbyszko in Athens in front of a crowd put as high as 65,000, the largest in wrestling history to that point; he was reunited with his father and called it one of the proudest moments of his life. Five years later, he returned to Athens and bested Kola Kwariani on October 22, 1933, to the roar of 60,000 spectators. What he meant to fellow Greeks, overseas and in the United States, was incalculable. Andrew Saffas, an American sculptor and artist, recalled how, as a kid, he persuaded his uncle Tony to take him to see Londos wrestle Everette Marshall in Kansas City, Missouri. By circumstance, Saffas' grandfather and Londos' father were cousins. The day before the match, Tony was driving his truck when he encountered Londos walking down the main street with an army of proud Greeks. "The Greeks, at that time in many areas of this country, were looked down upon as third-class citizens, so along comes a man who gave them something to be proud of. They worshipped him like a god. He in essence emancipated them from the ghetto of low prestige that many fellow Americans had put them in," Saffas recounted.

As alliances between promoters formed and splintered, Londos had to guard constantly against a double-cross in the ring. His fears were realized on April 7, 1933, when a fast count by referee Bob Managoff in Chicago moved the title belt to Joe Savoldi and eventually back to Lewis and his clique. The hijinks sullied the sport's already dubious reputation and led in December 1933 to a formal profit-sharing trust among major promoters, many of whom were Greek and all of whom were ready to restore Londos as wrestling's kingpin. But the trust cut out Jack Pfefer, a New York promoter, who responded by holding Londos personally responsible. His correspondence, collected at the University of Notre Dame, is full of plots to smear Londos. Dan Parker, Pfefer's ally at the *Daily Mirror* in New York, published embarrassing details of Londos' run-ins with the law over alleged swindles of countrymen in Ohio in 1918 and Tennessee in 1927. At one point, Pfefer and old-time manager J.C. Marsh hatched a scheme to leak damaging information about Londos and his wife Arva to a Communist newspaper called *The People's World*.

By far, though, Lewis represented the biggest threat to Londos. Usually hale and hearty, the "Strangler" seethed whenever the topic of Londos arose and derided him as gay, according to wrestlers who drove him to his gigs, for reasons Lewis never fully explained. The most intimidating shooter of his era, Lewis issued repeated challenges to Londos, who sidestepped them and actually lost championship recognition from some state commissions for his evasions. During one tempest in 1931, Londos said he'd be glad to get in the ring — for a quarter-million dollar guarantee and a vow that match profits would be donated to an unemployment fund. Lewis had a well-earned reputation for amassing and losing fortunes, and on behalf of Londos, White quipped, "I want to aid charity. But I do not want to aid Lewis."

Matches of the century seem to occur every few years, but when Londos and Lewis stepped in the ring on September 20, 1934, at Comiskey Park in Chicago, they truly closed the book on a rivalry that started with their first match in 1917. Londos put up his title, which he'd regained from Jim Browning before 25,000 fans in New York in June, but the curtain call in the series was less about mastery of the world championship than mastery of each other. Lewis needed the money; Londos, endorsed by the new wrestling trust, needed a win as a career-capping achievement. Eighteen minutes passed before either man went to the mat. Londos, as was his custom, let Lewis wear himself out before pinning his exhausted foe at the forty-nine minute mark. The attendance of 35,625 set a U.S. record, and the gate of $96,032 would not be eclipsed for seventeen years. Londos' cut was about $50,000, but there was no gloating. Reflecting on the match years later, Londos simply smiled, "Ed may have been a little old by then." Lewis was just three years older than Londos.

There were differences of opinion as to Londos' sheer wrestling ability, but he clearly understood that he was in a business, not out to prove who was the toughest guy in the room. "Don't let no one shit you, boy!" said Heidemann. "He was a little man, but he was smart. He was a businessman. If you wanted to shoot with him, he'd say, 'Meet me in the gym. I don't want to do it in the ring because I don't want to ruin things.' But if you wanted to meet him, he'd be there at four o'clock in the morning if you wanted." Jules Strongbow, an institution as a wrestler and promoter in California, recalled the first time he worked out with Londos in Detroit. He thought he'd throw a knee at his smaller foe. "Next thing I knew, I was stretched out every way but the right way. I tell you, even though I was a pretty fair rassler, he made a complete fool out of me. I almost decided to quit rassling."

Jim Londos ties up Sandor Szabo.

The secret, according to Phil Melby, whom Londos trained, was his under-standing of balance and leverage. Melby was a schoolboy in Phoenix, Arizona, when he started working out after school with Jerry Graham and Londos, who owned the local Madison Square Garden in the 1950s. "He'd tell me to get a headlock and try to take him over. Impossible. Whatever he did, he did it with his balance. I'd stretch it to say he was five-foot-six, he was short, he weighed 200 pounds and he had a great build," Melby said. "He beat my butt regularly every day. Many a night I went home on the verge of tears after being stretched by Jim Londos." In the ring, though, he was light as a feather. "There was nobody like Chris," said the old-time footballer Herman Hickman, calling Londos by his birth name. One night, Hickman was shrieking in pain to the audience's amuse-ment, unaware that Londos had broken his toehold. "He could rip your arm from your socket and you'd never know he had laid a hand on you."

Londos remained champ until Danno O'Mahoney upset him in June 1935 in Boston; $50,000 reportedly exchanged hands and Londos got some much-needed time off. He never again lost a match. In 1938, he defeated Bronko Nagurski for one version of the world title in his familiar haunt of Philadelphia. Various state commissions eventually vacated the championship for the lack of defenses, but Londos, based in California after he married Arva Rochwite, the daughter of a St. Louis architect, in 1939, carried the claim to the end of his career, even as he tended to his avocado ranch north of San Diego. He continued to put on his trunks throughout the late 1940s and 1950s against big names of the days such as Gorgeous George and Buddy Rogers. He was more name recognition than action as he passed his prime, if wrestler Bobby Bruns' critique of a poorly attended 1941 match in Chicago against Olaf Olson is any indication: "The bout only went twenty-nine minutes and stunk. Londos couldn't even get Olson in an airplane spin." On the other hand, Jerry Christy watched him wrestle his uncle Ted Christy in San Diego in October 1953. "Considering his age, the match was passable. When he took his robe off, the fans would sort of ooh and ahh — he had a great body," Christy said. Londos worked most often with ex-boxing champion Primo Carnera, who was not a good wrestler but was a decent attraction, and finished his career in 1959 touring Australia and New Zealand in tortoise-paced matches with "Da Preem."

Cain was wrestling in Arizona when he got to know Londos, who traveled from California to pick up the gate proceeds from little Madison Square Garden. As the temperate Londos admonished him not to put beer in his system, Cain came to an unshakable conclusion — that promoters would never again allow a wrestler to dictate to them the way Londos did. "You know, Londos proved one thing, that a top babyface could travel. He could travel and draw and this is something that they nipped in the bud because the egomaniacs that owned the territories made themselves top babyfaces. They stopped touring the great attractions . . . and those guys could have been contenders."

Londos' years of charity work were recognized in 1961, when King Paul of Greece awarded him the Cross of the Golden Phoenix for his work with orphans on Cyprus. President Nixon honored Londos in 1970 for his charitable contributions, and Londos donated a trophy to the winner of the National Hellenic Invitational Basketball Tournament in Chicago, which was known for a time as the Londos Invitational. In 1972, he received the Hellenic Civic and Humanitarian award in Long Beach, California, and the annual Jim Londos Memorial Wrestling Tournament is still conducted in Escondido, California. In failing health, he died August 19, 1975, at Paloma General Hospital in Escondido at eighty-one.

Don Leo Jonathan never wrestled "Jeemy," but knew him as a kid through his wrestling dad, Brother Jonathan, and visited him in his declining years at his avocado ranch. What impressed Jonathan was that Londos rarely stayed in hotels, preferring, when he could, regular folks who opened their homes to him — the common touch of a great man. "As far as the wrestling was concerned, every Greek was his cousin," said Jonathan. "In that case, Londos had a lot of respect; he had a lot of fans. That's a lot to say about a person, if every place that he went he found some place to stay. There's not many guys that could do that, if you stop and think about it."

BILL CUBITT

Brother, Hulk Hogan ripped through a lot of T-shirts in the 1980s.

2. HULK HOGAN

What can possibly be written about Hulk Hogan that hasn't already been written, *brother*? Whether wearing the red and gold, tearing off his T-shirt, or in the black of the villainous Hollywood Hogan days, he is the most popular wrestler ever, the best known on a global scale, and, conversely, the most overexposed.

For every positive triumph that can be spotlighted — portraying Thunderlips in the career-making *Rocky III*, MTV's *War To Settle The Score*, which led to the first WrestleMania and established the World Wrestling Federation, his charity work, Hollywood Hogan as the leader of the New World Order — a demeaning failure can be trotted out — denial of steroid use and his subsequent humiliating admittance, a stinker of a film career, over-the-top stage fathering on *Hogan Knows Best*, a high-profile, tabloid divorce.

In short, Terry Gene Bollea's Hulk Hogan character, with the rippling muscles, ever-receding hairline and trademark Fu Manchu mustache, is at once the most adored, famous, marketed, and transcendent professional wrestler of all time, and the most vilified, scrutinized, and criticized one as well.

"I'm recognizable enough that I think you'd have to live on Mars not to have ever heard the name Hulk Hogan, or not to have caught a glimpse of this Fu Manchu mustache on TV at one point or another," he wrote in his second autobiography.

The Hulkster can be in *People* magazine one week and *Rolling Stone* the next, with the *National Enquirer* taking its jabs too. Surely, he'll forever be the only pro wrestler to ever appear on the cover of *Sports Illustrated* (in 1985) and take part in an eleven-page pictorial with naked gals in *Oui* (pre-fame, in 1982).

"The only time I'm not Hulk Hogan is when I'm behind closed doors because as soon as I walk out the front door, and somebody says hello to me, I can't just say 'hello' like Terry," Hogan told *Forbes*. "When they see me, they see the blond hair, the mustache, and the bald head, they instantly think Hulk Hogan. My response is 'Hey Brother, how ya doin'.' Sometimes it's not that animated, but usually 24/7 I'm Hulk Hogan. Nobody at the mall or at the airport calls me Terry."

In the ring, Hogan soaked in the adulation. "The fans give you so much energy you forget who you are. You forget about your kids. You forget about your wife. You forget about your cars. You forget about everything. The past is over. The future is distant. You live in that moment. It's easy to deliver the smiles and the positive vibes."

His influence on wrestling is perhaps more measurable than his effect on pop culture and the perception of professional wrestling itself.

Hogan was on top at eight WrestleManias, and countless other WWE pay per views. According to research by Dave Meltzer and Matt Farmer, Hogan was the top drawing wrestler in the world from 1984 to 1991, and Hogan and Ric Flair, "because of the eras they worked and their longevity, have headlined more shows that have drawn 10,000 fans than any wrestlers in history." He's written two autobiographies, and his ex-wife penned one; three other books have been done about him. There are his leading roles in movies: *Mr. Nanny, Suburban Commando, No Holds Barred, Santa with Muscles, 3 Ninjas: High Noon at Mega Mountain*, and his TV shows: *Hulk Hogan's Rock 'n' Wrestling, Thunder in Paradise, Hogan Knows Best, Hulk Hogan's Micro Championship Wrestling*, not to mention his guest spots on everything from *The A-Team* to *Saturday Night Live* to *American Idol* and *American Gladiators*. Merchandise-wise, you could have your Hogan action figure, foam finger, bandana, any number of T-shirts, ice cream bars, and trading cards. Or maybe you saw him hawking Right Guard, or Hitachi, or Trivial Pursuit or Foot-Joy tennis shoes, proving that he didn't always back a winner.

Less quantifiable are the youngsters who chose to follow his lead and say their prayers and eat their vitamins, aiming to have their own twenty-four-inch pythons for biceps.

One of those was WWE superstar John Cena. "When I was a child, the most influential character to me was Hulk Hogan," Cena said. "He was as large as a comic book superhero. He had that same sort of superhero-type swagger about him. He wasn't like every other person you saw on the street. He was truly larger than life in everything that he did. I think that was the attraction of Hulk Hogan, and that's what made him transcend everything. He exuded the aura of being a superstar so well."

Yet when Hogan is queried about being a hero, it's not what happened in the ring he thinks about, but the impact he has had on sick kids through the years — and the effect they have had on him.

"It got to a point where, when I say a role model thing, where the kids wanted to meet me, and especially the Make-A-Wish kids that were dying. They had a chance to see Mr. T or Michael Jackson, or Mickey Mouse, and the kids wanted to see me more than anybody else," Hogan said. "Before the matches, they'd bring three, four kids to me, and some of them didn't have long to live. But you get used to it. Then I went through the final phase, where, 'Thank God, it's still happening.' It got to the point where I realized how important this was, and it was much more important than wrestling or anything else. I got myself in a situation that I could help someone, and help these kids that, when you think about it, they've got one final wish, and they want to spend time with you? If you can truly take that in, you thank God it's still happening."

Hulkamania is still running wild, and shows little sign of stopping, though he is a shell of his former self, eight surgeries leaving his back a trainyard of scars, his six-foot-seven body shrunken to six-foot-four with wonky knees, arthritis, and scoliosis.

But stepping out of the spotlight and living a quiet life in retirement does not seem an option for Hogan, who craves the attention.

Bollea was born August 11, 1953, in Augusta, Georgia, but he grew up in Tampa, Florida, where he'd attend matches with his father, Pete. His other love was music, and he played bass guitar in bands. Needless to say, a six-foot-seven, 270-pound young man with rippling muscles and long, blond hair stood out, whether at ringside or on the stage.

Brian Blair became friends with Bollea at The Other Place, a Tampa bar where Hogan played, and would see him at the matches. Former National Wrestling

Ric Flair begs off from Hulk Hogan in a strap match.

Alliance world champion Jack Brisco saw him there too, and recalled their meeting for the *Wrestling Perspective* newsletter. "During the break, I came over to him at the table for a beer. He was just so impressive. He was only like twenty-one years old at the time. I couldn't believe my eyes. I asked him, 'Did you ever think about being a wrestler?' [He said,] 'It's what I've always wanted to do. I'm a big fan of yours and I've been watching you for years. It's what I've always wanted to do.'"

Brisco told Bollea about the training sessions that went on at the Sportatorium. Bollea's first attempt to break into the business resulted in an actual break — the local shooter Hiro Matsuda busted his leg. "Terry had this long, bleached blond hair down to his waist, he was wearing all the hippie regalia, he was a musician, he talked the talk," said Florida veteran and former Olympic wrestler Bob Roop, adding that promoter Eddie Graham despised Bollea from the start. "He *hated* him worse than a leper; he *hated* him worse than having syphilis," said Roop. "I just knew he was going to tell me to hurt the hell out of the guy. If I didn't do it, he was going to do it." Instead, it was Matsuda.

After the leg healed, Bollea returned and earned a little more respect just by showing up. Blair was one of the youngsters who worked out with him on the mat as he learned the trade. "When we worked, I kind of took it easy on him, because I was way ahead of him as far as amateur wrestling and things like that. But he was very strong. And a lot of people don't realize what he really did learn on the shoot wrestling type side. He could handle himself pretty darn well at the end of that. He still had charisma, that size, and that look."

What he didn't have was a name. In his initial matches in Florida, he was under a mask as Super Destroyer. He quickly understood that it would take seasoning, and suffering, on the road to make it. Bollea went to Alabama, where booker Louie Tillet came up with Terry the Hulk. "He looked real great, despite the fact he was really green. He learned pretty quick though," said Tillet.

In Memphis, he was Terry Boulder. Musician and future wrestling manager Jimmy Hart said he and Jerry Lawler watched him one day. "I said, 'Oh my God, he's awesome,'" said Hart. Lawler replied, "Jimmy Hart, trust me. He will never draw a dime in this business." Hart laughed, "That's a true story. Lawler will say, 'I never said that.' But he did."

As with Hart, who would become one of Hogan's trusted allies over the years, the musical background helped with his performance. "I played music for about ten years before I ever got into the wrestling business, so I was used to being on stage and being in front of people," said Hogan. "I got over any shyness I had in the music business before I ever got into wrestling. Then when I got into wrestling, it was all about that scientific stuff and rolling around on the ground and putting each other in arm locks and leg locks, but the first time I ever looked out into the crowd — I was wearing a mask back then and they called me The Super Destroyer — the reaction from the crowd was a lot louder than I got for the actual wrestling. So the reaction from the crowd made the wrestling easier for me, and I worked that in my whole career. Most of the time when I wrestled, the crowd wasn't just cheering, they were standing up and cheering or carrying on, and that's what's cool about this game, it really plays up that entertainment aspect."

Many people have claimed to be the one who sent the golden goose up to Vincent J. McMahon in the World-Wide Wrestling Federation, and history may never truly know who made the call or sent the package. But Hogan was definitely sent packing from Georgia by booker Ole Anderson. "I booked him back in 1978 when he first started. I called him Sterling Golden. He was the shits. He was a great kid . . . he had the look but what would you do with it?" asked Anderson. "The only way you could possibly use him was if he went to a territory like New York or like Minneapolis, because we used to run towns on a weekly basis." A weekly crowd would grow tired of such a limited performer.

McMahon Sr. definitely came up with the name that launched a million lunchboxes. "You look like a Hogan. I want you to be an Irishman. Your name's going to be Hulk Hogan. Here's two bottles of red dye, and when you come back tomorrow, I want you to have red hair," is how Hogan remembered the conversation. "I told my manager, Fred Blassie, 'Look, I'm already bald-headed. I put this red dye in my hair, the party's over.' Fred Blassie says, 'Oh my gosh, you're going to get fired! He wants you to be a red-headed Irishman.' I came in there the next day, and Vince Sr. looked over his glasses, looked me over, and said, 'I guess the blond hair's okay.'"

The potential was there, and he was protected, said Dominic Denucci, who went around the horn with Hogan in the WWWF. "The old man came in and said, 'Dominic, we have to try to push this kid,'" said Denucci. "I said, 'Okay. That's all you have to say, don't worry about it.' . . . Hogan said to Vince, 'Vince, book me with Dominic in all the big arenas.' He did, from Pittsburgh to Bangor, Maine. I think that's the best money I ever made."

It was in the Midwestern-based American Wrestling Association, though, where Hogan learned to be a star. "[McMahon] couldn't get him over! He didn't know how to do it," Gagne said in 1999, explaining that Hogan was calling from Tampa, where he had almost given up pro wrestling. "So we brought him up, and the rest is history."

In the AWA and with a couple of trips to Japan, Hogan matured, learning that less could mean more, and the fans would erupt at the smallest things, especially after *Rocky III* hit theaters. "In a way, that was the start of Hulkamania right there. It was the audience that made that happen, the crowds that decided Hulk Hogan was someone they wanted to cheer for rather than boo," Hogan wrote in his book. "So I embraced it. I wouldn't fold with one punch. It would take three or four punches to make me fold. I would really play it up, combining bad-guy and good-guy elements all in one." Adding Survivor's "Eye of the Tiger" as his entrance music, a rarity at the time, put Hogan on the road to superstardom.

It just wouldn't be in the AWA.

Having bought his father out, Vincent Kennedy McMahon needed a hero to lead his vision of "sports entertainment" and he chose Hulk Hogan. On January 24, 1984, Hogan beat The Iron Sheik for the WWF world title in New York's Madison Square Garden, and started to change the world. Wrestling became cool and hip, attracting a younger demographic and new advertisers.

"Wrestling fans will always be wrestling fans, but this allowed us to branch out into another mainstream part of entertainment . . . Rock 'n' Wrestling. It was just not going to be rasslin' anymore. We were sports entertainment. More

No one in history used the television medium better than Hulk Hogan, here cutting a promo during a Hulk Hogan night in Chicago in 2009.

families came to the arenas. More kids," ring announcer Howard Finkel told WWE writer Kevin Sullivan. "I have a belief in my mind that a lot of people believe wrestling was invented on the night Hulk Hogan dropped the leg on The Iron Sheik . . . Anything before that doesn't exist, which is a shame, because it does. But I'm not gonna quibble or complain about that. But the night Hulk Hogan dropped the leg on The Sheik, that opened a whole new avenue . . . we became a worldwide entity that one night."

He developed a formula that worked: a pumped-up ring entrance with the original song "Real American" drumming through the arena, posing for the crowd, the heel beats him down, Hogan "Hulks up" and vanquishes his foe with a leg drop, which allows for more posing and an early shower before the trip to the next town — all the while merchandise goes flying off the shelves.

Hogan has many detractors, and always will, as he was content to make do with less. With creative control of his character, he never saw the need to change his act or cater to the hardcore fans who derided his lack of wrestling ability and routine matches. His opponents, however, knew that time with Hogan meant a big payday.

"Of all the guys I saw through the years, nobody was over like Hogan. A lot of people can say a lot of things that they want about Hogan, I mean, let's face it, we're all in the same business and the idea is to draw money and make money, and all you have to invest in is a pair of tights and a pair of boots. This mother-fucker was drawing money like fucking crazy. Isn't that the idea of the business?" said Pat Patterson. "It's the fucking truth. Hogan was not a good worker. He had the personality; the people fucking loved to see him. His promos were different and very aggressive. Other wrestlers should not be jealous of him, they should be saying, 'Goddamnit, how the fuck did he do that?'"

The ying to his yang was Ric Flair, always praised by fans for his wrestling ability; when Flair was wrestling sixty minutes every night in the NWA, Hogan was posing for ten and wrestling for five. When they did finally hook up in the WWF of the 1990s, Flair found that Hogan sure knew their business.

"He was the easiest match I ever had. He was a guy who could really perform and never fuck around. He was easy as shit," said Flair. "I respected him so much. He was over so big that the match could go one minute or it could go twenty minutes. But he could hang in there too. He never backed down. I used to smack the shit out of him. He used to go: 'Last call for room service. Let's do it.' Bingo. The boot and go home. But it was the easiest night I ever had. He wouldn't give me a bump. He wouldn't slam me off the top. He wouldn't press slam me. I just bumped around."

Hogan opened doors in Hollywood that were later smashed down completely by The Rock and Steve Austin. "We're not just big dumb jocks who beat up on each other," Hogan said during the publicity tour for No Holds Barred, a WWF-financed failure that did, remarkably, lead to more roles.

The 1994 jump of Hogan to World Championship Wrestling was a calculated risk, with the politically astute Hogan anticipating that the ownership of Turner Broadcasting would help him outside wrestling. It did, with Thunder in Paradise, and other TV vehicles complementing his lessened wrestling schedule.

Even his transition to villain in the summer of 1996, aligning with Scott Hall and Kevin Nash in the invasion New World Order storyline, shrewdly meant more TV time, another golden run. He parlayed the Hollywood Hogan days to messing with Jay Leno and claiming that he was running for President of the United States on Larry King Live.

"Hulk's the man. Anybody who ever doubts that doesn't know anything about wrestling. Hulk made the nWo," Hall told the Pro Wrestling Torch. "I tell you one thing that is cool about traveling through the airports. One time me and Kev are traveling through L.A., we're walking through the airport with Hulk. We were invisible. No one even said a word to us. We walked straight to the counter. Hulk got stopped a hundred times. I mean, it's kind of cool to not be hassled. Hulk's the man. I don't care where you go. You can go to any city in the world. You know what's cool, is people who don't know wrestling, they know Hulk."

The transition to icon was fully complete at WrestleMania 18 in Toronto in 2002, facing The Rock; with World Championship Wrestling a failed memory, Hogan returned to the Promised Land, reprising the nWo. But the fans wanted the red and yellow again. "I had been positioned as the worst person in the world. I'd hit him in the head with a hammer, put him in an ambulance, I ran him over with an eighteen-wheeler," said Hogan. "He was positioned as the hot babyface, Hulk Hogan–ish, he had *The Scorpion King* coming out. All of a sudden, I went out in Toronto, and they booed him out of the building. So the fans were loyal to a fault."

Perhaps that goes back to that day in 1989 when Vince McMahon testified in a New Jersey court that pro wrestling was, in fact, sports entertainment in an attempt to change the level of taxation on the gate. While one could argue that it wouldn't have been necessary if Hogan hadn't been bringing in so many people, what it really did was open up new avenues, which no one exploited better than Hogan.

"Instead of insulting the fans, Vince McMahon decided since the fans are intelligent and very smart, and they're living vicariously, the fans would be more interested if they knew the matches were predetermined," mused Hogan. "We would tell everybody that it was predetermined, but still, in the ring, after eight back surgeries and knee replacements and hip replacements, and my nose being broken thirteen times, and not being able to see out of this eye, that fake wrestling does get a bit testy."

3. BRUNO SAMMARTINO

Bruno Sammartino was not about sports entertainment. Maybe the undercard was, where the midget wrestlers or the gimmick guys frolicked. But when Sammartino's name was on the marquee at the old Madison Square Garden off 8th Avenue in New York City, thousands of people nervously milled around the lobby, anxious about the challenge their hero was about to face. "The anticipation was unreal," Davey O'Hannon recalled. "Maybe it was Gorilla Monsoon, and they'd say, 'Oh, look at the size of him. This is going to be bad.' Then it was Mike Scicluna. Mike was built differently, a lot taller than Bruno, 275 pounds

Japanese press catch up with WWWF World champion Bruno Sammartino in Toronto.

with that lean body. 'Oh no, this is not going to be good. He's going to put that hangman on Bruno.' You were so involved in this stuff. The entertainment was Fuzzy Cupid and Sky Low Low. They entertained us, other guys would entertain us, but boy, I don't think I could ever describe Bruno as entertainment. This was serious business, man, this was serious business."

Ask Sammartino to explain that emotional connection with fans, and he brings it back to a basic principle. "I never kidded myself about the realities of life," he said. "There's only one reason that you're a star and that's because of the people who bought the ticket to come and see you wrestle. . . . Any time I went in, I gave it my all because I felt I owed it to those fans and that was the least I could do because it was they who made me a so-called star in wrestling."

To cynics, that sounds corny beyond belief. But to his legions of fans and admirers, Sammartino stands apart because of that sincerity, rooted in the old-world values he brought from a childhood in war-torn Italy. Dr. Tom Prichard, a respected wrestler and trainer, said the first time he saw Sammartino wrestle live was against Mike York in the Summit in Houston, Texas, and he couldn't figure out what the fuss was about. "I thought it was horrendous. Then as I got older and realized more about the business, I said, 'Well, wait a minute. It wasn't

Bruno. It was Mike York.' If you gave Bruno a match that meant something, Bruno was a man's man." After watching the last great program of Sammartino's career, the 1980 feud with student-turned-backstabber Larry Zbyszko, Prichard believed, too. "I got the emotion, I got the feeling. It was the fact that Bruno was so over just by his actions and by people believing in him in his honor and doing what's right. And after meeting him and talking with him and having dinner with Bruno a couple of times, that's him. It was real because that's him."

When Sammartino hoisted "Nature Boy" Buddy Rogers on his left shoulder for a submission backbreaker to win the World Wide Wrestling Federation title in 1963, he started a new era in pro wrestling. He was twenty-seven years old at the time, twenty years younger than National Wrestling Alliance champ Lou Thesz, and the youngest world titleholder since the 1930s, depending on how "world" is defined. His presence on the cover of New York–based magazines helped the WWWF extend its reach far beyond the Northeastern states it pro-moted. He was the first of the modern-day strongmen to hold a major world title, projecting a sense of invincibility during a nearly eight-year reign. Yet his blue-collar work ethic, friends say, helped fans feel that he was one of them. "I think people really related to him because they could see him at their level and they could really connect with him because he was a foreigner," said Ivan Koloff, who upset him for the WWWF title in January 1971. "When he did his interviews, he spoke with that broken accent, the idea that he was somebody they could look up to because he looked the part. When you're 290 pounds, look in shape, he had that broken nose, he looked like he was in some fights, cauliflowered ears, and everything."

If Sammartino had never taken a fall, his life story would still be as compelling as anything Hollywood could fabricate. Born in October 6, 1935, in Pizzoferrato, Italy, in the central part of the country, he fled his village in 1943 when German SS troops overran the area during World War II. His father Alfonso had emigrated to Pittsburgh for work before the war, and was stuck there when Sammartino, nine, escaped with mother Emilia, a sister, and a brother to a mountainous area called Valla Rocca for fourteen months. Sometimes, they ate nothing but snow for days on end. Emilia snuck into the village to snatch food when Nazi guards were not looking, and once was shot in the shoulder. Returning to the mountain in October 2010 as part of a documentary, Sammartino reflected: "I'm over-whelmed by it because I put myself in her place and wonder if I was man enough if I could have ever done it." Long-time friend and former wrestling announcer Chris Cruise was with him as he revisited his past, and said those horrific experiences unquestionably forged Sammartino's sense of right and wrong. "It's a story of a little boy who was put up against a wall, and the Nazis were ready to fire and shoot him and his family. If he just came to America and became a carpenter and a family man, it's an extraordinary story," Cruise said.

After the war, Sammartino was so sickly with rheumatic fever that it took three years before medical authorities would clear him to travel and reunite with his dad in America. When he did, in 1950, he was a poor, skinny, eighty-one-pound weakling, bullied at school and barely comprehending English. A friend helped him get a membership at a gym, and lifting weights and wrestling became child's play compared with living a life of fear in Italy. "I can tell you that I became addicted almost immediately to physical fitness. They had a wrestling program, amateur wrestling, and they had weight training," he said. "My gym teacher was friends with a guy named Rex Perry, who was a wrestling coach at the University of Pittsburgh. Perry wanted to know if I'd be interested in going up there and working out with the big wrestlers. I started going on that program six days a week, religiously, no matter what work I did, like summertime when I was working construction." He went from weighing 130 pounds to 270, and bench pressing more than twice that amount. Sammartino was an apprentice carpenter, but sports announcer Bob Prince spotted him, referred him to Pittsburgh promoter Rudy Miller, who in turn sent him to see Vincent J. McMahon in Washington, D.C.

So much for the hammer and nails. He debuted in the fall of 1959 and made his first appearance in Madison Square Garden, which he'd make the Mecca of wrestling, on January 2, 1960, beating Bull Curry in five minutes. Jackie Fargo was wrestling there at the time and remembers how protective promoters were of a young Sammartino, wanting to build him as a superhuman force. "I worked with him when he first started in New York. Gawd, was he green! They told him, they said, 'Don't go off of your feet. Don't go down for nobody.' Well, my manager Jack Pfefer, he told him, 'Jay-kee will dropkick you and you will go down two, three times.' Oh, he did, and boy, they raised hell about that. They said, 'We told you not to go down.' He said, 'Well, Fargo dropkicked me and Pfefer told me to go down.'"

Sammartino was quickly on the top of the cards and just as quickly off them, winding up on promoters' "don't hire" list in 1962, after a rift with McMahon and a missed booking he didn't know about. With some help from Yukon Eric, he ended up with promoter Frank Tunney in Toronto, where his appeal to a large Italian population led to a boom in business before he returned to New York. "He told me he got a call from Vince McMahon and Vince wanted to

Bruno Sammartino pulls the neck of "The Russian Bear" Ivan Koloff.

bring him in, and Bruno was doing well for himself in Toronto, and then Vince told him, 'I want to make you my next world champion,'" said Pete Sanchez.

Sammartino won't speak ill of Rogers, but there was bad blood between the two. "Look, Buddy's gone now. I will never tell you that he wasn't great because that wouldn't be true. But he and I, I don't know how it happens in life, I don't know, Buddy and I never liked each other from the first time we ever met," he said. The Rogers-Sammartino bout on May 17, 1963, might be the most famous forty-eight seconds in wrestling, but less known is that the rivalry continued to simmer behind the scenes. In early 1964, "Wild Red" Berry brought Bill Watts to the WWWF, and the big Oklahoman quickly rose to become the number two hero behind Sammartino, and close friends with the champ. Behind the scenes, though, Berry had been spiriting Watts away for mysterious visits to Rogers' house. Then, in a confidential meeting in his Washington, D.C., office, McMahon told Watts he'd patched up his disputes with Rogers and wanted the Cowboy to visit the ex-champ to discuss a big money deal. As it turned out, Rogers planned to manage Watts in a heel turn against Sammartino. "He was going to come out of retirement and I was going to become his discovery, his protégé," said Watts, who felt compelled to tell Sammartino, though he'd been admonished to keep matters hush-hush. "He'll come out of retirement and he'll manage you but he'll end up working in on the deal and he'll drop you," Sammartino told Watts. "The whole deal is for him to get the championship back. I won't work with him.'" In the end, Watts pitched the bad-guy switch without Rogers and the result was box office gold for months. Sammartino also became a businessman, owning the Pittsburgh area promotion for about six years as his father-in-law, an accountant, handled all the bookwork.

For most of the 1960s, the WWWF formula was simple. Monster heel, meet Bruno. Have a three-match series, usually with a count-out, disqualification, or bloodletting thrown in, and then be vanquished. Hans Mortier, Professor Toru Tanaka, Killer Kowalski, Crusher Verdu . . . it was a simple but effective script, and it played off the schisms society was experiencing at the same time, Cruise said. "In the '60s and into the '70s, it seemed like the bad guys were ascendant, the Russians and the remnants of World War II. And especially in the '60s, where the world went from black and white to gray, Bruno represented the triumph of good over evil. I think that was part of his attraction."

One of the criticisms leveled at Sammartino is that he was a kick-and-punch wrestler for much of his career. "Pretty Boy" Larry Sharpe said he's shown tapes of Sammartino to non-wrestling fans. "I would say, 'Which one is the good guy?' They'd always pick the other guy because Bruno would start out punching and kicking right away. He was no babyface with his moves. He always had the heel come in, and they had such a grudge that he just went right to work on him, which worked for them back in the day, but he really wasn't a babyface." John Quinn, a challenger to Sammartino in 1968 as the "Kentucky Butcher," took a harsher view, calling him "a Hollywood wrestler." Said Quinn: "He worked, I guess he was taught like the camera was always behind him, and never going to expose him. Whereas the camera wasn't going to expose me, no matter where it was. I didn't throw anything that didn't land."

Vincent J. McMahon, Toots Mondt, and Bruno Sammartino.

Koloff, probably his greatest adversary, considers that unfair, saying Sammartino appreciated adapting to his opponents' styles. In fact, Koloff almost felt guilty when he dropped a knee on Sammartino on January 18, 1971, to win the WWWF title, because Sammartino was his hero. "What really surprised me, even in those big rings, boxing rings back then, twenty-four-foot rings compared to eighteen- or twenty-foot rings, he liked to do the spots, tackle, drop down, hip toss, reverse, double kick-up, non-stop type of matches. He impressed me with the idea of trying to be in more good shape. We'd get there early and he'd be running around in the wintertime inside the arena, he'd be running around before the people even got there. I'd say, 'Oh man, I've got to wrestle this guy?'" Dominic Denucci, a good friend, also regarded Sammartino as more versatile than he was often credited. "Why do you think Bruno lasted that long in New York?" Denucci asked. "Because he would adjust to each heel coming in. When Koloff was coming in a little later, that was all believable because Koloff could wrestle and do different things. Now, when he would wrestle with Superstar Billy Graham, that was all different, completely different."

Could the Sammartino formula have worked elsewhere? Sure, albeit to different degrees. St. Louis promoter Sam Muchnick, the head of the NWA, was

In January 2010, Larry Zbyszko and Bruno Sammartino meet again.

not known to pal around with wrestlers, but he liked Sammartino, used him as a special attraction, and publicly took Bruno and wife Carol to the well-known Ruggeri's restaurant. Sammartino went to an hour draw in St. Louis with NWA champ Harley Race in front of 10,043 in June 1973, though a return as WWWF champion in 1975 and 1976 drew crowds of less than 5,000 against Stan Stasiak and Dick Murdoch. "Even though he was not the prototypical NWA champion, he could have been NWA champion for Sam, because what he didn't bring maybe in some certain refined wrestling skills, he brought in his power, skills, and class. He could bring respect for you," said Larry Matysik, Muchnick's right-hand man, who also booked and called the matches in St. Louis. Sammartino's strength and conditioning might have saved him from a life in a wheelchair. Stan Hansen broke his neck on April 26, 1976, not with a clothesline, as promotional material contends, but with a missed scoop slam. "That's what broke my neck, not the lariat, and I did break my neck. In fact, my doctors told me that I came within a millimeter of being paralyzed from the neck down," Sammartino said. His comeback was part of the closed circuit Antonio Inoki–Muhammad Ali telecast and drew about 32,000 fans to Shea Stadium. Hansen was probably fortunate to avoid the wrong kind of retribution. "Bruno said some of the 'connected' people he knew told him, 'Let me know if you want me to take care of this,'" Hansen said in 2011 while promoting his autobiography. "Thank God Bruno said, 'No. That's all right, because I'm going to get him.'"

Sammartino's first WWWF title reign was singular, lasting a record seven years, eight months, and a day. In the same amount of time, the WWE title had thirty-six champions after it was reformulated in 2002. He came back in December 1973 for a second reign of three years, four months, and twenty days, before falling to Billy Graham on April 30, 1977, in Baltimore, Maryland. Put them together and it'd be among the top ten longest-running shows on Broadway. Fifteen years after the Watts heel switch, Sammartino was in semi-retirement as an announcer when Zbyszko, who grew up cheering him in Pittsburgh, played a similar card, bloodying his mentor's head with a chair during a supposedly scientific workout on TV. More than 36,000 fans turned to Shea Stadium in August 1980 to watch them settle their score in a cage match, the largest crowd in New York wrestling to that point. "Because of what I had learned from Bruno, I realized that, number one, the fans wanted to see Bruno back. I was a big Bruno fan. I wanted to see him back," Zbyszko said. "He was great to work with because there was so much emotion. You didn't have to really do a lot to blow the ceiling off of the arena. If Bruno would give you a couple of arm drags, the people'd go nuts. If Bruno died, people died."

Sammartino by and large retired after the Zbyszko angle, but Vincent K. McMahon wooed him in the ring again in 1984 after he took over the company from his dad. It was a decision Sammartino still regrets. He thought he was going to be able to win a push for his son, David, but that never materialized. He and David have been estranged for years because of David's steroid use and other issues, and Sammartino said he's put that last comeback out of his mind. "Those were very unhappy times. I didn't go in there with a great feeling like previous matches because this was after I had retired, circumstances were not the same, and I have no good memories of any of those matches," he said. There's been no more high-profile critic of steroids, vulgar story lines, and McMahon than Sammartino. He wants no part of the WWE Hall of Fame, though he's the cornerstone on which the empire was built. With a wave of his hand he dismisses critics who regard him as a bitter old relic. How can someone be bitter when his childhood town of Pizzoferrato, Italy, honored his small stone boyhood home with a historic plaque and named a sports facility after him? "I've said this and I say it a hundred times — I wish that most people in my age group that were in this business were as happy as I am. I'm an extremely happy guy. After all these surgeries and everything, I train six days a week, I'm in good shape, I go back to the old country once a year where I came from, my wife and I. . . . If you enjoy it, enjoy it. But don't criticize me for hating it because I have the same right as anybody else."

Sammartino underwent successful heart surgery in 2011; naturally, he was back on his feet and lifting weights within a few weeks. He has remained an icon in wrestling and in Pittsburgh, where he received a lifetime achievement award in 2010 from the Dapper Dan organization, the city's premier sporting organization, for the respect he brought to his profession and to his city. "I thought when I left [wrestling], I would go on with the rest of my life doing whatever and people would go on to new interests," he told journalist Alex Marvez in 2006. "I didn't expect years later for people to know or care who Bruno Sammartino was. I was quite pleasantly surprised that it's been different."

HOWARD LAPES COLLECTION

Dusty Rhodes, if you will . . .

4. DUSTY RHODES

Dusty Rhodes is a veteran now, and, like most stars from the past, his stories get exaggerated. "Mine are always embellished, they started out like that," he admitted with a laugh. "Everything starts with three things, always: I was the champion, it was sold out, and I went over."

In Dusty's case, however, it was true.

The magic of "The American Dream" is the stuff of lore. It is the story of a plumber's son born October 12, 1945, in Austin, Texas, who rose to become one of the most famous wrestlers in history, a man who oozed personal magnetism, vanquishing foes with elbows and jiggles, his doughy arm raised in victory more often than not, blood clotting on his scarred forehead, blond, curly hair a sweaty mess. Behind the scenes, he brainstormed, created, encouraged, and manipulated, making him one of the most influential minds as well.

"He was the most charismatic athlete I ever wrestled in my life . . . bar none," said Ric Flair, whose career intertwined with Rhodes' both inside and outside the squared circle.

Florida announcer Gordon Solie likely saw more of Rhodes' matches than anyone else in history. "Dusty Rhodes has a little bit of everything going for him," Solie said in 1984. "He's got more charisma in his little finger than most people have in their entire body."

Naysayers will decry Rhodes' monstrous ego, which, when challenged, would result in a flaming fury, and his pathological need to be in the spotlight, the chiseled, steroided bodies of the 1980s making his six-foot-one, 302 pounds of Jell-O look downright laughable.

J.J. Dillon confesses he was one of those who thought that way, but in retrospect, he has no problem reconsidering. "It just took me a while to understand that that ego was what drove Dusty Rhodes and what made him so successful." The ego, the belief in himself, that he was it, has meant that Virgil Runnels has long played subservient to his alter ego.

That confidence was there from the start, said Johnny Powers, who met Dusty Rhodes and his Texas Outlaws partner Dick Murdoch in Detroit in the early 1970s. "Dusty was Dusty then. I told [Buffalo promoter] Pedro [Martinez], 'That boy's really cocky.' He says, 'Cocky? Fuck, when he comes in the room, there's no more room for anybody else!'"

Contrary to popular belief, The American Dream was an evolution, and not the product of an immaculate transformation.

Many want to take credit for the 1974 turn that spun millions of turnstiles, including Eddie Graham, Bill Watts, Louie Tillet, and Gary Hart, but Rhodes says that, plain and simple, the fans had chosen.

"The people just turned me themselves, and I didn't change anything I did in the ring, nothing," Rhodes swore. Florida promoter Eddie Graham had laid the groundwork, smartly putting Rhodes in a position of a rising star. "Eddie was way smart enough, but he didn't know it was going to be as impactful as it was," Rhodes added. "He had an idea, and he guided me that way with Jack [Brisco], in my matches with Jack. Once he decided to pull the trigger, he had the guy in place, the Korean Assassin, Pak Song Nam, with Gary Hart, the Wino from Chicago, against the American Dream Dusty Rhodes."

Hart was more than instrumental in Rhodes' superstardom than just the 1974 turn. Working in Dallas, he met a young Virgil Riley Runnels, fresh off an aborted stint as a center and linebacker for the Hartford Charter Oaks of the Continental Football League, a league most notable for its instability. Returning to his Texas roots, where he'd gone to the matches in Austin with his father, and where he'd worn number 50 for West Texas State, Runnels headed to the Dallas wrestling office to pitch his services, following in the footsteps of West Texas alumni like Dory and Terry Funk.

"I helped him get booked, and I watched him a few times and the guy was excellent. He had fantastic charisma, and I told him the name Virgil Runnels wasn't very good," said a proud Hart, explaining that he had just watched the Andy Griffith movie *Face in the Crowd*, where the lead character's name was Dusty Rhodes. "I kept him in Texas with me for about five or six months."

Gaining experience in Texas, Ohio, and Kansas City, Rhodes said there were some key, unsung heroes who really helped him out. He'd watched Nick and Jerry Kozak as a fan, and now he was being ribbed by them. "I got back to the Alamo Plaza Hotel in El Paso, and they'd broken into my room, and I didn't know it. I turned back the covers and in the bed, they had taken a sack of potatoes and emptied them all in my bed," laughed Rhodes. "I went to somebody and said, 'What does a potato mean?' They told me, 'It means you've got to loosen up a bit.' Then I had to go to somebody else and find out what loosen up meant." In the car, he listened to the advice of The Beast, Yvon Cormier. "You cannot imagine how instrumental this guy was in my career," said Rhodes. It was Cormier who taught him to single out a fan in the crowd who was dragged there by his buddies, and was reluctant to get caught up in the act; that was who you aimed to get out of their seat. "I would pick out one guy that was a real asshole, you could tell it, and I would watch him. As the night went on, I could see if I got him for that moment, that he suspended his disbelief and really believed in what was going on in there."

But it was "The Great Mephisto" (Frankie Cain) who really saw great things in Rhodes. "He knew, and what I didn't figure out back then as a [heel], was that I was going to be a babyface, so he was taking care of his big babyface without me knowing it. He was kind of pre-loading my brain for what he wanted to do to get over. You know what I mean? They were cagey motherfuckers."

In Kansas City, he began teaming with Murdoch, and learned to live life to the fullest. Though both were twenty-two years old, Murdoch, the adopted son of wrestler Frankie Hill Murdoch, had been wrestling since he was sixteen, and was able to teach as well as raise hell. Rhodes learned to really work the crowd in between the two cases of beer a night. "The fans, the audience, the universe, they're not going to let you come back until you're ready. It's like tuning a guitar by ear. I know that Murdoch and myself in a tag match, when it would be time for the babyfaces to make their comeback, if they, the fans — Murdoch taught me this — if they weren't ready, he'd cut them off," said Rhodes. "He'd just cut them off until it was right for that huge explosion at the end of

Dusty Rhodes casts another spell during an interview with Gorilla Monsoon in the WWWF.

the movie. There's a fine line there. You can sell your ass off to where they wanted you to come back, but you went too far to where you just died and they've lost interest in you. That's the art of the game."

There was only one member of the Texas Outlaws headed for superstardom, said Powers. "When Dusty Rhodes came with Dick Murdoch, and they worked for me as brand-new kids in the Buffalo territory, I could sense Murdoch was a better technical wrestler, but Rhodes was so pushy, so in-your-face with a smile and a smirk."

Leaving the cold of the Midwest behind, Rhodes landed in Florida in the summer of 1973, claiming the Southern Heavyweight title and the area's tag belts (with Dick Slater) almost immediately; when he would return to AWA strongholds like Chicago years later, he would be the headliner.

To Rhodes, his success was because he was so different than everyone else, and appealed to the masses. He billed himself as "The Common Man," and went out of his way to stand up for himself — but didn't cater either.

"I didn't look like the white-meat babyface. I was anti-establishment, I was anti-everything. People loved that," said Rhodes, comparing himself to Robin Hood and Jessie James. "If I made a comeback, I wanted them to come back with me. If I was bleeding, I wanted them bleeding with me. If I won, I wanted them winning with me. If I accomplished that through the whole match, the roller coaster ride, to where everything I was feeling, they were feeling, then I had what I considered a really good match and they got their money's worth. That's what I wanted to accomplish."

Taking the audience on a memorable journey was fun, said Rhodes, admitting he was not the greatest worker inside the ring. "It's the idea that he's a guy that I can sit down and eat with here at the table, he'll go to a bar and fight with us, he looks kind of how my dad used to look, he talks with a funny lisp."

And boy, could The American Dream talk. "He talked the smack. Nobody had ever heard interviews like that before," said Brian Blair, who grew up in Tampa. "Dusty was just made for this business. All the interviews he did, 'The Tower of Power, the Man of the Hour, who's Too Sweet to be Sour.' All that stuff. He could put rhymes together before there was rap. He just had soul, a white guy with soul."

"I loved to listen to Dusty Rhodes. He reminded me of a southern preacher," Scott Casey told historian Scott Teal, acknowledging that he stole some of Dusty's schtick. "The way he'd open his eyes real big, or he'd lick his lips and look off in the distance, them come back and point his finger at you."

Gordon Solie, whether talking up his performances in the ring or holding the microphone in the TV studio, was key to the development of Dusty Rhodes; they are as intertwined as Howard Cosell and Muhammad Ali are in boxing. "We fed off each other," said Rhodes.

Given his popularity in Florida, where he virtually owned Tampa, before there were any other professional sports teams in the area, it was natural for other promoters across the country to seek him out. Featured in all the magazines, he'd be in the AWA one week, do a couple of shots in Atlanta or Houston, head back to Florida, and then on to Oklahoma, the Carolinas, or even Japan.

He was overwhelmed by New York, where the Florida tapes aired unbeknownst to him, on the Spanish station. "It was like a cult following. It was like Elvis when I came in there and they hadn't seen me before, except for that," Rhodes said. Former Ring of Honor champion Homicide understood the appeal of a fellow Puerto Rican, like Pedro Morales, in his Brooklyn home, but Rhodes was something else. "Dusty had everybody, yellow, black, brown, he just had everybody, just his charisma," Homicide said. "He's a soul brother, you know? You can't beat Dusty Rhodes."

Challenging WWWF world champion "Superstar" Billy Graham, Rhodes talked the talk, and made the masses walk into Madison Square Garden for epic bouts with the equally loquacious Graham, who said his matches with the Dream were the most fun of his career. "He's the most entertaining guy on the face of the Earth! You don't want to boo Dusty, even as a heel. The guy's too entertaining."

The popular perception of Rhodes changed with his peers, especially when he was given the chance to book the Florida territory. He was a fan of bloody feuds and hot-shotting angles, and, without any major investment in the pro-motion itself, didn't always stick to budget. Still, he had an eye for talent and a great feel for the business.

The reckless spending continued in the Charlotte, North Carolina–based Jim Crockett Promotions, which was in a furious fight to keep up with the powerful WWF. "If I made two million, I'd spend three," Rhodes has said about the heyday of JCP, which would evolve into WCW, referring to his personal life as much as business. "He was a big spender who enjoyed having a good time," said Flair.

In the NWA/WCW days, Rhodes fought the Four Horsemen, perhaps the best-known faction in wrestling history. "I've got groups of people here that I can beat, to make myself money, to make them money, and they're going to make me money because they're even more important than the actual babyface is. In the end, the babyface goes over. Period," said Rhodes. At various times, he gave his rub to the likes of Magnum T.A., Ronnie Garvin, Nikita Koloff, and Barry Windham to make that next level.

Critics just see the out-of-shape star with backstage stroke keeping himself on top, and that's the wrong view, said Dillon, manager of the Four Horsemen. "Oftentimes, he took a lot of criticism from people who didn't really know how hard he worked and how talented he truly was."

To become the NWA world heavyweight champion on the first two of three occasions, Rhodes had to play to the power brokers who controlled the title, and he wore the title briefly each time. A third reign, after the NWA title had come to be controlled by Jim Crockett Promotions, was lengthier.

Flair explained it would be a mistake to knock Rhodes' in-ring skills. "We'd wrestle for an hour. At 300 pounds he was never lazy in the ring with me," said Flair. "I wrestled . . . probably 200 hour[-long] broadways [with him]. He never

Dusty Rhodes drops a bionic elbow on Ron Bass during a bunkhouse match.

got tired. We didn't go full pace like me and [Ricky] Steamboat, but he never got tired and he was over so good, it didn't matter. I just kept at him. Let me put it like this. I was in good shape. Whenever I took that elbow, they were blowing the roof off."

Right. The Bionic Elbow.

"That just came, because I don't remember a lot of guys doing that back then," started Rhodes, explaining its genesis in his football days. "I started using some forearms and football shivers and stuff, and then it all came into play. I dropped it a couple of times, and named it 'Bionic,' and the rest is history. That's how people just trip over shit. That's how it happened. Yeah, I didn't really plan that."

Something few saw coming was Rhodes' jump to the WWF in 1989. Many took it as WWF boss Vince McMahon humiliating his rival, but Dusty didn't see it that way. "I enjoyed the polka dot times, because it was a time I got away from the Crockett thing, and I just wanted to relax and have some fun for a year and a half."

"It didn't matter what you did with Dusty, Dusty could make it work," said WWF referee Jim Korderas. "We talk about pro wrestling becoming sports entertainment. He knew how to be entertaining before anybody ever coined the phrase 'sports entertainment.' He knew how to get a crowd to react just the way he wanted them to. You talk about that intangible 'it' factor, he had it."

That "It Factor" never left him.

The perfect example is his brief run in ECW, a rebel promotion that seemingly despised the status quo and the legends who established it. ECW mastermind Paul Heyman, who had chafed under Rhodes' booking in the NWA, decided to bring the Dream in to feud with "The King of Old School" Steve Corino. To start it off, Corino called out Rhodes, who was sitting at ringside. "He took off the hat, but he took it off so slow, like Old West–style," recalled Corino. "Then he started the walk to the ring. Here's a thousand smart-marks in Atlanta, Georgia, 'Dusty! ECW! Dusty!' You would never have thought it. He came in, elbow, elbow, and it's, whoom, whoom, like I had heard for years at the Philadelphia Civic Center. He was over in every city we went to. It didn't matter if it was Orlando, Milwaukee, Philly, or everything, it was just amazing. He knew how to feel a crowd, he knew when to come back; he knew when the heel had to put the heat on him. He taught me so much without teaching. He taught me how to be a babyface even though I was a heel."

These days, Rhodes is enjoying teaching, out of the spotlight for the most part, at WWE's training facility in Florida — though he gets more fan mail there than anyone else. Naturally, Rhodes is often called upon to teach the art of the interview. "I like seeing young guys do well, whereas before it was me, and about me, I took the credit, but now it's about our developmental system," reflected Rhodes. "I've really changed. Age can do that to you."

With two sons who have followed him into wrestling — Dustin, who wrestled as Goldust, and Cody Rhodes — Dusty leaves a different kind of legacy behind with their successes. "I don't serve anybody or do anybody good trying to be Dusty Rhodes Jr.," Cody Rhodes told a New Brunswick newspaper in 2010. "There's just a vast difference between the character that was the American Dream and Cody Rhodes, across the board. I get asked if I'm adopted a lot."

Looking back on an incredible career, Rhodes reminisces about the simpler days, before fame changed his life and catapulted him into a stratosphere few wrestlers ever reach.

Those days, traveling with Murdoch, a cooler filled with beer, heading to the next town, are still very special to him.

"The happiest I was would be when we would get in the car, it would be over, and I would be lying down in the back with the Styrofoam cooler, and maybe a baloney blowout or something, country music on the AM radio, or an old 8-track, going to the next town with my partner," he concluded. "The biggest thing, I think, for my industry, that I can take from that are the most enjoyable times. It was not the thrill of the victory. [Only at] the Garden, with the trilogy with Superstar Billy Graham, did I really recognize that I didn't want to leave the ring. But any other times, I wanted to get in my car and move on to the next town. I wanted to make my shots, to have my beer, laugh and joke and sing and be happy."

5. VERNE GAGNE

As difficult as it may be, set aside all that you know about Verne Gagne and his American Wrestling Association, which he ran out of a Minneapolis hotel from 1960 until 1990. Instead, concentrate on the Vern(e) Gagne that headlined cards from coast to coast in the 1950s, a handsome star, seen by millions on the DuMont network. "You take this kid Vern Gagne," Jim Londos once said. "Well, he could have tied most of the wrestlers of twenty years ago in knots."

That Gagne might have been the top pure babyface of the early years of professional wrestling on television. He had it all, ballyhooed *SPORT Magazine* in its *Annual* 1953, "Vern Gagne Is No. 1 Wrestler": "In the opinion of most unbiased observers, it is the dark-haired, good-looking Gagne who had made the greatest strides during the year. Regarded by most experts as a genuinely competent wrestler, and scorning the 'ham-actor' role embraced by so many grapplers, Gagne was gaining on Thesz. It might not be long."

In his autobiography, Thesz gave props to Gagne. "He and I worked a 'feud' for several years in the early and mid-1950s when he was the junior-heavyweight champion, and those matches did big box-office wherever we appeared. I guarantee you they wouldn't have drawn a dime if Verne hadn't have been so credible."

Gagne's authenticity was indeed his biggest calling card in the early days.

Born in Corcoran, Minnesota, in 1926, Gagne can trace his lineage back to France in the 1600s, when his forefathers came to Canada, then settled in Minnesota in 1854. Gagne grew near Hamell, toiling on the family farm. In high school, he claimed a pair of state heavyweight wrestling championships, despite only weighing in at 185 pounds, and was also all-state in football.

Recruited by the University of Minnesota Golden Gophers, Gagne played each side of the field as a defensive end and tight end. But it was in wrestling that he made his name, winning a Big Ten wrestling title at 175 pounds in 1944

AWA World heavyweight champion Verne Gagne.

as a freshman. Up next, he enlisted in the Marine Corps, and was assigned to Santa Ana, California, where he played football for the El Toro Marine team and taught hand-to-hand combat to soldiers. With World War II concluded, Gagne returned to the Gophers and became the first-ever four-time Big Ten champion. To top it off, the three-time All-American also won two NCAA championships.

For the 1948 Olympic Games, Gagne made the U.S. Greco-Roman team, but, in one of the greatest frustrations of his life, didn't get to grapple. "I made the team, but they wouldn't let us compete, they wouldn't let us wrestle," Gagne said. "We came right down to the night before we were supposed to wrestle Greco and they pulled us out. They said, 'We don't think you guys know enough about Greco-Roman wrestling.' This is '48, right after the War, and we really didn't, but we sure as heck trained hard and wanted to wrestle. We were in the parade and weren't in the Olympics."

Yet he always treasured the memories, and it was there that he first met an eighteen-year-old Maurice Vachon, competing for Canada, who would become one of his notorious adversaries as Mad Dog. "It was a great experience. Wembley Stadium was the big parade. It was the first Olympics after World War II and it was a real focal point for the world at that moment in time and most of the world was there," he said. "It was a big disappointment not getting to wrestle."

Back home, he listened to the overtures from the NFL's Green Bay Packers and Chicago Bears, with the teams feuding over who had his contractual rights, but opted for pro wrestling, debuting in 1949. Gagne's first stop away from home was traveling between Texas and Oklahoma, living with his young family in a trailer.

"When I came out of amateur wrestling, I didn't know the submission hold," Gagne said. "But you learn it quick." (They also didn't teach the sleeper hold in school, but by the end of 1951, Gagne was using it as his finisher.) In his rookie year, he won the tournament to crown a new NWA world junior heavyweight champion, as the title was vacated when titleholder Leroy McGuirk lost sight in one eye.

In 1951, he was invited to compete in Chicago. "Fred Kohler didn't think he was big enough. He was the junior heavyweight champion down in Oklahoma at the time for the NWA. And he was about 215," said his son, Greg. "They brought him in Chicago and Fred told him about the big TV network and said, 'What I want you to do is we're going to dress you up what we think a Martian would look like and have you come out of the ceiling into the ring. We're going to lower you down." Naturally, Gagne balked, listing his credentials for Kohler and vowing, "You can line up everybody on the card and I will take on every one of them, one after another. If I can't beat them, I'll quit wrestling. But if you want me to go in the ring, I'm going in with my wrestling boots and my tights and if I can't make it as a wrestler like that, I'll give up the sport."

The reach of television through Kohler's show on the DuMont network surprised the wrestlers. Gagne often told a story about traveling to Buffalo with Pat O'Connor. A snowstorm prevented them from getting to the arena, which they expected would have been empty anyway. Instead, thousands had been turned away. "That's when he knew what the strength of the network TV was," said Greg Gagne.

Wrestling historian Mike Chapman was a ten-year-old boy when he first got to see the speedy Verne Gagne live, at the Hippodrome in Waterloo, Iowa, in 1954. "I had watched Verne Gagne several times on the DuMont Television Network out of Chicago and could not wait to see him in person. My dad took several neighborhood boys and me to see Verne wrestle Hans Schmidt," said Chapman. "Schmidt

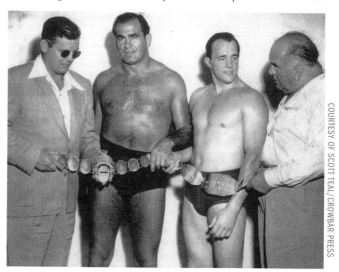

A quartet of champs: Leroy McGuirk, Lou Thesz, Verne Gagne, and Strangler Lewis.

arrived first, walking down the aisle to a chorus of boos and jeers. He stood towering in his corner, wearing a short, black jacket. He had his arms folded across his chest and scowled as Verne came down the aisle, waving to the wildly cheering fans. Verne leaped into the ring, did a little spin around with a wave, and the place went wild. My dad leaned over to me and said, 'Verne was an NCAA champion at Minnesota. You'll get to see some real wrestling tonight!'"

Well-spoken in his interviews, Gagne talked about the sport of wrestling, competition, and his desire to be the best; he spoke as an athlete, not as a performer. That led to him being one of the first athletes — not just wrestlers — on mainstream TV, appearing on shows with the likes of Art Linkletter, Arthur Godfrey, Steve Allen, and even Howdy Doody.

Olympians Ken Patera and Chris Taylor support Olympic supporter Verne Gagne.

His son said it was the real thing with his dad. "I think the way he was projected back in the '50s and throughout his career was that who you saw on TV was who he was. He was a good guy, he loved being around people, he was very charismatic."

Football star and coach Bud Grant was a friend of Gagne's at Minnesota, meeting on campus after the war. "I can remember him borrowing a shirt when we wanted to go somewhere. I don't mean a dress shirt or something fancy — just something to cover himself," Grant told the *Minneapolis Tribune* in 1981. "Verne didn't know where he would sleep some nights, or how he'd eat. Whatever he's got now, I don't begrudge him one cent of it. And he's the same person he always was, a great companion, always enthusiastic, always helping somebody. He puts somebody on his feet and never mentions it. You hear about it by accident."

Not one to brag, Gagne did master the marketing aspect of the pro wrestling business. Always friendly with the media, he also lent his name to any number of products, from a doughnut shop in Minneapolis to fishing equipment, to years later, "DynaPower!" on AWA broadcasts. Some promos are a little less clear, such as this March 1957 ad from Syracuse, New York: "Hi, this is Verne Gagne. I have recently entered into a business that is growing by leaps and bounds. I would like to extend an invitation to my friends in the Syracuse area to attend a meeting at the Onodaga Hotel today and tomorrow at 2 p.m. or 7:30 at night. At this time we will present an opportunity to qualified people to become associated with us in the greatest business in the world. This may well be the most important meeting you have ever attended."

Perhaps Gagne was searching for investors in his planned American Wrestling Association, which he ran with Wally Karbo. Gagne started out by acquiring the rights to Minnesota from Tony Stecher, and followed that up by buying Chicago from Fred Kohler, as well as Omaha, Winnipeg, and other Midwest locales. It was a massive territory, dwarfing the Northeast-based WWWF.

Gagne was careful about what was shown on TV. "Kids love wrestling and they've always been a big part [of it]. I know with our ratings that if we could get the kids, then the parents. And once they start watching, they're into it also," he said in 2000. "Although a lot of people didn't want to admit that they liked wrestling, right here in the Twin Cities, we beat the Vikings' ratings, and the Twins', and all the prime-time sitcoms. We had a twenty-six rating with a sixty-five percent share in our timeslot. That was in Chicago, Milwaukee, Denver, Omaha, Salt Lake, San Francisco, Vegas. We were in a lot of places. If the timeslot was right, we could generate interest."

As the '60s turned into the '70s, though, Gagne's hairline receded and his body lost that sporting definition. Despite still having much of the skills that he did, if not the speed, he became a prime example of a promoter keeping himself in the spotlight long past his prime. Off the record, wrestlers will complain that he hogged the spotlight, dispatching those getting over to smaller towns. Larry Hennig swears that Gagne, known to hold a grudge, once wrote him a check for zero dollars and zero cents.

"Gagne was Gagne," said Billy Robinson, who Karl Gotch had warned him was a "bald-headed, spindly-legged old gat." Robinson, who helped train wannabes on Gagne's farm, was one of the tough guys Gagne liked to have around him. "He was the promoter; he made himself the big star, like most of the promoters did in America."

It was important to differentiate between the promoter and the person, said Eddie Sharkey, who once put fourteen bullets from his 9mm into the walls of Gagne's office in frustration. "You get him outside of wrestling, and he's the most charming guy you're ever going to meet in your life. Everyone, his old football playing friends, the people he meets, just love him. Greatest guy in the world, as long as you don't have to work for him."

And when you did work, he was the boss. "See, Verne liked athletes, and Verne was a hell of a wrestler," said "King Kong" Angelo Mosca. "I'll never forget the night I wrestled him in Denver, Colorado. The referee says to me, 'Boy, you made that old man look good.' I said, 'That old man signs my fucking checks!'"

From 1960 to 1981, Gagne held the AWA world title ten times, for a cumulative reign of a decade. His last run ended on May 19, 1981, when he retired as champion. While he fought all the greats, from Dick the Bruiser to "Mad Dog" Vachon to Fritz Von Erich, it was Nick Bockwinkel who probably was his greatest foe. "I had great matches with Verne Gagne," said Bockwinkel in *Whatever Happened To . . . ?* "Verne always had an intense tenacity. He was very much a firebrand in the ring and he'd get frustrated very easily if things that he was trying to do weren't going as smooth as he would like them. What would happen was, he would get so mad at himself, and so angry, that he would trip and stumble and fall all over himself, because of the frustration he had mentally because of something that didn't go right."

In 1982 and early 1983, with Hulk Hogan on the top of the cards, the AWA was perhaps the biggest, most popular promotion in North America. When Hogan jumped to the expanding World Wrestling Federation, and Gagne ignored the warnings of Vince McMahon, his fate was sealed. The AWA limped along until 1990, a shell of its former self, despite a strong spot on ESPN. In August 1993, he declared bankruptcy, some of his real estate ventures having gone sour.

All through his years as a promoter, he propped up Minnesota Olympic athletes financially, including Ken Patera, supporting their dreams. He fundraised for the Minnesota wrestling team, and supported local charities. The rewards flowed back to Gagne later, including the University of Minnesota Hall of Fame (1992), the Pro Wrestling Hall of Fame (2004), the WWE Hall of Fame (2006), the George Tragos/Lou Thesz Professional Wrestling Hall of Fame (inaugural class, 1999), and the Minnesota Museum of Broadcasting Hall of Fame (2007). The Cauliflower Alley Club gave Gagne the Lou Thesz Award in 2006.

His story turned tragic, though, as his memory faded.

On January 26, 2009, the eighty-two-year-old Gagne, confined to a Bloomington, Minnesota, facility for people with Alzheimer's and dementia, threw Helmut R. Gutmann, ninety-seven, to the floor during an altercation; Gutmann, a former cancer researcher who came to the U.S. after fleeing Nazi Germany, died twenty days later. Police investigated the incident, which drew much media attention, but did not press charges. "You can't blame the person that did it," Gutmann's widow, Betty, told the local newspaper. "[Gagne] doesn't know what he's doing. I feel so sorry for his family, because they are faced with a terrible problem of what to do." Quietly, the Gagne family moved Verne to another location.

"The focus should not be on Verne's health, his family, or personal hardships after leaving the business," stressed AWA historian George Schire. "As for today's fans, very few appreciate the greatness of Gagne or old school wrestlers in general for their contribution to wrestling. Much less care."

6. "STONE COLD" STEVE AUSTIN

For the record, it wasn't intentional. "Stone Cold" Steve Austin was meant to be a villain, someone the fans despised. Instead, they found a hero who did what they always dreamed of: beating people up, flipping off the boss, driving everything from a monster truck to a zamboni, all the while drinking on the job. "Hell, yeah!"

"It wasn't deliberate. I was trying to be a heel and that's just the way the world took me. We never did change what Stone Cold Steve Austin was," explained Austin. "We just transitioned the people I was working with; I started working with heels rather than babyfaces. People wanted to be entertained . . . they were ready for that ride.

"Had I come along ten years earlier than I did, I'd have been a total heel. But at the time I came around, that's what people were looking for, and that was the flavor that became the hottest thing to ever sell tickets and merchandise and pay per views. You look at what's going on today, hmm, don't think it would fit — especially with the PG-climate that's the WWE right now."

Austin was the lone wolf in black boots and black trunks, preaching "Trust Nobody" while punching and kicking his way through the ever-loosening definition of heel and babyface dressing rooms.

Like most great characters, Stone Cold was really just Austin with the dial turned up.

"When he got that big push, and everybody started looking at him different, and he was the top guy and all that, he was very paranoid, and very suspicious of everybody. He was very difficult to get along with," recalled Terry Taylor, later a TNA executive. "Austin didn't want to get cheered though; people just dug his gimmick, which was pretty cool actually."

At the height of his popularity, from 1998 to 2003, the goateed bad-ass with the shaved head was bringing in millions of dollars off his merchandise sales alone. The "Austin 3:16" line — a smart-ass response to a Bible-thumping Jake "The Snake" Roberts at the 1996 King of the Ring tournament — probably made more money than any other T-shirt in wrestling history.

Born Steve Anderson in 1965 in Austin, Texas, his name was changed to Steve Williams when his mother remarried. A wrestling fan from the fifth grade on in Edna, he was trained in wrestling the old-school way in Dallas, by star "Gentleman" Chris Adams and journeyman Chico Cabello. "I was the one that broke him in, taught him eighty percent of the wrestling. Then the twenty percent, Adams took him to the next level," said Cabello of those early days. "He was the biggest guy, beautiful body, strong guy. He was ready. He had the hunger. Out of thirty students, he's the only one that made it to the top."

It wasn't an easy ride, however. He couldn't use his real name because of the already-established "Dr. Death" Steve Williams. There were rough times in Texas and Tennessee when he survived on raw potatoes. His blond hair pulled back in a ponytail — while his hairline receded — "Stunning" Steve Austin made it to World Championship Wrestling, where he established himself as thoroughly valuable in the mid-card, holding the promotion's U.S. and tag team titles, and learning in the ring against masters such as Ricky Steamboat.

Teaming with Brian Pillman in the Hollywood Blonds, cranking imaginary movie cameras on the ring apron to capture their greatness, there were definite hints that Austin was destined for more. "Brian would say, 'Goddammit, kid, you're a babyface.' And I'd cuss at him and say, 'Bullshit. I ain't no babyface, I'm a heel.' He goes, 'Aw, listen to the people. You're a babyface.' And that was a sign of things to come."

At thirty years of age, on the sidelines because of a detached tricep, he was released from his WCW contract. Thrown a lifeline in the upstart Extreme Championship Wrestling though he couldn't wrestle, Austin started cutting real-life promos that hinted there was a lot more to him.

Stone Cold stuns "Rowdy" Roddy Piper during a segment of "Piper's Pit."

Finally, the World Wrestling Federation dialed him up, and pitched him as being the "Ringmaster," a technical whiz guided by "The Million Dollar Man" Ted DiBiase. "It sucked," Austin would later recall. Fascinated by a TV show about the serial killer "Ice Man" Richard Kuklinski, Austin started mulling new nicknames. His wife made him tea, warning him to drink it before it got "stone cold," and a multi-million dollar man was conceived. Adding the unique Stone Cold Stunner — back-to-front with his opponent, Austin would put their head over his shoulder as he dropped to the mat — only solidified things.

Then add the memorable crashing glass entrance music, and you have a crowd popping and merchandise flying off the shelves.

But to truly have had the success he did, the unplanned anti-hero needed an antagonist.

As Austin's rise in the WWF was beginning, the company's owner Vince McMahon had decided to sever ties with long-time champion Bret "The Hitman"

Hart. At the infamous Survivor Series in November 1997, Hart was screwed out of the world title when the referee rang the bell prematurely. On TV, the new character of Mr. McMahon said that "Bret screwed Bret" and he permanently stepped out from behind the announcer's desk into the spotlight as the boss that everyone hates.

"You know why Stone Cold got so over?" asked Al Snow. "Because Vince got so much heat. If Vince did not get all that heat, Stone Cold would not have been so over."

Austin acknowledges Mr. McMahon's role. "Vince is a classic heel. He's not athletic. But he loves to be hated, he thrives on it," he said.

The other great foil in the WWF heyday of Stone Cold was The Rock. Together, they headlined three different WrestleManias. A little more agile and far more dexterous on the microphone than Austin, Dwayne Johnson craved the people's reaction. Like Austin, however, his superstardom was never anticipated.

"I remember when he first broke in," Austin told *Rolling Stone*. "He put this cocky, arrogant character out there, and people just hated his guts, and then that started flipping right back around for him, and the people started loving the hell out of him. When he's being The Rock he's just an amped-up version of himself, just like Stone Cold is for me."

It did take some time to develop into Stone Cold, though. "It usually takes life experiences to go out and be real. Austin became a heel because he had been screwed over so many times," said Tom Prichard. "He knew he had talent, but he was getting the runaround. His frustration came out when he came to WWF, when he was The Ringmaster. He knew that wasn't working, it was Austin who knew who he was, and he got the idea with Jeannie when they watched the HBO special. But he had all these life experiences to back it up, from being Stunning Steve Austin to the Hollywood Blonds with Pillman and being screwed over by WCW. It wasn't just overnight that he became Stone Cold. It was an evolution that took place."

Though Austin retired from pro wrestling in 2003, he stayed involved, realizing that making guest appearances on *Monday Night Raw* or as a special referee helps keep his name fresh with those who love him best — and it can promote his latest film or television project.

Having made movies big — *The Expendables* with Sylvester Stallone — and small — *Damage, Hunt to Kill* — Austin knows he has a certain role to fill as a tough guy on the big screen, and doesn't quite have the same range (or *joie de vivre*) as his foil, The Rock, does.

"At the end of the day, if I make thirty action movies, I'm a happy guy. If I get to make twenty-five action movies and five comedies, I'm a happy guy. I want to work. I don't want to be put in a box. But the bottom line is, I want to enjoy the movies that I make," Stone Cold said. "I want my core fanbase to enjoy the movies that I make. I also want to grow a new fanbase that never even knew I wrestled. The bottom line is I want to make good movies."

7. ANDRE THE GIANT

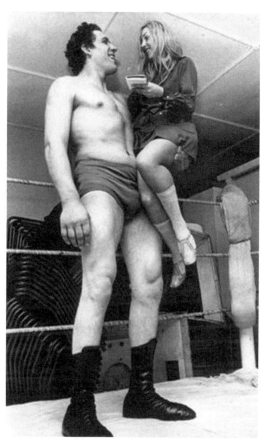

Andre Rousimoff in England 1969 at Dale Martin's Gym.

New Zealand wrestling guru Dave Cameron was touring the wrestling halls of England in 1969 when he became one of the first outside of Europe to glimpse Andre Rene Rousimoff, still a few years away from becoming the Eighth Wonder of the World. "He was a big man, but rather skinny, and he could move around the ring," said Cameron. "Everyone wanted their picture taken with Andre." He tried to hook up the twenty-three-year-old with New Zealand promoter Steve Rickard, but Andre's English skills and his passport time from his native France were both limited. Still, Cameron introduced him to the wrestling magazine world as "Monsieur Eiffel Tower" when Andre did tour New Zealand a couple of years later. "The first time he came out here he was just a sensation and they matched him with three opponents . . . The sight of thousands of people unable to gain admittance to our large stadiums is something that won't be forgotten for a long time to come."

Within a few years, Andre would become the best-paid and greatest wrestling

Andre the Giant is all smiles, dominating a heel Dusty Rhodes in 1972 in Milwaukee.

DAVID MACIEJEWSKI

attraction in the world. National Wrestling Alliance President Sam Muchnick called Andre one of only three wrestlers in history who could attract fans on his own, regardless of time, place, publicity, or opponent, along with Jim Londos and Buddy Rogers. So lasting was his fame that NBC's *Saturday Night Live* could pull off a light-hearted skit based on Andre mulling ice cream choices nearly nineteen years after he died. "You say, 'Well, he wasn't the greatest of workers, he couldn't move.' But he was a giant. People wanted to see that. Andre was the first like that," said friend and business partner Gino Brito.

Andre was born May 19, 1946, in Grenoble, France, with a condition called acromegaly, which causes the body to produce an unregulated supply of growth hormone, and can lead to serious illness and premature death. He ditched school after eighth grade, left home as a teenager, moved furniture for a while, and also became a boxer. If anyone got a finder's fee, it should have been wrestler-promoter Frank Valois, who brought him to North America. "I saw him at one of the arenas in Europe and I talked him into becoming a wrestler," he said in a February 1975 interview. "That was ten years ago. Andre was nineteen. I've been wrestling thirty-five years and I taught him everything I know. He's a natural: fast, agile, strong. I took him all over Europe wrestling; then to Japan, Australia, New Zealand, Brazil."

Working as "Monster" Rousimoff, Andre made his first trip out of Europe in January 1970, when he went to Japan, and that's when people learned he was more than just a big, tall Frenchman, according to Moose Morowski, who was there at the time. "They were going to sign him to a lifetime contract, but when he took his medical, that's when he found out, the doctor told him what his problem was," Morowski said. "The only people that knew at that time were the doctor, New Japan Pro-Wrestling and Andre the Giant, what his problem was. He never, ever said anything to anybody [about his condition] and he lived his life to the fullest till death."

In late spring 1971, Valois brought him to Montreal and Grand Prix wrestling as Jean Ferré. The story presented to Quebec fans was that Edouard Carpentier was driving in the French Alps when a giant redwood blocked his path. Ferré, a name lifted from a legendary French strongman, emerged from the woods Paul Bunyan–style to lift it out of the way, and Carpentier ushered him to Canada. "Carpentier had him as his tag team partner and Andre was the bump guy. That says something about Carpentier but it also says something about Andre that he was that agile to be the bump guy," said Sir Oliver Humperdink, who was managing in Grand Prix. The "Match of the Century" between Ferré and Don

Leo Jonathan sold out the Montreal Forum in May 1972. "I'd sooner be with him than against him . . . You never really knew how strong he was till you had a round or two with him," Jonathan said.

Ivan Koloff knew, which is why he did a doubletake when the Rougeau family brought him into Montreal in the '70s and directed him to whack Andre from behind with a chair during a TV interview. "I said, 'Does Andre know about this?' 'No, no, no, we're not going to tell him.' I said, 'What? Are you crazy?'" He did as he was instructed, though, and Andre responded with a huge, bloody bump over an announcer's table, teaching Koloff something in the process. "Andre was still a businessman. It was the type of thing where he knew it was him against me; if he didn't do something to make me look good on camera before then, that [the match] probably wouldn't do that good."

How do you wear a watch if your wrists are a foot in circumference? How do you type on a typewriter or dial a phone if the fingers on your sixteen-inch hands are too huge? How do you travel with friends? One time, Andre joined Rip Hawk and Swede Hanson on the way to Albuquerque, New Mexico, and the weight blew out all four new tires on Hawk's Cadillac. He hopped a ride with *World Wide Wrestling* announcer Rich Landrum after a show in Spotsylvania, Virginia. Landrum put the passenger seat in his Buick Riviera as far back as it would go. "He got in and he kind of folded himself up. He pushed with his legs to readjust himself and when he did, the back of the passenger seat just went 'Ka-bong!' and went over into the back seat. I looked at him and I said, 'That wasn't a reclining seat, Andre.' He goes, 'That's all right, boss. I pay for it.' So he rode in the back seat with his legs over the front seat," Landrum said.

Little wonder, then, that Andre — to whom everyone was "boss" — valued camaraderie above all else. "I think he felt normal in the locker room. Not an attraction; just one of the guys," said Bill Eadie, a close friend and one of the first men that the Giant allowed to bodyslam him. "I feel he felt most comfortable around the boys and felt at home. He liked the business and protected it. He had a good sense of humor and if he liked you, he would bend over backwards to help. If he didn't, then you knew it. No politics. Either he did or didn't." Rene Goulet, who met Andre very early in his time in Montreal, agreed that the Giant had no middle ground. "He had a little beef with Dino Bravo one time here in the Carolinas and Andre never talked to him after that. If he didn't like you, that's it. And he wouldn't go behind your back either. He'd tell you right to your face." Johnny Mantell was on the good side and cherishes a picture taken just after his daughter was born in 1982; her hand is in her dad's hand, which is in Andre's hand. "He was so much fun to work with and to play cribbage with in the dressing room. There was another guy that a lot of people didn't know away from the building," Mantell said.

When Andre signed on with WWWF in 1973, Vincent J. McMahon dropped the Jean Ferré pretext, and sent him from place to place, so his act wouldn't wear thin from overexposure. For the rest of his days on the road, Andre would wrestle and have fun. You could do a book on his drinking stories alone. Dick "The Destroyer" Beyer was ferrying him from Springfield, Illinois to Chicago, when, in his distinctive *basso profundo* voice, Andre announced, "We need beer." Recalled Beyer: "So I stopped and I had a case of beer and I set it in the front seat, just he

Everyone has an Andre drinking story.

and I. Seventy-five miles outside of Chicago, he says, 'We need more beer.' I drank three, he drank twenty-one. We stopped at a roadside bar at one in the morning and I got another case of beer, sitting between us. We get to Chicago and he says, 'We need more beer.' He drank another twenty-one. I had three. Anyway, what amazed me is that he drank forty-two beers in a hundred and fifty miles and he didn't have to stop to take a leak." Fernand Ste-Marie was the ring announcer for Grand Prix Wrestling and accompanied Andre to bars in Montreal. "Imagine you enter a bar [with Andre], a very popular bar at that time in downtown Montreal, not far from the Montreal Forum, and everyone would quiet. He used to call for six beers in a row. When he took the small Molson or Labatt beer with one of his hands, you didn't see the beer." Andre was said to consume 7,000 calories of alcohol a day. "Everybody always talks about Andre's ability to drink, but you just don't realize how big he was. A sixteen-ounce beer can in his hand looked like a three- or four-ounce can in somebody else's hand. A swallow to him was three or four gulps for any normal person," said Mantell.

Between the booze and Andre's habit of ignoring dental hygiene, he posed an ordeal for interviewers. Landrum darted away as soon as Andre was talking on camera. "I'd tell the camera crew, 'Once he starts, get the camera off me and go to a single shot.' I would take two steps back and hold the microphone. I went to [Jim] Crockett a couple of times and said, 'Look, this man's breath is killing us out there.' 'We know, we know,' he said. But what could they do?"

Hawk remembered another party time after wrestling in El Paso, Texas.

BILL CUBITT

A heel Andre in the WWF still towered over almost everyone.

"We went across the border to Juarez just to have a few beers and have some laughs. We got over there, we went in that bar and God almighty, there were so many hookers in that bar. They're looking at Andre and they can't believe it. Pretty soon, they started gathering around him and they look at him and this one spoke a little English. She saw the size of his hand and she said, 'Is your thing bigger than your finger?' And Andre says in that deep, rough voice of his, 'You will never know, darling. If you had my finger, it would be enough for you.'"

In fact, Andre did father a child, Robin Christensen, whom he barely saw during his life. "His doctors had told him that because of his glandular problems he could never father children. So lo and behold, he got a paternity suit. This went on for a couple of years. Finally, they had to go to court," said Paul Vachon, adding that Andre's lawyers thought he had a perfect defense because of his condition. "They walk into court, and a woman comes in with a little girl, about eight years old who looked just like him, but pretty though — the nose and the ears and the big lips and everything. He said, 'That's my girl, that's my daughter.' He's the one that told me that story, that's how I know."

The big guy was positively giddy at WrestleMania I in a bodyslam challenge with John Studd. Tom Buchanan was shooting photos ringside for WWE as Andre took the winner's purse, a bag full of $15,000 of real cash, and tossed it into the crowd. "Years later, I learned the cash was just a prop, and Andre wasn't to give it away at all," Buchanan said. "Vince McMahon was apparently going nuts backstage as his very real money was being shared with the crowd by the mischievous Andre the Giant."

A couple of years after Brito took over his late father's promotion in Montreal, Andre and Valois joined him as owners in Promotions Varoussac, an acronym of their three last names. Andre fought Hulk Hogan for the company in 1980, and Brito said the match put Montreal wrestling back on the map. Montreal was a second hometown to Andre, who owned a restaurant and had other investments there, but most of all loved the city's nightlife. "He was the only guy that Vince says, 'No matter how much he asks of you, give it to him,' because the Giant could go out one night and he'd spend two, three thousand dollars like I'd spend twenty." But Brito also had to watch Andre's back during those nights on the town because troublemakers figured they could make a name for themselves. "He hit one guy just one time in Quebec City and almost killed him. This guy had come in and he says, 'I'm not afraid of the Giant,' a big guy but not in shape, a guy who loved to street fight. The Giant gave him a backhand and the guy went flying and so I said to him, 'Giant, don't do these things.' I said, 'If I'm there, I'll handle it.'" Ox Baker can testify to Andre's strength, since Andre was only the second man to bodyslam the big Ox without his cooperation. "I didn't help him. He picked 310 pounds up off the ground. That's dead weight. That's like a 500- or 600-pound sack, and slam you," he said. "There were probably guys that could hurt him, but you couldn't beat the man. If you thought that, you were out of your mind."

His height was always a bit of a mystery because his afro hairstyle made him look taller, but Andre definitely got shorter as he got older — his seven-foot-four billing was all hype. By the time his back and body deteriorated, in bare feet, he was closer to six-foot-eight. To outsiders, he got rude and irritable as the acromegaly progressed. "Andre was a natural heel because he hated people," manager Bobby Heenan wrote in *Bobby the Brain: Wrestling's Bad Boy Tells All*. "While I would have memberships to all the airline clubs so I could go into the lounges and not be bothered, Andre wanted to sit in the hall. But everybody would bother him, and in turn he'd swear at them." Because he owned a farm north of Charlotte, North Carolina, Andre wrestled often in the Mid-Atlantic promotion, and referee Tommy Young was his designated custodian. Young saw the Giant growl many a time at a fan in a restaurant or a store. "He had his good side. He wasn't a total jerk, but he wasn't the nice guy you probably heard he always was," Young said. "He had to be a lonely man."

As a heel, his WrestleMania III main event against Hulk Hogan was the sport's first million-dollar live gate, a sellout with a pay-per-view buy rate estimated at eight percent, which no wrestling PPV has come close to touching. A rematch on NBC-TV on February 5, 1988, generated 33 million viewers, the largest U.S. TV audience ever for a pro wrestling match; that's when Andre won Hogan's world title in a famous referee switcheroo between the good and evil Hebner twins. At the time, he could barely move, wearing a brace for his surgically repaired back under his singlet, and holding on to the ropes to support his 500-plus pounds. "He never complained saying, 'Oh, I've got a bad back' or 'I can't do this or that,'" said Goulet, a WWF road agent during the last years of Andre's career. "But I know for sure he was in pain all the time, the back and the knees."

It's fair to say fans remember him during that time as much for his role as Fezzik in *The Princess Bride* as for being Hogan's foil. "That was before DVDs and he had several VCRs in his suitcase and he would always stay at a hotel as long as they could play it. And he would have people come in all the time. He must have seen his own movie a hundred times a day. And I'll tell you what. You could not have cast anyone better than him," said Lanny Poffo.

In January 1993, Andre returned home to France for his father's final days. Boris Rousimoff passed away on January 15, and Andre, forty-six, died in his sleep of an apparent heart attack twelve days later. He was returned to the United States for cremation and the ashes were scattered on his North Carolina farm. Terry Todd, who wrote a seminal article on Andre for *Sports Illustrated* in 1981, was among the eulogists. "The way Andre was, was hard for him to understand and contributed to his legendary fondness for beer. He told me late one night in a bar that he often wondered why a disease would make a man so large and strong, yet would weaken and kill him at a young age," Todd said in a radio commentary on the eve of the burial. "But even though Andre never understood the why, he made the most of his condition. Only rarely did the sadness show."

A classic pose by famed photographer Tony Lanza of a classy champ, Lou Thesz.

8. LOU THESZ

A lot of wrestlers claim they work the same way in front of eleven people as they do in front of 11,000. With Lou Thesz, it was demonstrably true. The site was a little National Guard armory in Urbana, Ohio, for a show that "Flying" Fred Curry was promoting. Jim Lancaster, who wrestled Thesz a handful of times, was on the card and said it was the smallest crowd he ever worked in front of. "We had eleven people there. And Curry decided he was still going to run the show. Thesz worked with one of the local guys that Fred had there, a guy by the name of Rick Jason. And he went out and I swear they went ten to twelve minutes and Thesz worked with him like he was working for the world title. Thesz, he put on a match there like he would if he was in the main event in any auditorium. And I was really impressed with that."

The question arises: What was one of the sport's greatest icons doing in a setting that looked like a scene out of the *The Wrestler*, the 2008 movie about faded glories of the business? The answer lies in the way Thesz thought about himself and wrestling. It was a profession, not an avocation or sideshow, but a profession to be practiced to its fullest, no matter how meager or uninspiring the circumstances. "I never heard him call it work because to him, it wasn't. He always trained me to look at the business as being competitive. He took everything seriously," said Mark Fleming, a Thesz protégé and trainer at his wrestling school in Virginia. "He wrote a note to me one time that he always considered me a wrestler. He said, 'You're a member of a small camaraderie.

Always remember that. If you have no respect for what you do, you have no respect for yourself.'"

There's no doubt that Thesz was wired differently, and his passion for wrestling was a reflection of a constitution that dealt with challenges by pouring everything he had into them. If something was worth doing, then it was worth committing heart and soul. "That's the way he was," said his wife Charlie, who met him in Tennessee in the early 1970s. "I used to say if I wanted to go to China, I'd give Lou a shovel because he was single-minded. When he set his mind on something, he had to conquer it. He raised chickens. He sailed. He had a furniture business. He had a carpet business, and whatever it was, it was all-consuming until he conquered it. Dogs — he got a Doberman and then he had to have best in show. He learned how to train them; he learned how to show them."

COURTESY OF SCOTT TEAL/CROWBAR PRESS

Lou Thesz has control of Assassin #1 (Tom Renesto).

The story of Lou Thesz, detailed in his autobiography *Hooker: An Authentic Wrestler's Adventures Inside the Bizarre World of Professional Wrestling*, is the story of wrestling. Thesz was never the flashiest wrestler, the most entertaining, or the best draw. But his death in 2002 broke the last remaining tie to the days of Ed "Strangler" Lewis, George Tragos, Ad Santel, and the founding fathers of professional wrestling. Tapping their accumulated knowledge, Thesz won his first world title in 1937 as an eager twenty-one-year-old, and his sixth and final one in 1963, when he was forty-six. Ten thousand Japanese fans greeted him in Tokyo in 1957, when he bestowed international legitimacy on mat idol Rikidozan and Japanese wrestling. In 1960, when he was forty-four years old, and nearly a quarter-century removed from his first world heavyweight championship, he was asked about retiring. Wasn't in his date book, he said. "The wonderful thing about wrestling is that age is no detriment. It's an asset. So long as you keep in top condition, you can keep on by using your knowledge and experience, relying on body language and a foolproof bag of tricks. I'll challenge any of these young kids." It wasn't a boast and it wasn't an old man rationalizing why he was still in the ring. Thirty years later, with an artificial hip, he'd be the first man to wrestle in seven different decades, against Masahiro Chono in Japan.

It's not hyperbole to say Thesz was obsessed with wrestling from the time he was in grade school. Aloysius Martin Thesz was born April 24, 1916, in Michigan's rural Upper Peninsula. The family moved to St. Louis, where father Martin, an immigrant Hungarian-German shoemaker with an amateur wrestling background, introduced his son to competitive wrestling at age eight. His education was on the mat; Thesz dropped out of school at age fourteen to work in the shoe shop and further his training. "I was seriously hooked by that time and realized it was just a matter of time before I was discovered," he said in 2000. "I kept showing an interest and I kept meeting people in wrestling that helped me get started." A junior heavyweight named Joe Sanderson was among his early mentors, and Thesz had his first recorded pro match in April 1934, two weeks before his eighteenth birthday. He fell in with some of the great shooters of the day, absorbing everything he learned like a sponge until Tragos and Ray Steele set him up with Lewis in a St. Louis gym. Thesz found he couldn't budge the old codger, about forty-six then, and made noises to his dad about heading back to the cobbling business. "Ed Lewis got wind of this, so he called my father, which would be like the president of the United States calling you to say 'Hello,' because my father had never talked with him," Thesz said in an interview with *TWC Online*. "He said, 'Tell the boy to come back, he did very, very well.' He said, 'But he forgot that he was wrestling me, and I've traveled the world and learned to take care of myself and that's what we were trying to teach him to do.' So I mulled that over a day or two and when I looked at the shoe repair shop again compared to the fantastic hype you get with the wrestling, I said, 'I think I'm going back to the gym.'"

The first of Thesz's six world titles came on December 29, 1937, when the handsome, dark-haired kid beat Everette Marshall by countout for one major version of the championship. Fans rushed into the ring to embrace their hometown prodigy, and Maurice O. Shevlin of the St. Louis *Globe-Democrat* heralded the dawn of a new era in wrestling. "Thesz, the youngster, had too much courage for Marshall, the veteran. He had too much stamina, and he knew all the tricks of the trade. He will not have to be 'protected' from the best the game offers in the way of wrestling ability." When the National Wrestling Alliance was formed in 1949, promoters voted Thesz as their first champion after his principal rival, Orville Brown, nearly died in a car accident that effectively ended his career. Thesz claimed that title for the next eight years, save an eight-month run by "Whipper" Billy Watson in 1956 and a couple of curious hiccups when the NWA and Thesz dabbled with the idea of using dual champions in different parts of the country to drum up attendance. "Lou kind of ran things in those days. He's the one who kept those promoters living for a long time. He was a very intelligent man," Dick Hutton, whom Thesz picked to succeed him as champ in 1957, told *Whatever Happened to . . . ?* in 2000. "In my opinion, Lou Thesz was Mr. Wrestling for twenty years. I think he kept it alive and moving ahead, and really kept it together. When everything else failed, Lou Thesz would always come in and pick things up. He had the reputation and everything. Everybody believed in him and respected him." But challenges always lurked around the corner. In an attempt to test Thesz, and perhaps double-cross him, Karl Gotch, another famous shooter, leaned forward to block a Greco-Roman backdrop during a 1964 match in Detroit. Thesz suffered the worst injury of his career — five broken ribs. The contest was over. Survival was on. "He came up to pop me and I hooked up with a double wristlock and took him over and that was it," Thesz recalled. "I made him howl." The injury was the lowest moment of his career. Thesz was out for a month, throwing a mattress on the floor of a Tucson, Arizona, lodge he owned and living in virtual solitude. "I wanted to see no one and wanted no one to see me," he told interviewer J Michael Kenyon in 1997. "After that ordeal, I was so out of condition I had to begin conditioning from square one."

Thesz was known for moves that still are seen every week on TV — the Thesz press, the stepover-toehold facelock. But as early as the 1950s, his on-the-mat style seemed like an anachronism compared with the flamboyancy of "Gorgeous" George, whom he liked, and the comedic antics of Antonino Rocca, whom he did not. His old trainer Santel acknowledged as much in a 1953 interview with the *San Francisco Chronicle*. "Most promoters would rather have someone else the champion. Thesz is dull. I can think of twenty others who are better showmen and not bad wrestlers, either. But they can't beat him. He is a throwback to the days when wrestling was on the mat, not on the feet."

Yet, it's essential to understand that Thesz's vision of wrestling didn't encompass bloody, wild-eyed beatdowns and stirring comebacks. He'd work a little rougher one night and a little gentler the next, depending on the requirements of the moment. Wrestling's fundamental hero-villain dichotomy held significantly less appeal for him than did competition. "Babyface, heel; he didn't dignify those terms. He didn't dignify that," Fleming said. "He dignified that as going out there and having a wrestling match. That's the way he put it over with the crowd. He didn't play to them with what they wanted. He showed them what he wanted. Other guys used to say, 'Listen to the crowd.' Lou never taught me that. Lou used to say, 'Go out there, grab a hold, have a wrestling match.'" Danny Hodge, regarded as the greatest amateur in history, fought Thesz seventeen times during his last run as NWA champ from 1963 to 1966 and loved every minute of it because of Thesz's tenacity. "Lou was, I'd say, fighting for his life. Can I put it more plainly than that?" Hodge asked. "I couldn't have had anyone better to wrestle with than Lou. I learned so much from Lou. I learned how to short-arm scissor you. Hey, it's a deadly hold. When you get something put on you, you learn from it. I used many things that he used."

The role of the NWA champion, especially during Thesz's final reign, was a complicated one. He had to travel from territory to territory, enabling the local challenger to shine like a star while maintaining his renown as the world's best. Buddy Colt, wrestling as Ron Reed, was the Central States heavyweight titleholder. But wrestling Thesz for the world title in January 1965 in St. Joseph, Missouri, was another order of magnitude. Imagine his shock when Thesz shook off promoter Gust Karras' suggestion that the champ take a fall and then finish the sixty-minute time limit match. "Lou said, 'Well, that won't do Ron any good. We'll take a fall apiece and go through [to the end],'" Colt said. "I was very nervous and intimidated by him because his reputation did precede him. But I had a fantastic match with him. The people were going crazy and at the time it was probably the greatest meaningful match I had ever had."

Thesz occasionally would give his opponents a love tap on the cheek — a bitch slap might be a better description — and Johnny Powers remembers when he got his in Hamilton, Ontario. "I said, 'Sir, I'm in front of my hometown. I'd really prefer seriously if you didn't slap me in the face one more time.' He looked at me and he laughed. He actually wanted to see if you had some grit. It wasn't so much he was going to try to damage me because from then on, he gave me seventy-five percent of the match and I looked like a champion." Powers would have gladly accepted a pinfall loss, but Thesz let him hook his foot over a rope, fall backwards and lose by a countout. "That meant so much because instead of beating me, it meant I just screwed up."

The championships and the Methuselah-like longevity don't begin to convey the esteem in which his co-workers held him. Tommy Gilbert got to work with him in 1974 in Tennessee, which was Thesz's home turf in his later career. Before the match, in the locker room, Thesz laced up his black wrestling boots and turned away. Gilbert figured he was in for a licking, a young 'un taking on a champion who had a reputation for roughing up rivals that he didn't respect. "He fooled me. We had the greatest match that I've ever had in my life that night. But he didn't say anything to me when we got back to the dressing room," Gilbert remembered. A week later, Thesz walked into the dressing room for a return match and thwacked his right hand across Gilbert's left thigh. Call it the slap of history. "Kid," he said, "You're going to have to help me . . . Once they've seen Thesz one time, they've seen him every time. You're going to have to call it from now on." Said Gilbert: "I never will forget that. That was the most precious night in my life in wrestling, when that gentleman told me that."

Wrestler Buddy Wayne booked Thesz as NWA champ in several small towns that he ran as part of the Tennessee promotion, always with spectacular results. One night in Jonesboro, Arkansas, Wayne estimated he had to turn away 2,000 people from a building that seated 1,400. He thought part of Thesz's drawing power came simply from the way he carried himself. "Let me tell you what he did in Memphis. He normally stayed at the Peabody, which was the nicest hotel in town at the time. If he couldn't get a room there, he'd stay at the Claridge. Most of the guys would walk two or three blocks, carrying a suitcase to the Claridge. Not Lou. He called a cab, drove those two or three blocks. And when he walked in, he had a suit on, or a coat and tie, and people just stood there and looked at him in awe," Wayne said. "He was the champion; there was no question about it."

Thesz never claimed to be perfect; there were times when he drank and partied too much, and the temptations of the road wrecked his domestic life until he settled down with Charlie. And few could hold a grudge like "Hunky," Lewis' pet name for his charge — the "Strangler" traveled with him from 1950 to 1956, helping him with interviews and ring presence. Buddy Rogers was the hottest heel in the country in the 1950s, but he once denigrated Lewis in front of Thesz, and that was it for the "Nature Boy." Thesz had the in-ring ability and the connections as NWA champ to call a lot of the shots. "The reason I would not lose a match to Buddy is because no one would have ever bought it. I was never that good a salesman," he scoffed. When Rogers aligned himself with the New York booking office to the exclusion of the rest of the country, Thesz was designated to beat him for the NWA world title in February 1963, though the ice between the two warmed in later years. "Lou Thesz, if he was working with a guy that for all intents and purposes didn't have any ability, Lou would just annihilate the guy, just grind him into the ground. The match would be the shits. The promotion didn't get its money's worth," said Nick Bockwinkel. When Lancaster wrestled Thesz in Tennessee, he admitted he was scared to death because of that reputation — that he'd lean on you if he didn't like you. "But I never had any problems with him. He was tough, he was stiff, he worked hard, but he wasn't the type of hard, stiff worker where you'd end up with a fat lip."

In 1976, Thesz teamed with Buddy Lee to run the short-lived Universal Wrestling Association in Tennessee in opposition to the established Nick Gulas promotion. Thesz had experience as a part-owner in St. Louis, but though the talent roster was impressive, the UWA's balance sheets were

Lou Thesz with announcer Sam Menacker and Mil Mascaras in the IWA promotion in the 1970s.

not, and they pretty much drained Lou and Charlie's bankroll. Thesz continued to wrestle occasionally in the United States and Japan through the 1980s before the final bout with Chono, when his hip replacement objected to the activity. "I was old enough to know not to do it, but I did it anyway," he told his hometown paper in Norfolk, Virginia. Fleming, a star amateur in Virginia, was barely grabbing notice in opening matches for Jim Crockett Promotions in the Carolinas when he caught Thesz's eye. That began a close relationship that reached across the Pacific, when Thesz was commissioner of the shoot-style Union of Wrestling Forces International in Japan in the 1990s and Fleming was one of its top competitors. In his late seventies, Thesz invited Fleming to swap holds on the floor of his home overlooking the Chesapeake Bay. "We'd train with different guys and he would make me get on the mat with them and stretch them before he'd take their money. 'I want wrestlers,' he'd say. 'I want guys who want to learn how to wrestle, not the TV stuff.'"

The wrestling world owes Thesz a debt of gratitude for keeping history alive, and unlocking mysteries to which only he held the key. In addition to his autobiography, Thesz fielded questions about his career on internet message boards and was always available for interviews from fans and historians until the last of the pure wrestlers died April 28, 2002, at eighty-six in Orlando, Florida, where he and his wife had relocated. "I never deluded myself," Charlie said. "Lou loved me. We had an incredible relationship but I never deluded myself into thinking he was more husband than he was wrestler. Wrestling, that's how he defined himself. He wanted what was best for wrestling and that was what was best for the fans."

9. ANTONINO ROCCA

At the height of Antonino Rocca's stardom in 1958, the writer Gay Talese followed him around the West Side of New York City to try to get at the essence of his appeal to the tens of thousands of Hispanics who elbowed their way into arenas for a chance to cheer him to victory. What he found was that Rocca was more than a wrestler — he was a ward healer, social worker, good Samaritan, and superhero all wrapped up in one. Talese wrote: "If the problem is unemployment, Rocca tried to find them jobs. When a woman is having trouble with her husband, she calls Rocca. Rocca breaks up street fights, arranges for doctors' appointments, lends money. He is invited to hundreds of weddings, parties and dinners. The food is not what he always likes, but he eats it anyway." Though he was Italian by birth, Rocca fully understood the psychology of his Latino constituency. "These thousands of poor, little Puerto Rican people — they have no hero," he said. "So I am their hero."

It would be a mistake to confine Rocca's popularity to the sidewalks of New York, though he certainly set the stage for the heroes such as Bruno Sammartino and Pedro Morales, who would dominate Northeast wrestling until the late 1970s. Since Angelo Savoldi spoke Italian — Rocca could handle Italian, Spanish, and some Portuguese — he was designated as his road manager, so the cash cow wouldn't stray or get lost. "Anywhere he went in the country, I don't care where he went in the United States, from the East to the West, North and South, standing room only for Argentina Rocca," Savoldi said. "When he got into New York, he made history there. Believe me, he was outstanding. Every match he had in Madison Square Garden, you couldn't get a seat, standing room only. He got so famous in New York, and then of course TV starts showing him all over the country, everybody wanted him, every part of the country wanted Argentina Rocca." Rocca's exuberant high flying had an effect on a whole generation of wrestlers. Tito Carreon worked side-by-side with him in Florida, Chicago, and New York and mimicked some of the things he did in the ring. "I was graduating from high school and he was wrestling in California when I first saw him. Everybody loved that guy and little did I know that a few years later, we'd be wrestling as partners," Carreon said.

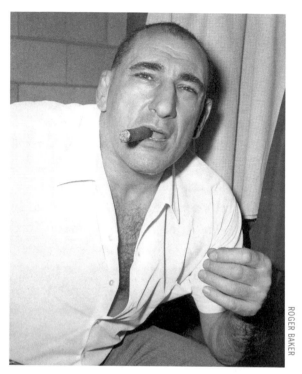

ROGER BAKER

The always successful Antonino Rocca enjoys a cigar.

"One thing he'd do, and I copied him, is he'd throw the fast dropkick. Boom! Before the guy can get up and go away, boom! He'd throw one-two-three-four and I started to do the same thing. Great personality on that guy."

A generation before Vincent K. McMahon rebranded wrestling into a form of cartoon-oriented, pop culture entertainment, Rocca was already there. In the August 1962 *Superman* comic book, he wrestled an octopus underwater, then threw the Man of Steel through the ropes during a charity wrestling match. He sat, smiling, in his well-furnished apartment on West 57th Street in New York while famed journalist Edward R. Murrow lobbed softballs at him for the *Person to Person* CBS-TV show. *The Tonight Show* with Johnny Carson, *David Brinkley's Journal* . . . Rocca was a ubiquitous presence on the tube. U.S. Senators Estes Kefauver of Tennessee and John McClellan of Arkansas numbered themselves among his fans, and Kefauver arranged for him to visit Capitol Hill one time. "I saw [Richard] Nixon and McClellan and others and I told them they must forget about every-thing," Rocca recounted. "They should relax. I told them to lay on the floor, lift their legs half-a-foot high, put on soft music in the dark, and relax."

Was Rocca a great wrestler? No way. His act consisted of a lot of butt-wiggling and lowbrow comedy, like when he'd jump on an opponent's shoulders and ride him like a cowboy, or extend his leg for a foot slap to the face or body. One of his stocks-in-trade was to lie on his back, wrap his bare feet around his opponent's head, and cartwheel him to the mat. A lot of wrestlers said they felt foolish standing there and letting Rocca go through his routine. "I'll bet I could pick out twenty-five rasslers today who could throw Antonino Rocca in a shooting match, and maybe more," Fred Bozic said in 1960. "Rocca is just a tumbler. He gets spectacular holds with his legs and feet, providing you stand still and let him do it. He's a big man because the Puerto Ricans in New York go for him at Madison Square Garden." Stanislaus Zbyszko, one of the pioneers of pro wrestling, tried to take the shine off Rocca in a 1953 interview with national columnist Harry Grayson. "That's why Antonino Rocca's dropkick, which seems

WRESTLING REVUE

Antonino Rocca dropkicks an opponent.

to impress the crowd, is so laughable. An honest wrestler could pin Rocca in five seconds by grabbing a foot and pouncing on him when he landed with his body out of control."

Rocca wasn't about trading holds, though. He was about money in the bank. Ted Tourtas understood that in New York, when Kola Kwariani, who discovered Rocca and was

one of his handlers, explained the facts of life. "He said, 'You good looking, nice. You work with Rocca. Match starts, you come out, Rocca dropkick, you get up. After Rocca dropkick you again, you get up. After Rocca dropkick you again . . .'" Shot back Tourtas, "'Wait a minute, Kola. All I've been doing is getting up. When the hell am I going to make a move?' It started to hit every dressing room. The guys would laugh about it. The Greek got tired of getting up. So anyway I called Rocca over and said, 'Rocca, how do you want to finish and how do want to start?' And we had a pretty good match and after that, Rocca wanted to work with me." "Crusher" Tom Townsend worked in Rocca's independent promotion in the 1960s and agreed that if you got past his inner circle, Rocca wasn't bent on stealing the whole show. "If you had some special moves, he'd let you do them. He wasn't always ninety-nine percent Rocca, one percent you. He'd give you a good opportunity to show yourself before he'd finish you off," he said.

Antonino Biasetton, the future Rocca, was as slippery about his birth date as he was to his onrushing opponents. When he died March 15, 1977, newspapers put his age at forty-nine. But the best available evidence, collected by researcher Tim Hornbaker from a signed Social Security application, indicates he was born April 13, 1921, in Treviso, Italy, meaning he shaved about six years off his age. Around 1939, he headed to Rosario, Argentina, where he and his brothers had contracted work. From there, the story gets murky, not least of all because Rocca was telling it. He definitely was a skilled swimmer, and a soccer and rugby player, and one of his versions has him captaining the Argentinean rugby team at age seventeen, though he might still have been back in Italy. What is clear is that he wrestled for promoter Karl Nowina in Buenos Aires, where Kwariani saw him at some point, perhaps as early as 1945, and filed him away for future reference.

Another wrestler, Nick Ellitch, brought him into the United States in July 1948. Rocca's debut in Galveston, Texas, that July 29 was sensational — he beat Gorilla Macias in two straight falls with dropkicks and flying head scissors, and was the Texas heavyweight champ within days. His visa expired after six months, and Toots Mondt of the New York office used the lapse to wrest him from Houston promoter Morris Sigel and Kwariani, who still got cuts of his paychecks as Rocca's agent and protector. Wrestling at Madison Square Garden had been black since 1938, save for a flop of a show involving Gorgeous George, but when Rocca took center ring on December 12, 1949, that all changed. His first house at the Garden drew 17,854, and he'd be a fixture through the end of 1962, appearing at one point in forty-eight consecutive main events there as a singles or tag wrestler. "I was jealous of him because he was so athletic and fast," said Billy Darnell, one of the country's top babyfaces of the '50s. "One night, we went to, I think, a Lebanese restaurant and he was sitting there with three or four people, and he had a jug of wine. He waved me over, we drank wine together, and became buddies." Rocca's income was into the six figures and it is no understatement to say he saved wrestling in New York. Dewey Fragetta, a legendary boxing matchmaker, summed up the front office perspective: "Wrestling was as extinct as the passenger pigeon until Rocca came along and gave the Latins in North America something to root for."

Though he was based in New York, Rocca traveled the country regularly, setting attendance marks in places as diverse as Waterloo, Iowa; El Paso, Texas; Petersburg, Virginia; and Ogden, Utah. "His tumbling ability and all-around ring speed have made Rocca wrestling's biggest attraction," said Mansfield, Ohio, sportswriter Fred Tharp, after a Rocca appearance breathed life into the sport there. Imitation was the highest form of flattery, and Rocca was flattered by spinoffs such as the Amazing Zuma, whom he fought in front of 20,000-plus in Madison Square Garden and a sellout in Newark, New Jersey. Willie Gilzenberg promoted in Newark and later wrote colleague Jack Pfefer: "Zuma, immediately after the Newark match, would have grossed anywheres from $1,500 to $3,000 per week for at least two years all over the country. Simply by trading on a simple slogan — Another Rocca."

"Freak of nature" — that's the term you keep hearing when others describe Rocca. In his heyday, he was six-feet, 225 pounds, with a fifty-one-inch chest and thighs almost the size of his twenty-nine-inch waist. "I guess you'd say he was kind of a freak of nature. This guy could jump up in the air and split and all that. We used to lock arms from the rear and he'd jump and squat with me from the rear. It's not an easy thing to do," Mark Lewin said. "He did some things I didn't like inside the ring, that didn't look right to me. He used to jump on guys' shoulders who were seven feet tall and bring them over. He did have some classic things that he did and he was a great athlete, but he was not a wrestler." Long-time foe Bob Orton Sr. offered the same analysis. "He was a nice guy. He was very athletic and agile. I don't know how much tumbling or tricks he could do like the gymnasts in the Olympics, but he was a specimen, a real freak of nature as far as health and power and quickness," he said. Equally impressive to Orton was that Rocca walked without shoes and socks in Central Park. "That was supposed to be good for him," he said.

Rocca explained that he started wrestling barefoot because he was too poor to afford shoes, and happily found his bare feet gave him more balance and stability. Equally plausible is the explanation that he would have required costly, specially crafted boots. His feet were 13E and Les Morgan got a taste of them in a tag match in June 1976 in West New York, New Jersey, teaming with Crusher Blackwell against Rocca and Gorilla "Gino" Monsoon. "I never realized how big his feet were. I'm five-eleven, okay? He jumped up to dropkick me. The bottom of his foot was in my bellybutton and his toes were in my mouth. They all start laughing. The referee was laughing, Crusher Blackwell almost lost it, and when Gino got Rocca in the corner, he goes, 'He bit my goddamned toe.'"

At times, the only thing more outlandish than Rocca in the ring were the

Rocca and Senator Estes Kefauver.

yarns he and promoters spun. While there was a kernel of truth in some of them, Rocca's boasts included earning a degree in electrical engineering at the National University of Rosario, composing lyrics for a slow waltz, winning the Carnegie Medal, defeating eighteen hulking tribesmen in the Amazon jungle, killing another wrestler who failed to submit to his backbreaker, running the 100-yard dash in ten seconds flat, owning a textile mill with 250 workers in South America, and perfecting a lifestyle that would enable him to live to be 100, or even 150. Eating green beans and vitamins for breakfast, based on a study of lab mice, was a component of that healthy living, he once insisted. "He embellished things a bit," Nat Loubet, the editor of *Ring Wrestling*, said after Rocca died. "Head to head, he almost would be a drab personality. His voice was low key. As soon as a third person came, his eyes would light up, his hands would begin to move. It was as if you turned a switch and the lights went on."

With Miguel Perez as his tag team partner, Rocca stayed at the top in New York through an infamous 1957 Madison Square Garden riot, when he got into a blood battle with Dr. Jerry Graham that led state authorities to cancel a subsequent show and fine the combatants. Pushed down the card as he hit forty, Rocca opened an independent, opposition office to Vincent J. McMahon called the World Booking Agency. Some friends in the Argentinean meat business backed Rocca, and Carolina promoter Jim Crockett joined in the endeavor for a while. "Even when we'd wrestle in the small places, he always used to say to everybody in that dressing room, 'We give 100 percent just like as if it was Madison Square Garden,'" said Townsend. "He'd go out and do the same thing, not an abbreviated match or a lackadaisical match. That was one of his qualities." The highlight of Rocca's company was a show at the 1964 World's Fair in New York, and that was probably the last big moment of his career.

Out of the limelight, Rocca wrestled occasionally, worked for a while as a physical therapist at a Florida hotel and as a night security guard at a toy warehouse in New Jersey. He didn't have the riches from his days as a $100,000-a-year earner. Promoters took bountiful cuts of his gross pay through the years and Rocca lost money in some bad investments. Several wrestlers said he had a private struggle with alcohol and Princess Little Cloud (Dixie Jordan) said she saw an ugly side after his heyday. "It's not even that he would hit on me, because he knew I was a kid in those days — even the older ones pretty much left kids alone — but he would say things like, 'You've got to sleep with the promoters to get ahead.' . . . He'd say it with very crude language."

In the fall of 1968, Johnny Powers and Pedro Martinez turned to Rocca as an attraction to shake wrestling in Buffalo, New York, and Cleveland, Ohio, out of years of dormancy. But Rocca no-showed a tag title bout in Cleveland in January 1969, causing Powers to convert veteran bad guy Moose Cholak to emergency babyface status. "Rocca had lost his time. He'd lost his 'jump up and down and look like Mr. Vitality' by the time he came to us," said Powers. "We used him to voiceover some Spanish tapes we sent to Mexico. Mostly, he'd sit in the corner and they'd let him make the comebacks but they weren't very enthusiastic. His era was gone." Rocca joined McMahon as a wrestling color commentator in 1975, and briefly reformed his partnership with Perez in the Caribbean before he died March 15, 1977, after a serious infection he failed to take care of apparently entered his bloodstream.

Graham was Rocca's favorite opponent; they worked together hundreds of times in Latin America and Cuba, as well as in the Northeast. "Doc" outlived his friend by twenty years, though he was as notoriously abusive to his body as Rocca was dedicated to his own. "He could have been elected mayor of New York," Graham told wrestler/interviewer Kurt Brown in 1991. "I made plenty of money with that man. He was a money maker. He was someone outstanding, someone who comes along once every hundred years."

10. RICKY STEAMBOAT

In the category of "you never lose it": Mid-Atlantic veteran George South was at his training center in Charlotte, North Carolina, showing Ricky Steamboat Jr. arm drags and other moves. Ricky Sr. was sitting on a couch, nicely attired in a dress shirt and pants from a previous appointment. "Next thing I know, big Ricky got in the ring and in a split second, he shot one of my guys off the ropes and it was like the heavens split open," South said. "He threw the prettiest arm drag that I'd ever seen in my life. We're all sitting there with our mouths open. I was so jealous that I wasn't the one that took that arm drag. He just went back over there and sat down. I don't know how long it had been since he threw his last one. It was the coolest John Wayne moment I've ever had. His shirttail didn't even come undone."

The irony, as Steamboat quickly acknowledges, is that much of his repertoire, like Ricky Jr., is second generation. He cribbed off Jack Brisco in Florida to develop his signature deep flying arm drag. "They never saw Jack do it because TV isn't the way TV is today, with cable. But that's where I first saw it and watched him do it and do it and do it down there and learned how to do it myself," he said. And he borrowed — with permission — a martial arts component from Dean Ho (Higuchi), when they were both working in Georgia in 1976. But Richard H. Blood Sr. was hardly a copycat. He possessed, many of his colleagues say, a unique ability to pick and choose, add and subtract, and then add his own special flavor to his character. Sgt. Slaughter feuded almost nightly with Steamboat for the Mid-Atlantic versions of U.S. heavyweight title and the world tag team title from 1981 to 1983. "Many times, when I wasn't the main event, when I came through the curtain after working with Ricky, under my breath I always said to the next two guys that were going out there: 'Follow that.' There wasn't anybody that made you look better than Ricky Steamboat."

Steamboat won't go that far. On the basis of a career that spanned about eighteen years as a full-time wrestler, he's convinced that diversity is what makes the business tick. "I don't think that you can bring up one name and say that he was the best. The bottom line in this business is you try to develop your own character because if everybody looked the same and did the same, there would be no business. Paul [Orndorff] did his 'Mr. Wonderful' thing. I was Ricky 'The Dragon.' Hulk Hogan was the Hulkster and everybody developed their own character and capitalized off it. We are all great workers — classified in our own niche that we created," he said.

Referee Randy Anderson lifts the arm of newly crowned U.S. champion Rick Steamboat.

If there is such a thing as a cerebral babyface, Steamboat is it, because he had a finely developed sense of how to play the chords that would resonate the most with fans. Before the gates opened, he often climbed to the top row of an arena and visualized his contest in solitude, as he once explained in a workout manual. "I would tell myself, 'This is what I did last week, so this is what the fans think I'm going to do this week. You always try to stay one step ahead because when they can start guessing what's going to happen, why even bother coming?" Early on, Steamboat said he sensed that selling his opponent's blows was job number one for a babyface. So, instead of trying to get all of his familiar moves in all at once — a common practice among today's wrestlers — he carefully orchestrated the moments when he'd shine, holding back bits and portions for later use. "I wanted to get the arm drags in and then get it over with within the first couple of minutes and then get right into heat," he said. Then, while his opponent was controlling the match, Steamboat would give his fans a little bit of hope with a cleverly timed skin-the-cat escape or a similar move. "I could sell for 30 minutes because I'd sprinkle in my shine. It would be during the heat. It would never, ever be in the front part" of the match.

WWE ref Jim Korderas admired the way Steamboat let fans know that although he was down, he was never out. "Like for example, when he's getting his butt handed to him in a match, you never see him lying still," he said. "He's never dead on the mat. He's always moving, he always looks like he's fighting, he's struggling to get to his feet, he's trying to do something. Just little things like that, that add to the overall match." South, who's been around Mid-Atlantic wrestling his whole life, said that Steamboat took the same approach with no-name television opponents as he did in pay-per-view main events with Ric Flair. "He sold for everyone; no matter if it was a job guy, it didn't matter. I don't think he ever went out and squashed anybody. I think Steamboat made a match out of every match he was ever in. Even if he let a guy get on him for just a little bit, he gave everybody something in every match. That's how classy he worked. That's how he showed he was not invincible and people cared for him all that much more."

Necessity was the mother that invented Steamboat's career path to the WWE Hall of Fame, where he was inducted in 2009. Born Richard Henry Blood in West Point, New York, he grew up in St. Petersburg, Florida, wrestling as an amateur against Mike Graham, the son of Florida promoter Eddie Graham, and earning a fourth place in the state tourney in 1970. Most of his attention went to football, though. He was a workhorse running back at Boca Ciega High School at five-foot-eleven and 180 pounds, part of a backfield dubbed "The Muscle Machine" by local sportswriters. He enrolled in St. Petersburg College, then a two-year school, intending to transfer to the University of Tampa and getting involved in coaching football. "This is in the early '70s and my [junior college] guidance counselor was telling me a lot of northern coaches were moving down to Florida to retire or coach a few more years. So the opportunities for a kid out of college without a whole lot of experience were pretty limited." At the time, Steamboat was dating a girl enrolled in flight attendant school in Minneapolis; by chance, her roommate was Donna Gagne, daughter of American Wrestling Association owner-champ Verne Gagne. Steamboat was eking out a living by peddling Kirby vacuum cleaners door-to-door, so he decided to give Gagne's training camp a shot. He trained for weeks by running barefoot on the beaches of Florida, but found the camp was the toughest cardio test he ever endured. Sixteen hopefuls laid down $1,000 each; after a week, only four remained. Gagne had moved his office to a twenty-story building, and trainees came to know every step, Steamboat said. "It was twenty-one stories counting the basement. We'd run up and down the stairs. Then we'd put a guy on your back in a fireman's carry and go up the stairs, switch positions, and then he'd carry you down. Then he'd grab your ankles and you'd go up the stairs on your hands . . . It was brutal."

Richard Blood's debut came in February 1976, and he worked in the AWA for about five months before Gagne sent him to Florida for Eddie Graham, with a careful directive to return ten percent of his paycheck as a fee. "You know, that Rick Blood, that's a hell of a wrestling name. Blood. . . . That's for a heel, though. You're just starting off in the business as a babyface," Graham told him. The promoter decided Blood, though born in New York to a father from Boston and a mother from Japan, could pass as the nephew of Sam Steamboat, a Hawaiian who'd done well in the Sunshine State. A side note to his Florida debut: the ring announcer in that West Palm Beach match announced "Rick Blood" was a no-show that night. "I'm here," Steamboat quietly protested, only to hear the P.A. man tell fans that one Ricky Steamboat was the replacement. "Smile and wave to the fans, kid; smile and wave to the fans," the announcer told him.

George Scott, the legendary booker in the Carolinas, first saw Steamboat on TV in Atlanta, where matchmaker Ole Anderson was using him in opening matches. "Ole was way, way off-base on this one. He didn't think Steamboat was box office and shipped him off over to us. George Scott couldn't wait to get him," said referee Tommy Young. He reffed a twenty-minute draw between Steamboat and Sgt. Jacques (Rene) Goulet at a spot show in Virginia and was an instant believer. "He brought the house down in a broadway [draw]. A prelim broadway. Goodness, that's not easy to do," Young said. Rich Landrum, later the announcer on the *World Wide Wrestling* TV program, was handling ring announcing duties in Richmond, Virginia, when Steamboat first appeared there. "He had not been on TV or anything. He came out billed as Sam Steamboat's nephew or some relative. And the crowd went nuts for him. I looked at him coming to the ring and I said to myself, 'Wow! This kid is really good-looking,' and his wrestling was as good as his looks, if not better. After it was over, I was talking to [promoter] Joe Murnick and I said, 'I don't know what you guys have got planned for Steamboat, but it'd better be good because he's going to end up being your franchise.'"

Rick Steamboat chops Harley Race.

DON FREEDMAN, PETE LEDERBERG COLLECTION

From 1977 to 1985, Steamboat rose to become the top hero in the long history of Mid-Atlantic wrestling; he was a part of the community around Charlotte, owning gyms and competing in bodybuilding contests. Jerry Brisco had been a regular in the region; he and his brother battled Steamboat and Youngblood for the region's world tag team title. "Ricky just had that intensity. Ricky would, I want to use the word 'hulk up,' but maybe 'bulk up' would be better for Ricky, when he'd show that fire, tense his body up. The people knew he was coming after you — and he delivered. He was really good at that," Brisco said. Every hero needs an antagonist, and Flair, another Gagne trainee, was in that spot for Steamboat. They started at it in 1977, when Steamboat won the TV title from Flair. The next year, Flair dragged Steamboat's face along a TV studio concrete floor, to the shrieks of sickened fans. That was no play-acting, Young remembered; abrasions left and right were part of Steamboat's commitment to selling his pain to the crowd. "They hard-wayed that. That was tough. That was brutal.

Flair just rubbed it and Steams said just go ahead and hard-way it and he just rubbed his face right across . . . it was ugly."

Young was the third man in the ring for their classics and probably refereed more bouts between the two than any other official. There's no telling how many times they wrestled; yellowed clippings and old results sheets suggest it was at least 225. "I've done tons of them and God, I loved them all, every one of them," Young said. "Flair told George [Scott], 'Give me Steamboat. I can work something with him.' The rest is history . . . Neither one needed the other. Either one could draw money and did draw money with many others. They certainly complemented each other, no doubt about that." The climax of their feud came in 1989 in a series remembered as one of the best ever. "Every time they wrestled, it was a different match. They were never the same two times and that's a sign of greatness," said journalist Bill Apter.

Steamboat joined the WWE in 1985, and it was a whole new experience, compared to his years in the Carolinas. Vincent K. McMahon overhauled him as Ricky "The Dragon" Steamboat, complete with a monitor lizard or South American caiman, a type of crocodile. "I'll never forget one time, I was sitting in the locker room. There was Jake 'The Snake' Roberts with this 150-pound boa constrictor, there was me with the crocodile, there was the British Bulldog over there with his dog, Koko B. Ware with the parrot Frankie shitting all over the place. It's a damn circus; somebody'll walk in here and think it's a zoo." The highlight of his first WWE run was his match with Randy Savage at WrestleMania III under a Hulk Hogan–Andre the Giant main event. "Savage and I knew at that time that Hogan and Andre were going to draw the show. They were going to be the ones to draw the numbers. Savage and I, we wanted to go steal the show." After fifteen minutes, he won the match and the Intercontinental belt, and the bout is considered one of the best in the annals of WrestleMania.

But his ceiling would be the Intercontinental title. Steamboat, considered better as the challenger, never got a long crack at the very top. He beat Flair for the National Wrestling Alliance title in the middle of their 1989 program and held it for seventy-six days. He took time off from WWE for the birth of Ricky Jr. and his upward push stopped dead in its tracks. "It's just the politics of the business," he said. "When it comes down to the world belt, whether it was NWA at that time, or WWF, when it comes to that call, it's strictly politics. And I just never figured into their political idea. I was good for the level I was at and keeping it at that level — taking it one more step, I was never figured in." He was back in the WWE in 1990 and 1991, breathing fire as he got to the ring, thanks to some training from a carnival act in Florida, before returning to NWA and World Championship Wrestling in early 1991 after the money and career advancement he expected from McMahon failed to materialize. Steamboat would have liked to try a run as a villain. Impossible, said Bob Roop. "As far as him never being a heel, nobody would have bought it. The fans loved him everywhere he wrestled, and he was perhaps the nicest guy I ever worked with. That was no act."

Though he planned to continue wrestling until he was forty-five, Steamboat's career was cut short after he suffered two herniated discs at the base of his spine in an August 1994 match with Steve Austin in California. "We're standing on the top turnbuckle together. It's a simple move where you get a headbutt and you do a flat back bump on your back. He gave me a headbutt and my foot slipped off of the turnbuckle and I came up and landed in a sit-up position on my tailbone," he said. Examined at the Duke University Medical Center, three doctors advised him against re-entering the game at a time when his matinee idol style of babyface was on the wane. "I had a good career in the business, I had a good name, I was happy with everything . . . I don't know how I could have played into the business and the direction it was going," he said.

Steamboat has had his fits and starts with McMahon through the years; he's now working with WWE as a producer and helping out in its feeder territory in Florida while living near Charlotte. "He was just an artist. I don't know how to explain it, other than that," said "Hollywood" John Tatum. "There were much better babyfaces as far as drawing money, I think, but just from the artistic part of it, watching it, being able to work seven days a week, 365 days a year, I would want to work with Ricky Steamboat."

11. EDOUARD CARPENTIER

Was Edouard Carpentier world champion on June 14, 1957, or not? He apparently beat Lou Thesz in Chicago at the International Amphitheatre for the NWA world heavyweight title, splitting the first two falls, with Thesz unable to continue in the third because of a bad back. Chicago promoter Fred Kohler and the National Wrestling Alliance sent notice that the title change had happened, yet politics soon scuttled the plan.

Carpentier did defend the title on a few occasions between the Chicago bout and the August NWA convention, at which point the powers that be decided

ROGER BAKER

Edouard Carpentier could cut an impressive figure anywhere, including a hallway.

that the world title couldn't change hands on an injury after all.

In a 2006 interview, Carpentier lamented the decision. "Although I am not an egoistical person, I would like to be recognized as Edouard Carpentier, the former world champion." Yet the backstage politicking, some of the most fascinating in wrestling lore, meant that Carpentier's claim to the title would indirectly lead to the formation of no less than three other world titles, breakaway promotions that used his accomplishment as a springboard to add legitimacy to their new champion's title.

He has one man to thank for the opportunity to achieve the sport's pinnacle, and the same one to blame for having a dream dashed. What Montreal promoter Eddie Quinn giveth, Eddie Quinn taketh away.

Over the years, many have laid claim to being the one who convinced Edouard Ignacz Weiczorkiewicz, a Frenchman of Russian-Polish descent who had been a teenage member of the French Resistance during World War II, to come to North America and wrestle. Weiczorkiewicz, born outside Lyon, France, on July 17, 1926, had been competing on the European scene since 1950 as Eduardo Weiczkorski (or Wiechorski) and Eddy Wiecz.

In Europe, Carpentier would meet many influential figures, big and small, in his future. There was Verne Gagne, who, like Carpentier, was an alternate on his country's squad at the 1948 Olympics in London — Gagne for the U.S. wrestling team, and Weiczorkiewicz an alternate for the French gymnastics team. Or Eric Tovey, who would become midget wrestling royalty Lord Littlebrook. "I used to be real good with a flying head scissors, and I used to do a somersault off the top rope," Tovey told historian Scott Teal. "You might remember Edouard Carpentier. I taught him how to do that son of a bitch when I was over in Paris for four months. He'd pick me up at the hotel in Paris on his bicycle and take me down to the gym. I'd ride on the crossbar of his bike. He wanted to learn the somersault, so I worked with him and worked with him. He finally got to where he was doin' it good and not hurtin' himself."

Montreal stars such as Yvon Robert, Larry Moquin, and Legs Langevin all crossed paths with him in France and sold him on coming to Quebec, to work with Eddie Quinn. Allegedly, Quinn said, "Who's the fucking midget?" upon laying eyes upon the five-foot-seven, 225-pound newcomer in 1956. Regardless of his initial impression, Quinn soon sunk his talons in deep, changing his protégé's name to Carpentier to capitalize on the fame of the French boxer, Georges Carpentier.

The newcomer's debut, against Angelo Savoldi, was April 18, 1956, at the Montreal Forum. Savoldi recalled that first match. "[The fans] went wild. I lost to him in about fifteen minutes. It was a thirty-minute match. In about fifteen, sixteen minutes, he jumped on my shoulder — how the hell he did it, I don't know — and he rolled me over, and that was it." Within months, Carpentier would revolutionize Canadian wrestling with his acrobatic moves and his impressive physique, shooting to the top of the wrestling world.

Mixing his gymnastic background with knowledge of judo, boxing, karate, aikido, savate, and Greco-Roman wrestling, Carpentier would be hitting front or back flips one moment, or kicking an opponent in the back of the head in the next. "He did the acrobatics that nobody else did. Ricki Starr did some of the things he did, but Edouard did things that a lot of other people couldn't do," said "The Destroyer" Dick Beyer. "When I looked at him, it was a person that I could wrestle with, because I was a wrestling heel. I was a heel and he did babyface things I could work with as a heel."

Quinn led his fan club, sending out press releases and convincing fellow promoters to take a chance on his new find, whom he managed protectively. For years, Carpentier would work three days for Quinn, and the rest of the week abroad.

Years later, Quinn's name was poison to Carpentier's ears. "Oh my, he ripped me off so much," he said in French. "I went to wrestle in New York in front of a packed house, Argentina Rocca was my partner, and Vince [McMahon] Sr. sent my check to Eddie Quinn who then called me to let me know that he had my check, $1,000, and I was jumping with joy as I had never made that much before. I go back the following week for a TV wrestling show and Vince Sr. asked me if I had received the check and I answered, 'Yes I did, thank you very much, wow $1,000, I never made that much for a match.' So following this rematch Vince Sr. sent the check directly to my house, $2,500. So I called Vince

Sr., and tell him there must be a mistake; my first match I received $1,000 and now, a week later, for the rematch, I get $2,500. So Vince Sr. answers, 'There is no mistake, it was $2,500 for the first match and $2,500 for the rematch.' It was Eddie Quinn, who pocketed $1,500 of my money from that first match!"

Quinn knew Carpentier was a moneymaker, and fought to protect his gravy train. A letter Quinn sent to NWA President Sam Muchnick in 1957 was leaked to *New York Daily Mirror* writer Dan Parker:

"Getting back to Carpentier you seem to overlook the fact that Carpentier is my personal property. He does not belong to you or the National Wrestling Alliance. He is not recognized by you and neither does he claim to be NWA champion. He met and defeated Lou Thesz June 14th in Chicago via disqualification. In a return match in Montreal he met and was defeated by Lou Thesz July 24th. You should be able to add two and two. I have consulted my attorney on the matter and they suggested that I write to you and have you return Edouard Carpentier's $10,000. What you are holding it for no one seems to know. If this money has not been returned within ten days from this date, I will have my attorneys turn this matter over to the U.S. Department of Justice and the St. Louis police, c/o the Bunco Squad. My attorneys seem to think this is a combination of blackmail, extortion or grand larceny. Hope this will clarify everything."

It's no wonder that the 1957 phantom title change with Thesz has remained a fascinating passion for historians through the years. The controlling Quinn was on one side, with Carpentier chafing to get away, and the never fully united NWA board on the other, having voted for the title change, apparently to lead to massive rematches after Thesz returned from a major fall overseas tour. The two did have a few rematches, including the aforementioned July 24th bout in Montreal where Thesz hid in the ropes and a frustrated Carpentier slugged special referee Yvon Robert for the DQ; three days later, NWA President Sam Muchnick ruled that Carpentier was still the world champ.

Though the controversy may have bothered Carpentier, it never affected his drawing power. There are few places in the world that he didn't work, but time and time again, he returned to Montreal, which he called home and where he could speak his native language.

Art Williams was a fan in Los Angeles, before becoming a referee. He was a heel fan who fell for Carpentier big time. "I thought he was fantastic, and I still do. Even as a fan when I'd go up to him in the parking lot in San Bernandino, he'd always shake my hand, sign my photo, and have a picture taken," said Williams. "On the mic, he spoke just enough for people to say, 'Well, this guy is the real deal' — which, to me, he was."

The complaints from his opponents, however, were that Carpentier was in it for Carpentier. "Very scientific, but very conceited," Freddie Blassie said in a 2003 *WrestleTalk* interview. "He thought there was only one wrestler and that was Edouard."

Pat Patterson let out a loud raspberry at the mention of "The Flying Frenchman." "You do the best you can. It's like working with a robot," spat Patterson, mystified by Carpentier's appeal. "In southern California, it's full of Mexicans, and it's full of different types of people, and

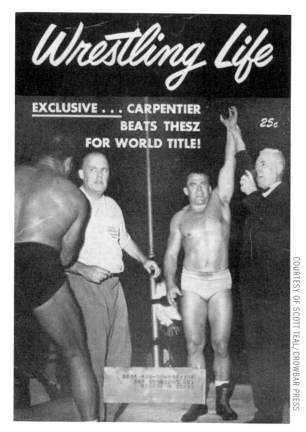

Wrestling Life on August 3, 1957, proclaims Carpentier the new NWA world champion.

you've got a Frenchman that can't speak English. What the fuck? How can you relate to that? You could relate to his look and his work. No, to me, I think Carpentier was very big in Quebec and that's about it."

But there is no denying that Carpentier had a big impact on the history of professional wrestling. Following the NWA world title non-event in 1957, his subsequent defeat in other territories would lead to more "world" titles. With Verne Gagne's win on August 9, 1958, in Omaha — with Chicago promoter Kohler as the referee yet — the American Wrestling Association was created. In January 1960, the Los Angeles promotion announced it was recognizing Carpentier as *its* champion, since he had met all the top title claimants. The World Wrestling Association made it more official on May 27 of that year when Carpentier beat Thesz in L.A.

In Montreal, Quinn would continue to bill Carpentier as the world champion into 1958, often pitting him against "Killer" Kowalski, who had been recognized as the champ in the Quebec territory. "I had a lot of matches with him," said Kowalski. "I did all the work in the ring. I carried him. He was a jumping bean. I'm not being mean here, but a lot of the things he did were not my ideas. But he was all right. He was another Polack." In May 1958, the Kowalski title and Carpentier's claim would be merged into the Atlantic Athletic Commission Big Time Wrestling world title for the Boston/Montreal axis, with Kowalski as champ.

Truly, it was a remarkable four years for a newcomer to North American shores. He would continue to factor into main events across the continent for years to come, winning countless titles — singles and tag belts — with much of his work centered in big-money territories such as New York, St. Louis, the sprawling AWA, California, Toronto, and, of course, Quebec.

He knew that there was a limit to his appeal in one location. "Here in Quebec, wrestling would slow down in late fall, early winter, I would wrestle once or twice a week, so I would go down to L.A. and wrestle for six months and then come back to Quebec," Carpentier said. "What happened was if you wrestled in the same area for too long, no matter how good you are, it seems the fans get bored."

With such a physical style, he kept himself in tip-top shape, and "The Human Trapeze" credited his fitness for keeping him from the wheelchair after wrecked knees and three slipped discs in his back, for which doctors recommended a spinal fusion. Instead he went into a body cast for three months. "I kept exercising with the few muscles I could still move," Carpentier said in a 1973 interview with the Montreal Gazette, "but I gained weight. So you know what I did? The last month, I lived exclusively on water. Two-and-a-half or three gallons a day of Laurentian spring water. It worked wonderfully. It cleaned out my whole system and I lost forty-five pounds. I was living in Côte Saint-Luc then, and one day I just cut off the cast myself, walked out onto the patio, and dived into the swimming pool. My neighbors thought I had gone crazy."

In 1964, he and Montreal frontman Lucien Gregoire were in a car accident, their Cadillac hit head-on by a "carload of hold-up men pursued by the police." That time, Carpentier was off nine months, and used acupuncture to make it through.

In 1971, Paul and Maurice Vachon, backed by Yvon Robert and his son, Yvon Jr., started the Grand Prix Wrestling promotion in opposition to the existing operation, As de la Lutte, run by the Rougeau family, which had featured Carpentier both in the ring and on commentary.

Carpentier is honored at a TOW show in Montreal in 2010.

Naturally, Carpentier was a key figure in the new company, and was its first champion. "He just had that 'it.' People *loved* Edouard Carpentier, especially in Quebec, Eastern Ontario, wherever our TV went from there. In Grand Prix, people just loved the guy," said Sir Oliver Humperdink. "He was a handsome bastard. He had a beautiful smile and everything. He was a great-looking athlete. He had everything it takes to be popular. And there wasn't anything he couldn't do."

Carpentier ended up buying twenty percent of the promotion. "There are two or three people in the wrestling business that I don't like, and he's one of them. He was very difficult," said Paul Vachon. "He was like a spoiled brat. And he was moody. You'd be talking to him or even wrestling him and having a good match, making him look good, and he'd be happy; then you'd twirl something and he'd curl and go sit in the corner and not talk to anybody for a while. He had an insecurity. It's funny. The guy had everything going for him, but the guy was jealous of everybody around him that had any success. And I ended up partners with the son-of-a-gun in Grand Prix Wrestling."

Carpentier felt he always deserved to be in the main event, said Vachon. "He wanted to run things. He would undo things that I did, and spoiled a couple of television contracts and licenses and stuff like that." The Vachons sold their share, while Carpentier stayed until the end, when the promotion folded a few years later.

With his Montreal base, Carpentier was called upon to train a number of French-Canadians right into the 1990s, namely Yvon Robert Jr., Michel "Le Justice" Dubois, who was also the Russian Alexis Smirnoff, Nelson Veilleux, and Luc Poirier. When Andre Rousimoff arrived in Montreal, Carpentier and Frank Valois helped train the Giant, Jean Ferré, at the Grand Prix gym. As well, Carpentier's nephew, Jacques Magnin, wrestled, capitalizing on the family name, sometimes working as André Carpentier and Jacky Carpenter, and in Grand Prix he was Jackie Wiecz.

During the early 1980s, Carpentier wrestled mainly around Quebec, but also, having filled in occasionally on the Rougeau's *Sur le Matelas* TV show and the Grand Prix show, got a gig as the color commentator on *Superstars of Wrestling* for the Gino Brito–led International Wrestling. "*A la semaine prochaine, si Dieu le veut*," he would wish his viewers. "He knew wrestling by heart, all the techniques and everything, so he was a very good wrestling commentator, that's for sure," said Grand Prix ring announcer Fernand Ste-Marie. When the WWF bought the International timeslot, Carpentier was the host of the show that went to all French-speaking markets, doing interviews and commentary until a falling out with the show's producer, Guy Hauray, sent him to the sidelines.

Carpentier's career in-ring was pretty well done by 1984, though he did make it out to a WWF legends battle royal at the Meadowlands in 1987, which was won by his old foe, Lou Thesz. In unpublished notes to his biographer, Kit Bauman, Thesz said that "Carpentier said some nice, hollow things" at the show that he didn't let affect him. "I could never understand why Carpentier left Quinn. Eddie found him living hand to mouth at a small circus in France, a bottom-of-the-barrel situation. Eddie was too good and too generous; he went overboard and overpaid him; he used his friends, including me, to get him over. Some people misconstrue kindness as weakness, and Carpentier began to believe his own publicity."

The last years of his life were spent in relative obscurity, as Carpentier was a shell of his former self, using a walker or a wheelchair and requiring regular visits from a nurse to his Montreal home in the Côte des Neiges district, where he had often shown off his culinary skills and art collection; his family had fractured years ago, his children scattered in France or Ontario. He survived a heart attack in 2000, and died a decade later, at home, on October 30. He had been hospitalized in August, and amputating a leg was discussed. The effect of his death was immediate in the Quebec media — one last run for the Flying Frenchman — as newscasts and newspapers celebrated his colorful life, his old colleagues getting their own chance to shine again. His passing was noted in Canadian Parliament.

His last appearance was for the TOW promotion in Montreal on March 5, 2010, where he was honored at ringside. "We were really nervous that he wouldn't show up," said one of the TOW owners, Marc Blondin, who replaced Carpentier on WWF French broadcasts. "I remember that night was crazy. The cab was there, he did not answer. Finally, he was there at the show. The fans really appreciated him. We were going to get his cab, because he was in a wheelchair, so we were sure that right after the tribute he would leave. But no, he stayed, he wanted to have his wheelchair just beside the ring. He watched the whole show and he was in the back with the wrestlers. A lot of people said he was so bitter with the business, but I didn't find that that night. He was such a star that to be in a wheelchair and not be able to walk, maybe that was what made him bitter. But that night he was feeling good. It was fun."

12. JACK BRISCO

Oklahoma City, Oklahoma. December 12, 1959.
Big Number 77 plowed through the line for nine yards, part of a rhythmic march down the field as Blackwell High School threatened to take the lead from Ada High in the Oklahoma Class A football championship game. Less than forty-eight hours earlier, Freddie Joe "Jack" Brisco was listed as doubtful with a sprained ankle he suffered in a semifinal the week before. But Brisco learned early in life how to take obstacles in stride and deal with them without fanfare. Part Chickasaw and Choctaw, Brisco helped raise brother Jerry, cooking, ironing, and supervising his homework, after his father ran out on them and his mother had to work to support the family in poor, rural Oklahoma. "He was able to overcome so much in his life, but none of it seemed to really get to him or bother him. From a young age, he really never let anything faze him," his wife Jan said. So Brisco, an All-State fullback and defensive tackle, recruited by big-time college programs, bit his lip and wrapped his ankle tightly. Against Ada, he turned in one of the best performances of his career, rushing thirteen times for sixty-four yards. But Blackwell's drive stalled when Brisco was stopped

The heir apparent: Jack Brisco prepares to defend his Florida championship.

for no gain on a key play and Ada pulled away in the fourth quarter. It was the last football game he ever played. He turned to his other passion, wrestling, a better outlet for self-reliance. "No matter what anyone else on the team did, if I was to have my hand raised, it was totally dependent on my abilities and what I was able to accomplish on the mat," he reflected in his 2003 autobiography, Brisco. "I didn't like losing at anything."

Ithaca, New York. March 28, 1964.

The losses ate at Brisco much more than the victories satiated him. He had rolled through the 1963–64 wrestling season at Oklahoma State, with only a draw against All-American Ken Hines of Colorado State marring his record. Three pinfalls sent him to the finals of the NCAA tournament against Harry Houska of Ohio University. By the time Brisco, trimmed to a wiry 191 pounds, walked onto the mat at Cornell University's Barton Hall, a World War I–era fieldhouse used as a military drill hall, the Oklahoma State Cowboys had already wrapped up their 24th national championship. Now it was time to add to the three consecutive state heavyweight wrestling championships he'd won at Blackwell High. For the first minute, Houska and Brisco barely touched, swatting hands and circling. Brisco went for his signature fireman's carry, intending to bring Houska to the mat and ride him, but his hands slipped off. A video of the match shows Brisco wiping his hands on his black tights; it was petroleum jelly and Houska had put it on his back and shoulders. An official wiped off Houska but foreign substance aside, he was much too quick for Brisco, reversing him and riding him for most of the match en route to a 6-3 win. Brisco would return to the NCAA tournament the next year to win the 191-pound class, finishing his Cowboy career with only one loss, to Houska. But the national title wouldn't dislodge what was stuck in his craw. Forty years removed from Ithaca, the subject came up with Bill Murdock, a North Carolina author with whom he collaborated on his autobiography. "When I interviewed him, he told me second-by-second of the match with Houska," Murdock said. "When I asked him about the guy he beat from Wisconsin for the national title, he said, 'I pinned him in the second period.' I said, 'Well, tell me more about the match,' and he just didn't recall that much."

Miami, Florida. August 11, 1971.

Miami News sportswriter Paul Kaplan captured the scene at the Miami Beach Convention Center. A young Asian girl had thrown herself backward in her ringside seat in exultation, her eyes rolling toward the ceiling. Men, women, and children rushed to the ring in celebration. Brisco's two-year pursuit of Dory Funk Jr.'s National Wrestling Alliance world championship had paid off. "My God, Jack won," the woman exclaimed. Only, he hadn't. Brisco beat Funk in two straight falls, but the second was on a disqualification when Funk tossed him over the ropes, and the title couldn't change hands on a DQ. Enraged, Brisco re-entered the ring and pummeled the champ until he was bloody, then beat up referee Leo Garibaldi.

Another night at the office for Brisco and Funk. During Funk's reign as world champion from 1969 to 1973, he fought Brisco forty-one times, mostly in Florida, and that's just the number recorded from clippings and old results sheets. It was wrestling's version of Ali–Frazier, with Brisco in the role as the favorite, the title just eluding him again and again. As Funk explained, "He was a hero to the rock fans, he was a hero to the working man, he was a hero to the old retirees. Eddie Graham, in the promotion of Jack Brisco, made sure he was a hero to everybody. He was a natural for me to work with, traveling to Florida as NWA world champion. I was absolutely the heel every time we went into the match, to work the match, but I didn't have to scream and yell on television. I could go on television and say, 'My opponent's a great athlete, he's an NCAA wrestling champion. I don't dislike him. The only thing about it is I'm a little better than Jack.' That's all the heat that was necessary and we let the match speak for itself."

As a kid, Jack always envisioned himself in a championship match, like the one in Miami Beach. "We became fans from going to the corner drugstore every Saturday morning and getting the wrestling magazines out and looking through the wrestling magazines till the store owner chased us out, so we were wrestling fans long before we were wrestlers," he said. Brisco turned pro less than two months after winning the NCAA title, with the help of Oklahoma promoter Leroy McGuirk, only to find a lot of the pro business was beyond his control. When he went to Dory Funk Sr.'s Amarillo, Texas, territory, he was used as fodder for Dory Jr. and ended up as a referee. His break came when Joe Scarpa (Chief Jay Strongbow) helped him get booked in Florida in September 1968. Graham groomed him for the world title, showing fans Brisco could be counted on to take care of himself. "What Eddie Graham did was to systematically, over a period of time, create impossible situations that you thought, 'He cannot overcome this.' And he overcame it," said J.J. Dillon. "He would have three guys jump Jack Brisco, one guy holding him down, another guy holding him by the head and feet. The other guy would reach out for him and Jack would small-cradle him and the referee went one-two-three. He's got three guys holding him down and he wins the match."

Houston, Texas. July 20, 1973.

Under other circumstances, the date might have been March 2, 1973. That was when Brisco was scheduled to take Funk's title in the Sam Houston Coliseum. But three days earlier, Funk was injured when he rolled his truck on his Texas ranch, and he was a scratch. Brisco, and many insiders, were convinced it was a ploy by Dory Sr. to prevent his son from losing in the middle of the ring to another wrestler, particularly an Oklahoman. Full-page magazine spreads of a hospitalized Funk did little to soothe Brisco.

Instead, his championship run would begin nearly four months later, after besting interim champ Harley Race in Houston. Race took the first fall — unusual because the challenger ordinarily wins it as a way of involving the crowd. But now Brisco was in the same predicament, fighting the odds, which Graham loved to dramatize. He broke out of a Race headlock and put him in a figure-four leglock for the second fall. In a tribute to his hero, former champion Lou Thesz, Brisco used a Thesz press, a modified front flying body scissors, to surprise Race, who was readying for a back body drop off the ropes, and won the match. Immediately, he was overcome with a sense of dread. "I was scared to death. It was something I had always dreamed of, something I worked years for and something I was finally going to get to attain and I was just scared to death that I wouldn't be able to maintain the prestige of the belt," he said. As a credential, Brisco quickly beat Thesz three times in less than three months. "It was really ironic because Lou Thesz being my idol and everything," he said upon his 2005 induction into the Pro Wrestling Hall of Fame. "When the announcer said, 'In this corner, the NWA heavyweight champion of the world,' I expected him to say Lou Thesz, and he said my name, and that's when I knew I was in trouble and had big shoes to fill."

With his smooth, quick-paced, athletic style, Brisco was probably the most gifted champ in NWA history to that point. But NWA protocol called for its titleholder to enter random territories and make the local hero — Jose Lothario,

Red Bastien, Johnny Weaver — shine by working as a subtle bad guy. "The only one that really had a problem with it was Jack himself. Jack was a babyface babyface, if you know what I'm trying to say," Race said. "He just looked so good, and he made so many babyface moves during a match that when they were trying to force him to be a heel, he was such a good babyface that it was hard to do." Another stumbling point — as champ, Brisco had to work with folks whose ringwork was a poor fit for his. "I never was a gimmick guy . . . It was not my style and whenever I had to wrestle one of them it was tough on me," he said. "Dick the Bruiser and The Sheik, I just never enjoyed being in the ring with them." He held the NWA title for two and a half years, except for a one-week swap with Giant Baba that netted him $25,000, but he acknowledged he was dragging at the end, waking up in the morning and grabbing his airline ticket to see where he was, and where he was headed. Regardless, Florida booker Louie Tillet said, Brisco carried himself like a champ. "He knew how to get over, he knew how to sell. Then when it was time for him to lose a match, we always found the right way to do it, but he was always there to do it. There was no complaints, there was no bad attitude. He was just great."

Atlanta, Georgia. April 9, 1984.

To some wrestling fans, it was like Chamberlain selling out at Munich. The Briscos owned about thirty percent of the stock of Georgia Championship Wrestling, and they were upset with the way co-owner and booker Ole Anderson was running things. On April 9, 1984, Vincent K. McMahon flew into Atlanta, where lawyers worked day and night to strike a deal selling GCW to the WWF for a reported $100,000 for Jack and $90,000 for Jerry. On July 14, WWF programming took over the NWA's timeslot on Superstation WTBS from Atlanta, a day known as "Black Saturday" in wrestling annals. Brisco was confident relying on his own judgment, which told him not to let Anderson handle his investment. McMahon was running wrestling territories out of business, and the Briscos were among the few to get out before they went under. "We saw the handwriting on the wall," Jack said.

To say they were despised by old-line NWA types would be an understatement. They became heels in and out of the ring; Jack and Jerry had switched to the dark side for the first time in their careers to swap the world tag team title in the Carolinas with Ricky Steamboat and Jay Youngblood. "I think the time was right. I was getting a little older and it's hard to be the babyface. When you

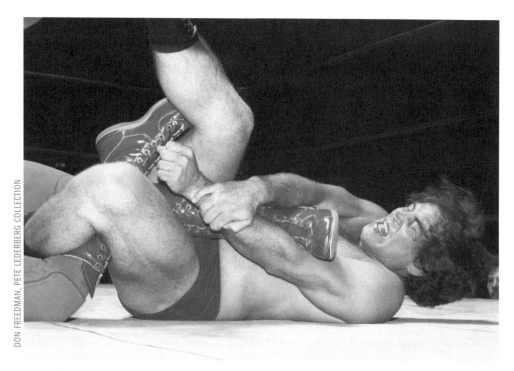

Jack Brisco ties up Austin Idol in a figure four leglock.

get to be a certain age, people would rather see you heel than babyface," Brisco said. Their betrayal led to their banishment from Jim Crockett Promotions, and at one point, Anderson called Brisco and threatened to have the Road Warriors come to his hometown of Tampa, Florida, and do a number on him.

It wasn't the first run-in they had with Anderson. One night in Columbia, South Carolina, Ole and Gene Anderson were scheduled to work against the Briscos when word came from referee Sonny Fargo to take it easy on Jack, who was suffering from stomach flu. "Ole says, 'Well, we'll see about that,'" said Boris Zhukov, who was wrestling that night and calls it a favorite Brisco memory. "When they got out there, Ole started messing with him and Jack started shooting on Ole and just turned him into a pretzel. Gene wouldn't tag in. He said Ole pissed off Jack and he wasn't going to get involved. What was neat was the way the dressing rooms were set up; you had babyfaces and heels on both sides of the auditorium watching the match. When Ole got to the dressing room, he was sweating like a pig and he says, 'God, it's hard to believe a guy with arms so small could make you hurt so bad.'"

Newark, New Jersey. February 10, 1985.

After the sale, Jack and Jerry went to the WWF. George Scott, their booker in the Carolinas, was running things in the federation by then, and talked Jack into working a program with tag team champions Dick Murdoch and Adrian Adonis. "I didn't really even want to go for George. My brother Jerry wanted to give it one more shot and he wanted to work that territory. I had worked there before — just doing shots, I never worked the territory. But Jerry wanted to do it real bad, so I just went back to please him," Brisco said.

From September 1984 until February 1985, they worked almost exclusively in tag matches, winding up against Roddy Piper and Bob Orton Jr. Jack was forty-three, wrestling twenty-somethings, when he sensed things were getting beyond his control. Self-preservation came on the heels of a miserable flight into the Newark, New Jersey, airport from Pittsburgh, amid sleet, snow, and 40 mph winds. Cars were buried under piles of snow and the Briscos walked around for an hour, unable to find their vehicle. "I kept hearing these airplanes taking off to the south and I knew one of them was going to Florida. I turned to [Jerry] and I told him, the next one of those planes heading south, I'm going to be on it," Brisco said. He went to Tampa and was cold turkey out of the business, working at his family's auto body shop, enjoying life, and spending a lot of time with wife Jan and a new love, stock car racing. "I've seen so many athletes stay too long, past their prime, then retire and come back out of retirement and continue to where they didn't really belong and I didn't want to be one of those people," he said.

He suffered a life-and-death back injury in June 1999 after a growth wrapped around his spine, leading to an agonizing surgery. Brisco and his wife joined a Tampa YMCA so he could rehab in a pool; when trainers told him after a year that he'd progressed as much as he could, Brisco said he knew better. As determined as ever, he tripled the weights he was lifting and cashiered his walker. He died February 1, 2010, at sixty-eight, following complications from heart surgery. After his death, members of the Y reached out to Jan, and their quiet condolences explained everything about Jack Brisco. "When I started hearing from people, they had no idea who he was," she said. "All they knew is that he was Jack from the YMCA. He was the guy who was on the treadmill next to them or riding the bike. I had so many people that told me they had no idea. He just enjoyed their company and enjoyed their friendship, and so his celebrity never mattered. It wasn't important to him."

13. BOBO BRAZIL

In 1947, Houston Harris was making fifty bucks a week punching a time clock in a foundry in Benton Harbor, Michigan, without much education under his belt. When he died more than fifty years later, it was not out of the question to mention him in the same breath with Jackie Robinson. Harris didn't have Robinson's sweeping cultural significance, of course, but as the sport's pre-eminent African-American wrestler, he confronted humiliating discrimination, yet his popularity and low-key manner helped to make promoters and fans less conscious of color. Killer Kowalski wrestled him dozens of times and remembered how he had to slip Brazil into hotels and restaurants that refused him service, even in the Northeast. "Some of these hotel managers had come to the arenas, and paid to see him wrestle me and cheered Brazil, but then when he wanted to rent a room to sleep for the night, they apologized and refused him. I'd later quietly sneak him into my room to share it with me later on, in the middle of the night which I did many, many times. It was very ugly, an ugly time and it happened in so many towns around the country," Kowalski said in 1993 at Mike Lano's *Wrestling Wreality* forum in St. Louis. "Bobo or Bearcat [Wright] or Sailor [Art Thomas] would act like it didn't bother them, but you always knew in your heart that it hurt them very deeply. I could feel their disappointment in their fellow man and the hurt."

The future member of the WWE Hall of Fame and the Professional Wrestling Hall of Fame didn't come from much. He was born on a cotton farm in rural Arkansas on July 10, 1924, and his father died when he was only seven. His family moved to East St. Louis, Illinois, and then he headed to Benton Harbor, where relatives lived, picking fruit for fifty cents a container and driving a truck that carried produce from the fields around the small city. Harris was working at a steel mill and exercising at a local armory, when he was spotted by "Jumping" Joe Savoldi, the famous wrestler and football player who promoted on and off in the Midwest. Savoldi saw something in Harris and worked with him in trade for menial labor — Harris hauled the ring and set it up at spot shows with Savoldi's son Joe Jr. A grandson, J.G. Savoldi, picks it up from there: "The ring was held up by a series of ropes, which were tied to spikes driven deep into the ground. As Houston would swing the sledgehammer to drive in the support spikes for the ring, Joe Jr. would hold them in place and pray that Houston wouldn't miss the mark." His first recorded match was March 29, 1948, in Benton Harbor, where he went to a thirty-minute draw with Armand Myers. There was no segregation in Savoldi's bookings; wrestling as "Huston Harris, The Black Panther," Brazil was in integrated matches from the start of his career against wrestlers such as Jim Spencer and Pete Schuh. "Joe Savoldi trained him to be the honest athlete in the ring and not to take short shots on anybody to win a match. Joe instilled in Bobo the ability to be a crowd's friend, right to the end," said former wrestler and manager Percival A. Friend, who knew Brazil for almost forty years.

A lot of the credit for developing Harris also goes to Rex Sheeley, who wrestled him multiple times in 1949 and 1950 in Benton Harbor and St. Joseph,

DAVE BURZYNSKI

Classic Bobo Brazil, with the Detroit-based version of the U.S. title.

Michigan. Sheeley helped with his training and eventually booked Harris into those towns after Savoldi left the business. "Houston looked far better than the average preliminary man the first time we worked out. Only experience gave me the advantage but it wasn't long before I was taking the falls and Houston set off for bigger opponents and prizes," he said in a 1953 interview. "Houston had trouble reading and writing, but you couldn't fool him in the ring and he learned holds fast."

Using a sequined satin cape stitched together by his wife Lois, Savoldi came

up with a ring identity of "Bubu Brasil" of South America, which morphed into Bobo Brazil when he started wrestling in Chicago in 1950. Recalling those matches in 1957, Brazil said he wasn't all that sure that he wanted to reach beyond his Michigan home. "I had a battered-up old heap and made twenty stops to pump air into the tires," he said. But television helped bring Brazil to a national audience, and fans could see that a black man could defeat a white villain without the sky tumbling down. He joined "Whipper" Billy Watson in a headline tag team in Toronto in 1952, and headed to California, where he held the International TV tag title with newcomer Wilbur Snyder. To wrestling writer Thomas Cummins, Brazil was about the only good thing going in the territory. "The year 1954 was one of many changes for wrestling in this area; not all those changes were for the better. Probably the best that can be said for it, is that it was the year of Bobo Brazil's entry into our mat scene," Cummins said. "This mammoth Canadian, who arrived just after the new year and had yet to suffer defeat in the territory as of Thanksgiving Day, was the difference between profit and loss for most local promoters." Brazil called his finishing headbutt a "coco butt," and it was his signature move for his entire career.

He had a big feud over the U.S. championship with Dick the Bruiser in Detroit in 1960, and headed to New York for Vincent J. McMahon in 1962. Willie Gilzenberg, promoting in New Jersey, had dollar signs in his eyes when he saw Brazil and initiated a scheme that would cheapen Buddy Rogers' National Wrestling Alliance world title. "You know how many places Rogers and Bobo could draw big — real big. In every city in the United States where there is a colored population. I would be willing to wager that Rogers and Bobo could draw at least $150,000 in Yankee Stadium or at the Polo Grounds," Gilzenberg wrote Jack Pfefer. No doubt with Rogers' acquiescence, Gilzenberg tried to pull off a fast one in Newark, New Jersey, that August, when Brazil beat Rogers by count-out and won brief billing as champ to set up a big-money rematch. No formal NWA recognition was forthcoming, though.

In Los Angeles, Brazil did win a world title, the World Wrestling Alliance championship, from "Killer" Buddy Austin, and never actually lost it. The Los Angeles promotion rejoined the NWA and decided to acknowledge Gene Kiniski as top man. To settle the score, Brazil and Kiniski, who fought dozens of times, went to an hour-long draw in the L.A. Olympic Auditorium in December 1968. In the end, the title probably meant less to Brazil, as Kiniski said he didn't need a belt to draw fans. "Bobo was a hot property everywhere he went," Kiniski said. "A very big man, but very agile. Handsome guy for his size." Jeff Walton, the long-time publicist, announcer, and promoter in southern California, said Brazil's unpretentious manner resonated with fans of every race and ethnicity. "What really got him over was his speaking. He was a big guy, but he was mellow. He'd be very low, very quiet, and he'd go on the interview and he'd say, 'Folks, come out and support Bobo. I cannot win this match without you being here.' Very simple, no yelling, no screaming. He came across very humbly. 'Just come out and support me and I won't let you down. I guarantee you that. You're the ones that won the matches for me.' And I think that's what got him over," Walton

COURTESY OF SCOTT TEAL/CROWBAR PRESS

"Bubu" Brasil early in his career.

said. "He was a big guy, but he didn't come across as a big guy. He came across as an average Joe and he truly was a nice guy."

And then there was The Sheik. Patton had Rommel, Eliot Ness had Al Capone, and Brazil had The Sheik. They fought as early as May 1956 and they were still going at it in the '90s. No one keeps such records, but if they didn't lock up as much as any two wrestlers in history, they're certainly in the top tier. Brazil was one of the few wrestlers allowed to pin The Sheik's shoulders to the mat and take his U.S. championship, once via a fast count from special ref Lord Athol Layton and another time in May 1971 in a chain match. "Supermouth" Dave Drason (Burzynski), who worked in Detroit for years and managed The Sheik at the end of his career against Brazil, said the blend hit just the right spot. "The best way I can describe the longevity is almost like a rock and roll band like the Rolling Stones. The same thing with Sheik and Bobo. Sheik was hardcore; there's no other way to put it. He was chaotic, no rhyme or reason, but Bobo brought wrestling into their matches, so it wasn't always the no-holds-barred kind of stuff. He would make it seem like a contest," Drason said. "Without a doubt, he was the greatest wrestler of color ever to appear in the squared circle."

Brazil did in fact break several color barriers. He was the first black allowed to wrestle a white man in Indiana — that was Hans Herrmann in 1960. Wrestler Mike DuPree knew Brazil well on the Indiana circuit later on, and said he helped make it acceptable for a white fan to root for an African-American. "He was pro wrestling's Jackie Robinson in these parts," DuPree said. "Growing up around a bunch of white bigots, I can attest to how over he was with that crowd, so yes, he was over." He also was in the first integrated match in Georgia a decade later. While Brazil didn't talk a lot about race, it had to be on his mind. When Rip Hawk got booked in two places at once in the 1960s, he missed matches with Brazil in Milwaukee and Indianapolis. They finally got together in Atlanta, and Brazil quietly asked if Hawk didn't like to wrestle him because he was black. "I said, 'Man, I hope you didn't get the wrong idea because one thing about you Bobo, I love to work with you and I think you're a great guy.' I meant that when I told him that and I still mean it today," Hawk said. "It's funny how little things could upset a guy as big as Bobo, over 300 pounds . . . He was one fantastic person."

Though a towering figure at six-foot-six, Brazil had ways to convince audiences that he was getting thrashed to within an inch of his life. At five-foot-nine, Roger Kirby strained to reach Brazil's chin. "How in the hell am I going to get heat? People are going to feel sorry for me," Kirby recalled thinking. "He said, 'Son, when I'm laying on my back, I'm only about fourteen, fifteen inches thick.' I looked at him, like, 'What are you talking about?' Bobo looked at me so serious. 'Just get me off my feet. Even if I'm on one knee, you're taller than I am.' That was the secret." Jim Lancaster first met Brazil when he was a young fan at Hara Arena in Dayton, Ohio, and worked up the nerve to ask if his head was so hard that he could knock a hole in a nearby concrete wall. "Yup, I sure could," Brazil said. In the '70s, Lancaster wrestled him and was impressed with the way Brazil could sell, spittle shooting out of his mouth whenever he was choked. "He'd pull you to the corner where it looked like you were pushing him, but he's actually pulling you. He'd sell, let you get your stuff in, clearly identify that you were the heel, and let you get your four or five minutes in. By that point, I was no longer convinced he could bust a hole in the concrete wall," Lancaster said. "When he did his headbutt, he always hit his thumb. He always put his thumb on your forehead and that was his target. He didn't take a lot of bumps; he didn't give you a lot of bumps."

Ricky O'Toole (Brogdon), agreed with Lancaster. "Bo did not have much of a wrestling finesse or background. His uniqueness, size, and finish to kick butt on a good heel is all that folks, blacks and whites, wanted to see Bo do," said O'Toole, who first met him at a TV taping for The Sheik in 1970. "I was the lucky one. He pulled part of the couch we were dressing and lacing boots up on, and treated me as though he and I worked over the last ten years. He always treated the new meat with respect." Drason said Brazil taught him an entirely different way of managing, one that made perfect sense after he thought about it. Drason was reaching into the usual bag of heel manager tricks, pulling trunks or tripping up the good guy. "He'd say, 'I know you're there. I know what you're going to do and I know when you're doing it. So don't pull my trunks. Put your hand there. Let me sell it. If you pull my leg, put your hand there. I'll sell it. Don't confine me.' That way, he was free and easy. With him, it worked beyond belief."

Brazil was laid back, cheerfully calling everybody he met "champ," with a cigar, deck of cards, and Canadian Club always at the ready. But you didn't want to mess with him. At Verne Gagne's direction, Ox Baker once roughed up a brawny skeptic who claimed pro wrestling was a bunch of garbage. "I rubbed a little skin off his head. I wrestled Bobo a week later. He brought a melon in his hand. He said, 'Ox, I don't like to get hurt.' I said, 'What do you mean?' He said, 'If you hit me too hard' — and he took that melon and slapped it against his head, smashed it. My eyes got big as saucers, and I thought I was a coward. I said, 'Mr. Bobo, you'll never know I'm in the ring!'"

Brazil toured nationally well into his fifties; he traded the U.S. title in the Carolinas with Blackjack Mulligan and Ric Flair in 1977 and worked for the WWE with Rocky Johnson as his partner in 1984. He ended up holding the Detroit version of the U.S. championship more than a dozen times before the city's wrestling business went under in 1980; he then headed to Indianapolis to work steadily for several years in the World Wrestling Association, winning the WWA title at one point. The paydays weren't great, but DuPree, who minded Brazil's wallet and his .38 chrome-plated gun for him, said "Bo" worked for the sake of working. "One time we were going to Warsaw, Kentucky, from I think, Carrolton, Kentucky. Anyway, the car we were in was a bit small for him, and as he was bending down to get in, he hit himself with the door, busting him open right between the eyes. He said, 'DuPree, in all the years I've been in the business, I never got color, now I juice myself with a car door.' I just looked at him and said, 'And you call yourself the king of the coco butt.' He had a pretty good gaff mark from that door."

As a promoter, Lancaster used him on independent shows as a goodwill ambassador who came early and stayed late, graciously meeting with the show sponsor and mingling with fans. By that point, Brazil's body was breaking down and he was suffering from diabetes.

Lancaster said he thought Brazil would not have minded dying in the ring. "He wanted to be so much a part of the business. He wanted to be taken out feet first; I honestly believe that," Lancaster said. "He was just the kind of guy that wanted to stay in the business and he was so loved." Brazil and his wife Lenora ran a restaurant in Benton Harbor, and a community center in his hometown was named for him. When he died on January 20, 1998, he was survived by four of the six children from his marriage to Lenora, and several other children, grandchildren, and great-grandchildren. "Bobo never knew the word color," Friend said. "He treated everybody on an equal basis no matter what he faced.

Two of the most intertwined names in wrestling history, Bobo Brazil vs. The Sheik, here with boxing legend Joe Louis as the referee in Detroit's Cobo Hall.

He was more than just a phenomenal athlete but he was a true gentleman from the word go. He loved the fans and they loved him back."

14. "WHIPPER" BILLY WATSON

The Whipper Watson Telethon, on the Barrie, Ontario–based CKVR television station in 1973, was advertised as a thirty-hour event, but the telethon had to take a three-hour hiatus for CBC's *Hockey Night in Canada*. Harold Ballard, the owner of the Toronto Maple Leafs, however, believed in "The Whip" so much that he not only allowed scrawls to run in southern Ontario on CBC affiliates to advertise the fundraiser, but he had the logo painted on the ice for all of Canada to see.

Ever a man of action, Billy Watson had suffered greatly when a car hit him as he was loading a fireplace screen in his car trunk on November 30, 1971, on an icy road in Toronto. It took him five months to recover from the three-and-a-half-hour surgery to the shattered left knee and leg that was nearly severed;

Whipper Watson was a huge supporter of Easter Seals and here introduces a young fan to the audience.

in a wheelchair for a year, Watson would use a cane for the rest of his life. Throwing himself into rehabilitation, he learned that the province of Ontario only had two therapeutic pools.

He approached CKVR about changing that, raising money through a telethon for a pool in nearby Newmarket, which had the largest hospital in the area. Whipper lined up the stars, calling in favors, and the result was $600,000 in donations, well above the quarter-million goal modestly set by the organizers.

"It was a true community effort rather than appealing to the altruism of individuals watching a show," said the telethon's producer, Bill French, recalling the initial pitch Watson made. "He was a very focused individual when he wanted to do something. I'll tell you, [at] the first meetings there was reluctance for doing it, because all of a sudden you're giving up all these broadcast hours, there's no remuneration, and, of course, the company was for profit." And Watson didn't just lend his name; he scrutinized the board members and made sure no one got any free lunches out of the money raised for years afterward. The Whipper Watson Rehabilitative Foundation was formed with the extra money, and until it was rolled into the hospital's larger foundation, ran the pool, named after Watson, until 2009.

There are similar traces of Watson throughout Ontario. In Keswick, there is the W.J. Watson Public School. He's a Member of the Order of Canada (1974), a recipient of the Ontario Medal for Good Citizenship and a member of the Order of Ontario; the City of Toronto gave him an award of merit, and York University presented him with an honorary degree. Whipper worked with the Easter Seal Society of Ontario for 37 years, the Ontario Society for Crippled Children, the Canadian Paraplegic Association, the Multiple Sclerosis Society; did hospital fundraising, championed weight loss with Pounds for People — where he slimmed down in exchange for donations. And there are more than a few old-timers who still proudly have their Whipper's Safety Club buttons, or a Whipper weight set, or maybe an empty bottle of Whipper Watson soda.

"People say I give a lot of my time and effort but they don't understand that I get back far more than I give," Watson said in 1984. Two decades earlier, while unsuccessfully campaigning for federal office as a member of the Progressive Conservative party, he talked about charity, a lesson he learned decades earlier from the legendary Conn Smythe, owner of the Toronto Maple Leafs. "I feel anybody in the public eye — with influence in any way — and who can afford it, should contribute some service to the community. I am lucky to have found my way into such work."

Watson would never have had his pulpit to spread his charitable works without professional wrestling, though.

Born William John Potts in East York, Ontario, on July 25, 1917, his father was killed in France two weeks before the end of World War I and he was raised by his mother and step-father, whom he resented. An outstanding athlete in everything from swimming to hockey to softball, a thirteen-year-old Potts landed in the local YMCA, where trainer Phil Lawson taught him amateur wrestling skills; Lawson also suggested heading to England to wrestle where lightweights were valued, which Potts did in 1936.

Sailing over on a cattle boat bound for Cardiff, Wales, the four Toronto friends, all under 200 pounds — Whinnet Watson, "Hangman" Bill Potts, Al "Krusher" Korman, and Kenneth "Tiger" Tasker — would find themselves linked for years to come, though somewhat confusingly in the case of Watson and Potts. At one point, with Whinnet at the top of the bill, he was unable to perform and Potts stepped in. The Watson name stuck, and adding the Irish Whip (learned from a Japanese wrestler) to his repertoire, Potts became forevermore Whipper Watson. Whinnet Watson became Pat Flanagan, a life-long friend to the man who stole his name. "He was Uncle Whinnet to me when I was a kid growing up," said Phil Watson, The Whip's youngest son.

Watson worked around England from 1936 to 1940. In July 1940, he escaped with a new bride, Patricia Utting, their convoy of passenger ships escorted across the Atlantic by British warships as the bombs were dropping.

Back in Canada, unable to serve his country because of a misplaced thumb to the eye that left him with only ten percent vision on one side, he pitched his talents to Toronto mat mogul Frank Tunney. His advance publicity had gone unheeded. "Frank didn't even pick up the box at customs," chuckled Watson. "Hadn't even heard of me. I had to show him what I could do before I got anything but preliminary bouts." Initially working the Toronto-Cleveland corridor, Watson quickly moved up the cards. In 1941, Tunney had Watson win a tournament to challenge for the NWA world title, and his 1942 battles with Nanjo Singh gained Watson a whole new following and respect for dealing with the madman, who, years later, would end up in prison for killing his wife in Philadelphia.

Lord Athol Layton, an Australian import to Toronto, learned the hard way what it was like to oppose The Whip. "When I first came to this country, I was like a lamb being led to slaughter, so to speak," he told radio host Larry Solway in 1974. "That is to say that I didn't realize the power of the local boy, and the local boy in this city, as you know, was Whipper Billy Watson. So that whatever I did in the ring, I couldn't do the right thing. If I am to throw a big judo chop at somebody, like The Sheik, everybody would cheer. But if you hit the Whipper with a chop, then it was like signing your death warrant in this city." And that trickled down to Layton's two sons, too, who would be forced to fight "the lads at school [that] belonged to the Whipper Watson Safety Club."

The rest of the country would follow with the national broadcasts by CBC out of Toronto after World War II ended, and Watson's drawing power across Canada was unparalleled.

Emile Dupre was a young wrestler on cards in Atlantic Canada. He said the first time Watson came to New Brunswick, the show was almost an hour late starting because "the lineup was about a quarter of a mile long to get into the old stadium in Moncton." Ever the opportunist, Dupre had gotten someone to print up postcards with Whipper's picture, and hired kids to peddle them to the people in the line-up at fifty cents a piece. "It had only cost me twenty bucks. They sold the whole thing and came back knocking on the dressing room, 'Do you have any more of them pictures?' As a matter of fact, I made more money with my pictures than I did with my payoff for wrestling on the card. They were asking, where did they come from? Because everybody would go get them autographed. Watson would ask, 'Where'd you get these pictures?' 'Some kids were selling them in the lineup out there.' He didn't know it was me."

While traveling the country, Watson was always on the lookout for new talent. In Calgary, Stu Hart said Watson was intrigued by "Bulldog" Dick Brower. "I sent him down to Toronto then, and Bulldog Brower became a superstar. He wrestled Whipper Watson about 500 times," said Hart in 1997. "Watson got rich wrestling him, the same with [Gene] Kiniski."

Ah yes, Kiniski; their names are intertwined like Funk-Brisco, Piper-Hogan and Gagne-Bockwinkel.

"I wrestled him so many, many times. I think I wrestled him in every city and village in Canada. In fact, the first time we met in Newfoundland, my God, you couldn't get near the airport. They had the largest

A young Whipper Watson, with an early title.

crowd in the history of Newfoundland to welcome him," recalled Kiniski.

Well past their days in the ring, with Whipper in Vancouver for a fund-raiser, Kiniski took his old foe to his son's bar across the border in Pt. Roberts, Washington. "We had a nice visit about the old days. I said, 'My God, Whip, it's just unreal. Seeing you now, it was a gift to wrestle you.' He said, 'What do you mean?' I said, 'I took a shit-kicking, but the bottom line is we all went to the bank, and we were always putting in and not taking out.' He said, 'Yeah, but you were always a smart businessman.' It paid off for me."

Like Kiniski, Watson could work with the media. The subject of countless profiles, he always dressed dapperly and shone on TV talk shows. Jim Coleman, a Canadian sportswriting legend, called Watson "the living embodiment of all

Elvis Presley meets The Whip during one of Elvis' 1957 Canadian shows.

the ideals of the Boy Scout movement and the Legion of Decency. Watson is as handsome as Robert Taylor, as powerful as the *SS Queen Mary* and as persistent and uncompromising as Dick Tracy in his efforts to exterminate evil. In moments of supreme exasperation he is likely to mutter 'Oh, fudge!' but otherwise conduct is exemplary," wrote Coleman in *Maclean's* in 1944. "Watson destroys his opponents with the air of Sir Galahad repelling scorpions, and the customers love him to pieces."

With his stardom in Canada and Tunney's strength in the promotional brotherhood, Watson was accorded two runs as the world champion, beating "Wild Bill" Longson in February 1947 for the National Wrestling Association title, and losing to Lou Thesz two months later, and, in March 1956, taking the National Wrestling Alliance crown, beating and losing to Thesz, who had been sidelined by a fractured ankle.

Tunney's son, Eddie, said that while Watson never had a percentage of the Toronto office, he did go in with Tunney on a percentage of St. Louis, and owned the promotional rights to a number of smaller Ontario cities outright. "He was the main event pretty well all the time, so he got paid pretty well, but no, he didn't have a part in the ownership," said Tunney. Watson invested much of his money in real estate, and had homes in Toronto, a farm north of the city in Keswick on Lake Simcoe, and a cottage.

Both of his sons, John and Phil, wrestled, but only Phil stuck with it for any length of time. "At sixteen, I was driving doing summer shows," said Phil Watson. "My job was to set up the ring, tear down the ring, and referee the bear match. Then when I was seventeen or eighteen, I had my first pro match." Actually, he really debuted at fifteen, when he wrestled a friend during an intermission. The crowd was dead, so The Whip's son turned heel. "I definitely took a verbal beating from my dad when I got back into the dressing room for having crossed the line," he laughed.

As his skills eroded, Watson relied more and more on young protégés, like Dewey Robertson, Murray Cummings, or Rocky Johnson, to do all the work in the ring. "I would go in and sell and sell and try to get to him. He'd come in and do the highspot and the finish," said Cummings.

Watson's health was an issue, said Wes Hutchings, who was Hartford in the Love Brothers team. "I used to love

A Watson Snowarama placemat.

wrestling him. The guy didn't do much, he was so big," said Hutchings. "He used to have to lay down until his blood pressure went down a bit. Then they'd let him go in the ring."

"Whipper was past his prime. When I was twenty-two and he was fifty-four or whatever and he had arthritis and his back was so blown out like my back is now, I had to hold him up for fifteen or twenty minutes but they still adored him," said Johnny Powers. "It was like a Babe Ruth at the end of his days, or Bob Hope. When you looked at him you didn't see just his current performance; you saw the last twenty years of performances represented by just one time in the ring. And I think all of us, myself included, gave him that extra depth even when he didn't have the game anymore."

Though he couldn't work as well, he never forgot who paid the bills, said Tunney. "He was always with the fans, signing autographs, at any time — after matches, before matches . . . he'd always stop and talk with fans. It was just a part of his personality. He was good, very, very good. Just a wonderful man."

And Watson never could escape his fame, said Joe Persechini, who befriended The Whip while organizing his Persechini Run/Walk-a-thons in Newmarket, which started in 1977. Not too long before his death from a heart attack while in Florida on February 4, 1990, The Whip was taken to a strip joint by Persechini and some buddies. Not having been to a similar establishment since the dancers were required to wear tassels, Watson made a suggestion. "On the way in, he says, 'Call me Harry, boys.' The bouncer says, 'How you doing, Mr. Watson?'" laughed Persechini, who then proceeded to have a T-shirt made for his pal: "To Harry, from your fishing buddies."

15. BRET "HITMAN" HART

It can be debated whether Bret Hart is "the best there is, the best there was, and the best there ever will be." There's little argument, however, that "The Hitman" was one of the most important figures in the wrestling business during one of its most pivotal periods.

The "Excellence of Execution" was more than just a nickname that announcers gave to Hart; it is probably the most accurate description ever given to any professional wrestler.

"Bret Hart has always called himself the Excellence of Execution," said Steve Austin, whose classic battle with Hart at WrestleMania XIII is regarded as one of the greatest in WWE history. "He lives that, he breathes that, and he truly believes that in his heart, and that's why he was so good."

The eighth of twelve children of famous Canadian promoter Stu Hart, Bret grew up surrounded by wrestling. Stu, a feared and dangerous shooter, stretched hundreds of aspiring grapplers in the fabled Dungeon, a training room in the dark basement of the family's rambling twenty-room, twin-gabled Victorian mansion perched in the hills of Calgary, where the gruff family patriarch would make the toughest, most macho of men squeal like children, begging for escape from one of his torturous, terrifying submission holds. "My father was two different people," Bret wrote in his 2007 autobiography *Hitman: My Real Life in the Cartoon World of Wrestling*. "At an early age, I began to call one of them Stu, and I was terrified of him. Dad was the father I loved."

The Hart house, a Calgary landmark for almost 100 years, was filled with pets and invited strangers who had an affinity for wrestling and an interest in Stu's never-ending stories. The estate had a labyrinth of a yard piled high with the husks of beat-up Cadillacs that had been driven to death in places like Moose Jaw and Yellowknife. Bret once jokingly called the house "a cross between a big hotel where the housekeepers had quit, a cat and dog refuge, and an orphanage for troubled children." It wasn't far from the truth.

His mother, Helen, a prim and proper New York socialite, was the antithesis of this rough and rowdy world. She balanced the books, signed the checks, and dealt with the wrestling-related headaches, but con-

WWF world champion Bret Hart makes his way through the crowd.

stantly begged her husband to get out of the business. Wrestling may have been Stu's mistress, but Helen would become Stu's constant companion for life. They were the truest of tag team partners, and would bring twelve children into the world, with Helen pregnant nearly every year from the time they were married until 1965 and the birth of youngest child Owen.

To say Bret's upbringing was "different" — even by pro wrestling standards — would be a gross understatement.

From his early twenties as a star for his dad's Stampede Wrestling promotion until his retirement at the age of forty-three, Hart lived and breathed wrestling, despite early aspirations to become a film director. "As a favor to my father, I went out for the wrestling team. One thing led to another, and all of a sudden I was winning championships."

After winning a city and provincial amateur wrestling championship and capturing a collegiate title while at Mount Royal College, Bret took on the family mantle in the ring. Under the tutelage of his dad, Bret mastered the fundamentals at an early age. Trained by respected Japanese veterans Mr. Hito (Katsui Adachi) and Mr. Sakurada (Kazuo Sakurada), who didn't leave out any detail in their sessions with Bret in the Dungeon, Hart learned at an early age to be a solid performer in the ring, but also to be safe with those he was working with, all the while making it look as realistic as possible.

Hart, who took the moniker "Hitman" from boxing great Thomas Hearns, was an exceptional ring technician. But his size — six-foot-one and 230 pounds — held him back during the WWF's era of chemically enhanced giants. Caught in the undercard, there was no definitive role or position for Hart, who set his sights high. Having idolized NWA world champs like Dory Funk Jr. and Harley Race, Hart envisioned himself as an international star with world title ambitions of his own.

Slicking back his hair and wearing mirrored shades during his interviews, Hart eventually gained traction in the tag team ranks during the late '80s as part of The Hart Foundation. With brother-in-law Jim "The Anvil" Neidhart as his partner and Jimmy Hart as their mouthpiece manager, the Pink and Black Attack went on to win the WWF tag team belts on two different occasions. But in the early '90s, Neidhart was set aside while Bret was pushed as a singles act, only to see his star rise when Vince McMahon was forced to go with superior in-ring performers in the wake of the steroid scandal.

Bret Hart's illustrious career can be summed up in two words: triumph and tragedy. While he captured the most prestigious titles in the sport and achieved the industry's pinnacle of success, the Canadian legend also experienced rock-bottom lows: the pain of losing his youngest brother to a WWE stunt gone tragically awry, the anguish of watching his dysfunctional family split into warring factions, his premature retirement from the ring due to a career-ending brain injury, and a massive stroke at the age of forty-four.

He was so good that he would equal Hulk Hogan's then record of five reigns as WWF heavyweight champion. His notoriety reached such levels that he was a recognizable celebrity in every corner of the globe where the WWF appeared, from Israel to the Taj Mahal, and was a guest of President Bill Clinton at the White House. His popularity had propelled him to an acting role as cowboy Luther Root on the *Lonesome Dove* series and guest stints on TV shows.

For better or worse, though, the WWE Hall of Famer ultimately will most likely be best remembered for his role as a victim in the "Montreal Screw Job" at the 1997 Survivor Series, one of the most infamous double-crosses in the modern era of pro wrestling, where company owner Vince McMahon conspired with

Shawn Michaels to take the WWE title from Hart in what was to have been his farewell match with the company. To the fourteen-year WWE veteran, it was the ultimate betrayal, a devious and ruthless act orchestrated by a man he had considered more like a father than a boss. The fallout from that match would last for years, and the "screw job" storyline would take on a life of its own as McMahon would attempt to capitalize on its notoriety in future matches and storylines. An unintended but fortuitous consequence of the match — the emergence of the evil "Mr. McMahon" character, spawned from the real-life hatred many wrestling fans had for McMahon following the screw job, and his high-profile feud with Stone Cold Steve Austin — would serve as a catalyst for WWE's "Attitude Era," one of the most productive and profitable periods in wrestling history.

WWE itself describes Montreal as "arguably the most controversial, most jarring moment in the annals of sports entertainment." Indeed it was a pivotal point in pro wrestling history and one that would lead to a dramatic shift in the Monday night wars.

To Hart, who was the highest-paid performer in the company at the time, "It was as if they murdered me, right there in front of the world." To McMahon, Hart simply wasn't willing to do "what was good for the business" at a time he thought was necessary. "We need people who understand this business and don't get so carried away with it that they believe their own publicity. He thought *he* was a Canadian hero. *His character* was," McMahon shot back.

Although a victim, Hart has been portrayed both sympathetically and otherwise. Until recently, bitterness over Montreal colored Hart's career and his life.

"Unfortunately, I believe the Montreal screw job permanently tarnished Bret's legacy," opined *Pro Wrestling Illustrated* senior writer Dan Murphy. "While he initially was seen as a sympathetic figure in the whole fiasco, he never quite managed to put it behind him, and he eventually came off as a bitter, sulking person with an ax to grind. He was still finger-pointing and playing the victim after he signed a huge contract with WCW and long after the rest of the world had moved past it, which made him look childish and self-important."

The Hitman remains a polarizing figure even among his own family.

"I think his legacy will be compromised by his egocentricity and his taking himself too seriously and putting himself above the business," said Bret's older brother, Bruce Hart, who contends the unseemly affair in Montreal didn't do much for the images of Bret, McMahon, or Michaels. "The thing that Bret will forever be remembered for — not unlike Shoeless Joe Jackson in the 1919 World Series — will be Montreal. Neither Vince nor Bret had any business

Bret Hart's bouts with AWA world champion Nick Bockwinkel did plenty to establish him as a Stampede Wrestling headliner.

taking any bows or being credited with doing anything for the business for that abortion. I think that's Bret's biggest shortcoming. It's too bad that he invariably put himself ahead of the business."

Younger brother Ross Hart, however, feels one match shouldn't overshadow a brilliant career.

"I don't think you can overlook the matches Bret had with Shawn and how good they made each other look in the ring. For all the bitterness and dissension between the two, they had fantastic matches right up until Survivor Series. The quality of their matches over a two- or three-year span shouldn't be focused on that one match."

While many pundits and historians will point to the Montreal Screw Job as the defining moment in Hart's career, it may have never even occurred had another seminal event not transpired several years earlier. In 1993, as McMahon was facing a possible conviction and prison term in his steroids trial, he summoned Tennessee promoter Jerry Jarrett to New York for a planning session. McMahon, said Jarrett, was blunt and to the point. "[WWE legal counsel] Jerry McDevitt said this is a serious lawsuit, and I have to plan in case I have to go to jail."

"I went up there . . . mostly because I had promised his dad," recounted Jarrett. "I had told Vince Sr. that I would help his son if the time ever came." The company, at the time mired in sex and steroid scandals, was wallowing in a down period of business. McMahon's penchant for pushing musclemen as his top stars was no longer paying off in the wake of increased scrutiny and stringent drug testing.

"Vince was scratching his head saying the Lex Express was a bomb," said Jarrett, referring to the mega-push given to Lex Luger. "He had this advance team and this big beautiful bus with Lex's picture all over it, and when they pulled into a town, after the advance team had been there four or five days, there wasn't enough people there to even get any film. And Vince couldn't imagine what was wrong."

To Jarrett, a long-time proponent of smaller, skilled mat technicians who could perform at high levels and relate to an audience, the answer was apparent. "Vince, you are the greatest promoter that has ever lived," he told McMahon. "Don't tell me that you don't know what's wrong."

"Well, I don't," replied McMahon. "Lex Luger's got a body, he's good-looking and his work is passable."

Jarrett's reply was brutally honest. "I told him that Luger had the charisma of the turd I shit every morning."

"Park the bus and stop the bleeding," was Jarrett's short answer to McMahon's dilemma. The longer version was a recommendation that McMahon reverse direction. "We're seven million dollars in the hole. We can't afford to blow this kind of money. You're not going to like my suggestion because you've got a big-man fetish. But you need to put the belt on Bret Hart. Bret is as big as Jerry

Lawler, and Jerry Lawler's drawn more people to the matches than Hulk Hogan has. I can tell you that Bret will be a great champion because he can work with the big man and he can work with the little man."

It was a recommendation, Jarrett said, that McMahon took to heart, and the change would signal a new direction in the business. Hart, who had won his first WWE title the previous year from Ric Flair, would be given a major push this time around and would become the company's most popular star. Hart and Shawn Michaels would introduce a more athletic ring style.

"The wrestling business changed then," said Ross Hart. "It marked a real change in the industry and for the WWF. Prior to that, you saw the larger-than-life types like Hulk Hogan and The Ultimate Warrior, the ones who were very large physically and in stature. For the most part, they were big superstars. It was a different era. When Bret won the title, it was a change in the industry where you saw the more talented technicians and versatile performers who could work with the smaller guys like Shawn Michaels or Rick Martel, or still work with somebody like Bam Bam Bigelow, Yokozuna. Bret was consistently having great matches with all those guys."

That, said Ross Hart, will be Bret's lasting impact. "It changed the direction of WWE . . . less emphasis on size and more on in-ring ability. Bret paved the way for a lot of others after him including Shawn, Owen, and some of the smaller performers who years ago would probably have never gotten past the undercard. I think that will be Bret's legacy . . . the consistently good matches he had night after night with a wide range of opponents, and more of the emphasis on ring work instead of just size and brawn, color and showmanship. All of those things are important, too, but Bret paved the way for guys to get over on the basis of their work."

Nowhere was Bret's solid ring style more apparent than his 1992 Summer Slam Intercontinental title match with brother-in-law Davey Boy Smith before more than 80,000 fans at London's Wembley Stadium. It was a bout Hart would later call the favorite of his career and one that solidified him as world championship material. "It was a classic matchup with an element of family conflict," said Ross Hart. "He was having very good matches with guys like Curt Hennig and Roddy Piper, but the magnitude of this match established him as a lead worker. I don't think there's ever been a Summer Slam match to eclipse this. It elevated him to a higher level, since three months after this match, he won the world title from Ric Flair."

Bruce Hart lifts the Hitman's arm in victory at WrestleMania XXVI, when Bret beat up Vince McMahon.

In an era filled with brawlers and high-risk artists, the achievement Hart was proudest of was that he never seriously harmed one wrestler in the ring. "To me, there is something bordering on beautiful about a brotherhood of big, tough men who pretended to hurt one another for a living instead of actually doing it. Any idiot can hurt someone," Hart wrote in his autobiography.

In recent years Hart has mended fences with WWE, including his relationships with McMahon and Michaels, and occasionally appears on WWE shows. The thawing of relations began with a call McMahon made to Hart after he suffered his stroke.

"It took a lot of diplomacy," Hart told the SLAM! Wrestling website. "But I think we just softened. Vince McMahon called me up when I had my stroke in 2002, and I think that was a big step towards where we are now. I always appreciated the fact that he called me, and that softened a lot of the bad feelings between us." Michaels also apologized for his part in the double-cross, and the hatchet was buried.

Bret was finally inducted into the WWE Hall of Fame in 2006 and was granted creative control over an anthology of his career. He surprisingly admitted at his induction speech that, despite the fallout with McMahon at Survivor Series, he had made a promise to himself that day that he'd be at the Hall of Fame if he were ever asked. "While I'll never forget what the WWE took away from me, I'll never forget all the great things that they gave to me," said Hart, thanking McMahon for allowing him "to work on his canvas."

"If there is a 'national family of wrestling' in any country on this planet, it would be the Harts of Calgary," said wrestling historian Bill Murdock. "And although the entire family was involved in wrestling, it was Stu and Helen Hart's eighth child that propelled the Hart name to a new level in the sport of wrestling."

Hart made his first live appearance on Raw in more than twelve years on January 4, 2010, and later that year reprised his "feud" with McMahon at WrestleMania XXVI. The storyline with his former employer has given him peace and closure, even though he will never be an active in-ring performer again due to his lingering physical issues.

Hart finally seems to be at peace; the bitterness over Montreal has subsided. "I believe that Shawn and me shaking hands buried the hatchet and it really did set him free. At the same time, I felt deep relief myself. And I'm sure Vince felt it, too," he told the Ottawa Sun. An emotionally charged DVD that revisits "the most controversial match in WWE history" was released in late 2011.

Hart also has recovered nicely from a stroke he suffered on June 24, 2002, one week after the death of brother-in-law Davey Boy Smith. He suffered total paralysis on his left side, which required months of physical therapy, but made an amazing recovery, through sheer force of will and determination, and regained much of his mobility.

The other, deeper pain — from Owen's death — will never fully go away.

"There still seems to be a lot of suffering over that," said Ross Hart. "Thinking that had he never left WWE or if Owen had maybe joined him at WCW, things might have turned out differently. The reconciliation with WWE and the DVD they released, which showed some of his greatest matches and moments, is how he would want to be remembered, not just the Survivor Series debacle. A big part of him still misses Owen, like all of us, and it pains him tremendously because they had great matches and great road trips together. That's probably more painful than for any of us in the family because he and Owen spent so much time on the road together. They really revitalized each other's career. That's most likely a pain that will always be with Bret."

If triumph and tragedy do indeed sum up Bret Hart's career, then perhaps "survivor" should be added to the resumé, since Hart has persevered in the face of tremendous odds.

"Nothing ever came easy for Bret. He always had very high goals for himself, yet he had to work very hard to achieve them," said brother Ross. "It was a struggle when he first broke into the wrestling business. There was a lot of pressure for him to follow his dad and brothers' footsteps and be successful as a second-generation wrestler. He certainly did that. His legacy is now being celebrated, and it isn't all focused on what happened in '97."

To Bret Hart, wrestling was real life on a stage.

"I never got into wrestling thinking that some day I would be rich or famous and never in my wildest dreams did I imagine I'd be where I am today. I am truly grateful to all my fans around the world who have allowed me into their hearts, lives, or on TV, to be their hero."

16. WAHOO MCDANIEL

"Who was Wahoo McDaniel?" Florida sportswriter Dave Hyde asked after McDaniel's passing on April 18, 2002. "Who wasn't he? An American Indian, an expansion Dolphin, a legendary wrestler, an old-time carouser, a full-time personality, an Oiler, a Bronco, a Jet, a guard, a linebacker, a kicker — he was the kind of figure we lost long ago on the sports pages: an original."

Some wrestlers have to work for years to attain a charisma that others come by naturally. Wahoo McDaniel was certainly in the latter category.

In fact, Edward Hugh "Wahoo" McDaniel was an American original, the likes of which have become a rarity in today's cultural landscape. His death at the age of sixty-three officially closed the chapter on an era of professional wrestling that long-time fans still talk about in reverent tones; an era when grapplers were judged according to their grit and toughness as opposed to their catch phrases and Q ratings.

But Wahoo was much more than a professional wrestler. His exploits both inside and outside the squared circle and off the gridiron are the stuff of legend.

Part Choctaw, part Chickasaw, and fiercely proud of his Native American

An intense Wahoo McDaniel meant pain for opponents.

heritage, "Chief" Wahoo McDaniel was one of those larger-than-life characters that you never forget. A pioneer in the early days of the American Football League, he left pro football when he discovered the wrestling business was far more lucrative for a star of his caliber. He didn't even have to put his last name on the back of his pro football jersey. Long before "He Hate Me" became just about the only thing the late XFL was noted for, McDaniel simply had "Wahoo" on the back of his jersey. His antics outside the field of play more than matched his antics during his tenure with the Jets, where the announcer noted each tackle he made with a loud "Guess who?" To which the crowd shouted back, "Wahoo!"

Off the field, Wahoo lived fast and lived hard, attacking each day like there was no tomorrow. That lifestyle, though, came with a receipt. He was married five times to four women, and a normal family life was virtually nonexistent. His "work hard, party harder" philosophy led to diabetes and other health problems (he lost both of his kidneys during the late '90s) that kept him from enjoying his favorite diversions — hunting, fishing, and golf, which just may have been his best sport.

Even Wahoo admitted that had he known he would have lived as long as he did, he might have taken better care of himself.

Perhaps it was because everything came easy to him on the athletic field. He caught the attention of none other than former President George Herbert

Walker Bush, who coached McDaniel's Pony League team in Midland, Texas. In later years Bush would continue to visit with his protégé whenever Wahoo stopped in to work in Houston. "I'll always remember him as a wonderful kid who captured the imagination of West Texas in the 1950s. He was idolized and worshipped by everyone who knew him," Bush would later say.

In addition to baseball, Wahoo also excelled at track, and, of course, football, where legendary coach Bud Wilkinson recruited him to play for the University of Oklahoma.

The five-foot-eleven, 280-pound McDaniel was impressive at Oklahoma, where he still holds the record for the longest punt return, a ninety-two-yarder against Iowa State in 1958. He also kicked a record ninety-one-yard punt that still stands, and boasts one of the Sooners' longest touchdown receptions at eighty-six yards. The Sooners posted a 27-5 mark during Wahoo's three years as a letterman there.

Wahoo's college career was somewhat marred by injuries early on but by his senior year, he was one of the top players on the team despite being caught drinking after games and skipping classes. Wilkinson once threatened to kick Wahoo off the team if he didn't follow the rules and get good grades. Every time Wahoo missed a class, he had to run up and down the bleachers twenty-five times. By the end of the season, he had run those bleachers more than 700 times.

Wahoo graduated from OU in 1960, just in time to join the brand new American Football League. He played linebacker for the AFL's Houston Oilers and Denver Broncos, but reached another level entirely when he was traded in 1964 to the New York Jets. A crowd favorite who once made twenty-three tackles in a single game against the Broncos, Wahoo rivaled rookie teammate "Broadway" Joe Namath in popularity and media coverage. Years later Namath wrote in his autobiography that Wahoo scared him to death.

He was selected by the expansion Miami Dolphins in 1966 and played there for three years, earning a reputation as a practical joker and party animal. It was his exploits in the latter field that resulted in his being traded to San Diego after an altercation during the 1968 season in which he knocked out two off-duty police officers. Summing up his life, he decided it was time for a change. Unlike many other players, who hang on until told they would have to leave, McDaniel walked out on his own. He was twenty-nine years old and making $42,000 a year, but he knew he could easily double that amount in his off-season job. That job was wrestling.

McDaniel, trained by Amarillo wrestling star and promoter Dory Funk Sr., first got involved in the business in 1960 during the off-season of football. He fit right in with the violent style that marked the Amarillo promotion. Among his initial matches were those with Dutch Savage and Don Jardine, whom he took on in singles bouts building to a tag team match. "Wahoo hit me with a chair and potatoed the living crap out of me," recalled Savage. "I didn't need to use my blade. I had blood running all over me, and there's a sheriff standing by me. Wahoo's behind me with a chair arguing with another sheriff. He was a pretty hot-tempered kid."

Wahoo cashed in not only on his football fame, but also his Native American heritage. It could well be said of him that he was not just a Native American who wrestled, but a wrestler that wrestled as a Native American. This subtle distinction bit Wahoo in the pocketbook years later when he was denied a regular run with the WWWF. "He was always bothered by the fact that he could never get into New York," said former WWWF champ Superstar Billy Graham. "That was because Chief Jay Strongbow was always there. That always bothered him. I didn't have any answers for him, but I knew that pained him. That would have been a crowning achievement for his career back then."

If he took it hard, it never showed in his work for other promotions, where the name "Wahoo" usually meant "Yahoo" at the box office.

One of the most amazing things he did in the wrestling business was to help booker George Scott turn around his fortune in the Mid-Atlantic area in 1974 by building up the Jim Crockett–run company as a singles territory in a blazing feud with Johnny Valentine. Known for his rugged, bloody matches, many of which involved an Indian strap, Wahoo was snug and stiff in the ring, making his work that much more believable. "Those were some of the toughest matches ever," Ole Anderson recalled. "When he wrestled Valentine, you could hear the chops and the fists outside the building."

"All I would hear is Valentine saying 'Harder! Harder! Harder!' Wahoo would say, 'My hand's about busted!'" recalled the late Sandy Scott. Wahoo found himself in another money-making program with Valentine's son, Greg, in 1977 when the younger Valentine broke McDaniel's leg in a memorable angle.

But perhaps no rivalry captured Wahoo's warrior spirit more than his epic bouts with "Nature Boy" Ric Flair. Few wrestlers knew Wahoo McDaniel better than the sixteen-time world champion.

The two worked against each other hundreds of times, and Flair estimates that he took thousands of Wahoo's trademark tomahawk chops during the course of their classic rivalry, which spanned from 1974 until the late '80s. "I didn't give nearly as many as I got," said Flair, who considers Wahoo to be the toughest man he ever fought. "Wahoo was just an incredibly tough guy. Not just the way he wrestled, but the conditions he wrestled under. He wrestled hurt, he wrestled sick. I remember he had a vasectomy at four o'clock in the afternoon, then wrestled at eight o'clock that night. Wahoo would wrestle under any conditions. He had an incredible work ethic. He wrestled long matches and was as tough as anybody in the ring. He was a real man's man."

Wahoo delivers a chop.

Wahoo, however, was more than just a drawing card to Flair. He was a teacher and a friend who was instrumental in Flair's arrival in the Carolinas in 1974. "To me, he was the one guy most responsible for me getting my career off to a good start. He was probably the most influential person in my career for the first ten years," said Flair. "I respected him so much. If something was going down in the business, I'd always ask Wahoo's opinion. He was responsible for bringing me down to the Carolinas. I asked him all the time and learned an awful lot about working from him."

Flair and Wahoo's exploits transcended the wrestling ring. "We went up and down the road a lot, going 100 miles an hour in my Cadillac chasing him or him chasing me," recalled Flair. "It was incredible. Of course, it was so kayfabe, and you couldn't ride with each other. You had to really be careful back then, because there was a big penalty."

That didn't stop them from being involved in their share of barroom brawls, the most notable occurring in Charlotte, resulting in Flair and Wahoo going to court and paying $3,500 in fines. The incident occurred when Wahoo was showing a friend his brand new diamond ring. The ring fell on the floor, and Wahoo bent over to pick it up.

"This female lawyer thought Wahoo was being fresh with her, and that's how it all started," said Flair. Three male friends, including another attorney, confronted Wahoo, who began putting the boots to the trio. "That's when she jumped on his back and Wahoo flying-mared her," said Flair. "That was it."

Flair remembered once coming into the back entrance of the old Greensboro Coliseum when a man tried to steal his bag: "I said, 'Man, let go of my bag,' and he started cursing and kicking me." Wahoo slapped the man and broke his jaw. The man sued and won $18,000. Another incident saw an unlucky fan among a group of hecklers and on the receiving end of a punch from Wahoo that shattered his nose in two places. Wahoo pleaded no contest to an assault charge, and the man was awarded more than $35,000.

His temper landed him in the middle of a number of locker-room fights as well. "He hated for anybody to touch that [Indian] headdress," recalled Ole Anderson. "For a short period of time he and I were partners, and when he'd get into the ring, I'd tug on a feather. I'd turn around real quick like I was chewing somebody out. Wahoo would come back over, and I'd have to calm him down."

Wahoo's ferocity and competitive spirit even spilled over to the golf links, on occasion. George Scott recalled a fight he had with Wahoo on the very first hole. "He hit me over the head with his golf club. I turned around and whacked him with mine. So we're standing there looking at each other. I put my hat on because I had this big bump on my head. But we went ahead and played nine holes after that."

Among other favorite golfing partners were country singer Charlie Pride and football coach Mike Ditka, but he also played with Arnold Palmer, Jack Nicklaus, Lee Trevino, and Gary Player. When he lived in Dallas, he'd play regularly with Yankees great Mickey Mantle.

"Old Wahoo used a hickory-shafted putter," golf great and frequent playing partner Trevino told *Sports Illustrated*. "One time he missed a high-dollar putt and smashed the thing against a fence post near the green. The putter snapped back and the clubhead split his lip open. That was the angriest man I have ever seen on a golf course."

But his antics outside the ring never cost Wahoo the love of the fans, or the admiration of his fellow wrestlers. When it came to his profession he was a no-nonsense guy who had time for everyone from the Jack Briscos to the untested rookies. His advice was always there for the asking.

"I never heard anyone anywhere that had anything unkind to say about Wahoo," Jack Brisco said in his autobiography, *Brisco*. "He always had time for the fans and would arrive early to a town to work in the ring with some of the new boys, demonstrating holds and sharing his knowledge of the ring. Not many wrestlers that had achieved the level that he did would take the time to help out the preliminary and mid-card boys. But that was Wahoo, and he never said a word about it."

"Wahoo McDaniel was my kind of man. He went into the territories and he wrestled his ass off," Terry Funk told the *Wrestling Perspective* newsletter in 2002. "He'd wrestle in those territories night after night. He'd bring that individual territory up damn near on his own. If something happened with any of the boys in that territory, if the promoter didn't treat them right, Wahoo would be right in the damn promoter's face for anybody and everybody. When a champion came in, he'd pump that territory up and he'd wrestle that champion and he'd draw those sellouts. Then the week after, he'd draw just as much or even more. He was good for the boys. He was good for his fellow wrestlers. He did well for them. He busted his ass and gave his life for them. That's the God's honest truth. That's what Wahoo McDaniel did for this business. He went into territories and the guys who were making $125 a week, he'd make them $400 a week because he'd up the territory that much by being in there. He'd be there week after week after week busting his ass. That's the kind of guy who really needs a feather put up his ass and sent to heaven as far as the boys are concerned."

"I always said that if I had to have one man to cover my back in fighting my way out of a building, I would pick Ed 'Wahoo' McDaniel," said Les Thatcher. "He was one of the most talented babyfaces ever in our industry. When Wahoo cut an interview that he was going to kick so and so's butt the next week in some Mid-Atlantic arena, there was no question in the viewer's mind that he was packing the gear to do exactly that, and in real life it wasn't in your health's best interest to provoke this former NFL linebacker either. Ed lived life at a hundred miles per hour, and often drove one of his Cadillacs the same way as I witnessed as a passenger when he attempted to set the record for the 200-mile return trip from Jacksonville to Tampa, Florida, back in 1967 without benefit of a complete interstate highway at that time, and through several small towns and over two-lane roads. As I recall we made it in under two hours and forty-five minutes and he said he could do better . . . I said maybe so, but it would be without me as a passenger! Wahoo

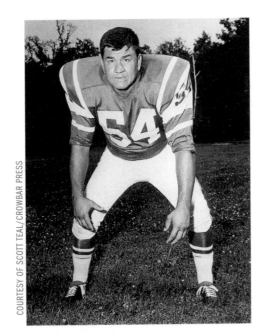

Football announcers would crow, "Tackle by Wahoo!"

should be put right up near the top when talking about the very best babyfaces of the '60s and '70s. A top-caliber athlete, and a legitimate tough guy."

His hard living and heavy drinking finally caught up with him in his late fifties and forced his retirement from the game he loved. He quietly spent his last years hunting and golfing, when his health allowed, and raising his youngest son, Zack. With his physical problems worsening, Wahoo moved from Charlotte to Houston to live with his daughter and son-in-law.

Wahoo was on the waiting list for a kidney transplant when he suffered a stroke and died of complications from renal failure and diabetes. His body was cremated and his ashes scattered over a lake near Del Rio, Texas, which had been the favorite fishing spot for Wahoo and his dad, a well-known West Texas welder and oil rigger.

Flair regrets that Wahoo didn't take better care of himself, especially in his later years.

"You couldn't even tell him back then. He'd say, 'No, don't worry about it, I'm fine.' When he got diabetes, instead of quitting drinking, he'd double up on the insulin and drink just as much . . . I'd say, 'Chief, let's go work out,' and he'd say, 'Boy, I've been working out thirty years, I don't need to work out any more. I'm tired of working out.'"

Flair remembers one of his last visits with Wahoo at a Charlotte hospital. "He was an incredibly tough guy, but he was clearly aware that he had some legitimate problems that needed to be addressed. It was probably the first time I ever heard him admit that he really needed help. It was really a sad day."

Even sadder, Flair said, is that many of today's fans will never realize just how important Wahoo McDaniel was to the business.

"I guess now I'm sad that not enough people knew enough about him or remember him. What bothers me is here we have probably the greatest athlete to ever be in our sport — the best athlete period to ever be a professional wrestler. Wahoo was such a legend to my generation. He'll always be that. That's what saddens me the most. It's called fleeting fame," said Flair. "They don't make men like that anymore."

17. DANNY HODGE

Everybody has a Danny Hodge story. Duke Myers' tale is set on a stage in Shreveport, Louisiana, where, at the champ's request, he put his open, flat hand between Hodge's legs.

"He said, 'I want you to pick me up.' This is without crossing his legs, just the muscles in his legs. He clamped down on my hand and at that time I was pretty stout and I picked him three feet up off the ground and he never flinched. The only reason I got my hand out was because he loosened it up. People don't realize how strong that guy is."

Jerry Brisco's story is as a kid in Oklahoma, where he snuck into a gym and crawled through the rafters for a chance to see his hero. Hodge's opponent that night was Victor, the wrestling bear. "I've never heard a bear scream so loud. That night, Victor was screaming. I always wondered, 'Why in the heck is that bear screaming so loud? That's Danny Hodge up there, I know, but man, that's a five-hundred pound bear!' Little did I know that fifteen years later when I was in the ring with him, I'd know why the bear was screaming."

And here's one from Jim Ross, who was awed as a young referee in the early '70s Oklahoma to be on the road with his idol. Hodge submitted to Don "The Spoiler" Jardine's claw hold one night in Shreveport, and ringside attendants carried him to the dressing room. There were cries of agony, but they were coming from the helpers, not the fallen wrestler. "Hodge has his arm over each guy's shoulder, and he's squeezing," Ross said. "They get him back up the steps to the back of the stage behind the curtain, and they are absolutely tormented and in anguish." Backstage, Bill Watts dressed down the playful Hodge, but found himself on the receiving end when Hodge snatched off a hot water faucet, leaving Watts to shower in the cold.

There are Danny Hodge stories, and then there's the Danny Hodge story. Hodge could squeeze apples until they burst into bits and break steel pliers with his gifted double-tendon strength. But those parlor tricks fail to capture the seething sense of purpose that drove Hodge to become the greatest amateur wrestler in U.S. history. At high school in Perry, Oklahoma, everybody would run three miles in training. Hodge was the last one out and the first one back, and later, out in the country, he'd run four more miles. "I put more in, I get more out; you see what I am saying? So I was different than everybody," he said. "If you do just what the coach says, that's fine. Your dad's happy, your family's happy. See, when I did that, though, I wasn't happy. I wanted to be happy for me."

There wasn't a lot of happiness in his childhood. Dan Allen Hodge came into the world on Friday the 13th, in May 1932, in the Dust Bowl that passed for Oklahoma. His family had no icebox and he had no boots, just gunny sacks wrapped around his feet, tightened with baling wire. His father, a hand in the oilfields, drank too much, and his mother, who suffered from severe depression, nearly burned to death when a fire destroyed their house. For amusement, Hodge and his friends took the round rings off wagon wheels, fashioned a "T" from the wooden slats, and ran up and down dirt roads with them. "You have no idea how many miles I'd run," he said. "I'd have tracks and I'd have to go across these ruts and once in while I would run into one and it'd knock the wind out of me, but that was my car; that was my toy." When the dust storms kicked up, he put a tea towel across his mouth to breathe. "People don't know what it's like growing up in the atmosphere like this. And I thought to myself then, 'Is this all the world I'm going to get to see?'" Shuffled from relative to relative, Hodge was regularly whipped with a cane by his alcoholic grandfather until he couldn't take it anymore. Eventually, he found refuge living at a fire house, sleeping on a steel cot, sweeping floors, and polishing trucks. Mike Chapman, the Iowa author and wrestling historian who worked with him on his biography, *Oklahoma Shooter: The Dan Hodge Story*, recalled how the normally agreeable Hodge got very direct when talking about the beatings he endured as a youth. "His eyes narrowed and he glared at me and he said, 'Mike, I made up my mind that I was never going to lose a fight again, ever,'" Chapman said. "I think he was born, and it was nurtured by his upbringing, with an incredible desire to never lose a fight."

In eighth grade, Hodge found he had a knack for wrestling. A career with the pros wasn't on his mind, but by 1949, he was analyzing their moves on TV on Saturday nights. He got a job in Perry at a Conoco filling station, and raced after work to the house of a coworker who owned a TV set. "Well, I think I could whip this one," he remembered thinking. "I could get out of that hold. I don't know if I could whip that one, not even knowing that I would ever have the opportunity to get in the ring." After losing a match as a high school junior, Hodge, driven by his inner fire, started crumpling up a newspaper page, one finger at a time, three times a day, to strengthen his grip. He won the state title in 1951 at 165 pounds and headed to the 1952 Olympics out of high school, placing fifth. He captured back-to-back national AAU titles in 1953 and 1954 at 174 pounds. A scholarship to the University of Oklahoma followed — the straight arrow never cut class, of course — and he became an undefeated, three-time All-American at 177 pounds. In three years, he was never taken down and his seventy-eight percent collegiate pinning percentage is regarded as the best ever. "When I stepped into the mat, when I shook hands with you, it was limper than a dishrag," Hodge said. "But when I grabbed you, I'd see the expression come over your face. Now you know why I'm here and I want all these people to let

ROGER BAKER

Danny Hodge makes a rare venture north to Toronto's Maple Leaf Gardens.

you watch the ceiling. And I was never happy with a win. I was a pinner. You see what I'm saying? And you can't do that until you get in shape." At the 1956 Olympics in Melbourne, Australia, he was well ahead of a Bulgarian opponent with a gold medal within his sights when the two became entangled. Hodge's shoulders grazed the mat and a judge called it a fall and a loss.

In 1957, America's best wrestler turned to boxing. An Oklahoma alum and oilman named Art Freeman sponsored him, hired a coach, and within five months, Hodge was the national Golden Gloves heavyweight champion, becoming the only person to hold national championships in boxing and wrestling. The pro fisticuffs lasted about a year; in July 1959, two months after losing to Cuban Nino Valdes, Hodge quit boxing and filed a $116,000 lawsuit against his backers, saying they breached a contract that was supposed to provide him with about thirty-five percent of the gate after expenses. He won a judgment in court. Fifty years later, he's still waiting for the check. "They told me, 'Danny boy, we need you.' 'No,

Danny Hodge, center, as a Golden Gloves fighter.

you don't need me.' I told them I can get all the fights I want here in Perry, Oklahoma, for nothing. And I don't have to train near as hard," he said. He didn't tell wife Dolores that he was changing gears to wrestle, but she'd been with him since their school days — they married in 1951 — and had no quarrels. "I figured it was his life and his choice and if he could make a living out of it, we would make it work," she said.

Hodge got top billing from the start and a helping hand from Ed "The Strangler" Lewis, the great champ who saw him on TV and asked if he could help manage him. On the road, Hodge soaked up tips from Lewis and wore out his famous spring-loaded headlock machine. "He showed me the leverage of the headlock," Hodge explained. "All I can say is it was pleasure to share my life with the last years of his life. He traveled with me and he would go to the towns and do the interviews with a radio station or TV and he says, 'I have a young man here that the world is going to want to see.'" Oklahoma promoter Leroy McGuirk had built his career on the National Wrestling Alliance junior heavyweight title, and Hodge, at about 220 pounds, held it regularly from 1960 to 1976. He made frequent world tours but, devoted to his home life, primarily spent his time in the brutally sprawling McGuirk territory, from Oklahoma City and Joplin, Missouri, to the Louisiana bayous and the Mississippi Delta. He had a championship tag team with Skandor Akbar in 1967 and 1968, and though he was top dog, he'd gladly take an initial whipping before tagging out, to build up his partner. "If I wasn't with Danny, the people hated me that much more. But if I was with Danny, then that made it," Akbar said. "He was literally Mr. Oklahoma and later on, when I turned against him, I had some very, very close calls with fans and things because they loved Danny Hodge." What Hodge calls one of the greatest thrills of life came in January 1968, when he defeated Lou Thesz for the short-lived Trans World Wrestling Association championship in Japan, becoming the only man to claim a world junior heavyweight title and a heavyweight title at the same time. "When he handed me the belt, I had almost tears in my eyes. You can't even imagine my thoughts. Here is the world's heavyweight champion and here I've got this prestigious belt."

Hodge is a gentle, God-fearing, family-loving man outside the ring. But inside, he could be a handful, sometimes intentionally, sometimes not. If you didn't challenge him, he'd find a way to make you, as Sputnik Monroe learned when he won the junior heavyweight belt from Hodge in 1970. He promptly offered to give it back. "Hodge would tie you up. If I'd squawk to the referee, he'd say he was just trying to make it look real," Monroe said in 1997 in Scott Teal's *Whatever Happened to ...?* "You know, you give him your body and he takes advantage of it. There's really no way that I know of to beat a guy that can break electricians' pliers with his hands." To Hodge, that was because Monroe and a few others failed to mix it up. "I'd ask him, 'You want to wrestle or not?' The people paid to see me wrestle." Gil Hayes, who called Hodge "an absolute gentleman," recalled another incident: "I worked with him and he made me look like a million dollars, but he potatoed me so hard that I woke up when the referee untangled our legs from the figure-four [leglock]. And he didn't even realize that he had knocked me out."

Hodge's career abruptly ended on March 15, 1976, and his life nearly did too, when he fell asleep driving from Houma, Louisiana, to Monroe. A crash jolted him awake; he had hit a bridge, felt his teeth breaking, and was overwhelmed by excruciating pain. The car flipped and suddenly Hodge was underwater with a broken neck, facing death at the bottom of a cold creek in the middle of the night. Then he heard a voice. "Hold your neck." He can still hear the voice today. "Hold your neck." How he managed to hold his head in place and get out of the car, well, only God knows that, Hodge said. "The doctor said if my neck had ever come down a quarter of an inch . . . that's why I guess God said for me to hold my neck." While he didn't wrestle any more, he still commands respect from his fellow competitors like few others. "The best wrestler I've ever met and I've met a hell of a lot of wrestlers," said Harley Race. He's been inducted into every hall of fame that amateur and pro wrestling can dream up, and had the ultimate honor bestowed on him in 1995, when the Hodge Trophy became wrestling's version of the Heisman Trophy, annually given to the top collegiate performer. Chapman thinks Hodge's profile is an intriguing parallel to that of boxing champ

Jack Dempsey, another product of a rural, impoverished childhood who rose to unimaginable heights. "He was like Dempsey. There's the gentleman side to him, the modest side, and the 'I want people to like me' side. But when that bell goes ding, something happened to Dempsey and something happened to Dan Hodge," Chapman said. "My feeling is he's a small-town kid who just had an insatiable desire to be somebody and to be respected."

So there's the Danny Hodge story, but then there are Danny Hodge stories, like the one he tells on himself. Jack Nasworthy ran a carnival based out of Hutchinson, Kansas, and once offered the cash-starved youngster $100 to take on all comers. "I'll be there before daylight!" Hodge eagerly replied. A $5,000 pot to anyone who could last ten minutes with him lured a couple of hopefuls from Chattanooga, Tennessee, with wrestling backgrounds. Hodge pinned the first in about thirty seconds, but the fellow protested the pinfall. Bad move. "Jack said, 'Get him back in.' I got him back down there, put a little tight squeeze on him this time," Hodge said, "and Jack said, 'Kill the son of a bitch, kill 'im!' He's looking like, 'God I just hope I get out of here.' I squeezed him and said, 'Pin,' but Jack's saying, 'Kill 'im, kill 'im!' You could hear him for four blocks. He got out and the other kid wouldn't come in to wrestle."

18. STEVE CASEY

November 10, 1940, was a brisk day in Boston, and fans gathered by the thousands along the Charles River to witness the most heralded rowing match race in the city in thirty years. Russell Codman Jr., a prominent broker and a highly decorated rower, put up $1,000 that he could outrace three immigrant brothers from Ireland, Tom, Jim, and Steve Casey, in single sculls along a one-mile course on the Charles. Interest ran so high that Governor Leverett Saltonstall donated a silver trophy for the winner. For the first quarter-mile, Codman stayed with the Caseys, but they quickly and convincingly pulled away. As they crossed the finish line, Tom edged out Jim, with Steve a couple of boat lengths back. Codman was fifteen lengths to the rear. "Codman was a real gentleman," Steve Casey remembered years later. "He never thought three clucks from Ireland could beat him, but he finished fourth."

What does a pair of oars have to do with wrestling? Only this: when he set out on the water that fall day, Steve Casey was between his third and fourth reigns as American Wrestling Association world heavyweight champion. The

Irish Steve Casey arrives in Boston.

Caseys are the preeminent sporting family in the history of Ireland, and in 2000, when a bronze statue of "Crusher" was unveiled in his hometown of Sneem, Irish journalist John Daly said it was not beyond the pale to call him "Ireland's greatest sporting hero." Bob Kennedy, a New England sportswriter, compared him with one of Hollywood's great leading men: "If television had been as popular in those late 1930 and early 1940 days, Casey would have become a matinee idol probably even greater than Ramon Navarro."

But it all began with rowing. The oldest of seven brothers, Casey was born December 4, 1908, with fresh water mixed in his blood. His parents, both rowers, presented their children with a unique choice of endurance. Either they walked several miles from their two-bedroom home in County Kerry across hilly terrain to school and Mass, or they rowed two miles across a bay. They chose the shorter route and by the early 1930s, different combinations of Clan Casey had wiped out the rowing competition in Europe. "There was no difference between the seven brothers rowing," brother Paddy said in 2002. "One was as good as

Steve Casey proved an immigrant could make it on American soil.

the other." Steve headed to London, soon followed by several siblings. He continued to row and worked as a bouncer at night, at one point dispensing of some rowdies in plain sight of Mick Howley, a boxing promoter, who knew athletic talent when he saw it. Steve brought along brothers Paddy, Tom, and Mick for workouts; all but Tom decided wrestling was less hazardous to their health than boxing. The fact that Steve and Paddy wrestled for pay, though, disqualified them from rowing as amateurs in the 1936 Olympics. "It would have been a sure thing, the gold medal," Paddy sighed. Still, at six-foot-two and 225 pounds, Casey was built for one-on-one combat. His hands measured fourteen inches across and could hold eight baseballs at once, so it wasn't long before he and his brothers dominated wrestling like they did rowing. "Nobody in England would take them on and pretty soon most of the European wrestlers felt the same way," said Irish matchmaker Gerald Egan, who helped arrange for passage to the U.S.

The boys of the Kingdom of Kerry seen glory on many a field,
But the brothers called Casey from Kerry at wrestling were surely the cream,
The most famous of all at the spin, flip and fall,
Was the famous Steve Casey from Sneem
— "The Famous Steve Casey" by Bryan McMahon, Irish playwright

Anxious to replace failed champion Danno O'Mahoney, Boston wrestling promoter Paul Bowser announced in 1936 that he'd shelled out $100,000 to import Casey. The pay, according to Casey's family, was actually $25,000, and his journey across the Atlantic was poignant. He snuck into the United States from Canada because he couldn't get a visa. His brogue, heavy even in later life, was probably borderline unintelligible to many Bostonians. "Being in a foreign country and ignorant of the world, Steve had never seen a telephone and had no family or close friend connections," said his daughter Margaret Marr. Steve had six years of formal education, but never completed a full year in any grade as Mick, his father, needed him as a worker. The working-class Irish sensed that he was one of them, and Casey became their hero during the hard years of the Depression. He debuted in October 1936, beating Wally Dusek, and became as much of a local landmark as Fenway Park or Faneuil Hall. Though he and his brothers continued to row for Riverside Boat Club in Boston, he was candid about why he went into wrestling. "There's no money in rowing, no pay, no gate," he acknowledged. "You have to depend on the side bets. In the States you can usually get a couple of thousand dollars here or there."

Casey's style was rough-and-tumble, and his best-known hold was the Killarney flip, an over-the-shoulder toss that was half flying mare and half hammerlock. Always the aggressor, he entered the ring as though he wanted to get the match over as soon as possible, and routinely took the action into the aisles and behind ringside seats. "Not since Londos have the mat moguls had a man they crown with any degree of confidence," said Lewis F. Atchison of the *Washington Post*. "Casey works and looks as though he actually can defend the title, successfully, in a 'shooting' match." While Casey wasn't skilled in hooks and submissions, he had other ways of making a point. In December 1936, when he was a wide-eyed innocent in the U.S., he took a fearful beating in Boston from George "K.O." Koverly, an ex-boxer known for roughing up unseasoned wrestlers. Though he won, Casey received treatment for facial cuts at a local hospital, and bided his time. It came in 1944 in San Francisco, when he gave Koverly a black eye, lacerations that required several stitches, and a half-dozen bruises. "Then and there Casey swore that he would get even," promoter Bowser said of the first match in Boston. "What he did to Koverly would put a drunken pier nine stevedore to shame."

Casey got his first world title run on February 11, 1938, when he beat Lou Thesz for the AWA championship, even though his hands were encased in gauze after he scalded them in a bath. His win heralded a mat revival in Boston, where attendance had been slumping since O'Mahoney's demise. Casey subsequently whipped O'Mahoney in Boston and New York City to cement his status as top Celt, though in August 1938, in a Gaelic unification match, the two went to a draw before 16,000 fans in Dublin. Fionnán O'Shea was part of the reception that welcomed Casey home as a national hero. "I can still remember traveling all the way with him from Cobh. Lines of men on horseback escorted him into Sneem and a party went on in the convent school until five o'clock the following morning. However, Steve was off training up the mountain at seven o'clock and not a bother on him."

Casey's greatest rivalry was with Maurice Tillet, the freakish French Angel who took the AWA title via a dubious disqualification in May 1940 in front of more than 8,000 fans at the Boston Garden. Casey and Tillet swapped the AWA title four times in Boston and San Francisco between 1940 and 1944 in one of wrestling's top feuds. In all, Casey held the AWA title six times from 1938 to

The Casey brothers, from left, Tom, Paddy, Dan, Jim and Steve, winners of the Salters Cup three years in a row.

1945, and though his home base was Boston, he had huge runs at the top in St. Louis, California, and western Canada. "Steve was a reserved man, but not at all stern. I think his ring presence was a function of his taking his vocation seriously, not as something frivolous. He was a very proud man and could never play the clown or be made fun of," his daughter Margaret said.

In February 1941, Casey enlisted as a private in the U.S. Army and was a mine sweeper at Camp Langdon in New Hampshire. During a training exercise, he ruptured four discs in his back while saving another soldier. The injury led to several surgeries and flare-ups that caused him to curtail his active career in 1947. He had a few matches in Massachusetts through 1950 and kept up with his other passion by handily winning the veteran's half-mile singles title at the 1954 New England Amateur Rowing regatta. While he spent much of his time operating "Crusher Casey's," a tavern in South Boston, hustling customers was hardly physical sport, so he trained packs of Plott hounds, beagles, and black and tan coondogs to hunt bears in the Maine woods. If they treed a raccoon instead, Casey simply climbed up and pulled the critter out with his oversized hands. "You can do it easy enough," he shrugged. "But once in a while, you come across a twenty-pounder. Then you are in for some fun."

Boxing great Jack Sharkey and Steve Casey.

In 1958, the forty-nine-year-old Casey mounted a comeback, setting his sights on younger stars such as Antonino Rocca and Edouard Carpentier. In his return, he bested Frank Shields and Bozo Brown back-to-back in front of the largest crowd of the season in Boston and later won a main-event disqualification victory over Dr. Jerry Graham before hanging up his boots for good. On New Year's Day 1968, he narrowly avoided death when he was shot twice below the heart by a man attempting to enter his lounge after closing hours; a bartender was killed. For months, Casey battled through surgeries, hemorrhages, and a staph infection, joking to the *Boston Herald*, "I'm still alive because Irishmen never die until they are dead." In retirement, he remained a local icon who taught young-sters self-defense at his home gym and the ways of the oar at his boat shed in Hull until he died of cancer in January 1987 at seventy-eight. "I believe he remained something of a sports hero long after his prime because he was a modest person who had many interests outside of wrestling," his daughter reflected. "He loved the attention and adoration he received in Ireland but truly loved his adopted country. His view was that America made him and he respected that, feeling he would never have done as well in Europe. America was his land of opportunity."

19. DORY FUNK JR.

When one considers Dory Funk Jr.'s greatest rivals, such as Jack Brisco, Wahoo McDaniel, or Johnny Valentine, one might conclude he doesn't belong in a book on babyfaces. But Funk Jr.'s style was such that he could not be outwardly hated by audiences; he earned their respect through his sheer wrestling ability and fabled Funk toughness.

Even before he was NWA world champion, Funk Jr. would be on the road, building his name and credibility far away from his home base of Amarillo, Texas, where his father, Dory Sr., ran the promotion. With time and effort, his name grew and grew.

Now, in retrospect, his NWA world title reign, from February 1969 to May 1973, might have been the greatest in modern history, with the variety of opponents, the distance traveled, the dignity exuded, and all for such a lengthy, uninterrupted period of time. He marked a generational change from the grizzled old veterans, like Gene Kiniski, Lou Thesz, and Dick Hutton, to a fresher, more handsome champion.

"It took teachings for me to understand Dory's greatest contributions to our business — that of the traveling world champion whose job it was to make everybody he came in contact with look better than they would have otherwise, and help everybody in every territory make more money than they ever would have," praised Mick Foley, the emcee as Funk Jr. was inducted into the George Tragos/Lou Thesz Professional Wrestling Hall of Fame in July 2011. "Dory personified being a champion."

Ever modest despite his accomplishments, Funk Jr. would sooner talk about students he trained in his Ocala, Florida gym than what he did in the squared circle. But he acknowledged it was a blast.

"I doubt there's ever been a time when I went in the ring and worked a match where I wasn't having a good time," Funk Jr. said. "The hard part is the politics and filtering your way through all the mechanics of the business, and the training and everything. But the actual matches, that's what we've done all the hard work for . . . I can't say it's easy, but it's the most enjoyable."

He will concede that the idiosyncrasies from wrestler to wrestler, territory to territory, did pose a welcome challenge.

"I wrestled so many different styles of wrestlers. There were many times when I was NWA world champion that I would walk in and meet an opponent for the first time ever in the ring," he said, using Abdullah the Butcher as an

Dory Funk Jr. signs an autograph before defending his title against Tim Woods in Tampa in 1972.

DAVID MACIEJEWSKI

example. "That's the challenge, but it's all what we're in the business for. What the people want to see is the clash of personalities."

There were different styles in the ring too, said Michel "Le Justice" Dubois. "He could be a heel one night and a babyface the next night. He could work any style," said Dubois. "He could work a street fight type, he could work a highspot type, flying stuff, and he could work the holds like Johnny Valentine, he could grab one hold on you and hold the same hold on you for thirty minutes and make it work, and the people would get involved in it. He was believable and people believed in him. He was all-around a wrestler."

Forced to be far-thinking, Funk Jr. had to always look down the road. "We had to pull off a great match every time. It couldn't be anything else, otherwise, just because we'd work back through six months later, and you had to draw a house then."

In Amarillo, given his pedigree, it isn't hard to picture him as a heroic figure. Born Dorrance Earnest Funk Jr., on February 3, 1941, to Dorothy and Dory Sr., he was a wrestler's son from the start, on the road, moving as often as every three months to better bookings. Eventually, the Funks settled on the Flying Mare Ranch in Umbarger, southwest of Amarillo, where Senior ran the Boy's Ranch, helping wayward youth find a direction. Funk bought into the Amarillo promotion with Karl Sarpolis in 1955.

"Other kids looked at my father as a hero," Funk said in a WWE documentary on famous wrestling families. "As a kid I used to dream I could do all the things my father could do. I wanted to be just like him."

With mats set up in the family garage, Dory Jr. and his brother Terry, three years younger, got a chance to see some of the greatest stars of the 1950s and '60s test each other's skills away from the spotlight. "It doesn't sound very dramatic: 'Let's go out to the garage.' You'd think to fix your car or something," laughed Terry. "My dad would bring them out to the house, my mom would give them a good steak late at night — Danny Hodge was one of them. In the morning, they'd go out there, and get in that daggum garage. The most wonderful thing about it is that they would also teach my brother and I. There were some greats that came out there and got in that daggum garage . . . I was sworn to secrecy about who did the best."

As much as the boys were schooled on the basics of amateur wrestling, football was important as well. At West Texas State University, Dory Jr. — nicknamed "Hoss" by a coach — was a starting defensive end and offensive tackle on the Buffs' 1963 Sun Bowl championship team. Having worked construction in the off-season, the six-foot-two, 240-pound Junior asked his father if he could turn pro; granted the chance, he debuted January 10, 1963, against Jack Dalton (Don Kalt, a.k.a. Donnie Fargo), in Amarillo.

Working against top names right from the start, such as Pat O'Connor, Gene Kiniski, Verne Gagne, Fritz Von Erich, and Lou Thesz, Funk Jr. learned very quickly, and added to his repertoire with stays in the Dallas, Vancouver, and Australian territories. Soon, his name was in discussion as a potential NWA world champion, and his father did the necessary behind-the-scenes politicking to make it possible.

He wouldn't have gotten the chance if he didn't have the goods.

Funk Jr. had a remarkable ability to do lengthy matches, breaking down the hour bout into six ten-minute segments in his mind. He always knew what he wanted to do, said Leo Burke. "Dory, he had a story. He didn't let the crowd dictate the match. He let the people come to him," explained Burke. "He never panicked. If people were chanting 'boring' or whatever, he stayed the course . . . The last ten minutes, trust me, he had them on their feet."

"He had that charisma. The fans liked him. They hooked onto him pretty good," said Kiniski, who Funk Jr. dethroned as NWA kingpin, and Kiniski stressed that Funk Jr. was "a tough son of a bitch."

The years 1972 and 1973 were key ones in the lives of the Funks. Funk Sr. helped Giant Baba with the start-up of All Japan Pro Wrestling, booking the U.S. talent and paving the way for the hundreds of trips his sons would make to the Orient. After an accident on the ranch derailed original plans for dropping the world title, Dory Jr. held the title until May 24, 1973, when Harley Race captured the crown. A little over a week later, Funk Sr. died of a heart attack on June 3, 1973, and the boys took over the Amarillo territory, and the arrangements with All Japan, further expanding their knowledge of the business.

"In terms of popularity, Terry Funk was (and still is) bigger than Dory in Japan, but for more core fans, like myself, Dory is much more popular," said Japanese historian Koji Miyamoto. In December 1969, Funk Jr. became the first to defend the NWA world title in Japan since Lou Thesz in 1957. On consecutive days, Funk Jr. worked sixty-minute draws against Antonio Inoki, in Osaka, and against Giant Baba, in Tokyo. "Those two matches completely made Dory's fame in Japan — sixty minutes in two straight days was absolutely unbelievable," said Miyamoto. The Funks were also entrusted with young Japanese talent, such as Jumbo Tsuruta, eager to learn the different style in North America.

Respected for his booking mind, Funk Jr. was tapped to run Florida for Eddie Graham in 1980, and the Mid-Atlantic area for Jim Crockett in 1983,

Dory Funk Jr. poses with Billy Robinson and Harley Race at a Charlotte fan fest in 2010.

stressing believability in his workers' performances. With the writing on the wall and the national expansion of the WWF inevitable, the Funks sold Amarillo to Dick Murdoch and Blackjack Mulligan and joined the WWF. Hoss and Terry Funk were featured performers, capable veterans put in a position to help the growing company, including a WrestleMania II bout against Tito Santana and Junkyard Dog; when Terry bolted, Dory teamed with a masked Jesse Barr, who was named J.J. Funk.

"I didn't like seeing the image of a respected former NWA world champion dumbed down to the point that he came across like a slightly punchy ranch-hand. I thought it was a shame that the average WWF fan had no appreciation for his accomplishments. As far as I was concerned, it was the WWF insulting the wrestling business yet again," said Harry Burkett, senior writer at *ProWrestling Illustrated*. "When I had a chance to discuss this with Dory many years later, he assured me that he was absolutely fine with it because he understood 'all the ins and outs of trademarking and what has to be done in the wrestling business.'"

In 1997, Funk Jr. partnered with the WWF in another way, setting up a fin-ishing school known as the Funkin' Dojo, where he polished future superstars like Kurt Angle, Christian, the Hardys, Test, Rhino, Lita, Steve Corino, Christopher

Daniels, and more. When the connection with the WWF ended, Funk and his second wife, Marti, set up their school in Ocala, and boldly leapt into the new medium known as the internet, with Dory-Funk.com, and their *Bang!* TV show.

"It was a very stressful time, as I felt like every day was an audition for a position on the WWF roster," recalled Daniels. "Although it never blossomed into working there, I was very fortunate to be able to work and train with Dory, and that relationship formed during my time there has lasted to this very day. It was also the place where I met and worked with men like Kurt Angle, Steve Williams, Steve Corino, and Devon Storm."

Still active on the occasional show and in the ring at his facility, Funk Jr. steers his students away from the idea that they have to be heel or babyface. "We have kids that come in here and say, 'I want to be a good guy; I want to be a bad guy.' The thing that you really want to learn is you want to learn the business; you want to learn to work. That includes everything that's necessary to attract wrestling fans to a promotion, to draw money for the company that you're working for, and to fill whatever niche that they need or they're looking for. I really don't believe that you completely know the business until you're a worker, not just a babyface, not just a heel."

20. "COWBOY" BOB ELLIS

The fans remember the blood. The wrestlers remember the toupee. Fortunately, "Cowboy" Bob Ellis isn't shy about talking about either of them.

He was always a good bleeder, and soon learned that it was instant heat with the fans.

"It got over so good. It made the match so easy. We got 'em where we wanted 'em," Ellis said. Having been hit with a chair or the ring bell or ringside telephone, Ellis would cut his forehead — or arm, or ear — and take a bump out of the ring, walking into the aisles so the spectators could see the crimson mask.

Not everyone was a believer, however. In April 1958, bleeding from a bout with Jim "Riot Call" Wright in Regina, Saskatchewan, Ellis — working as Bob Elliott — was confronted by a skeptical Arthur J. Cookson, chair of the Regina Boxing and Wrestling Commission — and the police chief. "He came up, 'We don't want any of that phony blood.' I took my hand, and I wiped it on his white shirt. That was the wrong thing to do! He had me suspended."

Bleeding was not without its dangers, he added. Once, working with "Killer"

A bloody and bandaged Bob Ellis walks through the crowd.

Tim Brooks, Ellis gigged his ear. "He bit it, and that got infected . . . it blew up, and I had to have it drained."

Another trick was blood in a condom, which Ellis admitted to pulling off a number of times. "We'd take a condom and draw my blood out a vein and put it into a condom. You'd put in this stuff that keeps it from clotting. You'd make a little ball out of it, and put it into your mouth, in your cheek. Then when the guy jumps off the top rope, then you'd burst it and start spitting it. It's really impressive," he said with a chuckle. "You'd swallow the condom. We had it all rigged up." Often, Ellis would be wheeled away on a stretcher or into a waiting ambulance. The return match a few weeks later would be a barnburner.

What didn't draw money so much was his hairpiece, though it was an obvious asset in appealing to the female set for the good-looking Cowboy from San Angelo, Texas. "It looked like one of those duck's tails," recalled Rip Hawk. "I didn't know and I grabbed it and it rolled right up the back of his head."

In the IWA, where Ellis was one of the renegade promotion's lead performers, he was taking on Ernie Ladd. "Ernie hit Bob with a big chop, and Bob's head went back like this into the turnbuckle, and his toupee goes, 'Whoosh!'" laughed Phil Watson, who was in the territory at the time. "Then Ernie puts his hand on his head and 'Whack!' knocks it back into place."

Having the toupee go askew was one thing, Ellis admitted, but it was nothing compared to the suffering his opponents went through when he just tried to cover his bald spot. "I put shoe polish on a lot of the time. Some of the guys I worked with didn't like it, because sometimes you'd get your head on them or something, and it comes off."

Born on March 15, 1929, Ellis was no natural athlete, even though his father had played football at the University of Texas. "I was so big and awkward, I never was a star at anything," the 6-foot-2 Texan said, though Ellis did participate in football, basketball, and track at San Angelo High School. Despite overtures from his father's alma mater, Ellis' poor marks and local girlfriend kept him in Abeline at nearby McMurray College.

He was drafted into the U.S. Army before he'd finished school — though he did finish his degree on USOC courses. He and a friend already had their pilot licenses for small airplanes, but an inability to hear high frequencies in his right ear kept Ellis from flying. As a foot soldier in the 101st Airborne — never a paratrooper, despite what those rasslin' mags might claim — Ellis spent half a year in Korea and the rest of his three-year stint in the U.S.

Upon his discharge, he was surprised to find a contract waiting for him for pro football — he still had a year of eligibility left for college ball, and Georgia Tech, Georgia, Alabama, and Florida State had all been in touch. The Philadelphia Eagles offered $5,000 for the season, and a $250 bonus; some of his army buddies had spoken highly of Ellis, who had made the All-Army squad on a stacked army team. He wasn't impressed with the Eagles. "These rookies weren't nothing compared to this army football team I'd been playing for," he said. Fed up with taking orders, and his bride and new baby at home, Ellis left after a couple of exhibition games. He set up a small gym in San Angelo, mod-eled on the pioneering bodybuilding gyms he'd seen in Los Angeles.

Ellis' father was the wrestling commissioner of the city of San Angelo, which the Amarillo territory ran every Tuesday. The wrestlers began frequenting Ellis' gym, and he befriended Pepper Gomez. "I kept bugging him, like most guys trying to get in. 'How do you get in, how do you get in?' And to get rid of me — I'd asked him so many questions — he gave me Sandor Szabo's address in Santa Monica, California. He said, 'He's got a school out there.' I just packed up and went on out there. He didn't even think I would go. Anyway, the next time I saw him, we were working together, in, I think, the Dallas–Fort Worth area. He got a big kick out of it, telling all the boys, 'I didn't smarten him up; I just sent him out there.'"

After training with Szabo, and getting a few local matches under his belt, Ellis began working as Bob Elliott. But they needed a cowboy in Albuquerque, where there was opposition running against the established promoter, Mike London. "I fit the bill pretty good. I had some cut-off Levi's, because I didn't have much money when I started — cut the Levi's off, went barefooted; wore boots to the ring and took them off."

Cowboy Bob Ellis honed his image. "It just happened when *Gunsmoke*, all those things on TV came on. It really got over. It got over so well, St. Louis called, and they were the big one."

Wrestler, matchmaker, and promoter Joe Blanchard said Ellis was a great babyface. "The people liked him, he had a good gimmick, he worked it, and he lived it. He was good at it. They bought it."

There were few places that Ellis didn't work — and he was almost always a headliner. But he wasn't always a babyface. In Puerto Rico, he was a hero until he turned on the promoter, the iconic Carlos Colon. "We did that, and I'm

Bob Ellis, in the white hat naturally, accepts a trophy for his horse, Candy, in a 1970 race in Arizona.

telling you, here comes these Puerto Ricans — that's the hottest bunch over there. You know, I made more money on the main event in Puerto Rico at the ballpark, than I did in Madison Square Garden, on any sellout we had."

Even though he worked for a number of renegade promotions over his career, Ellis always had work. "I'll tell you one thing, in professional wrestling, if you ever make it, or are in top in several places, it's hard to get looked down on. I even went against Vince McMahon one time when [Antonino Rocca] went opposition against McMahon. I worked a few shows with him, but I came back anytime to work with McMahon. Once you're lucky enough to get established, then the promoters look the other way."

Then, in 1982, Ellis quit wrestling. "I had enough money," Ellis said of his decision to retire, while on tour in Nigeria. "After I got through there, I just thought it had been long enough. I just went out very nicely. I was in there right at twenty-six years. I didn't miss many days. I broke a few bones and had to lay off a night or two."

Wrestling helped fund his other passion for ranching, and he bought two separate ranches while still active. "They weren't these million dollar things. They were just things to run cows on or something. It was just cheap land. It wasn't *Bonanza* or anything like that," he laughed from his Oklahoma home. Raising quarterhorses led to thoroughbreds and the horseracing business.

Having taken many shortcuts in the staged pro wrestling game, Ellis was caught on charges of criminal conspiracy involving race-fixing in 1983. Racing in Kentucky, he and his partners had substituted an untattooed Mexican thoroughbred named *Gallant Viking*, who had won three races previously, for *Data Up*, an unraced horse.

Like the blood and the hairpiece, Ellis doesn't mind talking about it. "We were just running horses. It wasn't a fixed race. We'd put in a better horse under another name. It was the wrong thing to do. It was just a sideline, something to do for kicks, and everybody else was doing it." Because it was a federal case, he was tried and found guilty in Rochester, New York. The case cost over $80,000 for a lawyer, and Ellis was put on probation for three years.

But it wasn't all bad, even though he had to sell his racehorses.

"My probation was so good, they let me off in a year and a half," he said. "It was business and all, but I had to report back once a month to the probation officer. He got real lenient too; he was a big wrestling fan."

THE NEXT FIVE

JUNKYARD DOG

At the peak of his popularity in the Mid-South wrestling territory, the Junkyard Dog would make more money off his photo sales than he would make for his appearance in the ring.

"He didn't even have to get paid. He could take his pictures and his stuff and they would take his stuff, and he would sell, and he would make thousands and thousands of dollars on one show," recalled "Mr. Olympia" Jerry Stubbs, who was JYD's tag team partner before turning on him — a common theme in JYD's career.

"There was probably no one ever more popular in the Mid-South area than the Junkyard Dog," said Ted DiBiase. "At one time there was a survey done in New Orleans, and JYD was picked as the famous person people would most like to see. He was that hot. My memories of JYD down here were great. It was a time Mid-South wrestling was flourishing. We were the 'salt and pepper' team. He was the black babyface, and I was the white babyface."

Born December 13, 1953, and raised in Wadesboro, North Carolina, Sylvester Ritter played football at North Carolina's Fayetteville State University, where he was a two-time honorable mention All-American, and graduated in 1975 with a degree in political science and a minor in geography. While a part of the Green Bay Packers organization, Ritter's knee surgery ended his pro football career. Adrift in his home state, he was directed to Sonny King.

"He came to High Point, North Carolina. We met together, and I started talking to him and helping him. My friend owned a boxing gym in Winston-Salem, North Carolina. I used to go and work out with him there," recalled King. "He had what I thought would make him a success without having to

Junkyard Dog is ready to thump his next opponent.

work real, real hard after it . . . He had a unique style and I gave him an idea about how he should go about it."

Ritter debuted in Tennessee in 1977, working as Leroy Rochester, and did a subsequent tour of Germany. His first proper territory, with a push, came in the Calgary-based Stampede Wrestling, where he was the heel Big Daddy Ritter, managed by John Foley. Ritter would reign as the area's North American champion for six months, dropping the belt to Jake Roberts for a short while before regaining it for one last run.

In the Mid-South territory, where his father Grizzly Smith was entrenched behind the scenes, Roberts put in a good word for Ritter with promoter Bill Watts and booker Buck Robley. According to Robley, it was a rocky start for the heel Ritter, now redubbed The Junkyard Dog, playing off a line in Jim Croce's popular song "Bad, Bad Leroy Brown."

"He couldn't work, he couldn't do anything. But he had a lot of charisma," recalled Robley. "Watts owned the company and he said, 'Fire him.' I said, 'No, I'm not going to fire him. He's got a lot of charisma. I think I can make money with him.' So that's how I got him started."

Heading to the ring with a wheelbarrow overflowing with salvaged parts, the chiseled six-foot-three, 260-pound JYD would throw the junk in the corner of the ring, beat his opponent in two or three minutes, toss his foe in the wheelbarrow, and roll him out of the ring. A big steel chain became a trademark that stuck with him. "It's the same chain I've carried with me since I started wrestling professionally," said Ritter in 1991. Terry Orndorff was another championship partner who later turned on the Dog. "He used to pull me out of the dressing room; I'd just hold on to the chain and I'd waterski out to the ring," Orndorff recalled. "He had a great gimmick."

The angle that shot him to superstardom is still revered as one of the most dramatic, emotional angles of all time. The Fabulous Freebirds, Michael Hayes, Terry Gordy, and Buddy Roberts, "blinded" JYD when Hayes rubbed Roberts' hair cream into Dog's eyes. Adding to the personal issue, JYD's wife was pregnant and fans were told that JYD didn't get to see the birth of his daughter. (A son had died earlier when in Calgary.)

Announcer Jim Ross recalled the incident on his blog. "This matter wasn't about titles but was simply a well constructed, personal issue that got many fans to emotionally invest in what they were seeing unfold episodically on weekly TV." Brian Blair was in the sprawling Mid-South territory at the time. "He was getting money in the mail," Blair said of the sympathetic fans. "He was on fire."

A 1980 match at the New Orleans Superdome drew 26,000 fans who came to watch JYD take on Hayes, the foes wearing dog collars and linked by a chain so the "blind" JYD could still get at Hayes.

For the next few years, Ritter headlined the territory. "He was a six-minute man; if he went past that, he didn't know what to do," said Gene Petit. "The Louisiana territory was basically a black face territory. He was over like a million dollars. Watts was smart enough to know that you couldn't go past six or seven minutes with him because [while] physically he could do it, he didn't really know *what* to do."

In 1984, Ritter abruptly left Watts for Vince McMahon's expansionist WWF.

"When Vince took him out from under me, there were some real hard feelings because [Ritter] owed me a lot of money, number one. Number two, I had built everything on him," said Watts. "We'd surpassed the racial thing and had really done some things with him because he was just that special person." Tony Atlas takes Watts' side. "Junkyard Dog was making $250,000 a year. Bill Watts bought him a brand new Mercedes-Benz, the big 450, the real deal . . . bought his wife a beauty salon, helped him get a house, did everything for him. Vince made one phone call to Dog, and Dog was gone."

In the WWF, the Junkyard Dog was a natural fit, simplifying his character to catchphrases and growls. Wearing white boots and full-length red tights with "Thump" on the rear, JYD would drop to his knees for headbutts. The kids loved him, pouring into the ring after his matches to dance with the Dog, to Queen's "Another One Bites The Dust" initially, and then the funky "Grab Them Cakes," which he sang.

Facing family issues and drug problems, Ritter became unreliable, his workrate deteriorated, and his nickname became "Junkfood Dog" for having gained so much weight. By August 1988, he was gone from the WWF. "JYD ended up with a drug problem. But to his credit, he's one guy that tried to fight it off and beat it," said DiBiase.

JYD had two less-than-memorable runs in the NWA/WCW, including a June 1990 main event against Ric Flair on the Coastal Crunch Clash of Champions special, and a 1992 stint as one of the "Dudes With Attitudes" along with Sting, Lex Luger, and Paul Orndorff. Just one month before he died, JYD appeared at ECW Wrestlepalooza, honored as a hardcore legend and receiving a massive pop from the notoriously cynical crowd.

In the last years of his life, Ritter wrestled on independent shows and was a part-time car repossessor. He died in a single-car accident on June 2, 1998, on Interstate 20 near Forest, Mississippi, in a repossessed car. He had been returning home to Magee, Mississippi, having been to his daughter Latoya's high school graduation in Wadesboro, North Carolina.

"Over the years my dad had worked with juveniles who had committed serious crimes and had been put in juvenile homes," said daughter Latoya, the youngest of Ritter's three children, after his death.

"Part of his life was tragic, at the end I know he lost a lot, he lost his family. I mean that's why when he died he had driven back to North Carolina to see his daughter graduate from high school, and it was on the way back that he had the car accident and was killed," said DiBiase of Ritter, who was the best man at his second wedding. "As a wrestler, he was one of those guys, as a character in our business he will never be forgotten. But as a human being, we all have our flaws and certainly I wrote a book about mine, but JYD as a person, as a man, was a man of his word, he was straightforward, he would literally give you the shirt off his back. And he was just a good man."

Watts regrets not making true peace with Ritter, even though he brought him into WCW.

"Buddy Landel asked me to write a eulogy for him that he could read at the funeral. When I sat down and wrote that eulogy, it broke my heart because I realized that I was so blessed to have had the time in my life with him," Watts concluded. "The fact of the matter was that he died without me getting to tell him how much he meant to me personally, and how much I benefited from his life."

MIL MASCARAS

How legendary does one have to be to boast his own postage stamp? Just ask Mil Mascaras.

One of the most famous stars in the storied history of *lucha libre*, Mascaras was honored in May 2011 by the Mexican Postal Service with a series of stamps bearing his likeness. The set belongs to a collection called "Icons of Lucha Libre" that includes the original El Santo and El Hijo del Santo.

To a generation of *lucha* fans, Mascaras was the messiah of the squared circle, a legend who symbolized fair and clean living, a masked marvel who is timeless and enduring.

"The Man of a Thousand Masks" was one of the industry's top stars of the

'60s and '70s and one of the most celebrated masked performers of all time. Known for his barrel-chested, Olympian physique and seemingly endless array of colorful masks, Mascaras stood five-foot-eleven and weighed 230 pounds, yet moved with the grace and speed of a junior heavyweight.

For most masked wrestlers, wearing a hood was part of their job. For Mil Mascaras, wearing a mask was part of his life.

A star in the ring and on Mexico's big screen, Mascaras became a larger-than-life figure, a masked luchador who was flashy, flamboyant, and acrobatic. And to many of his opponents, the descriptive "arrogant" might apply as well.

Was it arrogance or simply being misunderstood? Probably a little of both, but there's no denying that the international superhero's rock-star appeal

HOWARD BAUM

Mil Mascaras' flying – here against Frankie Lancaster – was ahead of its time.

made him one of the most sought-after performers in the wrestling business.

To gain a clearer picture of Mil Mascaras, though, one must look at his culture and his lofty standing in that culture.

Born Aaron Miguelito Rodríguez in 1942 (some sources list the year as 1938) in San Luis Potosi, Mexico, Mascaras has maintained a strict separation between his personal and professional life throughout his career. The fact that he does to this very day underscores the significance of the mask in his culture.

Masked wrestlers have been a unique cultural phenomenon since the 1930s in Mexico, and Mascaras followed in the footsteps of legendary luchadores such as El Santo (Rodolfo Guzman Huerta) and Blue Demon (Alexander Munoz

Moreno). In Mexico the mask is a mystical symbol and a projection of the soul. "I try to keep my privacy as much as possible. This is just part of me," Mascaras explained.

Mascaras, unlike most of his hooded contemporaries, has never worked without his mask and has no plans to take it off. "The mask means everything," said Mascaras, who sports one of his trademark hoods everywhere he goes. "It's a very important part of our culture. At that time in Mexico, it was only El Santo, Blue Demon, and me wearing masks. And now everyone has them."

That unwavering connection to the significance of the mask and Mascaras' confident demeanor has sometimes been interpreted as arrogance and aloofness by his colleagues in the business. Mascaras was a major draw but, according to some of his peers, was egotistical and often uncooperative.

"In the ring, he refused to sell his rivals' moves," noted the late Fred Blassie, one of Mascaras' most famous rivals. "Doing a job to elevate an opponent was the furthest thing from his mind. If it didn't benefit Mascaras, you could go fuck yourself."

Dutch Savage found the easiest way to earn Mascaras' respect was to force the issue. Savage remembers chopping Mascaras during a six-man match. Mascaras, however, didn't budge. "Well, Duchess, he doesn't seem to want to sell any of your stuff," Don Leo Jonathan chuckled to the six-foot-four, 275-pound Savage. "He will," Savage assured his partner. "I threw a punch at him on the ropes and I uncorked one. It caught him right in the clicker, and he went down. I said, 'Whoops, potato,' and went back to the corner. He sold for me after that," laughed Savage.

"Mascaras was never one of the boys," said Superstar Billy Graham. "After his matches, he'd shower with his mask on. I understand protecting your image, but the guy was kayfabing us. I'm not the first person to say that it wasn't fun wrestling Mascaras. He was mechanical, and because of his mask, fans couldn't read his facial expressions . . . Mascaras was also an absolute prima donna, prancing around on his toes and sticking out his chest. He hated to sell your moves; whatever you got, he gave grudgingly."

"He was miserable to work with . . . typical babyface, didn't want to do anything," said the late Don "The Spoiler" Jardine, who appeared in a historic match against Mascaras at Madison Square Garden, marking the first time a wrestler (Mascaras) had ever worn a mask into a ring in New York state. "He wanted everything for himself. He wouldn't do anything for you. He wanted all his classic stuff done, but not for anyone else."

Mascaras, though, was the kind of performer promoters loved to book on their shows because he drew big crowds. The key to Mascaras was knowing how to use him and, to an extent, understanding his culture.

"I never had a problem with Mil, because I understood that Mil represented a portion of my audience — the Latinos — and I never used Mil for angles," recalled the late Gary Hart, who was booking the World Class Wrestling territory at the time. "I brought Mil in, and put him as high to the top of the card as I could, and always put him over right in the middle, and instructed the guys who were wrestling him to remember that Mil has got to look great. Because if Mil didn't look great, what was Mil? I understood that. I could put Mil in the Sportatorium, or the Houston Coliseum, or the Reunion Arena, and put him with a top guy, and the Mexicans would turn out in droves, and the Anglos liked him too . . . I saw no reason to bring Mil in and beat him down, and try to work angles. That would be like bringing in Antonino Rocca or someone like Dusty Rhodes or someone like Hulk Hogan and trying to get a heel over. Nobody wants to see that."

While there's more than a grain of truth about Mascaras not liking to do jobs, you'd never convince Tennessee-based promoter Jerry Jarrett that Mascaras was anything but a consummate professional. Mascaras did a stretcher job for area legend Jackie Fargo at the Mid-South Coliseum in Memphis in 1979 and even allowed the fifty-one-year-old Fargo to run down the aisle, turn over the stretcher and put the boots to him to further sell a rib injury. Jarrett revealed the back story that he thinks might have led to Mascaras'"benevolence."

Salvador Lutteroth, known as the "father of lucha libre" and at one time the most powerful man in Mexican wrestling, had helped launch the career of lucha libre's first breakout superstar, El Santo, and transformed the masked star into a national pop-culture phenomenon. "[Mascaras] knew that Salvador Lutteroth thought very highly of me," said Jarrett, who had befriended Lutteroth at an NWA convention. "[Lutteroth] could have bought and sold me and half the people in the Alliance. We'd always have dinner together. My wife Deborah and I went down and stayed at his house in Acapulco. The manager of the El Presidente Hotel worked for Salvador, and Salvador assigned him as our driver. I think that Mascaras appreciated that relationship, and for that reason liked us."

Jarrett said he was very impressed with Mascaras' professionalism. "Arrogance begets arrogance, and kindness begets kindness. I told him that I appreciated his contributions to the business, and that when he got here that whatever he wanted to do we'd do. I think he saw we respected him and that

On the mat, Mil Mascaras was no slouch, and here ties up The Texan (Raul Mata) in Miami in 1983.

HOWARD BAUM

he had heard the same thing from Salvador. He said he was passing through and that he would like to do something to help us. At the time I didn't realize how significant it was."

Jarrett wasn't the only official who witnessed Mascaras' selflessness up close and personal.

Art Williams, who worked in the Los Angeles office when Mascaras was on fire in California, remembers refereeing a match where Mascaras did the honors. "I had the privilege of refereeing a match where Mascaras actually put someone over right in the middle of the ring, and I wish I had a video to prove it, because that hardly ever happened before or since. But at the Olympic, sometime in 1968, on a Friday night, for the America's title, Mascaras versus El Mongol, two out of three falls. In the third fall, Mascaras actually put Mongol over one, two, three, right in the middle. Little did I know at the time that history was being made."

Long-time wrestling magazine editor Bill Apter is a staunch Mascaras advocate who believes that many wrestlers simply just didn't understand Mascaras. "There were many top wrestlers throughout the years who would tell me that Mascaras was not all I thought he was in the ring, but I chalked that up to their insecurities that they couldn't do what he did and get the reaction from the crowd each and every time. As for Mascaras the man, I can tell you that we shared many a dinner table, many a theatrical event, and many flights and car rides. He is a classy man who I have been proud to be associated with during my career."

The mask was a symbol of something greater than Mascaras himself. He used the mask to cross over to a successful movie career in his native Mexico, breaking into the acting business about the same time he began wrestling professionally nearly half a century ago. A well-conditioned athlete who was training for a spot on the Mexican Olympics team in judo, Mascaras passed on the opportunity when Mexican magazine mogul Valente Perez convinced him that he could make big waves, but in a different direction.

The Mil Mascaras character was invented to fill a movie void when El Santo jumped to a rival studio following a contractual dispute and Blue Demon was injured and unable to work. Rodríguez was picked to play the character because he was athletic, and had an impressive physique.

Mexican movie producer Enrique Vergara, looking for a new character to star in his wrestling/horror movies, saw Mascaras as a natural and gave him the starring role in a 1965 flick aptly titled Mil Mascaras. Although production values were cheap and the campy films resembled B-movies made in the United States, the genre had become the rage of Mexican cinema, combining elements of Gothic horror, science fiction, sex, and comedy, with some wrestling matches thrown in for good measure.

Mascaras and fellow luchadores battled dastardly sorts that included everything from evil scientists to monsters to robots. His film with El Santo and Blue Demon, The Mummies of Guanajuato, was one of the highest grossing domestic films of all time in Mexico and throughout Latin and South America.

With Mascaras' amazing physique, colorful attire, and flamboyant personality, he became an instant hit in the ring as well as on the silver screen. Trained by Diablo Velasco, Mascaras sold out arenas throughout Mexico and did the same in Central America before making his U.S. debut in 1968, four years after his first pro bout in Guadalajara, where he worked sans mask under the name Ricardo Duran. Mil Mascaras first used that name on July 16, 1965, at Arena Mexico, partnering with Black Shadow, with whom he would regularly team along with his idol, El Santo. He won his first title on June 12, 1967, defeating the original Espanto for the Mexican light heavyweight title in Mexico City.

Unbeknownst to most, said mat photojournalist Mike Lano, wrestling's patriarchal Lutteroth family had someone else playing the "Mascaras" character for a while, but it didn't work out. Rodríguez, he said, was then plucked out of a gym as a bodybuilder and was a much better fit.

Like Santo, perhaps the most famous and iconic of all Mexican luchadores, Mascaras became a major star in his homeland. Unlike Santo, however, Mascaras would travel abroad extensively and become the biggest wrestling export his country ever produced. He became an international superstar years ahead of his time who helped revolutionize the sport and inspired a countless number of future stars ranging from Jimmy Snuka to Rey Mysterio.

"If it weren't for Mil Mascaras, there would be no Jushin Liger, no Ultimo Dragon or the Great Sasake," Satoru Sayama once said about Mascaras. Sayama, who as the original Tiger Mask inspired the likes of Liger, Dragon, and Sasake to become pro wrestlers, was himself inspired as a youth by the high-flying Mexican superstar.

"I made something completely different," said Mascaras. "The masks were different; I had beautiful, elegant clothes, and a different style with different combinations of moves. I changed the wrestling in the United States, I changed the wrestling in Europe, I changed the wrestling in Japan, I changed the wrestling all over. I was different from anyone else. The guys who started doing flying body presses and such were copying me."

Mascaras was one of the biggest drawing cards in the United States, particularly in southern California and Texas, during the late '60s and '70, and became this country's biggest name masked wrestler along with The Destroyer (Dick Beyer), with whom his series of matches helped put him on the wrestling map in Japan.

"Of all the wrestlers that I ever wrestled against, Mil Mascaras was the toughest, best-conditioned," Beyer said at a 2010 Pro Wrestling Hall of Fame induction speech. "When I want to watch a wrestling match at home, I take out a wrestling match where I wrestled against Mil Mascaras. And I can still get excited because Mil Mascaras was a wrestler who never gave you a hold. I learned quick that if he wasn't going to give me a hold, I wasn't going to give him a hold. We went sixty minutes in Japan, and in the Olympic Auditorium in Los Angeles, with the same type of match. We never talked. We never talked in the ring. It just came as the match went along."

The refined and patrician Mascaras, who rarely resorted to rule-breaking and used his repertoire of moves and counter-moves, was an innovator and trendsetter inside the ring who introduced aerial maneuvers such as planchas, topes, and suicide dives to new audiences. His visage routinely graced the covers of the era's top wrestling magazines.

Along with Bruno Sammartino and Dusty Rhodes, Mascaras became one of the most frequent and popular covers for Apter's newsstand magazines. With his colorful masks and ring outfits, Mascaras was a natural. To this day, the luchador remains one of Apter's all-time favorites.

"Back in the mid-1970s I used to watch the NWA wrestling shows from Los Angeles in my apartment in Queens, New York," recalled Apter. "Although the commentary was in Spanish, it didn't matter as the action and the roster of colorful characters broke the language barriers. The one standout on those shows was a masked man who captured my imagination with his in-ring style.

His colorful outfits meant lots of space in the magazines.

He made it all seem so easy. Every move he was put in, he had a counter for and eased into it with such a smooth, fluid movement and it was magnificent. That man was Mil Mascaras. Years later I would get the opportunity to photograph so many of his great matches right from the ring apron — and catching him flying through the air and trading holds made for some great images for the magazines I worked for back then. The sight of Mascaras perched high on the top turnbuckles and then so gracefully diving off onto his opponent for the pin was always the highlight of his matches. I always looked forward to catching that move, to be just in the right position with my camera, to get that fabulous shot."

Still wrestling occasionally, Mascaras stays busy and likes to write and paint, but more than anything, he maintains a solid physique through a strict daily training regimen. "When you love the profession, you take care of yourself. I stay active and I stay in great condition. Today I'll run five kilometers and I'll lift weights for about an hour. I eat good food and get good sleep. I don't take any drugs, I don't smoke, and only drink an occasional glass of wine or a beer or two. The body is like a clock or a good car. You have to take it to the mechanic and keep it in tune."

Mascaras also still protects kayfabe and goes to great lengths to keep the Mascaras mystique alive. "They all unmask in the locker room, save Mil," said Lano. "After all these years, he still keeps his mask on while showering around the boys, at restaurants far away from fans or the venues."

Mascaras was awarded the IWA world title in late 1974, defending the title at big shows in New Jersey against Ivan Koloff and Mexico City against Lou Thesz, and never lost it. He was allowed to keep the strap when former Chicago White Sox owner Eddie Einhorn's outlaw promotion folded. He still defends the title in Mexico and Japan and wears the old belt to the ring. "Japan is, oddly enough, his primary bread and butter other than mark fests here in the States now," said Lano, noting his history-making match against The Destroyer at Korakuen Hall in 1973. Mascaras had made his Tokyo debut in 1971 and was called "Kamen Kizoku," or the masked noble, by the Japanese fans for being a paragon of the luchador fighting spirit.

Mascaras is a member of one of Mexico's most prominent wrestling families — his brothers José and Pablo respectively wrestle as Dos Caras and Sicodélico; José's son, Alberto, worked as Dos Caras Jr. in Mexico and, most recently, as WWE superstar Alberto Del Rio. Pablo's son Aaron is better known as Sicodélico Jr.

The wrestling business has taken Mascaras from Pakistan to Japan to Nigeria, where he claimed a record for a crowd of 93,000 in a football and soccer stadium, and has allowed him to travel the world many times over. "I got the chance to go to the best museums in the world, to see other cultures, to visit homes of many friends. I've had a beautiful, beautiful, beautiful life in this profession."

JOE SAVOLDI

On a moonless August night in 1943, four American spies disguised as peasants launched rubber rafts from a patrol torpedo boat off the southern coast of Italy, paddled ashore, and vanished into the darkness. The sweep of their mission was breathtaking: to orchestrate the surrender of the Italian fleet in World War II. To execute their orders, they had to sneak through German-controlled territory and

Joe Savoldi demonstrates the "airplane whirl hold."

pass a note hidden in the slit cover of a book to a ranking admiral in the Italian navy. "The MacGregor Project," as it was known, was possibly the oddest and most hazardous assignment ever undertaken by a pro wrestling champion. Joe Savoldi, one of wrestling's top draws of the 1930s, was working for the Office of Strategic Services as bodyguard for Marcello Girosi, part of the spy team and brother of the Italian admiral. "His wrestler's face had been mashed against the ring canvas a thousand times. He was enthusiastic; I thought he would be perfect," recalled Michael Burke, another member of the undercover team and future president of the New York Yankees. "He would terrify Girosi and maybe the entire Italian fleet."

The operatives got their message across; the admiral thought about it, but decided to wait for formal negotiations with the Allies, which soon followed. By then, the team was culling information about weapons from inside sources and helping to smuggle anti-fascist scientists and naval officers from Italy. When Savoldi's eighteen months of cloak-and-dagger work were revealed in 1945, he was, like any good spy, totally circumspect. "Let's just say," he told Jack Cuddy of the United Press, "I was working for the government on special assignment."

Football star, international wrestler, entrepreneur, war-time spy, witness to labor strife — Joe Savoldi didn't live just a dual life; he lived four or five or more, and had a knack for always being on hand when history called. "He was, according to my father, the most competitive person in the world. Whether it was playing sports or cards or checkers — campus champion at Notre Dame — he had to be the very best," said his grandson, J.G. Savoldi. "He also realized fairly early that he was blessed with many talents and he felt like he had an obligation to live up to his potential. His service in the OSS was not born out of a sense of adventure as much as a sense of duty. His personal notes make mention of living knowing how great his life had been and of wondering if he was going to run out of luck and die during one of his missions in Italy."

Born May 5, 1908, near Milan, Italy, Savoldi spent most of the first twelve years of his life with relatives in Italy because family predicaments, illness, and World War I kept him from joining his immigrant parents in Three Oaks, Michigan. He was decidedly rough around the edges when he landed at Notre Dame to play football in 1927; quarterback Frank Carideo sometimes had to repeat signal calls to him in Italian, and Coach Knute Rockne told one southern sportswriter that Savoldi was the most awkward player in America. That changed on October 19, 1929, when Savoldi reeled off touchdown runs of forty-five and seventy-five yards in an important game against Wisconsin, and added ten tackles on defense. Suddenly, the wavy-haired Savoldi was a national hero whose awkward gait was simply a way of feinting defenders. "He has a deceptive hip-shaking gallop when underway and his high bobbing knees clip off tackles like a scythe," wrote Walter Brown of the Associated Press. "Jumping Joe" led the undefeated Irish to consensus national championships in 1929 and 1930. But romance, or the lack of it, got in the way of a good story. With four games left in the 1930 season, a judge in South Bend, Indiana, filed divorce papers that showed Savoldi had been secretly married for eighteen months. Marriages outside the Catholic Church, and especially divorces, were verboten, and Savoldi withdrew from the Catholic school on November 17 before it could expel him.

This was Joseph A. Savoldi Jr., though, which meant he simply passed from one moment in history to the next. Within a week of leaving Notre Dame, he inked a contract with George Halas, founder of the Chicago Bears, to play in the pros for $1,000 a contest, plus a cut of the gate. But Savoldi only appeared in two games for the Bears. Less than three months after his pro football debut, he was a marquee wrestler, at the urging of manager Billy Sandow and Ed "Strangler" Lewis, who were as important to wrestling as Rockne and Halas were to the gridiron. Money played a role in his change of heart; the reported $3,500 he got for his first match, a victory against Don Delaun — Don Leo Jonathan's dad — in Kansas City, Missouri, on February 16, 1931, represented a hefty downpayment on his avowed plans to finance his two siblings' education.

In later years, Savoldi explained that he turned to the mat because he wanted to get his head beat in on his own dime. The Bears' linemen, he said, stopped opening holes for him once they realized they were pulling in $25 to $100 a game to his $1,000-plus. "Shucks, I'd probably have done the same thing myself if I were playing with a guy getting twenty times as much dough as I did," Savoldi said. "I didn't mind playing against eleven guys but twenty-one was too many. When I found I had to play against my own team, too, I quit and took to pro wrestling."

At first, Savoldi's wrestling wares were mostly headbutts and flying tackles, but given his national celebrity, that was enough. During his first few months in the business, he scored main event victories in Los Angeles against Abe Coleman, Doc Sarpolis, and Everette Marshall. "Give Joe Savoldi another year in the wrestling game and he'll be the most popular and colorful performer in the sport not excepting Jim Londos, Strangler Lewis, or other famous groaners," Joseph "Roundy" Coughlin of the *Wisconsin State Journal* predicted in December 1931. "He's a trifle short of pained expressions, but he groans fairly well and eventually he'll master this end of the business." As Savoldi developed, he incorporated a dropkick into his arsenal, and while he didn't originate the maneuver, he became more associated with it than any wrestler of his time. "Jumping" Joe delivered a traditional dropkick, back parallel to the mat, with his feet thrusting into his foe's chest or chin, depending on the rules of the particular state athletic commission overseeing the bout.

But a fast count, not fast feet, elevated him to the top of the profession. On April 7, 1933, Savoldi won the world championship from Jim Londos at Chicago Stadium via a controversial pinfall that apparently only referee Bob Managoff Sr. saw. Londos and the 6,800 fans were bewildered by the sudden stoppage of action, but behind the scenes, New York promoters Toots Mondt and Jack Curley had been trying to spirit away the title from the Greek and place it around the waist of someone less independent-minded. Londos protested long and hard about the double-cross, and Illinois authorities temporarily suspended wrestling in the state, but Savoldi remained the champ. "Even if it was a 'cross' as some of the evil-minded have suggested, it was a victory for Mr. Savoldi," sportswriter Damon Runyon concluded. "As a wrestler he is one of the best showmen in the game, with plenty of color and personality." For his part, Savoldi agreed to a reported $100,000 pact with a Toronto syndicate and bought himself a new overcoat. "It was all right to go without a coat and a hat when I was just a wrestler," he explained. "Cold never bothers me. Now it's different. You've got to look like something when you're champion."

Life was good for the new champ. On May 22, 1933, he married Lois Poole, an art student, in a ceremony in La Porte, Indiana, and headed straight to New York City, where he felled the aging Lewis after forty-three minutes of work. His reign was brief; Jim Browning took the title claim from him June 12 in New York. Savoldi went on to tour North America, with regular and successful appearances in Toronto and other cities. The following February, he fell to Londos in a rematch in Chicago when the Illinois athletic commission deprived him of his signature move by barring the dropkick. Doubters yelled "fake" at Londos because his victory was so brief at twenty minutes, but the important number was the size of the crowd — a whopping 20,200.

While wrestling in the United States dissolved into competing factions, Savoldi capitalized on his success with long and profitable overseas tours. He spent ten months in Australia and New Zealand in 1936 and 1937, made side trips to India, Greece, and Singapore, and wired sportswriters back home that business was simply too good to return to the States. In 1938, he starred in Europe, and Cecil B. Brown, later a famous World War II correspondent, found him living comfortably with Lois and son Joe III in an apartment on the Left Bank of Paris, still exuding an undeniable charm. "The hair is receding from his forehead, and there's a sunflower spot on top. His eyes have lost the luster of youth, except when he starts to demonstrate a pet hold, or how he starts his famous flying kick. Then they become adolescent, mischievous, completely boyish," Brown wrote.

Savoldi plowed his payoffs, estimated at $50,000 annually before expenses, into a handsome house in Michigan, and announced plans to manufacture a new soft drink called "Drop Kick." The venture faltered because war-time sugar rationing impeded production, and soon enough, he found himself at age thirty-four drawn into World War II. The OSS recruited him in 1942, gave him the code name of "Vic," and shipped him off for training in the mountains of western Maryland. One day, Savoldi stunned a close combat instructor when he lunged at him, grabbed his legs, knocked him over, and pinned him.

As Rutgers University historian John Whiteclay Chambers II recounted, the stunned instructor, Jerry Sage, spit out grass and asked "Vic" where he learned that. "'That's my specialty in the ring,' Vic replied, 'It's called the flying scissors.'" On duty with a provost marshal's office in Italy, Savoldi was credited with breaking up a black-market ring in Naples and interrupting the hijacking of military trucks.

Savoldi lost most of his earnings because of the aborted soft drink venture, so he returned to wrestling after the war. He also promoted matches in Chicago and Michigan, where a barnstorming baseball player named Houston Harris was his greatest find;

Joe Savoldi, football star.

Harris became Bobo Brazil, the best-known African-American wrestler in history. Though he showed the rigors of his years, Savoldi remained a headliner and was a frequent victim of Gorgeous George's evil ways in places as distant as Iowa and western New York. "When he returned to the ring he had a ridiculous schedule, and it seems to me that I counted 280-plus matches in a single year as he traveled mostly from Michigan to the East Coast and up into Canada," grandson J.G. said. "He was proud to be a wrestler up until the 1970s when he thought that the sport had digressed." A reprise of his feud with Londos in Chicago drew only 1,200 in 1950, and Savoldi curtailed his active career in 1952, just as Joe III matured into a conference champion in track and field at Michigan State.

Never far from the headlines, though, Savoldi wound up testifying before a congressional committee in 1953 probing a strike at a Benton Harbor, Michigan, plant where he worked. Even then, he had one more accomplishment left to check off his list. At the suggestion of a friend, Savoldi resumed the studies that he dropped at Notre Dame. After a thirty-year absence, he returned to school, and received his bachelor's degree from Evansville in 1962 at the age of fifty-four. Savoldi became a high school science teacher in nearby Henderson County, Kentucky, and wife Lois said in 1972 that he finally closed the book on a lifetime of adventures. "He loved it. He had found his true calling at last," she said. "He used to say the only thing he regretted was that he wasted all those years before getting into teaching." He died in January 1974 at sixty-five in Cumberland Shore, Kentucky, and sports pages across the country gave him one final wink. "There are many more Savoldi stories," said Joe Doyle of the *South Bend Tribune*, "but Joe was a guy who beat the odds with such an involved background."

MR. WRESTLING II (JOHNNY WALKER)

A simple phone call may have changed the course of wrestling history.

What would Georgia Championship Wrestling — or the wrestling world in general — have been like without Mr. Wrestling II? It might be hard to fathom, considering the masked man's tremendous impact on one of the most visible territories in the country during the '70s, but we might have never known had it not been for Jerry Jarrett.

The Tennessee-based promoter, who was being brought in by Jim Barnett to take over the booking job from Bill Watts in the Atlanta office, was looking for a masked man to replace the popular Mr. Wrestling (Tim Woods). Jarrett had asked Woods, a headliner working for Eddie Graham in Florida at the time, to return to Atlanta where he had been one of the top stars.

"Tim Woods was probably the most famous wrestler in Atlanta at the time. He was the Jerry Lawler of Atlanta," said Jarrett. "I asked Tim to come back and be my superstar. He said he appreciated my offer but didn't think he'd come back."

It didn't take long for Jarrett to come up with the name of a wrestler he thought just might fit in Woods' place. Ironically the wrestler Jarrett had in mind was pushing forty and had been considered more of a journeyman for most of his career. But Jarrett had experienced some success revitalizing the careers of Jackie Fargo and Don and Al Greene in Memphis, creating a second major run for those veteran stars, and was confident he could pull off that same magic in Atlanta.

Within minutes of ending his conversation with Woods, Jarrett made a call to Johnny Walker, who had semi-retired from the wrestling business and was running a gas station in Knoxville, Tennessee. Jarrett had first met Walker several years earlier in Tennessee where the latter had enjoyed a nice run and regional tag team reigns with area favorites such as Ken Lucas, Len Rossi, Bearcat Brown, Dennis Hall, and Tojo Yamamoto, along with holding the territory's NWA U.S. junior heavyweight crown.

"He had these smooth escape moves that really intrigued me, but he was very much an undercard man," said Jarrett. Still, Jarrett was convinced it could work, age be damned. "They were about the same size, and I believed that Johnny could pick up the Tim Woods mannerisms. It clicked. It worked. It was just one of those things that I was very lucky on."

His marching orders to Walker were clear: "Go out and buy yourself a white outfit and a white mask. You will be Mr. Wrestling II in Atlanta."

And the rest, as they say, was history.

"He came down and got over like a million dollars," said Jarrett. So much, in fact, that Woods, who had long been established as the Mr. Wrestling, placed a call to Jarrett asking to return. "Well, you son of a gun, you've kind of replaced me," Woods told the new Atlanta booker. "Oh no, we just put a two after his name," Jarrett joked.

Lillian Carter, mother of U.S. President Jimmy Carter, chats with her favorite wrestler, Mr. Wrestling II.

What resulted was the creation of one of the greatest runs in Georgia wrestling history, and one of the most beloved icons in the business.

Mr. Wrestling II, simply known as "Two," initially was introduced as the tag team partner of the original Mr. Wrestling (Woods), but would achieve even greater success than his talented predecessor. Sporting a white mask trimmed in black, Walker would become the top star on the nation's first SuperStation, Channel 17 out of Atlanta, and would be a staple in Georgia for the next decade. With cable TV still in its infancy, Mr. Wrestling II would become one of the most recognized performers in the wrestling business, garnering national attention in matches aired via satellite on WTBS.

Walker was so popular that police officers would sometimes pull him over just to get an autograph. "I was one of the few guys who could walk into a bank with a mask," he chuckled. "It was over big time in Atlanta."

He was even invited to the White House. He shared a close bond with former president Jimmy Carter, who considered Mr. Wrestling II his favorite wrestler,

HOWARD BAUM

Mr. Wrestling II slaps the sleeper hold on the Assassin (Joe Hamilton).

and was personally invited to attend the Georgia native's inauguration in 1977. Walker, though, reluctantly declined a seat with the Carter family when the Secret Service told him he would have to remove his famous mask due to security concerns.

A wrestler's mask stood for something in those days, and Walker took the values symbolized by the white hood he wore quite seriously. "But I understood why they did it," said Walker, who was rightfully concerned about the damage it might have done to his career had he revealed his identity for all to see.

The president understood, and so did his mother, Miss Lillian Carter, a down-to-earth, devout grappling fan who religiously attended the weekly matches and was perhaps No. 2's No. 1 fan. "She used to come down to Columbus, Georgia, to watch me wrestle," recalled Walker, who was even invited to her home in Plains, Georgia. For that visit, anyway, Walker got to keep his famous mask on. "If you folks don't mind, I'll just leave the mask on," he told agents who accompanied him to Miss Lillian's home. "She didn't want anyone coming in while we were talking. We probably talked more than two hours. We discussed all kinds of stuff. And the whole time I was in there she never cracked about wrestling. And I appreciated that."

There are many stories of Walker being extremely protective of his identity.

He tells the tale of an inquisitive black lady who approached his wife during a show at the SuperDome in New Orleans many years ago. "Mrs. Walker, can I ask you a question?" the fan asked. "Have you ever seen your husband with his mask off?" "My wife looked around at the woman and said '. . . No.' She told me about that later and I almost wet my pants."

Born in 1934 in Charleston, South Carolina, John Francis Walker was the grateful recipient of a second chance in the wrestling business. And, unlike many others, he converted that second chance into a remarkable career.

Walker was a Marine brat who bounced around quite a bit during his early years. He spent most of his life in Hawaii, having moved there in the late '40s before leaving in 1958 to go on the road. He returned to Honolulu in 1989 after retiring from the wrestling business and has lived there ever since.

Walker "got sidetracked" as a 191-pound sumo wrestler before breaking into the pro ranks in 1956. Going up against true super-heavyweights such as the revered 528-pound Azumafuji Kin'ichi, Walker routinely found himself at a definite weight disadvantage, quickly discovering that the more conventional art of pro wrestling was more to his liking. "I got bounced around like a toy," he laughed. "I was very strong and I gave everything I had, but even with my strength it didn't matter."

The sense of balance and coordination that Walker developed in sumo would help in amateur and pro wrestling, and he used the experience to train with established stars such as Pat O'Connor, Dick Hutton, Don Curtis, and Tony Morelli. "Those guys would really work me over," said Walker. "I guess I was a real glutton for punishment back then. But I was a young kid and I loved it."

Walker, whose incredible flexibility and double-jointed, contortionist moves prompted Houston promoter Paul Boesch to dub him "Rubberman," appeared throughout the country and in Japan and Canada, proving himself to be a reliable hand if not a main-event act.

Veteran heel Rip Hawk was one of many opponents who found Walker's double-jointed antics a little disconcerting. "I'd have a hold on him, and all of a sudden he would slip out of it. Boy was I surprised," he recalled of his first encounter with Walker, not realizing he was double-jointed.

"I first saw Johnny Walker wrestle as 'Rubberman' during my training time in Boston in 1960–61, and then we became friends and travel companions in the Nashville territory in the late '60s, and Tampa in '71 when he was 'The Grappler,'" recalled Les Thatcher. "Then we both were with the NWA during 'The War of Atlanta' where he drew big as Wrestling II. A solid worker who made the wrestling fans believe with his realistic interviews and his 'Big Knee' finisher. John fit any role he was asked to play."

Walker, in fact, toiled more than fifteen years as a journeyman before reinventing himself as one of the most successful masked babyfaces in mat history. Shortly before his emergence as Mr. Wrestling II, Walker donned a mask in Florida for the first time in his career as The Grappler. "Eddie Graham had asked me to come down with a mask, so my wife made me a mask that was purple and yellow." Initially he hated it so much that he ran to the dressing room after his first bout and promptly ripped the hood off his head.

"I took that damn mask off as fast as I could. I couldn't get my breath," Walker recalled. "How was I ever going to get used to wearing this thing?" Fortunately he did get used to wearing the mask, and eventually began to even enjoy it. It didn't hurt that the hood seemed to bring him a renewed feeling of confidence that would translate into bigger payoffs and greater success. But it never even crossed his mind that he would spend the rest of his career behind the hood.

It was less than two years later, after he thought he had hung up his wrestling tights for good, that fate came calling. Jarrett and former booker Leo Garibaldi had both lobbied to bring Walker in, and the idea intrigued Walker. He had just purchased a house and a Tenneco gas station in Knoxville, but he left both behind and headed for Georgia.

The gimmick became an instant moneymaker for Walker, and was so successful that he never appeared again without the hood. "It's strange how that worked out. Folks liked me better with the mask on than they did with my plain old face. I guess I was just so damn ugly," he laughed.

His masked bookend, Mr. Wrestling, would play a big part in Walker's success. Walker would both team with Woods and work a major program with him. The two formed one of the top duos in the business during the '70s, drawing sellout crowds at Atlanta's Omni and throughout the Southeast for matches with such formidable teams as The Assassins and The Anderson Brothers. "We made a good team and complemented one another very nicely," said Walker. "We got along fantastically. He was an old-time wrestler like myself and we just clicked."

Because of their close relationship outside the ring, Walker wasn't overly happy about "feuding" with his friend and partner in a major angle that popped the territory. "I liked the angle to a point. I didn't really like the idea of me turning on Timmy because Timmy and I were closer than brothers. I did it because they thought it would do business. But I wasn't that crazy about it."

Walker, as Mr. Wrestling II, was quick and explosive in the ring, his signature "million-dollar kneelift" becoming one of the most popular finishers in the business at the time. Fans would pack Atlanta's City Auditorium and Omni to pop for the masked man and his coup de grace.

Woods actually had been the first recipient of Walker's kneelift when Walker introduced the maneuver while working as The Grappler in Tampa. "Timmy was my guinea pig," laughed Walker. "It busted him all to hell. He got two black eyes and a knot on his forehead. That was the only time he ever took it. People just bought that hold like crazy. It kind of followed me around."

Journeyman Johnny Walker.

Mr. Wrestling II also enjoyed feuds with other masked heels such as "The Spoiler" (Don Jardine). "Mr. Wrestling II was truly a legendary figure of Southern wrestling, much like Bruno Sammartino in New York, Fritz Von Erich in Dallas and Dusty Rhodes in Dallas, and he was far better and much more over than the first Mr. Wrestling, Tim Woods, ever dreamed of being," said manager Gary Hart in his book *Playboy Gary Hart: My Life in Wrestling*. "The feud between Mr. Wrestling II and The Spoiler was one of the best businesses I ever did for a singles run."

Walker retired from the business not long after Vincent K. McMahon's national expansion in the mid-'80s and returned to Hawaii. His wife, Olivia, a talented, Dublin-born seamstress who designed exquisite costumes and ring robes for such wrestling stars as Ric Flair, Dusty Rhodes, Greg Valentine, and Paul Orndorff, as well as for celebrities such as Dolly Parton, Porter Wagner, Charo, and Liberace, passed away in 2000. "She was not only a tremendous seamstress, she was a tremendous woman," said Walker.

The two enjoyed forty years of marital bliss. "My wife was very special. How many wives would polish your shoes when you're not there? Mine did. It's hard to imagine that she's even gone. I sit here sometimes and think to myself where is she? I have pictures of her here and there. It's hard. We'll be together again, and I look forward to that time."

Walker, as Mr. Wrestling II, came out of retirement in 2006 and helped train a group of wrestlers for a Hawaiian promotion run by Don Muraco. He actually worked a short match the following year and, at the age of seventy-three, used his signature kneelift.

Walker, who suffered a heart attack following a Fanfest event in Charlotte in 2010, takes it a little easier these days. "It was the first heart attack I had ever had, and I didn't even know I had it then. I had a hard time breathing, but I didn't have any pain." Walker ended up undergoing triple bypass surgery. "The doctor did a fantastic job on me. I'm on a regimen of pills now, and they're keeping me going. I feel fine." The scenery, he added, doesn't hurt either.

The man with two careers wouldn't have traded either for the world. "I had a fantastic career. I loved every minute of it."

YUKON ERIC

The marriage began with a lopped off ear and ended with a wife hiding in fear, protecting their three children.

Then the father shot himself in the head in a church parking lot.

This is not a standard wrestling tale, yet the first half of the saga — "The Ear" — is one of the most retold stories in the history of the business. In 1954, Killer Kowalski leaped off the top turnbuckle during his singles bout with Yukon Eric at the Montreal Forum, and the villain's shin bone grazed the hero's cauliflowered ear, tearing it off.

While the accident meant big business down the road between the two colossal stars, in the short term, the forced time off allowed for Eric Holmback to marry his girlfriend of a couple of years, Aileen, who he had met through Toronto photographer Michael Burns.

"When he had his ear knocked off, he had to take some time off. So he said, 'Let's get married.' We went and got married and went to Florida. We were there for quite a while," recalled Aileen, who wasn't there that night in Montreal. Eric never dwelled on the accident, she said. "He just wore his hair long over it. He had really nice hair, and it was thick. He just had it covered. The lobe was still there."

The recollections of Aileen and two of their three children allow for fascinating insight into one of the biggest wrestling stars of all time. There were three distinct sides to Eric, she said: his public persona, the attitude he had with friends, and his very private home life. "His professional personality was not like his real personality," she said, calling him "moody" and "a loner." Eric loved hunting and fishing, but also reading and writing poetry. "He was smart and he was more intellectual, I think, than people realize. But he didn't want that known."

COURTESY OF SCOTT TEAL/CROWBAR PRESS

Classic Yukon Eric, his pants held up by a rope.

Of Swedish descent, Holmback was born April 22, 1916, in Monroe, Washington (and not Fairbanks, Alaska, as was ballyhooed), and died by his own hand on January 16, 1965, in Cartersville, Georgia. Between those dates lies the bulk of the tale, but not all of it. The family is still searching out answers to some questions, in particular the early years. "There's still a lot of gaps in his history," said son Erik Holmback. "I'll ask my mom about things, and I think he just didn't share a lot of details with her, as far as the specifics. She tells me what she knows. I try to find out as much as I can."

In 1935, Holmback was a freshman on the Washington State college football team, but doesn't show up on the roster until 1939, when he's billed from Gray's Harbor and six-foot-one, 231 pounds. His son suspects that the missing years were filled at a two-year college in Aberdeen, but the press guide says that he took at least one year off, giving weightlifting demonstrations at Lake Aberdeen and the Hoqulam YMCA. According to his wife, he was bounced from his scholarship after being caught playing poker for money.

Holmback first makes headlines in 1942. "It required only a few minutes to induct Erik Holmback into the army at the Presidio of Monterey but it is going to take four months to provide him with a uniform," reads a wire story. "A size-nineteen neck and a fifty-seven-inch chest measurement are two of the reasons for the delay. The quartermaster department at the Monterey Presidio took one look at Holmback and reported there was nothing on the west coast to fit him." Assigned to the special services division, Holmback never had to see any action overseas.

Though the wire story asserts that Holmback wrestled prior to his stint in the army, if he did, it was nothing notable. After the war, having met and befriended Man Mountain Dean, Eric "The Chest" Holmback's career started in earnest in Texas in 1946. Within a few years, he had started to cultivate the Yukon Eric character: Reared in a lumber camp, he trapped, hunted, and fished for his family's livelihood along the mighty Yukon River.

Based out of the Toronto office, Yukon Eric became an attraction, like Andre the Giant would be a decade later, heading into a territory for three or four shows, then off to the next destination. Promoters could count on him to draw based on his national name and a curiousity factor. In the ring, he was no

ROGER BAKER

Yukon Eric hoists Duke Noble into a shoulderbreaker.

Thesz, but he didn't have to be. His huge, muscled look demanded power moves.

Yukon Eric could lift a giant like Sky Hi Lee up into a shoulder back-breaker, in a hold called the Kodiak Crunch. "It's a simple little ditty in which the Klondike Kid hoists his opponent to his shoulder, and then goes bouncing about the ring with the body limply bouncing along out of 'tune,'" reads one report.

As a traveling attraction, Yukon Eric never held many titles. He did not need the belts to get over with the audiences. He was the world champion based out of Montreal in 1950 for a time, and he held titles in Texas and Toronto, but that was about it.

Holmback gave a rare, out of character interview with famed Atlanta scribe Furman Bisher in 1961. "A large passel of man, stripped to his vast, stove-shaped mid-section, and clad only in a pair of faithful dungarees held up by an equally faithful piece of rope, stood at one end of a large packing box and I on the side," is how Bisher described his subject.

"I've got this image," Yukon Eric told Bisher. "I didn't create it. Those fans did. I'm only being what they think I am in the ring. When I get dressed and walk out that door, I don't want anybody invading my private life.

"I'm antisocial. I'm sorry I'm that way but I am. I'm a peace-loving man, but I'm antisocial.

"People ask me if hunt and fish anymore. When I can go to the butcher shop or the fish market and get what I want to eat, I don't see any point in going out and killing. I had to do that when I was a kid, because that was how we got our food.

"People want to know about my hobbies, and my wife and my family, and it's none of their business . . . I like eating, and sleeping, and lying in the sun, but that's nobody's business."

In restaurants, having pulled up in his open-topped, big-finned Cadillac convertible (no matter the weather), his year-round tan showing through his undone lumberjack shirt and frayed, cut-off jeans, Yukon Eric would demand whale steaks and buffalo milk. "The waitresses' mouths would drop open. They thought he was nuts," said Aileen. "That was just his type of humor."

Eric Holmback's gravesite in Ogallala, Nebraska.

He was a natural Pied Piper, added his wife, who once sought out tennis lessons. "I think we were there about five minutes, and I was just learning the basics, and a group of kids came along. That was the end of my tennis."

Reta Holmback is the oldest of the couple's children, and was ten years old when he died. "I think he truly liked children, and I don't think a lot of adults do," Reta said. "He really looked in your eyes, and not just because we were his children, but I talked with some of the other wrestlers who were young guys at the time, and he liked to have the young boys around him."

One of those young boys was Nick Bockwinkel, whose father Warren was a contemporary of Yukon Eric's.

"It was fun to travel with him," Bockwinkel remembered of his days as an eighteen-year-old football player. "He had a soft eloquence." On one occasion, while traveling to Boston, they entered a restaurant and encountered a gaggle of well-dressed, elderly matrons. Everyone knew who Yukon Eric was. "Their jaws, they weren't dropping as much as they were just open. They were in awe of this massive man with his shirt open, and this massive chest. And he was handsome; he had this chiseled face, with this wavy, blondish hair. He came right up to them and he stopped. They were looking at him — they didn't know what to make of him. He says, 'What a lovely group of ladies. I surely do believe that you will have a delightful lunch, because that's all they could do for someone as nice as all of you. Have a good day.' Then he walked towards our table that the guy was showing us to."

Then there is the sad story of his dog, Tex, a boxer, who drowned. Aileen was visiting Eric in the trailer he had established in the Buffalo territory, and a teenager knocked on the door, yelling that the dog was in trouble. "Eric flew out of the trailer. His trailer was parked by a small quarry," recalled Aileen. "This is the wintertime, and it was covered with ice. But there was a hole in the ice. Tex had gone in that. Erik went out, and all he threw off, he took his wallet out, and jumped with his boots and everything else on, and tried to save him." The teen and Aileen formed a chain, and used a hockey stick to pull Erik in, but the dog was gone.

Despite his love for kids and dogs, his ex-wife asserts that the homebody Eric Holmback was something else entirely.

"I had to make myself scarce until we were divorced," she said. "The reason I left is because I was scared to death . . . I left because I didn't want to end up dead." There were a lot of rumors that persisted, especially following the suicide. "I had good reason to leave. Let's just leave it at that. I was terrified for quite a long time that he'd even find me," Aileen said. "I was accused of taking all his money, but I didn't. I didn't have hardly any money, but I managed. It wasn't pleasant. I was sorry about the whole thing. It was a bad situation, that's all, and there wasn't anything that could have been done about it."

Erik Jr. was four when his parents split, and confirmed that the children and Aileen went to "an undisclosed place." His father chose not to stay in contact with his children after the divorce. "I know that he was devastated because of the break-up and the suicide note he left reflected such," he said.

Besides the letter, the car contained a number of clippings of Yukon Eric's career, which now are part of his son's ever-growing attempt to piece together the tale of his father's life. The man known as Eric Holmback now rests in a small cemetery in Merna, Nebraska, where his sister Ellen brought him to rest. But the character of Yukon Eric will never go away.

PRE—WORLD WAR II

ORVILLE BROWN

COURTESY OF SCOTT TEAL / CROWBAR PRESS

Orville Brown at the top of his game.

A few weeks before his death in 2006, Bob Orton Sr. ran a well-worn index finger across his chin and pondered the most famous wrestling match never to occur — the November 25, 1949 bout between Orville Brown and Lou Thesz to unify the world heavyweight championship. Orton wasn't interested in the outcome — Brown was in line to win — but instead in the grand order of the wrestling hierarchy: What would happen if you put the two most respected wrestlers of the day together in an unscripted match? "Thesz was great, but Orville was so big and had such good balance and was so strong," Orton said. "I watched every match locally he had when I was a kid. There was nobody to compare with him in my book." A split second on a dark road changed everything. Less than a month before the match, Brown was in a horrific car accident that ended his career and nearly killed him. Friends and family said the Kansas blacksmith refused to let the mishap define him; though he failed to become first universally recognized world champion in fifteen years, Brown settled into a successful life as a promoter, businessman, and civic leader. But his exit from the scene came just as the budding TV industry turned to wrestling to fill its content void, so thousands of fans never learned who he was or what he was all about. "Orville Brown was one of the greatest wrestlers that I ever saw," said veteran Sonny Myers. "He was a great wrestler, number one. Number two, he was a very, very . . . well, he was a hell of a guy is what he was. Everybody respected him because everybody knew that the guy could wrestle."

Brown was built for wrestling at six-foot-two, with short legs and a long body, but he stumbled into the sport strictly by chance. Born in 1908 to a Kansas farmer and his wife, he was orphaned at eleven and worked a succession of odd jobs on relatives' farms while picking up a few tricks as a cowhand. He had some success riding broncos and bulldogging steers at rodeos, though the prize money was hardly enough to support him and wife Grace, with whom he had eloped in 1926. In 1931, Brown was working as a mechanic, blacksmith, and all-around handyman at a garage and shop in tiny Wallace, Kansas, living with his wife and son Dick in a one-room cabin, and grateful to be gainfully employed during the Great Depression.

One August afternoon in 1931, Brown was sharpening plow shears for wheat harvesters when a passing wrestling scout named Ernest H. Brown — no relation — spotted him working shirtless and convinced him to give the mat a go. The work couldn't be any more laborious, Orville reasoned, than hauling loads of coal through blinding snowstorms or standing all day over a red-hot forge. In the morning, Brown put in three miles of roadwork before his daily labors; at night, a local wrestling coach taught him the basics of the sport on a high school gym mat. Brown debuted with small fairs and carnivals in 1931 and his ascension was swift. According to logs that his wife meticulously maintained, he won his first seventy-two starts and laid claim to the Kansas title in September 1932 by beating Alan Eustace. From the beginning, Brown was groomed as championship material, a humble Midwestern farm boy in the mold of Frank Gotch and Joe Stecher, with a sturdy frame and even sturdier constitution. In 1933, he headed to St. Louis for seasoning, and, backed by a $5,000 stake from promoter Tom Packs, went from challenging locals in Kansas to semi main-event status in cities like Baltimore and Philadelphia in less than eight months. "We decided it was time to try our wings again and Orville should have his chance at the 'big time,'" his wife wrote in a family recollection. "Come what may, he could go no further if he stayed in Kansas." The day the Browns left Wallace, the first of a series of debilitating dust storms hit, leaving co-op farmers and ranchers broke.

Reviews of Brown's early work were laudatory, as sportswriters approved of his aggressive, assertive style. "Brown's ability to counter enemy offenses with his own offensive holds has caused fans to liken him to Frank Gotch, who originated and became world champion with this style of wrestling," the *Kansas City Star* said in 1934. Brown continued that pattern throughout his career, a bit of a ruffian even when he was the fan favorite, and a bit of a bully when he was the designated bad guy. "Orville Brown was a bull of a man. He would miss a flying tackle and wind up eight rows deep in ringside, push aside the debris and climb back into the ring and finish off his opponent," said iconic Midwestern sportscaster Bill Grigsby, who worked for Brown in the Kansas City, Missouri, booking office.

Orville Brown oversees the brief career of his son, Richard.

Brown's attacking style was never more on display than in 1935, when a hot three-match series with Jim Londos in Detroit rocketed him to national attention. In April, the two went to a ninety-minute draw before the largest crowd and gate in the history of the Olympia Arena. Londos won the third match, an outdoor affair in June that attracted 11,572, but when the Greek lost his world title that month, Brown was viewed as an eventual successor. His payoff came in 1940, when he beat Dick Shikat for the Columbus, Ohio, version of the Midwest Wrestling Association world championship, adding it to a branch of the MWA title he'd picked up in Kansas City. In addition to the adulation he received from fans, Brown earned important credibility among mistreated wrestlers as the top "policeman" in Al Haft's sprawling Columbus promotion. "They had a fellow who came in there named Jack 'Sockeye' McDonald. He'd hurt some of the boys intentionally. The office told him to back off, ease up. He wouldn't do that," recalled long-time wrestling official Al Mandell, a friend of Brown. "So they put him in a match with Orville. When he got out of the hospital, he left the territory. Orville did a number on him."

Brown left Columbus to keep an eye on his farm in rural Centropolis, Kansas, and work as matchmaker for Kansas City promoter George Simpson. He was the top star in the regional promotion and had no qualms about coming up on the short end of a match. Knowing profitable rematches were in the cards, he turned over the various versions of the MWA title almost a dozen times between 1940 and 1948 in feuds with Lee Wykoff, Bobby Bruns, and The Swedish Angel, among others. In November 1944, he became champion of Des Moines, Iowa promoter Pinkie George's ambitiously named National Wrestling Alliance. The alliance went big-time in July 1948, when a group of Midwestern promoters, meeting in Waterloo, Iowa, formally organized the group as a wrestling coopererative, with Brown as its nationally touring champ. Behind ex-sportswriter Sam Muchnick, the new NWA gained a toehold in wrestling-rich St. Louis in 1948 when it added box-office sensation Buddy Rogers to its stable. That cut into the profits of the old-line St. Louis promotion, controlled by Thesz, who was the National Wrestling Association — not Alliance — champion, and his allies. In late July, representatives of both sides decided to join forces, establishing the NWA as the dominant force in the sport, and setting the unification match between Brown and Thesz.

In the early morning hours of November 1, 1949, Brown was returning from a card in Des Moines when he suddenly came upon a stalled transport truck in the middle of U.S. Highway 69 near Bethany, Missouri. He jerked the wheel of his 1948 Cadillac to swerve out of the way, but the car lodged under the truck bed, shearing off its top. Brown's head crashed into the truck frame, resulting in severe brain trauma, major wounds, and multiple lacerations. Passenger Bruns, whom Brown had defeated hours earlier, suffered a fractured shoulder and upper arm injuries. The sedan was a $218 piece of gnarled salvage. For five days, Brown lay unconscious at Research Hospital in Kansas City, and while he survived, he never was the same; he abandoned a brief comeback attempt in 1950. "He never regained the ability to respond automatically. He had to think about every move," his son Dick said. "No matter how hard or how much he worked he was simply unable to react with the speed necessary to do what he wanted to do most — to wrestle again." Brown promoted for years in the Midwest, keeping an eye on his son's brief wrestling career and fending off a takeover attempt by Bruns and other promoters before he retired in 1963. He tended to a variety of successful business interests and investments and died

January 24, 1981, at age seventy-two. Brown was inducted into the Professional Wrestling Hall of Fame in upstate New York in 2005.

In later years, Thesz acknowledged that Brown was supposed to win the unification match and hold the title for a year before they swapped roles as champions of the world. Left unanswered was the more intriguing question of who was champion of whom. Muchnick leaned toward Thesz, and in 2000, Thesz belittled Brown as "a mediocre wrestler," leaving no doubt that he felt he could handle him in a straight-up contest. On the other hand, Myers, who wrestled him about twenty times, called Brown "one of the greatest things that you ever touched." And Mandell, Brown's old friend from Columbus, spoke on the basis of nearly seventy years in and around wrestling. "Now, personally, I don't think Thesz could have beaten Orville in a shoot. I've seen them both work many times, and Thesz was good, but again, I quote Bobby Bruns, that when Brown was in his prime, nobody could beat him."

COURTESY OF SCOTT TEAL/CROWBAR PRESS

Jack Claybourne was the rare specimen during his era: championship material.

JACK CLAYBOURNE

On a July day in 1939, a new wrestler popped up in the Cincinnati Music Hall Sports Arena looking for work. In halting Spanish, the slender, dark-skinned Latino explained that his name was Pablo Hernandez, and he had recently wrestled in Cuba. Hernandez appeared in a few matches until, during training one day, he slipped up, spoke a few words of English, and blew his cover. He was not Pablo Hernandez and he most certainly was not Cuban. He was Jack Claybourne of Missouri, and he assumed the Latino guise because that ethnicity was not as high a hurdle to overcome in professional wrestling as was the fact that he was black. As Claybourne recalled, local authorities were tolerant, and permitted him to continue wrestling. But the incident encapsulated the life and hard times of a talented wrestler, who got his biggest break outside the continental United States, and, knowing no life other than wrestling, killed himself when his career ended. "What I'd seen was kind of unjust and to say the least was startling," said Frankie Cain, who met him as part of Al Haft's Columbus, Ohio promotion, where Claybourne worked in the late 1930s and the early 1950s. "Jack really stood out. He looked the part and he made beautiful moves. The preliminary boys Haft had were beating Claybourne in the opening matches and they were strictly job guys. Guys that couldn't work at all, he was putting them over and I thought, 'Jeez, what an injustice.' It was really a misuse of talent."

During a career that spanned more than a quarter-century, Claybourne was one of the best known wrestlers in the world, thanks in part to an aerial style that was borderline revolutionary and included a signature move in which he leapfrogged a referee and dropkicked his opponent square in the kisser. The Press-Telegram of Long Beach, California, proclaimed him "the first man to introduce jumping and acrobatic techniques to wrestling. It only remained for Argentina Rocca to make the most of it . . . he originated the style that made the South American famous." That was an exaggeration, but Claybourne incorporated ballet-style moves into his routine a decade before wrestling sensation Ricki Starr. As the Fitchburg Sentinel put it for one Massachusetts bout: "A sepian ballet master, [he] demonstrated all types of steps and dances, doing a Charlotte Greenwood leg-lift over [George] Linehan's bald head a short time after the match started."

Born March 8, 1910, in Missouri, Claybourne started boxing as a teenager in the Kansas City area, but quit after a few months. He got into amateur wrestling at sixteen as a lanky six-footer whose frame would eventually fill out to 210 pounds. Claybourne credited St. Joseph, Missouri promoter Gust Karras with launching his pro career. Karras used Claybourne on traveling carnivals during the summer and gave him prominent billing as "Happy Jack" on wrestling cards in Missouri and Iowa as early as 1932. Claybourne left the heartland in 1935, heading to the Pacific Northwest and northern California with moderate success against light-heavyweights like Danny McShain, and Rod Fenton and Mike London, future promoters for whom he'd later work. But he was always looking over his shoulder at Jim Crow. In December 1937, a white Indiana athletic commissioner refused to license Claybourne and another black wrestler for a bout in Gary. Cain talked to him during one swing through Columbus and thought he seemed lonely and ill at ease. "I thought, my God, what talent this guy has got, not just from the high flying but the selling and just his all-over work," Cain said. "If there was anybody they could have made money with, it certainly would have been him because he didn't get in and wiggle around and do the things the promoters had the black guys do later on. He was a solid worker and a hell of a worker."

In northern cities such as Boston, Toronto, and Chicago, Claybourne earned decent standing in the late 1930s and early 1940s, with title shots against stars like British Empire titleholder

Jack Claybourne chats with Tom Mortimer.

"Whipper" Billy Watson and Salvatore Balbo, a junior heavyweight claimant. Often, he was advertised as the colored world champion, though no official wrestling organization sanctioned the title. In September 1941, when he beat Seelie Samara to regain the "Negro world heavyweight championship" in Louisville, Kentucky, local newspapers derided the match as a "novelty," along the lines of a 400-pound wrestler or a women's contest. During World War II, Claybourne wrestled on USO tours to entertain the troops, but he didn't become a phenom until after the conflict, when he went halfway around the world to Australia and wrestling-starved New Zealand. "Being the first black to ever appear here, an athlete who could vault the top rope in 1946; that was something to behold," said New Zealand historian Dave Cameron, who enjoyed talking with the visiting star. "His leap over the top rope was sensational at the time and his dropkicks were perfect and always landed on target. When he wrestled another dropkick artist, George Pencheff, the house was in an uproar as they traded dropkick after dropkick at one another."

In April 1948, a year after Jackie Robinson broke the color line in major league baseball, Claybourne went to Hawaii, known as a racially hospitable territory, and enjoyed the biggest run of his career. On October 31, he won the Hawaiian junior heavyweight title from Hisao Keomuka in two straight falls and headlined weekly main events in Honolulu constantly for almost a year, in between visits to Australia and New Zealand.

Sportswriter Hubert H. White of the Associated Negro Press held him up as an exemplar of the black athlete, crediting him with "unquestioned ability to use holds and tactics far superior to many of the wrestlers seen here." Claybourne returned to Australia and New Zealand in 1951, and again for long stretches in 1956. Back home, Boston was as close as he came to having a base, and he feuded there for years with Bull Curry. On March 15, 1955, Claybourne integrated wrestling in Texas, beating Danny Plechas by disqualification in El Paso in the first mixed bout in the state. Yet, Beatrice Tyler, his sister-in-law and a long-time Boston resident, said he was hardly a militant, by background or bearing. He was an affable sort who carried around a collection of lucky charms, including a silver talisman on a chain that he often wore to the ring around his neck. "He was a gentle soul. He had a very tiny voice for a big man," Tyler said. "He did do well here in Boston because he was the only black. He was the only black one and he was good and people enjoyed seeing him. But, they only let him get so far also." When Claybourne wrestled in Virginia for the first time in the early 1950s, his attitude was one of resignation. "It's too bad that the colored fans of the South cannot get to see more of us," he said. And he maintained that the rise of nationally televised wrestling in the early 1950s worked against black wrestlers. "If a match is going to be on TV, you can be dead sure that it will be two whites in the ring. Sure, boys such as myself, Jim Mitchell, Bobo Brazil, and Buddy Jackson will be on the card, but our grappling will be through when it comes time for the cameras to pick up the ring action," he said forcefully in 1954. "We know that many of the bouts are seen in the southern states via TV and I believe that is the reason. The promoters do not want to offend any of the would-be-paying fans."

A by-the-books competitor, Claybourne was not given to histrionics and flashy behavior, and he acknowledged that the sport's drift toward showmanship hurt him as his career wound down. "Personally, I wish the game stayed the way it was back when I started. Wrestlers were idolized, not ridiculed in those days," he said. He finished up in 1958 for old friend and promoter Mike London in the Albuquerque, New Mexico area. In 1959, a planned swing through Europe failed to materialize. "During the later years, they were deciding what to do and where to go," Tyler said of Claybourne and her sister. "They didn't want to go to Australia because it was too far and they didn't want to come back to Boston because it was too cold. Then they settled in California but he didn't have any success there at all." On January 7, 1960, Claybourne set a championship trophy in the bathroom of his Los Angeles house, sat next to it, turned a loaded .12-gauge shotgun on himself, and squeezed the trigger. Friends said he was despondent about the end of his livelihood and was drinking heavily. He was forty-nine.

THE PRICE OF HEROISM

It's not enough to be a hero in the ring. It's important to be a hero outside of it, even if it comes at a high cost.

More than a century ago, a wiry youth named Elmer D. Brown learned how to wrestle by tussling with his dad and his brothers in the hard dirt of wrestling-crazy Taylor, Texas, north of Austin. Nicknamed "Pet," he became such a marvel of endurance, tenacity, and strength that traveling carnival wrestlers bypassed Taylor, knowing they couldn't hold their own, or make any money, with the locals. By the time he turned 21, in 1909, Brown, who stood 5-foot-11 and weighed about 160, had copped Jim Downing's Texas title and claimed a victory over William Demetral, frequently billed as the Greek champion. Working with the legendary Ad Santel and lightweight Joe Savini as his trainers, Brown mowed through the competition to earn a shot at Mike Yokel of Utah, who held a version of the world middleweight crown. In May 1914, before a packed hometown crowd at the Taylor opera house, Brown won the middleweight belt when Yokel forfeited after allegedly suffering a concussion during the bout.

Pet Brown was a Texas idol.

Brown mostly stayed close to his Texas roots, but his ring work was known far and wide. On March 2, 1915, he beat Joe Turner, a future East Coast promoter, in two straight falls at the city auditorium in Houston. In the sweat of defeat, Turner praised Brown as the greatest wrestler he'd ever seen at 158 pounds. In 1916, John Kilonis, later a world light heavyweight champion, declared that he'd pay $100 to anyone who could produce a challenger that he refused to wrestle. His challenge contained a Brown corollary. "I bar no one except Pet Brown of Texas. I take my hat off to him," Kilonis said.

What made Brown so capable, besides a seemingly endless wind, was his ability to casually slip on a variety of holds, half-nelsons and hammerlocks among them. The secret to that was a pair of powerful hands that could wrench the life out of the unsuspecting. A sportswriter for the *San Antonio Light* discovered that when he met Brown before a match with Walt Evans. "This piece of triple distilled energy has a lunch-hook with a grip like a vise. I didn't need anyone to tell me he was in condition to put up the bout of his life. I knew it when that No. 12 hand of his closed over mine in his hearty greeting."

Brown met his match in the form of Clarence Eklund, a Wyoming rancher who specialized in using his legs as weapons. In 1917, Eklund handed Brown what was believed to be the first clean pinfall loss of his career. By then, change was coming to Taylor. The hardscrabble earth that Brown tumbled on as a youth was rutted with tire tracks from Model T cars. Seeing a business opportunity, Brown opened a contracting firm with four mules at his service. Soon, his road-building business expanded to packs of forty and fifty mules, with blacks and convict labor supplying most of his grueling manpower. By the standards of his day, Brown was remarkably colorblind. His protégé and workout partner "White" Nobles, who helped to maintain order among the road crews, was one of the few blacks who wrestled professionally in Texas.

In December 1919, Brown stopped wrestling regularly to concentrate on business. Even in semi-retirement, he was a figure of awe. Texas writer Langdon Richter recalled that he and his friends once mustered the gumption to ask Brown if he was strong enough to lift a discarded sledgehammer. "Pet just stuck out his hand and said, 'Put it up there.' Several of the larger boys responded and managed to get it high enough to where his hand was, and there it was, all muscled out. Pet said, 'How is that?' Then after dropping it to the ground, he walked off laughing."

On May 5, 1923, Brown got into in a verbal battle with L.J. Sharkey, a constable, who tried to arrest Brown's black employees for shooting craps at their camp. To the principled Brown, the intrusion smacked of a shakedown — Brown contended that lawmen were collecting money from his workers and pocketing it as their own. Like any benevolent boss, Brown agreed to go to court and pay the fines, as long as the authorities promised not to jail his men. But tempers flared. As Brown reached for Sharkey's arm to escort him through a door, the constable pulled a gun and shot him through the heart. Brown was 34. The next day, 1,000 citizens showed up at a memorial service. Sharkey later was acquitted of murder, successfully arguing that he acted in self-defense because he feared for his life.

Brown's legacy lives on; he's still noted in local chamber of commerce literature and a bust of him sat for many years in a fire hall. But his death was a blow to a sport he loved.

As *The Wrestling News*, a magazine of the era, eulogized: "Pet Brown was for years without doubt the most popular wrestler in the South and Southwest. And all through the state of Texas he was the idol of the fans."

Man Mountain Dean's fame exceeded wrestling.

MAN MOUNTAIN DEAN

Frank Simmons Leavitt was nearly forty and going nowhere fast. An overweight ex-soldier, he had taken a stab at boxing but discovered it was too hard on his eyes. He hooked up with a fledgling pro football team, but it went belly-up after two games. As a pro wrestler, he was a flop whose repertoire was limited to giving his opponent a bum's rush. A stint as traffic cop in Miami, Florida, ended when he was canned for cozying up to underworld kingpin Al Capone. So, in 1931, at the height of the Great Depression, Leavitt and his wife Dorris were relegated to selling eggs, a dozen at a time, from a tiny chicken farm in Georgia. He was out of shape, out of work, and out of money.

But he was not out of luck. What happened next is the stuff of legend, excess, serendipity, and, above all, opportunism, for Leavitt stumbled on to a gimmick that made him the toast of the pop culture world within two years. Reinventing himself as the porcine hillbilly Man Mountain Dean, he became a 300-pound license for promoters to print money. He raked in as much as $1,500 a pop for hauling his bulbous frame into rings for a few minutes of action, or, more commonly, inaction. Hollywood beckoned, and he squeezed film appearances between mat gigs, promotional stunts, and product endorsements, en route to becoming a household name. "I say that seriously I, as a child, sat on the lap of somebody who was as famous as Hulk Hogan in those days . . . Man Mountain

Dean," said California wrestling veteran Jerry Christy. "He was in the Haystacks Calhoun category, a big fat guy that drew money."

Everything about Dean was oversized — his britches, his fame, and his ego. In November 1934, *Los Angeles Times* sportswriter Bill Henry calculated that the bearded behemoth was attracting about $2,000 in paid attendance per minute of work at the Olympic Auditorium. "That's a lot of dough for a side show," Henry mused. Just as important, Dean blazed a path for all manner of oddities to become box office draws, like Eddie Civil, an ex-prizefighter who took Houston by storm as country bumpkin "Whiskers" Savage, and Marvin "Blimp" Levy, to whom Dean spotted a couple hundred pounds. "He practically pioneered the business of

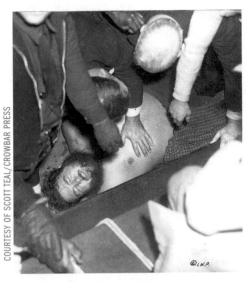

COURTESY OF SCOTT TEAL/CROWBAR PRESS

Man Mountain Dean is tended to after being thrown from the ring by Jim Londos in October 1932.

hokum, whiskers, and phony groans," wrote Scripps-Howard columnist Robert C. Ruark. "I loved the old fraud."

Separating the wheat from the considerable chaff in Dean's life is maddening because under his toneless flesh beat the heart of a publicity hound. At various times, he claimed to have played football at five colleges; coached under gridiron legend John Heisman; became the first U.S. soldier wounded in World War I; lost just seventy-eight of his 6,383 pro matches; beat nineteen wrestlers in sixty-one minutes, including one in two and three-fifths seconds; won a ten-mile swim race; and narrowly escaped persecution by Adolf Hitler. Whether the boasts contain a sliver of truth is incidental; taken together, they defined a towering character who relished the spotlight. "Man Mountain made no secret of the fact that he loved publicity," said Paul Cox, who covered him for the *Anniston Star* in Alabama. "He always wanted an even dozen papers when his name was mentioned, and we always sent them to him because somehow Dean was different. He had that touch of immortality that lives with only a few athletes."

Born June 30, 1891, in Manhattan, Leavitt spent most of his youth in the Westchester County town of Eastchester, where his formal schooling ended after fifth grade. He enlisted in the U.S. Army in April 1911, when he was nineteen, and he served during World War I in Europe under the command of

Gen. George Patton. Around 1916, he started wrestling for dough as Soldier Leavitt. Adolph Majower, who served with him at Fort Slocum near New York City in the 1910s, remembered Leavitt as a unique blend of slough-off and showoff. "That guy hated Army routine so much, he went out for every team at the post, football, basketball and baseball — and I think he even boxed a little," Majower recalled years later, when Leavitt was at his peak as a celebrity. "Finally he went to New York and took up wrestling to earn a few pesos on the side. I used to go down to watch him every week, and was he awful. He didn't know a half-nelson from a handshake but he was big and tough and afraid of nobody."

Leavitt kicked around the Eastern wrestling circuit for several years, but never got off the undercard. He scaled back his activity in 1924 after breaking his hand against Hans Steinke in Chicago and bombing in a tournament in Montreal, where the *Gazette* newspaper declared his wrestling to be "nonsense." In 1928, he wrangled a job as a traffic cop in Miami and played it to the hilt, admonishing motorists to "watch the chandelier," his stock wisecrack for a traffic light. He even found time to marry a pretty blonde office manager from Georgia named Dorris Dean. But Leavitt's penchant for ballyhoo cost him dearly. On May 6, 1930, Miami's public safety director fired him for three unauthorized visits to Capone's Palm Beach home. "We were friends all right," Leavitt murmured, "but I wasn't any gangster like they said." After getting sacked, he returned to the mat in New York, Salt Lake City, and California, reprising his Soldier Leavitt gimmick to little fanfare.

The many accounts of Leavitt's life and times crisscross, overlap, diverge, and contradict each other. But if sportswriters, wrestling promoters, and colleagues agreed on one thing, it's this: Dorris, a strong and forceful woman, was the one to give him a kick in his ample butt. Securing a few matches in Atlanta in 1931, Leavitt became "Stone Mountain" Leavitt, a hat tip to a nearby granite dome summit. At his wife's suggestion, he was "Man Mountain" Leavitt during a 1932 swing through the upper Midwest, since Stone Mountain meant little to the folks in Wisconsin. Kenneth R. Kennedy of the *Wisconsin State Journal* thought he resembled nothing so much "as a 315-pound beer keg mounted on broom handles." That led to a brief gig in Europe, where according to legend, he acted as a stunt double for actor Charles Laughton in *The Private Life of Henry VIII*, and grew his famous whiskers because a fake beard fell off his face.

In a rare moment of candor in 1935, Leavitt confessed that it didn't happen that way. As part of the tour, he went in Germany to wrestle, only to find that authorities in Hitler's regime considered "Leavitt" to be Jewish, and ordered him to leave the country. With five bucks to his name, he hopped on a freighter bound for Florida and started a long trip across the Atlantic with stops in South America and Mexico. According to separate reports from Leavitt and ship officer Henri Oden, the whiskers debuted during the journey, and they had nothing to do with the portrayal of a dead regent. "The reason I didn't shave in all that time was not because I wanted protection from the sun and wind but because sailors are super-stitious about lending their razors, and I'd lost mine in Germany," Leavitt said.

At home in Norcross, near Atlanta, inspiration struck the Leavitts. Before he broke out a new razor, his wife sent publicity pictures to Paul Bowser, the pro-moter in Boston, with the new look and a new name. "It was Mrs. Dean who urged him to grow [the beard] and to change his name by way of disguise, because under his old name and modest fame he was dated with the profession — a man of thirty-nine, and no star, either," said columnist Westbrook Pegler. Bowser bit and told him to hurry up to Boston, and not to touch that bristle. As a 300-pound monster, with Dorris as his meddlesome manager, Dean started drawing decent paychecks. They started a near-riot in October 1933 against Sandor Szabo in Newark, New Jersey, when Dorris whacked a timekeeper over the head with an umbrella. In Cleveland the following April, she broke out her pocketbook and clobbered Farmer John O'Dell when it appeared her husband was in danger of being pinned. "Surely I take credit for a great deal of the suc-cess of my husband," she told one interviewer, describing her duties as cook, chauffeur, and accountant. "Why should I settle down and be just a housewife? I love the wrestling game just as much as Frank does."

In July 1934, Dean hit the West Coast and became the biggest thing going. Fans who ducked away to the concession stand might have missed his matches; his first three appearances at the Olympic Auditorium went six minutes, sev-enteen seconds, combined. His finisher was a running . . . well, waddling . . . broad jump, in which he leaped into the air and landed in a sitting position on his rival's back or chest. Dean's first dozen appearances at the Olympic netted promoter Lou Daro $130,000, or more than twice his standard take. A much-hyped bout with Jim Londos drew a whopping 23,765 to an outdoor stadium in Los Angeles. When the mountain returned home to a sellout audience in 1935, the *Atlanta Constitution* proclaimed that the prodigal son had turned into the fatted calf. "When opportunity knocked at his door," Ralph McGill wrote, "he used brass knucks to make sure the big guy heard him."

There was an ulterior motive to his westward ventures. Dean parlayed his minimal role in *HenryVIII* into a lucrative side career. In Hollywood, he appeared in a number of flicks, thirty-eight by his count, though the real number seems to be closer to a dozen. Once living a hand-to-mouth existence, Dean claimed his net worth approached $300,000. "I have grossed more money in four years than Ruth, Dempsey, Londos, or any one else in sport over that same period of time," he announced in June 1936. Typically, he exaggerated his bank account, as he confided privately to promoter Jack Pfefer just two years later: "Bad eyes, broken legs and bones . . . a few bucks is all one makes out of it. It's also true I made some but the big shots made twice as much out of me."

Officials try to fit Dean for a military uniform in 1942.

Dean alternated egos in the ring. In California, he started out as a bombastic rogue who shat-tered Bill Longson's back when a running broad jump went amiss in January 1937. Amid Dean's huffing and puffing, the state athletic commission banned the move twice and suspended him in 1939. In New York, though, he delighted fans by beating tough guy Rube Wright in two minutes through the simple tactic of sitting on Wright's face. In St. Louis, roughhouser Ernie Dusek fell in five minutes after he tried to pick up Dean for a slam and crumpled under his girth. In truth, Dean was neither a hero nor a heel. He was a spectacle, and he made no bones about it. "Funny is everything," he told the Associated Press' Paul Mickelson. "When I was a fine wrestler I almost starved to death. Then I lost my holds, grew whiskers and look at me today." Dean's beefiness, which reached 360 pounds, was perfect fodder for pranks. In the locker room, he always wore a pair of slip-on shoes, so as not to mount the exertion to tie shoelaces. As Jim Coleman, the esteemed Canadian sports columnist, recounted, Dean showered after one show in Toronto's Maple Leaf Gardens, unaware that prankster Ray Steele was driving spikes through his shoes, fastening them to the floor. "After the bout Dean dressed and then having admired himself in the mirror, stepped into his moored slippers. As he attempted to stride forward he fell to the floor with a crash which permanently damaged the Gardens."

While he was a magnet for fans, Dean had his share of detractors. Alan Ward of the *Oakland Tribune* berated him for callously disregarding Longson after he broke his back. "Plenty of good men in the wrestling business never forgave Dean for that neglect," Ward said. Dean also had a reputation of running out on matches over perceived slights. In 1935, he bewildered fans in St. Louis by returning to the dressing room in the middle of a match with Strangler Lewis. According to an unpublished Lewis account, Dean had boasted before the match that his stardom eclipsed that of the Strangler. Once in the ring, Lewis let him have it, and Dean decided that the dressing room represented a safer haven. "I never wanted to work with Man Mountain Dean," veteran Fred Bozic confessed in 1960. "He was just a big tub of blubber and it made me sick."

A stab at a political career fizzled in 1938 when Dean mounted a futile candidacy for the Georgia legislature. As World War II dawned, he saluted and transformed back into Soldier Leavitt, serving with a tank unit in Georgia, supervising trash pickup at a base in Maryland, and working as a recreation officer in California. Though he was fifty, the army overlooked his age and considerable belly on the recommendation of Patton and other high-ranking friends. "I beat every Jap I ever wrestled and I can still do it," Dean bellowed. He was in the service from January 1942 to October 1942, when he was discharged because of a kidney ailment. Undeterred, he re-enlisted in May 1943 and served until December 1945 as a master sergeant. Out of the army for good, Dean returned to wrestling in 1946, working with another misshapen phenomenon, Maurice "The French Angel" Tillet, to massive crowds. An affair in Cleveland in February attracted 10,439, the largest wrestling audience in the city in a dozen years. He finally called it quits that fall after a swing through western Canada.

By then he was fifty-five, but hardly ready to disappear from the scene. In 1949, the grade school dropout enrolled at a University of Georgia branch in Atlanta. His goal was to accumulate enough coursework so he could apply for a physical instructor job with the Veterans Administration. But the back-to-school story was a natural for feature writers, and Dean eagerly revealed he studied psychology, sociology, and English so he could write his autobiography. Tinseltown rang again, and though he had to dye his gray beard to keep it black, he landed a strongman part in *Mighty Joe Young*. "We gotta wrestle a monkey and we gotta lose. He's supposed to drag us into a creek. I don't know how that'll go on the beard dye, but I'll take a crack at anything once," he said.

On May 29, 1953, Dean died of a heart attack at his house near Norcross. He made almost as many headlines in death as he did in life, remembered as a football player, serviceman, actor, wrestler, politician, policeman, and personality of the first rank. Dorris, who lived until Christmas Eve 1982, saw her husband's fame extend long after his passing. Case in point — in 1960, Democratic presidential contender Hubert Humphrey declared that he was the poor man's candidate against Sen. John F. Kennedy, who "looks as much like an underdog as Man Mountain Dean looks like a pygmy." Probably, Dean would have delighted in that reference. "I don't guess anything could be quite like wrestling," he reflected the year before his death. "Wrestling was pretty good to me."

DAVE LEVIN

A Sunday morning in 1934, in the middle of the Great Depression, and George W. Wenzel Jr., a young butcher from Brooklyn, had bigger dreams than anyone had any right to have in a time of breadlines and mass unemployment. Citing his amateur wrestling background, he earned an audience with pro wrestling impresario Jack Pfefer at the Times Building in New York City. Pfefer instructed Wenzel to strip to the waist, eyed him like a piece of fresh meat, and sent him to scrap with tough guys Tony Morelli and Herbie Freeman at a nearby gym. Wenzel knew he didn't stand a chance with the pros, so he mostly kept up his guard, tossing in just enough moves to suggest that he might be able to hold his own, given some hard work and a lot of training. Pfefer, a Polish Jew with a laundry basket full of idiosyncrasies, liked what he saw. But the name George Wenzel just wouldn't do. No, it would be have to be something else . . . a Jewish champion, perhaps, to appeal to the ethnics. Maybe Dave Levin.

For the next twenty years, Levin was one of wrestling's biggest stars. He claimed the world championship at a time of mass promotional confusion, stared down death, and got along with Pfefer to the exclusion of almost everyone else in the industry. He was the prototypical babyface across the country because, his friends recalled, that's the way he was in real life. As Vic Holbrook, a California-based star of the 1950s, explained: "Dave was like a gentle rain falling on an arid desert. Where he found no integrity, he brought his own; when gentlemanliness was at a premium he had enough for us all . . . I am proud to say that I wrestled in the era of Dave Levin."

Born in October 1913, Levin molded himself, hour after hour, with homemade ropes attached to a little pulley in a garage at his family's home in Brooklyn. On Saturdays, he hopped on his bike to deliver wurst, kraut, and pigs' knuckles

George Wenzel became Jewish champion Dave Lewin.

from a butcher shop. Eventually, he learned the trade — he'd be billed as the "Jamaica Butcher Boy" for years — but he had other things in mind. "I saw the professionals come in and 1934, you know, was pretty much of the Depression days and butchers weren't making an awful lot of money," he reflected in a 1995 interview. "I'd go down to the wrestling matches and see these guys and think, 'By golly, maybe I can handle one or two of them. I'm going to get myself a professional match and forget about the Depression, you see.' And that's how I became interested in wrestling, going down and watching them and working out."

As his father approved and his mother cringed, Levin spent his early career around New York City. To capitalize on his faux Jewish character, he tussled in an endless series of matches against real and make-believe Germans like Frederich Von Schacht, Wilhelm Wagner, and Ernest von Heffner. On June 12, 1936, he upset Ali Baba, a mustachioed Armenian who claimed the most widely recognized version of the world title, in a match in Newark, New Jersey, when referee Frank Sinborn disqualified Baba for kicking his foe in the groin. New Jersey had banned dropkicks, following the 1934 lead of the New York State Athletic Commission. Behind the scenes, Pfefer and promoter Toots Mondt were seeking to lift Baba's crown through some chicanery and turned to Levin as their vehicle. Regardless of the double-cross, the Associated Press declared Levin "had the better of his opponent from the start."

Perhaps it was because he had a token of good fortune with him. His mother attended one match, watched her son get tossed out of the ring, and begged him to find another line of employment. Still, she sewed a single penny in his trunks for good luck. "As much as she hated wrestling, there was a note in there that said, 'May the best man win,'" Levin's wife, Virginia Wenzel, recalled. Mondt acquired his contract from Pfefer for $17,000 and sent the new champion westward for one of the most anticipated set-tos of the era — Levin, recognized as champion in the East, against Vincent Lopez, billed as world titleholder in California.

One of the pre-match publicity stunts paid off handsomely. During a photo shoot on the beach in Santa Monica, California, a hostess recruited Virginia Tyler, a distant relative of President John Tyler, to spice up Levin's matinee idol appeal. Levin was smitten with her, though her nickname of Ginger translated to "Ginja" in his heavy New York accent. Neither knew it at the time, but they'd eventually be married for sixty-five years. In addition to a future wife, Levin got another title. Before more than 15,000 onlookers at Wrigley Field, he stopped Lopez in three falls. Influential *Los Angeles Times* columnist Braven Dyer, who usually looked at the sport with a jaundiced eye, was more than satisfied. "I doubt if he weighs more than 185 pounds, which is pretty small for a heavyweight bone bender, but he's a good actor, knows the value of speed and fairly oozes personality," Dyer wrote. "His ability to retain the title may be questionable, but his drawing power cannot be doubted."

What would be the first of many championship runs for Levin was short-lived. In the wee morning hours of September 29, 1936, he dropped the title to Dean Detton in a grueling two-hour match in Philadelphia. Levin lost eight pounds from bell to bell, and he fell a few days later in a rematch with Lopez before 10,400 fans. But the losses were nothing compared to what he was about to endure. On January 21, 1937, Levin squared off with Bobby Bruns at the Hippodrome in New York. Physically and mentally, he was feeling miserable; he'd just lost his mother to cancer. The next morning, he struggled to get out of bed and hobbled downstairs to call his father. By the time his father and a doctor arrived, Levin was delirious. Unknown to him, a minor rope burn he suffered on the back of his leg against Detton had become infected. He developed a case of hemolytic strepto-coccus, blood poisoning in a virulent form. At St. John's Hospital, he received a transfusion from Bruns, was bound with chains and lived on liquids as his toned body wasted away. Only his conditioning saved him; he spent three months in the hospital. "I guess I just wasn't good enough to die just yet and join [Frank] Gotch and all those other good wrestlers," he later joked. But he was not out of the woods. The drug employed to restore him to health, Prontosil, drew the toxicity toward his ankle. His doctor fused the ankle, hobbling Levin throughout his career because of the unnatural stress on his hip. After eighteen months, he returned to the game with pockets as empty as the day he started. "He ended up broke," his wife said. "Not only did his mother have cancer and the specialists, he paid all the expenses for her. Then he got sick and had nurses around the clock. When we got married, he had nothing." And the illness robbed him of some of his mobility. "He never was quite the same," she said.

It was Levin's fate to return to the mat just as the business was petering out. He jumped from Los Angeles promoter Lou Daro to Hollywood promoter Hugh Nichols, because Nichols paid $20 a shot to Daro's $10. He earned a comparative fortune when Oregon's Ted Thye agreed to fork out $150 a week, plus train fare in November 1939. His 4-F physical impairment kept him out of World War II, but he found work in August 1941 at a shipyard near Casmalia, California. "The payoff is good and I am learning a trade which will always be a good thing to know," he told Pfefer. But his love of wrestling showmanship won out and he bolstered his skills by taking matches on nights off. By 1944, he was back on top of the heap. On May 4, he beat Orville Brown for the Midwest Wrestling Association world championship, and felled Ray Steele, advertised as the National Wrestling Alliance world champion, six days later in Des Moines, Iowa. Though titles were tossed around like confetti in those days, the twin victories gave Levin a firm grasp on top billings. His Midwest title runs lasted about a month, and he struck out from his California base on trips to the East Coast, Australia, Hawaii, and New Zealand.

In the ring, Levin was an innovator, with an impressive mix of aerial action, holds, and counterholds. "Dave was a creative worker in which he had the attention of everyone in the audience," said veteran wrestler Bobby Christy. "Dave was a credit in every aspect of wrestling, both in and out of the ring." Working with 600-pound Marvin "Blimp" Levy in Galveston, Texas, on one July 1945 card, he was confronted with the nearly impossible task of coaxing a convincing match from a slow-moving bulk. After getting squashed in the first fall, Levin reached into his tool kit, catapulted from the ropes, did a momentary handstand and kicked Levy in the face. Against the gifted Buddy Rogers, he shined, winning the third and final fall of an October 1946 match in Salt Lake City with a dropkick in only eleven seconds. As sportswriter Ed McFadden recounted, the bout "had ringside spectators nudging and pawing at their ringside neighbors. They couldn't believe that it was true." What little video remains of Levin shows him hamming it up with the audience and covering up from attacks like an ostrich. "At one time, his waist was small, and he could get in a scissor hold and rest. So he'd pretend like he was really being killed while he was resting," his wife said.

Joe Jares used Levin as one of the sources for his classic 1974 book, *Whatever Happened to Gorgeous George?* "He was a good-looking babyface. He was very popular, a very handsome guy. As I said in the book, he was not a Jew," Jares said. "The classic Dave Levin story is that some rabbis were brought back into the locker room to meet him and he had to cover up quickly because he wasn't circumcised."

Pfefer loved Levin above all his other finds; his letters to wrestling confederates, usually dripping with venom over some real or imagined slight, displayed an uncommon touch toward Levin. As he pecked away on one, "I will say and honestly mean it and you can believe me if there ever was a Prince Charming in our game you are the undisputed Prince and nothing in the long years has changed you or your way of life and to me my dear Dave, you are still the undisputed and incomparable Prince, as I have never found another one like you and I quit dreaming that I will ever find another Dave."

His body aching and his heart yearning for home, Levin stopped wrestling regularly in 1954. He landed a job as a salesman for a liquor outfit, promoted wrestling in a small town, and worked on TV handling interviews and substitute play-by-play. But his later years were excruciatingly difficult. Years of wrestling with a rebuilt ankle placed an enormous strain on his hip; he required an artificial joint at a time when the procedure was so novel that his doctor, Charles Bechtol of UCLA, wore a space suit during the procedure. His hip later became infected and had to be replaced; at one point Levin spent five months in a hospital bed in his own living room. The indignities never affected his chipper personality, and he explained that his positive attitude went back to his brush with death so many years before. "I was so far gone at one time I prayed to die. I was just so down," he reflected. "When I pulled through, I was so grateful for that, that I think I've just been so glad I've been alive ever since and I'm tickled to death to be alive and be happy out here. If you just get to the place where you're almost dead, then you realize you want to live."

Levin died in 2004; he was ninety. While the staph infection eventually left his blood, wrestling never did. Frequently, he reminded Pfefer how much he yearned to be back in the ring just one more time. "Do you remember that Sunday morning when I came to see you at your office in the Times Building? I wanted to get started in professional wrestling and you told me to see you that Sunday morning," he wrote in 1966. "All that took place thirty-two years ago in 1934. But I can remember it like it was yesterday."

EVERETTE MARSHALL

It seemed like a good idea at the time. On Thanksgiving Day 1930, Everette Marshall tried to drum up publicity for an upcoming match by holding a sparring session with his 400-pound black bear Gotch at the Swope Park Zoo in Kansas City, Missouri. For several years, Marshall had tussled with the bear, whom he named for wrestling icon Frank Gotch, in a pen on his family's ranch in Colorado. But now it was time for them to go their separate ways. Marshall was getting to be a big star, away from home more often than he was there, so he wanted one final go-around before he donated the bear to the zoo. Only Gotch had no intention of being the fall bear. As a crowd of 1,500 and a battery of newsreel crews watched in amazement, Gotch bared his teeth, howled, and threw a wild haymaker in Marshall's direction. At the suggestion of the zoo superintendent, Marshall ducked out of the makeshift ring to safer ground.

The handsome Everette Marshall as world champ.

Perhaps it was a case of nerves, Marshall mused, or maybe the lower altitude unsettled Gotch. Regardless, Marshall thereafter stuck to two-legged opponents, and his success against them earned him acclaim as one of wrestling's top stars of the pre–World War II era. Harnessing the speed of a welterweight inside a chiseled heavyweight frame, Marshall packed a lot of accomplishments into a relatively brief career. "Marshall is an underrated former champion, for he suffers by comparison with Strangler Lewis and the other great stars of the era who were on the wane when Everette won the title," said Lou Thesz, who took his first world championship from Marshall in December 1937. "But make no mistake about it. He was a good, exceptionally tough wrestler."

Born November 4, 1905, Marshall grew up on a farm in La Junta, Colorado, but an unhappy family life led him to run away and join the Marines at fifteen. Eventually, the service figured out his true age and sent him back to Colorado, where life calmed down after his father remarried. In high school, he was an all-state lineman and helped his football team to the 1925 state title. More importantly, veteran middleweight wrestler Pete Jordan, who was helping to coach football in the area, took a shine to Marshall and worked with him on wrestling basics. Marshall enrolled at the University of Denver for a year, and his impact on its wrestling program was so great that the school inducted him into its athletic hall of fame in 1999. From there, he went to the University of Iowa, where he ranked as the school's top heavyweight before he decided to turn pro in December 1928. His interest in pay-for-play was strictly business, because he wanted to buy a farm with Harriett Dunham, a teacher whom he married in December 1929. "What I had always heard from my mother was they decided he would go into pro wrestling just to earn money to buy more land," said his daughter, Ann Marshall Schomburg. "That's exactly what he did, and he got a lot right across the road from his father."

His exploits in the ring soon eclipsed his plans to cultivate the property. In May 1929, he beat Joe Severini in La Junta for his first title, the Rocky Mountain Heavyweight championship. His hometown paper proudly proclaimed: "La Junta and vicinity take great pride in the new champion. He has played the game squarely and fairly, as all his opponents thus far have testified, and it is the hope of his legion of friends here and elsewhere in the state that he will be able to go higher in his chosen profession." Also taking notice were Strangler Lewis and his manager Billy Sandow, a founding father of modern pro wrestling. Lewis traveled to La Junta that November for an hour-long standoff with Marshall, and the newcomer was on his way. Heading to Los Angeles under Sandow's management,

Marshall's fresh face meshed perfectly with promoter Lou Daro's plans for a big money-making show. On January 8, 1930, he beat Joe Malcewicz in two straight falls, and the *Los Angeles Times* explained: "Although local mat fans considered Malcewicz fast, Marshall was so speedy that he made the Panther look slow. Joe had four holds on the youngster during the evening and each one lasted about four seconds." On April 16, Marshall beat Lewis in a two-out-of-three falls bout, winning the third in thirty-three seconds, to set up a match with world champ Gus Sonnenberg. Their May 5 outdoor contest at Wrigley Field drew 17,580, including about 500 fans from Colorado, and a gate of nearly $70,000. Given the buildup, it was a bit of a surprise when Sonnenberg, an ex-football player who popularized the flying tackle, won the match and kept the title.

Marshall continued as a regular in California in the early 1930s, and barnstormed across the country for a few months at a time, wowing fans with a blend of quickness and power. He contrived a wooden dummy with a spring-loaded head and foot stirrups for leverage, and hours of applying full nelsons on the contraption turned his forearms into oaks. His pleasing style and handsome appearance reminded fans of Jim Londos, the reigning champion of the era, though Marshall never got the measure of his rival in more than a dozen matches. In December 1933, for example, he was disqualified against Londos in Philadelphia, when his histrionics included attacks on referee Ben Paul, Sandow, and a police officer. Marshall's antics got the desired effect at the gate, though. A rematch in February 1934 drew a city record reported at 15,000 to 17,000 fans.

When Londos took a break from wrestling in 1935, Marshall seemed like a logical heir to his mantle, but he ran into a series of political roadblocks on the way. When an article in the *Saturday Evening Post* appeared to slight his skills, citing his multiple losses to Londos, Marshall slapped a $1 million lawsuit on the publication and six promoters whom he charged were in cahoots to undermine his good name. Relocating to Ohio, Marshall was awarded the Midwest Wrestling Association championship, the result of manager Sandow's ties with Columbus promoter Al Haft. On June 29, 1936, Sandow and Haft booked Marshall in Columbus against Ali Baba, who had a claim to the badly fractured world title. Before a wildly enthusiastic crowd of 8,763, Marshall used a series of three full nelsons to soften Baba for a slam, a body press, and a victory. That still left the title picture murky, but according to national columnist Harry Grayson, it had the virtue of putting the world championship, or part of it, around the waist of a no-nonsense traditionalist. "Earnest Everette has restored wrestling to the wrestlers — taken the leadership of it at least out of the hands of the acrobats and buffoons.

With Marshall on the program, clowning and tumbling is restricted to the pre-liminaries," Grayson wrote. Marshall added Illinois to the states that considered him kingpin in January 1937 by beating local hero Jim McMillen in Chicago. The championship run was profitable, as Sandow estimated in 1937 that Marshall earned $500,000 in wrestling and regularly got $1,000 for a main-event bout.

Health conscious before it was in vogue, Marshall eschewed white bread and tobacco, stayed free of scandal, and refrained from incendiary statements in the press. St. Petersburg, Florida, sportswriter Dick Blalock watched him quietly cast a fishing line while on vacation one day in 1937, and decided that he didn't fit the wrestling stereotype. "The writer found Marshall a surprisingly quiet and unas-suming individual and vastly different from the general run of gnarled-ear behe-moths of the mat world. He is one person who has remained idealistic toward the sport." As Marshall told Blalock, "There are others just like me who have spent years in training and then have to suffer when some clown decides to turn wrestler behind the backing of some wealthy or political figure. It's that kind of people who destroy the confidence of the public on the legitimacy of the sport."

On December 29, 1937, Marshall lost his title to twenty-two-year-old Lou Thesz in St. Louis. Typical of the promotional kiss-and-make up game, billing for the match emphasized not the MWA championship but American Wrestling Association honors, with a new $10,000 belt studded with diamonds, rubies, and sapphires to be awarded to the winner. Thesz attempted an airplane spin, lost his balance, and tumbled outside the ring with Marshall, who was counted out. Sandow and Marshall protested that Thesz illegally tossed his opponent over the top rope, to no avail. Marshall had one more run with a major championship. The National Wrestling Association, at its 1938 meeting in Montreal, voted 8-6 to rec-ognize him as champion, replacing John Pesek, a legendary shooter who was as difficult to control as he was talented. Marshall lost that title to Thesz in February 1939, again in St. Louis, in an hour-long skirmish in which two referees were knocked out. "He left a kid some big damn shoes to fill!" Thesz said on his mes-sage board at WrestlingClassics.com before he died in 2002. "He was one of the encounters in wrestling that kept me going when I was tired and lonely."

By the end of the 1930s, Marshall's mind was on his farm and not on the mat, his daughter said. "Mother got tired of traveling. Even those two years in Columbus, they made good friends and we'd see them later on but they both just wanted to go back to La Junta. I think he was proud that he had seen our country and he was ready to come home and that's exactly what he did," Schomburg said. Marshall dabbled in promoting wrestling, and made a brief comeback in 1946 and

1947. But mostly, he threw himself into his land. He started with a small dairy operation, and then turned to harvesting onions and cantaloupes on several thousand acres of Colorado farmland. He employed more than 300 people, and proudly announced a banner crop of more than five million pounds of onions in 1943. He expanded into feeding about 7,000 cattle for Hansen Packing and American Stores and was headed for a comfortable retirement in 1963, when he got overextended, and sold $3 million of land, cattle feedlots and produce warehouses to an investment group. The deal flopped and Marshall landed in bankruptcy court. He lost almost everything he had, and he started to deteri-

Every wrestler needs a workout partner.

orate physically and mentally. Doctors later found substantial scar tissue on his brain, a residue of his years in the ring and a possible cause of his disorientation, his daughter said. During a procedure for kidney stones in February 1973, he failed to come out of anesthesia and died at sixty-seven.

Gone, maybe, but not forgotten, because his work touches the lives of troubled youths to this day. In 1959, Marshall was approached to be a co-founder of the Colorado Boys Ranch, an orphanage for abused and abandoned boys near his La Junta ranch. He'd been generous with time and donations for youth programs as an organizer of the Arkansas Valley Athletic Association, and the ranch afforded him a cause that he worked on for the rest of his life. The organization, now CBR YouthConnect, has become a nationally renowned residential treatment facility, providing mental health, education, and life skills services for as many as 175 at-risk boys annually. Fittingly, it's where Marshall's wrestling mementoes are on display. "He was key to getting the Colorado Boys Ranch up and running because everybody knew him," said Bob Cody, a member of ranch's first board of directors. "The people we needed support from didn't recognize Bob Cody or anybody else on that first board, other than ol' Everette. And there was no talking him into helping. He signed on immediately." CBR YouthConnect's highest honor is the Everette Marshall Distinguished Service Award.

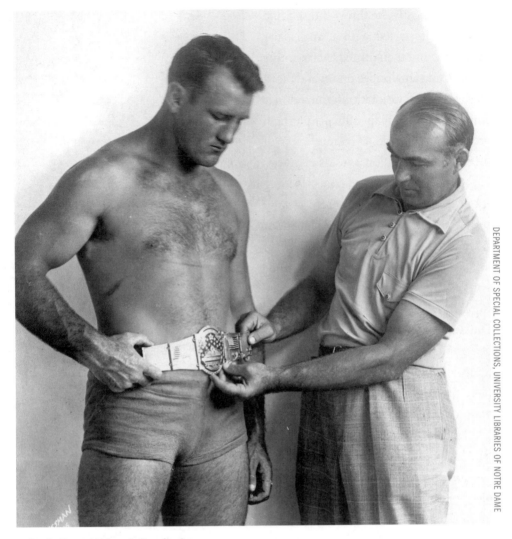

Bronko Nagurski tries a belt on for size.

BRONKO NAGURSKI

The clippings now are old and faded, and there are few around who really knew him as a contemporary. But that doesn't stop the rich tales from flowing; even a brief brush with Bronko Nagurski is a story to share for decades to come.

Take "Gabby" Gil Hayes, who would become a mainstay of Stampede Wrestling. He was about seventeen years old, drinking underage in International Falls, Minnesota, a border town with Fort Frances, Ontario. A fight broke out with his friends and some Americans, and Hayes took off as the police arrived. "Here I am, an underage Canadian drinking in the United States, and the cops can nail my ass. So I am really booting it, and I run around this corner and into this guy that is right behind a little garage. He's putting something in a big garbage bin. It was Bronko Nagurski at his garage." Calmly, Nagurski took the future wrestler into his garage, and allowed him to hide out in the grease pit. "He talked to me for a little bit. He said, 'Okay, you can go now.' Away I went, and I snuck back across the border to Fort Frances. That was the only time I ever met Bronko Nagurski."

Or Alex Karras, who had a photo of Nagurski on his dresser as a youth, and grew into a feared defensive tackle for the Detroit Lions, and later an actor in movies and on TV. As George Plimpton recounted in 1973's *Mad Ducks and Bears: Football Revisited*, Karras met Nagurski in Minneapolis the season he was suspended from football and tried pro wrestling.

"I was late, and I came running into the place and the promoter said, 'You're on the tag team tonight.' 'Wonderful,' I said. He didn't mention my partner on the tag team. So I went down to the locker room. Locker rooms that wrestlers use are different from any other — dingy and small and dirty, and always with this very distinctive smell, a body smell that's worse than anything you find in places where football and baseball players have been. I don't know why. Maybe it's because a lot of wrestlers are big, haystack guys that sweat a lot and maybe take a bath once a month. The smell of wrestlers lies in these little rooms in layers," said Karras. "Well, I went down there to change my clothes, and in the shadows I saw this older man practicing with a pair of dumbbells, pumping his arms. I kept looking at him. A much older man. Suddenly it came to me that it was Bronko Nagurski, my childhood idol, standing over in the shadows and pumping these barbells toward the ceiling. I could hardly believe it. I went over and introduced myself; sure enough, it *was* Nagurski. He was my tag team partner. I stared at him, bug-eyed. Hell, I knew more about him than *he* did."

And Lou Thesz told the story many times about meeting Bronko at the Wabash train station in Chicago — and changing Nagurski's life.

"We recognized each other, had breakfast together. I was making twice as much money as a very young journeyman wrestler than he was as a football player," Thesz wrote on the WrestlingClassics.com newsboard in 2001. "I told him how much Tony had helped me, and I suggested he to talk to Tony Stecher about a wrestling career. I did them both a favor. Bronko was a good man, and Tony was the very best."

Such is the legend of Bronko Nagurski. Not only does he inspire stories, his feats are used for inspiration in movies (*Hearts of Atlantis*), he was on a U.S. stamp, the top college defensive player each year gets the Bronko Nagurski Trophy, and his name is used on the hometown football team (the International Falls Broncos), where a museum in his honor stands — believed to be the only museum in the world dedicated to a sole football player (or wrestler, for that matter).

Born Bronislau Nagurski on November 3, 1908, in the small town of Rainy River, Ontario, to parents Michael and Amelia Nagurski, Bronko moved with his family across the border in 1912, where they operated a farm, sawmill, and corn store. There was nothing to the name, stressed his mother. "Bronko is a common name in that part of the Ukraine from which we come and as far as I know it has no particular meaning."

But back to Nagurski lore. He was into sports growing up, and liked to run the four miles to school, but how did he end up at the University of Minnesota? International Falls, on the northern end of the state, is not exactly on the regular recruiting path, and Bronko's high school time on the varsity did not get much press.

The story, as it goes, has an alumnus getting lost and asking a young man plowing the field — without a horse — for directions back home. "It's that way," said Bronko, picking up the plough in one hand and pointing in the general direction of Minneapolis.

With the University of Minnesota Gophers, the six-foot-two, 230-pound Nagurski was an All-American from 1927 to 1929, the only player in history to make first team All-Pro at more than one non-kicking position: fullback and defensive tackle. When he wasn't running the ball, he'd be an offensive tackle rather than sitting out. "It would be a mop-up if you put eleven Nagurskis on the game field with any other eleven men," Grantland Rice once wrote. Over his three seasons, the Gophers lost only four games with Bronko in the lineup. "And we lost those four games by a total of five points," said Bronko. "In 1928 we lost to Iowa 7-6 and Northwestern 10-9 and the next year Iowa beat us 9-7 and Michigan by 7-6."

There were no college scholarships in Bronko's day, so he worked for a law firm, serving papers three nights a week, and later as a watchman in a lumber yard, sleeping on a cot.

Bronko's exploits were known across the country, because, at the time, college ball was far more popular than the pros. But Nagurski, who joined the Chicago Bears in 1930, was one of the men who changed that as well. He played nine seasons for the Bears, spread out over fifteen years, helping the team win two titles. "When you hit Bronk, it was almost like getting an electric shock," said Bears teammate Red Grange. "If you hit him above the ankles, you were likely to get killed."

The details of his salary with the Bears, under George Halas, are key to understanding his decision to go into pro wrestling at the peak of his career. He made $5,000 the first season, talking Halas up from the initial offer of $3,500.

"But then I took cuts. I played four years with Red Grange on the Bears. I don't know what he got. It was hard to go up with Halas. It took me seven years to get back to $5,000. In 1938 I tried to get $6,000 and quit," Nagurski recalled in 1965. "I was asked to come back in 1942. It was a war year. In the last game I gained over 100 yards and scored two touchdowns, and it put us in the playoffs. Linemen were getting $6,500 then but I only got $6,000."

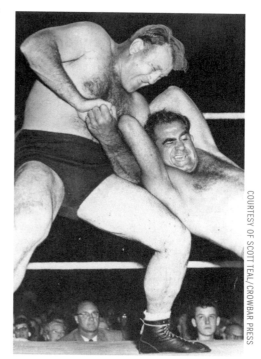

Lou Thesz struggles to get out of Bronko Nagurski's grip.

In February 1933, Nagurski tutored under Minneapolis promoter Tony Stecher, and began wrestling when time allowed. Other regular workout partners would include George Sauer (Ray Steele's brother), Jack Sampson, and Henry Ordermann. "I went in without too much experience, depending on strength and condition," said Nagurski in 1971. "I wasn't wrestling any of the top boys until I had a couple of years under my belt, and my seasons were short because football cut in, so it was a couple of years before I was wrestling better opponents."

Right from the start, his travel was intense, going north to Winnipeg, and south to St. Louis, east to Detroit, and west to Los Angeles, where sportswriter Jack Singer poetically penned, "Bronko Nagurski, a primitive symphony of bone and sinew, mightiest mammal of the mat."

"At one point in three weeks, he had five football games and ten wrestling matches, and was on both coasts of the country. He had sort of an iron man schedule at the time," said his son, Tony Nagurski.

After a year marred by a hip injury, the Bronk moved up the card upon his return in 1937. On June 29, he knocked off Dean Detton for a version of the world title. His chance meeting with Thesz in the Chicago train station led to Nagurski's decision to stop playing football and concentrate on wrestling, starting in 1938 — the Bears' contract proposal required him to give up the grunt and groan business.

"For years I've been waiting for a man who really can catch the popular fancy," said New York promoter Toots Mondt, who took Nagurski to court to reclaim the "World" title Bronko had lifted from Detton. "Nagurski is the man. Such demonstrations as they give him in Minneapolis and Los Angeles reflect his ability to win popularity. The country will be mad about him. He has every-thing . . . a physique which makes you catch your breath when he peels off his robe. He's the strongest man I've ever seen on a mat. He's as fast as lightning and has the earnest manner and the obvious love of rough competition that excites the crowd."

Knowing that Nagurski was a great draw, Thesz agreed to drop his NWA World Heavyweight title to the football great. The match, in Houston on June 23, 1939, was marred by Thesz suffering a broken kneecap and struggling through the third and deciding fall. On March 7, 1940, Ray Steele toppled Bronk for the title in St. Louis. Bronko had one more three-month run with the belt in 1941, beating Steele and losing to Sandor Szabo.

During World War II, Nagurski only worked a handful of matches in and around Minneapolis, choosing to stay home in International Falls and raising chickens for the war effort. "He didn't think he should be participating in sports because he was ineligible to go into the service," said his son.

The war-depleted Bears got one more season out of "The Nag," where he played tackle, but Bronko wrestled for another seven years. "I went on with it until 1950," he said in 1969. "It wasn't fixed on the scale it is now, but I prob-ably wish I hadn't done it. I wasted a lot of time."

Indeed, in later interviews, Nagurski did not speak highly of his wrestling days. "I think that goes back to the purity, where wrestling had been," said Tony Nagurski, who traveled with his dad at the end of his career, and still has his autograph book to prove it. "Had it stayed more of a pure sport, he prob-ably would have thought a little more of it. But yet he did it. He was involved for twenty-five years."

After getting off the road, Nagurski kept the family farm going and ran his gas station, where fans would seek him out, getting a handshake that was once compared to "grabbing the bottom half of a boat oar." Bronko and Eileen had four boys and two girls; his eldest son, Bronko Jr., was a successful football player in the Canadian Football League, and another, Ron, made it to hockey's minor leagues.

Though Nagurski's body gave out January 8, 1990, the laurels never did. A charter member of the Professional Football Hall of Fame, he is also in the College Football Hall of Fame and the Professional Wrestling Hall of Fame — an unparalleled three-peat.

"Of course I'm very pleased to be among the charter members, but naturally after a long period of years as these honors keep piling up you get kind of used to receiving them," said the modest Bronko upon learning of his Pro Football Hall of Fame honors. "And then the first awards you get are the biggest because you're not accustomed to it."

Now in the process of studying his father's amazing career, Tony Nagurski marvels at it all, and the modesty that remained throughout his life (Bronko refused to ever even be feted in his hometown). "He could never play football today, because of the attitude and the way these players react. They showboat so much," concluded Tony Nagurski. "He just wasn't that type of person, which is interesting when you read about his wrestling career, because that's part of wrestling. The articles do talk about him getting into it and doing some of the things that he had to do, essentially the acting part of it. That's different from his personality. I guess he did it quite successfully."

YVON ROBERT

"Just who is this Robert kid, who has brought the mat sport out of the doldrums and, apparently, has wrestling addicts all over the country humming his name?" The Ring magazine was an early supporter of Yvon Robert, writing the advance praise for the twenty-one-year-old Montrealer in 1936. That praise never really stopped for Robert, who addressed the hype twenty years later: "During the years since I began to wrestle as a professional there have been millions of words written about me. Some were true while others were publicity agents' pipe dreams."

His celebrity in Quebec was such that when he died of a heart attack on July 13, 1971, at fifty-six, that newspapers led with the news on front pages and columnists opined on what he meant to Quebecois culture — at one point, he was probably the most famous French Canadian in the world. A book toasting the closing of the fabled Montreal Forum gives Robert two whole pages, and tells a story about Robert's fanbase encouraging him to run for the mayoralty of Montreal. "I am highly flattered but . . . I don't think it would be fitting for Montrealers to read in the sports pages that Mayor Robert is wrestling tonight at the Forum."

Such was his love of wrestling that Robert, born the youngest of five children on October 8, 1914, in Verdun, a suburb of Montreal, never wanted to be far from it. He was a strapping young lad, delivering groceries by bicycle, when fate

COURTESY OF SCOTT TEAL/CROWBAR PRESS

Yvon Robert, Québécois legend.

intervened and he crashed into a monstrous specimen of a man who, unhurt like Robert, suggested he try wrestling. Robert heeded the advice, and threw himself into the training. Encouraged by a coach, the seventeen-year-old went into the Laurentian Mountains, thirty miles north of the city, seeking a wrestling camp run by Emil Maupas. Campers would be expected to work hard all day — running ten miles, swimming two miles, using a medicine ball — on top of whatever it was they were studying with the specialists. Besides wrestlers such as Tony Lanza, Legs Langevin, and Harry Madison, Maupas took in the Montreal Canadiens on one occasion, plus other hockey players, cyclists, runners, boxers, skiers, and fencers. Everyone was expected to be in bed by 8 p.m. and rise early. Robert came to the camp in 1931, stayed ten months, and became a prize pupil, quickly getting up to 200 pounds on his six-foot-one frame.

Turning pro before he was nineteen, Robert gained popularity around Quebec for his winning style and handsome visage, and was given the chance to face and draw with, though rarely beat, huge names such as Earl McCready, Ed Don George, and Strangler Lewis. But it was in Beantown, under the guidance of promoter Paul Bowser, that Robert gained the experience to become a star and met his future manager/business partner, Eddie Quinn, a former Boston taxi driver and Bowser confidant. He also met his wife, Leona Brunelle, in Boston, with whom he would have three children.

On February 28, 1936, Robert fell to champion claimant Danno O'Mahoney in a controversial two-hour epic before 20,000 fans at the Boston Garden. It had been a masterful build to the bout, with Robert showing up for months during O'Mahoney's matches to heckle and challenge the Irishman, including an incident in January when Robert collared O'Mahoney and threw him to the mat, pinned Danno for thirty seconds, and, after letting the Irishman up, KO'ed him, knocking him from the ring to be carted back to the dressing room. "The wisdom of this angle is suspect and it may have been the first and most humiliating stunt ever pulled on a willing world champion," said historian Steve Yohe. "I can't believe it helped O'Mahoney's image in the national press, but it did serve Bowser's plan of making a star out of Robert."

That July, Robert took the American Wrestling Association world title from O'Mahoney, the first of many belts he would claim, including seventeen runs with the International title, the top belt in Montreal. Outside of Quebec, his month and a half with the National Wrestling Association title, beating Bill Longson with a Japanese arm lock in Montreal on October 7, 1942, and losing to Bobby Managoff in Houston, on November 27, cemented his legacy. Robert also did three tours of Europe, facing top grapplers like Henri Deglane and François Miquet. "In Europe, we called Yvon Robert the Gentleman of the Ring," said Edouard Carpentier, who met Robert on one of those tours and was encouraged to come to la belle province. "Yvon had a lot of charisma. It's not for nothing that he was a wrestling god in Montreal."

In 1939, Robert partnered with Eddie Quinn to reopen wrestling in the Montreal Forum, which had banned the grappling game following a riot a few years earlier. Their partnership, which lasted until Quinn's death in 1964, made each very wealthy, allowing for other ventures, including nightclubs, horses, restaurants, and a share of the St. Louis wrestling office. "They were able to accomplish it because ego and vanity had no place in their partnership; they were only interested in doing what was best for their business," wrote Lou Thesz in Hooker.

"We managed pretty good," Robert said of Quinn in 1956. "He couldn't speak French, and I couldn't speak English, but we were both out to make a buck, and I guess that's what you call a universal language, eh?"

Protecting his interests, Robert was careful who was on the cards. "In those days, it was Wednesday night wrestling at the Montreal Forum," recalled Paul Leduc. "Most of the time it was one, sometimes two, outsiders. The rest of the crew was Quebecers. There was a clique, they were his friends, like Larry

Moquin, Ovila Asselin, Yvon Racicot, Eddie Auger." It was Bowser's crew from Boston that generally filled out the bill.

Still, Robert was smart enough to know that he needed new stars in Quebec. Johnny Rougeau was his greatest protégé, and he made room for Carpentier on the top of the cards; both benefited from the rub. "They were there doing the set-up and let Yvon Robert do the finish," said Leduc.

Rene Goulet was one of the wide-eyed youngsters who got to work with

TONY LANZA

In the last wrestling photo of Yvon Robert Sr., he accompanies his son to the ring in Montreal.

his idol. "He used to always have a brand new Cadillac convertible. When he'd come to town, he'd have the top down. Everyone said, 'Look! Yvon Robert!'" said Goulet.

Emile Dupre had Yvon Robert in his corner as his manager when he first hit Montreal in 1957, and soaked in the coaching and advice, while never forgetting his mentor's fame. "When we walked into a restaurant somewhere, and they saw him, it was like the pope came in. Oh, the people loved him. The funny thing about it, he never threw a dropkick, he maybe could do a tackle, but he didn't do much in the ring. But what he did, the few moves that he made, whatever it was, the Montrealers really liked him."

Robert's son, Yvon Jr., entered pro wrestling, well aware that it would be impossible to live up to his father's fame. "I knew I was going there to give the best of myself, but I would never be the equal of my father," said Robert Jr., who also worked as Bob Brunnell. "So I did not have the complex of the son of an athlete trying to match him. I said I could be as good if I have an organization that promotes wrestling." Instead, he heeded the advice his father had shared: "The man that smokes the cigar makes the money, not the guy who puts on his tights." The Roberts were key figures behind the scenes in the ascension of Grand Prix Wrestling in the early 1970s in Montreal, though with Senior's death so early in the promotion's existence, he does not get much credit.

By 1960, Robert Sr. had stopped wrestling, but not participating, and was often used as a guest referee. One time, while wintering in Florida, Eddie Graham used him, and Goulet was in the bout against the Funks in Tampa. Robert knew his health was precarious after a few earlier heart attacks, said Goulet. "He told me in the dressing room, 'Man, if you see me out of breath and down, my pill is right here in my pocket.'" His last time in the ring was as a guest referee for a barnburner between the Vachons and Leducs at Lansdowne Park in Ottawa.

Robert's life ended at his home at Havre des Iles, Laval. A biography on his life, eight years in the making by author Pierre Berthelet, *Yvon Robert: Le lion du Canada français*, came out in 1999, with a foreword by the man he was most often compared to — the iconic, fiery hockey star "The Rocket" Maurice Richard.

"There's nobody like Yvon Robert. You've got a legend there," said Gino Brito. "You figure what Maurice Richard was to the people here, so was Yvon Robert. The same thing. Yvon Robert was phenomenal. There's no Canadians, never mind French-Canadians, there's no wrestler that came close to Yvon Robert. To watch him, he didn't do that much in the ring. You know that he never threw a dropkick, a tackle, or something like that. But he had something about him. You know when you've got charisma? When you're Humphrey Bogart or something? They were the same thing."

LEO "DANIEL BOONE" SAVAGE

Well, c'mon in, sit a spell and lissen up 'bout Leo Dan'l Boone Savage. Yes sir, ol' Whiskers — that's what ev'rybody called 'im — was 'bout the biggest thing down here, least as far as the rasslin' was concerned. He come from up Kentucky way, but said his kinfolk weren't none too happy 'bout his scufflin'. So he headed down to Texas instead and found hisself a callin'. Lemme tell you, when one of them rasslers got in there with 'im, they was on the business end of a whuppin'. He'd wrap them arms 'round 'em like a grizzly bear and 'bout pop the eyeballs right out of their heads. And ol' Whiskers, he was a sharp 'un. See, everywhere he went, he carried a lantern with 'im, just in case the 'lectricity went out. Then he'd be able to see where he was a-headin', whilst ev'rybody else was stumblin' and bumpin' into things. He sure was somethin', Whiskers was. Why, Mr. Boesch said he done saved rasslin' in Houston. Saved rasslin' in Houston! Pretty good, fer a country boy.

On March 7, 1934, Ed Strangler Lewis beat an ex-boxer named Eddie Civil in a nondescript wrestling match in a Brooklyn arena. A brawny heavyweight at six-foot-four and 250 pounds, Civil had been boxing professionally since he was 1921, with mixed results, and a foray into wrestling in the early 1930s didn't work out much better. So when he disappeared from the athletic landscape after the loss to Lewis, the world was apparently out one thirty-four-year-old, third-tier pugilist. But it was about to pick up one first-class character. A face full of bramble, a coon dog, and a couple of roosters later, and Leo "Daniel Boone" Savage took Civil's place on earth for the remainder of his sixty-six years. At his peak in Texas in the mid-1930s, it was commonplace to see Savage sitting outside an arena hours before a match reading, if that's the word, the comic pages, his lop-eared dog tied to a pole. He'd take up residence at a local Salvation Army, and fans would follow him through the streets like a pied piper, trying to barter chickens or eggs for tickets at the City Auditorium box office, just to see him wrestle. "It may have been that the average fellow had been beaten down for so long he was ready for something that could make him cheer," Houston promoter Paul Boesch wrote in *Hey Boy, Where'd You Get Them Ears?* "He was reaching for something to pull him out of his own personal depression. He reached up and grabbed Whiskers. And Whiskers was equal to the occasion."

He represented hope to the down-and-out because he identified with their plight; if anyone was ever a man of the people, it was Savage. "What you saw and what you talked to is what you got," said his son Bob Savage. "I think people sensed that. If he had a roof over his head and three meals a day, he was happy. He wasn't into monetary items." Born in March 1900 in East Liverpool, Ohio, to a day laborer and his wife, Civil was raised by grandparents in Kentucky after his mother died at a young age. He snuck into the U.S. Army when he was about sixteen; he got kicked out, but rejoined the service when he came of age and served in Europe. Based out of Ashland, Kentucky, Civil started as a pro boxer at age twenty-one, a strapping puncher who had less wind than the doldrums; only two of his recorded fights ever got past the fourth round. The closest he got to squaring off with a big name was a second-round knockout in 1927 at the hands of Young Stribling, a contender in the '20s and '30s. By 1933, he was wrestling a little and boxing preliminary bouts in places like Zanesville, Ohio.

But this was the era of wrestling's Man Mountain Dean, who proved great riches could accrue to even the most unlikely of candidates, given the right gimmick and dedication. In the summer of 1934, Civil grew a briary beard, like Dean, and became "Whiskers" Civil, a Kentucky wildman to whom the rule book was just so much fancy talk. He headed to Florida, which became his real-life home, and terrorized the state as Bob Savage, a bearded beast who was equal parts wrestler, boxer, and entertainer. Boasting that he could outbox or outwrestle anyone, he put on the gloves to take on King Levinsky, a respected

Whiskers Savage was one of wrestling's greatest characters.

heavyweight, in Tampa in February 1935. Levinsky dropped Savage in the second round, whereupon Savage staggered to his feet and, appearing only marginally conscious, swung wildly at the air and knocked out both of his seconds.

It was, then, something of a surprise when Savage materialized in Beaumont, Texas, in May 1935 as a well-meaning bumpkin from Boyd County, Kentucky, who naively entered the ring during the middle of a match to have a go at things. To a disappointed Savage, the referee explained, no, you can't unilaterally decide you want to get in a few licks. If you want, come back another time and we'll hook you up in a sanctioned contest. The scene was repeated in Houston the next week, and Savage was on his way to becoming the biggest thing in Texas since Sam Houston sent General Santa Anna packing. Clad in faded overalls with a bandanna around his neck, wearing a coarse burlap sack as a robe, Savage drew a dozen standing-room only crowds for promoter Morris Sigel in Houston in 1935. Exuberant sportswriters claimed he attracted an extra quarter-million fans to the city's turnstiles. That's probably a stretch, but the scribes can be forgiven because they rarely stumbled on such good copy. Savage lived his character every day, every moment, as though he'd been rebaptized in a jug of corn mash. His training, he said, came from restraining the hind legs of ill-tempered mules, while whittling strengthened his hands for combat. Some knowledgeable reporters recognized the switch from ex-boxer Civil, but it was more fun to go along for the ride because Savage was as faithful to his persona as anyone who ever hitched up overalls. "Never lived in no town at all. Lived just acrost the mountain from Nubbin Ridge, nigh the folks of Turkey Creek," he informed Ward Burris of the *San Antonio Express*. "Ah fished some, hunted possums more, and in the daytime slept and did a whole lot of whittling." Asked a bemused Jack Cuddy of the United Press, "Is he a genuine hillbilly? I don't know. If he isn't, he's a swell actor and in a line where acting really counts. Anyway he's the strangest bozo I ever met in sports."

There was not much to his wrestling, a few body blows and a finishing bear hug where he squeezed his opponent with all the force he applied to greased pigs and tree stumps back in Boyd County. Like a boxer, he crouched low, long arms extended, and he was several weeks into his career in Texas before anyone even knocked him to the mat. Referee Art Crews recalled what Savage told him in the ring during pre-match instructions one night in St. Louis: "Mister, I don't care nuthin' 'bout these here city rasslin' rules. I just aims to scuffle a little."

If fans took him seriously, so did the powers that be. On May 10, 1936, the Texas athletic commission recognized Savage as its heavyweight wrestling champion when titleholder Danno O'Mahoney no-showed a match. In September 1936, the National Wrestling Association declared Dave Levin, Everette Marshall, and Savage as its top contenders, even though Savage professed little interest in championship gold. "Ah don't want none of those titles. Ah jus' likes to scuffle and pick up a few dollars," he said. "Always felt sorry for the other feller after ah beat him and told him he could keep his championship — fellers like that O'Mahoney from Ireland." True to his word, Savage abruptly bolted Texas and headed for the Hollywood hills in 1937, leaving behind a vacant world title. In California, he landed a part in *Swing Your Lady*, a 1938 Humphrey Bogart–Ronald Reagan flick, and unsuccessfully pursued a battle of the hillbillies with Dean, indignantly announcing he'd seen a paper where the Man Mountain admitted to being a city slicker.

Savage went national in the late 1930s, touring from St. Louis to New York City to Atlanta, where an indignant Babe Zaharias balked at wrestling him on the grounds that Savage's coon dog Roscoe might take a bite out of his backside.

Tommy Fooshee, later a referee, watched Savage as a teenaged wrestling fan in Houston and eagerly sought his autograph. "He'd look like he was saluting you; he'd have his hands over his eyes and that's the way he would go into the ring. He was just a very, very good draw." As a youngster, Savage's son Bob followed him around the Texas circuit, and said his dad possessed a natural magnetism that enraptured men, women, children, and critters, with the exception of monkeys. "I witnessed it on more than one occasion, and monkeys were petrified of him," Bob said. "One time, we were at a circus and the guy came out with the monkeys doing tricks and they wouldn't do anything. All they'd do was stare up at Dad. Finally, somebody came up and asked him if he would go outside or go behind where they couldn't see him, so the monkeys would perform. I don't know if they thought he might be a gorilla or what. That's the only explanation I can come up with."

Savage ended his active touring in 1952, but he continued to wrestle part-time in the Houston–San Antonio–Galveston territory through the late 1950s. During the winter months, he worked close to his Florida home, his heinous antics as Bob Savage long since forgotten. Never out of character, he was invited on a Houston TV cooking show, and brought along a live possum he intended to simmer up; the varmint escaped the clutches of his son and enlivened the studio for a spell. Savage was still taking a pet rooster to the ring for appearances in Daytona Beach, Florida, a month shy of his fifty-ninth birthday. He operated a roadside fruit and gift stand in Anthony, Florida, for many years, and died of a heart attack in nearby Ocala on January 7, 1967. Long after Savage's heyday, talent scout Jack Pfefer visited promoter Sigel's office in Houston and saw picture after picture of wrestlers lining the walls. There was none of Savage, though, and asked to explain, Sigel said he reserved a place for Savage, alone in his inner sanctum. "The camera shot of Savage is not with the other pictures of wrestlers in the anteroom because he made me more money than any grappler in my long history as a promoter," Sigel said. "He had the golden touch."

THE UPSIDE-DOWN MAN

If wrestling was conducted upside down, Joe Tonti would be a first-ballot hall of famer. The Pennsylvania strongman could do more on his hands than most people could do on their feet, whether it was hauling an automobile with his teeth or walking, palm by calloused palm,

Joe Tonti, right-side up . . .

down the Washington Monument. Though Tonti's mat career was secondary to his feats of strength, he packaged them together to become one of the most unusual gate attractions of the 1930s and early 1940s. "He was just a showman. He loved show business," said his wife, Helen Tonti Weaver.

Born in May 1907, Tonti was the third of twelve children of Italian immigrants and grew up in the small steel town of Midland, Pennsylvania, south of Pittsburgh. His father was a beer distributor and Tonti developed muscles when he was in grade school by hauling beer cases. But strength is one thing — lots of old-time wrestlers built their physiques with makeshift devices. To be inspired enough to do everything upside down, and have the ability to pull it off — that's something else. In 1926, his father opened a three-story hotel in Midland, and the creative Tonti started to amaze. He walked along the bar on his hands, pushed off, and landed on his hands. "When we were kids, he used to pick us up by the collar and carry us around with his little finger, just for kicks," said nephew Caesar Colista. "He was that strong."

Tonti played football at Midland High School, before going to Geneva College and then Temple University, where he was on the team from 1931 to 1933. He left to go into pro wrestling in 1934, hoping to earn a few bucks to help his family keep its hotel during the Great Depression. Only 5-foot-8 but a muscular 200-plus pounds, Tonti mostly accrued wins or draws against preliminary wrestlers from the New York–Pennsylvania–Ohio circuit south to Memphis, Tennessee, and New Orleans. He sparred with Max Baer and James J. Braddock before their famous 1935 heavyweight boxing title fight, then headed west in 1937, with an eye on Hollywood. "NY acrobat, stunt spec. wants a No. 1 agent," read his classified ad in the *Los Angeles Times*. Coming up short in the representation category, he went to Hawaii, where he stayed for about six months. Touring the Pacific, he used his prowess to promote upcoming matches. An astonished New Zealand scribe wrote after one display: "Tonti amazed a large crowd of spectators on Saturday morning when he pulled a heavily laden motor-car up an incline while holding the towing line in his teeth and walking on his hands and there will be an opportunity tonight to see how this brilliant matman came to be nicknamed 'Londos the second.'"

. . . showing off his remarkable talents.

Accounts of the time suggest Tonti was regarded as a good wrestler. Les Goates of the *Deseret News*, who usually treated the business tongue-in-cheek, described him as "a human dynamo" and, after a 1940 draw with George Harben in Salt Lake City, explained, "The fans really fell for the stocky Italian's sturdy aggressiveness and attention to the business at hand." Wrestling was not lucrative, though, and his wife nudged him to quit after they got married in 1943, concerned about injuries. "That wasn't his thing. He said it was so much 'put-on,' " she recalled. "It didn't turn out the way he thought it would."

But it did raise his profile, and his celebrity provided Ripley's "Believe It or Not" and John Hicks' "Strange As It Seems" with some choice fodder. A Tonti sampler:

- In 1934, he played a piano with his nose while doing a handstand on the piano bench.
- In 1940, he pulled an automobile with his teeth, using a homemade leather strap, while standing on his hands before a Long Beach, California, match with Lee Wycoff.
- In 1944, he walked 50 feet on his hands with a 175-pound weight on his neck.

Always eager to lend a hand to others, Tonti was stationed during World War II at Will Rogers Field in Oklahoma, where he trained GIs in physical fitness and appeared in exhibitions on behalf of war bonds. A workout fiend, he opened a fitness center in Oklahoma City, though his indifference toward billing customers led to its demise. Tonti graduated from chiropractic school and returned to his hometown of Midland, planning to set up a practice. On October 24, 1959, Tonti suffered a fatal heart attack near the bench of a high school football team he was training. He was fifty-two. "I guess if he would have had some sort of mercenary attitude, he probably could have made money, but that wasn't him. He just was a big-hearted guy," Colista said. Tonti is still remembered today by his local sports hall of fame as "one of the most versatile athletes ever produced in Beaver County."

RUFFY SILVERSTEIN

COURTESY OF SCOTT TEAL/CROWBAR PRESS

Ruffy Silverstein.

In wrestling, timing is everything. Take the case of "Ruffy" Silverstein, a son of Russian Jewish immigrants, who rose from the playgrounds on the west side of Chicago to become an NCAA wrestling champion. Ed White, the manager of Jim Londos, thought he had another winner on his hands when he signed Silverstein out of the University of Illinois in 1937. "What we need for the game is the same kind of build-up we developed for Jim Londos," White wrote promoter Jack Pfefer in July 1940. "Not a clown, but one who has natural showmanship and a certain appeal for the public. I have that man in Ruffy Silverstein." In 1941, Silverstein responded with convincing appearances in St. Louis for promoter Tom Packs. "He got a better hand, entering and leaving the ring after his match, than Tom's top notchers, including his champion," White related. Within weeks, though, Silverstein would trade in his trunks for military fatigues, and tote a gun instead of a championship belt. World War II had arrived, and it would consume Captain Ralph Silverstein of the U.S. Army for five years, in what would have been the prime of his career.

Whether the barrel-chested Chicagoan would have realized White's ambitions is open to question. Wrestlers who worked with him in later years found him to be stiff and too serious in the ring, and dependent on a charismatic rival — say, Buddy Rogers or Bill Miller — to draw big money. The thing is, though, the convivial Silverstein probably didn't mind because he was too busy breaking ring floorboards, working with blind children, or spinning yarns for anyone within earshot. In later years, he'd regularly hold court at a B'nai B'rith lodge in Chicago, sportswriter David Condon remembered, and, planting his tongue firmly in cheek, let the courtiers egg him on. "Oh, there have been so many greatest sporting events, ever. And I'm proud to have been the shining knight hero of them all," he announced. And memories of Silverstein's thirty years of battles, Condon said, flowed like wine.

If you could have molded the perfect amateur, Silverstein would have served as the cast. Built low to the ground, with a five-foot-eight frame that would carry as much as 225 pounds, he resembled a seawall and was about as difficult to move. Born March 20, 1914, in Chicago, he was just nine years old and barely sixty pounds when he made it to the finals of the Chicago Park District wrestling tournament, and he turned into a standout at Crane Technical Prep High School. "He had a very low center of gravity and tremendous strength in his upper body. There wasn't anybody he couldn't take down from the standing position," one teammate, Ralph Gradman, explained. Wrestling with older brother Max sharpened his skills; Max placed second in the nation at 158 pounds for the U.S. Naval Academy at the 1932 NCAA tournament. Ruffy stayed closer to home at Illinois, where he was Big Ten and NCAA champion at 175 pounds in 1935, and Big Ten heavyweight champ in 1936. He missed out on a chance at the 1936 Olympic team, losing to Orville England. After he got out of school, Silverstein was matched with fellow Illini Jim McMillen, an ex-footballer, to win a hastily conceived Illinois state pro title, which he never actually lost; the state athletic commission dissolved it after a couple of years.

In 1941, Silverstein came as close as he ever would to a major world title with a big push in St. Louis. He got a main-event victory over ex–world champ Everette Marshall in May, and hundreds of fans, according to White, milled around the new star after he whipped Ernie Dusek. He was scheduled to meet Bronko Nagurski on June 5 for a widely recognized version of the championship, but promoter Packs instead substituted the more established Sandor Szabo, who captured Nagurski's crown on a disqualification. During the war, Silverstein was stationed in Okinawa, the Philippines, and Japan, working in intelligence and dabbling in athletics, learning the judo and kendo styles as a counterintelligence officer in Honshu, Japan.

The war exacted a terrible toll, though. Brother Max was killed in the Battle of the Coral Sea in May 1942 when his ship sank under Japanese attack. The U.S Navy later named the USS *Silverstein*, a destroyer escort, in Max's honor. When Silverstein exited the service in 1946, he tried his hand as a plumber's appren-tice in Chicago. But that went nowhere, and two promoters who worked in cahoots, Fred Kohler in Chicago and Al Haft in Columbus, Ohio, got him back in the game. Silverstein became a mainstay of their promotions throughout the 1950s, always as a good guy to whom fans could relate. Karl Pojello also used him at his Chicago gym to break in young wrestlers, or convince them to find another line of work. "On Sundays, our day off, he would bring in Ruffy Silverstein who would kind of run us through the mill. He would come down and literally beat the hell out of us every Sunday. I wrestled Ruffy Silverstein several times and I still feel it," said Rip Hawk.

In July 1951, Silverstein beat Frankie Talaber in Dayton, Ohio, for a TV title that was a Haft creation, but had a big-time payoff since the show was broadcast by more than thirty stations across the country. That year, he also became the American Wrestling Association world champ, a vestigial title that had its ori-gins in the Boston area. A 1951 program with Bill Miller, the Ohio State football and wrestling star, was a natural — Buckeye versus Illini, Ruffy versus a rough house. To drum up interest, Silverstein put up $1,000 weekly to anyone who could pin him within thirty minutes. The pot reached $2,400 in August, when Miller tossed him from the ring ninety seconds before the magic thirty-minute mark to take Ruffy's money and his AWA title. Ruffy regained the title, though not the cash, in a December rematch at the Rainbo Arena in Chicago.

Still, Silverstein needed to be paired with a star attraction to draw a big gate, according to Ed Francis, who frequently traveled and wrestled with him. "He had to be with somebody," Francis said. "He was no great performer, but being that he had the great amateur background, Buddy Rogers took him under his wing. Rogers made a lot of money for him. Rogers wrestled him and maneuvered him around the ring so that they had some pretty good matches." Silverstein and "Nature Boy" wrestled more than fifty times from the late 1940s through the early 1950s, in arenas from Chicago to Montreal to Baltimore, and

Ruffy became Rogers' muscle, just in case somebody tried to get cute with him. Rogers explained the origin of the relationship in an interview with Max Jacobs for a famous college term paper: "I tried to teach him showmanship but this guy was not a broomstick you could sweep around; he was a crowbar. He was the best wrestler I ever worked with after Ed Lewis and probably the greatest Jewish wrestler that ever lived. We got in the ring together to try out some holds and after he almost broke my arm, the fourth time, I said, 'Hey, Ruffy, you know the difference between "working" and "shooting"? You want to make a living? You want to be my "policeman"? You want a piece of my gates?' He said he did. 'Then stop murdering me!'" Their series for the AWA belt took an odd twist when Silverstein bodyslammed Rogers and broke the ring at a July 1952 outdoor program in Chicago. Rogers disappeared three feet below the mat, and officials called off the match. Rogers finally took Silverstein's title a month later in a more solidly constructed ring.

In the Army, he was Ralph Silverstein.

What became Silverstein's passion, though, and what kept his memory alive for years, was an encounter in 1951, when he swung by the Ohio State School for the Blind in Columbus, which housed boys aged six to eighteen. Silverstein was a local sports celeb making the holiday rounds when he heard a performance of Handel's "Messiah" — "Then shall the eyes of the blind be opened." He was touched by inspiration. Why not teach them wrestling? Silverstein asked viewers of Columbus TV wrestling to pitch in for equipment and got $600, a regulation mat, and several small practice mats within a few weeks. So twice a week for forty-five minutes for several years, Silverstein worked with boys on all kinds of techniques and became, in the delicious words of Chicago columnist Charles Bartlett, "a fall guy for blind kids." With that, Silverstein had no need to tour nationally beyond his Midwest comfort zone, since Columbus, as Haft's booking office, was easily accessible from his Chicago home. "To those who are receptive I can do a lot of good. I can inspire them to improve themselves physically. I give them a concrete example of how right eventually wins out and that science can offset brute force. What higher goals can anyone have in life?" he asked in a 1952 interview.

Silverstein last wrestled as a pro in 1964, but kept close to the amateur side of things and was a coach in the 1965 Maccabiah Games in Israel. He earned the rank of patrolman for teaching self-defense to Cook County police reserves, and also taught physical education at a local high school. In later years, he suffered from Lou Gehrig's disease and died April 5, 1980, at the age of sixty-six. Condon, the famous *Chicago Tribune* columnist, tossed him a final garland, accepting his wrestling as light entertainment, and regarding him as a hero beyond the squared circle. "Ruff Silverstein was a humanitarian. He was a kind man, a person with high ideals, and a patient teacher. He believed in sport for the sake of sport and loved pure wrestling more than any other athletic endeavor."

SANDOR SZABO

For all his accomplishments in wrestling — an amateur standout in Europe, a multi-time world pro champion — it took a broken thumb to promote Sandor Szabo to the top rank of pop culture. In late 1952, Szabo, who left the word "bashful" back in Hungary when he emigrated to the United States, announced he'd croon "White Christmas" on a TV wrestling show in Los Angeles if he lost a match. As it turned out, George "Zebra Kid" Bollas beat him that December 23, taking Szabo's TV title and breaking his thumb in the process. Pained, and needing to seek treatment, Szabo blew off the vocals. That was all that critic Walter Ames of the *Los Angeles Times* needed to accuse him of setting up the whole thing as a cheap publicity ruse. Chastened, Szabo appeared on the Jack Owens show on KCEA-TV to sing "Hold Me in Your Arms."

Call it Hungarian Idol. A Hollywood recording company liked what it heard, and signed Szabo to do a couple of numbers for a special label called Hammerlock Records. The 78 rpm, featuring "Hold Me in Your Arms" on one side and "It's All in the Game" on the other, was a surprise hit, getting national attention and a favorable review in *Time* magazine. "We must admit that we were completely unprepared for what we heard when playing the record. This guy is great," chimed in Bob Foster of the *San Mateo Times*. "He has a fine, deep voice, an accent which adds much, and a great deal of Old World feeling." Szabo said he picked up about $4,000 in earnings from the record, and with only one drawback.

SANDOR SZABO
Hungarian Champion

Sandor Szabo, the hero to Hungarians, in his prime.

When he lost a fall, he told United Press in 1954, ringsiders mocked him with the flip side title, crying out, "It's all in the game."

Part wrestler, part businessman, part humanitarian, and part ham, Szabo represented the fusion of serious wrestling and show business. More than any other pro, he popularized suplexes and throws from Greco-Roman wrestling, where below-the-waist holds are barred; his halch hold, a quick double-arm suplex, was a devastating finisher in a match. He laid claim to being the longest-running wrestling hero based on the West Coast; his career there extended for three decades, always as a headliner. "My association with him was just great, and to me, he was just a first-class guy. He was synonymous with wrestling in Southern California," said Gene Kiniski, a regular opponent in the 1950s, who said Szabo's charisma reached beyond his Hungarian fans. "He had a good amateur background, and the guy was a technician in the ring."

Hobnobbing with Hollywood types was about the last thing one could have expected when Szabo was born January 4, 1906, in Kosice, then part of Hungary. The city was overrun in World War I, becoming part of Czechosolvakia. His parents spirited their seven children to Budapest, and Szabo later said he learned to box and wrestle in return for bread during lean war-torn years. Promoters would overbill him for years as an Olympic great, but there was no need to exaggerate Szabo's amateur accomplishments. He was a top-flight Greco-Roman wrestler, winning a bronze medal at eighty-two kilograms (about 180 pounds) at the European championships in 1926 and a gold medal a year later. Szabo came to the United States as a member of the 1929 Hungarian Greco-Roman national team, and saw enough to make it his permanent home. In New York City, a large Hungarian community helped him to speak English and wrestling bird dog Jack Pfefer helped him get matches for money.

Szabo debuted as a pro in October 1930, and promoters pushed him to the moon as a hunk of a man with legitimate wrestling credentials, who also appealed to various ethnicities. He rattled off wins in his first forty-eight matches before Karl Pojello, later to become handler of the French Angel, went off-script and double-crossed him in a February 1931 match in Philadelphia. Szabo stayed mostly on the East Coast and in Canada, wrestling the likes of Jim Londos and Ed "Strangler" Lewis until 1935, when he took his first trip west to participate in Los Angeles promoter Lou Daro's international tournament. Though he didn't win, Szabo fared well in the competition and won tongue-in-cheek praise from the normally skeptical Jack Singer of the *Los Angeles Times*: "Szabo is likely to revolutionize the entire bone-bending industry. He has some brains which he doesn't carry around in the seat of his pants, the place where most rasslers deposit theirs." Just as important, Szabo was no less transfixed than the discoverer Balboa upon seeing the Pacific for the first time. He brought wife Lillian west and made Santa Monica, California, his base of operations for the rest of his life. His name was synonymous with the Pacific Coast title, which he held thirteen times from 1937 to 1951.

In June 1941, Szabo won the first of his world championships, beating Bronko Nagurski by disqualification for the National Wrestling Association belt in St. Louis as an eleventh-hour replacement for the allegedly ailing Ruffy Silverstein. He'd eventually achieve an unparalleled grand slam as the only wrestler to hold the National Wrestling Association title, the Boston-based American Wrestling Association world title, the Montreal version of the title, and the Minneapolis version of the NWA title. His career peaked before the creation of the modern National Wrestling Alliance, but he held that belt vicariously through close friend Lou Thesz. They'd met in 1938 at Zimmerman's Hungaria, a restaurant in New York; Szabo spoke in Hungarian, Thesz in German. Neither man understood each other, but they bonded as Szabo, about ten years older, acted as something of a big brother to the wrestling legend. "He was a great wrestler, had a good singing voice and could keep a party going into the next day," Thesz recalled on WrestlingClassics.com. "He was on the board of the Santa Monica swimming club and became more interested in showbiz than wrestling. He had small parts in many movies and really became the entertaining darling of the movie industry."

While he was full of life, Szabo at times was full of himself, with humorous consequences. "Szabo was another character. He used to pose in the mirror," said California mat vet Ted Tourtas, mimicking Szabo's thick accent. "'Mirror, mirror on the wall.' He'd say, 'Szabo, with your beautiful body and a pretty face, handsome, you are great wrestler.'" Tourtas rolled his eyes. "Who the hell would pose in the mirror and say you're beautiful unless he had ego? No one would do that." And Szabo's ability to make female fans swoon came back to haunt him, as his daughter Alexandra Radtke remembered. One woman named Lucky wrote him flowery fan letters, which Lillian Szabo dutifully answered on behalf of her husband. Lucky even sent him a belt buckle with his initials in diamonds. One night, Szabo returned to his home in Santa Monica, red-faced and distraught. Recounted Radtke: "He said, 'I met Lucky tonight. She was like 300 pounds, she had all these kids.' And my mother said, 'What did you expect, Marilyn Monroe?' He was so upset." But he had a soft spot, too. When Hungarian dissidents rose up against Soviet bloc control in 1956, Szabo, who became an American citizen in August 1938, helped many of them escape persecution and enter the United States. His sponsorship of some of the estimated

200,000 refugees who fled Hungary earned him letters of commendations from President Dwight Eisenhower and Vice President Richard Nixon. "He was very good about helping bring people to this country," his daughter said.

As the 1950s rolled on, Szabo lived a comfortable life on the West Coast, pulling in about $50,000 annually, by his estimate, through wrestling, bit parts in TV shows and movies, singing gigs, and investments in apartments and other properties. He opened a wrestling school for youths and would-be pros in Westwood, California — Cowboy Bob Ellis was among his trainees — and was assistant booker to Jules Strongbow for the Los Angeles territory. Trying to guess Szabo's age in 1960, Oakland sportswriter Alan Ward was impressed by how little he'd changed since he burst onto the Southern California scene in the pre–World War II era. "An all-around athlete in his youth, Szabo has retained most of his Frank Merriwell dimensions and attitude. He employs a classic wrestling style, free from the obvious hippodrome of less talented performers. Women fans dote on him," Ward said.

Rarely was Szabo upstaged, but he had no control over what happened on the night he was supposed to retire. In January 1962, an edition of the popular Los Angeles wrestling show was set up as his sendoff. The featured match ended about twenty minutes early, so Antonino Rocca was sent out to kill some time by demonstrating his warmup ritual. Dave Levin, who was there, explained how Rocca crashed the party. "It's a wonderful routine but I bet Szabo could have killed him. Rocca took up so much time that after a few commercials and the reading of a few telegrams from guys who couldn't make it, they had to sign off before Szabo got the chance to make a speech. So I guess he'll have to make a 'comeback' and do it all over again." Sure enough, Szabo had several more matches that year in Las Vegas and toured Japan in 1963 for the 5th World League Tournament, returning to Tokyo to help with the U.S. wrestling team at the 1964 Summer Olympics. On October 13, 1966, he suffered a fatal heart attack at his home, bringing down the curtain on a personality who'd been in the spotlight for so long that California wrestling fans considered him an extended family member. "You know how it is when you've been around for years; everybody thought they knew him," said Don Leo Jonathan. "To all the fans, he was, 'My friend Szabo.'"

AFRICAN-AMERICANS

TIGER CONWAY SR.

It's two hundred and fifty miles from Shreveport, Louisiana, to Houston. But for Tiger Conway Sr., it was the journey of a lifetime. Born and raised in meager circumstances as the son of a sharecropper, Conway became a rich businessman and respected leader in his adopted hometown of Houston through a combination of pluck, hard work, and a couple of breaks along the way. Even more remarkable is the fact he achieved his station in life as an African-American wrestler in the segregated South, where he was largely confined early in his

A young Tiger Conway Sr.

career to same-race matches. "I tried to represent myself and all of them [other black wrestlers] with respect. Because Lord knows, we didn't always get respect depending on where and when we were rasslin'," he told Mike Lano's *Wrestling Wreality* in 1993.

Even as a child, Conway displayed a fierce determination that he'd carry into the ring for more than twenty years. Plasee Dennis Conway was born March 4, 1932, in Shreveport, and shared a one-room sharecropper-style house on a cotton farm with ten brothers and sisters. Years later, when he took his own children back to see his roots, they couldn't believe their eyes. "Why are we going down this road?" Tiger Conway Jr. remembered asking. "There's nothing but corn over here. Oh, my God!" There was a stove, an icebox, a big washtub where parents poured water on dirty children, and that was about it. No plumbing. An outhouse. Conway only made it to about seventh grade in school, and spent most of his youth picking cotton and learning how to fight a little.

As a teenager, he headed to Houston in 1947 and took jobs as a busboy and cook at Weldon's Cafeteria and the DeGeorge Hotel. There, legendary wrestler Danny McShain befriended him and got him odd jobs hanging around matches. Paul Boesch, who helped to promote Houston for Morris Sigel, also had a hand in advancing his career. Debuting in 1956, Conway beat Tex Brady to win billing as the Texas Negro heavyweight champion. Quick and agile, he was a small heavyweight at five-foot-ten and about 220 pounds, and Sigel liked enough of what he saw to recommend him in 1959 to national talent scout Jack Pfefer as "an awfully good colored boy . . . an excellent worker."

McKinley Pickens and Willie Love, a pair of blacks, were Conway's regular opponents, and the fact that he didn't get a wide range of experience definitely stunted his development, according to Paul "Butcher" Vachon, who wrestled him during a tour of Australia in 1962. "He was sort of green. Working with a white guy was different for him. Up until then, he'd been working with black guys and he had to learn to trust you in the ring," said Butcher, who, with brother "Mad Dog," was instrumental in getting Conway booked in Quebec.

Conway was a fixture on Texas cards in the 1960s, with main-event shots against "Killer" Karl Kox and Fritz Von Erich, but there was a definite glass ceiling to his career. Gary Hart, later better known as a manager, said he proposed a match with Conway in Fort Worth, Texas, but found that was a non-starter. "Not only did a lot of white wrestlers not want to get in the ring with black opponents, but Texas promoters didn't think the fans would want to see a black wrestler face a white wrestler," said Hart, who taunted Conway at ringside on TV until promoters booked the two. "I really loved Tiger. He was a great guy and a true friend of mine until the day he died." Conway especially liked pictures and clippings of tigers, and egged photographer and radio host Lano to send them to him. "I was named 'Tiger' because I was relentless like a tiger. A tiger is loyal, too. In the ring, I stayed on you and never gave up. As your friend, I defended you to the end," Conway said.

After he was in the business for a few years, a local entrepreneur approached

Paul Diamond, center, with Tiger Conway Sr. and his son Tiger Jr. at a Cauliflower Alley Club reunion in Las Vegas.

him about getting involved as the front in a fencing company to capitalize on his name recognition. Conway became as well known for his fencing and construction work as for his wrestling, and any time the City Auditorium in Houston hosted a cage match, it was inside a Tiger cage. If anything, Conway spread himself too thin between his professions, said his son, who speculated that was a product of an unwillingness to trust others. "My daddy was the first black fence contractor in the area. He'd work and wrestle on the same day. Three o'clock, pick me up from school. We'd take off to Dallas, San Antonio, Fort Worth, up and back. Then he'd load the truck for the crew for the fencing. Then he'd come back home." Investments in real estate followed and Conway ended up as a millionaire, though he never moved out of his home in Houston's Fifth Ward. Conway also served on the board of directors for the Christian Alliance for Humanitarian Aid, Inc. "He always went first-class. He always had a brand new truck. He always had a diamond ring, always smiling, always happy. He was a big credit to the profession," said Tommy Fooshee, a friend and wrestling referee.

When Junior entered the business, the two often formed a tag team, usually in Texas, but also during a swing through the Carolinas in the fall of 1977.

Conway's last matches were in early 1979. In 1995, he achieved an honor he could not have imagined when he was picking cotton in the fields — the Texas Senate passed a resolution commending him on his wrestling career, memorializing him as "a man of uncommon strength and talent." A regular at Cauliflower Alley Club reunions, Conway suffered a stroke and died November 15, 2006, at seventy-four. "Wrestling was a tool," his son said. "He brought the family from the sticks to the city. That was his biggest goal for his family. He accomplished that. And that's the respect that I had for him."

BRIAN BERKOWITZ, PETE LEDERBERG COLLECTION

Rocky Johnson demonstrates his boxing skills.

ROCKY JOHNSON

Rocky Johnson owes his trademark shuffling of his feet before his high dropkicks to old age. It turns out that some of his early opponents, often long-in-the-tooth veterans like Fred Atkins or Joe Christie, couldn't do the up-and-down moves that were required; therefore there was a need to fill time. "I started dropkicking, and they were taking their time in getting up from it," recalled Johnson. "I just started doing those little shuffles and all of a sudden people were going nuts. That's all it took."

Other than actual boxers turned wrestlers, such as Primo Carnera or Scott LeDoux, no grappler took the sweet science further into the ring than Johnson, who filmed vignettes with Muhammad Ali and George Foreman, among others, over the years. He had "boxing matches" with everyone from Jerry Lawler to Roger Kirby to Jim Dillon, and actually had a boxing license in Ontario while he was starting to wrestle.

Though he was born Wayde Bowles on August 24, 1949, in Amherst, Nova

Scotia, when he was a teenager, his family — his mother, three brothers, and a sister — moved to Toronto where the wrestling (and boxing) bug caught him. He was actually at the NWA world title change at Maple Leaf Gardens in 1963 when Lou Thesz toppled Buddy Rogers.

Working out at the Trinity Community Centre in Toronto's west end, he would come in contact with the wrestlers, and was soon dispatched to Jack Wentworth's gym in Hamilton to learn a new trade; by day, he drove a forklift.

Johnson would debut in 1966, having just trained six weeks and weighing 217 pounds. "I taught him the business very quickly, with no horseshit," said Hamilton's Murray Cummings. "I showed him the moves, I showed him how the takedowns work, and everything. You showed him once and he had it."

Turning pro was a politically expedient decision; Toronto's top dog, Whipper Billy Watson, was campaigning for a federal government seat.

"He was looking to get the black vote, so he called Jack Wentworth and said, 'Do you have any black guys there?' He said, 'I've got one. He's young. Pretty good body, pretty good athlete.' But naturally, no matches, right? So they put me on CFTO-TV. Channel 9. I worked with Firpo Zbyszko in my very first TV match. When you don't know nothing, you can't go wrong, you can't make no mistakes. We went a 1:40, Firpo jumped me, bam bam, and I could always throw a decent dropkick. He backdropped me, I landed on my feet, threw four dropkicks, sunset flip. I'll never forget this, and I'll tell you why later, sunset flip, one, two, three. Nervous, couldn't talk. He [Whipper] came out to talk for me. He said, 'I've been training this guy for the last two years. He's my protégé' — because he was trying to get the black vote. When I went home, my mother said, 'But you just met him!'"

While the Whip lost the election, Johnson excelled with the quick promotion. He was sent to the Dungeon in Calgary for further schooling. "That's where Stu Hart stretched me," said Johnson. "He broke a blood vessel in my eye."

Toronto promoter Frank Tunney acted as a de facto godfather to him, advising him on his next career steps and talking him out of trips to the U.S. where he would have been eaten up and tossed aside. Instead, in Vancouver, he was given the chance as Don Leo Jonathan's tag team partner.

"He had a lot of potential. He was just a young guy then. The only thing that was holding him back was his size. But later, he bulked up, muscled up, and looked pretty damn good after a while," said the Mormon Giant.

"The Soulman" acknowledged that he was an anomaly. "They never had black wrestlers in Canada. There was a bunch of diamonds, and I was that black diamond in the middle. That's the only way I could put it." His upbringing in

Canada meant that, unlike a lot of his peers in the U.S., he had never experienced outright racism and stood his ground when confronted by any prejudice.

"I never let it happen. They tried it in the South, but I stopped it," he said, mentioning Nashville promoter Nick Gulas specifically. "My name is Rocky, not 'Boy.'"

Getting to California in late 1969 was the key to his success, Johnson said. "I had already learned to wrestle, but I didn't have the psychology until I went to San Francisco. You can teach a six-year-old kid a headlock, but you can't teach him psychology."

Having gotten his name out there, Johnson dropkicked across the continent for the next decade. According to Dave Meltzer of the *Wrestling Observer*, Johnson doesn't get his due because he did travel so much. When pitching Johnson as a candidate for the newsletter's hall of fame, Meltzer wrote: "Headliner and champion in nearly every territory he worked from the late '60s into the early '80s, particularly big in the '70s when he had incredible agility and speed. In particular, is the best wrestler of the past forty years when it comes to doing a dropkick series, and that's considering he was a 255-pound powerlifter type with a boxing background. One of the business' top athletes of the '70s with a career record that is far more impressive than most realize."

BOB LEONARD

Rocky Johnson launches one of his patented dropkicks while in Stampede Wrestling.

Johnson held titles everywhere he went, but the one that most cite as his crowning glory was the WWF world tag team titles in 1983, alongside Tony Atlas. The irony is that Atlas and Johnson didn't get along and rarely actually worked together outside of TV tapings. "They couldn't put us together because I wanted to smack him in the mouth every time I saw him," Atlas said in the *Shooting With the Legends* newsletter.

Today, Johnson is known mostly as The Rock's dad. It seems every contemporary has stories of young Dwayne — "Dewey" — hanging out backstage. But Dwayne wasn't the first family member who followed in his father's footsteps. Rocky's brother, Jay, broke into the business in 1978 in Toronto as Ricky Johnson. In Hawaii in the early '80s, the Johnsons were a hot team, where Rocky was promoting with his in-laws, Peter and Lia Maivia, having married their daughter, Ata.

The Soulman's career ended in 1987, but always in superb shape, he came back for a few matches on the indy scene in 1993, 1994, and 2002. In 2000, Johnson was the physical fitness and recreation coordinator for the South Florida town of Davie, working with the city's Police Athletic League and conducting pro wrestling fundraisers. In 2003, he was hired by WWE to help develop young talent; after all, his first trainee, The Rock, did okay. Brock Lesnar, Orlando Jordan, and Sylvain Grenier all went through his finishing school. Another interest is draft horses, which he raises on a ranch in Missouri with his third wife, Sheila. At its WrestleMania extravaganza in 2008, WWE inducted Rocky Johnson into its Hall of Fame, with his son doing the honors.

RUFUS R. JONES

His name was Rufus R. Jones and, as the colorful wrestler was wont to declare in his vintage spiels, "The R stands for guts!"

Long before Jerry "The King" Lawler claimed the title, South Carolina native Rufus R. Jones was the undisputed "King of Wrestling."

It wasn't a self-proclaimed moniker either — he was actually presented a crown by a legion of fans one night at the Greensboro Coliseum. It was a crown and title that he would proudly wear throughout his career.

Jones was a beloved babyface in the midst of troubled times, during a racially segregated era when black wrestlers had to play stereotypical roles to gain bookings. The balancing act between staying gainfully employed in the wrestling business and maintaining one's dignity was a difficult one at best, but Rufus managed to not only survive but also prosper in a profession that was sometimes unfair and biased.

"Rufus was extremely popular," recalled Charlotte promoter Jim Crockett. "He had one of the most unique styles of interviews I had ever seen. The first time I heard him do an interview, he was talking about a watermelon in his pocket, and I didn't quite understand what he was talking about. But I later found out it was just a slang term that I had never heard, and I'll never forget, that meant having a lot of money."

"Everyone loved Rufus," echoed Tennessee-based promoter Jerry Jarrett. "He would say to me, 'Jerry, when I leave here, my billfold's gonna look like footballs

The "R" in Rufus R. Jones stood for guts.

in my ass.' I'd say, 'Rufus, if you have footballs in your side pocket, I promise you that I'll have basketballs in mine.' He was a real character and I loved him."

When Carey "Buster" Lloyd, a.k.a. Rufus. R. "Freight Train" Jones, died of a heart attack in 1993 at the age of sixty, he left behind a lifetime of memories for friends and fans. It seemed almost fitting that he would pass away while on a hunting trip near his Kansas City home. "He went out doing what he liked to do — hunting — because he sure loved to hunt," said Jerry Brisco. "Rufus was just a great personality and an outstanding person. I loved being around the guy. He was so funny all the time. And you knew you could trust him."

If there was anything Jones liked doing more than wrestling and hunting, it was cooking. His specialties weren't exactly the type of fare you might find in your neighborhood eatery.

"He really did like those pork chops and collard greens and the country food he ate as a boy," recalled Melvin "Burrhead Jones" Nelson. "He was born and raised in the country, and he always loved his home cooking. To prove the point, after he got out of the business, he got himself a great little rib shack."

Among Rufus' favorite dishes to cook were Southern "soul food" — pig feet, ham hocks, hog jowls, chitlins, cornbread, and fatback.

Abe Jacobs recalled Jones living in a Charlotte motel where he would routinely cook for the boys. "He had a friend who used to bring him raccoons. He'd kill them and skin them. Rufus absolutely loved them."

"Guys used to come over after getting back from wrestling," recalled Nelson. "He fixed food for all the boys — heels and babyfaces. It was sometimes four in the morning. Rufus used a slow cooker so it would be ready by the time we got there. It was very seldom that we'd eat at a restaurant. Rufus could bake very well . . . that good old Southern cornbread. He was a barbecue king. All the boys loved it."

Rufus was such a good chef that he taught his wife, Brooksie Lloyd, how to cook. "I thought I could cook when we first got married, but after tasting his food, my food was nothing compared to his," she said. "He used to tell me, 'Most people won't tell you. But I'm going to let you know.' And he did. He let me know I couldn't cook. It hurt my feelings at first, but then again, it made me a better cook. There even got to be some things I could outdo him on."

Rufus R. Jones was born Carey Lloyd on July 4, 1933, in the small town of Clio, South Carolina. The Lloyd family, who were sharecroppers, moved to a tenant house in the Little Rock community in Dillon County when Rufus was a young boy. "The Lloyds grew tobacco, cotton, corn and the other basic crops. Like most poor folks of that day, they probably grew most of what they ate," said South Carolina historian Carley Wiggins. "Rufus was remembered as a big husky fellow with broad shoulders and very strong . . . He was born with the tools that would take him into the world of professional wrestling — size and strength." Like his father, Rufus was an avid coon hunter who loved the outdoors, and also worked as a logger when he was a young man. Most of his relatives would move north to New Jersey and New York, because there was not much future in the South for African-Americans in that day, said Wiggins.

Looking for a better life, Rufus also left for New York City in the late '50s, and it was there that he would meet Nelson, a cousin by marriage. "I met Rufus at a birthday party for my wife in New York City," said Nelson. "He'd come over to my house and we'd run around town together. We became very, very close because we were looking for the same future in life. We weren't wrestling at the time, but we both liked the sport."

Rufus secured employment as a carpenter and found additional work putting up steel beams on high-rise buildings. "We got along real good right from the beginning," said Nelson. The two began working out together at a 42nd Street gym, meeting wrestlers such as John and Chris Tolos, Mark Lewin, and Don Curtis, and decided that it was a line of work they'd like to pursue.

Rufus, a large, lumbering specimen, weighed 250 pounds before he went into the gym. Some pro grapplers, including black superstar Bobo Brazil, told him that he would never make it as a pro because he was "too big and clumsy." Brazil, though, would discover in later years that while Jones might not have been the smoothest worker in the ring — "Wrestling Rufus for an hour was no walk in the park," Ric Flair would later claim — he had an ability to relate to fans, especially those in the South, that few could match. "He really made Bobo out to be a liar," laughed Nelson. "Rufus was just down to earth. He got over way better in the Carolinas than Bobo did. Bobo had no showmanship, no color. He couldn't talk that talk that the people wanted. When you're from the South, you understand the way that Southern people live."

It was that type of connection that endeared Jones to blacks and whites alike during an era punctuated by racial tension. And Jones, like his cousin, realized that "getting along" would only serve to benefit him in the wrestling profession where a limited number of black wrestlers found steady employment.

Jones, who played college football briefly at South Carolina State and who as a Golden Gloves boxer notched an impressive record of thirty-two wins and three losses, began his wrestling career under the name Big Buster Lloyd and moved to Kansas City in 1970 where he worked for Gust Karras' Heart of America Wrestling Promotions. Portraying the stereotypical black wrestler, but adding his unique style to the mix, Jones rose to main-event status working in the Carolinas and even headlined a show for Sam Muchnick at the storied Kiel Auditorium in the NWA wrestling capital of St. Louis where he held Dory Funk Jr. to a one-hour draw in a world title match.

It was in the Mid-Atlantic area where Rufus would rejoin Nelson, now known as "Burrhead" Jones, for a memorable program involving Flair, Blackjack Mulligan, and Gene and Ole Anderson. "We made a heck of a team and we drew some good money together," said Nelson. "He was one hell of a good wrestler and a great drawing card."

The personable Jones, who used running shoulder blocks known as the "freight train" to soften up his opponents for his finishing head butt maneuver, was known for his colorful, yet sometimes disjointed, television interviews. While much of his broken English was a shoot, it was part of the charm that endeared him to his sizable legion of fans.

Rufus R. Jones wants the crowd's approval before punching Jerry Lawler in 1974.

Jones' entree in the Mid-Atlantic area almost didn't happen. The role had initially been reserved for Bearcat Brown following Bearcat Wright's health issues. Since there wasn't room for two black babyfaces, Jones was given the nod since local promoters decided the South Carolina native could relate better to fans in that territory.

Bill Howard recalled a lively discussion with Rufus and Wahoo McDaniel in Florence, South Carolina, over who was more popular in the territory. "Wahoo was bragging to promoter Henry Marcus about how much he drew and how everyone paid to see him. Rufus was in on the discussion and he grabbed the promoter, took him outside, and asked him, 'Do you see any Indians out here?' They were all black. I thought that was funny as hell."

Jones held an assortment of titles during his career, including the Mid-Atlantic heavyweight title, the Mid-Atlantic TV title, the Mid-Atlantic tag team

COURTESY AL FRIEND

Rufus was the king.

title with Bugsy McGraw, the NWA world tag team title with Wahoo McDaniel, the Central States heavyweight title, the Central States tag team title with Bulldog Bob Brown, Mike George, and Dewey Robertson, and the North American tag team title with The Mongolian Stomper, Steve Bolus, and Bob Geigel. It was Rufus' portrayal as "one of the people" that helped sell tickets, said Geigel. "Rufus was one hell of a guy. The fans bought everything."

Geigel continued: "One day I said to Rufus, 'Go to the V.A. with me, will ya?' He said, 'Sure, Bob.' Rufus and I were going on Veteran's Day. We walked in the door, and Rufus went to the left, and I went to the right. Now there's a white guy on the left and a black guy on the right, and Rufus went to the left, and I went to the right. He wasn't a one-way person. If everybody in the United States . . . had the same attitude Rufus R. Jones did, there would be no white-black animosity."

Rufus retired from wrestling in 1987 and worked for a couple of years as a security guard at a dog-racing track before opening a restaurant in 1991 at 23rd and Vine in Kansas City called the Ringside Restaurant and Bar. And, like most things he took on, the restaurant was a success.

When Rufus R. Jones died in 1993, he was given a send-off befitting a man who had many friends and had left a lifetime of wonderful memories.

His son, Kenneth Johnson, a Texas pastor better known in wrestling circles as The Rev. Slick, conducted the service. A song composed by Rufus called "Lilacs Today" was performed at the funeral. "The service was absolutely beautiful," said Brooksie Lloyd, Rufus' wife of thirty years. "It had everyone spellbound. It was like nothing you had ever experienced before."

"My daughter, who is a strict Catholic, was with us," recalled Howard, who served as a pallbearer. "She had never attended a black funeral before. When they started the hallelujahs and went running up and down the aisles crying and screaming, she was amazed."

Howard was just one of a number of Rufus' mat contemporaries who attended the standing room-only service. Many, like Roger Kirby, Bob Geigel, Bob Brown, Mike George, Benjy Ramirez, and Sapphire, were part of the wrestling crowd who would come down once a month on Mondays to have lunch at the Jones' restaurant. Former NWA world champion Harley Race had been on hand for the restaurant's opening, and Bruce "Butch" Reed had ridden a horse into the establishment at midnight.

"When he lay in state at the funeral home, Roger Kirby came up to the casket and placed his hands on Rufus and said the words, 'Rufus, you were the only guy I could trust in the ring and I am retiring right now.' Kirby never wrestled after that," recalled manager Percival A. Friend. "Those words were a true respect for a ring giant that looked after the guys he wrestled."

The restaurant is now long closed, a relic of the past, but memories of happy times there linger. "The restaurant was our home away from home," recalled Rufus' widow. "When he finally got wrestling out of his system, the restaurant got to be his life. He had something else he could do, and that made a difference."

Cousin Burrhead Jones could only smile when he recounted a prank pulled on Rufus while on one of his tours of Japan. "They gave Rufus this big trophy that (supposedly) said he was the greatest black man who ever wrestled in Japan. He was so happy about it. But the boys over there pulled a rib on him. The writing was in Japanese and really said he was the biggest cocksucker in Japan. Rufus was really proud of that trophy. When Rufus came back here, he was in one of the territories and there was a Japanese wrestler, and he was trying to explain about this award. The Japanese guy said (with a Japanese accent), 'Rufus, trophy say you greatest cocksucker.' Rufus never lived that one down."

Fun-loving and happy, proudly wearing his crown as "The King of Wrestling," is how many of his friends remember Rufus.

"Rufus R. Jones the jovial personality you saw on television and in the arenas was the exact same Rufus away from the wrestling business," said Les Thatcher. "A laid-back gentleman if there ever was one. I thoroughly enjoyed my social time with Rufus, and watching him with the children that came up to him in public was a joy as well. I don't believe Rufus ever met a stranger."

LUTHER LINDSAY

Luther Lindsay.

Luther Lindsay could do pretty much anything in a wrestling ring ... except wear a world championship belt. His dropkicks were sky high, his uppercuts threatened to separate opponents' heads from their torsos, and he routinely whipped world-class amateurs in workout sessions. As a black man in a white man's game, he couldn't win a world title. But he could earn respect. In the late 1950s, Lindsay was healing from a broken leg when Calgary, Alberta promoter Stu Hart wooed him into his infamous "Dungeon" for some sparring. On the mat, Hart, always testing his partners, drove his knee into the back of Lindsay's bad leg. In a flash, Lindsay snatched Hart, spun around on him, ensnared him in a front facelock, and drove him into the wall. "Stu says, 'Ehh, ehh, Luther — I think I hear my phone ringing upstairs,'" said friend Abe Jacobs, one of many privy to the account.

Still, respect doesn't pay the bills, and Lindsay found he was better off leaving his home in North Carolina and spending a chunk of his twenty-one-year career in the more racially tolerant Pacific Northwest. "Whenever he wrestled here in North Carolina, it had to be with another black wrestler and that's why we did not stay here," said his wife Gertrude Goodall. "He was up in Oregon and Washington state. He was a champion out there. You were treated like a human being. Down here, you still felt second class, back at that time."

Born December 30, 1924, in Norfolk, Virginia, and raised on a farm, Luther Jacob Goodall was a hero long before wrestling fans started to cheer for him. As a U.S. Army corporal in July 1944, he spotted a private struggling for his life in a heavy undertow behind 5th Army lines off the western coast of Italy. Goodall plunged into the treacherous surf and swam 100 yards to join a rescuer and bring the man safely to shore, earning the Soldier's Medal. Stateside, he enrolled at Hampton Institute in Virginia, now Hampton University, and rival colleges wished he'd stuck to swimming. A bull of a man at five-foot-eight and 250 pounds with nary a trace of fat, he was an All-American guard on offense and defense, and an intercollegiate wrestling champion. He and Gertrude married in 1950 and headed to New Jersey, where Lindsay played football for the minor league Jersey City Giants of the American Football League. But what he really wanted to do was wrestle, and he wrote letter after letter in the hope that some promoter would give him a break.

Al Haft, who loved collegiate stars, brought him to his Columbus, Ohio, promotion in 1951, and quickly decided that Gertrude's maiden name of Lindsay flowed off the tongue smoother than Goodall. Lindsay debuted in September 1951 in Columbus, and got main-event shots almost from the start. In 1953, he had his first extended run in the Northwest, where he first met National Wrestling Alliance world champion Lou Thesz. They had four matches that year, and three the next, with Lindsay losing by a clean pinfall only twice. In his autobiography *Hooker*, Thesz called Lindsay the greatest black wrestler ever. "His place in history is not because he was black; it is in spite of the fact he was black," Thesz wrote.

His Jackie Robinson moment came in December 1955, when Lindsay integrated wrestling in Dallas, Texas, quietly slipping in as an unannounced sub for Larry Chene in a tag team match. Two nights later, he beat Duke Keomuka in the first mixed-race bout in Galveston, Texas. "I think he's the strongest wrestler that I ever wrestled. He was super-strong," said Tony Borne, who met him in Columbus at Haft's gym. "Luther pioneered wrestling in the South for the Negroes. I was in the car with him several times when we'd stop at restaurants and he'd have to go back in the kitchen to eat." Lindsay never viewed himself as a trailblazer, though, and was fearful that his skin color could cause hardships for his friends. On a winter night in 1968, Lindsay agreed to Les Thatcher's invitation to join him at his Charlotte, North Carolina townhouse, rather than drive in blizzard conditions to his home in Gibsonville, North Carolina. The next day, Thatcher found him awake before dawn, packing his bags. "He finally came around with a sheepish look and said, 'Well, I wanted to get out of here before daylight because of your neighbors.'" Thatcher shot back that Lindsay could sleep till noon, then kiss him on the lips in the middle of the parking lot for all he cared. "But this was the South in the 1960s. He was looking out for me. That was still the way he had been raised right back when he was a kid," Thatcher said.

While he compiled an impressive travelogue, Lindsay kept returning to Don Owen's Portland, Oregon–based office, where he held the regional singles title three times and the tag team title ten times with partners like Pepper Martin and Shag Thomas, another black ex-footballer who found a home in the Northwest. Jerry Christy, a long-time friend of Lindsay, recalled that Thomas had somehow rubbed some patrons the wrong way at a black bar in Portland. One night, three boxers went to the bar to confront Thomas. "They mistook Luther for Shag. Bad mistake — Luther took one out right away. Another one ran. I forget what the fate of the third one was," Christy said. "He had everything — great worker, tough shooter, and a rugged, well-built body."

Then there was the time at the Boston Catholic Youth Organization hall when Lindsay was working out with Bill Miller and Don Leo Jonathan. In

came an Olympic wrestling coach, who told his charges to ignore the sham pros. Lindsay got on the mat with the coach and, if you blinked, you missed the pin. In a second go-round, Lindsay was on the bottom position. "Luther was out from under him, behind him and pinned him just as fast as he did the first time," Jonathan said with a chuckle more than forty years later. "You

Karol and Ivan Kalmikoff, Luther Lindsay, and Sputnik Monroe find a diner they can all eat in.

should have seen the looks on those kids' faces. I don't think they had much confidence in their coach."

In 1967, tired of life on the road, the Lindsays headed back to Gibsonville, and Luther wrestled in Jim Crockett's Mid-Atlantic territory for most of the rest of his life. But the return was bittersweet. Though well-regarded among colleagues and fans, he was confined to undercard matches and took a job at a Greensboro country club to supplement his income. "Jim Crockett didn't care for Luther too much. Luther was no fool. He was a smart guy," said Jacobs, Lindsay's best friend and tag team partner. "[Crockett] used Luther because I think he was scared that if he didn't use him or book him, Luther might go to the authorities and make a news thing. He didn't want any problems. But he never liked Luther too much."

Lindsay started having health issues after a serious single-car accident in fall 1963 in Portland. The crash left a deep laceration from his thumb joint to his wrist, and his left arm atrophied for the rest of his life, no matter how hard he hit the weights. In the last year of his life, Lindsay experienced fits of coughing. After a series of tests, a doctor felt his lower leg; it was so swollen that the physician's fingers left deep imprints — a sign of serious heart-related issues. Lindsay was a poor patient, saying he couldn't let the news get out because it might cost him his career. "I couldn't get him to go the doctor," his wife said. "I would drive past the same area where the doctor's office was, but he would not go in there. He would not get out of the car. And therefore that last Monday when he went to wrestle, he didn't come back." That Monday was February 21, 1972, at the Charlotte Park Center. Lindsay beat Bobby Paul in ten minutes with a dropkick and signature big splash. When he went to get up, he collapsed. Thatcher and Jacobs went to the ring with Johnny Weaver, but they were too late; a heart attack had claimed him at forty-seven. At the funeral, Thatcher ran into Larry Hamilton, the Missouri Mauler, who was well-known for his racial prejudices. "Larry said, 'Les, everybody calls me a racist but I came here to pay my respects to Luther.' This tells you something about Luther. No matter what their differences were, he respected what Luther was and came to pay his respects."

THUNDERBOLT PATTERSON

Claude Patterson remembers toting his gym bag every week to the wrestling shows at the old Hippodrome in Waterloo, Iowa, in hopes that someone might take him under his wing.

Much to his dismay, though, there never were any takers, and it left him feeling ignored and neglected. It would be a feeling he'd experience again and again in a business that, ironically, he would excel in. It was also a business that would ostracize and blackball him for his outspoken manner and his push for change within the industry.

Take the politics out of the equation, and what you've got is one of the most colorful and controversial characters in the history of pro wrestling.

A number of performers would attempt to imitate Patterson's inimitable style. Dusty Rhodes and Blackjack Mulligan both admit drawing from his soulful,

Thunderbolt Patterson rants as announcer Gordon Solie watches.

shuck-n-jive interviews. But let there be no mistake. There was only one Thunderbolt Patterson.

"If cutting promos and interviews were all a wrestler was graded on, then Thunderbolt Patterson would have been in the top five of everyone's best of the '60s and '70s," said Les Thatcher, who spent time on the road with Patterson during his Mid-Atlantic run. "Not the best technical wrestler around, Claude mesmerized fans with his glib patter during his time on the microphone and with his fire and charisma while in the ring."

Patterson could turn it on just as effectively as a heel when promoters needed someone to play the role of a rebellious, headstrong black man claiming to have been used and abused by the system. It was eerily similar, though, to what Claude Patterson was feeling, and dealing with, his entire career.

Born in Waterloo in 1941, Patterson found employment with the town's major employer, John Deere Tractor Works, but left for the larger confines of Kansas City in pursuit of a career in wrestling. Ray Gunkel, an All-American from Purdue and pro star, was the first to take an interest in Patterson, giving him an address where he could obtain some wrestling boots. Patterson would repay the favor years later when he went to work for Gunkel's widow, Ann, who was waging a wrestling war in Georgia against the established National Wrestling Alliance.

"I never did get anybody who was coming through to train with me," lamented Patterson, who eventually worked out with Pat O'Connor and Steve Kovacs. But, he added, "O'Connor and Kovacs couldn't beat me, and that just blew their mind. It was a joke." The raw-boned rookie was impressive enough for promoter Gust Karras to offer him his first wrestling gig thirteen miles from his hometown. "Gust was very instrumental. They kind of just threw me out there. But I whipped my first opponent real quick," he boasted.

Patterson brought some experience with him, having grappled at a boys camp run by Jack Crawford, who trained Patterson and Doug "Ox" Baker, from nearby Evansdale. Doing occasional TV shots in Omaha and Minneapolis, while waiting for Sonny Myers to book him in Japan, Patterson said he was "starving to death" until a phone call gave him his first big break. Bob Geigel was on the phone with Dory Funk Sr., and asked Patterson if he could be an Indian. "I told him I'd be any damn thing you want me to be to make some money and get some work."

Though no Indian, Patterson would be the first major black heel to hit Amarillo. To this day Patterson has great respect for the late father of Dory Funk Jr. and Terry Funk: "The only individual who ever stood up for the racial part when the guys started acting funny was old man Funk. He called a meeting and told them all that if someone was drawing money and they didn't like it, they could leave. Dory Sr. took what they called a joke and turned him into a good worker."

Throughout Patterson's career, it was feast or famine, with the political machinations of the profession usually determining his level of success in any particular territory. He experienced tremendous highs in the business, but unfortunately the memories that stand out the most were the ones in which he claimed he was mistreated.

"I was always there when they needed something different," he said, alluding to working territories where promoters would "use and abuse" him. His first hints at inequality began when he met fellow black stars Edward "Bearcat" Wright and Bobo Brazil for the first time in Los Angeles.

"I didn't understand what was going on. They were bitching and complaining with one another. Bobo was the 'good guy.' Bearcat was the one that they didn't care for. Both were fantastic workers in the business, but Bobo was the one everyone could get along with. He would do anything they (promoters) wanted him to do. As long as he made $500 he didn't care. But Bearcat questioned things. He wanted his money and he wanted his due. He was the one who drew more money than most of them and could outwork pretty near all of them, but they didn't want to fool with him. He liked white ladies, and they didn't like that."

Patterson soon discovered what Wright — who also had been blackballed for his controversial stance — had been talking about.

"The roughest part was when I understood I was a crowd-pleaser and was drawing money, but couldn't have the opportunities to work the big shows and make the money like all the big-time guys were. They were doing to him exactly what they wanted to do to me. People were calling for me from all over the country." Even Funk Sr., whom Patterson admits had made him more money than he had ever made in his life, couldn't hold on to T-Bolt. "He was fair. But he was trying to hold me in there and I wanted to get out and go different places."

Patterson was a huge star in Texas where he enjoyed high-profile programs with the likes of Johnny Valentine and Wahoo McDaniel. But, according to Patterson, Fritz Von Erich's church asked the promoter to run Patterson, one of the territory's top heels, out of town. "They wanted him to 'get that nigger out of town,'" said Patterson. Von Erich promised Patterson he could return and "get in on some of the business" if he would help Eddie Graham out in Florida. Once again, said Patterson, "those words were nothing but empty promises."

"A lot of the guys were let in on all kinds of different deals. None of those so-called friends let me in on any of those deals. They had all kinds of deals going, but they never let me in."

Patterson was the Florida heavyweight champion when he got hurt during a riot in San Juan, Puerto Rico, while helping Dale Lewis. "He got scared and ran and I went back to get him, and the people cut us off. I dove into them and I started kicking. I ended up breaking my foot. Eddie Graham was across the hall and he did not come and say one word. I don't know what I would have done had it not been for The Missouri Mauler [Larry Hamilton]. He stayed with me. If you've ever been in a hospital in a place like that, which at that time was Third World, it's pretty scary."

Patterson said he received nothing while recovering back in Tampa. "I never will forget one day Lester Welch called me and said, 'Thunderbolt, you've been off for a long time. If you're off for a long time, people will forget you. I want you to come out on TV without those crutches.' I told him, 'If I haven't done any more than that and the folks forget me, I'm supposed to be forgotten.' I wasn't going to get off those crutches until the doctor told me. I stayed off a little while, but when I went back, it went boom. We drew a lot of money, but we didn't get any pay. Me and Jack Brisco sold out everything they had down there. Brisco was just like a machine."

Patterson recalled talking to long-time Florida promoter Cowboy Luttrall, gravely ill at the time, about buying into the Florida territory. "I went to his bedside and asked him if I could buy into Florida. He laughed in my face on his dying bed," Patterson remembered. "His words to me were: 'Ain't no nigger going to be in this.'"

"There were some harsh things," continued Patterson. "I stayed down there

Thunderbolt Patterson acts as a Pied Piper for Detroit admirers.

as long as I possibly could. I got a lot of slaps in the face, but I kept on pushing. I went to bed many nights with tears in my eyes because of the way I was treated."

It was the same everywhere, said Patterson, who continued to draw big houses but got left out of what he calls the big payoffs. "Every territory I went in, once I got the people hanging from the rafters, then they want to deal with the six-man, the three main events, split the money up because they got their boys. Bearcat and I found out in San Francisco they were paying different a long time ago. I left Florida and went back to Texas. Fritz apparently didn't know anything about the deal we had talked about when I left."

A major turning point in Patterson's career came when Grizzly Smith arranged for him to work for Jim Crockett Sr. in the Carolinas. "Once I got to Charlotte, everything just bloomed," said Patterson, who formed one of the hottest teams in the area with Ronnie Garvin, and worked lucrative singles pro- grams with Ole Anderson and veteran Rip Hawk.

The territory, however, experienced a changing of the guard when Crockett Sr. died in 1973. "John Ringley (Crockett's then-son-in-law) and the kids (Jim Crockett Jr. and David Crockett) took over. They called me one morning, and

STEVEN JOHNSON

Thunderbolt Patterson and Robert Fuller at a 2008 reunion in Charlotte.

John Ringley asked me to come down to the Coliseum Hotel in Charlotte. They were at the point of talking about changing bookers. I didn't see the point of it then. George Scott, a friend of mine who had gone through Texas and different places with me, called me up and asked what needed to be done. I told him the first thing he needed to do was to let me wrestle with whoever the champion was so I could whip his ass and take that belt and do something. His very words were, 'A black man doesn't need any belt,' and that he could just as easily get 'a nigger off of a dump truck.' It blew my mind. He was supposed to be my friend. I had problems from that point on."

Meanwhile, in Mid-Atlantic's neighboring territory, Georgia promoter and star Ray Gunkel had died nine months earlier, setting the wheels in motion for a torrid wrestling war in that state, led by his widow Ann. Patterson recalled getting a call from his old friend, Ernie Ladd, asking him about his availability. "I had Jack and Jerry Brisco, Bill Watts, David Crockett, and Jimmy Crockett in my apartment in Charlotte when I got the call. I used to ride with Watts. We used to scuffle together. Ann took it and Ann wanted to pay me a percentage. That's something no one had ever done. They told me if I went, I would never work again. I told them I was going and that was that."

Patterson agreed to work for Gunkel Enterprises' All-South Wrestling promotion that ran opposition to the NWA in Georgia. He also used the opportunity as a platform to speak out against poor working conditions for wrestlers and would later sue on grounds of racial discrimination. Joining forces with another disgruntled worker, former NFL star Big Jim Wilson, Patterson soon found himself blackballed by NWA promoters. It would be years, with Patterson taking a job at the *Los Angeles Times* in the interim, before he would be called back into service. Dusty Rhodes, the biggest star in Florida, came down with gout and needed a replacement. Graham was in a bind, said Patterson, who agreed to replace Rhodes on a major show. "I went back there and boom. Same old thing. Dusty got sick again, and I came in back up here." All the while, said T-Bolt, he was negotiating with Jim Barnett about buying in or even becoming a booker himself. But in the end, it was another opportunity, and another door slammed in his face.

"'My boy, if you want to be a booker or run something, you need to start your own [territory],'" he said, imitating Barnett's effeminate voice. And when Rhodes recovered, it was the end of another run for Patterson.

It was yet another demoralizing blow to the frustrated star. "Dusty was now my replacement. I was the originator of the shucking and jiving. They brought Dusty in as the blue-eyed soul brother with that dream. The dream means a home and a job for people. From that it got to the point I couldn't work with any of the alliances. The only places I could get to work then were places I had never been."

Patterson went to work for Ron and Robert Fuller when the brothers took over Tennessee. "They did as much as they possibly could. Robert was as much of a friend as anyone could be for dealing with my ability, but he could only go so far."

Labeled a renegade and a troublemaker, Patterson would continue to hit one brick wall after another.

"He was always trying to bring civil rights into wrestling," said long-time referee Tommy Young. "Blacks don't get discriminated against in this business. If they get over, they're put on top because they're going to draw money. He always cut his own throat. He was his own worst enemy. Here's a guy who the people loved, but he alienated everyone, including the other black wrestlers. It should have been better than what it was."

Patterson shrugs at the notion he was hard to get along with. "I was hard to get along with because I wanted a job. I wasn't going to let those guys beat up on me . . . I hate to say or believe that it was all because of racism. I hate to think that they say I was hard to get along with, because I was no harder to get along with than the Dusty Rhodeses or the Ric Flairs. I think they owe the fans an answer."

Patterson, who joined Ole Anderson as a tag team partner in the early 1980s and briefly shared the NWA National tag team title, would wind down his career during that decade, serving as a commentator on the *Georgia Championship Wrestling* program and a trainer of young talent. "Ole was the only one who would give me work regardless of whatever," said Patterson. "He was a straight shooter. You knew how he felt."

He retired from the business in 1994, with his last official match coming at Slamboree '93 where he teamed with Brad Armstrong to defeat Ivan Koloff and Baron Von Raschke.

Patterson, though, never really quit fighting. He boycotted, he marched, he railed against the establishment and status quo in the name of equal opportunity and better working conditions. Black or white, it didn't matter, Patterson would rattle cages even when the odds were solidly against him. The labor organizer once threatened to drive his old Cadillac up the steps of Atlanta's City Hall and burn it down if the city denied him equal access in renting the Omni. He eventually got into the building, but had to endure heavy-handed tactics from his NWA opposition as well as unfair regulations imposed by the city and a lack of cooperation from some area civil rights leaders.

Patterson will always love the wrestling business, he said, although it was years ago when he discovered that "the wrestling business wasn't quite for me."

"It's a white man's business. It was and it still is. There's just more diplomacy about it now," he claimed.

His wrestling days long gone but not forgotten, Patterson is involved these days in a higher calling. An ordained minister, Patterson is working with Tony Evans, a pastor and founder of the Youth Dynamics ministry in Georgia, to promote Kingdom Championship Wrestling. The goal is to incorporate family-oriented pro wrestling as a springboard to spiritual causes, with free shows and motivational speaking that promotes church and community.

"I can't question anything that God has done," said Patterson, who also ran a foster home for troubled boys in Atlanta following his retirement from wrestling. "I forgive everybody and I love them all."

Patterson, though, feels he could have been relevant in the business for many more years. "They put me out. If you treat a dog bad at home, he's going to leave. I wanted to work. Nobody has called me about a job. That's hard to believe."

He refuses to stay down for the count. An abiding faith has been his strength. The wonderful part of his career, and life, he said, was that he "found Jesus."

"That made up for everything in my life. When I really look back over it, everything I did I did to myself. I didn't do it to people. I didn't do anything wrong, at least intentionally, to anybody. I didn't harm anybody. I loved the business. I think I was one of the better team players . . . they just didn't want me on the team."

Thunderbolt Patterson's legacy will be one of greatness, albeit diminished, fairly or unfairly, by controversy and activism. It will be a career marked by not what he did, but what he might have done.

"I just want to be remembered as a down-to-earth individual that was able to come through wrestling," he said. "I just want all of the fans to ask the questions: Why was Thunderbolt not figured in? Why was Thunderbolt not the world champion? If I was given the opportunity, I could have been. Why didn't these so-called promoters and so-called friends call me? I was Thunderbolt Patterson — the People's Champion."

SAILOR ART THOMAS

In his prime in the 1960s, there was perhaps no better body in professional wrestling than Sailor Art Thomas. His chest and arms rippled with muscle, his big hands suited for a crippling bear hug. The fans were in awe of him, said Rocky Johnson. "People said, 'We know how you got your muscles — you pumped air in!'"

He came by the muscles honestly, starting a weightlifting regimen after his discharge from the Navy in 1947, serving twenty-seven months in a construction battalion, building an airstrip in Guam, and delivering ammunition to other outposts.

Having grown up in Arkansas as one of six children, Thomas moved to Madison, Wisconsin, in 1935, following his mother who had moved there the year before. When she died, he dropped out of high school and began working various jobs, shuffling in and out of an orphanage and foster homes.

Naturally blessed with strength, his physique developed quickly, and he competed in bodybuilding contests. Often the only African-American, he was therefore denied any titles.

"I was a big, black fellow, and there wasn't too many blacks in Madison anyway. I'd go downtown on the square and people would just stare, which did make me feel good. I started working out that much more and got pretty cut up," Thomas told historian Scott Teal in 1997.

Sailor Art Thomas makes sure he is on the card in West Hempstead, NY.

At the YMCA, Jimmy Demetral, a local old-timer and promoter, spotted Thomas and convinced him to learn pro wrestling while still working at Greyhound greasing buses. Thomas debuted as a pro in 1960 and quickly rose to prominence, but he had worked on Demetral-promoted carnival shows before that.

Buddy Rogers met Thomas in Chicago and told WWWF promoter Vincent J. McMahon about him. McMahon sent him to Fred Atkins for almost a year of schooling, and told him to get a sailor's outfit.

Thomas debuted on TV out of Washington, D.C., as a fan out of the audience that host Ray Morgan asked to show off his muscles. "I took my jacket and shirt off. At that time, I was about thirty-three inches in the waist and had a twenty-inch arm. He says, 'Whoo! Man, look at the chest and arms on this guy! Will you strike a pose for us?' I tightened up, sucked up my stomach, and posed a little. They said they got hundreds of calls. 'Who is that big guy?' 'Why don't you put him in the ring?' They had me come into the ring, then one of the heels came in and got a little rough with me to steam things up. Overnight . . . I was made."

Launching into a program with Rogers, he put the "Nature Boy" into a bear hug on TV and immediately faced his fair share of resistance from wrestlers who thought he'd gotten too much too fast. "There was a lot of jealousy. I was an easy-going guy," Thomas said. Though he wasn't a shooter by any means, Thomas could hold his own since he was so strong. A few guys tried him in the ring, like Don Curtis, Bill Miller, Larry Hennig, and Blackjack Mulligan, and none could really budge him. "A whole lot of 'em tried me. But the thing was, I was so nice about it. I didn't push things, or carry through with it. I just let 'em know and then, 'Hey, let's forget it.' I think because of my attitude, I got a lot of guys in the business that love me to this day, and I love them, too."

One of those buddies was Bobo Brazil. There's an oft-repeated story in which the two were on the New York subway heading for Madison Square Garden, and Brazil leaped from his seat and exited the car, putting Thomas — with his sea bag — in a panic. Then Brazil zipped right back on, laughing. "You do that again, you won't get to Madison Square Garden," threatened Thomas.

Whether he was "Seaman," "Hercules," or "The Body," Thomas was a draw. "He was a box office attraction. Good performer, but he had to have a leader in the ring to have a good match," said Kansas City promoter Bob Geigel. "We'd bring him in for a week and draw like hell."

The Carolinas at the end of the 1960s were where Thomas claimed he made the most money. "He got over like a house on fire," said Abe Jacobs. "Art was a great draw, so they would draw a hell of a house."

While Thomas might have been a success in the South, the racial tensions prevented him from traveling with his Caucasian wife, Juanita, said Jacobs, who on occasion was asked to accompany her to events posing as her husband.

Not happy with the way he was being used in Florida, Thomas quit the business (temporarily) and returned home to Madison. He got a job at Oscar Meyer, working in the bacon department, spending nineteen years there, and enjoying a proper pension, unlike many of his peers. Taking bookings that would complement his full-time job, Thomas wrestled until 1983, staying close to his seven children and their families.

"I know no one who loved his family more than him," wrote Ox Baker on his website in tribute to Thomas, who died in March 2003, only a month after being diagnosed with cancer. "He would always talk about them, always talk about his wife and kids when we were working out."

BEARCAT WRIGHT

The always colorful Bearcat Wright.

To some, Bearcat Wright was a civil rights crusader. To some, he was an opinionated blowhard. To still others, he was the wrestler who rose from the grave. "Bearcat Wright is Dead!" the October 1973 edition of *Inside Wrestling* sadly announced. "The familiar sight of the tall man in the dashiki gracefully leaping over the top rope and then waving his hands to greet his fans is no more. Bearcat Wright is dead. He was cut down by sickle cell anemia, a disease that slowly kills black people," the magazine reported. Supermouth Dave Drason (Burzynski), working for The Sheik's promotion in Michigan at the time, accepted it at face value. "I look back and I think Bearcat Wright was almost like the Abe Vigoda of professional wrestling because everybody thought he'd died," he said. "Then all of a sudden, here comes Bearcat Wright into Detroit in 1973 and it's like, 'Are you kidding me? The guy's still alive?'"

He did have sickle cell, and it would claim his life August 28, 1982, in Tampa, Florida, but the misunderstanding epitomized the mass of contradictions that was Edward M. Wright. In 1960, he stared down an unwritten color barrier in Indiana; a few months later, the New York athletic commission yanked his license after a no-show. In 1961, he became the first black to win a world heavyweight title, and then he got suspended in Michigan and Indiana for blowing off a March of Dimes benefit. He won a higher profile version of the world title in California in 1963, decided he didn't want to lose it, and hightailed it out of town. Sweet Daddy Siki was his tag team partner in the early 1960s, and even he didn't profess to know what made the Bearcat tick. "I didn't question him on a lot of things. He wanted to be alone most of the time. He was particular about associating with any of the other guys," Siki said. "Whatever he thought, he wanted me to think that way too. But, like I said, I could never do it . . . It must have got him more money or whatnot."

At almost six-foot-seven and with the reach of a tree limb, the towering Wright was a boxer until he switched careers. Born January 13, 1932, he followed in the footsteps of his dad, the original "Bearcat," who fought out of Omaha, Nebraska, as a defensive-minded heavyweight, and battled such greats as Jack Dempsey and Sam Langford during a nearly twenty-year career. Young Bearcat was so much taller than his teenaged opponents in the Golden Gloves that he was punching downhill. At seventeen, he boxed in main events on amateur cards on shows run by Donald Van Fleet, the old-time touring carnival wrestling promoter. The record books credit him with an undefeated 8-0 mark and five victories by knockout in 1951 and 1952, and he almost certainly had more unrecorded bouts. He attracted attention because he might have been the tallest heavyweight in the game at the time. But Iowa sportswriter Jim Rose summed up Wright the fighter: "He is too big to step across the ring very fast and would have to rely on a knockout because a faster opponent would wear him out before fifteen rounds were over."

Wright was learning to wrestle at the same time, sometimes in the same match — he lost a three-fall, combo boxing-wrestling bout to Danny O'Sullivan in Burlington, Iowa, in August 1951. Much to his dad's chagrin, he decided there was no reason to pinch pennies in boxing when it was raining dollar bills in wrestling. "My father was disgusted," he said to Boston columnist Jerry Nason in 1958. "But in my first two bouts, on successive nights, I earned $225. That was more than I cleared in twenty-two bouts as a pro fighter." He was wrestling full-time in 1952, working a lot in Minneapolis and Ohio, and wrestling under a mask in Minnesota as the Black Panther. It's hard to determine what he could conceal — Wright was all legs and arms and fluctuated around 260 pounds. Diana Hart Smith, meeting him in Calgary, Alberta, thought he looked like an otter. "His neck was the same width as his head and it was fleshy so it looked as if he was wearing rings around his neck," she wrote in her memoir. When he wasn't wrestling, he was chilling. "One time out of Minneapolis, I seen his car. He had a big Cadillac," said Stan Holek. "I thought, 'That's Bearcat's car. Maybe it broke down.' So I stopped and pulled over, and he was in the front seat, sleeping. I said, 'What are you doing?' He said, 'I'm just having a catnap.' That kind of just blended right in with the Bearcat, taking a catnap."

By 1960, he was the hottest babyface in the country. In April, police estimated that between 15,000 and 30,000 people roamed the streets outside the International Amphitheater in Chicago, frustrated that they couldn't get tickets to see Wright against Johnny Valentine. On July 29, a crowd of about 31,000 paid nearly $90,000 to pack Comiskey Park in Chicago, where he fell to Buddy Rogers in the semi main event under a world title match between Pat O'Connor and Yukon Eric. Six weeks later, he beat Killer Kowalski in the main event at Comiskey before 26,371, with an $82,000 gate, and his tag team with Siki drew huge numbers to indoor cards in the Windy City. That also was the year, *Ebony* magazine reported, when a disgusted Wright rose up after a match in Gary, Indiana, and broke what was termed "an unofficial ban" against mixed-race matches in the city. Wright said his declaration against arenas that prohibited mixed bouts earned him support from the NAACP and a brief athletic commission suspension, but he found he didn't have to pursue the matter. "Surprisingly enough, there was no real problem. My suspension was lifted and slowly mixed wrestling has been opening up everywhere," he said afterward.

Wright became the first black to hold a world championship when he wrestled for Tony Santos and Jack Pfefer in 1961 in their small-scale New England promotion. Willie Gilzenberg, the New Jersey promoter who'd be a partner in the WWWF, was frothing at the mouth for a piece of the action. "If it is true that you put your hooks into Bearcat Wright, you have made the best snatch of your entire career in wrestling," Gilzenberg wrote Pfefer. "Again, if it is true, I must congratulate you on grabbing the best drawing card wrestling has ever had and that included Jim Londos, Strangler Lewis, Antonino Rocca, or any wrestler in the history of the game."

But Wright wouldn't be the Bearcat without controversy, as Freddie Blassie learned when he urged promoters to bring Wright to southern California in 1963. Wright got a mega-push that saw him win the World Wrestling Alliance world title from Blassie via a third-fall countout on August 23 in Los Angeles. The victory was historically significant; the WWA title was a bigger catch than the one in Boston, and it came just five days before Martin Luther King's "I Have A Dream" speech in Washington, D.C. Writing in his autobiography, *Listen Up, You Pencil Neck Geeks,* Blassie said Wright promptly started putting himself ahead of business. "Bearcat was a big drawing card, but he was no Jackie Robinson. Very quickly, he let the win get to his head, and he became very delusional. To hear him speak, he was America's number one role model for the black race, and now that he had the title, he wasn't going to give it up." Blassie's powers of perception were right on the money, according to Violet Ray, a woman wrestler married to carnival promoter Van Fleet. "Bearcat called us and said he just won the world title," Ray said in *Whatever Happened To . . . ?* in 2001. "He said, 'Let them go ahead and poke me now. They'll have to take it away from me.' The guys were all scared of Bearcat after that. Bearcat always said that Van was the only white guy he had a lot of respect for. I think it was because Van knew him since he was a little boy."

In early December, Blassie underwent an emergency appendectomy just before he

Later in his career, Bearcat turned to managing the likes of Buddy Colt.

was scheduled to regain the WWA championship from Wright. Booker Jules Strongbow tried to talk Blassie out of the match, but the "Hollywood Fashion Plate" insisted he could work with Wright. In the dressing room at the Olympic Auditorium that December 13, Wright informed Strongbow he had no intention of dropping the strap, according to long-time Los Angeles publicist and announcer Jeff Walton. "Bearcat said, 'No, I don't want to, I've got a lot of fans out here.' And it was almost a Bret Hart type of thing — 'I got here and I got the title and I don't want to lose.'" Wright double-crossed Blassie, holding down his weakened opponent for a pin after a headbutt, and triggering a commotion in the front office.

Three days passed, and Wright was scheduled to work at the Valley Garden Arena in North Hollywood. Walton was there and still can visualize the night's events. Strongbow had gone to promoter Mike Lebell to enlist brother "Judo" Gene LeBell, wrestling as the red-garbed Hangman and known for good reason as the "toughest man alive," to force Wright to surrender the title and teach him a lesson in the process. Wright and the Hangman never got in the ring. "Bearcat didn't know who he was working with," Walton said. "I was in the parking lot and I saw him pull up. And then, I saw him go in. It wasn't more than, oh, five minutes, he came running out into his car and took off with the belt. Somebody clued him in as to who he was going to work with. Somebody tipped him off." The promotion stripped Wright of his title claim and Strongbow urged other promoters to boycott Wright. Part of the problem might have been rooted in Wright's complaint that he couldn't work as a bad guy and draw even bigger money. "It's a heel's business," he confided to Pulitzer Prize–winning sports-writer Jim Murray in 1963.

Wright bounced from territory to territory — if he could burn bridges, he also could attract fans. Right after the brouhaha in Los Angeles, he did an extensive run in San Francisco. He split off to the Pacific Northwest as a tag team champion in 1966 and returned to northern California as U.S. heavyweight champion in 1968 and 1969. He spent much of 1971 in Hawaii, where he and Sam Steamboat were tag team champions. He did a successful turn in upstate New York for Pedro Martinez in 1961 and again in 1972 before heading to Detroit and the Carolinas. Wright relocated to Tampa, and got to work as a bad guy for a while, winning the Florida tag team title with Bobby Shane.

With Wright, the line between pride and arrogance was always blurred. When Buffalo publicist Earle F. Yetter wrote a story on him for The Ring in 1961, Wright went ballistic, ridiculing the piece and saying he didn't talk the way Yetter make him sound. He appeared to have a legitimate gripe — one passage apparently attributed to him read: "'Man alive, that's the kind of life I wants,' said Big Ed Wright. 'Yes, sah, I loves to eat like those boys do . . . that's for me, sure 'nuff.'" But at the end of his career in 1975, when disease curtailed his wrestling, he was Buddy Colt's "advisor" in Georgia. Colt rode with Wright for a few months and got along fine with him, but said there was an unmistak-able chip on his shoulder. "He thought everybody was against him. He was working New York back when I was still a fan. I'd see him on TV and they'd call him from Jamaica, Bearcat Wright from Jamaica. He thought there were a bunch of bigots and prejudiced people in wrestling because they said he was from Jamaica. I said, 'Well, Joe Scarpa is really an Italian, and they're calling him an Indian [Jay Strongbow]. The Von Brauners are supposed to be German and they're not any more German than I am. They're just trying to give you personality by saying you're from Jamaica.' But he thought they were all out to get him." In fact, even the offending Yetter piece in 1961 identified him from Omaha. "He didn't help himself with promoters," Colt concluded.

Ironically, it was Gilzenberg, so excited about him in 1961, who prematurely interred Wright. The promoter had called Bill Apter, the legendary wrestling magazine writer and photographer, to report Wright's demise. Apter checked with other promoters and wrestlers; they confirmed the news and he penned the obituary. "About a month later, I got a letter from a fan in Toronto and the wording of this is precious — 'You've made a grave error,'" Apter remembered. He phoned Gilzenberg and Vincent J. McMahon, who still insisted Wright was dead; the magazine ran an appropriate retraction. "We never heard from Bearcat," Apter said. "When I saw him years later in Florida, he said, 'You know, I was going to sue you guys for that.' And I told him what happened and he said he didn't know where anyone got the idea he was dead. He had no idea."

POST-WAR TERRITORIAL ERA

Bob Backlund, with his trademark towel around his neck and WWWF world title around his waist.

BOB BACKLUND

Larry Matysik was sitting in the wrestling office in St. Louis when the phone call came in. Vincent J. McMahon had built his New York wrestling empire on the shoulders of main-event ethnic attractions, but now he wanted something different, and he reached out to St. Louis promoter Sam Muchnick for a hand. "Vince wanted an All-American boy. That's what he wanted and Sam was the one who suggested Bob Backlund. It was before the Von Erichs really clicked here and Ted DiBiase was still a little behind, so he was the option. So Sam is the guy who, I won't say sold Vince on him, but certainly touted him," Matysik said.

It would be hard to argue with the premise that Robert Lee Backlund was everybody's All-American. He earned that status in amateur wrestling in junior college and NCAA Division II, where he was a national champion at 190 pounds. But questions about whether McMahon's choice was a good fit for Northeast audiences used to the likes of

Bruno Sammartino, Antonino Rocca, and Pedro Morales linger to this day. "I was surprised that they put the belt on him in New York, because usually they had either a Latin or Italian in New York. He was a tough guy to work with because nobody really believed in him," said Angelo Mosca, one of Backlund's principal challengers in 1981. "Working with a guy like Bruno Sammartino or Pedro Morales was a piece of cake . . . They were what they called 'over' in the business, and Bob Backlund was not really over. He was a nice guy; don't get me wrong. He was a good guy, very powerful man." Backlund acknowledged that he harbors some of those same doubts. "I don't know if I was even a 'good' good guy," he said. "I don't think I was, really. I don't think I was as over as I could have been. But I'll tell you — I was over as a bad guy, but I was never over as a good guy."

That's not to diminish his accomplishments. When Backlund pinned "Superstar" Billy Graham on February 20, 1978, in Madison Square Garden to become the World Wide Wrestling Federation's eighth heavyweight champ, he was an earnest, athletic, eager-to-please, twenty-eight-year-old with the endurance of a marathoner. He'd hold the company's championship longer than anyone except Sammartino, just two months shy of six years. Unlike a traveling National Wrestling Alliance world champion, Backlund had to thrive in a smaller geographic territory and didn't have the luxury of varying his style his style from night to night. "I believe Bob Backlund was a great WWF champion. I was the most difficult opponent Bobby Backlund faced. Bobby was a pure wrestler and that is not what I was about," said George "The Animal" Steele, who fought him dozens of times. "The key to success in the wrestling business is selling tickets. I did not adjust to Bobby's style. I forced Bobby to adjust to me and my wild brawling style. Our matches were far from a cakewalk and out of Bobby's comfort zone but the fans got their money's worth. The promotion was happy. That is why we had so many matches. I enjoyed working Bobby and the pay was great."

Backlund is proof that diligence and hard work can move just about any mountain. He was born August 14, 1949, to Normal and Bernice Backlund, and he didn't have a lot growing up on a farm in Princeton, Minnesota. He struggled in school and took out his frustrations fighting with other kids before redirecting his activities to wrestling and football. He attended Waldorf Junior College in Iowa before going to North Dakota State, where he was a two-year starter at defensive tackle in football and the second Bison wrestler to claim a national championship, winning the NCAA Division II title in 1971, and placing fifth nationally to finish as a heavyweight the next year. He probably could have taken his amateur wrestling further but he didn't want to give up football — not to mention the joys of weighing 230 pounds as a lineman and the harshness of cutting to 190 as a wrestler. "Football was always in the fall and that's when the Olympic trials and things were going on, so I had to make a decision for one or the other and so I decided I wanted to play football." He hoped to have a pro football career, but when that didn't pan out, he trained in Minneapolis and turned pro wrestler in 1973.

Backlund headed to Bill Watts' Mid-South territory and almost instantly suffered his first serious injury. "When I started wrestling I was in the Seventh Street gym. Eddie Sharkey was training me there . . . The ring, it was down on the floor so when you got thrown over the top rope, you didn't have a drop. My first battle royal was in Baton Rouge, Louisiana. At that time I had just started. I was going to get thrown over the top rope — I wasn't going to win — I got thrown over the top rope and I hit my hip on the side of the ring," he said. "I got a bruise from under my arm pit down to my knee and I had to wrestle the next night, but I still have repercussions from that injury." Backlund also spent time in west Texas and the American Wrestling Association before getting a big break in St. Louis. He started there as a regular in December 1975 and won the Missouri state championship, considered a stepping stone to bigger things, from Harley Race the following April. He stayed there until the end of 1976 and then joined the then WWWF. Three days after he beat Graham, Backlund went to a sixty-minute draw with NWA champion Race in a rare interpromotional title match in Jacksonville, Florida. "There's probably never been another athlete in pro wrestling who kept himself in the physical shape that he kept himself; not monthly, not yearly, but daily," Race said. "Vince Senior recognized that he had a white, Irish piece of gold and nobody deserved it more than Bob Backlund."

At a time when Graham, Dusty Rhodes, and Ric Flair oozed braggadocio and charisma, Backlund was a throwback, a shy man who came across as a square peg in a round hole. WWWF veteran Davey O'Hannon worked with Backlund in St. Louis and was taken aback when he became the federation's anointed one, because he didn't see the skill set. "He's a tremendous athlete; he's a fantastic credit to our business and he made it easy for us to say we are professional wrestlers," O'Hannon said. "But a lot of his stuff was simply not believable. A big, big, big part of this business is talking and he was just dreadful on interviews. He would get exasperated and get lost. Could he have gotten over big time? Probably not with the tools he had." Compared with his

Antonio Inoki ties up with Bob Backlund.

over-the-top contemporaries, Backlund was painfully introverted to the point of being suspicious. "He was a different style of worker, and he was very paranoid that somebody was going to screw him all the time," said Pat Patterson. "He had the old school in him. You had to educate him to what the business was all about." Outside of his closest circle, he was polite, but wrestlers describe him as withdrawn, an uneasy fit in the backslapping fraternity of the wrestling dressing room. "I was very sort of outside the business, almost," Backlund said. "I'm not sure why, but when I look back, I wasn't really 'in' like I should have been."

It's hard to assess Backlund's drawing power as the face of a franchise. The attendance numbers at Madison Square Garden during his reign are outstanding — 22,000 for Swede Hanson in October 1979; 21,000 for Stan Hansen in 1981; 22,000 for Adrian Adonis in 1982. "We were selling out. It's not like Backlund didn't do anything, or it was somebody else on the card. With a good heel, and a good program, and the respect he had as champion, we did as good a business, as good attendance-wise, as they're doing now — sometimes even better," said Don "The Rock" Muraco. Still, there was the suspicion that McMahon kept extra angles in his pocket to keep the houses packed. In 1980, the Sammartino–Larry Zbyszko feud was the hottest ticket in town, and the WWF always had its fill of Andre the Giant, Rhodes, Sgt. Slaughter, or Jimmy Snuka on the undercard. "If

Bob Backlund gets his chicken wing hold on Bill Alfonso at a reunion in 2009.

you really look at it, they were afraid he couldn't draw, so they loaded those cards with Dusty, with Mil Mascaras," concluded wrestling journalist Bill Apter. "It wasn't proven that he didn't draw. I think after a while, people started coming to see him. But I don't think the promotion was ever secure enough in him without loading up the card. It's a shame because the concerns about whether he was colorful enough overshadow his legacy as a great technical wrestler."

In fact, Backlund was easily the best technical wrestler of any WWE champion until Kurt Angle, though he could be as stiff as he was smooth to work with. "It was like grabbing hold of a parking meter. He was the strongest kid I'd ever seen," Jack Brisco said in *Wrestling Perspective*. "He had so much amateur in him. I don't think for several years he felt comfortable working. That's my own opinion." Greg Valentine was one of his top challengers, and said Backlund busted his eardrum with a slap from nowhere. "I don't know where he got this idea. I had a short-arm scissors on him and he picked me up," Valentine said. "All of a sudden, I'm sitting on top of the rope and he hauls off and slaps me in the face — but he slaps me in the ear, and he blew my eardrum out. I'm sitting up there on the top, and I don't even know where I'm at . . . It's not a lot of fun." Backlund once dislocated O'Hannon's right thumb — not intentionally, of course — but had to work at sliding into pro orthodoxy from his competitive amateur days. "You'd never know which way he was coming from," O'Hannon said. "I used to take big, crazy bumps and I'd tell him before, 'Bobby, you just kind of guide the body. I'll take care of the bump.'"

Some things might have been beyond Backlund's control, but conditioning was not one of them, and the stories about his staying power are legendary. Jerry Brisco was his tag team partner in Georgia and decided one night it would be great fun to see if he, Dick Slater, and Bob Orton Jr. could tire out Backlund — "blow him up," in wrestle-speak. "Bobby Backlund was Howdy Doody. He was a character in himself and he didn't realize he was a character at that time," Brisco said. "So that night, every time Bobby'd come to tag me, I'd just take a walk down the aisle way, and I was never there for the tag, and they were switching in and out and we never blew him up. When Backlund finally got to me, he slapped my hand so hard I thought he slapped it over in the next county." Backlund used to do the grueling Harvard Step Test for the full hour of TV wrestling programming and remains a fitness freak today. In 2011, he was a guest instructor for the Springfield, Massachusetts police academy. Sgt. Brian Keenan, a staff instructor at the academy and friend of Backlund, organized the workout. "Mr. Backlund, at sixty-two, blew up every single police recruit, some of which said that they were in better shape than when they were in Marine Corps boot camp at Parris Island. No one could hang with him with pushups, squats, pullups, situps, leg lifts — and he was just getting warmed up. Unbelievable."

It was more effort for Backlund to get his mind to catch up with his body. As an athlete, he was pushed through school and college, and he called his diploma from North Dakota State just a "piece of paper." When he left wrestling in 1984, he worked a succession of unfulfilling jobs that included stints as a bail bondsman and drywall installer, in part because of his poor reading skills. "I was able to cover up that skill in the sports world," he told the *Hartford Courant* when he ran unsuccessfully for Congress in 2000. "I was struggling outside the sports world because of my laziness." In time, he forced himself to improve, using flash cards, studying speed reading, and listening to memory tapes to the point that he'd drop ten-dollar words in the middle of conversation — even if they didn't necessarily fit. His self-improvement efforts have led to Backlund Energy, a heating oil business he runs in Glastonbury, Connecticut.

When Vincent K. McMahon took over from his dad, Backlund knew he was yesterday's news. McMahon once dissed him as "black and white movies with no sound" and wanted Backlund to turn into a bad guy at the dawn of the Rock 'n' Wrestling era. Backlund was working with youth groups and his daughter was just starting school; sensing he was about to be mocked as a cartoon figure, he left the WWE not long after losing the title to The Iron Sheik on December 26, 1983. "I think I took it personal, what happened back then, but he believed everybody should be more of a character, and that's when I was into doing the stuff with the kids to me that was very serious. I made a lot of promises and that's when I had to make a decision," he said. He came back to the company in 1992 and found a niche as "Mr. Backlund," a hyper-maniacal, overbearing, goody-two-shoes. He claimed, not without some justification, that fans had changed, not him. Backlund beat Bret Hart at the 1994 Survivor Series for his second world title, a three-day interregnum to pass the title to Kevin Nash, and worked on and off in the WWE for several more years, and briefly for TNA. "Let me be bad by being good," he said. "I learned more being a bad guy in two years, about life, about people, than I did my whole career trying to be a good guy."

BILLY DARNELL

"Physician, heal thyself." Billy Darnell took the proverb to heart. He busted backs, and then he healed them. Darnell wrestled for twenty years until he retired to open up a chiropractic office, which he maintained to the end of his life in 2007. There was no contradiction between the two practices, Darnell said; in fact, one led naturally to the other. "We never went to doctors, they couldn't help us much," he explained in a 1988 interview with the *Philadelphia Daily News*. "Chiropractors could do us some good. That's how I became interested in it." In all likelihood, he is the only doctor of chiropractic to appear on national television wearing a single-strap, Tarzan-style, leopard-skin singlet that made the girls swoon. "Billy worked very hard. He was very well built and had a wonderful body and he told me about all the girls who used to wait at those Stage Door Delis [in New York] for him," said Ida Mae Martinez. "One of the greats of all time."

William L. Darnell got into wrestling strictly by accident. Born February 25, 1926, in Camden, New Jersey, where his dad worked on a railroad, Darnell was a teenaged lifeguard when promoter Al Mayer eyed him as a fill-in for wrestlers who had been pulled away by World War II. Years later, Darnell explained, "I didn't know that much about it, but I worked out, was pretty athletic and it was a way to make a couple bucks." On his eighteenth birthday, he fell in for the first time with another Camden product, a sometimes-cop named Herman "Dutch" Rohde. They wrestled several times in 1944 as a good-guy tag team before Darnell headed to the army that December. His tour of duty included a stint with the Corps of Engineers in the Philippines. When he got out two years later, he spent some time at Temple University and reconnected with Rohde, by then Buddy Rogers,

The ever-photogenic
BILLY TWO RIVERS in 2009.

Andrea Kellaway

ORVILLE BROWN. Courtesy Dick Brown

BRUNO SAMMARTINO turned announcer post-career, and here interviews **ANDRE THE GIANT** and **PAT PATTERSON** in the WWWF.

Brad McFarlin

The People's Family: Ata Maivia, son Dwayne — the future **ROCK** — and **ROCKY JOHNSON.**

Brian Berkowitz, *Pete Lederberg Collection*

A young **HULK HOGAN** already knew how to pose.

Brad McFarlin

JOHN CENA meets his admirers at WWE Fan Axxess at WrestleMania XXV in Orlando, Florida.

Mike Mastrandrea

The man of honor is celebrated at the opening of Tiger Jeet Singh Public School in Milton, Ontario, in September 2010.

Greg Oliver

When being the greatest babyface of his generation didn't prove to be enough, **RICKY STEAMBOAT** was asked to be more dragon-like.

Howard Baum

GEOFF PORTZ and ARCHIE "THE STOMPER" GOULDIE try to take away DORY FUNK JR.'s NWA world title.

Bob Leonard

The feud between SHAWN MICHAELS and BRET HART went from the top of the cage to the dressing room.

Ed Russino

DUSTY RHODES looks for fan approval as he battles **THE SHEIK** in a cage.

Howard Baum

THE CRUSHER celebrates a 1972 brawl in Chicago with a cigar.

David Maciejewski

who hooked up Darnell with his own manager, Jack Pfefer. For a while, Darnell was billed as Rohde's younger brother since "Dutch" was about five years older; the two worked out together at an athletic club in Camden.

You can't begin to discuss Darnell without Rogers. Friends until the day Rogers died in 1992, their "rivalry" was one of the greatest of all time. After their initial pairing in 1944, they squared off more than 250 times in singles or tag affairs, often night after night after night, through 1961. "Rogers and Darnell could wrestle twenty times and never repeat themselves," Boston promoter Tony Santos said in a 1981 interview. "The Leopard Boy" even wrestled for a brief time as Billy Rogers in Texas in 1947, before heading to California, scene of some of their most memorable matches. "Then [Pfefer] took me out to Hollywood and I became junior heavyweight champion, then Buddy came in. That's where we really hit it big, when we wrestled a few shots out there. But after that, everybody wanted that match," Darnell said. One example: a sportswriter for the *Bakersfield Californian* called their February 1949 match the "most sensational card of the year," as they split the first two falls. In the third, Darnell flung Rogers through the ropes and into the aisles, where he pounded on his prostrate opponent until a policeman intervened, allowing both men to climb back into the ring. Rogers caught Darnell with a knee to the chin for the winning fall. Rogers usually got the best of Darnell, though not always; Darnell beat him for Pfefer's version of the world title in October 1948 in San Diego.

In 1953, Darnell and Bill Melby became the first tandem to hold a world tag team championship acknowledged on a national level, defending the title for Fred Kohler's Chicago-based promotion on TV and around the country. As a singles competitor, Darnell worked in every corner of the country, always as a good guy. Dick Brown, the son of former world champ Orville Brown and himself a Central States heavyweight champ, said the image was no gimmick. When Darnell was booking in Indianapolis in 1957, Brown sandwiched a trip to the famous Indianapolis Motor Speedway between a couple of wrestling appearances. "The week of the Speedway, we got to the hotel with no reservations about 2 a.m. The lobby of the hotel was packed. A lady working at the desk was a good wrestling fan. She called Bill over and gave him the key to her house and told us to go there and go to bed. I couldn't believe it, but Bill Darnell was the kind of guy you could trust with your house keys."

The naturally inquisitive Darnell had his finger in many pies. He learned how to scuba dive and took up aviation at the suggestion of Ray Stern, for a while flying himself to matches in a small open-cockpit plane. Later in life, he had a large

Billy Darnell and the singlet that made girls swoon.

hypnosis practice, as well. But talk about wrestling outside of the fraternity was verboten; he was old-school on that point. "He wouldn't even discuss it with the family," said his daughter Linda Spiegleman. "I tried to talk to him about it lots of times. I used to make a joke, 'Did you take the Hippocratic oath of wrestling?'"

In addition to booking in Indianapolis, Darnell took over as promoter in Hagerstown, Maryland, in 1956. He started to eye a career as something other than a full-time wrestler because his body wasn't holding up. In one match in 1954, Rogers accidentally injured Darnell, crushing discs in his neck during a piledriver that went awry. He wasn't a chiropractor yet, so he did what he thought best, wearing a support collar and stretching himself daily before returning to action in a few months. "I used to hang myself, I had a chinning bar I carried with me everywhere. I put the thing on my neck and hung myself with pulleys," Darnell said. If the broken neck was worst, an incident in Pittsburgh was a close second. Darnell beat Ali Pasha in a TV match on May 20, 1961. "I picked him up and slammed him down. I heard him groan. I thought he was just out of gas. I could feel him melting. He died right there. He must have had a heart attack. The doctor tried to shoot adrenalin into his heart in the dressing room, but it didn't work."

Darnell was one of the few wrestlers who walked away on his own terms. In 1957, he started chiropractic school in Glendale, California, a departure George Bollas noted in a letter to Pfefer from Hawaii. "Darnell left on the moment's notice. He's going to college in L.A. to become a chiropractor. We all wished him luck . . . Billy got over like a million dollars here." He transferred to Lincoln Chiropractic College in Indianapolis, and got his degree in 1961. That was his last year of full-time action, though he had a few bouts in 1962 before he put the Tarzan gear in the closet for good. He owned a bar in Woodbury, New Jersey, from the late 1960s into the early 1980s, and his daughter said he never formally took down his shingle, working with patients out of his home in Maple Shade, New Jersey, until he died in September 2007 at 81. "He could cure you when nobody else could cure you," Spiegleman said. "One time, he had to go into surgery for a hernia. He came to my house, in the bedroom, and he set up all these different colored lights. He did light therapy and magnet therapy and he was out of here in two days. He was able to cure himself."

ABE JACOBS

If ever one hold were more closely associated with a professional wrestler, Abe Jacobs' Kiwi Roll would be right at the top of the list.

The maneuver was the venerable New Zealander's "best friend" in the business for many years, winning him the vast majority of his matches and forever linking Jacobs to his famed coup de grace. "I learned the hold coming along as an amateur," he said. "One day I was working out with someone in the gym, and I happened to grapevine a leg and kind of rolled with it. The guy screamed, 'Hey, hey, hey, my knee, my ankle!' That's when I knew I had something special."

Jacobs' career, though, wouldn't be defined by a single hold. His athletic career started back in New Zealand where he was an amateur standout in both wrestling and rugby. Born and raised on a sprawling ranch on the lonely, ocean-washed Chatham Islands, he rode to school on horseback and acquired a love for the rugged outdoors. But wrestling was his first passion, and Jacobs pursued a dream in the late '50s when he arrived in the United States.

His first official pro match had been in his native country in 1958. Jacobs, a former New Zealand amateur wrestling champion who won seven provincial titles and was a runner-up to the nationals and a winner of the national championships, immersed himself in the business and locked horns with top names such as Dick the Bruiser, Big Bill Miller, Ray Stevens, and Whipper Billy Watson his first couple of years in the U.S. and Canada.

Twenty-five years and more than seven thousand matches in hundreds of wrestling rings would leave Jacobs with broken ribs, dislocated shoulders, neck and back injuries, fractures in his leg, and a number of turned ankles and knees. But Jacobs has absolutely no regrets about his decision to get into wrestling. "I've done a lot of traveling . . . four times around the world. You name it, I've been there. And it's great to watch TV, especially the Discovery Channel or news from overseas, and say, 'I've been there. I know what's around the corner.' It's been a wonderful experience."

Among Jacobs' favorite opponents were the great Lou Thesz, whose five meetings included a sixty-minute draw for Thesz's NWA world title, and "Nature Boy" Buddy Rogers. "Buddy was a good pro wrestler, but he wasn't a wrestler," said Jacobs. And, he added, you had to watch out for Rogers, "a great man for himself who would accidentally hurt you on purpose," as was the case the last time the two wrestled in Norfolk, Virginia. After fifty-five minutes, Jacobs missed a flying tackle, fell from the ring, and injured his shoulder. "If I hadn't have caught that top rope, I probably would have landed on my head."

"Look, don't book me with Buddy, because the last time I wrestled him he tried to hurt me," Jacobs told booker George Scott, a close friend of Rogers. "You book me with him, he's not going to be in a position to hurt me, but I might be in a position to hurt him."

Some of his greatest successes in the wrestling business would come in the tag team ranks. Since Jacobs knew how to legitimately wrestle, and his conditioning was beyond reproach, promoters liked to pair him with big men whose skills were often limited but whose drawing power was strong. Jacobs teamed with the 601-pound Haystacks Calhoun in a number of territories including the Carolinas, Los Angeles, and the Pacific Northwest, with the two driving cross-country and the enormous "Stacks" behind the wheel of a station wagon. Other "special attractions" partners included Man Mountain Mike, "Haystacks" Muldoon, Sailor Art Thomas, and "Klondike" Bill.

There also were skilled partners like Don Curtis, whom Jacobs first met in the mid-'50s when Curtis was touring New Zealand. Jacobs, by then a pro, next saw Curtis headlining at Madison Square Garden during the late '50s. The next time their paths crossed, in Florida in 1964, promoter Eddie Graham paired the two. The smooth-working duo took the Florida version of the world tag team belts from the Japanese heel combo of Hiro Matsuda and Duke Keomuka in 1964, losing them later to Chris and John Tolos.

Jacobs always took great pride in calling himself a "real wrestler," an ath-

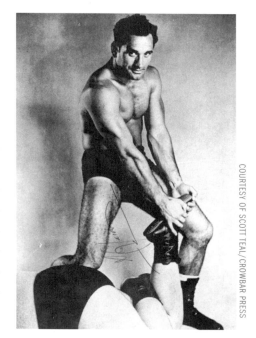

Abe Jacobs demonstrates a hold.

lete that could not only "work" in the ring, but could actually "wrestle."

"You have to look like an athlete," he said. "In wrestling you have to be able to get heat, and you do that by getting the other guy over at the right time. You do a move that looks good to the people."

He was so good that he once hit the lights with a dropkick during a TV match. "You had to do things that were spectacular. They were always calling for me to put the Kiwi Roll on my opponent. At that time it was one of the most spectacular holds in wrestling."

He's been asked by dozens of wrestlers who just couldn't pull off the maneuver. At this stage of the game, he'll probably take the "secret" to his grave. "I could teach you, but then I'd probably have to kill you," he laughed.

Jacobs made his biggest impact in the Carolinas, falling in love with the area and eventually buying property and setting up a home base that lasted beyond his in-ring retirement in 1983. With Jim Crockett's Carolinas-Virginia territory serving as a hotbed of tag team wrestling during the '60s, Jacobs formed formidable combos with the likes of Sandy Scott, George Becker, Nelson Royal, and Luther Lindsay.

Rip Hawk, who was a frequent opponent on the tag side, teaming with Swede Hanson against Jacobs and his partner of choice, has nothing but fond memories

Abe Jacobs at the podium for his induction into the George Tragos/Lou Thesz Professional Wrestling Hall of Fame in 2008.

of the New Zealander. "You couldn't find a nicer man to know and to deal with. He's aces all the way. I don't think anybody could ever say a bad thing about Abe." Their era was one in which heels and babyfaces rarely fraternized, so most of their interaction occurred within the ropes. Still, said Hawk, "Abe was a class act all the way."

Dubbed "Honest Abe," Jacobs was well-liked and respected by his peers.

"Abe was an excellent athlete and a very skilled mat wrestler," said Les Thatcher. "Easy to travel with and a guy who could have a good match with anyone. I always felt he should have been pushed more. The only things he may have loved as much as wrestling would be his golf game and his horse."

In his latter years in the business, Jacobs was used primarily in the role of the aging veteran who would put over the younger stars and help teach them the ropes. He was a young Ric Flair's first opponent when the future "Nature Boy" first hit the Carolinas in the spring of 1974. "Green as grass" is how Jacobs remembers Flair's first match in Charlotte, a win for the newcomer.

"Abe treated me like a million bucks when I was young and new to the business," said Charlie Fulton. "He always took care of me and took me to school in the ring and never hurt me. He taught me a lot of things on the go and it was like on-the-job training." Fulton was a ring rookie when Jacobs told him to execute a relatively simple kip-up as he held Fulton in an arm bar. Fulton had never done a kip-up, and was reluctant to try it until Jacobs gracefully lifted him up and completed the spot.

Jacobs, who was once billed as the "Jewish heavyweight champion," was named one of the "Top Ten New Zealand–Born Wrestlers" by *Fight Times Magazine*. He was inducted into the George Tragos/Lou Thesz Hall of Fame in 2008. His status in the Chatham Islands was celebrated when his likeness graced its commemorative special edition Millennium ten-dollar bill in 2000 and 2001.

Jacobs served as an instructor at Ricky Steamboat's gym in Charlotte for eleven years after retiring from the ring, and still keeps in tip-top shape. He still lives in the Charlotte area with his wife, Evelyn, and shuttles cars for Avis four days a week.

Jacobs' exact age remains a running joke among his friends and colleagues.

"I can't tell for sure, but he looks and gets around a hell of a lot younger than he is," laughed Paul Jones. "You really can't put your finger on how old he is. It's a mystery to all of us."

Jacobs supports a number of charitable organizations in the area, taking part in numerous golf tournaments to raise money for various causes.

"The only thing that exceeds Abe's incredible wrestling ability is his tremendous heart," said Bill Murdock, executive director of the western North Carolina–based Eblen Charities, an organization that assists children, adults, and families in times of need. "Since retiring from the ring, Abe has been involved in innumerable charitable endeavors including being instrumental in the beginning of the Eblen Charities. If Abe Jacobs isn't in a class by himself, it certainly doesn't take long to call the roll."

GRIDIRON GRAPPLERS

Football and professional wrestling have a long, intertwined history. One is a sport and the other the ultimate in self-promotion and salesmanship, though given the over-hyped media world of today's NFL, it might be hard to establish which is which.

"I find that both sports pay well but most of all one puts me in fine physical condition for the other. Playing football is fine training for my wrestling matches and engaging in a mat bout puts me in fine physical trim for the gridiron game," said Herman Hickman in 1934, a former All-American guard at Tennessee University who never really amounted to much in the squared circle.

Through the rich vein of football, promoters have mined many of the biggest names in wrestling's history, including Gus Sonnenberg, Bronko Nagurski, Joe Savoldi, Leo Nomellini, Wilbur Snyder, Dick the Bruiser, Wahoo McDaniel, Ernie Ladd, Blackjack Mulligan, and Bill

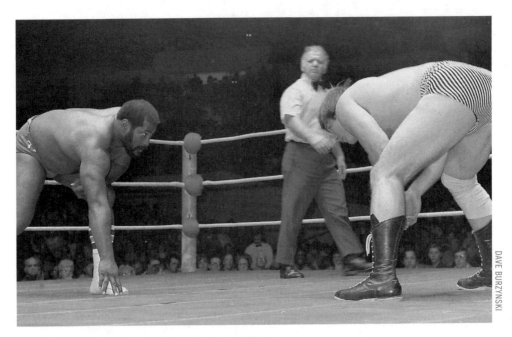

Walter Johnson lines up across the ring from Ron Pritchard.

Goldberg. Some wrestled while playing, while others were forced out of football by injuries or age.

But what brought those gridiron giants (and not-so giants) to the ring? Usually, it was a friend.

For Otis Sistrunk, it was "The Big Cat" Ernie Ladd. "I knew Ernie and when I got into the NFL, he said, 'I think this will be a good second career for you.' I said, 'I'll try it and see what the deal is,'" recalled Sistrunk, who played for the Oakland Raiders.

While at Stanford University, Don Manoukian used to housesit for Nomellini. "He lived in Palo Alto, and I went to school there in Palo Alto. When I'd be around during the holidays, or for summer school, I would look after his home while he went back to Minnesota to visit friends and relatives. So Leo's the one that got me started in the business. That's how that began — much to my university's chagrin. They were very unhappy that one of their notables went into this shoddy, unacceptable business of professional wrestling. And worse yet, being on TV as a heel! Holy Christ, it made them crazy."

Bob Bruggers roomed with McDaniel when both backs played for the Miami Dolphins. "In the off-season a couple of times, him and I would take a road trip in a car and go to wherever he was going to wrestle, and then we'd go play golf. I'd watch the wrestling matches with him. But basically that's how I got involved in it," said Bruggers, who turned to Verne Gagne for training when the general managers stopped calling. His career famously ended in the October 1975 plane crash in Wilmington, NC, that also saw the pilot killed,

Johnny Valentine get crippled for life, Tim Woods banged up, and Ric Flair to the sidelines for a year with a broken back.

Arizona's Ron Pritchard went north to Calgary to visit his friend Bob Lueck, who was a star for Stampede Wrestling in the off-season, and ended up wrestling a week later, spinning that into five off-seasons of competition. "I had the privilege of being trained in the Dungeon for a couple of hours, with Stu Hart of all people, and he never stretched me. He liked me for some reason. I think it was because I kept my mouth shut and was really serious about his business, and I wasn't trying to be a big shot as an NFL player."

As for Sistrunk, all told, his wrestling career lasted only a few months in 1981, done in by the travel. Big names like Ric Flair, Rufus R. Jones, Ricky Steamboat, and Blackjack Mulligan had a hand in training the defensive lineman. "You had to get in wrestling shape before you wrestled. I went to school for three months. I had to learn how to fall, learn how to hit, learn how to do different things."

Sistrunk, who now manages Cowan Memorial Stadium in McChord, Washington, scoffed at any likeness between the two athletic endeavors. "Wrestling compared to football? There's no comparison. The thing about it is both of them are hard to do. Football, you've got to train for one thing and in wrestling, you've got to train for another one. With wrestling, it's individual, it's an individual sport. It's just tough to learn. The biggest thing is learning how to fall, learning how to take a punch, and learning different things in the ring. In football, whatever position you're playing, you've got to turn around and try to be the best at the position you're playing, whether defense, the offense or whatever."

Ring of Honor star Kenny King was a strong safety in college at Florida State, and the University of South Florida. He took a chance on wrestling while redshirting at UNLV, having scoffed at the training he saw on the first season of WWE *Tough Enough*. "On my way to class, I saw an ad for *Tough Enough 2*, and I remembered watching the first *Tough Enough*, and remember thinking to myself, 'Man, those guys aren't even athletes. I could do that,'" King said. Light on his feet to chase speedy receivers, King agreed that some of his football skills translated well. "I found that some of the things we did, the agility drills and having quick feet, and being able to think on the fly, those are some of the things that immediately translated well into wrestling. The other thing is that football is reckless abandon, wrestling not so much. So that didn't translate. Just the agility and the skills that I learned, balance, and some of those things are what I utilized mainly in my wrestling game."

What did translate, Bruggers found, was loyalty to teams. "People liked the fact that I used to play football. When I went into the ring, especially when I was in North Carolina, back in those days, the Miami Dolphins were a big deal. I used to wear my Miami Dolphins jacket." It was different in other territories, said Bruggers, who has worked as a bartender for years. "When I was wrestling Dick Murdoch in Texas, there they hated me because I was a Dolphins

Don Manoukian.

guy. They're all Dallas Cowboys fans. So now I'm the bad guy. You don't dictate good or bad, it's just the way people accepted you." (He never wore his San Diego Chargers jacket.)

Pritchard didn't have to travel the territories and was primarily brought in as a special attraction, playing off his time as a linebacker for the Houston Oilers and Cincinnati Bengals. In Walter Johnson of the Browns, he took on a fellow NFLer. "In Cleveland, I was the bad guy and he was the good guy. In Cincinnati, he was the bad guy and I was the good guy. It was great," Pritchard reminisced, recalling their teammates often at ringside egging them on.

Though hard to understand in today's world, where a lockout derails an NFL season as owners and players bicker over how to split billions of dollars, there was a time when a good athlete could make more money in wrestling than in football.

"That's why I didn't go back to football after my first year with the Raiders," said Manoukian. Hall of Fame center Jim Otto was sent to Portland to convince Manoukian, a guard, to return to Oakland for the second season of the AFL. "I told him, 'Jim, there's just not that much money in that football. I can't do it.' I was making $8,000 to $10,000 playing football. So they promised me many more dollars. But I'd made a commitment to go to Japan in the fall. I could not renege on that commitment."

Did Manoukian, now a real estate maven, miss football? "Very much. I really enjoyed the sport immensely, but it was strictly an economic decision."

Mike Webster, a British Columbia native who played college ball at Notre Dame and wrestled for a short while in the early 1970s before getting a master's and a doctorate from Western Washington University in clinical psychology, and becoming one of the world's most sought-out experts on hostage negotiations, has a unique take on both sports.

"The biggest thing for me was the camaraderie. I loved that about football, being a part of a team. You're getting paid to be with the guys, you go out and you play a game that you love, you play hard and you lose hard too. You do it all as a group, and everybody's supportive of each other, mostly everybody's supportive of each other — there's always some elements on a team where they're pulling in another direction. Mostly it's like a big family. Boys will be boys, goofy at times, immature and haven't grown up, but it was a wonderful, wonderful experience," Webster opined. "And then going to wrestling, that was the thing that I liked best about wrestling. I liked the idea that it was, to me, wrestling was an art. To be able to, through the thing that I did in the ring, affect people who were not connected to me in any way, emotionally or relationship-wise, or anything — I'm speaking of fans. To be able to just by choreographing something in the ring to be able to get people to have an emotional experience, an emotional reaction to that, I liked that."

DON LEO JONATHAN

JIMMY CARUSO

The great Don Leo Jonathan puffs out his chest for a 1973 Grand Prix Wrestling promo photo.

Don Heaton is quick to dispute the placement of his alter ego Don Leo Jonathan in any book about heroic wrestlers. "There would be a lot of fans in certain parts of the country that sure wouldn't agree with you!" he said in his squeaky, high-pitched voice that belies his hulking six-foot-six frame.

Yet time and time again, Jonathan would be in a territory as a bad guy, terrorizing the local heroes, when something happened to put him on the right side of the law.

And a great hero needs a great villain. It was often Killer Kowalski.

"He was the most athletic wrestler I ever came across. He comes up the steps, stands on the apron, hands on the rope, does a flip right over top, and lands in the middle of the ring," recalled Kowalski. "We were a tag team, all over, everywhere. And what did I do? Quite a few times, just to make sense of a match, I double-crossed him. So called, anyway. We'd wrestle one another that way. We enjoyed it, wrestling one another. We'd go on the road, we'd be a team again and I'd do the same thing again and we'd wrestle one another here, there, and everywhere.

BOB LEONARD

Don Leo Jonathan drops onto Klondike Bill.

We're acting like more than family. He was my brother, I was his brother. We wrestled like that all over the country. We'd just keep on going. We became really close as friends, very, very close, as two wrestlers rarely become."

To Jonathan, it was never cut and dried. "A lot of the matches I had with Kowalski, we had a split fan base, some liked me and some didn't. You really never know how the fans are going to take you, but if you're an outsider coming in, and you're wrestling some-body that they know, that's been there a while, automatically they go for the guy they know."

He philosophized a little further on how fans react.

"You take two guys the people don't know, and you put them in the ring for five minutes, and the people will have made up their mind what they want. Sometimes, you just can't do what you want to do. You just go with the flow. Why fight it?" he said, adding that you just have to feel it. "Nobody can really tell you. What you do is you watch. You pay attention and you watch. I've prob-ably watched twice as many matches as I was ever in — especially when I was younger. I studied Kowalski like a book. He was the best. And if you want to be the best, you have to work with the best."

Well, many people would put Jonathan on the list of the best as well.

Though he was born Don Leo Delaun Heaton on April 29, 1931, and always billed from Hurricane, Utah, he grew up in nearby Harmony and Kanab. His father, Jonathan Delaun Heaton, entered pro wrestling in 1927, and worked as Brother Jonathan, Don Delaun, and Sparrow Condelmedis. "Hurricane was a small place, and everybody who was there during my time, they would remember me, but they wouldn't remember me as Don Leo Jonathan or Don Heaton. All they would remember would be my nickname 'Mutsy,'" laughed Jonathan. His father gave him the nickname. "He was good at nicknaming everybody."

At Cedar City High School and Hurricane High, Heaton excelled in shot put, wrestling, and football, where he was a tackle, and, as a part-time job, worked as a butcher. His success in wrestling wasn't a surprise to his father, who had the family on the road often, and young Don Leo learned the amateur moves at age five in his dad's heathatorium in Phoenix. As a child, Don Leo also appeared in a few episodes of Our Gang but not in any sort of featured role; as an adult, he would appear in numerous films as well, and in a 1963 TV commercial for Wheaties, Breakfast of Champions, which aired during the World Series.

After he graduated in 1949, he had scholarship offers for college, but elected to enter the Navy Special Services, training in San Diego in deep-sea diving. It would become a life-long passion. In 1963, he went back to school to learn how to drive a submarine, and followed that with lessons in bell diving and deep-gas diving. The result? His Vancouver-based business, Can Dive Ltd., which built and operated diving equipment, and DLJ Enterprises Ltd., a parent company to oversee many ventures.

His partner in the company, Dr. Phil Nuyten, said that some old truisms describe Jonathan best. "The thing that comes to mind is a whole string of clichés. Those clichés are 'strong as a bull,' 'straight as an arrow,' 'smart as hell,' 'you get your money's worth,' 'one face for your face and the same face for your back,' most unusual, and 'one of nature's gentlemen,' 'his word is his bond,' and all that sort of thing. Those old clichés epitomize Leo because they are fundamental, old-time values."

Still recognizable now, both because of his bulk and his now-grey mut-tonchops, Jonathan is happy to be stopped for the memories. "Guys fifty, sixty years old that I talk to, 'Oh, I used to come and see you with my grandpa. My grandpa would take me every week to go see you' . . . makes you feel kind of good, especially those that say, 'You signed my autograph when other guys wouldn't.' To some of the kids, that little thing that you do, you stop and give them an autograph — it's nothing to me, but they, some of those kids remember that and they tell me about it. One of the kids told me he got my autograph ten times and sold each one for a dollar," he laughed. "That's how he kept going to the wrestling matches! He'd always manage to get several autographs from me."

Of course, for many years, young Don was one of those kids going to the matches. After getting out of the navy and giving up on his aspirations to compete in judo, Don's wrestling career overlapped his father's for a couple of years, beginning in California before moving worldwide. On a handful of occasions, he strayed from the name inherited from his dad, including El Loco in Baltimore and El Diablo in Columbus.

While he was world champion in Montreal in 1955, and held numerous other titles, Jonathan avowed that titles never meant much to him. "I always seemed to be more interested in learning as much as I could," he told Scott Teal. "There were times I wrestled and it didn't even occur to me that it was a title match." To prove his longevity, Jonathan would reign again in Montreal, under the Vachon's Grand Prix banner, in 1974. He really made an impression earlier in the territory with his "Battle of the Giants" against the newcomer to North American shores, Jean Ferré, later Andre the Giant.

Ever adventurous for travel, Jonathan would headline from New York City to Vancouver, from Tokyo to Sydney, from Cape Town to Berlin. "I loved the travel, I loved foreign places, I loved foreign languages. I just liked the atmosphere and it fed my ego to a great degree also. But to get that recognition, you had to do the work," he said.

Jonathan's stardom meant bookers would often pair him with up-and-coming stars for the rub, or create interesting Mutt and Jeff pairings, the giant and the shrimp. Consider the mayhem-causing paring of Don Leo and Gene Kiniski (champs in Toronto in 1959), or a rookie Rocky Johnson, in Vancouver in 1967, where The People's Father listed Jonathan as his brother on a car lease.

"To me, Don Leo Jonathan was probably the greatest human that ever lived," said John Quinn, who held the tag titles in B.C. with him in 1979, and faced him countless times. His strength was only matched by his sense of humor, said Quinn. "He'd pick me up . . . and start to giggle. Ever hear him giggle? He's worse than a fucking girl!"

Then there's the brawny tale of Don Leo bodyslamming a braggadocio Haystacks Calhoun, who claimed it couldn't be done. That night, in the battle royal, Don Leo instructed all the boys to head for the ring ropes at once, leaving him alone with a stunned Calhoun, who had only just met the Mormon Giant. "Calhoun turns around and Leo is facing him and he crotched him. When he crotched him, Calhoun tried to sit down," explained Dutch Savage, a tag partner in '77. "Leo picked him up with his right arm, picked him up in the bodyslam position and bodyslammed him. When he did, [Calhoun] crapped himself. The big fat guy, his stomach went, wobble, wobble, like a rubber ball. You know those overalls he used to wear, the cutoff overalls? Crap went all over the audience, people were screaming, yelling, laughing." Back in the dressing room, Calhoun was mumbling to himself about revenge, and Jonathan, chew in his mouth, calmly said, "Well there, 'Stacks, if you ain't careful, I'm going to do it here on the concrete." (Naturally, Jonathan and Calhoun would be championship partners later, in 1966, in B.C.)

Ever the free spirit, Jonathan would plan his bookings around hunting season, or great places to fish or dive. He'd bring friends along, whether it was taking Red Bastien diving for octopus, ribbing Dutch Savage with wacky dishes on his first trip to Japan, or killing a deer with his bare hands while hunting with Killer Karl Kox, who was hesitant to get blood in his car.

The boys loved him for a reason, said Moose Morowski. "He always gave credit to the guys underneath that put him over. He never said, 'I'm this, I'm that.' He always gave credit to everybody else. It makes a big difference."

At his induction into the Pro Wrestling Hall of Fame in Amsterdam, New York, in 2006, Jonathan put everyone over but himself. "To learn, I was hoisted on the shoulders of many, many, many great men," he said, thanking everyone from his wife, Rose, to his three children, to his half-brother, who was in attendance and whom he had only met four times in his life. Lastly, he thanked the fans.

"A lot of times people don't take the time to look back and consider, 'Why did I get here? How did I get here?' There were a lot more people that deserved credit for me. I didn't do this by myself. And anybody who tells you they did it my way, they done it themselves, it's not reality," Jonathan said afterward. "The thing is the fans don't get enough credit, because without them, we wouldn't have had a business."

MARK LEWIN

By his own description, Mark Lewin was a chameleon, able to change his character or even his physique to meet the demands of a situation. One time, he was wrestling Jimmy "Superfly" Snuka at a massive and muscular 280 pounds. "Oh, you're so big," Snuka told him. "Next time — we were both coming back in three months to Singapore — I said, 'How do you want me?'" Lewin recalled. "'How do you want me to be built? I'll change my physique for you.'" Like an actor prepping for a movie part, Lewin worked out in Hawaii, carved his body with every rep, and morphed into a hard, lean 220-pounder. That required an almost indescribable

A young, babyfaced Mark Lewin.

intensity and single-mindedness, which is exactly what Dr. Tom Prichard saw when he was just sixteen and pumping iron with Lewin at a Houston gym. They were doing forearm curls, for reasons Prichard couldn't fathom. "But then I got it," he said. "He was so intent on this. This was all he was doing, this was all he was going to do, and this is the way he was going to make money like the old carnival mentality, the only way he knew how. He was a different breed altogether from anyone I've ever been with."

Charismatic, enigmatic . . . if a psychoanalyst tried to get a read on Lewin, he'd throw in the towel, though he'd have to figure out first who he was throwing it at. In the 1950s, Lewin was a teenage heartthrob who fibbed about his age for a chance to begin a pro career. In the 1960s and 1970s, he was one of the best babyfaces in the business when he wasn't flipping out, sometimes in the very same match, as "Maniac" Mark Lewin. In the 1980s, he was the bizarre Purple Haze, a wrestler in perfect sync with "Purple Haze," the classic Jimi Hendrix psychedelic drug song. "I'm believable because I am the Purple Haze. And I am the Maniac. And I'm the guy that delivers brownies. All of these personalities," Lewin said. There was no picking and choosing between them, either. Early in his career, Bob Roop wrestled in Australia, and thought the world of the way Lewin was booking the promotion there and operating the business. Later, when Roop was booking in Florida, he fired Lewin along with Kevin Sullivan for freelancing their matches with antics that made no sense. "There were some extra-curricular activities going on . . . I had my share of mistakes when I was in the business, but for these guys, it was a lifestyle," Roop said. "It was a shame because I had worked with Mark in Australia when he was the booker, and I was only in the business about a year or so. I looked up to him. I thought he was a good talent, good booker, and everything."

Lewin was barely old enough to shave when he started wrestling as a pro at sixteen. Born in March 1937, the youngest of three wrestling brothers from Buffalo, his passion for the sport was unbridled, and when brother-in-law Danny McShain took him under his wing, it was goodbye, Lafayette High School; hello, world. The vagabond spirit beat deep in the soul of the Lewin family; father Sid went on the road at age fifteen as a drummer selling jewelry and Donn, the oldest brother, quit high school at fifteen to enlist in the Marines in World War II. "So Mark leaving home at sixteen in our family was not a big deal," said brother Ted, who wrestled before launching a prodigious career as an author and illustrator; he wrote *I Was a Teenage Professional Wrestler*. "There was Mark sitting at home, second year in high school, making my parents' life miserable. He was

Mark Lewin rolls his eyes as the mad Purple Haze.

not going to stay there." He went across the country with McShain in 1953, lied about his age to get a California license, and started wrestling in opening matches in southern California, Washington, Texas, and Arizona. The *Tucson Daily Citizen* tried to smoke him out, saying he "looked like a husky teen-ager but set his age at twenty-one." For a while in 1955, he wrestled as Skippy Jackson, a preppy name given to him by Buddy Rogers that made him sound more like the vice president of a college fraternity than a pro wrestler. No matter — Lewin was doing what he wanted. "I was so crazy about wrestling I was dropkicking in the backyard, I was dropkicking on cement. I would let people throw me through trees. Wrestling was my whole life. I was just raised in it," he said.

Working with McShain, one of the greatest heels in history, Lewin was studying with a master and he soaked it all up. His call to New York came in 1958 and Vincent J. McMahon referred to him as his top babyface; unusual for the day, in that he had no gimmick like Ricki Starr or no ethnic appeal like Antonino Rocca. What helped him stand out were the mini-lessons he picked up from McShain and then imparted to his own wrestlers down the road. Jerry Brisco, who worked under him in Australia, regards him as one of the best ring psychologists ever, with a million little tricks that spell the difference between an

The princess and the chameleon at the Pro Wrestling Hall of Fame induction in May 2011.

ordinary and a compelling presence. "Just how you walk to the ring, how you hold your head, hold your head up, and the way you look when you walk to the ring, when you leave the ring. Just the little details, not so much the technical part of the business, the moves and the physical part of it, but the psychology of thinking about a match," Brisco said. Where'd he get those tics? From just about everybody, said brother Ted, who noticed that Lewin took on the mannerisms of whomever he was with at the time. "He hung around Danny McShain long enough to emulate Danny McShain, not only in the way he talked and the way he turned his head, but even the way he would get up in the morning with his briefs on. He'd put his thumb in the elastic part of the brief and snap it, like Danny always did," he said. "Then he hung around Red Bastien and he sounded like he was from Minnesota because Red was from Minnesota. He had all the inflections and the pronunciation of words down pat. He hung around Rito Romero in Texas and he sounded like a Mexican. He had that knack for picking up things about other people and emulating them."

Don Curtis and Lewin were U.S. tag team champions and a mainstay of the then WWWF for about three years before the "Maniac" started to surface. The full flowering came in Texas in 1963, when Lewin found himself surrounded by a surfeit of fan favorites and wanted to distinguish himself from the pack. Call it a wrestling case of cognitive dissonance. *Wrestling Revue* magazine showed him smilingly tending to a family poodle and teaching neighborhood kids to swim. These photos appeared alongside pictures of him whacking Jerry Kozak in the head with a chair and cutting open Cowboy Bob Ellis. Promoter Paul Boesch put out a picture of Lewin with a caption that asked whether he was a good guy or a maniac. The answer, of course, was both. "I was believable and when you're believable in a contact sport, you have that roughness," he said. "Was I Mark Lewin? Was I the Haze? Was I the Maniac? It just depended on what personality I wanted to get into at the time, or all of them at the same time." Either way, the business became his life, and his life became the business. As Tiger Jeet Singh, who also worked with him in Australia, put it: "Mark is a mark; the name sounds good."

The highlight of Lewin's career had to be putting Lou Thesz to sleep in the middle of the ring on October 28, 1966, in Los Angeles to win the World Wrestling Alliance world championship. Months later, he was defending the belt in front of one of the largest crowds of the decade, a reported 48,000 in Seoul, South Korea, against Kintaro Oki. The Maniac was back. Before the bout started, Lewin kneed him in the back and cut him open. He remembers it with a trace of a smile: "And they rioted. It took about twenty minutes to get the people under control. I remember I had to go under the ring because they were throwing things . . . chairs were flying. Everybody got hurt but me, naturally. It was outdoors and they had all these geishas dressed up, and flowers. They were going to make a nice little thing out of this and I spoiled their whole parade."

Fans of the nWo take note: Lewin hasn't gotten full due as the godfather of every wrestling "army" of the last forty years. Walking to an Australian arena among fans, feeling the moment, he spontaneously yelled out, "Let's lock arms, brother," and realized he had put together The People's Army. "I had read in the newspaper, you know, we were going to Hong Kong and I read about the People's Army in China. So if you read the newspaper, you never know where you will get ideas." Best buddy and running mate King Curtis was a part of the army, which peaked in 1973; so were Wadi Ayoub and Spiros Arion, as they fought Big Bad John's army of heels.

If Lewin was known for his creativity and imagination, he also gained infamy for living the psychedelic, drugged-out life of the '60s. Without going into detail, he acknowledges that's a part of him, too. "Let's face it, I'm out there no matter how much of an athlete I've been. I'm from the Timothy Leary era," he said. It proved to be too much for Donn, who retired to Hawaii after a long and successful career in wrestling and the Marines. "The trouble with him, it breaks down into one sentence: Too much, too soon. He had great gifts. He didn't know how to handle it," said Donn, who died in 2010. Through the years, Lewin also gained a reputation for burning bridges as he went from territory to territory. Stewing over payoffs, he started up an opposition group to The Sheik in the Cincinnati, Ohio, area in 1969 that lasted a few months. When promoter Jim Barnett was getting ready to sell his interest in Australia, Lewin and some members of The People's Army tried and failed at a breakaway group. It caught up to him — when Prichard worked out with him, Lewin was living in an apartment in a dumpy section of Houston, down to once-a-week bookings from Boesch. "Very few people in the business I was negative about, but he was one of them. Shot himself in the foot with too many guys throughout his career," said Dutch Savage. On the other hand, Gary Hart defended Lewin, saying he approached business the best way he knew how. "Mark Lewin would go to Houston, Texas, cut his head open, and you'd beat him 1-2-3 right in the middle if Mark thought he could make money for you. Mark Lewin was only difficult when promoters made him difficult," he said.

James Beard said Lewin reminded him of wrestler/booker Eddie Gilbert, who came a generation later but also wowed people with his creative genius while ruffling feathers just about everywhere he went. "Mark probably could have been a great booker if he had been in the right situation and been of a mind to just do that. He had kind of an Eddie Gilbert–type mind." Beard refereed for Lewin during a 1990s tour of Singapore and knew all the horror stories, but came away impressed. "I couldn't imagine anyone being more honest and straight up even though I've heard the tales from other people who had different situations with him."

In 2009, Lewin was inducted into the Pro Wrestling Hall of Fame with Curtis. He lives in Washington state with his wife, Princess Lynda, who is actual royalty in Singapore. He spotted her while he was wrestling in a match in Singapore and it was love at first sight. Lewin said he turned his life around in the 1990s after reading Arnold Schwarzenegger's *The Education of a Bodybuilder*. "I was doing some evil things to myself and when I read that, I said, 'I'm going to go along with this thing. I'm going to do this program for a year and not mess with it.'" Just like that, he flipped the switch — looking fastidious, sharp, and trim, he had a different outlook on life. Like a chameleon.

PETER MAIVIA

Going home to Western Samoa for the first time in fifteen years, "High Chief" Peter Maivia knew that it was a good chance to make a buck. He talked his friend, The Destroyer (Dick Beyer), into a match for the U.S. title just before Christmas 1970, in a bout promoted by New Zealand's Steve Rickard.

"We could have wrestled three times in one day and still packed the house," Beyer recalled with awe. It was one of the easiest nights he ever had. Though the fans were packed so tight their arms reached into the ring, they were putty in the hands of the skilled mat veterans.

"You talk about wrestling somebody and not having to do anything, and have the people want to come in the ring and kill you, that was the kind of match it was," said Beyer. "All I had to do was grab an arm hold on him, boom! Maybe I grab a little hair, pull him down, and those people are halfway coming in the ring." Naturally, Maivia went over, winning the U.S. title and setting off pandemonium. "I worked to where I got disqualified and he won my belt. We went out to dinner later — the promoter threw a dinner for his family, my family. I said, 'I need that belt, because I'm leaving for New Zealand tomorrow, and I'm taking that belt with me.' I got the belt back, and nobody in America ever knew that, or that the match ever took place."

So while that particular bout may have been on the hush-hush, "High Chief" Peter Maivia never was. The tales of his strength, his appetite, his love, have

Vince McMahon Sr. with Chief Peter Maivia in the dressing room at Madison Square Garden.

grown and grown through the years, perhaps necessary to keep up with the rising fame of his grandson, Dwayne Johnson, a.k.a. The Rock.

Though High Chief Fanene Leifi Pita Maivia died June 13, 1982, of cancer at the age of forty-five when young Dwayne was only ten, Dwayne had lived in Hawaii for two solid years as the entire family — grandma Lia, mom Ata, dad Rocky Johnson, and uncle Ricky Johnson — tried to make the Hawaiian promotion work again. He'd gotten to know his grandfather and the lifestyle associated with being a wrestler.

"When my grandfather passed away in 1982, he was running the wrestling promotion in Hawaii and his dying wish was that my grandmother continue with the business, and she kept it going," said The Rock. "She kept the business going, but at that time, there wasn't a million-dollar contract. There wasn't a lot of money to be made. You know, the wrestling business at that time, and essentially for us, was like a very hippie-esque lifestyle. So it was tough. It was really, really tough in Hawaii. It was tough, kind of all over. Like the movie, things are tough all over. But again, it was everything that life is to us today. It was awesome, it was the shits. It was wonderful and beautiful, and it was tough too."

And tough is a word thrown around a lot when talking about the High Chief. Though he was only five-foot-ten, at his greatest fame Maivia packed a whopping 320 pounds onto his frame, which was often adorned with colorful grass skirts and traditional accessories of his Samoan culture. Later, much of his body would be covered with imposing tattoos as well.

Less discussed is his prodigious appetite. Bill Balch was a go-boy in the Los Angeles office in the 1960s, shuttling the wrestlers from the airport, to the doctor for their physicals, to the office for their licenses. Sometimes he took them to eat, and none compared to Maivia.

At the Pantry, a well-known eatery, Maivia first devoured a plate of roast beef, potatoes, vegetables, coleslaw, and homemade sourdough bread. The waiter brought the bill, and Maivia ordered a T-bone steak, which came with identical fixings. The waiter approached again, and was dispatched to get some pork chops. "That is what he ate at the Pantry. A steak, pork chops, roast beef, three loaves of sourdough bread and three or four plates of coleslaw," said Balch, swearing that the High Chief out-ate the likes of Andre the Giant and Haystacks Calhoun.

Maivia's only daughter, Ata, loves to tell the story about how the family was kept in the dark about how professional wrestling worked.

"My father was so protective of the business that for the first few years he even protected it from my mom and I," she said. "Hence during a match in

London, England, during the early sixties, my mom jumped in the ring, her stiletto heel in hand, to beat the pulp out of the guy that was beating my dad — and my dad selling so fantastic that she was convinced he was done for." The next day, Maivia was instructed to smarten his family up.

Maivia was born in Western Samoa, one of three sons, and raised in New Zealand, where he worked as a plumber and began his wrestling career in 1958 as Peter Fanene Anderson, training under the light heavyweight champ Doug Harding. He got to England for the first time in April 1963, and stayed, off and on, for four years. Initially known as Peter Anderson, he was given the Peter Maivia name (to confuse everyone with the original Prince Maiava, who also wrestled as Neff Maiava), and became a star, in part because of a small role as a thug fighting Sean Connery in the James Bond film *You Only Live Twice*. In England and on the continent, he was known for lying across the ropes in between rounds. "With his pure wrestling skill and smiling face, Peter Maivia was a very popular figure in Great Britain," said British historian and former referee Ray Plunkett. "I must admit he was one of my favorite foreign stars to watch."

In North America, his first major port of call came in San Francisco.

"Peter was a great wrestler; in fact, he was a great amateur wrestler," recalled Fritz von Goering, a frequent foe in California. "He made a lot of good moves. He wrestled barefoot. He moved like a lightweight or a middleweight." Maivia begged von Goering for a run with the Beat the Champ title, which meant taking on amateurs and tough guys on behalf of the office, proving that the sport was legit. The Samoan took the belt in October 1972. "Peter called me up a couple of weeks later, complaining about the bookings. 'Do you want it back?' I said no," chuckled von Goering.

Pat Patterson was both friend and foe in San Francisco. "He had a big following, so that made a big difference. Boy, if you're in the ring and you beat the shit out of Peter Maivia, here come the Samoans. They attacked me a few times, believe me. I thought I was going to die," Patterson said. "He had a look and he was believable. When he got mad, that son-of-a-bitch, you could see that motherfucker's mad. And when he got mad, the Samoans would get mad."

"I never realized how many Samoans lived in San Francisco until I saw the crowds that turned out when Peter wrestled," wrote "Superstar" Billy Graham in his autobiography. "Afa and Sika Anoa'i were two gargantuan Maivia supporters who believed that everything they saw in the ring was real. They'd come to the Cow Palace with their families and literally rip out chairs bolted to the floor. The heels were petrified of them. Maivia kayfabed the Anoa'is for a long time, but eventually smartened them up and trained them for the business. As the aptly named Wild Samoans, they became World Wrestling Federation Tag Team Champions."

Indeed, Maivia inspired many from the islands to give wrestling a try, and though his bloodline in the business only really consists of his cousin, Papali'itele Siva Afi, and grandson, The Rock, many others from the Wild Samoans' family tree consider him the patriarch of the family.

"When I am being interviewed on television, I generally like to say a few words in Samoan to my people. I feel that I owe them a lot of respect," Maivia said in 1969.

The tribal tattoos became Maivia's calling card, and they made good copy in the programs. "Peter had the tattoos, eventually, and that really intrigued a lot of people," said "Moondog" Ed Moretti, who grew up watching Maivia in San Francisco. "Once in a while in a program, they'd show a still picture of Peter laying on a table with a guy with a shark's tooth. They had the announcers talk at length about how tough Peter was because he had that whole body tattoo done with a shark's tooth, with poisonous ink that could have killed him at any moment."

A babyface for most of his career, he did have a high-profile heel run, betraying WWWF champion Bob Backlund in late 1978. After the WWWF stint, Maivia settled in Hawaii. Promoter Ed Francis had sold the territory to Steve Rickard of New Zealand, who sold twenty percent each to Rick Martel and Maivia. The plan was to rotate talent from New Zealand to Hawaii every six months or so, to keep things fresh. The partnership lasted only three months, with Martel and Maivia having differing opinions on what was needed in Hawaii.

"He was a great guy. I loved that guy and everything, but he wasn't business. For him, it was about having a good time, his friends and all that. When it came down to business, we really didn't get along," said Martel. "He was over in Hawaii. He'd come in once a month for the big show, the Blaisdell, and he was really good. But Lia, heh heh, Lia was staying in Hawaii when I was there, and oh man, she'd come around, ugh, she was really tough to have around."

Following her husband's death in 1982, Lia kept the promotion going until 1988. She died in October 2008. That same year, Peter Maivia was twice honored, with induction into the Samoan Sports Association Hall of Fame in Auckland, New Zealand, and the WWE Hall of Fame.

The Maivia legacy would live on, of course, through grandson Dwayne Johnson, who took the name Rocky Maivia as a tribute to both his father Rocky Johnson and his grandfather. In 2002, The Rock made his first appearance in Hawaii at the Blaisdell Center, which sold out in four hours.

"It was his first time wrestling in Hawaii, in the same arena that his grand-father High Chief Peter Maivia, and his father Rocky 'Soulman' Johnson, and his uncle Ricky Johnson wrestled in years before him. The same arena that his grandfather tried so hard to sell it out . . . and now seventeen years later, his grandson comes in and makes his grandfather's dream come true," recalled The Rock's mother, Ata. "I was sitting at ringside, surrounded by family and most of my father's former wrestlers and students, as my son entered the ring, to a thunderous, emotional crowd. His body was covered with goosebumps as he pumped his heart and pointed upward, toward my father's resting place on Diamond Head, as if to say . . . Grandpa, this is for you. There wasn't a dry eye at ringside. We all felt my dad's smiling spirit."

THE MIGHTY IGOR

Many of pro wrestling's top babyfaces were multi-layered characters who could adapt to different styles and change from territory to territory. Dick Garza, though, employed a gimmick that was simple yet successful.

A former Mr. Michigan who parlayed his bodybuilding background into a successful career in which he was billed as the world's strongest grappler, Garza hit wrestling paydirt when he created the beloved character of The Mighty Igor.

Igor, initially known as Igor Vodik, was the ultimate babyface — a symbol of an innocent era in pro wrestling. The name alone conjures up an enduring image of the friendly, bearded, shaggy-haired Polish strongman, wearing cut-offs, a tattered tank top and a black beret, chewing on a kielbasa (Polish sausage) and waving to fans with a childlike naiveté.

Portraying a kind but simpleminded wrestler whose shoulders resembled oversized grapefruits, Garza knew what it took to connect to his audience, even if it meant dancing the polka, waltz, or a rousing Watusi. Sometimes he would bring a stuffed animal or a children's toy to the ring, and along the way would plant kisses on the foreheads of fans and ring personnel. And after a few weeks in a territory, he would amaze audiences with his feats of superhuman strength.

The Dearborn native, who was born July 16, 1931, began bodybuilding as a teenager in Detroit and was named Mr. Michigan in 1954. With pro wrestling not on his radar at the time, he went on to try out for the Mr. America and Mr. Universe titles.

"To enter those contests, you have to have a pretty good physical shape to yourself," said manager Percival A. Friend. "You need to be proportioned to the other athletes on the stage with you, and then you have to satisfy the judges in a multifaceted display that you were better than the rest. Unfortunately for bodybuilding, but fortunately for wrestling, the judges disqualified Dick in the Mr. America contest due to his huge arms. They measured twenty-one inches and did not fit proportionately with the rest of his body. He was also below that six-foot mark needed to make his spectacular body equal to other parts that were also hugely muscled."

Garza would soon after break into the wrestling business after punching

ROGER BAKER

Photographer Earle Yetter scurries out of the way of an angry Mighty Igor.

out the rugged Brute Bernard while the two were exercising at a local gym. "He was working out in George Jacobs' gym on the incline bench with 120-pound weights when Brute Bernard walked past a couple of times and finally whacked him (for no reason apparently), despite Garza's warning," wrestling historian Mike Lano recounted of a 1998 conversation with Garza. "Garza did not like Brute. Brute was a bully who'd spit on a guy's steak if he wanted to eat it. At any rate, Garza rose and clobbered Bernard on the jaw, laying him out."

"He's layin' there and he don't get up," recalled Garza. "I thought I'd killed him."

"Evidently," said Lano, "Bernard lay unconscious for five minutes until Jacobs got him to come around. When he did, Brute was furious and demanded Jacobs, 'Get that S.O.B. to meet me at the Park Avenue Hotel.' Garza showed; Brute never did."

Bert Ruby, a wrestler-turned-promoter, heard about the incident and recruited Garza for the ring. Ruby had seen the bodybuilder at the Mr. America contests during a talent hunt and, while Garza was not impressed with the thought of traveling to make a living, preferring to stay near his Dearborn farm, the lure of making big money was appealing.

"Fans loved him and were constantly running up to him to grab onto those twenty-one-inch arms," said Friend. "He neither wore fancy outfits into the ring nor was he explosive on the microphone during interviews. Later in his career, when Bert Ruby went on WXYZ-TV in Detroit, Dick's career really took off. He was exposed to more of an audience than ever before and began making more money than he had ever made."

Years later Ruby's son, Rob, would recall just how strong Garza was in recounting an incident that had occurred forty years earlier. The then sixteen-year-old was driving Garza to a show and, glancing into the rearview mirror, observed his passenger perform his customary stress-relieving ritual in the back seat: popping the links off a thick, steel chain with his mammoth thumbs. By the time Ruby had driven Garza to his match, the car was littered with busted links. "They were like worry beads for him," said Ruby. "The other wrestlers thought he had the strongest hands in the world."

Ruby also recalled his brother, Allen, driving Garza to a wrestling show. "They got cut off by some people who were taunting them — it was a very bad scene. Dick reached into their car and pulled off the steering wheel, which was pretty effective."

Garza, who won a regional title in Michigan in 1957, captured his first major title, the Los Angeles version of the international tag team championship, with Eric Rommel in 1962. But his career would take off just a couple of years later when he met Ivan Kalmikoff (Edward Bruce), an old veteran who had been part of a successful Soviet heel duo in the '50s and early '60s with "brother" Karol Kalmikoff (Karol Piwoworczyk). Kalmikoff would help create the "Igor" gimmick along with Garza and AWA champion/promoter Verne Gagne, and would serve as Igor's spokesman, confidant, and "father figure," taking his pro-tégé from territory to territory where Igor would perform his strongman stunts at matches, television shoots, shopping centers, and fairs.

One of his favorite feats of strength involved a car. "Richard would put his back against a wall, and his manager would get in the car and start the car," recalled his widow, Donna Garza. "Richard would keep it from crushing him by pushing back with his legs." Igor also would lift a truck on a pulley, break chains, bend iron bars, and have cement blocks broken over his head with a sledgehammer.

A 1967 *Wrestling Revue* profile on the wrestler reflected just how popular Igor was. "Who needs Batman and James Bond anymore? We've got Igor. He's a live folk hero, and lively. Wants to give everybody he meets a big bear hug. Can Batman pick up a 1,850-pound Volkswagen by himself? Igor can. He can even lift it when it weighs 2,350 pounds with two men in it. What would happen if somebody tried to break a cement block on Bond's head with a sledgehammer? Well, 007 might be a little worse for wear. But it doesn't even faze Igor."

Garza, five-foot-nine and nearly 300 pounds of pure muscle, was limited in the ring because of his gimmick, but with his amazing strongman act, it really didn't matter. "He would play tug of war with as many as ten people from the audience and win," recalled Friend. "He also did as many as ten push-ups with huge farmers weighing as much as 350 pounds on his shoulders. Then, he would rise and clap his hands together like a kid that had just been given a present at Christmas time."

Using the bear hug as his finisher, Igor held the Omaha version of the AWA world heavyweight title for a week during 1965 before dropping the belt back to Maurice "Mad Dog" Vachon. A year later he took the AWA Midwest heavyweight title from Bob Orton Sr.

He was a star in virtually every territory in which he appeared, including his home area of Detroit where he worked major programs with brawlers such as The Sheik, Bull Curry, and Pampero Firpo. He held that area's version of the NWA tag team title with Hank James in 1975. Titles were few and far between, though, since Igor was considered more of an attraction who didn't need to wear a belt to draw.

He was a top star for Eddie Einhorn's IWA in the mid-'70s, where he was most noted for his bloody feud with Bulldog Brower, but was recruited by Jim Crockett in 1977 in a raiding of the remnants of the IWA, which by that time had become a small independent in the Carolinas running opposition to Crockett.

In the Mid-Atlantic area, Mighty Igor is fondly remembered for his 1977 feud with The Masked Superstar (Bill Eadie) and manager Boris Maximilianovich Malenko (Larry Simon). A red-hot angle in which The Superstar smashed Malenko's lit cigar into Igor's eye spurred one of the top moneymaking programs in the territory. Garza sold it so well that his vision suffered as a result. "Even when it got better, he went and got sandpaper and scarred up his eye," said Eadie. "He wore this big patch to the extent that it almost cost him his vision. He wore it for almost six months. But people sure remember that angle."

Garza's "Mighty Igor" character was childlike, simple, and innocent, and the formula got him over wherever he appeared. "He lived the gimmick," said Eadie. "When he was out in public, he was Igor. When he was in the ring, he was no different. I have nothing but good memories of him. He was a very good businessman. We didn't have that much time to talk, but I know that over the years he made some good purchases in Florida. He made quite a few good investments and bought up a lot of property."

"Behind the goofy lovable character that Dick Garza brought to the ring as The Mighty Igor was a soft-spoken man with the mind of a Wall Street stockbroker," echoed Les Thatcher. "For all the craziness displayed in the ring and on camera, the former Mr. Detroit bodybuilder invested in the stock market and worked toward an early retirement."

Dick Garza celebrates a birthday in 1961.

"He was a very gentle man," Garza's wife told the *Detroit Free Press*. "Kids just loved him. When he was down in the Carolinas, there was a young boy who had leukemia and was dying, and his big wish was to see my husband. Richard went up to the hospital to see him, and they said it helped make the boy live longer."

Ivan Putski (Joe Bednarski) later adopted Garza's gimmick and became a star in his own right during the '70s. But it was never as effective as the original. "He stole it," claimed Eadie. "It was something good, but Ivan was never as good as Igor. Ivan was a very obnoxious person. He just saw the gimmick. The most important ingredient was liking people, and Igor liked people. I guess it's flattery if somebody stole it, but he didn't do well with it."

One of Garza's last major programs was with an up-and-coming Hulk Hogan in Florida in 1981. "Mighty Igor could draw money quickly," said Dory Funk Jr., who along with promoter Eddie Graham brought Igor into the territory for a program with Hogan. "We put him on television sitting in the audience with the wrestling fans. He cheered for the good guys and booed at the bad guys and loved waving at the camera . . . Everyone loved Mighty Igor from the start.

"On the third week, The Mighty Igor performed his feats of strength,"

ROGER BAKER

Ivan Kalmikoff slams a sledgehammer down on a concrete block on Igor's skull.

Funk continued. "With great fanfare, he bent a steel bar between his teeth, charged a trash can with six wrestlers bracing against it (naturally they all fell on their rear ends), and stood steadfast in the ring while three men on each side pulled on a rope wrapped around his neck. While pulling with all their might, The Mighty Igor reached out and grabbed the rope and gave it a mighty pull, and all crashed into each other. Now the need was there for someone strong to face The Mighty Igor."

Funk made the call to Hogan, who lived in Tampa at the time and was in between tours of Japan, but still wanted to have a successful run in the Florida territory where he grew up as an athlete and musician. "Hulk shook my hand and said, 'Brother, I will work my tail off for you. All I want is the opportunity to work in my home territory and be free to show what I can do.' What more could a new booker ask for? Hulk and Mighty Igor popped the territory drawing sellout crowds all over Florida and giving us time to establish other wrestlers who could take over later."

Garza spent the latter years of his career working in the Midwest and the Caribbean. His final stint with a major company was with Puerto Rico's WWC in 1987 when he feuded with Kareem Muhammad (Ray Candy) and briefly held the Caribbean title.

Garza, who battled heart problems at the end of his life, died of a heart attack at the age of seventy on January 7, 2002, in a Detroit hospital, leaving behind his wife Donna and a son Eric.

"If you were his friend, you were a friend for life," said Friend.

SONNY MYERS

The stitches on Sonny Myers' stomach constitute absolute proof that no matter how many people love you, there's always someone out there who doesn't. The knifing — perhaps the most gruesome and best-known in professional wrestling lore — took place in Angleton, Texas, on June 23, 1951, after a match with Rito Romero. It's a tale that has grown through the years. "His intestines dropped to the ground," claimed Mad Dog Vachon. "He held his guts and he walked maybe 200 yards to the dressing room, which was in another building," said referee Tommy Fooshee. Neither Mad Dog nor Fooshee was there.

Myers' own recollection of the stabbing, which resulted in more than 100 stitches (a number which grew over time with every retelling), is as colorful and cantankerous as he was. "The son of a bitch was about eighteen inches, right around my belly," he recalled in 2006. "I beat him and I was walking to the dressing room and this goddamn Mexican or whatever he was — I think he was a Mexican — he run by me and put a knife in me and cut my tights, cut my jockstrap, cut my pants off. I've got the pictures of it. Shit, there was no hospital around there. I waited until somebody took me to a doctor's office and then he put me in a hospital in another town."

There was always another town for Myers, who would parlay his wrestling success into the traveling Sonny Myers Carnival; a controversial stint as sheriff of Buchanan County, Missouri; a job at a car dealership; various wrestling promotions and gyms to train wannabes; and even time as a greeter at a Wal-Mart.

Harold C. (Sonny) Myers was born in 1922 in Savannah, Missouri, and grew up on a farm. As a youth, the six-foot-two, 235-pound Myers played a lot of basketball at the local YMCA. One night in 1943, he stopped to watch the wrestlers work out, which led to a chance meeting with the local promoter. "I walked in there and said, 'Jesus Christ, let me out of here!' And Gust Karras looked at me, and he laughed. He used to smoke a pipe all the time, and, boy, he started puffing on that pipe, and I said, 'My God, how does anybody get a breath in here?' He said, 'They do. Pretty soon, you'll never know it. Once you get in a building where you've got three, four, five thousand people, everybody's smoking, you don't pay any attention to it.' And he was right."

It took some time and convincing for Myers to make it, however. After two years at the University of Missouri, and while employed at the Swift's meat packinghouse, he started attending the matches in 1947 (the same year he would marry another wrestling fan, Elaine), and would get so enthralled that he and a friend would get kicked out week after week for getting overly excited and trying to get into the ring. Eventually, both youngsters were invited into the fraternity.

The clean-cut, fair-fighting Myers succeeded where his friend didn't. "I can't think of anybody who did more with less of a body than Sonny Myers," recalled Dick Brown, son of Myers' hero, former world champion Orville Brown. "They used to call him 'Bag Of Bones.' He got over very well in St. Joe, and he did in other places too. He really was a junior heavyweight, and should have been a junior heavyweight probably."

Mad Dog Vachon said that he was often asked if he knew Sonny Myers, but he didn't meet him until Sonny was old and refereeing in Kansas City. Vachon later saw tapes of Myers and knew why they asked. "He was so handsome. That's why so many women asked me, 'Where's Sonny Myers?' They loved him, he was such a nice looking man." *Wrestling Revue* once plugged Myers as "college-bred, smooth, and handsome as porcelain."

Agile and quick, the "Missouri Meteor" was known for his Atomic Drop and the dreaded Japanese Sleeper. Myers was always willing to demonstrate the mysterious sleeper on newsmen and non-believers. It was his way of proving, as he swore in 2006, that his "wrestling wasn't pre-determined." In Indianapolis in 1961, he became Sonny Weaver, partner to another upstart youngster, Johnny Weaver, who stole the sleeper — er, Weaver Lock — from Sonny the same way Myers had lifted it from the Japanese villain Mr. Moto.

Myers built an incredible in-ring career. He was a fourteen-time Central States champion, the NWA Missouri champ, a five-time champ in Texas, and held tag belts with Dizzy Davis, Pat O'Connor, Leo Garibaldi, Larry Chene, and Bobby Graham. "I wrestled and had so many belts, so much that you forget," Myers admitted.

Forgotten by history and circumstance — and devious promoting, perhaps — was Myers' brief run as a recognized world champion. He defeated Orville Brown in November 1947 for a version of the belt. However, in early 1948, the National Wrestling Alliance was formed, and recognized Brown as its first champion, leaving Myers' reign confined to the history books.

His legacy lived on through a lawsuit, however. Myers sued Des Moines promoter P.L. (Pinkie) George and the National Wrestling Alliance for $600,000 in an anti-trust action. Myers' contention was that the alliance and George had a monopoly on wrestling and had caused him financial damage. The feud with George dated back to 1953.

More than forty years later, George's name still irked Myers. "The no-good son of a bitch, he would try to book everybody upside down. I just got goddamn tired of it. You just can't do that. If you're a wrestler, you're a wrestler; you're not a goddamned shotgun man. The idea that he was doing wrong because he'd book you with somebody, and then when you'd go up there, you're all cranked up for your opponent, and what do you think

Sonny Myers signs another autograph.

he does? He changes them all the time. You just can't do that. He was just a no-good S.O.B."

Myers lost the first court case in December 1958, won the retrial in January 1962, and was awarded $150,000, but then the entire case was locked in appeals and dismissed in March 1964.

Lou Thesz, like many of Myers' peers, followed the trial(s), and in an interview in *Whatever Happened To . . . ?* in 1999 talked about what he had heard: "Pinky George did a stupid thing. He said, 'I'll see that you never wrestle anywhere again.' That's it . . . bingo! After that, they all had to sign a consent decree that they would not be involved in any restraint of trade."

But historians like Tim Hornbaker contend that the trial really didn't make a difference, and it is unlikely that Myers ever saw any settlement monies. "Myers winning the court case [in January 1962] looked like a monumental achievement, evidence that a single wrestler could stand up to the powerful NWA monopoly, but in reality, his actions had little impact on how the Alliance did business," said Hornbaker.

It wasn't Myers' only run-in with the law, either. Colleagues can throw out tales of Myers' shiftiness with a restaurant check, or sleight of hand in a convenience store. "There was a bandito from the word go. I've got a thousand, million stories on him," claimed Ed Wiskoski (Colonel DeBeers, Mega Mararishi), who grew up knowing of the legend, and then got to spend time around Myers. "You talk to the old guys that were in the business with him, and he was just a con artist."

So perhaps it is not a surprise that his election as sheriff for Buchanan County ended badly. In January 1974, after five years on the job, thirty-four indictments were handed down by a grand jury against the sheriff, as well as more indictments against his son and selected deputies. According to Mark Sheehan, editorial page editor of the St. Joseph News-Press, "The heart of the charges accused the sheriff of billing the state for phantom guards during the transportation of inmates. Ultimately, Sonny agreed to leave office. The authorities agreed to seal the case against him."

Like his wrestling career, Myers' years as a public servant bring out stories as well. The one told the most, perhaps, is his bust of a long-tolerated illegal cockfighting ring in southern Buchanan County. "I went there one time. You couldn't even see the building until you were right up next to it. It had black tar paper around it. But inside it, it was all bright lights and everything else," said Wiskoski. Myers decided to go after the illegal cockfighting and get some publicity; he and his deputies busted it and arrested thirty-five people. "The magistrate court was overflowing Monday morning," Bob Slater, former St. Joseph News-Press managing editor, said in Myers' obituary following his death on May 7, 2007, after a two-month illness. "Sonny was not one of the good ole boys."

The dead roosters went into storage. "By the time it was all said and done, and about a year's worth of trial, all the county ended up getting out of it was a big bill for the cold storage of the dead cocks," laughed Wiskoski. "He ended up with egg on his face there."

As a wrestler, Myers competed off and on up until about 1980, at which time he helped out here and there as a referee in the Central States territory based out of Kansas City. (Having had both knees replaced, Myers was not exactly known for flying across the ring.) He also trained wrestlers — using the gym at Lord Littlebrook's St. Joe home — and promoted the occasional show. Myers figured he had fifteen to twenty people come through his door asking to be trained. Myers shared a tale of his own: "When I put the squeeze on them, they say, 'Hell, what are you trying to do, kill us?' 'No, I'm not trying to kill you. I'm trying to make things so that you can win.'"

PAT O'CONNOR

January 9, 1959, saw the crowning of a new National Wrestling Alliance world heavyweight champion, as New Zealand–born Pat O'Connor beat Dick Hutton in Kiel Auditorium in St. Louis. It says a lot about the state of the business at the time that the title change was witnessed by a crowd of only 4,896. But the swap was about more than putting the belt around the waist of a more popular performer. O'Connor brought a new and absorbing style to the championship, combining a solid amateur background with a flair that drew fans to the edges of their seats, much like Dory Funk Jr. and Jack Brisco, whom he'd help train as future NWA champions. He wasn't a high flyer, but came across as a skilled athlete who excelled at slipping in and out of holds and creating something out of nothing. Based on the reviews, the NWA brass had to feel it made the right call in O'Connor when he wrestled in Toronto a week after dropping Hutton. "Yes, Virginia, there is a Santa Claus. How else can you account for O'Connor replacing Dick Hutton as NWA champion?" wrote *Globe and Mail* sportswriter Steve York of Toronto. "O'Connor bounces around, has more color and is more expressive than the phlegmatic, stolid Hutton, who does everything deliberately. Besides which, Pat is as good a wrestler as Hutton."

When you talk to O'Connor's friends and opponents, the little things he did to draw audiences into his matches become clear. Long-time star Paul DeMarco, who called him "a beautiful wrestler to watch," described a favorite stratagem. "Most people will just take a hold and they hang on to it. But he didn't do that. He put emphasis on it," DeMarco said. "Like if he grabbed your wrist to twist your arm, then he'd walk around your body to twist it even more. So he was adding more to it than anybody else could even think of doing. He was very dramatic, very, very dramatic in wrestling . . . And very simple. No bumps." Ed Wiskoski worked a lot with him in the late 1970s and early 1980s in St. Louis and Kansas City, Missouri, where O'Connor owned a piece of both offices. O'Connor was fifty-five at the time, but "Easy Ed" said he still had the magic touch, at least if he wanted to. "Starting out, he'd do a couple of cute moves on you, and he'd say, 'Cut me off and get a hold, and then we'll go to work.' He'd sell the hold, be it a front-arm scissors or a front facelock, and he'd try 10,000 times to get out of it; he'd make it once, and you'd snatch him back in somehow with a heel move. He had little gimmicks; he'd do one to you, and you'd go, 'How'd you do that, Pat?' 'Ah, it's an old secret.' But he was the only one that did 'em."

O'Connor's decade-long ascent from the reaches of amateur wrestling in New Zealand to the top of the pro world culminated with his NWA title win. Verne Gagne outranked O'Connor in national prestige as a fan favorite, but Gagne's claim as U.S. champion sharply divided NWA leaders and sparked a rivalry with former world champ Lou Thesz. O'Connor had NWA President Sam Muchnick of St. Louis in his corner, and his background suggested he could discard potential troublemakers if he had to defend himself. Just ask the sheep back in New Zealand. After he won the title, he attributed his success in a New Zealand sports magazine in part to the strength he gained from shearing sheep. "If you think it's easy to wrestle one of those squirming, twisting, 200-pound sheep to the ground and then clip it — just try it," he said.

Born August 22, 1924, in Raetihi to a strict Catholic family, O'Connor served briefly in the New Zealand Air Force, and then took a job as a black-smith in Wanganui to finance his interests in wrestling and rugby. Little known nationally, he started to turn heads as a runner-up at the 1947 New Zealand wrestling championships and then moved to Wellington so he could work with Anton Koolman, a one-time Olympic wrestler from Estonia and New Zealand's top trainer. Koolman helped him beef up to about 230 pounds, and O'Connor won the New Zealand heavyweight championship in 1948 and 1949, though a quick and surprising loss to Australian Jim Armstrong at the 1950 British Empire Games exposed his lack of experience on the international scene. No matter — veteran pro and agent Joe Pazandak was touring New Zealand in the summer of 1948 when he spotted O'Connor and marked him down as a find for the Minneapolis wrestling office. Dave Cameron, the authority on New Zealand wrestling, skipped school in 1949 to go to Gisborne and watch him in the New Zealand amateur championships; he followed O'Connor during his whole career. "He was immensely popular with the ladies as a good-looking young wrestler with a terrific body and he could fly around the ring," Cameron said. O'Connor came to the United States in August 1950, working for Tony Stecher's Minneapolis-based promotion and training with Gagne, Len Levy, and David Bartelma, the wrestling coach at the University of Minnesota, before his first recorded match on September 14, 1950.

He stayed almost exclusively in the Stecher territory through April 1952, when his career took off thanks to exposure on TV wrestling from Chicago. In June, he was the fan's choice when he wrestled and lost to Thesz before 12,283 in Chicago's Wrigley Field. He became a familiar face in the United States and Canada — one paper called him the "beau ideal" of the game — and he toured across

North America in the 1950s. He held the British Empire title, a Toronto-based championship, for more than a year in 1956 and 1957, and was greeted as a hero during a two-month undefeated swing of New Zealand where he wrestled Don Beitelman (Curtis) nine times in four weeks.

Nineteen sixty-one marked the first time two New Zealanders squared off for the NWA world title when Abe Jacobs wrestled O'Connor in New York. "In my opinion, not because he was from New Zealand or anything like that, he was one of the best pros," said Jacobs, who wrestled O'Connor several times after that, including matches where

COURTESY OF SCOTT TEAL/CROWBAR PRESS

The classy Pat O'Connor.

O'Connor worked as a subtle heel. "Every move he did looked great. I never saw Pat in a bad match." But O'Connor's time on top saw the NWA pinched in several strategic places that affected perceptions of him as the top wrestler around. In the Midwest, Gagne and his backers bought Stecher's operation, formed the American Wrestling Association in May 1960, and in something of a ruse identified O'Connor as its first champion. He didn't defend that title within ninety days and Gagne took it over. Montreal promoter Eddie Quinn was feuding with the NWA, so O'Connor never worked in that hotbed as champ. In the East, O'Connor wrestled for Vincent J. McMahon's Capitol Sports promotion a few times. But flashier attractions like Antonino Rocca, Ricki Starr, and Rogers ruled that roost. A dig from Oscar Fraley of United Press International, one of the country's best-known sports columnists, summed up the situation. "Bulletin! Pat O'Connor is the current world's wrestling champion," he wrote two years and two days into O'Connor's reign. "That's the word from [promoter] Willie (The Beard) Gilzenberg, who led a troupe of panting pachyderms into action

Pat O'Connor slams Buddy Rogers during their famous 1961 bout in Chicago's Comiskey Park.

in Miami. And I'll bet you thought it was Antonino Rocca, the shoeless Argentinian who makes $100,000 a year." On June 30, 1961, O'Connor put his belt on the line against Rogers in a Match of the Century at Comiskey Park in Chicago. Even then, a week of newspaper pre-match hype was all about Rogers' endearing smarmi-ness — he got a full magazine-style profile — while O'Connor, who actually lived in Chicago at the time, didn't garner a single quote. Rogers beat O'Connor in three falls in front of 38,622 fans, the largest crowd in the U.S. since the 1930s, with a whopping gate estimated at $141,000.

O'Connor received a consolation prize in 1962 when the NWA sanctioned him as U.S. champion, a title arranged by Muchnick, and he toured North America and Japan for the next two years. He and Thesz drew a sellout crowd to Kiel Auditorium in 1965 during Thesz's final run as NWA kingpin, and he gradually slid down the card in favor of in-your-face roughhousers like Fritz Von Erich and Dick the Bruiser. Even so, his work stood out from his contemporaries. "We all have heroes, right, and to me, Pat O'Connor was number one. He was so smooth, he was like silk. I really enjoyed working with him," said Canadian Leo Burke, who loaned him some wrestling gear one night; O'Connor in turn helped him get his work permit in the United States. "O'Connor would take your ear, or your finger, you'd swear he was tearing it apart. He was that good. And a very good storyteller as well." Roger "Nature Boy" Kirby fought him regularly after the championship reign and is full of praise for O'Connor the wrestler. "To me, he was a hell of a wrestler, almost strictly business," Kirby said. "He was so far above my head, especially at that time, but yet he was strictly business."

He bought a part of the Kansas City, Missouri territory with Bob Geigel in 1963, and added shares in St. Louis in 1972, so he had little reason to stray far from his home bases. As he aged, he lost the sharp tone of his youth, and Percival A. Friend, the infamous manager, said O'Connor was sensitive about it. "He got a little upset at me the first day I was in Kansas City. We were doing promos and I called him 'Fat Pat.' Phew. Wrong thing to do. Geigel, he laughed. He thought it was really funny. Pat turned around and smacked him, and said, 'I don't think it's a bit funny. I ain't fat!'" Friend said. "Some days he could be the greatest thing in the world, and the next day he'd be the biggest old fart you'd ever set your eyes on." After his 1968 divorce from his first wife, Pat wandered through a string of failed relationships and marriages with hangers-on to the point that his three daughters are older than some of their stepmothers. "I think he was a difficult man to get to know," said Larry Matysik, who liked him and worked side-by-side with him for years in the St. Louis office. "You would be wrong to call him outgoing. For him to do an interview today would have been very difficult. You would have had to script him."

You didn't want to cross him though. Wiskoski learned that when he saw Chuck O'Connor, the future Big John Studd, boast on TV that he would beat "that old man" in no time at all. The match was supposed to go twenty minutes to a draw, and Wiskoski shivered at the memory of what happened that night in Kansas City. "Poor old Studd, at the end of about six minutes, he was puking outside the ring. O'Connor dragged him back in to do some more shit to him, and he'd go outside and puke again. He couldn't beat him in twenty minutes, but the old man certainly made an example out of him."

If O'Connor was reserved and protective of the business, to his friend he was intensely loyal. Tom Andrews wrestled frequently as his tag team partner and they became close friends; Andrews accompanied him and other wrestlers on hunting trips for deer, antelope, and other game in Wyoming, where O'Connor sometimes served as a guide for celebrities. O'Connor started calling Andrews "bludger," and Andrews responded with the same line. "That's how we started every conversation — 'Hi, you dirty ol' bludger,'" Andrews said. When Andrews asked him the meaning of the word, the reserved O'Connor just waved off the question. Mervin O'Connor, Pat's brother, was more forthcoming when he flew into St. Louis from New Zealand for a memorial service after O'Connor died in 1990. Andrews, who'd made a hat band for Mervin at

Pat's request, noted that O'Connor never would explain what a bludger was. "He said, 'Well, a bludger is a leech.' I said, 'Oh, my gosh! He was calling me a leech?' He said, 'No, no, it had a little secret meaning to it — it was blood.' It was like blood brothers. So that really made me feel good."

In the end, O'Connor pretty much lost everything he had. Geigel, O'Connor, and Andrews owned a bar in the late 1970s and early 1980s in Kansas City that did well until a recession shuttered local businesses and factories and wiped out their client bases. Muchnick retired in 1981 and made O'Connor matchmaker in St. Louis, but the territories went bust and he did too with tax and financial problems. "I think it hurt him deeply. He had poured all his money into it," said his daughter Carly O'Connor, who was very close to him. In the last seven years of his life, though, he settled with Julie Browne in St. Louis and seemed quite content, especially when he had a pot and pan in hand, his daughter said. "After he retired, he did all of the cooking. He was happy about having a family life again." His last big moment in the ring came in November 1987 in an old-timers' battle royal at the Meadowlands in New Jersey, when he and Lou Thesz were the last two men standing; Thesz won. O'Connor also was a judge for a Ricky Steamboat–Ric Flair title match in 1989. A few months later, he was diagnosed with advance prostate cancer and died on August 16, 1990, at sixty-four. O'Connor was cremated and his brother returned his ashes for burial to New Zealand, where countryman Cameron said he still is a national wrestling hero. "I prefer to remember him as a young superstar from the early 1950s and I shall never forget him winning the world crown when world titles actually meant something."

JOHNNY POWERS

In 1965, Simpsons-Sears Limited created a Sport Advisory Council, choosing some of Canada's most famous athletes to endorse its sports equipment. There were hockey stars "The Golden Jet" Bobby Hull, Glenn Hall, and Pierre Pilote, the brother-sister figure skating team of Otto and Maria Jelinek, CFL lineman John Barrow, and a few others. The athletes had a say in the store's fitness line and made appearances at stores across the country.

Professional wrestler Johnny Powers, all of twenty-two years of age, was on the Council as well, and not only was it his first real introduction to the business world outside of wrestling and the wonders of retail marketing, it was also his justification for turning babyface in his home territory, the

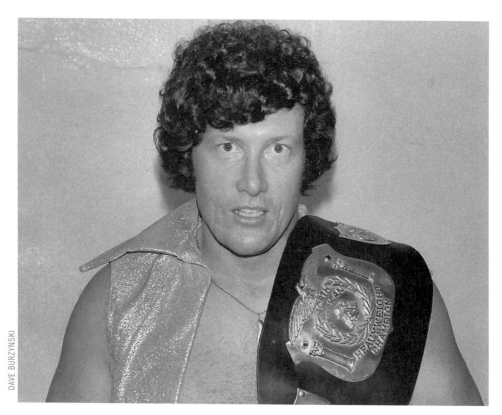

DAVE BURZYNSKI

Johnny Powers poses with the North American title.

Toronto–Detroit–Buffalo corridor. After all, you can't have someone designing sports equipment for Canadian youth and then whacking wrestlers with chairs.

"I got a good-sized contract with the sports equipment and they wanted me to be the Canadian Ted Williams, so I made the decision to go to babyface [in Toronto]," explained Powers. "But The Sheik was on top and [Bulldog] Brower was there and there weren't a lot of strong local on-top babyfaces that I had to compete against. Whipper [Watson] was past his prime."

The promotional jaunts made for a few memorable moments, too, said Powers. Getting disgusted with the "wrestling is fake" line of questioning, Powers, never one to keep his opinions to himself, would respond, "Off the record, fuck you. On the record, fuck you too." Soon, though, he had Pilote, the diminutive, battle-hardened Chicago Blackhawks defenseman on his side. "He sticks a finger right in the [interviewer's] chest and says, 'Let me tell you something, JP is one of the quietest nicest guys I've ever been around. He never brags on himself like that horse's ass Hull over here and he's just a cool guy to be around. If you don't shut up and ask him nice questions, I'll punch your fucking

Bruno Sammartino sizes up a young Johnny Powers.

head in.' He became my bodyguard," laughed Powers. With his "roadmap of a forehead" Pilote would warn the media ahead of time to avoid the other four-letter F-word, or they would face a punch to the head.

In all, it's a great example of how cerebral Dennis Waters was.

"He always had business in him. He was a smart guy anyway. It wasn't like he was saying, 'Ugh, I don't know what I'm going to do next.' He always had his finger in the fire for something," said Bruce Swayze, who in 1958 was covering the front desk over the lunch hour at Wentworth's gym on the east side of Hamilton, Ontario, when a tall, impressive kid from Delta Collegiate walked in with a towel around his neck, looking to learn how to wrestle. "Even when he was in the business, he was always looking to do something, and he always sort of kept his head above water like that. He was a bit of a chance taker, which you have to be in life to be able to be successful. You've got to take risks; you've got to take chances. He did that."

Waters was born March 20, 1943, and played hockey as a youth, until he grew into the six-foot-four wannabe — 285 pounds at age seventeen — who took a risk on an outlandish new career, his time at McMaster University studying geology having disenchanted him quickly.

After surviving the training in "The Factory," as Hamilton was known, he headed off to Detroit, still a teenager, where promoter Jack Britton dubbed him Lord Anthony Lansdowne, his Canadian enunciation apparently close enough to British royalty. At twenty, he was a full-time wrestler. On Detroit: "There were times when I really felt I was the mark, the kid from the east end of Hamilton going to the big city, downtown Detroit, the den of iniquity, with all the hookers and the hotel, giving five-dollar blowjobs to truck drivers and charging the wrestlers more, I think."

In Pittsburgh, he became Johnny Powers, with bleached blond hair, and got to the top of the cards, learning later in life that it was Bill Watts and Killer Kowalski who stood up to promoter Ace Freeman, saying, "Don't hurt the kid."

"He'd come in for the show and he was the driver for the midgets," said Watts. "Bruno and I were on a card and I said, 'Bruno, you've got to watch this kid. He's got a lot of box office.' So Bruno put a word in with Ace Freeman."

Powers created a style based on Lou Thesz's strong wrestling basics, Johnny Valentine's punch-mouth toughness, and Buddy Rogers' show-stopping pace. He meshed his tae kwon do skills with his natural frenetic wildness.

He was twenty-one years old when he was challenging WWWF champion Bruno Sammartino in Philadelphia, Pittsburgh, and Toronto. Young and ambitious, Powers was chomping at the bit. "I'm thinking, this is really pissing me off, this match, because I could do so much more with him if he'd only let me lead a little more or loosen up and trust me in the match, then we'd have a great match." Watts had a different take, saying the first bout with Bruno was great because Powers listened; the rest weren't because he didn't. "The second match, he goes in — Bruno worked a return [match] out of it — Johnny comes in and he's telling Bruno what to do. He's got the sunglasses on and he's like he's the damn superstar and he's not talking to any of us."

Having been exposed to a bigger world through the Sears sponsorship, Powers started thinking about promoting professional wrestling. He bought a couple of small Ontario towns from Toronto major domo Frank Tunney, and sidled up to Buffalo's Pedro Martinez for lesson after lesson. "Pedro Martinez was an unbelievable mentor to me. He taught me to shut my goddamn mouth and listen. Be a student. Be still, be a student. Be still, be a student. I did that for a long time. Then I was able to go into other businesses."

At this point, it becomes hard to differentiate Powers the promoter from Powers the wrestler, even though he continued to take bookings from St. Louis to Minneapolis to New York City. He was only twenty-four when he went into business with Martinez, and was the top star in Buffalo-based territory, which ran from central New York State through to Cleveland, Ohio, from 1968 to 1974.

Being a promoter so early meant "it overtook my career as a worker in the ring," admitted Powers, whom "The Boys" thought was standoffish — if they talked to him at all away from the ring. "I used to get heat — and I didn't try to get heat — but I'd walk into the dressing room, and I'm already thinking, 'This is match three, and the first and second matches weren't very exciting,' and I'm pissed at myself because I thought at least the second match would start to get the crowd going. I'd be walking in, thinking it's time to get my boots on. I never had time to socialize with the boys."

Through the *Championship Wrestling with Johnny Powers* program, Powers reached into the hearts of fans, facing down a wide variety of villains, utilizing his Power-lock leg hold to triumph. There were the traditionalists, like Johnny Valentine; the wildmen, like The Sheik and Abdullah the Butcher; and the unforgettable icons, like Ernie Ladd and Wahoo McDaniel. "I believe that separate from the fact I was an owner with influence, my longevity in a weekly territory primarily came from an adjustment to each heel's style," said Powers, "with me letting him play to his strengths and letting him get over."

The Buffalo/Cleveland promotion would evolve into the National Wrestling Federation and established its own world title in 1970 with, naturally, Powers as champ. Neither the title nor the promotion lasted long, but its influence continued.

In 1967, he did the first of more than thirty tours of Japan. Powers established a friendship/rivalry with Antonio Inoki, leading the Japanese star to gain control of the NWF title — and basically what was left of the NWF promotion — in 1973, making it a Japanese-based belt, the world title in New Japan Pro Wrestling, shut out from the NWA world title by rival All-Japan. "I had some great matches with Inoki, who was a heckuva guy, just from the ability to move in the ring and keep going. I had over fifty matches with Inoki through the years," said Powers, known as "The Iron Man" in Japan.

Back in the U.S., Powers and Martinez were presented with a major opportunity in the fall of 1975. Chicago businessman Eddie Einhorn had launched the first truly national wrestling promotion, the IWA, but he was having troubles and wanted out. With top-notch production values for its TV show and major names like Mil Mascaras, Ivan Koloff, and Ernie Ladd on board, the IWA is one of wrestling's biggest coulda-woulda-shoulda promotions. "At the end, they called me up because nobody could build a grassroots territory, [no one] understood that underneath a territory, underneath a television show, you'd better have some houses that are making some money," said Powers, who relocated to North Carolina and struggled for two more years to make it work, with almost as much action in the courtroom as the ring. He doesn't blame Einhorn for scooting "off into the bushes with his tail between his legs," protecting his interests in the TVS network, a group of local stations that began airing college basketball games nationally in 1960, and his minority ownership in the Chicago White Sox; but Powers does wish that Einhorn hadn't canceled a bunch of IWA TV contracts on his way out.

Unlike the NWF world belt, Powers kept the IWA one, and in 1982 lost it to Bulldog Brower in Nigeria, intending to retire. He was back the next year for a few matches in the Caribbean, capping a career of more than 5,000 matches in twenty-seven countries. For a time, he partnered with Sweet Daddy Siki on a wrestling school in Toronto, but by and large has had little to do with professional wrestling in the decades since.

Post-wrestling, he threw himself into various business enterprises, and sponsored and promoted pankration and mixed martial arts fights. Looking back, it is evident that Powers was on to a lot of great ideas, perhaps ahead of his time. He and Martinez formed a company to market their old wrestling footage, and syndicated their NWF show to Japan, Mexico, and the Armed Forces Network.

He learned the importance of consensus building from pro wrestling, and it translated into the business world. "You learn from the marketplace, and the storylines and a lot of products don't have that sense of emergency of every week you've got to come up with something to keep them tuned, keep them buying tickets," he said. "So I've been able to play that over into business. That's put me in good stead. I actually have lots of fond feelings for the business."

And he is certainly not forgotten.

Gene Weiss is the Chairman of the Ohio Athletic Commission, a former competitive amateur who ended up refereeing and wrestling a little for Powers in Cleveland, and lost some money on Powers' ambitious three-ring show at Municipal Stadium in 1972. Overseeing the couple of visits a year from World Wrestling Entertainment, Weiss harkens back to the NWF's glory days. "He was the guy that made it happen. Can you imagine the Cleveland Arena, our big arena, which is 10-12,000 people, and filling it every single Thursday? People were trying to break the doors to get in. There were riots, people were nuts," said Weiss. "He meant a lot to Cleveland."

Billy Robinson with the IWA title in Japan in 1974.

BILLY ROBINSON

The chess pieces move from territory to territory, and as fans, we see the results of the switch, but rarely the motive. Billy Robinson, the British star from Manchester, England, settled on Minneapolis and a home base of the AWA for a couple of reasons. For one, he didn't like the school system in Hawaii, where he'd been living for two years, or the easy availability of drugs, and with his son, Spencer, old enough to enroll, he sought stability. Robinson also wanted to be able to go east to Japan and west to Europe with relative ease.

His tour of Florida in 1975 was brought on not by a desire for sunshine but by the sad fact that the wife of his friend and "uncle" Karl Gotch had cancer, and he wanted to be nearby for support.

Earlier in his career, Robinson admitted that he would travel anywhere on the notion that there was someone there who could beat him. That explains trips to India, Australia, and just about every country in Europe. "These were the opportunities that were there," Robinson said. "They'd say, 'Well, this guy's pretty good over there, he thinks he's the best in the world.' So I went over and beat him."

Bringing it to the current day, the legend, who spent almost a decade learning the ins and outs of amateur wrestling and hooking in Wigan, England, now lives in Little Rock, Arkansas. It turns out that his son, Colonel Spencer Robinson, works at Camp Joseph T. Robinson, the 33,000-acre training facility of the Army National Guard.

Wigan's Snake Pit was the result of Great Britain's colonial history, said Robinson. "You had the greatest wrestlers of all time in that gym, basically caused by the British Navy. They went around the world, controlled most of the world for hundreds of years, and picked up stuff from all over the world and united it into one submission sport. When you got to the gym, all the old-timers would be there watching. If it was one of the old-timers, it was probably an ex-world champion, and if he took a liking to you, he'd pull you to one side and say, 'Try this, son, try that; don't do this, and don't do that.' It was just a great way to learn. They didn't teach you how to wrestle, they taught you how to learn."

Robinson, born in 1938, already had the pedigree, given that his great-grandfather was Harry Robinson, a bareknuckles boxing champion; his uncle Alf fought Max Baer and wrestled Jack Sherry in Belgium; and his father Harry was a light-heavyweight boxer. He seemed destined to become a boxer as well, until he injured his eye at age eleven and was unable to ever get licensed. At fifteen, he headed to Wigan from Manchester, where he worked in a wholesale fruit market, the biggest one in England, moving crates and bags of potatoes.

In 1960, he made his pro wrestling debut and quickly built a serious repu-tation. "Billy was one of a number of fighters who would never allow himself to be defeated unless he was convinced that man was capable of beating him," wrote the late Jackie "Mr. TV" Pallo in his autobiography. "A really gentle gen-tleman outside the ring, is Billy. But he could be a bit vicious inside it." He was constantly looking for a challenge, said Frank Earl. "He used to go around the dressing room and ask people, he said to Les Thornton and I, 'I hear you can block a bit.' I said, 'Yeah, not bad.' He said, 'Why don't you work with me?'"

"Billy Robinson was a first-class heavyweight English wrestler who had skill and strength and was a popular wrestler wherever he appeared," said British historian Ray Plunkett. "He was mainly a top-of-the-bill wrestler and was for a time British Heavyweight Champion, winning it from Billy Joyce."

In 1969, after meeting Dave Ruhl in Japan, Robinson left for Calgary, still the British Empire champion, where he was a hit. "His repertoire of quasi-amateur moves, such as suplexes and saltows, combined with the high-tech Euro style, made for a compelling hybrid — the likes of which fans in our neck of the woods had never been exposed to before and were captivated by," wrote Bruce Hart. But Calgary was where his reputation for being difficult to work with multiplied. Archie Gouldie walked out of the territory, giving up an NWA world title shot rather than work with Robinson.

"He wanted everyone in the world to think that wrestling was real because of his background," said Calgary headliner Dan Kroffat. "I hated the guy. He was a bully. He was an antagonistic sort of guy, he bullied guys, he stretched guys. He was really not a likeable guy. Then Robinson, if he had respect for guys who were shooters, of course he would give them great matches. He went to Minnesota where Verne Gagne was a shooter. He fit right in to Verne Gagne's thinking. But in Calgary, Jesus, nobody wanted to work with him. I had him seven nights in a row. It was the closest I ever came to quitting the business in my life. He just stretched me night after night."

Robinson will admit that he would shut down opponents he felt were unworthy of his talents. "Normally, it was the guys that were just showmen that were scared to death to get in the ring with me. It used to take me five to ten minutes to get them at ease so they'd work," he said. If they were scared to work with him, too bad. "That's their fault, not mine. I've never been scared of anybody. None of the guys from Wigan ever were."

After Calgary, Robinson spent two years in and out of Hawaii, and met Verne Gagne there, and the AWA promoter invited him to Minneapolis. There, Robinson was a genuine headliner, allowed to work with foes that could perform his style. "He was one of the real fine technicians. He was great on submission holds," said Gagne in 1994.

Nick Bockwinkel was one of those Robinson allowed to shine. "Nick was a genuine man, and a very, very good worker, excellent worker, one of the best," said Robinson. Bockwinkel told Whatever Happened To . . . ? that "Robinson was always a challenge, but I always looked forward to the matches I had with him. He was such an excellent technician. He would do things to me that sometimes I didn't know, and of course, one of his shortcomings was, he would always go for the extra move. It was like, no matter how well he thought he impressed the audience, he thought he had to make one more move to try to impress somebody." While based in Minneapolis, Robinson helped train wrestlers at Gagne's farm — including Ric Flair and The Iron Sheik — and was the co-lead, alongside Ed Asner, in the 1974 film The Wrestler. "Not only does he provide spectacular action in the ring, he shows excellent acting talents," reported Wrestling Monthly.

Foes often had a hard time adapting to his shoot/submission in-ring techniques. Ivan Koloff called Robinson "a real-life hooker, one of a kind," and put him in the same category as Edouard Carpentier and Mil Mascaras for their unique styles. "There were several guys like that who were in right great shape, and they're the type of wrestlers that you had to be on your toes and work hard to make a match. Not that they were difficult that way, it was just the idea that they were proud guys and you just didn't kick them around in the ring."

Besides his success in North America, Robinson is close to a deity in Japan, where he did countless tours, was the first ever International Wrestling Alliance

Billy Robinson uses a toehold, and pins the other leg with his arm, to add most of Paul Trudeau's weight to his own in a bridging press.

world champion, battled Antonio Inoki in a massive 1975 contest, and is a respected trainer. Karl Gotch was his entry into Japan, though the promoters didn't know that Gotch and Robinson's uncle had been great friends, and that Billy saw Gotch as an uncle. But that doesn't mean they always got along, stressed Robinson. "We had our differences, but we worked it out in the gym," he said. "If it had been in public, it would have been a street fight and we both would have been arrested."

Robinson's real fights are a big part of wrestling legend. The Rock likes to tell the story of his grandfather, Peter Maivia, brawling with Robinson in Japan in 1968, falsely crediting the High Chief for Robinson's eye loss. Then there's the incident with "Sailor" Ed White in the '70s. "Sailor White beat the shit out of him and pissed on him — and Billy Robinson was supposed to be the shooter," said Frenchy Martin. "Everybody thought he was a shooter, but once Sailor White beat him up, that was it. He had to go, and he left."

Robinson was always great friends with Lou Thesz, who always championed bringing legitimacy back to professional wrestling. Together, they started the Union of Wrestling Forces International in Japan. "Billy is a competitor to the core. It was his best asset and his worst enemy. He had to push himself and make everyone he wrestled look as bad as possible. Winning wasn't enough, Billy was into destruction," said Thesz in 1997, adding that he had "ultimate respect for his ability and spirit," and that "he is also more fun than a barrel of Aussies."

In North America, Robinson's career petered out in the early 1980s, just before the cartoonish WWF took off. "I'm a real wrestler. I believe in real wrestling. I believe in catch-as-catch-can wrestling. The show wrestling now has become pathetic. It's a complete show, and I just won't have anything to do with it," he said.

Instead, backed by trainer/author Jake Shannon, Robinson has carved out a living over the last number of years as a guest trainer at seminars from Japan to London, from Montreal to his regulars in Little Rock. He makes occasional appearances at fan fests, and was inducted into the Pro Wrestling Hall of Fame in 2011.

THE BIG, FRIENDLY TYPES

There's big and there's *big*. Wrestling has a long, rich history of pushing men that pushed the boundaries of their pants. Given its carnival roots, where the toughman competitions on the athletic shows led to professional wrestling's worked bouts, perhaps it was only natural for the carnival fat man to get invited along for the ride as well.

Haystacks Calhoun was indisputable king of wrestling's big men, if only from his ability to get press. After all, what reporter could resist trying to capture the ol' country boy in print? "Wa-a-l, let me put it this way. Ah'm too big to hide, 'n too fat to run. So 'ah only one chance. To stand and fight," the *Los Angeles Times* attempted in 1974.

The six-foot-four Country Boy Calhoun was usually billed from Morgan's Corner, Arkansas, at 601, give or take a couple of dozen pounds, and all his publicity listed him at 11-3/4 pounds at birth. Raised in Bloomdale, Texas, William Dee Calhoun played football in high school, and debuted in pro wrestling in November 1955, wearing overalls, with a horseshoe strung around his neck for luck. The bearded, scruffy hillbilly gimmick was hardly original in wrestling, but his size and friendliness helped keep him on the road until the 1970s, when his health failed, and diabetes caused a leg to be amputated in 1986. He died December 7, 1989, at age fifty-five.

There was a secret to using Calhoun, said Kansas City promoter Bob Geigel. "You'd bring Haystacks every week, and he wouldn't draw anything, but if you brought him in one time, every five or six months, he was an attraction." In fact, Calhoun even challenged Lou Thesz for the NWA world title on one occasion.

Haystacks Calhoun teams with the McGuire twins for a ring-testing bout in Detroit.

Abe Jacobs was Stacks' partner for years. "You used him in singles matches, and there was attraction there," he said. "If you used him in tag matches, somebody like myself could work around him, and then he could stay for a while." Matches would consist of bounces off his various doughy parts, leading to the inevitable Big Splash to end it all.

Jacobs said that Calhoun enjoyed piloting his custom-fitted vehicles, with the front seat way back and the steering wheel wedged in his massive belly. "He was a heck of a driver. He could drive for miles and miles."

Calhoun was well aware that he was in the public eye; after all, it's not like he could hide. "I try to be careful how I behave, particularly in front of kids. So many adults, particularly athletes, ignore the kids," he said in 1968. "I cater to them, which is why they love me. Kids look up to athletes, so I try to be nice to them and set them a good example. If I drink or cuss or carry on in public, I'm not setting a good example, am I?"

Other buildings with legs wrestled for years, like Man Mountain Mike, Haystack Muldoon, and Elmer Wiggins, but only a few ever approached Calhoun's fame — or frame.

Happy Humphrey's celebrity has endured during the years primarily because of his association with NWA world champion Harley Race, who, as a youngster breaking in, drove the 700-pound William J. Cobb from town to town in 1960, wrestling him frequently, and occasionally bathing him outside with a mop, liquid soap and a garden hose. "I drove Humphrey in a 1951 Pontiac that was custom made to fit him. The doors opened from the front to

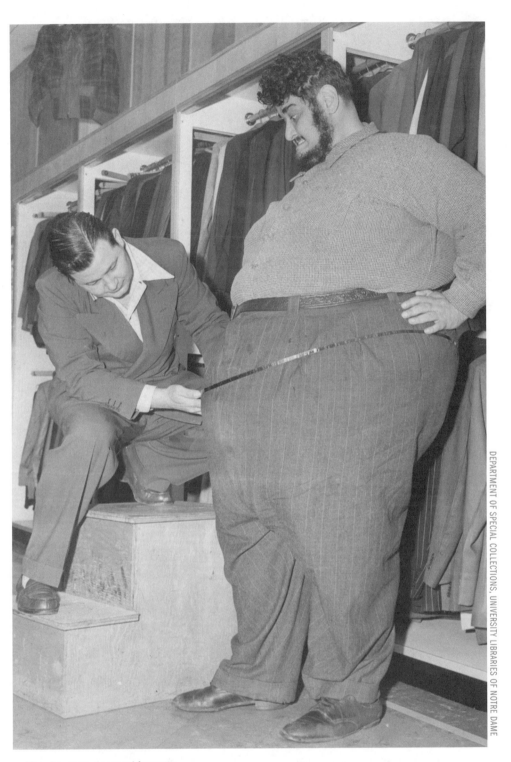

Blimp Levy gets measured for pants.

back, and the shock absorbers were re-enforced," wrote Race in his autobiography. A victim of a pituitary gland disorder, Cobb claimed to have weighed 23 pounds at birth and 150 pounds at age three. Humphrey started wrestling in 1953, and worked until the early 1960s, including a ring-straining series of bouts against Calhoun. In March 1963, while promoting small Texas towns, Humphrey wrote to Jack Pfefer: "Things here [in Texas] are fair, not getting rich, but eating good. You know I have to make the bundles to pay for my spaghetti & kosher pickles." Post-wrestling, he achieved fame for losing 570 pounds on a Medical College of Georgia diet, but later got back to about 440 pounds, where he felt more comfortable. Humphrey lived until 1989, working as a cobbler in the Faith Shoe Repair Shop — unable to go to school, he'd learned the trade from his grandfather at age six.

The tag team of twin brothers Billy and Benny McGuire (born McCrary) made for an unforgettable pairing, with the *Guinness Book of World Records* listing them at 814 pounds and 784 pounds respectively. The McGuire boys made papers by riding little Honda bikes to shows as a promotional gimmick. In a 1999 interview with Scott Teal's *Whatever Happened To . . . ?* newsletter, Benny McGuire said there was jealousy among the mountains. "Haystacks was jealous of me and Billy because there was two of us. I remember we'd go to the ring in a six-man tag and he would run to the ring to get ahead of us," he said, laughing. "We'd let him go ahead because he'd do all the match. He'd go to tag us and we'd just turn around on him."

As for The Blimp (Martin Levy), who had been working as the fat man in a Coney Island side show, he had the promotional wizardry of Jack Pfefer behind him in the 1930s and '40s. Pfefer pitched his services to the likes of Australia's Ted Thye in 1948: "Now, just remember that no living wrestler today can outdraw the human Blimp all that you have to do is use him as an extra few minutes exhibition and I am more than sure that the Blimp will sell out every arena where he will show as he has proven that in this country." The Boston-born Levy weighed around 625 pounds for much of his career. After he was forced to the sidelines, around 1950, he dropped from the limelight, and, when he died at age fifty-six in an Alabama trailer park, he was said to have weighed 900 pounds, with a 120-inch waistline.

In the 1970s and 1980s, big men like Jerry Blackwell (474 pounds), Abdullah the Butcher (360 pounds), and King Kong Bundy (400 pounds) broke the mold completely of what was expected of weighty ones, leading the way for world champion gargantuan grapplers like "Vader" Leon White (450 pounds) and "Yokozuna" Rodney Anoa'i (600 pounds).

With black hair, Reginald Siki was on the side of right.

SWEET DADDY SIKI

Sweet Daddy Siki is not one to reveal secrets. He won't tell his age or his real name. But when pressed, he will share hair tips.

"I was the first black guy to have blond hair. I was the first one. I could do commercials for Miss Clairol, because I've been bleaching my hair since '56, something like that," he laughed, praising the virtues of Lady Clairol Ultra Blue. "I am very fortunate with my hair, bleaching it that long and having a full head of hair — a full head."

Indeed, Siki is still as recognizable today in his late seventies (or is it his early eighties?) as he was in his heyday, memorably bumping around for his mentor "Nature Boy" Buddy Rogers, or strutting to the ring with his sequined vest, white gloves, sparkly, oversized sunglasses, and hand-mirror, "the ladies' pet and the men's regret."

Prepping for a booking in Toronto, he first bleached his hair while working in New York, heading into a Harlem beauty parlor to change his life forever. "I stepped out on the street, and you should have seen the cars stopping!" he remembered. "They're all looking. They'd never seen anything like me before, no sir, never seen anybody like me."

It was a long, segregated road to fame, however, for the native of Montgomery, Texas, who grew up in Los Angeles. Serving in the 2nd Division, infantry, in the U.S. Army, he rose to Corporal within two years, serving in Korea after the peace treaty was signed in July 1953, patrolling and keeping the peace. Before getting drafted, he had dabbled in wrestling lessons, having been a fan, but took it up in earnest after being discharged, enrolling in Sandor Szabo's wrestling school in Los Angeles. Though he never met Szabo, Siki learned the game from

Ray Ortega, and worked out with Louie Miller. After an initial hiccup with the California courts and trying to get his wrestling license despite his small size — 180 pounds, Siki got booked in Artisia, New Mexico, and made $13.50 in his debut in late 1955 under promoter "Elephant Boy" Tony Olivas, where he didn't need to be registered. Performing as Reginald Siki, the name of another black star from the 1930s, the five-foot-ten workout fiend got up to 230 pounds.

Athletic and blessed with stamina and bravery, Siki slowly started to make a name

DAVE BURZYNSKI

With a little peroxide, Sweet Daddy Siki is the man.

for himself. With his dark skin and dark hair, he was a babyface, teaming with other African-American heroes like Sailor Art Thomas on the broadcasts from Chicago's Marigold Arena. He was known for his leaping ability. "I used to practice, practice, dropkick, dropkick, dropkick," he said.

Siki was one of the first African-American heels, and wasn't scared to push the envelope. At one point, he changed his name to Mau Mau Siki, after the Mau Mau Uprising in Kenya, and was nearly hanged in Walla Walla, Washington. "I was the last one to leave the dressing room, and people were out there waiting for me. They had a rope up in the tree," he said. "When you're young, you do a lot of foolish things. I walked downstairs, laughing like hell. 'Ha, ha, you crazy people.' I walked right through them — I didn't run. One thing I learned, you don't run; you start running, that's a bad thing, they run after you and get you."

His villainy didn't develop in earnest until he mastered his craft as a babyface against his idol, Buddy Rogers, whom he'd befriended in Ohio. "He took me under his wing," said Siki, adding that it was Rogers who got him to the booming New York territory, and they spent three years in each other's company. Siki toppled Rogers for Columbus' Eastern Heavyweight title in February 1959.

The bout that stands out the most, however, was in Greensboro, North Carolina, with the Ku Klux Klan picketing outside and surrounding ringside. "When I walked out there, no lie, you could hear a pin hit the floor," said Siki. The referee told Siki not to throw even one punch. Rogers took it all in strut, and Siki was counted out in the finish.

Promoters weren't as forgiving when they learned of Siki's marriage to Ann, a Caucasian woman. His bookings dropped, as did his pay, and he retreated to the less prejudiced Toronto in late 1961.

In Canada, he earned his stardom with cross-country tours first in wrestling, then in his country and western band, The Irresistibles, in towns big and small, primping and picking away. And it was in Montreal where he was first dubbed "Sweet Daddy" Siki rather than Reginald Siki. He was a star in the Atlantic Grand Prix territory ("Ninety-nine percent of the women love me, one percent hate me, but they are the fat, ugly ones with no teeth; Leo Burke can have those ones"), throughout southern Ontario, and in Calgary, where Stu Hart used him regularly. "He did everything Gorgeous George did, except he was black," said Hart in 1997. "I'd never seen him in a bad wrestling match either." Mr. Irresistible was a wizard on the microphone, his nasal Texan twang enhanced by the arrogance.

Musically inclined, Siki cut a few singles as a whim when he was starting over in Toronto, and by the end of the '80s, he had four albums: three country and western and one rock 'n' roll. Both of his sons got involved in the music business. And Siki wrote his own theme song, too, "I Am So Proud Of What I See." The touring became a grind, though. "It's a big responsibility when you have to be the boss of three or four other guys," he confessed. Instead of touring, he bought himself DJ equipment and a karaoke machine, and took his act to parties and taverns across southern Ontario, hitting many of the little towns that he had wrestled in while working for "Bearman" Dave McKigney.

His wrestling career came to a close in 1987, but he stayed involved for a time, running a wrestling school with Johnny Powers and then Ron Hutchison. The biggest names to have benefited from his training were WWE stars Edge and Christian.

Looking back, Siki will say that one of the rare perks of the racially segregated life on the road was meeting other celebrities stuck in the same situation. Count Basie recognized him in a Chicago hotel, he partied with The Shirelles, and a young Cassius Clay hung around him for three days in Florida. He missed Muhammad Ali when the boxing great was in Toronto's Maple Leaf Gardens, but learned that George Foreman was a huge fan. "I went in the dressing room. George said, 'God, I remember you! I used to come see you wrestle in Dallas, Texas!' Can you imagine that?"

Ever careful of his money, Siki takes a calculator with him in the restaurant to figure out the tip. Though he doesn't actually have the first nickel he ever earned, as his friends are quick to quip, Siki is proud of what he has done. After all, it's a long way from hoping to find some fresh roadkill, like a rabbit, for dinner, or scrounging in garbage bins for food. "This is what I did to become who I am."

COURTESY OF SCOTT TEAL/CROWBAR PRESS

The graceful Ricki Starr.

RICKI STARR

Buddy Goldstein saw how Bernard Herman represented the improbable fusion of dance and fray long before Ricki Starr became a national sensation. Goldstein, Herman, and Don Emmons were scholarship students at Lalla Bauman's dance academy in St. Louis when they were tapped as stand-ins for a Russian Ballet performance of *Scheherazade* at the Kiel Opera House. They were essentially stage props clad in baggy pants, holding spears and lunging forward and backward on command. "I did not see Scheherazade signal to go back and I stood with my sword in her nose almost the entire ballet," Goldstein laughed. "She was really, really angry and the guy who was supposed to pay us our five dollars told us in his dialect, 'I'm not going to pay you.' Bernard picked him up and put him on the wall and said, 'I think you will.' He goes, 'Put me down. I'll pay.'"

Jete, body slam, glissade, drop toe hold, soubresaut, right cross . . . it was all the same to Starr, who delighted audiences in North America for a decade before taking his act to Europe for another long and successful run. Other wrestlers did not mind playing straight man to his elegant gyrations because he made them money. In one delicious quip, George Bollas, the Zebra Kid, wrote Starr's manager Jack Pfefer in October 1959, "Give Rickey Star [sic] my fondest, sexiest wishes. He's so cute, I wouldn't know if I should wrestle him or fu-- him. Ha ha." How entertaining was Starr at his peak? Dan Parker was a sports columnist for the *New York Mirror*, a crusader who did his dead-level best for years to expose the inner workings and unseemly practices of pro wrestling. But Starr brought a smile to his face. "He made the program jell," Parker wrote after Starr danced past Skull Murphy in February 1957. "Ricki Starr is different. There's nothing offensive about his routine. Besides being original, it is hilariously funny by comparison with the clumsy attempts at comedy that have become, like trachoma, a chronic disease of the mat."

Starr's gimmick was born of necessity. Pint-sized by the standards of pro wrestling, he struggled to get bookings from promoter Sam Muchnick in his hometown of St. Louis, despite an outstanding amateur wrestling background and the pleadings of his dad Joe, an ex-wrestler. "My size was against me," Starr admitted in 1961, putting himself at five-foot-nine and 199 pounds, which was decidedly generous. So he sought ways to stand out from the pack, and his interest in dance led him to the Bauman school around 1951. There, he trained strenuously five to six hours a night, alongside Emmons, a future Broadway star, and Goldstein, who said Starr actually wasn't all that great in ballet during their time together. "I think Bernard was a clever human being even back then," Goldstein said. "I think he knew exactly what he was going to do. He knew he wanted to be a professional wrestler and I think he needed that to step up into it, as an act. I think he thought about that, way back when."

Though he wasn't the Nureyev promoters made him out to be, Starr was remarkably lithe and supple, and continued to take lessons on his own dime while he was wrestling. His first regular appearances as a pro were in 1952, and there were times, he said, when he would have been better off as a waltz instructor. "The first year in this business I spent thirty-five percent of my gross income on medicine and hospitalization," he said in one interview. "I was constantly being treated for something — sprained ankles, shoulder separations, wrenched neck, and mat burns." Taking a deep breath, he accentuated his character in 1954, in west Texas of all places, by donning purple ballet slippers, a matching leotard, and slinking along the ropes like a cat rubbing its back against a wall. Bingo! "I've been mixing ballet and wrestling all my life," he told the *Los Angeles Times*. "But it wasn't until I put them together in the ring that I became a success." Starr's fame skyrocketed and he headed to the Big Apple to capitalize on it, lining up the quirky, hard-charging Pfefer as his front man. Promoter Willie Gilzenberg told Pfefer he'd landed the goose that laid the golden egg. "Ricki Starr is the biggest thing to hit New York in years. Properly spotted — not too often in the same clubs — he would sell out again and again. And, what a performer, when he wishes to be," he wrote.

Starr's name was on the marquee from the time he tripped the light fantastic on the East Coast in 1957. "He was fun to watch. He made people laugh with the way he'd outsmart the villains with his ballet moves," said Ted Lewin, a veteran of New York mat wars in the '50s. "He has this monster charging at him and

Ricki Starr takes the battle to Lenny Montana.

he pirouetted away and then dropkicked him or did those high judo kicks. He convinced you that he was really able to beat these guys even though he was half their size." There was a reason he projected that image — he really could beat them if he abandoned the theatrical pretenses. Herman grew up wrestling at the Young Men's Hebrew Association in St. Louis, following in the footsteps of his dad, whom an Alton, Illinois newspaper once called a "professional anguish artist." At fifteen, he sparred in Stillman's Gym in New York, according to one account, but went back to the Midwest after getting his brains beat in for little money. While his Soldan-Blewitt High School didn't have a wrestling team, Herman made a mark at the club level. He represented the St. Louis YMHA at 165 pounds in the 1949 AAU nationals, losing in the first round to a wrestler from Michigan State. The next year, again wrestling out of St. Louis, he placed fourth at 175 pounds. In 1951, he had his best showing in the nationals, winning five of six matches at 175 pounds, good for a third-place finish. By then, he was in Lafayette, Indiana, the home of Purdue University, and he'd be advertised in the future with exaggeration as a Boilermaker grappler. But he did hook up with Purdue alum Ray Gunkel, an All-American and AAU national champ, to hold the Texas tag team title, and father Joe captained Starr's team to win a $1,000 pot in a giant team match competition in May 1953 in Galveston, Texas. His brother Mark Lowell Herman followed him into wrestling, though with limited success. "Backstage, he was like any other guy," said Dick Steinborn. "He thought of himself as an artist. He'd go to the corner, stretch and check his nails, then he was on you like a caged animal. A guy would be beating on him and Ricki'd lean up against the ropes, and ask the audience, 'Can you believe what this guy is trying to do to me?'"

Starr has made himself scarce for years, informing old friends and schoolmates that he is out of the publicity game. But a number of his letters to Pfefer have survived at the University of Notre Dame library, and excerpts help to pull back the curtain on the phenom that was Ricki Starr, a guy whose inventiveness earned him $500 for a few minutes of work, as long as his bookings were handled with care:

- Just a note to make a few points I didn't make the last time we talked. #1) It's IMPERATIVE that you get all matches ONE FALL, at least for the time being. It's very important. #2) I'll leave it to you to pick out "cooperative" opponents, ones who'll go along with my "Dreck." (September 1958)
- There was a lot of this sweet talking you mentioned about coming back right after Milwaukee for two more weeks. Jack as I said there's not a lot going so I don't think it would be too advantageous to come right back and expose our novelty attraction too much. The people in all the places went WILD. They love me as long as they can't have me too much. Farshtaist! (November 1958; the term is Yiddish for "Do you understand?")
- I agree with you only 1/2 when you say I am a sucker. Let's compare bank books. Mr. America #1 [Gene Stanlee] — 0. Mr. America No. 2 [Steve Stanlee] — 0. Ricki Bean — $0,000. But here's where I agree when you say I am a sucker. Jack Pfefer (1 and only) — $000,000,000. When you teach me that trick, oh boy! (September 1960)

Starr knew that his routine had a half-life and when he noticed that the gate proceeds were slipping, he scratched his showbiz itch. A fall 1960 tour of Texas provided the impetus — $35 in San Angelo, Texas; $25 in Borger, Texas; $25 in Hereford, Texas; $20 in Santa Fe, New Mexico — "and I spent $22 flying in!" he sighed. "I'll be eating nothin' but pickles." He edged into the entertainment world by inking a record deal with RCA, and appearing at the Teenage Jamboree

Rock 'n' Roll Show in Long Island, singing his song, "Shooting Star." He landed a TV gig in an episode of *Mr. Ed*, a show about a talking horse, on January 7, 1962. Shortly after the episode ran, Starr embarked on a months-long world tour, with stops in Japan, Hong Kong, Thailand, India, Egypt, Greece, Italy, and Switzerland. Reappearing on *Mr. Ed*, Starr got a few chuckles as a skilled horse groomer too bashful to cut women's hair. Director Arthur Lubin said Starr was so well received that his production company attempted to develop a series centered on him for the 1963 season, though that didn't materialize.

In 1964, Starr promenaded to Great Britain, where his routine was fresh and delightful. Tony Rocco, wrestling in Europe at the time, was instrumental in his trans-Atlantic passage. He'd seen Starr during a swing through Canada in 1963, and told promoters Paul Lincoln and Ray Hunter to snatch him up. Coincidentally, Starr had been trying to get into Dale Martin's promotion, the largest wrestling company in the country. "He had called the big office, but they said they didn't want him. Especially for a small guy, it was very hard to get in . . . The wrestling, it was more rugged. In England in those days, you didn't take bumps. You had to work for the bumps," Rocco said. "He was fantastic. People loved him. I liked Ricki. He gave me advice when I started in wrestling." Starr stayed overseas when the competing offices merged a couple of years later. Adrian Street wrestled Starr dozens of times, and boxed him as well. "He was immense when he came over there at first. I can't say I was in love with the guy, he could be a cocky bastard; mind you, he had a right to be because he was good." Street witnessed the same side of Starr that Goldstein saw after the *Scheherazade* episode. "I don't know what the disagreement was over, but Wild Ian Campbell — he wrestled in the States before he wrestled in Britain — they had a disagreement in the dressing room, and bear in mind that Wild Ian was about six-foot-four and weighed well over 300 pounds. He tried to crowd Ricki in a corner but I'll tell you what, he got his bleeding clock cleaned."

Starr came back to the States for a handful of appearances in the early 1970s. Even though he was physically underwhelming and past forty, he could still teach young Dewey Robertson a lesson in humility in Lafayette, Louisiana. "When I saw him he weighed about 185 pounds, I weighed 240 pounds. This I thought would be no contest," Robertson said. "I learned an important lesson about judging a man [by] his size. His international stardom was because of his ballet dance maneuvers in the ring, combined with his wrestling ability. He out-maneuvered me during the match, and I learned a good lesson." Toward the end of his career, Starr grew his hair into something that resembled an Asian-style topknot and sprouted a Fu Manchu mustache, looking little like the clean-cut guy from the '50s. He excelled in tournaments in Germany and Austria as late as 1975 against familiar names such as Steinborn, Eric Froehlich, and Bob Della Serra before settling into a secluded life in London, cutting himself off from his past. When a group of old-time wrestlers contacted him recently, urging him to attend a reunion of Brit grapplers, Starr begged off, saying it would conflict with his belief system about not reliving the past. "He says, 'Oh, no, no, no. I can't have anything to do with wrestling or wrestlers anymore because of my spiritualism,'" Street explained. "He's a spiritualist now, and that's his religion sort of type of a deal. He was never right in the head, quite honestly."

Perhaps it's best then just to appreciate Starr, about eighty years old in 2011, in his past prancing glory, a one-of-a-kind act in the copycat world of wrestling. "How would you believe that you could take a guy who probably didn't weigh any more than 180 pounds, put ballet slippers on him, have him doing ballerina moves and make a babyface out of him?" Lewin asked. "It's almost unreal."

SAM STEAMBOAT

Beach boy, surfer, wrestler, announcer, teacher. These words and many more are used to describe Sammy Steamboat. Easily one of the greatest wrestlers ever to come out of Hawaii, Steamboat was a main eventer in the mid-to-late 1950s until the '70s, when he stopped life as a grappler.

"To different people from different eras, he was different things," his oldest daughter Samantha Moikeha told the Honolulu Advertiser. "To Mainland people in the 1950s, he was a big wrestler. In the '60s and '70s, it was Wrestling Hawaii. In the '80s and '90s, it was paddling and coaching. He was always doing something."

Like Richard Blood, a.k.a. Ricky "The Dragon" Steamboat, who inherited his name and legacy, Sammy Steamboat was seen as a perennial good guy.

It wasn't an act.

"The fans loved him. He was strait-laced. He was very sincere about his work," recalled Danny Miller, who teamed with Steamboat in Florida in the late 1960s.

"He was a nice person, very quiet and very shy. He really was about meeting people," said Lord James Blears, who was instrumental in getting Steamboat started in wrestling.

Born Sam Mokuahi (which translates to "steamboat"), he was a multi-
sport athlete at Roosevelt High in
Honolulu. His father, Sam Steamboat
Sr. ("Big Boat"), was one of the first
to offer canoe and surfboard rentals
on the famed Waikiki Beach. "His
family was on the frontlines," said
Don Muraco. "Steamboat Sr. was one
of the original beach boys."

The Destroyer Dick Beyer recalled
the same thing. "Sammy's father was
the king of the beach boys, really,"
he said. "When I'd go down to the
beach, I couldn't do anything wrong
because Sammy Steamboat's father —
you do something for the Hawaiians,
they'll bend over backwards to repay
the favor. I had great times in Hawaii."

Sam Steamboat done up in traditional garb.

Lord Blears stakes the claim of getting Steamboat into the grappling game,
just as he would later for King Curtis Iaukea. "I started him wrestling. He was on
Waikiki Beach, he was a beach boy, but he had a terrific body on him, worked
out surfing every day," said Blears from his nursing home bed. "I said, 'I'll teach
you to wrestle if you teach me how to surf.' So he said, 'Okay.' We went out
every day on the board and he taught me how to surf, and we went down to the
gym, and I taught him how to wrestle."

The young Steamboat would work out with the wrestlers in town, who
loved the territory — weekly pay for working only a day or two each week.
Among his early trainers and workout partners were Blears, Gene Kiniski, Sandor
Kovacs, Don Curtis (Don Beitelman), and Tony Morelli. "He used to have a neck
like a goddamn goose, and we used to work on his neck at the beach every day.
Finally, we got his neck worked up like it should be," said Kiniski with a laugh.

In February 2000, Iaukea shared his recollection of Steamboat with a
Hawaiian newspaper. "He was the best looking man I've ever seen walk across
the sand of Waikiki. And now he's horrible looking — he got two cauliflower
ears that look like two okoles sticking out of each side of his head, and not a hair
on top of his head."

By the mid-'50s, Steamboat was a pro wrestler, and claimed the NWA Hawaii tag titles with Billy Varga on August 5, 1956, defeating Tosh Togo and Ed Gardenia in Honolulu. He would soon hit the road, and in 1959, he made his way to the Toronto territory.

The Whip newsletter, dedicated to Whipper Billy Watson, had a feature on Steamboat in its September 1960 edition. "Sam is one of the most colourful wrestlers in the ring today and is also a fan favorite wherever he wrestles. Why is he a fan favorite? Mainly because his fans know when he enters the ring, he possesses everything a wrestler should have, is fast as lightning, and prefers the clean scientific style of wrestling. However if an opponent is rough and rugged, Sam is always equal to the occasion as many have found out."

Lou Thesz was Steamboat's friend and mentor. "Steamboat just idolized Thesz," said Kiniski.

"Lou always told me, 'Wrestle, do not be a clown,'" said Steamboat in July 1994.

"I used to say to him, 'You've got the wrong goddamn teacher. He taught you how to wrestle but he's goddamn left-handed!'" laughed Beyer. "Lou Thesz had a lot to do with training him. Lou Thesz, he loved to go to Hawaii too. He was good friends with Sammy's father."

In Florida, Steamboat aligned himself on the side of local hero Eddie Graham, and headlined countless cards. He became such an icon in the state that when a young Richard Blood started out, he was dubbed Steamboat's nephew Ricky. "The Steamboat name did obviously derive from Sam. But Eddie Graham and Jack Brisco when I went to Florida after I left Minneapolis, Eddie Graham gave me the name," Steamboat told writer Jimmy VanderLinden. He quickly made it up the ranks in Florida. "And it wasn't because of my work, it was only because of Sam Steamboat."

In the later '60s and '70s, Sam Steamboat came home to Hawaii. As the local promotion faded out, he drifted into coaching paddling.

That's the Sam Steamboat that Don Muraco knew. Steamboat and Iaukea were the two local legends that Muraco could turn to for inspiration. "He was a good, solid worker. He was a good draw around here and most of the places he went. He spent a lot of time with Eddie Graham and Lou Thesz," said Muraco. "He was a good guy, quiet, dedicated to the community. He did a lot of work with canoe clubs in his community after wrestling. He didn't have much to do with wrestling after he finished up here."

Steamboat's passion became outrigger canoe paddling, and he coached a number of clubs, including the Outrigger, Hui Nalu, and Waikiki Surf Club. His hard work promoting canoe paddling led to the sport becoming a sanctioned high school sport in Hawaii in 2000.

Alzheimer's tore out Steamboat's memories over the last years of his life, which ended May 2, 2006, two days from his seventy-second birthday. Fittingly, following Hawaiian tradition, his ashes were scattered in the ocean, and family members rode the wave in to shore.

Tim Woods was a top-tier performer unmasked.

"MR. WRESTLING" TIM WOODS

The trademark white mask, white trunks and white boots spoke volumes about the man. But it was his name — Mr. Wrestling — that told the story.

From collegiate champion to professional wrestling star, Tim Woods embodied the spirit of the game; so much, in fact, that he adopted the name "Mr. Wrestling" just a few years into his career. While the billing may have initially appeared presumptuous and even arrogant to some, it didn't take long for Woods to make believers out of the skeptics. No one was ever more tailor-made for the role than the man who would end up carrying it straight into the annals of wrestling history.

Woods' approach to professional wrestling was simple, and he stuck to the basics. "He is poetry in motion," legendary announcer Gordon Solie once said of Woods. "What he is doing out there is what the Greeks had in mind when they invented the sport."

His achievements in both the amateur and professional ranks were monumental. Before turning pro in 1962, he had been one of amateur wrestling's most decorated athletes, having won a number of state and regional titles in high school and later as a star at Michigan State, where he captured two Big 10 titles and twice finished second in the NCAA championships, along with being a three-time AAU national champion.

Born George Burrell Woodin in Ithaca, New York, and nicknamed "Tiny Tim" as a child because he was so small, Woods seamlessly bridged the gap between the amateur and pro styles. He captured his first AAU national title in 1955 at 191 pounds. He originally went to Cornell University, but didn't wrestle, concentrating on his studies, and getting a degree in Agricultural Engineering. He had firmly established himself as a top amateur nationally, placing fifth in the AAU nationals as a high school senior, losing to Syracuse University standout and future pro great Dick "The Destroyer" Beyer, who placed second that year. It would be more than just a little coincidental that years later Woods and Beyer would become two of the most successful American masked wrestlers of their era.

COURTESY OF SCOTT TEAL/CROWBAR PRESS

Under a mask as Mr. Wrestling, Tim Woods stood out.

He headed to collegiate wrestling power Oklahoma State to compete on the mat as well, as for post-graduate work, but ended up transferring when legendary coach Myron Roderick brought in another highly touted grappler, Iraqi national wrestling champion Adnan Alkaissy (the future Sheik Adnan El-Kaissey). Woods narrowly missed out on a dream meeting with Oklahoma's Danny Hodge in 1957 when Hodge, who was coming off a run in the Olympics, a record pinning streak, and a *Sports Illustrated* cover, pulled out of the tournament due to a neck injury. Woods, who had considered dropping down to the 174-pound class to face Hodge, decided not to cut weight and won the Big 10 title at 191. Ranked No. 2 in the nation the next year, Woods pinned his way through the Big 10 tournament before losing in the finals.

Woods won his second Big 10 title in 1959, this time back at 191, and was ranked No. 1 in the nation. He breezed through the tourney, including a semifinal victory over Oklahoma State's Alkaissy by an 8-2 margin. At the NCAA Finals, Woods would suffer only his second college defeat. His seventy-four percent career-pinning percentage was second in NCAA history to Hodge.

In 1962, he started working prelims as Tim Woods in the WWWF. He got his first break in 1964 from Dory Funk Sr. in Amarillo, before promoter Joe Dusek tried to copy the success of the black-masked, super heel Dr. X in Omaha from six years earlier, but this time coming up with a babyface, white-masked Mr. Wrestling. His decision to don a hood, conceal his identity, and work as a fan favorite after only three years as a pro was a risky move. Few in the '60s would have imagined a masked grappler as a babyface, since hoods in those days were exclusive to the profession's most hated heels. Then again, few had the credentials that Woods brought to the table.

The plan worked to perfection, with Woods drawing sellout crowds that culminated with him voluntarily unmasking before a match with "Mad Dog" Vachon. Woods won the match and held the Omaha version of the title for two weeks, but relinquished the belt in a rematch.

Woods would achieve his greatest success in Georgia where booker Leo Garibaldi was convinced that the man with the white mask could become as popular as the territory's two top hooded heels, The Assassins, were hated. His hunch was right, and after spending months on TV building up the arrival of Mr. Wrestling, hyping him as a mystery man that nobody could beat in a legitimate match because of his stellar amateur record, Woods would prove to be perhaps the biggest star of that decade in Atlanta. His vast repertoire of moves, including his unique standing head cradle that he developed by accident during a college match, made fans true believers.

It was that same confidence in Woods' wrestling skill that prompted promoters to issue a challenge to anyone who could stay in the ring with the masked man for ten minutes. The move would backfire in a famous incident in Columbia, Georgia, when a 280-pound street fighter, trapped in one of Woods' arsenal of holds, took matters literally into Woods' own hands and bit off one of the wrestler's fingers at the joint. Woods proceeded to pummel the local thug into oblivion.

A series of matches with then NWA world champion Gene Kiniski drew record business in Atlanta, including the fastest-ever sellout at the Atlanta City Auditorium, with the severed finger coming into play, and Woods becoming even more of a cult hero. A rematch planned for Atlanta Fulton Stadium, which would have been the biggest match ever in the state, was scrapped when Woods bolted for the Carolinas after getting a paltry $400 payoff for his match with Kiniski.

Woods would return for future stints in Atlanta, but his reputation had been long cemented as one of the territory's all-time greats. "Tim Woods was probably the most famous wrestler in Atlanta back then. He was the Jerry Lawler of

Atlanta," said booker Jerry Jarrett, who would bring in Johnny Walker as Mr. Wrestling II while Woods was headlining for Eddie Graham in Florida. It was in the Sunshine State where Woods enjoyed a stint working as a subtle heel, combing his mastery of ring psychology with his wrestling skill set, in a feud with Jack Brisco over the No. 1 contendership for Dory Funk Jr.'s NWA world title. Eventually Brisco beat Mr. Wrestling for his mask, and Woods turned back babyface, having a big 1972 program with Funk Jr.

With Woods the top star in Georgia during the late '60s and early '70s, Walker would assume that title for the rest of the decade. With Woods, by then working with and without the mask, the two would draw major business as both partners and rivals, including a series of twelve consecutive sellouts at Atlanta's City Auditorium, culminating in a mask versus hair match in which Woods had his head shaved. Walker and Woods would become best friends as well as solid wrestling partners. "It's strange how things work out," said Walker. "We made a good team and we got along fantastically. Timmy and I were closer than brothers."

Woods was a hero to a legion of fans who spoke of him in the same reverential tones reserved for the legendary stars of the business. Between his pro debut in 1962 and his retirement on September 17, 1983, against Mr. Wrestling II, before a sellout crowd at the Omni in Atlanta, he held a slew of prestigious titles and became one of the most respected professional wrestlers of his era. He held victories over every world champion over a two-decade span, a lofty list that included names like Lou Thesz, Pat O'Connor, Gene Kiniski, Harley Race, Terry Funk, Jack Brisco, and Ric Flair. Named wrestling's most outstanding performer in 1974, Woods held then world champion Race to a draw in October 1973, marking the first sellout in Atlanta's Omni.

Perhaps Woods' greatest accomplishment, though, was actually one whose value couldn't be quantified by mere numbers or level of prestige: when he was called upon to protect the business over and above the call of duty.

It was while working for the Charlotte-based Crockett Promotions that Woods was involved in the 1975 plane crash that ended the career of Johnny Valentine — with whom he was engaged in a torrid feud at the time — and broke the back of future legend Flair, as well as causing serious injury to football player-turned-grappler Bob Bruggers. The pilot of the twin-engine Cessna would die nearly one year later from injuries suffered in the crash.

In a crafty move that most likely saved business in the territory, and possibly in territories across the country, an injured Woods wisely gave authorities

Mr. Wrestling struggles in the leglock of Mr. X #2 (Geoff Portz) in Florida.

his real name and listed himself as a promoter so fans wouldn't discover in newspaper reports that he had been on the same flight as his "hated" ring rival. Despite being in tremendous pain, Woods quickly checked himself out of the Wilmington, North Carolina, hospital and was making televised appearances within days.

The revelation that Woods was aboard that plane with some of the territory's top heels could have caused irreparable damage to the promotion. When rumors started to circulate that Woods perhaps was on the plane, he bravely returned to the ring despite being in extreme pain. Woods was "more than just Mr. Wrestling that day, but was the man who saved wrestling," Flair wrote in his book, *Ric Flair: To Be the Man*.

Woods became a major force in the resurgence of Mid-Atlantic Wrestling in the '70s where he would clash with Johnny "The Champ" Valentine over the latter's thousand silver dollars, engage in memorable bloodbaths with Flair and Blackjack Mulligan over the U.S. heavyweight title, and challenge fellow amateur greats Jack Brisco and Baron Von Raschke in amateur rules matches.

One of Woods' personal highlights was being inducted into the prestigious George Tragos-Lou Thesz Professional Wrestling Hall of Fame in 2001 in Newton, Iowa (in 1996 he had been inducted into USA Wrestling's Hall of Fame/All-American Club at the World Championships in Atlanta). Woods, who considered his entry into the Thesz shrine as one of his greatest honors, had been long-time friends with the six-time world champion, who died six months before Woods' passing. Thesz listed Woods on his own elite "Top 25" all-time list. "His attitude was so welcome in the dressing rooms and his wrestling credibility sustained many a town," said Thesz, who lauded Woods' super upper-body strength, fantastic personality, and great pin record as an amateur.

If Woods had an Achilles heel, joked several of his colleagues, it was habitual tardiness. "He just couldn't be on time for a ride to the towns we wrestled in!" laughed Les Thatcher. "After coming close to being a late arrival because of waiting for Woods to show up to ride with me, I finally came up with the answer; so I started telling Tim to meet me thirty minutes before we really had to be on the road, and then maybe he was only ten minutes late!"

Woods also may have been the only wrestler in history to have ever been served a subpoena during a match.

Woods was teaming with Buddy Colt — then known as Ron Reed — against The Fabulous Kangaroos (Al Costello and Roy Heffernan) in New York City. "Tim apparently hadn't eaten right that night and had an upset stomach," said Colt. "He's leaning his head over the apron of the ring puking on the floor, and this guy slaps a paper in his hand, and a flashbulb goes off. Tim goes back into middle of the ring and hands the paper to the referee and asks him to hold it for him until the match was over. It turned out to be a subpoena from his ex-wife for child support. They served him right in the middle of the ring at Madison Square Garden."

He wasn't a big partier, though. While most wrestlers would buy six-packs of beer, Woods would get a six-pack of Pepsi-Cola. "He drank soda pops like it was water," said Walker.

When Woods retired, he never looked back, having spent more time in the profession than he ever imagined he would. With several degrees to his credit and a vast array of interests outside the wrestling profession, dull moments were few and far between. Woods was an accomplished musician, photographer, and also raced drag-type cars and motorcycles. He developed several patents dealing with air conditioning, heating, and refrigeration, and later managed a consulting business in Charlotte. "He was too smart to be in this business. He could have done anything he wanted," said Rip Hawk. "But he loved wrestling so much he stayed in it."

In later years Woods worked tirelessly for a number of charitable organizations, including the Asheville, North Carolina–based Eblen Charities, which assists disadvantaged families in western North Carolina. "The only thing, I believe, that could eclipse Tim's accomplishments on the mat or in the ring is what he accomplished out of it on behalf of countless children, adults, and families who were battling illnesses, disabilities, and may have been less for-

Lou Thesz and Tim Woods at a Cauliflower Alley Club reunion.

tunate than others," said Eblen executive director Bill Murdock. "Tim helped establish the Eblen Charities and the Eblen Celebrity Golf Invitational and was one of our most popular celebrities since its inception. Everyone wanted to golf with Mr. Wrestling."

Woods died of a massive heart attack November 30, 2002, at his home in Charlotte, at the age of sixty-eight. His passing evoked memories from a number of long-time local fans who followed his illustrious career. "Growing up in Georgia in the '70s, Tim Woods showed me the difference between good and evil, right and wrong," recalled one fan. "In a day when it is hard for kids to find a hero — I had mine in Mr. Wrestling."

ETHNIC HEROES

DORY DIXON

COURTESY OF SCOTT TEAL/CROWBAR PRESS

Dory Dixon twists El Enfermero.

There are heroes and then there are *national* heroes.

When Dorrel Dixon stepped off a Mexicana Airlines plane at the Palisadoes International Airport in Kingston, Jamaica, on July 4, 1963, the twenty-eight-year-old was junior world heavyweight wrestling champion, and he was returning home to the island he left eight years earlier, deserting his country's weightlifting team at the 1955 Pan-American Games in Mexico.

Kingston Mayor Leonard Curtis welcomed Dixon and gave him the key to the city. "Welcome back to Jamaica. You have done this country proud by your brilliant performances in the wrestling rings of the world as you beat star after star on your way to the junior world heavyweight championship," said Curtis. "On behalf of the Corporate Area, and indeed all Jamaica, I wish you a spectacular victory in your fight at the National Stadium on Saturday night."

That show, headlined by NWA world heavyweight champ Lou Thesz defeating Mike Padousis, had Dixon beating Duke Keomuka in the semi main event, refereed by former world heavyweight boxing champion "Jersey" Joe Walcott. Over 6,000 turned out for the first pro wrestling show on the Caribbean island.

"I went to Jamaica and the place was so packed, the prime minister, the governments, the people, they came from all over. Naturally, I was a national hero," said Dixon of the show, which celebrated Jamaica's independence from England, that he set up through Eddie Graham's Florida office. "It was lovely, lovely."

Lovely could also describe Dixon on many levels: his physique, as one of the first bodybuilders to make it big in pro wrestling; his technique, which included high-flying, inspired by his training with luchadores in Mexico, but rare for the day in North America; his personality, which is still easygoing and friendly, with a rich, deep laugh; and his speech, straight from the islands, but tinged with Spanish inflection and terms like si and exactimundo.

Born February 1, 1934, in Addington Hanover, Jamaica, Dixon got hooked on bodybuilding at just sixteen, having spent a short time in prison for youthful exuberances. He began training at home under a breadfruit tree. A year later, he began studying with Jamaica's famed bodybuilder Lloyd Young; two years later, he was Mr. Jamaica. Switching to weightlifting, Dixon represented his country at the 1954 Central American and Caribbean Games and the 1955 Pan-American Games.

The rest sounds like a Cold War spy story, but Dixon, now an evangelist for the Seventh Day Adventist Church, chalks it up to God's will.

"After the Games were over, in Mexico City, the people told me that, 'You should not go back to Jamaica.' So they took me and hid me away, from Mexico City to the state of Puebla. I came here to live, to hide away. I did not go back with the delegation or the team," he recalled. "The British Embassy looked all over for me, but they couldn't find me."

He befriended the local governor, Javier Comacho, who was the brother of the Mexican president Rapheal Avila Comacho.

"The governor said, 'Take your clothes off,' in the office with all the senators and big men. I started to pose and pose and pose. He said, 'You stay with me,'" said Dixon, thanking the kindness of the average people too, quick with a meal or a treat for the refugee who stood out because of his dark skin color. Soon, Dixon was teaching fitness at a Puebla university, serving as an occasional bodyguard, and officially on the books as a liquor license inspector.

Dixon would attend the local lucha shows with friends, and was often egged on: "You can beat that one!" The Mexican promoter, Salvador Lutteroth, heard about him and invited him to Mexico City in 1955. "He had looks, a physique, strength, and intelligence. Also, a personality," said Lutteroth in *Wrestling Revue* in 1962. "I gave him a chance in Mexico City — and I was right. He has everything."

But before Dixon became a star, he underwent a year of wrestling training. "I cried for one year, every day and night I cried from the pains and the bumps," admitted Dixon, adding that he got fifty pesos for his first match.

The initial gimmick didn't last, he sighed thankfully. "I was going to wrestle barefoot, like an African boy, and they said, 'Don't do that. Don't wrestle barefoot because they will say this little black boy has no money for shoes.'" In 1959, the 185-pound Dixon took the EMLL Light Heavyweight title from Al Kashey in Mexico City.

The shoed Dixon wrestled around Mexico until early 1961, when he sent an introductory letter with Danny McShain to Houston, Texas promoter Morris Sigel. Lee Stephenson Wood, Sigel's secretary in the Gulf Athletic Club, changed his tune on Dixon quickly in letters to promoter Jack Pfefer. "I haven't seen him work . . . but everyone says that he is sensational . . . he is from Jamaica . . . but he may just as well be from darkest Africa, because these people (wrestling fans) simply do not want Negro wrestlers . . . especially when you mix them with White . . ." he wrote in November 1960. Three months later, Dixon's complexion was no longer an issue. "The Negro boy . . . Dixon . . . has been drawing a lot of dark faces . . . doesn't go over too well with the whites . . . but as long as they come, to heck with the color!"

Dixon took on Paul Vachon in Houston. "They had a big deal in Houston, because they weren't sure if the black people and the white people and the Mexicans would take a mixed-race match. So in order not to have too much heat if the black guy was beating up the white guy, they hired a Russian, Nikolai Zolotoff," said Vachon/Zolotoff.

In Oregon, Dixon befriended a man unconcerned with any color but that of money, "Nature Boy" Buddy Rogers. Following a dressing room spat with another wrestler, Dixon was the only one to help Rogers to his taxi. A few weeks later, Dixon was summoned to the Big Apple, where Vincent J. McMahon, Rogers' greatest supporter, ran the show. "He said, 'Dory, I'm going to make you a lot of money.' But I didn't want to go, because I was afraid, I didn't really want to go. Finally, finally, finally, he kept calling, and I gave him an answer. I finally went to New York, and that was big, big television. I wrestled as 'The Calypso Kid' Dory Dixon."

Like Frank Sinatra sang, if Dixon could make it there, he could make it anywhere. "He was the prototype of Kofi Kingston and all these other guys," said writer Bill Apter. "I remember him so well, because when I was a kid, we used to go to the Sunnyside Garden in Queens. He was on every show."

"That was one of the special parts of my life, because I knew it might work, and I wrestled with Buddy Rogers, in Madison Square Garden and all those special places, then that opened the door," said Dixon. "Everybody welcomed me as a black man."

Rogers, married to an African-American woman, also bravely dropped a version of the world heavyweight title to Dixon in 1963 in Cleveland, Ohio, for promoter Larry Atkins — but the promotion itself didn't last.

Neither did Dixon's run in the U.S. After competing from New York to Los Angeles, Dixon was back in Mexico, wrestling regularly, with the occasional trip north. He'd compete until 1994. Mexico is still his home, with five children from his first wife and three from his second, though trips to Jamaica are frequent too; he has one daughter there.

He has followed his faith as well, studying in Jerusalem, and spreading the Word across the world. His wife, Viki Dixon, is an equal partner, expounding the virtues of her approach to weight loss and how her calling to the faith saved her from a fall from a three-story building.

Looking back, Dixon says each step in his life prepared him for the next. As for wrestling, he says, "It was a blessing for me."

PEPPER GOMEZ

Can a gimmick cost a hero his life? Pepper Gomez's widow thinks so. As "The Man With the Cast-Iron Stomach," Gomez demonstrated his toughness by having trucks drive over his stomach or opponents jump off ladders.

Naturally, the chance to hurt a prone foe proved irresistible to villains. In San Francisco, "The Crippler" Ray Stevens rose to the challenge — twice — but on the second attempt leaped onto Gomez's throat from the ladder, sending Pepper to the hospital and igniting one of pro wrestling's most famed feuds. It was a repeat of an almost identical angle done with Duke Keomuka in Houston years before.

Wrestlers were instructed to work the stomach sparingly, said Pat Patterson. "Whenever you hit him in the stomach, he would never register to it," he said, "but sometimes you have to do that to show that it didn't affect him."

While he was seemingly invulnerable in the ring, that was not the case in the hospital. In 2003, doctors discovered that he had a faulty kidney from the years of abuse in the ring. He was wheeled into surgery.

"He didn't have a disease. In fact, when he had his kidney transplant, they left both kidneys in, and put the new one in the middle," said Bonnie Gomez, his third wife. Things didn't go smoothly with the surgeries, however, and he never regained consciousness after the second operation on April 16, 2004. He died on May 6. According to Bonnie, though, Pepper, a life-long fitness fanatic, really faded when he had to quit working out.

Little Jose Felapio Palimeno Gomez Jr. — Pepi to his mother — started out bodybuilding in his native Los Angeles by putting cement in cans and tying them onto a bar for makeshift weights. He attended Los Angeles City College, studying

Phys Ed, running track, doing gymnastics, playing halfback, and pitching in softball; but what he was really doing was figuring out how to improve his own physique. A regular on Muscle Beach in Venice, California, Gomez placed in a number of bodybuilding contests, including Mr. Los Angeles (2nd, 1947) and Mr. Pacific Coast (4th, 1948), and was on the cover of a 1948 *Strength and Health* magazine.

Houston promoter Morris Sigel, center, oversees a contract signing between Lou Thesz and Pepper Gomez as Ed Lewis and Blackie Guzman look on.

After a stint in the U.S. Navy, a chance meeting with Blackie Guzman (Miguel Huerta) in L.A. would result in his eventual pro wrestling debut in January 1953.

"He liked to hang around wrestlers. He had big brown eyes and they sparkled like stars when he shook a wrestler's hand. I knew right away that this kid had stardust in his eyes and that if he didn't turn out to be a wrestler himself someday it would only be because he was crippled or dead," Guzman told Houston announcer/promoter Paul Boesch. "He stuck out his chest proudly and said, 'See, Mr. Guzman, how big I develop. And my arms and legs are big and very strong too.'"

Guzman took Pepper to Houston and acted as a father figure for the soon-to-be star. "I don't consider Pepper just another wrestler," Guzman said. "To me, he is my oldest son."

Despite blowing out his knee in his El Paso debut, Gomez would battle back to become an icon of Texas wrestling, holding the Texas heavyweight title twelve different times from 1955 to 1963, and later everywhere from Florida to New York, Minnesota to California, Kansas to Oregon, Japan to Australia.

Because he was billed from Mexico City, Hispanic fans identified with Gomez. Promoters would promise, "Pepper, you're gonna make a lot of money here, because there's a lot of Latin people." Gomez would gamely go in. "I could speak the language on TV and get over with them," Pepper told historian Scott Teal. But he also had a short fuse when it came to promoters, and didn't last as long as perhaps he should have in many territories.

He is most associated with the San Francisco territory, run by ex-wrestler Roy Shire. "I can always remember Pepper Gomez being there. Roy kept him around. He lived in the area. We were programmed just to like him, really," said Ed Moretti, who grew up a few miles from the Cow Palace. Shire had his announcers stress Gomez's Latino temper, and should he snap, opponents had better beware. Pepper's finishing moves were less fearful, laughed Moretti. "One was called the Mexican drop, and then he'd follow that up with the Mexican cradle. If you look at it today, you go, 'God, that's horrible,' because it was just a little cradle where he'd jump over the guy's legs and hook him and roll him up," mocked Moondog Moretti. "I think any amateur wrestler, watching that back in the day, would just say, 'That's ridiculous.'"

Though he is most tied to Shire, interestingly, in a post-career interview he didn't single him out. "From Szabo to Thesz to Buddy Rogers, I fought everyone," Gomez told radio host Dr. Mike Lano. "I thank everyone for my career, especially Morris Sigel, he was the best promoter I ever worked for. Sam Muchnick and [Giant] Baba too."

Gomez himself had a short stint as a promoter in Las Vegas, with his wife Bonnie. "He wanted to wrestle and you can't wrestle and promote too. So he put me in as the promoter," said Bonnie. "He was doing everything. I was just handling all the money."

Yet again and again he proved his sincerity and goodwill for the fans, never shortchanging them, even at the end of his career, his knees shot.

"After the matches, he wasn't one of these top faces who would tell the kids, 'Get away from me,'" Nick Kozak told the Cauliflower Alley Club website. "He

Pepper Gomez and wife Bonnie at a Cauliflower Alley Club reunion.

would take time for everyone when he was coming out of the dressing room at the end of the night. He would talk to everyone and sign autographs. I tell you, he treated those kids like they were his kids. A lot of guys didn't do that. They would forget that it's the fans who buy the tickets, but Pepper was great with them."

He was also great post-career as well, acting as the maitre d' and manager at Scoma's, a famed Fisherman's Wharf restaurant in San Francisco, after proving he couldn't mix a drink as the bartender.

"He loved to talk with the fans," said Pepper's stepdaughter, Teri. "He had such a big heart, and he never forgot the people who supported him over the years."

Gomez made a point to stay in touch with old friends, including Stevens, Lou Thesz, Red Bastien, and Kinji Shibuya, who, of course, he could never be seen in public with. Lighthearted and fun to be around, Gomez's best friend was Bobby Heenan.

"They talked on the phone all the time," said Bonnie Gomez. "He and Bobby Heenan used to be the two biggest goof-ups, they were something else."

Heenan wrote of his friend in his first autobiography. "I'd pull a lot of ribs on Pepper Gomez. He was short, and when we would get in the car to go on long trips, I'd put telephone books in the front seat so he could sit up and look out the window. He'd get embarrassed and mad," wrote The Brain. "When I wrestled Pepper, I never called 'high spots' in the ring, I'd call 'low spots.' When we would work, he would usually shoot me into the ropes and I'd give him one tackle, he would drop down, I would jump over him, and he would get it again. Then, I threw him into the ropes and he would tackle me. I would drop down, and he came back to jump over me, I'd raise my body up about an inch and he'd catch his toe and trip. I'd whisper, 'Can't you get those little legs up higher?'"

For all the mirthfulness, Gomez took his legacy seriously. Tearing up, his widow shared one last story of his impact. "I remember this one, and it just broke my heart. This little boy, his dad came to the matches all the time. His boy used to come with him, but he had cancer and he was dying. He had Pepper go to the hospital to see him, and Pepper took a picture. Pepper talked to him and everything and said, 'You're going to get better. And when you do, you're going to sit in the front row, and you're going to have to catch me when I come out of the ring.' Then the boy died," she concluded. "The father came to Pepper and said, 'Pepper,' — God, it brings tears to my eyes now — 'I put your picture in my son's casket, because he loved you so much.'"

THE GUERREROS

It's a double-edged sword to be a Guerrero, said Chavo Guerrero Jr. It was far easier to get your foot in the door, to get a break that others would have to work many times harder to get. But then there is the challenge of living up to the name. "You have to live up to your family a lot faster than just a regular person coming in; they expect you to be good right off the bat. Everybody heard it. My dad heard it when he first started: 'You'll never be as good as Gory.' Then Eddie heard it when he started: 'You'll never be as good as your uncles,'" said Chavo Jr. "I heard it when I started: 'You'll never be as good as Eddie.' We always have to live up to the person in front of us."

Or, in simpler terms, one Guerrero led to another.

Jeff Walton was the publicist for the Los Angeles office when the Guerreros were the darlings of the fans in the 1970s. "The Guerreros came in in waves. We actually brought in Chavo first. It was like a big tidal wave, is what it was. You had Chavo coming in, who was really kind of the mainstay, and a very good worker. Because we could emphasize his father — his father had a big following here

Mando Guerrero poses with WCW stars, his nephew Chavo Jr. and brother Eddie.

in the late '30s and '40s," said Walton, referencing the patriarch, Salvador Gori Guerrero. "As Chavo would kind of wind down a little bit, he'd say, 'Hey, I have my brother, Mando. You should see Mando. He's a really good worker.'

"After Mando came Héctor, and Héctor was a tremendous worker. So it was a non-stop tidal wave of Guerreros. We got a lot of mileage out of these guys, because we put them in tag teams, you put them in singles matches, you put them with other guys, besides the brothers, if they weren't all here at one time. It just made for great wrestlers. They were really polished, skilled wrestlers."

They excelled as sympathetic heroes, embracing it completely, said Superstar Billy Graham, recalling one bout with the Americas champion Chavo Sr. in L.A. "It was funny because he said, 'Listen, this is my house. You're out of the Garden and in my house. I'm a *babyface* here man, and you're going to be the heel. I'm going to win, you're going to get juice, they're going to take you out on a stretcher.' I said, 'Are you going to sell for me?'"

The diminutive Guerreros were true students of the game; willing role-players who excelled at making their opponents look good.

"I was a Mexican coming in from Mexico, I was a second-generation wrestler, I was short," said Mando. "That was nothing but ammunition for the heel to grab and use to dig at the people, because that's how the people identified themselves with me. There was no such thing as a fantasy, made-up character."

"It's the land of the giants, pro wrestling. All of us, not one of us were over six foot," said Chavo Jr. "We're sitting there, 200 pounds, wrestling guys that are 300 pounds, that are six-foot-eight. You have to be that much better than those guys, really, because you've got two things in the ring. You've got to remember that we've got to make these guys look better than they can make themselves look, but at the same time, not get eaten up. So we've got to be that much better than those guys. That's how we were taught our whole lives."

The Guerrero family tree has produced much fruit — and perhaps it is not done. Gory Guerrero (1921–1990), born in Arizona but raised in Mexico after age thirteen, started wrestling in 1937, and was one of Mexico's biggest stars from the '40s to the '60s. "Gori Guerrero's career in *lucha libre* history is proudly etched in large letters, carved out of decades of dedication and desire. Gori's talent and tenacity were legendary throughout Mexico," said Dan Madigan, author of *Mondo Lucha A Go-Go*. "His popularity soared into the outmost reaches of the wrestling stratosphere because the fans knew that every time he stepped into the ring he gave everything he had and every time he stepped out, he left a little piece of himself behind."

Gori and his wife Herlinda would have two girls, Maria and Linda, and four boys, all of whom became professional wrestlers: Salvador (Chavo) Guerrero Sr. (born 1949); Armando "Mando" Guerrero (born 1952); Héctor Guerrero (born 1954), and Edouardo "Eddie" Guerrero (1967–2005). Chavo's son, Salvador III, or Chavo Jr. (born 1970), turned pro in 1994; Eddie's daughter, Shaul (born 1990), is in training in WWE developmental, perhaps hoping to join her mom, Vickie, as a WWE personality.

"We never wanted to be Superman or Batman or the Lone Ranger in my era, we wanted to be wrestlers," Chavo Sr. said. The boys would train in a gym in Mexico with their father, where he stressed tumbling and the need to tuck their heads during falls. Having introduced submission moves and an aggressive technical style to *lucha libre* and its penchant for highspots, Gori also insisted that his sons learn amateur wrestling, competing successfully at the high school and collegiate levels.

Based out of El Paso, Texas, for high school, with upward of three rings in the backyard, the boys began their wrestling careers on local shows that their dad promoted. In 1974, Chavo Sr. headed west to Los Angeles and the World Wrestling Association. Mando would follow shortly thereafter and Héctor after that. With eighteen years between Chavo and Eddie, the youngest Guerrero wouldn't start until 1987. "Out of my whole life, there were maybe four months that I thought

Chavo Guerrero Sr. poses with his NWA World Junior Heavyweight championship along with (from left) Los Angeles booker Tom Renesto, his father Gori, and his brother Mando.

I don't want to be a wrestler," Eddie told his hometown newspaper, the *El Paso Times*, in 2003. "But I knew what I wanted to do all my life. I grew up watching my dad and my older brothers do it."

Through the years, the brothers' lives intertwined — Héctor was in Florida and brought in Chavo Sr.; Mando was in the AWA, and invited his brothers in; Eddie worked in Mexico and used his big brothers as backup. They all had their strengths and weaknesses: Chavo Sr. was the most polished; Mando, the smallest, could really fly and sell; Héctor had the greatest charisma, which makes the decisions to saddle him with the Gobbledy Gooker and LaserTron gimmicks all the more odd; Chavo Jr. was a key role-player in the WWE, with runs as ECW world champion and tag team champion.

"They were all good enough to be on top at different times," said Moondog Ed Moretti. "Chavo had the book in L.A., I guess, in the late '70s, but any one of his brothers could have filled that role — they were all that good."

Just about everyone agrees that Eddie was the best of the bunch.

The pinnacle of Eddie's career came at No Way Out 2004, when he beat Brock Lesnar for the WWE world title. A little more than a month later, one of his best friends in wrestling, Chris Benoit, also ascended to the top of the WWE as world champion at WrestleMania XX. The two world champions embraced in the ring following Benoit's victory. "You know how sometimes a dream seems too far-fetched and unreachable — well, WrestleMania XX was one of the moments where I realized that dream. Not only for myself but also for Chris," Guerrero told England's *Sun* newspaper. "Breaking that mould of giants was great — I'll take a pat on the back for that one. Being a smaller wrestler is something I've been dealing with all my life. But it's not the size of the dog in the fight that counts, it's the size of the fight in the dog. And that's what I'd say about me and Chris."

Eddie's sudden death in a Minneapolis hotel room on November 13, 2005, at age 38, was a tragic ending for someone who had been clean and sober for four years, and battled adversity and personal demons throughout his career. His passing, attributed in part to a weakened heart from steroid use, was one of the catalysts in the Chris Benoit double murder/suicide in June 2007, the Canadian star having admitted to being lost without his best friend.

Bill Anderson worked with all four of the older Guerrero brothers during his career, centered in California and Mexico, and attended the three-hour funeral in Scottsdale, Arizona, for Eddie, along with much of the wrestling world. "This was by far the most moving funeral I had ever been to," said Anderson, praising the Guerrero work ethic. "Their love and respect for life, family, and wrestling was always a bit more intense than the average person."

A couple of years after Eddie died, Madigan was working for WWE as a writer, and found himself chatting up a storm with "Chavo Classic," as Chavo Sr. was known when he came in for a brief while to second his son to the ring. The show was in El Paso, and before they knew it, everyone had left and they were miles from the hotel with no ride — so they started walking. "As we walked and walked toward the highway Chavo told me that 'in the day' the Guerreros ruled El Paso," remembered Madigan. "'Everyone knew us. My dad's popularity was off the chart. Everyone came to see the Guerreros wrestle. Everyone came into town to wrestle us.'" Despite Madigan's misgivings, they flagged down a large, dark van in the middle of the desert. "All of sudden several guys get out of the van. They look at Chavo and the following happened: 'Holy shit! It's Chavo Guerrero!' the guys yelled excitedly as they came up shaking Chavo's hands. Thirty years after he had wrestled in El Paso the fans still recognized him; recognized him on a lone deserted road late at night. Chavo asked if we could get a ride to the hotel. The guys couldn't have been nicer. We jumped into the van and drove around for awhile sharing the beers they had in the cooler and they were reliving the many times they had seen Chavo and his family wrestle. These guys were genuinely taken aback that one of their idols was with them driving around having a few beers and talking about the day. Chavo looked over to me and smiled and said, 'I told you, Dan, in the day the Guerreros ruled El Paso.' I toasted him with a beer and replied, 'The Guerreros *still* rule El Paso.'"

Jose Lothario, Texas Heavyweight champion.

CHRIS SWISHER COLLECTION

JOSE LOTHARIO

If Guadalupe Robledo had stopped growing and not ended up six-foot-one and 240 pounds, chances are the wrestling world would have been denied the fiery comebacks of Jose Lothario. Born in 1940 in Torreon, Mexico, into a family of ten kids, Robledo was a young boxer just moving into the middleweight class, making sixty-five to seventy pesos a bout, when he went to the *lucha libre* show. There, surprised by a grappler about to land in his lap, he swung his fist and knocked him out. The promoter saw the whole commotion and asked Robledo to wrestle. He found that he enjoyed that more — but quickly outgrew the luchador mold.

"I was gaining so much weight that I was getting to be a heavyweight," Lothario recalled. "They don't have Mexican heavyweights in boxing, so I tried to go to wrestling. I made it from there."

And made it he did. Debuting in the U.S. in 1957, Lothario paid his dues as Joe Garcia in the Carolinas until getting his first big break as El Gran Lothario in the Gulf Coast territory, where he was heavyweight champion. Following that, he mentored under Pepper Gomez. "The best tag team partner that I ever had was Pepper Gomez. I'd just come from Mexico," said Lothario.

After that, Lothario was one of the top headliners in Florida and Texas in the 1960s and 1970s, winning singles and tag team belts, as well as Brass Knucks titles in both states, tangling with notorious tough guys like Johnny Valentine and The Missouri Mauler.

Blackjack Mulligan said Lothario is underappreciated, calling him "probably the greatest Mexican star of all time as far as working ability. I mean, he was a big guy. He didn't fly like Mysterio and these guys. Those guys are little guys. Jose was a 235- to 240-pound guy."

"He was just a real tough guy, really believable," Mulligan continued. "He worked all over the Southwest. He never got up to the North, though, because he was never given the chance. He should have. He would have been a good Latino for New York if given the right time and the right place, like when [Pedro] Morales went in there. He could have worked in a situation like that."

Celebrated by his fan club, Pride of Mexico, Lothario's fame rose to the point that he was able to open the Casa Lothario restaurant in the early in 1970s in Tampa, Florida, with his brother, Salvador.

"I would have to list Jose as one of my favorite opponents. He was a fantastic worker and had a huge following in Florida, Texas, Puerto Rico, and everywhere he was booked," wrote Jack Brisco in his autobiography. "He was the perfect challenger. In all of his title matches with Dory, Harley, me, or whoever, Jose always looked like he was on the verge of taking the title away from any of us."

Referee Tommy Fooshee said Lothario was the best babyface ever in Texas. "He could throw punches and he had fantastic matches. The thing of it is, it's like Valentine said of him, you can beat him every week, and it doesn't hurt him because they're still for him."

That talent never left him, either. In 1981, a Dallas magazine profiled the local promotion, and backward complimented Lothario. "Lothario had a sagging midsection, but moved around the ring like the Russian dancer Baryshnikov while working over [Raul] Castro."

"Lothario's gotta be in his mid-forties, probably," said Fritz Von Erich in the article. "He's typical of a lot of guys. He's so skillful at what he does, he might be around another ten years. That's what I like about wrestling. Get to be this age in most other sports and, man, it's over with."

Later in the 1980s, Lothario trained one of the icons of modern-day wrestling, former WWE world champion Shawn Michaels. "Joe was a great teacher and always looked out for me. He was a nice, wonderful man, not that grumpy, mean aggressive old-timer that you hear about in this business. He really believed in me and he was very encouraging," Michaels wrote of his teacher. "He would let me learn and struggle, but when the time was right, he let me know it was time to move on. Jose didn't make a huge deal of the situation or tell me that I was being screwed or anything. He just said it was time to go. One thing Jose didn't do was stir things up." The association with the Heartbreak Kid, including being his second at the Iron Man Match at WrestleMania XII, has kept Lothario's name fresh with younger fans. Without Lothario's connections, Michaels might not have made the steps from the Mid-South to Kansas City to the AWA and finally the WWE.

Content to deal with his grandkids these days, Lothario acknowledged that he was well connected in his thirty-six years in the business. "I always got along good with everybody."

The star of the Amarillo territory, Ricky Romero.

RICKY ROMERO

It's the fundamental question of "Rapid" Ricky Romero's career: Why didn't he work anywhere else but the Amarillo territory, run by the Funk family, which stretched west into New Mexico?

He didn't need to.

"Ricky did so well in Amarillo as one of our top babyfaces that he never found it necessary to go anywhere else," said Dory Funk Jr. "Consequently, he didn't really get all the recognition that he deserves. But Ricky was truly a great, great babyface."

His brother Terry concurred. "In the summertime especially when the Spanish would come in — and they would come in to work the fields in the summertime — he would have 'em hanging from the rafters. I'm not kidding you. I mean, we would open towns up in the summertime like Littlefield, Hereford, Plainville, and we'd run those towns and they would do so well because we had Ricky Romero. Not all year long because they only came in in the summertime, but they were wrestling people. They just loved Ricky Romero. Lubbock was the number one drawing city in the state of Texas above Houston and Dallas basically because of Ricky Romero."

Romero had become friends with Dory Funk Sr. in the Arizona territory, and was made in Amarillo when Senior put him over. Having worked in Mexico and

California before getting to Amarillo, Romero knew there were other opportunities out there, but Senior always convinced him to stay. In a *Whatever Happened To . . .?* interview in 1997, Romero recalled telling Dory Sr., "I've been here for three years, man. It's time for me to go somewhere," to which the boss responded, "Well, I've been here fifteen, and I'm not going yet. You're not going no place, Mexican."

Enrique Gregory Romero was born in San Bernadino, California, in May 1931. He was a baseball player as a youth, but declined an offer by the Giants to enter the minor leagues. Tall for a Mexican at six-foot, he was recruited to be a wrestler by Professor Romero and Professor Diablo Velasco. After two years of training, he made his debut, and within a few weeks, had moved into main-event slots in Mexico.

After four years, he was invited to Los Angeles by promoter Jules Strongbow, but he never made the big time there. Danny McShain convinced him on Houston, but that didn't last because the territory already had Mexicans in El Medico, Blackie Guzman, and Pepper Gomez. So the call to go to Amarillo for promoter Doc Sarpolis would have seemed to have been a godsend. It wasn't.

The bookers in Amarillo, Al Lovelock and Tommy Phelps, kept Romero in the little towns, out of the big cities like Amarillo, Lubbock, and Odessa. "I was making twenty-five dollars in the little towns, and the other guys are making money," Romero told historian Scott Teal. "I finally couldn't take it no more." Romero quit wrestling and left for Los Angeles, where he worked painting plane parts.

When Dory Funk Sr. took over the booking duties in Amarillo, he convinced his boss, Sarpolis, to give Romero (whom he called "Mexican") a $1,500 per week guarantee — a lot of money in 1960. "If it hadn't been for Dory, I would never have made it," Romero told Teal. "Dory went all the way to help me the best he could, because he knew that I could produce."

Romero did more than produce; he changed a lot of the culture in Texas. "Pretty soon these Mexicans started coming into the arenas . . . like in herds. It was like I broke the barriers for the Mexican people," he said. Dispatched for public functions and charity events by the promotion, he put a positive face on being a Mexican-American. A naturally positive person with a smile on his face, his friendliness translated into the ring, where he'd wear colorful boots, jackets, and tights, topped off with a sombrero; he'd throw miniature sombreros to the fans at ringside.

Moose Morowski once worked an angle with Romero in Amarillo where "Rapid" Ricky destroyed his false teeth. "We drew like crazy. It was unbelievable," said Morowski. "Ricky was good to work with, and it was so easy — you didn't have to do nothing hardly with him, because he had such a following. He was the number one babyface there for all them years."

"Ricky's natural fire and emotion reminded me of Eddie Guerrero many years later," said WWE announcer Jim Ross. "Ricky was as smooth as Tito Santana and as reliable as anyone you would ever meet. He wasn't a bodybuilder but looked like an athlete and knew his craft expertly. In today's marketplace with his in-ring skills, Ricky Romero would be a huge star to his fellow Hispanics and other fans as well."

Through the years, Romero grew to be a part of the Funk family, helping to train Dory Jr. and Terry (and Ted DiBiase) for the sport, working in the office and managing many of the smaller towns.

MIKE LANO

Chris and Mark Youngblood with their dad, Ricky Romero, at one of Terry Funk's retirements, in 1997.

If loyalty to the Funks was the first word many think of in relation to Romero — he was a pall-bearer at Senior's funeral — family would be the second. Dario ("El Negro") and Alberto ("Lumberjack") Romero, Ricky's brothers, also worked in the business.

"There are a lot of fond memories of my uncles starting with my grand-mother, Florence Romero, who would pack up all the grandkids in her Chevrolet Impala and drive us to the San Bernardino Orange Show auditorium to watch my uncles wrestle," recalled their niece Rebecca Romero Gomez Mendoza. "My mother used to sew their trunks, jackets, and masks for them during their wrestling heyday. I loved to see my uncles come over and hear them talk about their bouts."

Ricky Romero had six children, and three got into wrestling as the Youngbloods (often wrongly attributed to their mother's maiden name, which was actually Marrujo): Mark, Chris, and Steve, who worked as Jay Youngblood. After Jay died in New Zealand in 1985 of a heart attack, his father lost his passion for the business. He was content staying home, having grown "tired of doing nothing."

In the late 1990s, Ricky's legs were amputated due to diabetes, and he passed away on January 15, 2006, in Amarillo, his home since 1958.

"Big" Bill Anderson was one of those kids who worshipped Romero growing up, watching the TV show from Amarillo in Phoenix, Arizona. "I never met Ricky until a few years ago at the Cauliflower Alley Club reunion in Las Vegas," Anderson said. After the dinner, someone pointed out Romero to him, sitting alone in his wheelchair. "There were at least 500 men and women in attendance, yet this legend sat alone. I went about five tables over and knelt down to introduce myself to him. I told him how I watched him thirty years ago on the old Amarillo tapes and he was my hero growing up and that he was a legend. Tears came down his face as he thanked me. He seemed to be a very humble man. He graciously posed for a photo with me."

THE ITALIAN CONNECTION

Like Don Corelone, Bruno Sammartino was always careful to keep *la famiglia* near him. While they may not have been quite as bloodthirsty as Michael, Sonny, and Fredo, they did serve a vital purpose in the heyday of Bruno's eleven-year WWWF title reigns through the '60s and '70s.

To get a crack at the world title, challengers would have to run the gauntlet, knocking off Sammartino's friends, such as Tony Parisi (sometimes billed under his real name Tony Pugliese), Gino Brito (who worked as Louis Cerdan in the WWWF), or Dominic Denucci. On the heel side, Italians included Tony Altamore, Lou Albano, and Gino Marella, a.k.a. Gorilla Monsoon. Hell, even Chief Jay Strongbow was an Italian named Joe Scarpa.

"My first match at Madison Square Garden took place on December 15, 1975, against Dominic Denucci. Like Bruno, Denucci was a native of Italy. This was not a coincidence. Vince [McMahon] Sr. wanted to create interest in my impending confrontation with the champ by having me whip his *paisan*," wrote Superstar Billy Graham in his autobiography.

"You know how you meet people in your lifetime, and you're supposed to be brothers and sisters? That's what happened with Tony, Gino and Dominic — and Bruno too," recalled Parisi's widow, Clara. "I remember when we first met Bruno, what a wonderful man he is too. They just connected. Bruno is the one that got Tony started in New York. They looked out for each other, but that's because they just connected."

There are similarities that go beyond the fact that three of the four were born in Italy (Brito, actually Louis Gino Acocella, is from Montreal; his grandparents came from France and Italy in 1911).

"They were on the road, they're Italian. They had a lot of things in common — their values, their lifestyle, that was all in consideration," said Clara Parisi.

Tony Marino, Bruno Sammartino, Tony Lanza, Ilio DiPaolo, and Dominic Denucci.

The connections as they weave throughout the years are remarkable. Brito met Denucci when Dominic immigrated to Montreal from Frosolone, in the province of Campobasso; in fact, Denucci trained with Tony Lanza, who lived on the same street as the Acocella family in Montreal. Brito's father was Jack Britton, and for a while, they lived in Windsor, Ontario, and Britton managed the midget troupe that traveled the world, and helped Burt Ruby and Harry Light promote in Detroit. Parisi started wrestling in Windsor, and had some of his earliest matches against Brito. Denucci would eventually settle in Pittsburgh and be one of Sammartino's confidants. After Parisi died from a heart attack on August 19, 2000, in Niagara Falls, Ontario, it fell to Brito to walk Parisi's daughter, Ida, down the aisle on her wedding day.

But in the WWWF, it was all about Bruno.

"Bruno, you might say I'm partial and everything, but he was nice to everybody," said Brito. "He wasn't up on that pedestal, looking down on the guys. He talked to everybody. You'd go out to eat with him, and he would pay the bill — he always wanted to be the one to pay the bill. Everyone was treated well with him, and they knew that he was the drawing card."

Denucci can only laugh at the memories, and agreed that there was an Italian mob in New York. Just not a very tough one — "You put all four together, they couldn't kill a bird!"

PEDRO MORALES

It all came full circle for Pedro Morales when he purchased the store where he first learned about professional wrestling.

"There was a business on my island, and they had a television. They used to put the TV outside to watch wrestling," Morales recalled. "We used to sit there, we would sit down on the sidewalk. It was amazing, because I bought the building. My first wrestling show that I watched was in that building, outside." Now, it's a pizzeria/bar on one side, and a luncheon counter on the other.

The transaction is a testament to Morales' shrewd business dealings throughout his wrestling career and his continued love for Culebra, a small island off the east coast of Puerto Rico, where he lived until heading to New York City as a teen.

And what promotion aired its shows in Puerto Rico? Ironically, it was the Washington, D.C.–based Capitol Wrestling, where Morales would later reign as World Wide Wrestling Federation champion for almost three years, and also held the promotion's Intercontinental and tag team belts.

"These guys were my heroes when I was watching wrestling. Then I was in the dressing room with them two, three years later, I can't believe it," he admitted, listing favorites such as Mr. Moto, Wild Red Berry, Primo Carnera, and Lou Thesz.

In the dressing room, surrounded by his idols, Morales said he kept humble, but was not intimidated. He attributes that to his upbringing in Culebra, where he was born October 22, 1942, and estimates that more than half of the island's population is related to him somehow. "I never was intimidated. We had a navy base. My mother had a business and the gringos used to come and drink. We used to associate with them. I was always in front of people." Morales was also an accomplished baseball player, though his move to Brooklyn derailed that.

It was a culture shock in the new country, going from an island of about 600 people, where the electricity only ran from 4 to 11 p.m. each day, to the bustling Gotham. Dispatched to live with his aunt and attend high school — since there wasn't one on Culebra — Morales soon joined a wrestling club, enticed by the brothers of his sister's friend.

The five-foot-eleven, 240-pound Morales had his first professional match in 1958 at the Sunnyside Gardens in Queens, and his father had to sign some paperwork to allow him to fight.

Though he was in some solid mid-card programs, often teaming with Miguel Perez or Argentina Apollo, it became apparent that he wasn't going to go very far in the northeast, and he headed out to get seasoning. In Amarillo and the Pacific Northwest, he was Johnny Como for a decent stretch, but in Hawaii, he worked under his real name.

"I think that was one of the best places, because I loved the beach," Morales said of Hawaii, where they wrestled only three or four times a week. "I was born and raised on the ocean, on the island of Culebra. Culebra is only twenty-eight square miles. My grandfather had a big sailboat, and could fit twenty-five head of cattle inside. I grew up in Culebra in a place right on the ocean. . . . Before I came to the United States, I was in the ocean all the time. I loved the ocean."

In California he became a star. The WWA world title found its way to his waist in March 1965. The *Long Beach Independent Press-Telegram* talked to him just before he knocked off The Destroyer for the belt.

"Outside Morales' dressing room at the Long Beach Auditorium, the cheers still resounded. For Pedro is the people's choice. Little tykes beg for his autograph and little old ladies jab pins into his opponents. And even his most dastardly opponents have learned to respect the twenty-two-year-old Latin hero," reads the story.

"He was a great talent," raved The Destroyer (Dick Beyer). "Everything you wanted him to do, he could do. We never had a bad match, that's what I liked about working with Pedro. You could go in the ring, you could go twenty minutes, thirty minutes, an hour, and you could do it with Pedro."

For the next number of years in California, Morales reigned as a singles star, and in tag teams with Luis Hernandez, Mark Lewin, Ricky Romero, and Victor Rivera.

"Pedro was a big crowd pleaser. He had that energy and that spark," said Jeff Walton, the publicist for the Los Angeles office. "He was one of the first Latino stars that really sparked the area and the crowds here. There were others before him that were here, but a lot of them were local guys, and he really came in and made quite an impression." The promotion was careful not to promote him as a Puerto Rican, however. "If you mentioned Puerto Rican to the Mexican population, they kind of tuned them out actually."

In Hawaii, ethnic makeup wasn't an issue, said promoter Ed Francis. "There's so many different kinds of people there, Filipino, Japanese, Chinese, so many different kinds of people, Portuguese, people didn't pay any attention to that kind of stuff."

Promoter Vincent J. McMahon knew his fanbase was heavily ethnic, and had his eye on Morales for years. With his world champion, Bruno Sammartino, demanding time off, McMahon needed a new draw. Morales returned to Madison Square Garden on January 18, 1971, the night Sammartino was dethroned by Ivan Koloff. Three weeks later, Morales knocked off Koloff for a title run that went until December 3, 1973, when Stan Stasiak surprised Morales, and subsequently lost the title back to Sammartino.

Photographer George Napolitano was at ringside when Morales beat Koloff. "Despite what people say, what I really remember is that there was a hush, it was quiet. Nobody really expected it to happen. It was more surprise than jubilation," he recalled. "They were happy, yeah,

Before he ruled the WWWF and the East Coast, Pedro Morales was WWA world champion in Los Angeles.

but they just didn't expect it. It wasn't like, 'Wow, look at this!' It was more subdued silence and respect, like, 'Wow, he really did it.'"

"Like Bruno Sammartino, Pedro Morales was an ethnic hero. When he wrestled in Madison Square Garden, the Bronx emptied out, and every Puerto Rican in the borough filled the arena," wrote Freddie Blassie in his autobiography. "If you were roughing him up, all he had to do was give the high sign, and he'd have twenty thousand tag team partners charging the ring."

Blackjack Mulligan, an early challenger for Morales' WWWF title, can attest to that loyalty. In 1972, the fans in Boston rioted when Mulligan and his manager, The Grand Wizard (Ernie Roth), snuck in a weapon.

"Ernie hands me a blackjack and boom, I nail the Hispanic, and there's seventy-five percent Hispanic in the building — they're going to go nutso. And they come unglued. They totally came unglued. We weren't ready for it," explained Mulligan, who was stabbed in the leg and chased back to his hotel.

Parade, a national newspaper insert, described the champ in April 1972. "Morales, whose soft-spoken, courteous manner contrasts with his bulging chest and shoulder muscles, is reflective of the growing interest in wrestling in cities

The epic battle of Pedro Morales against Bruno Sammartino in 1972 ended in a draw.

with big Puerto Rican populations. Portraits and posters of Morales are sold in Madison Square Garden almost like saintly relics, and his fans come armed with Puerto Rican flags which they wave furiously when he pins an opponent."

Not a big man, and surrounded by giants, the left-handed Morales relied on his fire and intensity to sell his skills to the masses. Slapping his chest to get himself motivated and rev up the crowd, his emotive face could convey feeling to the back rows.

After he dropped the title to Stasiak, he took it easy, settling into life in Woodbridge, NJ, where his wife, Karen, taught elementary school, and where their son, Pedro Jr., grew to six-foot-ten and landed a basketball scholarship at the University of North Carolina-Charlotte.

But the need to compete remained, and in 1980, Morales added to his legacy, claiming the WWWF tag titles with then world champ Bob Backlund — they had to relinquish, since the world champ was prohibited from holding both titles — and then the Intercontinental title on two occasions.

"I enjoyed working with Pedro," said Ken Patera, who dropped the IC title to him. "He had a good fan base other than the Puerto Ricans. Of course, when I worked with him, every Puerto Rican within 200 miles would show up, especially up there in Massachusetts, Worchester, Boston, Portland, Maine, New Haven, Connecticut. He had a good following."

"Irish" Davey O'Hannon traveled and wrestled with Morales around the Northeast, and witnessed both the ego — "Pedro would walk into a place and think that everything should stop and focus on him" — and the reason for it, like a twenty-four-hour sandwich shop, deep in the Bronx. "We pulled into a little Bodega and went in to get a sandwich, and the place went nuts. It was Pedro. And this was eleven o'clock at night, it was a twenty-four-hour place. Oh man, he hit that door, he could have walked away with the store if he wanted to. It was unreal. He was wildly popular here."

Later, Morales would challenge IC champion Randy Savage for the title as the WWF expanded nationally, with a viciously draining schedule. He quit in 1986, with a last bout in a legends battle royal in 1987, and became a Spanish commentator for the WWF and then WCW.

Having saved and invested his money well, Morales is content to manage his businesses, work out at the gym, and grow tomatoes in his garden. He isn't one to head out on the convention circuit or to gather up awards. "He is home in New York and doesn't like to leave," said Savio Vega, a star in Puerto Rico. "Even when [WWE] wanted to induct him into the Hall of Fame, I was the one that received the award for him because he didn't want to come."

TITO SANTANA

Merced Solis listened to the advice he got early in his career — "Everyone kept telling me how important it was to have fire, to learn how to sell, not to die" — and converted that into a lengthy career solely as a babyface.

It was a tricky line, he admitted, between selling and dying. "It's hard to explain to somebody, because you almost have to feel it in the ring," he explained. "The fans always have to see a little life in you, you couldn't just die and come out of the grave and all of a sudden be wide awake, make an explosive comeback." Instead, the key was showing a little life, fighting back, and having the heel stop you. Repeat. "What I took a lot of pride in is finally, when

I exploded, I wouldn't make a comeback until I was practically drained — that's why a lot of the guys said I had a lot of fire. When I made that comeback, I just kept going until I was exhausted."

Indeed, it was a familiar scene from 1977 until the late 1980s to see Tito Santana leave the ring dripping with sweat, whether in tag teams or singles competitions, having given his all in the ring for the fans. Outside of the ring, he was equally giving.

"Coming from such a poor family, and now to know that the fans were the ones that were making me a good living, more than I had ever expected in life, they were never a nuisance to me," Solis said. "I saw a lot of the guys that turned fans down. I never turned anybody down that asked me for an autograph. To me, if it wasn't for the fans, I wouldn't have had the career that I did."

Born May 10, 1953, to migrant workers in Mission, Texas, Solis would be pulled out of school in the fall and spring to help pick crops. It wasn't until his freshman year at Mission High that he actually completed a full year of education. "My grades were never up to par," said Solis, who at six-foot-two, 234 pounds excelled in football as a speedy tight end, and in basketball and track. "I would never have been able to get into a big school. West Texas State was the best that I was able to get accepted to."

The quarterback on that West Texas team was Tully Blanchard, son of San Antonio wrestling promoter Joe Blanchard. Though he wasn't a fan, Solis soon learned about pro wrestling, and kept it in the back of his mind through training camp with the NFL's Kansas City Chiefs and a season with the BC Lions of the CFL. He loved playing in Vancouver. "I was young and single and I thought it was a beautiful city, beautiful people, beautiful women. I had a great time. I lived there for a year and a half. It was a very good experience for somebody who came from way down south, a little town with 14,000 population. That was the beginning of my world tour, I guess."

The senior Blanchard told Solis of the riches of pro wrestling compared to football. "I told him that my first love was football. And he replied, 'Well, you have a chance to make $80,000 a year as a professional wrestler.' After that, I started thinking that football was such a hard sport, with no security, and with $80,000 in one hand and $20,000 in the other, it was a no-brainer. I started watching wrestling, too, and noticed how a wrestler's career seemed to be a lot longer than a footballer's, and I thought that I should go into wrestling." After consulting Terry Funk, another West Texas veteran, Solis gave himself four years to succeed or try something else. Solis needn't have worried.

After training under Hiro Matsuda in Florida, he debuted under his real name in 1977, and quickly made the rounds of Florida, Georgia, Amarillo, the Mid-Atlantic (as Richard Blood), the WWWF (where he was tag champion with Ivan Putski, and was renamed Tito Santana), and the AWA, where he stayed for almost three years. In 1983, Solis was back in the WWF, and in the perfect place for the national expansion, adding color, depth, and international flavor to the babyface roster.

It was always obvious that Tito Santana left it all in the ring.

"I never denied my heritage, and I always threw in some Spanish. I think that the true Mexican or true Hispanic knew that my English was too good to be a solid Mexican," he said. "I believe that I got over with everybody, blacks, Japanese, whites, everybody liked Tito Santana."

His opponents especially liked him, and the office relied on him to headline "B" shows without Hulk Hogan.

"Tito was a fabulous worker," said Greg Valentine, who knocked off an injured Santana for the Intercontinental title in 1984, and dropped it back to Santana in a famed cage match.

For all the fame, trading cards, cartoon characters, and action figures, Santana, who was also known as El Matador (having learned some bullfighting techniques for the role), was never given a chance at the WWF world title. "At the time, the reigning champion was Hulk Hogan. Back then, they didn't put a good guy against a good guy. I would have loved to have wrestled Hulk Hogan," he said, recalling a few matches they actually did have back in 1979. "At one time my popularity was pretty high up there with him. I think people would have enjoyed a match, me against him."

Solis also regrets never getting a chance at a heel run, something he pitched to the WWF powers that be; instead, his championship tag team partner, Rick

Martel, got the opportunity to go rogue. "I considered myself a better babyface than some of the guys who turned, who had become good heels. I used to say to myself, 'If that guy was able to make the transition, I have a complete understanding of the psychology of our business, I know I can become a good heel, because I know what makes the people pissed off, what got the people burning.' I just never had the opportunity to show that I can do it."

While Solis is content with his place in wrestling history, which includes a stint as a Spanish announcer and induction into the WWE Hall of Fame, he has the most pride in what he was able to provide for his family. Married for almost thirty years — his wife runs a hair salon, Santana's — the success of his three sons proves how far the farm laborer from Mission has come. "My oldest son's a lawyer, my middle one got his master's in International Law and went to Princeton, and my little guy got his master's in Accounting," said Solis, who has also taught gym and Spanish and coached basketball at schools near his Roxbury, NJ, home. "I always say, 'I'm the wealthiest wrestler around.'"

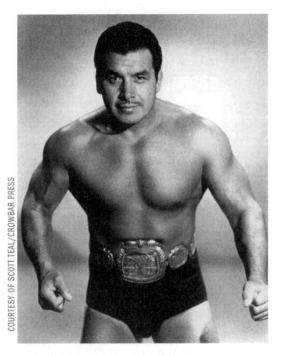

Enrique Torres was one of the biggest stars in the history of California.

ENRIQUE TORRES

It was a little over-the-top to proclaim, as *Official Wrestling* magazine did in 1951, that "the greatest gold mine discovered in Mexico since the days of Cortez is Enrique Torres." But not by much. The old National Wrestling Association used to issue a Top 10 list every year, and Torres was on it for six years in a row in the late '40s and early '50s, in there with Lou Thesz, Gorgeous George, and Buddy Rogers. While friends and co-workers said his Mexican heritage probably helped in places like Texas and California, it can't begin to account for the way Torres got marquee billing in places like

Georgia, Missouri, Ohio, South Carolina, and Quebec. "If I were to name the top babyface workers of all time, I would pick Enrique. The best clean match I ever had was with him in Portland, Oregon," said Jerry Christy, adding that his wrestling uncles Vic and Ted also put Torres at the top.

Torres came on the scene in 1946 and wouldn't leave it for twenty-two years. Along the way, he claimed a version of the world championship in California, had roughly forty runs as a singles and tag champ in every corner of the country, and shepherded his brothers Ramon and Alberto into the pro game. Frankie Cain was instrumental in getting the Torres brothers booked in Atlanta in the 1960s, where they had a legendary feud with the Vachons. The only thing that puzzled him is that Torres never got a big shot in the New York market; he was there only a few times. "He was very good. He had good moves. He was very convincing. You could have made money with him," Cain said. "It's remarkable that [the New York office] never brought that guy in there because he was handsome and tall and could move. They sure missed the boat there because if they brought Enrique Torres there in his prime, boy, what money he could've drawn there."

While Torres was the strong, proud type in person and in front of crowds, Kata, his wife of forty-four years, said he actually was shy. "He had a great depth of character, something that really didn't show to the public," she said. "He didn't much care to be talking on TV; he conveyed his methods by action. He could imply a threat where he didn't actually have to come out and say, 'I'm going to bash your head in.' He could convey menace without using the words."

On the mat, Torres was billed from Sonora, Mexico, but though his parents were born in Mexico, he was born July 25, 1922, in Santa Ana, California. Growing up, he didn't intend to make wrestling a career. After his father suffered a serious injury when Torres was about fourteen, he left school to support the family by driving a truck in the fields to carry crops to local markets. He wrestled as an amateur in and around southern California, turning pro against the wishes of his mom and dad. In 1946, he blasted onto the scene in California, winning one version of the world title from George Becker, which he'd hold — sometimes it was called the Pacific heavyweight title — until 1950. Trained by Benny Ginsberg, he was an absolute sensation with a flying scissors attack and few other accoutrements. "I didn't change my name or anything," he said in an interview in 2006. "I didn't have a gimmick of any kind. I was just Enrique Torres and that was it." In 1948, PAN magazine, Hardy Kruskamp's publication for California boxing and wrestling, had Torres third as an attraction behind only Gorgeous George and the Dusek

Enrique Torres at his Calgary home in 2005.

family, and would have had put him higher if he hadn't run off to other parts of the country. "He has class and ability. No one for the last ten years that has entered the game has had so much on the ball," the publication reported.

From there, he was in constant demand. In Montreal, Torres was regarded as the number one challenger to the great Yvon Robert in 1948. In Kansas City, Missouri, he feuded with Bob Orton and put the Central States heavyweight belt around his waist in 1952; he'd headline there again a decade later. In San Francisco, it was championship tag teams with Bobo Brazil, Leo Nomellini, Ronnie Etchison, and Johnny Barend. In the Carolinas, he hooked up with George Becker as Southern tag titleholders in 1959. Renowned wrestler and trainer Les Thatcher watched him as a kid, knew him as an adult, and always liked what he saw. "Ricky and I traveled together quite a bit in K.C. and I watched his work in Atlanta, and was a fan of his when I was a young fan," Thatcher said. "I have often wondered why he was overlooked so much. With back problems in K.C., his knowledge and timing still made him a money-drawing babyface. Very smooth to watch. I picked up pointers from him early on." Most telling, perhaps, is the fact Torres was one of the preferred challengers for the National Wrestling Alliance heavyweight championship. From November 1947 to November 1950, he worked almost two dozen main events, coast to coast, with Lou Thesz. Not until the days of Mil Mascaras would any wrestler of Mexican descent rival Torres' profile in the United States and Canada.

Despite that pedigree, Barend also thought that his old partner has been somewhat overlooked. "As a performer, he had a lot of talent, and he was a good showman, and a nice person." The record books make it sound easier than it was, though — he missed nearly a year in the late '50s with a ruptured disc in his back, and had to slip out of Cuba with Alberto aboard a Navy ship when Fidel Castro overthrew the Batista government. Kata said he didn't talk about it extensively, but it clearly was a harrowing moment. "It was scary. Guys were walking on the streets with machine guns and pistols, and they'd say, 'Viva Castro.' If you didn't respond, 'Viva Castro,' they shot you on the spot."

The battle for Georgia between the Vachons and the Torres brothers was Enrique's last hurrah, and he went out on top. It started in the fall of 1966 and ran for more than two years. The three Torres brothers paired off with Mad Dog and Butcher, as well as "wrestling brother" Stan (Eric Pomeroy), in every conceivable permutation; Ramon and Butcher donned masks at various times as an Avenger and a Japanese wrestler, respectively. Butcher credited booker Leo Garibaldi with laying out the unusual feud — Mexicans and French-Canadians fighting it out in the heart of Dixie. "Leo had something to prove with the Torres brothers because the guy who owned the territory was Paul Jones, but the real guys were his two partners. They had told him, 'Leo, those guys are like blacks. They'll never get over here.' So Leo took that to heart and he really got them over," Vachon said. Enrique finished up as Southern tag champion with Alberto in June 1968, when he retired to California to care for his mother after his father died.

During his career, Torres sent his mother money that was invested in residential rental properties, so much of his post-wrestling career was spent with Kata at his side tending to apartment buildings and a real estate portfolio in the San Fernando Valley. He sold them off a bit at a time and moved to Nevada with his wife before heading north to Calgary to help care for her relatives. He remained in excellent shape, losing weight deliberately after he retired, working out religiously, and managing diabetes for about thirty years. He was doing well after a kidney transplant, until he suffered a stroke in March 2007 and died that September at eighty-five. "He was very intelligent," Kata said. "I think if he had gone on to higher education, he would have done very well. He made the comment numerous times that he wished he'd stayed in school, and my retort was, 'To what end? Because you've achieved great things, and maybe you wouldn't have become the man you are now.'"

HOMETOWN HEROES

RUTH OMAN, PETE LEDERBERG COLLECTION

Never too showy, Bob Armstrong could grab the crowd, or Jack Brisco, with a headlock.

BOB ARMSTRONG

"I'm Southern-born and Southern-bred, and when I die, I'll be Southern-dead." Bob Armstrong has been saying that for about as long as he's been wrestling, and that's a long time. Armstrong, born Joseph M. James on October 3, 1939, had his first match on his birthday in 1961, and he's still on the mat more than half a century later, one of a handful of wrestlers to compete in six different decades. So although the agreeable Georgia native was inducted into the WWE Hall of Fame in 2011, he is definitely not going to be similarly honored by the Retirement Hall of Fame. "It does get in your blood and as long as I can do it, I can't see why I shouldn't," he said. "I always say this is my last year and I always lie to myself." Even after all that time, Armstrong still resonates with fans in the Deep South, according to veteran referee Mac MacMurray, who's known him for more than forty years. "It's the Southern redneck thing," MacMurray said. "He was over real strong. He's over strong now. If the independent [promotions] bring him in, he'll do good business. In fact, I try to make some of his indie shots when I know he's going to be there."

Be sure, though, to give assists to an understanding wife Gail and Dr. James Andrews, the noted orthopedist who's been putting Armstrong back together for years. Armstrong lives only a few miles from the renowned Andrews sports clinic in Gulf Breeze, Florida, and the doc, who first met him at wrestling matches in Columbus, Georgia, keeps rebuilding him, like Robo-wrestler. "I've got pins and screws and clamps and all kinds of parts, but every time I've gone to the Andrews Institute, it's been a success and they've kept me going," Armstrong said.

Armstrong is the patriarch of the first family of Southern wrestling. Sons Brad, Brian, Scott, and Steve all followed him into the business, and while they've had success, they've yet to eclipse their dad, who's held more than sixty individual and tag team championships in his career. Among his colleagues, you'll find nothing but admiration and respect for Armstrong, but they also know better than to cross the ex-Marine. Dr. Tom Prichard saw what happened to a motorcyclist who cut off Armstrong and his passengers at a left-turn light. "I've seen him jam the car in park, go in the back, snatch the guy off his bike, yank his helmet, put him back on, get back in the car, screech off, and we're all looking at each other, Brad and the rest of us, like, 'Holy shit, that just happened!'" Prichard exclaimed. "Bob Armstrong definitely had charisma and he definitely had that knowledge that he was a badass."

Armstrong was born and raised on a farm in Marietta, Georgia, and got interested in wrestling as a kid when his father took him to see Gorgeous George. You can still hear the wonderment in Armstrong's voice when he describes how the Gorgeous One tossed gold-plated bobby pins to his public. "I sat on my dad's shoulders and I thought this must be what an angel looks like. He was dressed all in gold with that platinum hair and it made such an impression on me." He boxed in the Marines, but said he was not allowed to lift weights because an instructor thought it would make him look muscle-bound. Once out of the service, Armstrong was a fireman and weightlifter in Marietta, and followed fellow firefighter Darrell Cochran into wrestling in Georgia. Around 1966, he committed to the sport full-time, mostly as big-biceped Bob Armstrong, a name promoter Charlie Harben gave him, though he'd also work under other guises as the masked Bullet and the Georgia Jawjacker. "When he first got over in Georgia, they really, really pushed that he was a fireman, like he was an everyday regular guy. I think the people really identified with that," said Southern veteran Davey Rich. When Ted Turner's superstation WTBS started beaming *Georgia Championship Wrestling* to a national audience in the 1970s and 1980s, Armstrong reached a whole new level of exposure. "I remember going to Grand Rapids, Michigan. Brad had just started wrestling. We couldn't get off the stage for fifteen minutes. The fans were grabbing him and the older people were grabbing me. That's when I realized what cable TV had done for us."

Armstrong could adapt his style to suit just about any opponent. He specifically recalls a fifteen-minute match with Abdullah the Butcher that packed the house in Macon, Georgia, as one of his favorites — that was a marathon compared to the minute or two melee for which the Butcher was known. But Armstrong also said he made a colossal blunder when wrestling his idol Lou Thesz in Miami, Florida, around 1974. "Thesz came in, he was about fifty-five years old and I was in my prime and I said, 'Lou, do you want me to slow down a little bit?' That was the biggest mistake I ever made. He made a pretzel out of me and just made me realize how great he really was. We went forty-five minutes and I don't think he drew a tired breath."

Davey Rich was wrestling under his real name of David Haskins when Armstrong brought him into USA Wrestling in Knoxville, Tennessee, where he was booking. He points to Armstrong's belief in continuing wrestling education as a key to his success. "He's a legend in the South," Rich said. "I think he was such a student of the game. He studied things. He was one of the few people who, instead of partying and having a big time, he was studying."

Armstrong was Southern heavyweight champion in Georgia and Florida, won the Georgia TV belt, and held the Macon and Georgia tag team championships a dozen times combined in the early 1970s, frequently teaming with long-time friend Robert Fuller. The low moment of his career came outside the ring, when he suffered devastating facial injuries during a 1980s weightlifting catastrophe. Armstrong was lying on a bench, doing two-arm pullovers with about 180 pounds when his world turned upside down. "The bench wasn't nailed down or bolted down. It was my fault completely," he said. "I had just started to pull it over when the bench slid and broke and all the weight came down on my face. It tore my nose off and broke every bone in my face." Ronnie Garvin, Pez Whatley, and Bob's son Brad helped him get emergency treatment. "My face was just about gone. It turned black, blue, and yellow with no nose. We put a sheet over my head so that people wouldn't scream. They put me back together but it took a while and I lost about thirty pounds, maybe more." The plastic surgeries and scars led Armstrong to don a mask as the "Bullet," and though healed, he's kept that trademark for more than twenty-five years. "It just got better and better. Now I wouldn't wrestle without my mask for anything. That's just a part of me."

Bob Armstrong's display at Fan Axxess before his induction into the WWE Hall of Fame.

In the ring, there was a definite restlessness and aggressiveness to his work. "Oh, he'd chop you in a heartbeat. He was, 'Come on, let's go,'" said Pat Rose, who worked with Armstrong in Alabama-based Southeastern Championship Wrestling, at one point hanging him from a rope with Prichard to the horror of fans. "It was all kinds of stuff. It was the body. It was the ex-fireman-turned-pro-wrestler. It was the Georgia Jawjacker. He knew how to get over. In his interviews he would say little corny lines like something about an old lady referring to the heels. It would be funny, but it would be realistic." One memorable Armstrong jab at Fuller and Jimmy Golden: "Birds of a feather flock together and these are two of the biggest buzzards I've ever seen." In fact, he traced his popular down-home mic skills to his youth on a farm, where the Southern-born-and-bred expression came from. "That was a saying down South. I heard my grandfather say it, I heard my uncle say it. So I heard a lot of old sayings, old Southern, confederate sayings and I just picked up on them. They just fit right in with whatever I was saying. They just popped right into my mind."

Armstrong also served as commissioner of Smoky Mountain Wrestling and has been on TNA Wrestling on and off for years. Konnan and the Latin American Exchange turned his real-life knee surgery into a hot angle in 2006 that ran for several months. In May 2009, a big crowd turned out at the Dothan Civic Center in Alabama for a final farewell to Armstrong and Jerry Stubbs. "I was really serious about retiring," he said. "And I sat at home for about a month and I got the itch, and a promoter called me and made me an offer I couldn't refuse." The bookings kept coming to the time of his WWE Hall of Fame induction, when he figured he'd wrestle through October 2011, the fifty-year mark of his career, and put the boots in the closet. "That failed," he said with a laugh. In fact, he marked his golden wrestling anniversary with an 800-mile round trip to Boaz, Alabama, for a big Halloween show. "I'm sure somebody will break a bone and that'll finish me," he laughed. "But until that happens, I'm probably going to keep it up."

TERRY DART

Leo Burke, ready for action, in one of countless arenas he performed in across Canada.

LEO BURKE

In the Canadian Maritime provinces, one hero stood higher than the rest, a grappling god worshipped by the locals on television and in person at the steamy hockey arenas during the summer-long wrestling season.

But you'll never hear him brag about it.

"It's not for me to say, but yeah, I was well respected, no doubt," allowed Leo Burke.

For 1980s Atlantic Grand Prix Wrestling announcer Gair Maxwell, one word — humility — stands out when he thinks of Burke, whom he worshipped himself as a youngster in New Brunswick. "Leo had a certain humility about him," said Maxwell, continuing. "That humility wasn't just something in terms of a put-on in front of a microphone or in front of a stadium or arena. I saw that humility many, many times over in the confines and the sanctity of the dressing room. Right there amongst the guys, I just remember how he was never affected by his own fame."

And famous he was.

"You would never understand how over Leo was until you saw him work," said Buddy Wayne, who grew up in Washington state and knew nothing of

Burke when he was booked to work out east as Wayne Gillis. "I witness him walk to the ring, no music, and the place goes wild. Every night, same thing. I tell everyone he was the Hulk Hogan of the Maritimes — meant as a compliment."

Leonce Cormier was born June 29, 1948, in Dorchester, New Brunswick. "I lived, ate, drank wrestling since I was six years old. And of course, I have two older brothers in the wrestling profession that made me want to follow in their footsteps," said Burke, referring to Yvon, who was The Beast, and Rudy, who was a promoter in the 1970s in the Maritimes and wrestled and managed as Rudy Kay. Brother Bobby is a year younger than Leo. After being trained by his older brothers, he chose the last name Burke after a friend, Jackie Burke, who was a boxer. "I didn't want to do it on my brothers' reputations. So I needed to do it on my own or not at all," said Burke, who turned pro in 1966.

Burke worked on top or near the top in Calgary, Japan (where he was under a mask as The Atomic), New Zealand, India, and in the United States as Tommy Martin in Kansas City and the Carolinas. Yet he always felt the call of the Maritimes, and would return annually for the summer.

Those grounded Maritime roots are undeniably part of who he is, and why he was so popular. "The thing of it is down home, and even out in Calgary, yes, I was a crowd favorite, no doubt. But I think it was because, sure, I was Leo Burke the wrestler, but I was always first and foremost Leonce Cormier. I never considered myself above anybody. That's one reason I kept my popularity — even today. When I went back for my brother's funeral, even after twenty years, people recognized me, wanted pictures and autographs. I had my son with me. He said, 'God, Dad, I can't believe it. You haven't been here in twenty years!' I said, 'Yeah, that's what it was like.' We were like movie stars, especially in the Maritimes, because that was the first time we had TV live. It was incredible. But good moments. I've always had a soft heart for kids and the older people. I would always, after a match, it didn't matter if I was tired or not, I always stayed there and signed autographs. As long as there were people there, I'd stay and sign."

But he wasn't without his quirks either. Burke loved garlic, would confuse the opponent and referee by speaking French if angered in the ring, and he didn't have the best vision in the world.

"You work with him, and everybody believes you're killing him," said Goldie Rogers (Dave Sherman). "Very nice guy to work with, but a little bit dangerous too. All the Cormiers were, because they all wore glasses, and when they wrestled, they took the glasses off — they can't see now! They go for your forearm and hit you in the nose instead."

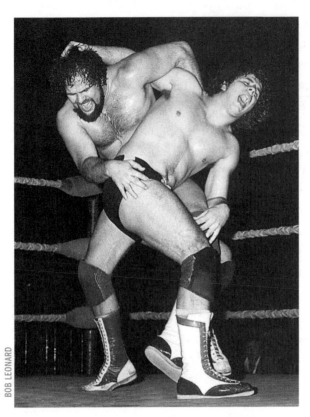

BOB LEONARD

Leo Burke ties up Bret Hart in an abdominal stretch.

In a career that saw him hold dozens of titles and compete against the best in the world, including challenging for the NWA world title against five different claimants — Dory Funk Jr., Harley Race, Jack Brisco, Terry Funk, and Ric Flair — and the AWA title held by Nick Bockwinkel and Rick Martel, Burke is still one to downplay his accomplishments.

After "retiring" in 1992, through his friend Bret Hart Burke got a job as a trainer in Calgary for the WWF. "Bret has a lot of respect for me over the years. I wrestled him maybe a hundred different times," said Burke. "They were looking for a wrestling coach, and he said, 'I've got one that you'll really like.' That's how I got in touch with Vince McMahon." He worked for the WWF for three years training names such as Test (Andrew Martin), Ken Shamrock, Glenn Kulka, Edge (Adam Copeland), Christian (Jay Reso), and Mark Henry. Other "real" jobs included tending bar and running a sandwich truck.

Yet the ring kept beckoning, as did the Maritimes. He would regularly return home to wrestle or for public appearances. Joe E. Legend (Joe Hitchen) worked with Burke in 1999, and Burke landed Legend a tryout with WCW after he had switched training allegiances. Legend said Burke commanded a great deal of respect without demanding it. "He might be the Ric Flair of Maritime wrestling. Never really lost a step, great psychology, and always was good to everyone. He didn't need to lean on the green kids to big himself up. He was a great ambassador to the business."

Maxwell, still based in New Brunswick, speaks on behalf of the Maritimes. "I think there's no question there's a real pride that this region associates with someone like Leo, who has traveled and who's done things at a world-class level. I don't think, though, that they truly grasp — still to this day — how good he was, to be honest. That he could literally get in the ring with the absolute best in the world, the best in the business, and have a terrific match that would really have people jumping out of their seats. And it didn't matter what role he played, either babyface or heel. That's the thing that made Leo Burke so great, is you could put him in any situation, and he was going to be able to deliver like a professional, because that's what a professional does, he was going to be able to give the audience every bit of what they paid for, and then some. He was going to give them their money's worth."

WHITEY CALDWELL

By 1970, a year into his reign as National Wrestling Alliance world champion, Dory Funk Jr. was living hotel to hotel, and frequently didn't even know who he would be wrestling until he got to the arena. As he scanned the dressing room one night in Knoxville, Tennessee, somebody pointed out his opponent du jour, a wiry, sandy-haired guy who looked like he should be carrying wrestlers' gym bags, not holding one of his own. Funk thought it was a joke. "I thought to myself, 'Surely by the time I go into the ring, somebody is going to tell me who I am wrestling tonight.'" And that's how Funk met Whitey Caldwell. Funk won a narrow victory, and came back for a sold-out rematch a few weeks later. "Whitey Caldwell did one hell of a job that night and earned my respect as one tough wrestler," Funk said.

In a lot of ways, it was tough to take Whitey Caldwell seriously. He probably weighed 190 pounds on a good day. He had no gimmick, no tan lines, no fancy ring garb . . . heck, no first name. He had a good day job to support his family, and seldom ventured far from home. But oh, did he embody the hopes and aspirations of everybody who loved rasslin' in east Tennessee, and in his hometown of Kingsport. "He was bigger than anything this town has ever had or will ever have," said Beau James, a wrestler and promoter in Kingsport. "Whitey worked a regular job and most everyone knew it. But every Wednesday night, he would be in the ring at the Civic Auditorium battling for the people of his town."

If there was a sport in Kingsport, J.C. Caldwell — that's the entry on his July 1935 birth certificate — was involved in it. He loved to swim, pitched in American Legion baseball and boxed in the Upper East Tennessee Golden Gloves tournament. But wrestling really caught his fancy. A group of about six boys,

Whitey Caldwell.

including future über-villains Ron and Don Wright, wrestled at the local Boy's Club and fell under the tutelage of promoter Mickey Baarns. Interest ran so high in the amateur bouts that they outdrew the professionals who came to town, and Caldwell had his first recorded bout for pay in January 1956, when he was twenty. For the next sixteen years, he wrestled in east Tennessee and surrounding areas at night, while working at a glass factory by day, where he was sergeant-at-arms for the union. "He had offers to go to Japan like some of the other wrestlers were doing but he wouldn't do that either. He loved his kids and he didn't want to lose his insurance at the glass plant," said his wife Nancy, who married her sweetheart when she was seventeen. "He didn't like a lot of praise. People didn't understand how he could be a wrestler and be so quiet."

If he was less of a homebody, Caldwell might have had an extended run with a light-heavyweight championship in some other territory. Though Baarns had a vested interest, he was not far off the mark in 1961 when he identified Caldwell as "the fastest wrestler in the South." Long before the missile drop-kick gained a formal name, Caldwell was launching it off the turnbuckle. He held the Southeastern singles championship and just about every other title in the region as he battled Frank Morrell, Sputnik Monroe, the Von Brauners, and Tarzan Baxter.

The Wrights, especially motor-mouthed Ron, were the Hatfields to his McCoy, and their rivalry stayed fresh for years on the strength of ever-more-imaginative bookings. In November 1962, Caldwell came from behind to win the final four falls in a shave-your-head match against Ron. A few years later, the Wrights resorted to a chloroform-laden rag during a televised match to knock out Caldwell and take the Tennessee tag title from him and Les Thatcher. In July 1970, when Ron relied on a loaded boot to kick his opponents into unconsciousness, Caldwell wore a crash helmet into the ring, and then clobbered Wright with it for the winning fall. Tornado matches, chain matches, strap matches with ten-foot-long-leather bindings . . . you name it, they did it, and the ensuing carnage was enough to propel the small territory to the cover of national wrestling magazines. Caldwell had a short fuse and Ron said he knew exactly how to light it, so their matches became even more believable. "The first match we ever had, I broke his shoulder.

Whitey Caldwell clotheslines Ron Wright and referee Mel Johnson.

I didn't mean to. It was an accident. I threw him over the ropes and he came down wrong. Every time I talked about that, that'd set him off," Wright said. "He didn't like it when I badmouthed him. That made me do it even more. So when he got in the ring, he was already mad." Even Wright knew where to draw the line, though. Tennessee referee Mel Johnson, who loved Caldwell liked a brother, referred to him as "Little Dynamite" one time. "Don't call him little!" Wright cautioned.

When Thatcher entered east Tennessee in the fall of 1968, he was as suspicious as Funk about the local hero, especially when John Cazana, who promoted Knoxville, campaigned for Caldwell as a possible tag team partner. "I didn't say anything to John at the time, but I was thinking, 'I don't want to be in a position where I'm putting over the local babyface.'" Also like Funk, Thatcher watched one Caldwell match and became a believer. "I said, 'Damn, this guy can go!'" he recalled. "He was a very soft-spoken man. He was not boisterous, he was not loud, he was not a bully. But I'll tell you this right now: None of those boys wanted to fight him. They knew enough to fear him."

Johnson, also a Kingsport native — at one point, he and Ron Wright worked at the same printing company — was third man in the ring for most of the rivalry's classic matches. Sometimes he wore old, tattered pants because he knew a Caldwell-Wright match would mean major bloodstains on his good referee's garb. "There would be a lot of matches where they got out there and they would shoot and just make sure they didn't do anything to the outcome," he said. "I'll tell you something — when I was in there working with these guys, I got to where I believed it myself. These guys worked that tight and that good, and of course, they beat themselves to death."

In one of the truly memorable angles in east Tennessee wrestling, Caldwell beat Ron Wright in Knoxville in September 1972 to win the Southeastern title and possession of Wright's walking horse, *Southern Perfection*, which he sold to a fan a week later. The next night, October 7, 1972, Caldwell was returning home shortly after 11 p.m. from a match in Morristown, about an hour away. Another driver veered to pass multiple cars in a single swoop, but failed to return to his lane and crashed head-on into Caldwell's car, mangling it beyond recognition. He was thirty-seven, and left behind a wife and three kids. So familiar was Caldwell to east Tennessee that the page one headline in the *Knoxville Journal* read simply: "'Whitey' Killed in Accident." The following week, Ron Wright took Caldwell's place in a tag team match, and there weren't a lot of dry eyes at Knoxville's Chilhowie Park.

Years have passed, and fans still place flowers on Caldwell's grave. Those memories linger, probably because there's not much in the way of visual images to capture Caldwell. He was almost averse to publicity and balked at selling his promotional pictures, except one time to raise money for a twelve-year-old girl who needed a kidney operation. "When he died," Nancy Caldwell said, "her mother wrote me a letter and sent me a picture of the little girl."

LARRY CHENE

He's been gone for many years, but the vignettes Larry Chene left behind are so striking that they defy the passage of time. Johnny Powers remembered one from a 1963 night in a Pontiac, Michigan armory, when he first saw Chene perform a Death Walk. Wrestling as the conceited Lord Anthony Lansdowne, Powers dropkicked Chene over the top rope. Staggering along the ring apron, unsure of his bearings, Chene took an errant step into thin air and fell in a full-body pancake on the floor, like a skydiver whose parachute failed to open. Powers was shaken. "Your heart stopped for a second or two because he hit it with such a thump. You walk over and he's flat out, lying like he's dead, no movement on the concrete. The people are standing up, they're not yelling, there's total silence in the armory," he said. "I come

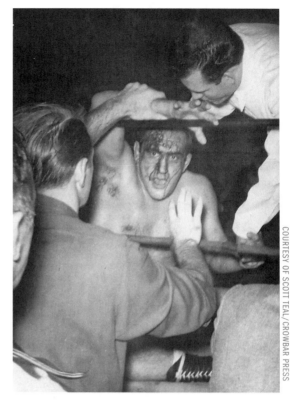

A battered Larry Chene is seen to by his colleagues.

over, 'Can you hear? Larry, can you hear me?' And there'd be a little tremor, a little death rattle. 'Aw, gee, say something, say something, baby.' A little tremor, he rolled over and the darned dude winked at me."

George "The Animal" Steele recalled an incident that led to his first full-blown riot as a pro. With Gary Hart, Steele was the masked Student in Michigan in the early 1960s against Chene and Lou Klein. The evil-doers tossed Klein out of the ring, and then thrashed Chene to within an inch of his life. Blood gushing from a head wound, a limp Chene was carried back to the dressing room. A few minutes later, he re-emerged, trooping down the aisle in the fashion of a Spirit of '76 soldier, a streamer of gauze flapping from his head bandage like the tail of a kite. The fans were on their feet, shrieking in glee, because they knew Chene would clean house. But he had something more compelling in mind. "Cut me off and do it right now. Beat me," Chene whispered to Steele. "That started a riot because they were so excited with him running down and boom!" said Steele. "You beat him; it was just a real downer. The people were frantic to help him and they rioted."

On an otherwise unmemorable night in Kalamazoo, Michigan, wrestler

Gino Brito witnessed Chene's remarkable hold over fans, the trance of a wrestling pied piper. It was an outdoor show, it was dark, and the rain was coming down in torrents. "People were starting to leave because it was raining so much, and all of a sudden, it's Larry Chene's match. And they all came back and everybody stayed in the rain, soaking wet, screaming, yelling, till his match was over. Then everybody was gone."

Arthur Lawrence Beauchene entered the wrestling world late and left it too early. But during a fifteen-year career, he redefined the standard for the hero in peril who absorbed unconscionable beatings and kept coming back for more. "Larry was the kind of guy that represented Joe the average guy," said Percival A. Friend, a Chene trainee who had a long career as a wrestler and manager. "He knew how to take a punch and draw pain from it. He knew how to be put into a wrestling hold and suffer a hurt from that. He knew how to fall from a ring onto the floor and lay motionless while fans nearly rioted. You don't see that type of wrestler anymore because the fans are conditioned to seeing more gymnastics than wrestling today."

Larry Chene listens to a question from host Lord Athol Layton.

Beauchene was born in 1924 in Detroit, the product of an unusual French and Italian union. He played football at St. Bernard High School, trained as a fireman, enlisted in the U.S. Army in November 1945, and worked for a while as a bouncer while raising a family that would number six children. One day, Detroit promoter Bert Ruby, always on the lookout for fresh talent, saw him swing onto a trolley car using a railing. Ruby had a rough idea of the young man's identity from frequenting a butcher shop run by Chene's uncle. It was a chance encounter, but Chene looked young and athletic, enough so that Ruby suggested he drop by his office and give wrestling a whirl.

"At that time I was losing my shirt in a small trucking business," Chene told the *Detroit News* in 1961. "Bert got me a match in Saginaw. For wrestling thirty minutes I was paid $27.50 — the easiest money I ever made. The next morning I folded the trucking business and told Bert to get me some more matches." In

1950, Chene broke in around the Ohio–Michigan–Indiana circuit as the "Flying Frenchman." From the onset of his career, he feuded with Ed Farhat, the Sheik of Araby, a young Ruby wrestler who became one of the most infamous heels of all-time. In fact, it seems implausible, like Lucifer and the archangel Michael shacking up together, but Chene and Farhat shared an apartment in Texas in the 1950s. "He was always my Uncle Eddie and she [Farhat's wife] was my aunt Joyce. She and my mom are still like best friends over some sixty years later," Chene's daughter, Donna Fletcher, said with a chuckle. "They had an apartment together for a while, the two young couples. Young Eddie [Farhat] was born and my sister Carol was born and they couldn't afford it on these wrestler salaries, so they lived together. But yet in the ring; forget it. The Sheik was the ultimate bad guy and my dad was the ultimate good guy."

Chene won the Texas junior heavyweight title in 1954, his first major championship, and held the Texas tag team title twice. The Lone Star State was his base of operations for six years, though a foray to the Pacific Northwest in 1956 earned him the junior heavyweight belt and a run as a tag champ there. He also was U.S. champion for Fred Kohler's International Wrestling Association late in his career. But belts were secondary. Though unimposing at five-foot-ten and 220 pounds, Chene knew how to put on a good show, and habitually egged on opponents like Steele in cramped arenas where ring lights hung ten to twelve feet above the canvas. "After he got comfortable with me, I would throw him into the ropes and give him a backdrop and he would say 'Hit the lights!' And I'd shoot him as hard as I could and if his butt, heels, or anything could make the lights swing, that was a big party for him. It'd motivate me to push him that high so he'd get excited about hitting the lights," Steele said. "Larry, in my opinion, is probably the best worker, the best psychologist that I was ever in the ring with."

Returning to Michigan in 1960, Chene became a hometown hero in a sports-mad city. He worked for Jim Barnett and Johnny Doyle on shows at Olympia Stadium, including a September 1960 battle with Dick the Bruiser that drew more than 15,000; predictably, the match was called because of excessive bleeding. "At the Olympia, we had the same ring they used for the boxing, which didn't give like today," Brito said. "It was just hard ring, with the two-by-fours and all of that. He didn't give a damn. He'd take the big backdrops right on his back and he got over big." Future wrestling manager Dave Drason Burzynski, who lived downstairs from Chene in east Detroit, said he really made his mark in smaller venues run by Ruby, Harry Light, and Jack Britton, Brito's father. "At the time, he was the biggest thing going in Detroit. Doyle and Barnett had the big names, but Ruby hit all the little spots across Michigan and had the TV on Channel 7. So his guys were well-known and Larry became the hero in those blue-collar towns," he said. At one performance in Pontiac, Chene inspected the ring and informed Powers that the planks were old, dry, and ready for some first-class bumps. "He told me, 'We can bust it,'" Powers said. "I thought he was crazy. But we busted it with me bodyslamming him relentlessly and the four corner posts fell in and they couldn't continue the last two matches. Just imagine how hard I had to keep slamming him. He wasn't going on last that night, so we went out with a bang, literally."

In the predawn hours of October 2, 1964, Chene was driving on Interstate 80 northwest of Ottawa, Illinois, following a match in Moline, when his car skidded and hit a telephone pole, killing him instantly. Police reported they found a speeding ticket in his car that had been issued near Atkinson, Illinois, five hours earlier. The Midwest wrestling community was in shock. His funeral was held four days later and fans observed a moment of silence that night at the Minneapolis arena, where he was scheduled to wrestle. "It was devastating, just devastating for all of us, for the family. It was like, 'Why?'" Steele asked, the sadness apparent in his voice forty-five years later. "The thing I remember most about going to his funeral was I'd never seen The Sheik before and he's a pretty strong legend. But he was wrestling out of Texas and other places. He flew in, and was dressed in a silk suit with real small glasses to cover his tears."

When an athlete dies prematurely, the "what if"'s never end. With Chene, though, there's no "what if," only a "what would have been." Not long after Chene's death, Farhat acquired the Detroit booking office and turned it into one of the hottest wrestling promotions in North America. Chene would have been his foil for years, probably always bloodied and certainly unbowed. "Larry was very free with his emotions, and if someone fell on bad times, he would give them what he had in his pocket, never thinking about when he would get a return," said Friend, his one-time trainee. "I miss him with a lot of feelings and hope that he will be the one holding the tag ropes when I am called to that big ring in the sky."

ILIO DIPAOLO

When wrestlers remember Ilio DiPaolo, they recall his huge hands. When the citizens of Buffalo, New York, remember Ilio, they think of his huge heart.

He was taken from the world on a miserable, rainy night on May 10, 1995,

Ilio DiPaolo and Billy Red Lyons try to keep up with the demand for autographs.

hit by a car when crossing the street in Hamburg, New York. Only with his death did the true understanding of his impact on the community become evident.

At least 6,000 people turned out for the two-day visitation alone, patiently waiting in long, snaking lines to pay tribute to a man who had touched their lives, whether through his wrestling, his pizzeria, or his charitable works, both publicly, such as his wrestling tournament and the Rotary Club, and privately.

"It was fascinating in the sense that you talk about a guy that was a professional wrestler. Well, what the hell does that mean, 'professional wrestler'? People didn't know anything about it other than watching a little bit of it on TV, and had fun with that. You then realized the magnitude of what he had done in his lifetime, and the number of people that he had touched," said Bud Carpenter, the head trainer for the Buffalo Bills and a long-time friend of DiPaolo's.

"Anybody who was anybody was there, but it wasn't just the VIPs," said broadcaster Bob Koshinski. "[Ilio's son] Dennis told me stories afterward that people would come up and talk about the things that his father had done for them that he was never even aware of. Somebody was down and out on his luck, where he gave them a meal or gave them a few bucks, these were people

The Destroyer, Giant Baba, and Ilio DiPaolo enjoy a round of golf at one of Ilio's golf tournaments.

who were complete strangers to the family who felt they had to come by and pay their respects."

His death was front page news, and led all the newscasts. The funeral was equally packed. "You would have thought that the governor of the state of New York had passed away," said Koshinski. "The coverage was unbelievable."

"The Bruiser from Abruzzi" was born November 8, 1926, at a whopping thirteen pounds. As a boy, he was stricken with polio; while he battled back to full health, his Italian province was occupied by the Germans during the Second World War, making it difficult to find enough to eat. Post-war, prospects bleak, he left for Venezuela when he was twenty-three years of age. At six-foot-two and 240 pounds, he found work on a road crew, and legend has it he single-handedly lifted more than one truck out of the mud.

New York promoter Toots Mondt was in Venezuela and came across DiPaolo, inviting him to give professional wrestling a try. Ilio met and married Ethel, stepdaughter of Buffalo promoter Pedro Martinez in 1952, and eventually they settled in Western New York and had four children. From Toronto to Minneapolis, from San Francisco to Australia, Ilio was always a babyface — the only exception was a tour of Japan where he participated in the last match of Rikidozan's career on December 7, 1963.

"He was just like a racehorse. He was so damn tough, you'd hate to even touch him! He would touch you and he would hurt you!" recalled Sweet Daddy Siki, laughing at the memories.

Dominic Denucci chose a different equine. "He was like a godamn mule. He was. Big-boned, like Bruno [Sammartino]. Actually, Ilio did have bigger hands than Bruno," said Denucci of his friend who wore a size-eighteen shirt and a size-fifteen triple-E shoe. "He had a natural, good body on him. He was like a machine. He'd just keep going and going and going."

Approaching his forties, and slowed by injuries, Ilio decided to branch out into another career. He opened a small pizzeria in Lackawanna, New York, in 1965, but it was destroyed by fire. The second pizzeria, in nearby Blasdell, grew into what today is the 10,000-square foot Ilio DiPaolo's Restaurant and Ringside Lounge.

"There's something about Blasdell. He loved the small town . . . [and] small-town atmosphere," Dennis said of his father. "We never wanted to move, and we had many offers. 'Come to the north side, we're really expanding, we're doing this . . .' We said, 'Nope, this is where we started, this is where we grow our tree, right here.'"

Being family with the local promoter meant that DiPaolo still meant some-thing locally, even after he retired in 1965. "He had a bad leg, and he was hurting. He was tired of being on the road. Because Pedro was a relative, he was allowed to continue to be positioned," said Johnny Powers, who later bought into the Buffalo promotion. "But also, Ilio was a natural host as an Italian . . . He was a natural host figure. Because he did so much work in the community, that resonated."

DiPaolo had a way of making young and old feel welcome, and was a sur-rogate father for many of the Buffalo Bills players, who trained nearby.

Hall of Fame quarterback Jim Kelly was one of those who fell under DiPaolo's spell, learning to play bocce, or hanging out at the restaurant, where Ilio would know everyone's name, circulating the room and having genuine dialogue, not just small talk. "I'd be sitting there just with Ilio, just having conversations with him, if it was a tough game or whatever, he always had those encouraging words to never give up, you're making Buffalo proud, continue to do what you're doing," said Kelly. "People went to his restaurant because it was good food. But people also went to his restaurant because he was such a people person."

When DiPaolo died, it was evident that something longer lasting than flowers would be needed, said Carpenter. He and Dennis DiPaolo came up with the idea of a scholarship fund, not knowing exactly what that would mean. A quick call to an attorney and the Ilio DiPaolo Scholarship Fund came into existence. The first big donations came from the Bills players. To date, more than $750,000 has been raised to help an area children's hospital and the handicapped, to start up a high school football program, and to send kids to college.

Kelly is proud to be one of the spokespersons for the Fund. "You talk to the recipients, and even though they're kids, [they are] reading about Ilio and talking to their parents, and understanding what he was like," he said.

With a monument in Blasdell, and two more in Introdacqua, Italy, there are permanent tributes to DiPaolo.

But just as Ilio's tongue would loosen and the colorful stories would flow easier with a couple of glasses of wine, his friends love to share stories of the larger-than-life figure who always wanted to demonstrate he still had it.

"He still wanted to prove that he was flexible, putting those size fifteen or sixteen triple-E width shoes up over your shoulder, over your head," marveled Kelly. "Man, this guy was unbelievable. You never wanted to make him mad, that's for sure."

For Koshinski, it was Super Bowl XXVI in Minneapolis, where Kelly was leading the Bills into action against the Washington Redskins. Ilio and Ethel had a hotel room that opened into the courtyard. "Each night, it became a regular routine, media and fans, family members of the Bills players, would gather outside the DiPaolo room," Koshinski said. One night, he started bragging to Koshinski that he could still do his age in push-ups: "So he took his shirt off, got down on the floor and started doing push-ups. Then he insisted that I sit on his shoulders to demonstrate just how strong he was. I balked at that. I'll never forget Dennis and his mom coming over and telling him to get up, didn't want him to hurt himself. Witnessing what I saw, there was no way he was going to hurt himself. Even at the age of sixty, he was incredibly strong."

TOM DRAKE

Tom Drake just might be one of the most influential men to ever lace up a pair of wrestling boots.

While his pro wrestling resumé is impressive, Drake's accomplishments outside the squared circle place him in some pretty lofty company. He coached with the likes of the legendary Paul "Bear" Bryant, served nine terms in the Alabama state legislature, and even had an audience with the pope. A chance meeting with a former Golden Gloves boxing champion (and future governor) named George Wallace set him on course for a law degree and an illustrious career in politics.

Much like another University of Alabama product, the fictional movie character Forrest Gump, Tom Drake — farmer, attorney, politician, wrestler — seemed to always be in the right place at the right time.

The "Cullman Comet," as Drake was affectionately known, carved out a nice career por-traying "a man of the people," but it wasn't a work. Inside the wrestling ring, there was never

COURTESY OF SCOTT TEAL/CROWBAR PRESS

Tom Drake in his prime with a world tag team title.

any question as to whether Drake was a babyface or a heel. His political life dictated that he be a fan favorite. And he did it quite well.

A product of the Great Depression, Drake was born December 5, 1930, in Falkville, Alabama. His father, a tenant farmer, was killed on a railroad when Drake was only five years old. He had three younger siblings who he said "almost starved to death" during the dark days of the Depression.

Sports, however, proved to be a life-altering outlet for Drake. He took to wrestling as a junior in high school in the late '40s when he'd go to the local drugstore on Saturday afternoons and crowd around a small television with his friends, watching the athletic theatrics with amazement and awe. The teenager knew then that he had a bright future waiting for him in pro wrestling.

"I couldn't whip everybody at boxing or all that kind of stuff, and I didn't necessarily have more strength than them. But I had one thing they didn't have, and that was the God-given talent of balance," said Drake. "You can't learn balance. You inherit it, and I knew I had it. I could always whip everyone in my class because I could outwrestle them."

Drake used that same sense of balance to outmaneuver larger players on the football team's offensive line at Cullman High School by simply picking them up over his head. There was no wrestling team at the school, but Drake was good enough on the line to earn a football scholarship to University of Tennessee-Chattanooga. He became so confident in his ability that he asked his football coaches if he could watch the wrestling team and try out.

The college didn't offer wrestling scholarships at the time, but Drake remained undeterred. When football season was over, Drake got his chance. In a span of only three weeks he whipped the team's heavyweight and took over that position. His third opponent just happened to be someone named Dick Hutton.

"They said, 'Well, hell, you can whip him. If you can whip the heavyweight here at Chattanooga, you can whip this fellow,'" Drake recalled. "And they convinced me that I could. I went out there and found out that I couldn't whip him." Hutton, a three-time NCAA champion at Oklahoma State, disposed of Drake in fifty-nine seconds. The quick loss earned Drake the dubious nickname "Fifty-Nine-Second Man" as a takeoff on a popular song from that time called "Sixty-Minute Man." The two later would become close friends.

A small All-American guard who played in two all-state football games, Drake placed third in the division in the Southeastern Conference wrestling tournament his first year in 1949. The last three years he went undefeated in the light heavyweight division and won the conference championships three consecutive times without a defeat.

Drake qualified for the United States Olympic finals in 1952, and his coach gave him $25 and bought him a train ticket to go to Ames, Iowa, with the promise that Drake would return to play football the following year. During the stopover in Chicago, Drake met another young wrestler named Danny Hodge. "He wrestled at 167 pounds, and I was a much bigger fellow and looked a lot older," explained Drake. "He had a plaster of Paris cast covering up his ear, and I couldn't believe it. I'd never seen anything like that before. Back then they didn't know how to treat cauliflower ears." They established they were both destined for the trials. "I'm going to win it, too," Hodge boldly declared. "Well, I guess if you are, I will too," Drake shot right back. The two shook hands and forged what would become a lasting friendship. Forced to take a part-passenger and part-freight train because of tracks that had been washed out by a flood, the pair almost wasn't allowed to compete due to their late arrival. With neither having a coach, they cheered one another on throughout the trials. Drake went to a draw with Dale Thomas, who coached at Michigan State at the time and was seven or eight years older, but Thomas' seniority earned him the Olympic bid. Hodge would go on to place fifth in Helsinki.

Back on the football field, Drake was the first player in the history of UT-Chattanooga to be selected to play in two college all-star games (Senior Bowl and Blue-Gray game), and the NFL's Pittsburgh Steelers made him a draft pick on the strength of stellar showings in the all-star games. In 1952 he received the Templeton Trophy for the "Best All-Around Athlete" at Chattanooga for his accomplishments in football, wrestling, and track.

But Drake never relinquished his dream of becoming a pro wrestler. While in Chattanooga he had met up with a 168-pounder named Eddie Gossett (later Graham), who had worked his first pro match in 1947 at the age of seventeen and was paid off with a twenty-five-pound turkey. Drake even signed a "letter of intent" with "Cowboy" Clarence Luttrall in 1952 after impressing the long-time Florida promoter with his performance in a football game in Tampa.

Drake, who earned his degree in 1954, would take a detour with a stint serving in the U.S. Army in the Korean War, but not before working his first pro match in Dyersburg, Tennessee, for promoters Roy Welch and Nick Gulas. He would coach the Special Troops Command football team while in the army.

It was while stationed at Fort Benning, Georgia, that Drake noticed a news-paper ad plugging a wrestling show promoted by Fred Ward. With only three months under his belt and making $59 a month, Drake offered to do some wrestling. Ward thought he might be a local drawing card and billed him as a Fort Benning judo instructor, although Drake knew little about judo. But he became an instant hit with the military crowd and the 64,000 troops at Fort Benning, making more money in one night wrestling than he was making in a month in the army. A three-day pass would allow him to wrestle in the sur-rounding area, including Friday nights in Atlanta, where he'd make as much as $150 a show. Not only did he love the sport, but he found out he could make a good living at it as well. Drake was soon able to buy a new Mercury as a private, and before long was loaning money to his company commander.

Drake had intended to return to Alabama to get his doctorate degree in education, until he ran into a former Golden Gloves bantamweight champion named George Wallace who encouraged Drake to switch to law and help him get elected as governor of Alabama. Drake campaigned for Wallace in 1958,

Tom Drake in 2009.

his first full year in the wrestling business, and became one of Wallace's closest friends and key campaigners.

The two enjoyed a mutually advantageous relationship. Drake liked the fact that Wallace was an athlete himself and a rising star on the political scene, and Wallace liked the fact that Drake was a popular athlete who wielded considerable influence with the wrestling crowd.

"We were making a lot of money," recalled Drake. "We went to Ladd Stadium (now Ladd Peebles Stadium) in Mobile and drew more people than the University of Alabama football team did there." The strategy was simple. Drake would invite Wallace to the wrestling matches and introduce him to the crowd for a rousing ovation while Drake would hand out campaign material at ringside. He would even hand flyers to local heels who would tear them up, stomp and spit on them, inciting the crowd into more of a frenzy.

At Wallace's urging, Drake entered law school in 1960 at the University of Alabama, where he earned a master's and a J.D. During his time there, he served as a student assistant for legendary football coach "Bear" Bryant. Drake had made a good enough impression playing for Bryant in the 1954 Senior Bowl that he asked him to coach the school's first wrestling team as well.

During his last semester at the University of Alabama Law School, using some of the money that he made from professional wrestling, he successfully campaigned for a seat in the Alabama Legislature, representing Cullman County. Drake thought if he could do this well, he could go back home to Cullman, a German community fifty-five miles northeast of Birmingham, and turn this into something good. "There was 11 of us running, and I beat every damn one of them without a runoff," said Drake.

Drake, with nine terms in the Alabama State Legislature, would serve longer in the House of Representatives than all but three of its members in the history of Alabama politics. He was Speaker of the House from 1982–87, and practiced personal injury law and general civil law for half a century, handling many high-profile cases in the North Alabama area.

Using the dropkick as his signature maneuver, Drake wrestled professionally for twenty-four years before retiring in 1978. Tangling with such greats as Gorgeous George, Buddy Rogers, and Fred Blassie, Drake won a number of titles and wrestled Lou Thesz for the world championship in 1962. "Tom Drake has brought more respectability to professional wrestling than any other man: his rise to Speaker of the House and his strong reputation as a no-nonsense politician and his open pride and admission it was pro wrestling that made it all possible," praised Thesz.

During an appearance on the *What's My Line* network television show where the panelists tried to guess his profession, Drake was asked, "Do you do what you do standing or lying down?" "I looked at him and said, 'A little of both,'" he replied.

Drake has had plenty of formidable tag team partners over the years, but without question his most valuable partner has been wife Chris, a noted politician in her own right. They shared more than fifty years of wedded bliss, as well as a lucrative law practice, until her death in 2011. "We've always worked, and I don't know if we'd be happy if we didn't have something to do," commented Drake. Two sons practice law: Tommy, who has tried some of the top criminal cases in Alabama, and Whit, one of the top trial lawyers in the state. A daughter, Mary Frances, is the head pediatric doctor of nursing at the University of Oregon Hospital in Portland. Another daughter, Christy, teaches Greek, Hebrew, and Latin at the University of Western Oregon.

Always loyal to his grappling fraternity, Drake has represented many a wrestler in legal matters and can't even begin to remember exactly how many speeding tickets he helped them with. He's taken a lot of licks playing football, wrestling, and in politics, he jokes, but wouldn't trade any of it.

Drake remains active in the Cauliflower Alley Club, where he serves as the organization's vice president and legal counsel, and the International Wrestling Hall of Fame (now named after Dan Gable) in Waterloo, Iowa. "Tom and Chris Drake have probably been the two most important reasons for our continued success and growth over the past twenty years. Always available and willing to give of themselves to the club and others," said CAC executive vice president Karl Lauer. "They have taken care of any and all club legal needs for over twenty years and never charged a penny."

The Alabama Legislature commended Drake for his exemplary legislative service for his three decades of service to the people of this state in the House in 1998. His role as professional wrestler, noted the Legislature, "may explain his tenacity and longevity in the Legislature; on more than one occasion members of the House have felt as if they had been body slammed after an engagement with Speaker Drake."

In 2008, Drake was the recipient of the Senator Hugh Farley Award, given to an individual who has distinguished himself both inside and outside of the ring, at the Professional Wrestling Hall of Fame and Museum in Amsterdam, New York. In 2001, he was awarded the second-ever Frank Gotch Award at the George Tragos/Lou Thesz Professional Wrestling Hall of Fame in Newton, Iowa, where he was reunited with long-time friend and then Minnesota governor Jesse Ventura who, like Drake, went on from the wrestling ring to the political ring.

"Jesse and I did a lot of wrestling and tumbling in our younger days, and we've proved that we're not through by taking our acts into politics," Drake told The Decatur Daily (Alabama). "A lot of people say wrestling is fake, but I would like to see them out there doing what we did. Fake or not, it was hard work and a lot of fun. We even made some money doing it."

"Tom is one of the nicest guys that I've ever met," said Ventura. "I know he is a popular person in Alabama, and I would not want to run against him if he does decide to enter the political arena again."

THE WORST TRAFFIC TIEUP

They came, they saw, and then they couldn't move.

If there were any doubts about how much of an impact a wrestling hero can have on his fans, they were erased in the late-night hours of July 30, 1935, as devoted followers of Danno O'Mahoney locked Boston traffic in a submission hold.

Thirty-six thousand fans, a U.S. attendance record that would stand for half a century, packed Braves Field that night, and the '30s-era Boston infrastructure was inadequate to the task. For hours after the match, the city was on its knees, as 20,000 motorists tried to leave all at once, creating what the Boston Herald headlined as the "Worst Traffic Tieup."

Along Commonwealth Avenue, the main access road to the cavernous ballpark, cars were snarled, bumper to bumper, for a mile in each direction. On the side streets around Kenmore Square, the scene alternated between bedlam and bottleneck. Trolley cars had no hope of getting past vehicles double- and triple-parked in the main drags south of the Charles River.

The twenty-two-year-old O'Mahoney, a pro for just seven months, was the reason for the gridlock.

Boston promoter Paul Bowser struck gold with Boston's Irish community when he tapped the 220-pound ex-soldier from Cork County, Ireland, as his world champ. "If you were wondering where all the Irish were last night here's the answer — they were at Braves Field," Bob White wrote in the *Boston Post*.

The problem began even before O'Mahoney entered the ring to square off with Ed Don George in a world title unification match, the highlight of an eleven-match card. The *Herald* later described the scene as something out of a disaster movie: "Panic stricken lest they miss the main event of the evening, motorists began to abandon their cars

DEPARTMENT OF SPECIAL COLLECTIONS, UNIVERSITY LIBRARIES OF NOTRE DAME

Danno O'Mahoney demonstrates a slam for the camera in 1930.

shortly before 10 p.m., parking beside hydrants, in forbidden areas, two and even three deep, climbing curbings, and entering private yards, lawns, and driveways."

After ninety minutes of wrestling, O'Mahoney strengthened his claim to the world when special referee James J. Braddock, the heavyweight boxing champ, counted George out of the ring. At a nearby police station, Captain Joseph McGrath was sitting at a desk at 11:30 p.m., assuming that thirty police and four sergeants would suffice to handle the exodus from Braves Field. When the phone on his desk rang with news of the impasse, McGrath mobilized as many extra officers as he could.

What they found was enough to send any self-respecting traffic cop back to desk duty. Thirty-one trolley cars stood immobilized. Taxi drivers with paying customers honked and screamed because they couldn't budge. Cars were parked at all angles along Commonwealth and its tributaries, blocking every avenue of escape. Along an area known as automobile row, cars sealed off the entrances of salesrooms, and blocked doorways of garages.

For the next two hours, more than 100 police officers from Brookline and Boston tried to redirect traffic by turning thoroughfares into ad hoc one-way streets, keeping cars and motorists off trolley tracks, and clearing out side streets to relieve the crunch on main arteries. Authorities reported traffic was under control by 1:30 a.m., though it wouldn't return to normal for several hours.

Pre-match hype suggested a crowd of 55,000 was possible, so police had advance warning that they might be facing an onslaught of Depression-era roadsters. But baseball's lowly Boston Braves attracted just 4,000 to the ballpark two days earlier, and Brookline police later confessed that they had never encountered the kind of traffic volume that O'Mahoney instigated.

The attendance — accounts put it as high as 45,000, but "about 36,000" was the official reported count — stood as the U.S. record until WrestleMania III in March 1987. O'Mahoney didn't last as long. Challengers lined up in the correct belief that he lacked the skills to protect himself in an unpremeditated match. "He would grab you by the hand and pull you back and forth until you were supposed to get dizzy. He really couldn't have thrown my little boy," said veteran Fred Bozic. Dick Shikat took O'Mahoney's title in an infamous 1936 double cross in New York City, and the bloom was off the wild Irish rose. But for one night in 1935, his fame brought Beantown to a standstill.

LEE FIELDS

Rasslin' and racing were the two staples of sports in the Deep South and nobody embodied both of them better than Lee Fields. As its main attraction and later owner, he spent twenty years building Gulf Coast Championship Wrestling into a top territory. Then he spent another twenty-plus years breathing life into Mobile International Speedway, the South's fastest half-mile, high-banked oval. Two professions, but a common denominator, in the view of his widow Ida — a talent for promotion and a love of crowds. "He understood how to promote things," she said. "He had a way with people. It was how friendly he was. He didn't walk away from his fans. He wasn't rude to his fans. He knew that was his living."

The wrestling part of Fields' career was all but ordained. Born August 18, 1930, in Pawhuska, Oklahoma, Albert Lee Hatfield was part of the Welch-Fuller-Hatfield family tree that played a role in just about every promotion in the South for half a century. His father, Virgil "Speedy" Hatfield, a referee, married Bonnie Welch, the sister of Jack, Herb, Roy, and Lester Welch. They moved to Tennessee in 1946 and Lee, one of their three wrestling sons, was a teenaged phenom, debuting in the ring before his twentieth birthday. His earliest recorded match was in June 1949 in Kingsport, Tennessee, against veteran Jack Bloomfield, and though he lost, *The Kingsport News* claimed he "stole the show with his aggressive action." Fields stayed in the Ozarks, and got his first turn with a championship title in May 1952, when he and Edward Welch, a.k.a. Buddy Fuller, won the Southeast Missouri tag team titles.

In the late 1950s, Fields dominated the Gulf Coast title, which he held three times, and the Mississippi state title, which he held five times, in a series of wild matches that had Southern hardcore written all over them. Working for promoter Skip Wetjen, who'd figure in his racing career as well, Fields started one Mississippi reign in January 1959 with a fifth-round boxing match knockout of Joe McCarthy and ended it a month later when the state athletic commission vacated the title because he'd smashed a chair on the noggin of Sputnik Monroe. In 1959, Fields bought the Gulf Coast territory from Fuller, relinquishing his Gulf Coast title at the behest of the Alabama athletic commission. In the process, he had the biggest match to that point in Mobile, Alabama, as Eduardo Perez beat him bloody for the Gulf Coast title and a Cadillac. He was best known for his tag teams with brothers Don and Bobby; various combinations ruled the Gulf Coast and Southern tag scene from the late

COURTESY OF SCOTT TEAL/CROWBAR PRESS

Lee Fields is set for a 1959 outdoor show at Ladd Memorial Stadium in Mobile, Ala.

1950s to the mid-1960s, and Fields also held the Mid-America version of the world tag title with Mario Galento and Lester Welch. As the oldest of the boys, Fields was everybody's big brother, and Tennessee star Tommy Gilbert said the bond between the brothers was so strong that it tugged on fans. In a tag team match, for instance, Gilbert said Fields' expressions told the whole story: "'That's my brother in there. You shouldn't be doing him like that. Don't do that to him with me out here. I'm going to get a hold of you and there's going to be payback,'" Gilbert recounted. "You could see that in his eyes and face, and it was not just me; it was what the fans saw."

Ida Fields, a beauty school student in Louisiana in 1966, was a fan who went to the matches, met Fields, and eventually married him. That's the good memory of Lafayette. The bad memory is a match there with the Dalton brothers for the territory's tag team championship that nearly cost Fields his ear. As the heels threw him out of the ring, his shoulder caught one of the ropes, blocking his momentum and nearly slicing off his ear in the process. Ida was sitting in the audience aghast. "I thought he was going to lose his ear. They had to sew it back on. That's the only one he could hear out of," his wife said. "They left me sitting there when they went to the hospital and they wanted to lock up. I said, 'I don't have a ride home!'" Fortunately, a ring crew member gave her a lift.

Growing up in Mobile, Joe Turner looked up to Fields as a hometown hero even before he got a chance to wrestle him with Bill Bowman as the original masked Interns. "I grew up around him. The Fields brothers, they were it as far as I was concerned back then," he said. "Lee was a heck of a worker. He was very agile and he had a lot of guts out there. They did well because a lot of times they didn't have TV in Mobile and they still drew good houses."

Fields started to wind down his active career in 1966, and tapped Cowboy Bob Kelly, then a ref, to succeed him as Bobby's partner and the promotion's top good guy. During his apprenticeship, Kelly was having trouble grasping the nuances of dying, when a wrestler is down the count, and selling, when a wrestler credibly registers his opponent's blows. Fields, always serious about business, said he'd show him the difference. "So he hits me with a working punch. I took a bump, and went down like I was almost knocked out. He said, 'See, that's dying.' Then as I got up, he slapped me hard as he could, bang, real quick. Man, he spun me around. 'See,' he said. 'That's selling.'" Fields wrestled occasionally and promoted full-time in Alabama and the Florida panhandle when he came back in 1971 as part of the most famous angle in Gulf Coast history. Bobby Shane, arrogance oozing from every pore, picked a feud with Fields, mocking him as "Leroy" and slapping him on TV. Their bad blood enraptured the territory for most of the summer, and culminated in a Fields victory in August before a sellout crowd in Mobile. "He could wrestle, but the fans knew he would fight down and dirty when he was pushed far enough. Even when he lost, the fans knew he had given everything he had and they respected him for it," said former wrestler Michael Norris, the Gulf Coast's leading historian.

Kelly considered Fields like a brother, and said he excelled at using his hard-earned reputation to pass the torch to younger wrestlers. To entice fans to accept Kelly as a main eventer, Fields had open workouts with him in Lafayette. "It got me over. I didn't win those first matches but I was getting close and the people'd think, 'Hey that was close,'" Kelly said. "Lee was just an honest-to-goodness, ol' country boy who believed in a handshake."

In the early 1970s, Fields was branching out into the world of racing. He was partners in a car lot with a friend who suggested he try his hand behind the wheel. As much a natural as he was on the mat, he steered a late-model Chevy to victory in 1970 at Five Flags Speedway in Pensacola. In 1972, Fields purchased the Mobile track from his old friend Wetjen, and mixed racing and wrestling for about six years. The track business started to grow, and with his back feeling the effects from years of bumps, Fields sold his interest in the wrestling promotion to a group led by Ron Fuller in January 1978. With Ida, he turned Mobile into a huge success, even rebuilding it by hand after Hurricane Frederic ravaged the property in 1979.

Fields died of leukemia in June 2000 at sixty-nine. "We were like a team. It was like I lost my teammate. We weren't husband and wife; we were best friends," his wife reflected. She still owns the Mobile track and the Lee Fields Memorial 150 weekend is its signature event. Fittingly the winner of the race in 2011 received a leather and silver championship belt designed by wrestling belt craftsman Dave Millican. "I grew up watching Lee wrestle and then I had the great opportunity to race for him here at the speedway," said Rick Crawford, a veteran NASCAR Truck Series driver who is manager and promoter at Mobile. "Without Lee, none of us would be here. The belt is the ultimate prize for our biggest race weekend of the year."

EDDIE GRAHAM

There was a Jekyll and Hyde quality to Eddie Graham. The Hyde side was one of Florida's top favorites in the ring, the brains behind one of the sport's legendary promotions, and a civic leader committed to dozens of charitable causes. The Jekyll side was capricious with his talent, bogged down by alcohol, and ensnared in a bad business deal that ultimately would lead to his suicide in 1985 at age fifty-five.

Frankie Cain saw both sides of Graham from the time he wrestled under his real name of Eddie Gossett to his glory days as head of Championship Wresting from Florida. Back when Graham, fresh out of the army, was struggling to make ends meet in the early 1950s, he was with Cain and Buddy Fuller, picking cotton to earn enough gas money so Cain could make his fight in Cape Girardeau, Missouri. "I got I think a dollar and a quarter, Graham got seventy five cents. And we went over and asked Buddy, 'Buddy, you have a dollar you can loan us?' And he said, 'Let me take my last bundle in first.' He had a sack so damn long that it needed a taillight for the end of it. That's how broke we were." Years later, when Cain joshed about the episode — in private — Graham would have none of it. "You know what he said? 'I don't remember anything like that.' How the hell do you forget being broke and picking cotton? He didn't want that mentioned," Cain said. "That wasn't like him when he was younger. I don't know what happened to him."

Maybe he was trying to push his childhood into the recesses of his mind. Born January 15, 1930, in Dayton, Tennessee, Eddie dropped out of school at an early age, and lived a poor and difficult upbringing. Graham's mom worked as a clerk and in lunchrooms, and his dad was an itinerant laborer who regularly beat him and took the money Graham earned as a newspaper boy in Chattanooga, according to Graham's son Mike. Graham was in fights long before he was into wrestling. "You know you can get into trouble on the street. The newspaper gave all of us memberships to the YMCA. It was a gift to me; otherwise I wouldn't have been able to go," he reflected in a 1967 interview with a Florida newspaper. "That's the way I got to be an athlete and it is where I had my first encounter with wrestling." Graham hung around the Y with "Lucky" Gilpin, who'd also wrestle as a pro, when Florida promoter "Cowboy" Clarence Luttrall spotted him and encouraged his progress. Graham's first match was in 1947 with Gilpin at a benefit run by local restaurateurs; he said he got a turkey as a payoff.

Through the early-to-mid 1950s, Graham, blind in one eye, worked for the Fuller-Welch family promotion in small towns like Blytheville, Arkansas, and Hopkinsville, Kentucky, usually as an undersized favorite at five-foot-nine and about 210 pounds. In Amarillo, Texas, he was the heel Rip Rogers for Dory Funk Sr., and alleged kin to Buddy Rogers. His second big break came in the form of the bulbous Dr. Jerry Graham, who figured he'd make an ideal wrestling "brother" as "Golden" Eddie Graham. Eddie started in the Capitol Sports Promotion in the summer of 1958, and the Grahams became the top heel team in the Northeast for about two and a half years. "That was probably the turning point in his life because he met another senior, Vince McMahon Sr., and Vince took him to the next level," Mike Graham said. "Through Vince, he learned fancy robes, showmanship, big venues." It couldn't have hurt the Grahams' image as ruffians when they were busted on concealed weapons charges in Wilmington,

Delaware, in 1958, after authorities found a .22-caliber pistol in Eddie's car and a .45 automatic in Jerry's car; they promised not to do it again, paid court costs, and got the charges dismissed.

Graham had wrestled off and on as Eddie Gossett for Florida promoters Luttrall and Pat Malone since 1949, and his parents moved to Tampa. When he went to the Sunshine State full-time in 1961, he kept the Graham name but turned into the top baby-face in the territory at about the time Luttrall's TV programming kicked in, so the promoter could run shows year-round. He had a tag team with Hans Schmidt, then became his rival after a late spring 1961 switch, and started tagging with Dick Steinborn,

Eddie Graham was a wrestling mastermind.

Don Curtis, and Sam Steamboat. "Eddie expected perfection. He was a perfectionist," the late Skull Von Stroheim said in 2001. "When you wrestled with him, you had to build your match slowly. At first, you wrestle, then you start heeling a little with him, and you build the match to a climax. Then, when he made his comeback, the place exploded." Graham's top feuds were with Bob Orton Sr. and Boris Malenko. He was a four-time Southern heavyweight champion and set up a Brass Knucks title he'd trade with Malenko. "Eddie was a good seller but you couldn't work high spots with him," Cain said. "You could if the heel was taking some kind of a bump, but a lot of things he was limited in what he could do, but he could sell good and he could bleed."

Less known to fans was that Graham had bought into Luttrall's company with the money he saved from the big stage in New York. In a 1991 interview, Dr. Jerry recalled that Luttrall had lost a son in the Korean War. "He then accepted Eddie as his son. Luttrall offered Eddie to be 'in,' and I said, 'Eddie, go! You're in like Ali Baba and the forty thieves. Go show them how it's done!' And he did." L&G Promotions would be the result, and Graham was another one of many territorial owners who wedged themselves in as their company's top hero. Luttrall retired in 1970 and Graham became the official head of Championship

Eddie Graham returns to the ring in his later years to fight Joe Leduc.

Wrestling from Florida, a spot he'd essentially held since 1961. He promoted Jack Brisco as NWA titleholder, and Bill Watts, Dusty Rhodes, Terry Funk, Ricky Steamboat, and a host of champions regarded him as one of wrestling's true creative geniuses. "The real education began my second year in the business when I went to Florida Championship Wrestling and went to work for Eddie Graham and he was a master," said Magnum T.A. "He was a master of psychology in the ring, he knew all the ins and outs and mechanics of telling a story, painting a picture, what it takes to make a success in the ring."

Though he was rough around the edges, Graham's civic resumé reads like a Chamber of Commerce biography. He contributed more than $100,000 to the Florida Sheriffs Boys Ranch, was a founder, served on its board of directors, and was named the organization's "Our Friend" in 1977; he was a trustee of a similar support group for disadvantaged girls. He poured money in AAU wrestling and was recognized by the Tampa Sports Club as its sports citizen of the year in 1978; he's a member of the group's Hall of Fame. With the University of Tampa, he sponsored a youth wrestling camp — Brisco and Bob Roop were among the instructors — and pumped $10,000 into the wrestling program at the University of Florida, which, to his consternation, dropped the sport a couple of years later. Undeterred, he set up a wrestling scholarship at the University of Tampa. Mike was an outstanding amateur and teamed with his father as a pro. Eddie wrestled through 1979, hanging up his boots just short of his fiftieth birthday.

But there was a down side to Graham, too. One example: Joe "The Assassin" Hamilton moved to Florida in 1976 to take over as his booker and found himself enormously frustrated. In one case, Graham pushed out Rock Hunter, who was doing well for the promotion, for no apparent reason. At times, the bottle was interfering with his business. "His judgment was clearly impaired when he was drinking. When Eddie was sober, he was one of the most intelligent people in the business, but when he was drinking, it was diminished and he became very paranoid," Hamilton wrote in *Assassin: The Man Behind the Mask*. Mac McMurray, known best as a referee and part-owner of the Knoxville, Tennessee promotion, worked for the office in Florida and got along with Graham. But McMurray said the feeling wasn't mutual, because Graham felt "Mac" hadn't been born into the business, as opposed to much of his talent. "I had tremendous respect for Eddie but he had no respect for me whatsoever," McMurray said. "There were two Eddie Grahams. There was Eddie Graham the businessman and Eddie Graham the party man." By the early '80s, Graham had alienated some of his moneymakers and became more and more withdrawn. Said Roop, "He had driven off every guy he ever gave a break to. Even the boys who had made a fortune with him had no use for him."

Orton, Florida's top heel for years, was the one who got Graham into flying, and he became a skilled pilot. One day in the '60s, Graham invited Orton into the heights over Orlando — Disney World was still under construction — to scout out places where he could build his own arenas, so he wouldn't have to rent from cities and the state, and could own the concessions and parking rights. "He couldn't take a rib, you know. I said, 'Boy, you seem like a man that can see his own destiny and control it.' Boy, he didn't like that at all. Just gave me that look and all that," Orton said. "But I just wonder, after all the trouble he got in — he knew Vince McMahon and Cowboy Bob Jr. were coming in and going to take his territory — I just wonder if he thought that he couldn't control his own destiny." A bad deal with a convicted felon over a dirt-hauling business threatened to ruin his reputation — about half a million dollars was coming due — and that deepened what his friends believe was almost certainly depression. On January 20, 1985, he pointed a loaded .38-caliber revolver at the right side of his head and killed himself.

It was a sad ending, but Graham was acknowledged posthumously when the WWE inducted him into its Hall of Fame in 2008, bringing his life story to a generation that never knew him as the face of Florida wrestling. Bruce Tharpe was a ring announcer in Championship Wrestling from Florida, following in the footsteps of his father Chet, who worked for Graham's office. As he put it, "He was a guy who rose from humble beginnings in Tennessee, uneducated and poor, who rose to the top of his business, headlined Madison Square Garden, became a wrestling promoter and had one of the most successful companies in history, became a millionaire, and eventually the president of the National Wrestling Alliance. That just about says it all."

JERRY "THE KING" LAWLER

Though Jerry Lawler has been "The King" since 1974 when he got his crown from the late Bobby Shane, his majesty has displayed an uncommon ability to connect with his subjects. "Nightmare" Ken Wayne, who's known Lawler from the start of his career, would ride with him to, say, Louisville and stop off at a place like Bowling Green, Kentucky, to get something to drink. "He'd buy the local newspaper. I'd say, 'Jerry, why are you buying the Bowling Green news-paper?' 'Because we're going to be working here next month and I've got to cut an interview for it and this way I can relate to something here in town, some-thing that's going on in local government or a ball game.' So, as a babyface he was able to say, 'Hey what about that championship football team?' He was able to personalize it," Wayne said. "Jerry understood his audience. He understood what they would buy and what they wouldn't buy."

Mike Samples saw that same logic when he was working with Lawler in the Memphis, Tennessee territory in the 1990s. "The King," he said, was a man of the people, and he came across just like one of them, in large part because his interviews were confident and believable. "He always used a truthful back-ground. For example, when the Moondogs were there, they brought in 'The Big Black Dog,' a black guy from the St. Louis area that wasn't very good. But Jerry Lawler gave a great interview about how when he was a kid, his dad was trans-ferred to Cleveland — true story — and worked at an automotive plant. Every day, Jerry had to walk to school and he had to cut through a yard that had a big black dog that always tried to bite him," Samples said. "This is how all of his interviews were. They were based on actual facts, and the fans could easily relate to what he was saying. He made a mental connection with them."

That, friends and colleagues say, is the most important thing to know about Jerry O'Neil Lawler. At six-feet tall with some pudge around the midsection, he looks like a guy you could share a beer with, though "The King" is a teetotaler. But he knows how to get himself and his programs across, be it as a young, gumsmacking upstart challenging the Fabulous Jackie Fargo's top spot in Memphis in 1974, or as a credible sixty-one-year-old contender for the The Miz's WWE title in 2011. "Jerry Lawler's psychology is second to none. His flawless ability to tell a story in the ring, whether it's in front of 500 people or a

"The King" Jerry Lawler was never too proud to mix with his commoners.

crowd of 50,000, is on par with the greatest of all time," said Scott Bowden, who watched Memphis wrestling as a kid before becoming a heel manager in Lawlerland. "He didn't have to take potentially career-ending bumps or death-defying falls to build the drama. His superior psychology is just one reason why he's endured for so long while others' careers have been cut short far too soon because of neck and back injuries." As Lawler put it in *It's Good to be the King . . . Sometimes:* "I was never a flashy wrestler myself but I always knew the value of selling. I've always thought that the best match you could have is when you get two wrestlers going against each other, and each one is trying to outsell the other."

Lawler's story is familiar to most fans, thanks to his nearly twenty years of exposure on national TV, mostly as the color man on WWE Raw. He grew up in Memphis, except for a few childhood years in Cleveland. He was pretty much a goof-off at Treadwell High School, but he did have a knack for art, and started drawing caricatures of Fargo and some of the wrestlers who filled up Ellis Auditorium on Monday nights. Lance Russell, the voice of Memphis wrestling, got a hold of them, displayed them on TV, and Fargo and business partner Eddie Bond set up Lawler in a sign company they were opening. His artwork was impressive, but his command of religious denominations was not — Lawler misspelled one project for the Church of the Nazarene as "Nazirene." Despite the gaffe, Bond let Lawler hang around his radio show and run a graveyard on-air shift at county radio station KWAM. Meanwhile, after Lawler started wrestling for outlaw promotions, Fargo took him under his wing and brought him into the sport.

Billy Wicks, the fresh-faced champion of Memphis wrestling in the early 1960s, recalled getting a letter from an inquisitive Lawler about becoming a wrestler. Lawler didn't have any wrestling background, but Wicks, a legendary catch-as-catch-can combatant, gave him a few pointers and urged him to get with Fargo and promoter Nick Gulas. "He was a sharp kid and I have a lot of respect for Jerry Lawler. He never fooled with drugs or alcohol and he was a good guy as far as I was concerned," Wicks said. Even Wicks' one and only match with Lawler, in Batesville, Mississippi, didn't disabuse him of that notion. "Jerry don't remember this but I do very well. We locked up and he had a wad of bubble gum in his mouth. He took the wad of bubble gum and stuck it in the hair of my chest. I said, 'You son of a bitch!' Anyway I pulled the big wad of bubble gum out of my chest and went and slapped it on his head. It didn't stick."

If that sounds sophomoric, well, in some ways Lawler has always had a goofy, frat-boy quality. Though Jerry Jarrett is about the same age as Lawler, he was already booking, promoting, and running towns when Lawler was still learning the ropes. "There was a kid who was an artist and a lot of people thought he'd never make it as a wrestler because he had this terrible habit of grinning and chewing gum," Jarrett said. Samples said one of Lawler's pranks consisted of loading up on soufflé cups of coleslaw at a fast food joint before he hit the road. "Then, as he passed you on the highway, with him doing over 100 mph, he would bomb your car with cups of coleslaw. This became a game and was quite a challenge to some of us. Nobody could beat him. He was the king of road warfare." And then there was the time Lawler, who always drove like a speed demon, got pulled over by a police cruiser. In the meantime, James "Kamala" Harris zipped by him. As Tom Prichard related, Lawler decided to pull a fast one by sticking a revolving blue light on the hood of his car and stopping Kamala. "Lawler says, 'Get out of your car and face the front of your vehicle.' Lawler grabs his package and Kamala stands there without even turning around," Prichard said. "Kamala chased Lawler for the next fifty miles."

Lawler's first official contest was a match with Tojo Yamamoto in Jonesboro, Arkansas, in 1970. Russell said he knew early on that Lawler had the ability to go somewhere in wrestling because of his interview skills, which stemmed from his stint as a disc jockey. "In his early days, he got every gag book he could get and committed most of them to memory so that if somebody said something to him, he had a reply, one, two, or three. It's what I call working at your trade," Russell said. Lawler was in a tag team with Jim White for the first couple of years of his career, and earned the first of his hundred-plus championships with him as Southern tag team titleholders in 1973. In 1974, Lawler as a heel became the key guy in the Memphis promotion, selling out the city for weeks against Fargo in a new guard–old guard feud. Memphis fans still talk about a 1977 mock concert angle in which Jimmy Valiant facilitated Lawler's turn from heel to hero by busting a guitar over his head in front of his horrified trio of teenaged girl backup singers. Only a broken right leg suffered running a quarterback keeper in a pickup football game at his old high school in January 1980 slowed him down. "Oh man, this is killing me," he told the Commercial Appeal at the time. "This is only the third day and the doctor tells me I'll have the cast on for four months." It ended up being much longer than that. Annoyed that the cast limited his movement in the bathroom, Lawler cut it back from hip to knee and then all the way off, and started to put weight on the gimpy leg. In September, he worked a "cast" match with Karl Krupp in Memphis, screwed up the mending process, and the leg had to be reset. He wouldn't be center stage again in the Mid-South Coliseum until December 29. In retrospect, the break probably helped Lawler in that it gave him time out of the spotlight. "You can only chew the same flavor of gum so many times," Wayne said. "It was one of the best things that happened to him as far as drawing power. It gave an opportunity to get somebody else over. When he came back he was hotter than ever. It was a bad thing, but it turned out to be a good thing in the big picture."

Maybe "The King" wasn't as ubiquitous in Memphis as Elvis Presley, but it wasn't for lack of trying. His image was on billboards, he hosted his own TV show, and he served a commercial spokesperson for all kinds of local businesses. "Memphis fans were as emotionally invested in Lawler as Florida fans were in Dusty Rhodes, and his chase of the world championship was a program the promotion could always go back to, to spark the houses after the wild brawls and grudge matches," Bowden said. One key to that, he added, was the relationship between Lawler and with Russell, who served as the straight man for so many of his zingers. "Memphis was known for its outrageous gimmicks and unusual matches, but Lawler and Russell had a way of making it all seem logical . . . WWE likes to think they introduced comedy to the business, but the exchanges between Lawler and Russell, with Jimmy Hart later added to the mix, helped make Memphis TV the most entertaining show in the business for at least ten years."

Lawler eventually became partner in the promotion with Jarrett, and said he kept himself on top for business reasons — it's fair to say no wrestler has drawn more people in a single city during the last thirty-five years than Lawler has in Memphis. That meant there was always going to be a glass ceiling for aspiring workers there, but the record of guys who were developed in Memphis on their way to the big time is still a roll call of top talent — The Fabulous Ones, The Rock 'n' Roll Express, Kamala, Eddie Gilbert, and, of course, Andy Kaufman. The entertainer-turned-wrestler's 1982–83 feud with Lawler put "The King" on a national map for the first time and laid the groundwork for the fusion of celebrity and wrestling that's so common today. "Jimmy Hart and Jerry Lawler weren't household names in New York or the rest of the country," Hart wrote in his 2004 autobiography. In fact, they had to push levers to get Lawler on the David Letterman show with Kaufman, who was supposed to be a solo comic guest on July 28, 1982. A hard slap and a string of profanities later, the Lawler–Kaufman pull-apart landed as number 83 in TV Guide's list of the 100 top TV moments. "And that, as they say, is how we made television history," Hart said.

Lawler never got a run with the National Wrestling Alliance world heavyweight championship, though Jarrett built up a program called "Quest for the Title" in 1974 that saw Lawler knock off a variety of wrestlers en route to a disqualification loss to then champ Jack Brisco. "I campaigned unsuccessfully for years to get the NWA title for Jerry," Jarrett said. "But some people on the NWA board felt that he wasn't tough enough. I was always saying, 'Tough? What do you mean tough? This is show business.'" He'd have to wait until 1988 for a world title, when the Memphis office aligned itself with the American Wrestling Association and he beat Curt Hennig for the strap. It made front page news in Memphis. "The only great worker ever, in my eyes, to come from Tennessee was Jerry Lawler," said manager "Playboy" Gary Hart. "I think Jerry Lawler would have been big anywhere he went. He could work, he could perform. He never had a bad match. He would do whatever it took."

His two sons, Brian and Kevin, entered wrestling with considerably less success than their dad; they didn't use his last name and for years he went to lengths to avoid mentioning the family ties. Sixteen years after the battle with Kaufman, "The King" was still convincing enough when he played himself in the production of *Man on the Moon*, the movie about Kaufman's offbeat life, that the Hollywood trade press asked "Was it real?" when he allegedly jerked around lead actor Jim Carrey, who had spit in Lawler's face. Back home, Lawler ran unsuccessfully for mayor in 1999 and 2009, though he was taken credibly as a candidate. He never left the art realm; a gallery in Water Valley, Mississippi, ran a six-week exhibition in 2011 of four decades of his illustrations and oil paintings of wrestlers, comic-book heroes, and other subjects.

Lawler joined the WWE as a commentator in 1992 and, though he once walked away when the company fired then wife Stacy Carter, he has been there since. Sitting next to him every Monday night as part of WWE's best-ever announcing combo, Jim Ross gained insights into what makes "The King" tick. "He does not portray a TV character; he is merely an enhanced version of himself. He's a lifelong fan, therefore he's able to understand the psyche of the audience and more importantly knows how to connect with the fan base," Ross said. "As a fan favorite or villain or broadcaster, Jerry is in a handful of the business all-time greats. He's a natural born entertainer and an extremely underrated athlete."

In 2007, Lawler was tapped for induction into the WWE Hall of Fame. When WWE CEO Vince McMahon asked him who he wanted as his presenter, Lawler requested Russell, his long-time friend. Not a big enough name, McMahon answered. Maybe somebody else. Russell said he wasn't hurt by the snub, but he knew Lawler would find some way to capture the moment. "It popped in his mind that there is so much competition for air time on that presentation. So he knew a guy who knew William Shatner, and he got William Shatner to do it because he knew the name would attract the camera and they wouldn't cut a bunch of his stuff out. That probably points out the difference as much as anything I know about what Lawler. He just had a mind that worked that way."

LEN ROSSI

December 8, 1972, sticks out for Len Rossi because it was the day everything changed for him. Cowboy Frankie Laine was driving along Interstate 40 near Jackson, Tennessee, with Rossi nodding on and off in the passenger's seat. Suddenly, they came over a hill right into the middle of a multi-car crash near a bridge, and Laine couldn't swerve in time. Rossi was crushed like an eggshell — broken feet, arms, ankles, and legs. For forty-five minutes, he lay in a ditch in miserable, damp weather until an ambulance could rescue him. "I went over to Madison County Hospital to see about him," his son Joey, also a wrestler, recalled a few years later. "I remember I walked down the corridor. They had some beds out there. I walked right by him. I didn't recognize him at first. It hit me like a bomb . . . The doctors said at first they didn't know if he would make it."

From the challenge comes the commitment. Rossi survived his calamitous injuries, and though he made a couple of brief comebacks, his wrestling career was over. But the accident started him down a path he still is on today as a holistic counselor and health food store operator in Nashville, Tennessee, relying on diet, exercise, and lifestyle changes to help patients cope with a variety of medical conditions. "For me, this is my ministry. That's what I think God wants me to do, to help people, counsel them, advise them. We work with cancer patients, heart disease, anybody who is interested in a natural approach."

COURTESY OF SCOTT TEAL/CROWBAR PRESS

Len Rossi demonstrates a Boston crab in a publicity photo.

Still, you scratch Rossi, and there's a warmup jacket and a Boston crab underneath. He was one of the most popular stars ever in promoter Nick Gulas' Kentucky–Tennessee–Alabama territory, and he delighted in playing the crowd like a conductor. After all, not many wrestlers could get as much mileage out of a single hold for two straight falls. It happened in Chattanooga, Tennessee, with "Mean" Don Greene during one of Rossi's seven runs with the Southern junior heavyweight championship. Greene and Rossi came on after a red-hot tag match that turned into a chair-throwing melee. "I told Don, 'Here's what we'll do. You grab a headlock on me and you hang on to that headlock the whole first fall.' He had a headlock on me and every time I'd pull away, he'd grab my hair, whatever. Before you know it we had the people hooked, just oohing and aahing. Then I finally lost the first fall, I submitted, I gave up with a headlock. One hold." At the start of the second fall, Rossi kept retreating to the floor and shaking the cobwebs out of his head to accentuate the punishment he'd taken. "I finally got back in the ring and you know what the big high spot was? I got a headlock on him and the people came out of their seats. That's the honest truth."

With apologies to Mark Twain, Rossi is the story of an Utica Yankee in Colonel Reb's Court. "He was different than what they were used to seeing down here," said Billy Wicks, who counts him as a close friend. "He was a Yankee coming down to Tennessee and that wasn't easy. I think he was a good Italian — 'Len Rossi, eh, eh' — and everybody likes a good Italian. That was part of it and then he was a good, clean-cut wrestler who believed in the rules, was polite and respectful."

The son of Italian immigrants, Len Rositano was born September 24, 1929, in Utica, New York. He worked out at the local YMCA, where he had to pass by the wrestling mats to get to the weight room. A local coach kept goading him into wrestling, and Rossi, outweighing him by fifteen pounds, figured he'd give it a shot. "He mopped the floor with me," Rossi said. "But I took it as a challenge. I was always strong for my age but I realized there was more to it than that." Rossi started wrestling for the Y at fourteen; there was no high school wrestling program in Utica, and he wound up in unsanctioned "smoker" matches for a couple of bucks at a time.

Still he was hooked, and he embarked on a pro career for promoter Ed Don George in upstate New York after two years in the military. "That was my intention from the very beginning. I didn't know how much money they paid. It was rough. I remember, somewhere around Spokane, Washington, or somewhere up there, I didn't get any bookings. I lived on peanut butter and bread. Couldn't even afford to go to the restaurant. I was sending my late wife money orders, two dollars, three dollars, anything I could afford. I just kept plugging, kept plugging." Rossi — a Boston promoter informed him "Rositano" wouldn't fit on a poster — got into his first big feud in 1954 and 1955 with Gypsy Joe in the Utah–Idaho area. It culminated in a scheduled ten-round boxing and wrestling match in Provo, Utah, with Rossi winning on a sixth-round knockout. From there, he wrestled in the Illinois–Wisconsin region, Texas, and New York before heading to Tennessee in May 1958 for what was supposed to be a two-week stint.

With Joey nearing school age, the Rossis decided to settle in for good. "I would leave once in a while and go to Oklahoma or North Carolina. I went to Japan one time on a tour, but we headquartered here and I've been here ever since."

In the late 1950s and early 1960s, his tag team with Tex Riley was the most popular pairing in Gulas' territory, which sprawled from Kentucky to just north of the Gulf Coast. Riley had been a regular in Tennessee for years and Rossi credits him for advancing his understanding of audiences, at least when Tex was sober, which he was not one night in Jackson, Tennessee, against Don and Al Greene. "We were going to go two out of three falls, I think they beat us the first fall, whatever. At the end of the last fall, I go over to tag Tex Riley and he's sound asleep in the corner. Honk-shoo! So the Greenes beat me and on the way out, an old farmer yells, 'Hey, Riley, what's wrong with ya?' I said, 'Oh, he's sick.' He said, 'Oh, he's sick all right — I can smell it from here.'" If the Riley–Rossi tandem was popular, the Rossi–Bearcat Brown tag team was the most socially important because it represented the first regular integrated tag team in the South. The two held the territory's world tag team championship five times from 1969 to 1972. "Bearcat, all the black people could come to see him. And Rossi, all the white people could come to see him. So when Rossi would tag Bearcat, the black people would go crazy and vice versa. It was a great combination," said Buddy Wayne, who wrestled a lot with and against Rossi. "Len is a good guy. He knew what he was doing in the ring."

Some 600 callers flooded a TV station switchboard after Gulas announced Rossi's car crash, but the outpouring of sympathy didn't compensate for his personal struggle. With no formal trade and no post–high school education, he was at a loss. He spent seven weeks in the hospital, underwent multiple surgeries, developed colon problems, and started drinking too much. A bedside visit from a radiologist alerted him to the work of Denis Burkitt and Neil Painter, who had done epidemiological studies in Africa and attributed low incidences of diverticulitis, colitis, and heart disease to high-fiber diets. "This is in the '70s, not like today, where we didn't know what fiber was. So that's when God hit me in the head with a hammer, woke me up. I changed my lifestyle; I quit drinking because I was worried about my future and what I would do in my old age." He studied nutrition at Belmont University in Nashville and completed distance-learning classes for a doctor of naturopathy degree. Save a brief return to the mat with son Joey, who died in 2003, he has been working in natural healing ever since. "I'm blessed because I did wrestling for about twenty-two years and I loved when I was doing it, and I love what I'm doing now. In a way it's more rewarding because you're helping people's health and I think that's the most precious thing in the world. So it's more fulfilling, but at the time, I loved what I was doing."

CHRIS SWISHER COLLECTION

Being a cowboy suited Nelson Royal . . .

NELSON ROYAL

Few in the wrestling-rich Mid-Atlantic area would ever believe that a pompous, arrogant "Englishman" known as "Sir" Nelson Royal, replete with tails and top hat, would one day emerge as a cowboy who would steal their hearts. But that's exactly what "Nellie" — as he would become affectionately known to a generation of fans and friends — did.

Royal first arrived in the Carolinas in 1964 as half of a heel tag team with The Viking (Bob Morse). Sporting a black beard and black vest and billed from London, England, Sir Nelson Royal was a perfect complement to his white-bearded, Scandinavian teammate. Royal had refined his heel gimmick working in the Pacific Northwest and the Amarillo circuit, where he feuded with the territory's owner, Dory Funk Sr. "Nelson loved Texas so much he became a cowboy," said Dory Funk Jr., who had his second match as a pro with Sir Nelson Royal in Albuquerque, New Mexico.

Bringing Morse with him to the Carolinas, the two headlined against such established duos as The Kentuckians and George and Sandy Scott, but eventually went their separate ways. Morse, whose late-night, hard-living style didn't mesh with the milder-mannered Royal, left for Kansas City, while Royal grabbed a cowboy hat, abandoned his rule-breaking ways, and hooked up with lumbering, six-foot-nine Hugh "Tex" McKenzie as part of a wildly popular big-man, small-man tandem.

McKenzie, whom Nellie would jokingly refer to as "one big, tall sucker — he

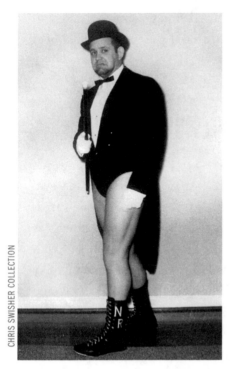

... far better than being a "lord" did.

stood seven foot tall if he stood up straight" — towered over the five-foot-nine Royal, whose hard-nosed mat style was in sharp contrast to that of McKenzie, a jovial and easygoing performer who was all legs and arms in the ring,

While Royal was more than proficient in singles competition, he became a workhorse in tag team wrestling, first pairing with McKenzie in 1966, then adding a young Paul Jones to his side in 1968. Jones, who accompanied Royal to Los Angeles in 1969 to capture the international tag team title, tapped into his more experienced partner's popularity to help establish himself as a solid main eventer in the Carolinas. "I learned so much from Nelson. We were partners for about four years and never had one argument," said Jones.

Royal, who became one of the top draws for promoter Jim Crockett Sr., was a tag team specialist in a territory known for tag team wrestling, and would enjoy other successful partnerships with the likes of Sandy Scott, Klondike Bill, Les Thatcher, George Becker, and Johnny Weaver. Between long runs with McKenzie and Jones as partners, Royal would be involved in some of the territory's most memorable programs.

Just how good was Nelson Royal? Royal, said Les Thatcher, was one of the greatest ring generals he ever encountered. "He could judge the pulse of a crowd and switch directions to emotionally pull them in as smooth as anyone I ever encountered. He was a very genuine person and gave so much to his craft."

Abe Jacobs also worked with and against Royal. "Nelson was as good a pro as there was in the business," said the New Zealand native. "He was a good heel and a good babyface — he could work either way. He was maybe one of the best all-around performers in the business."

Royal, as scrappy and tenacious as they came, could "go" with anyone. Dutch Savage (Frank Stewart), who teamed with Royal in Oklahoma and Japan, called Royal "a human dynamo." "He was constantly going," said Savage. "He worked a completely different style than I did. I was a slow, methodical, center-of-the-ring guy. Nellie was all over the place. He was a whirlwind who just never stopped."

Born Nelson Clark Combs (he later added the name Royal) in Wheelwright, Kentucky, on July 21, 1931, Royal started wrestling at the age of seventeen under the watchful eye of Native star Don Eagle. For nearly two years, he trained with Eagle and wrestled in nightly events held at National Guard armories for $5 to $10 a night. He was told by promoters that he would never make it to the main event due to his height. Undaunted, Royal broke in with Al Haft's prestigious Columbus promotion, and quickly hit the road to Idaho, New Mexico, Washington state, Oregon, Maryland, and the Carolinas.

Royal, who came from a background that emphasized tough, realistic mat work, would achieve his own level of success for his realistic, hard-hitting style. One of the most respected technicians in the business, he held the world junior heavyweight belt several times between 1976 and 1988. For that style, though, Royal's body would pay a price.

He once said there wasn't a rib in his body that hadn't been broken, and if it weren't for anti-inflammatories, he would never be able to sleep. "I've got more stitches in my head than I want to think about," he said. Royal, however, considered his numerous scars and ring injuries a badge of honor.

Perhaps nobody went at it harder and longer than Royal and veteran heel Rip Hawk (Harvey Evers). Hawk was one of Royal's fiercest rivals in the ring, and the two battled hundreds of times over their careers, leaving blood spilled on mats throughout the Southeast. "Nelson and I really wrestled," recalled Hawk, who once broke Royal's leg during a singles match. "There were no cartoons or anything like that. Nelson was great as a single wrestler or in tag teams. He was a leader and he was fun to wrestle. It was hard, but it was fun. The people couldn't believe some of the moves we made. Nobody could 'see daylight.' It was all very tight."

As capable a worker as Royal was in the ring, his greatest gift may have been as a trainer and molder of talent. With former ring adversary Gene Anderson, Royal helped break in a number of young wrestlers, including rookie Ken Shamrock, who moved with his father to Royal's ranch in Mooresville, North Carolina, during the late '80s while Royal was training wrestlers and running his Atlantic Coast Wrestling promotion after Jim Crockett Promotions folded. Royal and Anderson trained aspiring grapplers in an aluminum building on Royal's property with no heating or air, and on a ring that was that rock hard.

Those who survived the training would become better men — and women

— for it. And that included Royal's two sons and even his daughter. "Dad was very tough on us," said Shannon Lloyd McCrary, who worked as valet Sha Sha in Royal's Atlantic Coast Wrestling promotion. "I wanted to be a valet like Baby Doll, but Dad told me I had to learn how to wrestle first." McCrary, who trained alongside another second-generation performer, Rockin' Robin Smith (daughter of Grizzly Smith), said the experience gave her "a whole new perspective" on what her dad did for a living.

Neither McCrary nor her two brothers would make wrestling their livelihood, although the experience would last a lifetime. "I gained a new respect for him and wrestling. I wouldn't trade any of those days in the ring with him. Besides having my children, that was one of the best times of my life," McCrary said.

Brad Anderson, son of co-trainer Gene Anderson, also earned his stripes at the camp. "Dad would usually be on the outside and tell us, 'Looks like shit, do it again,'" recalled Anderson. "We bumped our asses off, learned wrestling holds, learned to listen in the ring to who was calling the match. The whole time the 'psychology' of how to put a match together, how to get heat, and how to sell was introduced and reiterated over and over."

Trainees such as Johnny and Mark Laurinaitis, Rikki Nelson, Curtis Thompson, Todd Champion, Robbie "Stro" Kellum, Tommy Angel, Trent Knight, David Isley and the late Colt Steele, and Jammin' Mitch Snow learned that making it through the grueling camp would be no easy task.

The training was arduous, Isley recalled, and consisted of running laps through rows and rows of unplowed cornfields and putting fellow trainees on your back and going up and down a steep hill, followed by freehand squats, pushups, sit-ups, and then getting stretched on the mat. "It was probably one of the toughest things I've ever done in my life, and I knew if I could get through that, I could get through anything."

It wasn't just wrestling Royal was teaching, said Isley. "He taught us about life. He told us that this business would open up our eyes to so many things and to people in general. It does because you live this carney life. He was giving us life experiences that taught us things we never would have learned anywhere else. He also taught us how to take care of ourselves in the ring. He taught us not to let guys push us around and to give it right back to them if they tried."

If Nelson Royal trained you, you were as good as gold, said Isley, who recalled being part of a group of Royal–Anderson trainees booked to work some WWF shows. "They were so amazed at how good we made their guys look . . .

Bobby Heenan came up to us and said, 'Guys, I just want to tell you something. We haven't had any good guys come through here in a long time that got our guys over and made them look so good.' He took a hundred-dollar bill out of his pocket and told us to split it amongst us and grab some beer on the way home, and that he really appreciated our efforts. That's the kind of respect we got." That respect, said Isley, would later open doors for him and others. "I got a lot of my breaks on down the road because of who trained me," said Isley. "It opened a lot of doors for me, including extra tours like All Japan, because of Nellie. They all knew we were trained the right way. Nelson taught us locker-room etiquette."

Royal took pride in the fact that he was a legitimate tough guy and a genuine cowboy. It wasn't a gimmick. "He was a real cowboy, and if you actually were to question his toughness, all you had to do was watch him on the back of a ton of bucking, snorting bull to realize that was more than a show as well," said Thatcher.

Royal loved his horses and his ranch. "He was always riding when he was home," said son David Combs Royal. "He had two or three stallions at different times, and showed on the circuits and so forth when he had an opportunity."

As aggressive and relentless as Royal was inside the ring, he was just as kind-hearted and giving outside it. "He was nice to everybody," said Hawk. "Some guys feel like they're big shots and too good to shake hands with somebody or talk to some kid. Nellie was never that way. He was always courteous with people and a real fan favorite."

"You couldn't find a better guy. He's probably the best human being I ever met," said Ronnie Garvin, whose nickname for his friend was "Grandfather." "He called me 'Grandson' for years," he joked.

Royal, who was involved in a number of community efforts such as the DARE drug awareness program and Crime Stoppers, operated his western supply store in Mooresville for more than thirty years, selling boots, belts, and saddles, and raising horses. The store remains in operation today.

Alzheimer's disease slowed Royal in the latter years of his life, but he continued to work in his store, where fans and old wrestling buddies would drop by to talk about the old days. Royal died at the age of sixty-six of a massive heart attack on February 3, 2002, after returning home from church one Sunday morning.

"He was a real hero," said his daughter. "He'd never turn away a fan who wanted to talk to him about the business. No matter how tired he was, no matter what we might be doing as a family, he always had time for his fans. It got hard sometimes to share your dad with the fans, but he always told us that they loved wrestling just like he did and they paid for what we had. Of course, when you're young, sometimes you're jealous and you're angry because you don't want to share your dad. But as an adult, you look back and see what a great man he really was. He wasn't just someone who wrestled and didn't want to talk to the people who came and watched it."

TIGER JEET SINGH

Having succeeded through the years in his Toronto booking office by promoting a series of ethnic heroes, from Italians like Bruno Sammartino and Ilio DiPaolo, to Irishmen like Pat Flanagan, and Scotsmen like Andy Robin, Frank Tunney was on the hunt for something different.

Enter Jagjit Singh Hans, a six-foot-three, 265-pound athletic Indian immigrant, from Ludhiana, a small village in the state of Punjab, who was fated for bigger things as Tiger Jeet Singh.

"When I came here, I had no dream that I was going to be what I am today. I was just an ordinary person, no dream. But it was written in my destiny," Singh said. "And everything came, and God showed me the path to Frank Tunney, then Fred [Atkins] came in my life, from there, Japan came into my life, Jim Barnett came into my life."

Singh's honesty clicked with Tunney, and he immediately took a liking to the young Sikh. Tunney called the ornery old-timer Fred Atkins to his side, and they privately discussed the young Indian wrestler. "I don't know what they talked about in the back. Next thing I know, he gave me a contract. He said, 'Five-year contract. We take care of your expenses. You stay at Crystal Beach with Fred.'"

Looking back now, Singh is still amazed at the chance that Tunney took, especially given that they never discussed targeting the ever-growing South Asian community around Toronto. "As a businessman, maybe Frank, he thought a lot of Asian people are coming here and there's no Asian talent here. Maybe he should make me one, train me properly, and have me under his wings for five years, and let's see what he can do."

While training in Crystal Beach, Ontario, on the shores of Lake Erie, Singh lived in a garage across the street from the Atkins family, with a bed and a heater. They quickly fell into a routine, and Singh obeyed. "He'd wake me up early in the morning, take me to the beach, and make me run in the sand with the heavy shoes." In the basement, Singh learned how to fall and build his stamina. "Stamina was his main key. He pushed me just to get in shape and train properly." Professor Hiro was another trainee when Tiger was there.

Though Singh debuted in 1964, after six months of training, he would stick with Atkins, off and on, for the five-year contract. "I learned very fast. If you showed me something, I would listen very carefully to what you are telling me, and pick it up very fast. I have that good ability; I pick up everything very fast."

What Atkins neglected to do, insists Singh, was teach him the inner workings of professional

A young Tiger Jeet Singh with the North American title during a bout in Detroit.

DAVE BURZYNSKI

wrestling. "[Atkins] never let me talk to anybody about our match. No fixed matches. 'You're just going over that guy. Just go beat the shit out of the guy.'"

A trip Down Under changed that. "I got smartened up in Australia, not in Canada. In Canada, I fought for my life," said Singh. "In Australia, I learned how to work, because I worked with Mark Lewin, and he was the champion and he was the booker for Jim Barnett. I had a match with him. I used to chop so hard that I'd leave five fingers on people's chests. People used to hate my guts."

But back in Toronto, Tunney had struck gold.

"Ethnicity played a huge role," recalled Jim Korderas, a fan who would become a long-time WWE referee. "Tiger Jeet Singh, no matter what he did, he was so revered by the East Indian population, especially here in Toronto, that he could do no wrong." Singh admits that he did face racism, chants of "Paki go home," and the occasional lawsuit outside the ring for standing up for himself.

In May 1968, Singh's career took off when he captured a version of the U.S.

An older and much wilder Tiger Jeet Singh attacks Giant Baba in Japan.

title in Maple Leaf Gardens. "I remember when I wrestled right here in Toronto, Johnny Valentine for the U.S. title. I was a nervous wreck, and didn't know if I was coming or going. I just went wild. And after that I never looked back," Singh said. He would speak Punjab on TV interviews with Lord Athol Layton, imploring his countrymen to come see him fight. "People used to be glued to the TV and next day, they couldn't wait."

The crowning achievement was a February 21, 1971, bout in Maple Leaf Gardens. "We drew 20,000 to see The Sheik fight Tiger Jeet Singh this spring at the Gardens. It's the largest wrestling crowd we've ever had. We turned away 5,000 people," said Frank Tunney in 1971. Singh had similar, though briefer, successes in Vancouver and Montreal, and was a regular on the road from Buffalo to Detroit.

"I knew right away this guy was going to be a star in the business," said Bruce Swayze, who kept his Ontario ties throughout his wrestling career. "I talked to many people that were of his faith . . . I wouldn't say he was a god to them, but he was a superhero, bigger than Superman. They loved this guy. I used to get a charge out of that because, anybody I ever talked to, sometimes I'd just fool with it, and I'd ask somebody, 'You ever heard of Tiger Jeet Singh?' And they'd go, 'Ooh, Tiger Jeet. We love Tiger Jeet Singh. We love Tiger.'"

That love has continued and been returned ten-fold. Having invested his money well, Singh has been heavily involved in the South Asian and Sikh communities in southern Ontario for decades, raised money for charities large and small, and the neighboring cities of Milton, where he has a 14,000-square foot mansion, and Brampton, have relied on him as an international business ambassador. In 2010, Tiger Jeet Singh Public School was opened in Milton, believed to be the third school in the world named after a pro wrestler; there are schools named after Whipper Billy Watson, in Keswick, Ontario, and strongman Paul Anderson, in Vidalia, Georgia.

But the story of Tiger Jeet Singh, of course, is an international one. And it is one of fear and hatred.

In Australia in 1971 and '72, Jim Barnett had Singh as a villain, wearing his turban and traditional outfit, playing on the anti-Asian immigration fears of the time. "I never got to see many sites in Australia because I was a heel and people hated my guts. I was always worried and had to watch myself," he said. "My heat was so good that sometimes I never even got to take my costume off for the match." Singh was naively fed a few lines to say on TV, like an infamous one directed at Australian icon Spiros Arion: "I'm going to punish you like the Turks did to the Greeks for years." Yet, in a city like Perth with a heavy Indian population, Singh was revered.

It was a similar tightrope act in Japan, where he first landed in 1972 and immediately was thrust into a supermarket brawl with Antonio Inoki, establishing a stardom that continues today through public appearances and his Tiger Jeet Singh Curry Houses.

"Singh became a cult figure there and superceded The Sheik from the standpoint of the wildness, and so did Abdullah," said Johnny Powers. "They built unique personas over there. You'd have to be there actually to appreciate how huge they were. Their wildness and uniqueness and exoticness for the Japanese really caught on. They became huge stories over there."

Brandishing a sword, Singh would often spend more time chasing the fans than in the ring. "I can go slap people, I can go kick the people, I can go spit on the people, they'll still come and worship me," he said. "Even when I was a heel, people bought my shoes, my shirts. I slap the people, they just bow down, sit down, I'm kicking them, everything. They're still, 'Tiger-san, please sign T-shirt?' They paid $45 for my T-shirt and they want my signature on it."

All that merchandise money has made Singh, who has always maintained that he arrived in Canada with six dollars, a wealthy man, in more ways than one. His family is incredibly tight, living close by and working for him. His son,

Mick, who wrestled for a decade as Tiger Ali Singh, is his right-hand man in just about any venture.

"They ask, 'How much your net worth?' I say, 'Enough,'" concluded Singh. "I'm living very simple. I like to do a lot of charity work, like helping children. And God is great, he gives us his blessing, like I never expected in my life."

DAVID MACIEJEWSKI

Billy Robinson and Wilbur Snyder await their opponents.

WILBUR SNYDER

After dropping out of the University of Utah following his junior year, where he had tackled and kicked for the football team and served as a heavyweight on the Redskins wrestling squad, Wilbur Snyder found himself back in Van Nuys, California, driving a cement truck for his father's business. Unable to be drafted and play pro ball until his college class graduated, Snyder begged Benny Ginsberg to get him into wrestling. Ginsberg took him to meet Los Angeles booker Jules Strongbow, who promptly said, "We don't need any more football players in wrestling."

For a less determined man, this might have been the end of the story. Instead, Snyder latched on to Jerry Christy, nephew to L.A.'s famed Vic and Ted Christy, who had only debuted himself in 1951. "I refused many times," recalled Christy of Snyder. Though both had gone to Van Nuys High School, they were too many grades apart to know each other. Eventually, Christy caved, and began unteaching some of the lessons Ginsberg shared. "I got him and taught him the right things, like he had a hard time when he was selling. He said, 'I just can't do that!' . . . But he learned." Christy convinced Don Sebastien, a small-town promoter in the shadow of Hugh Nichols in L.A., to watch them work out; Snyder's debut at the Valley Garden Arena in early 1953 followed.

Having heard about the local product, the big-time promoter headed to the rinky-dink show. "Hugh Nichols saw him, and oh my God, Hugh Nichols just fell in love with him," summed up Christy.

From there, Snyder shot into prominence very quickly, challenging top stars like Mr. Moto and, most surprisingly, NWA world champion Lou Thesz, in the summer of 1953, less than a year into his part-time career.

"The same Wilbur Snyder who couldn't quite make the first team at the University of Utah football camp several years ago will be wrestling for the world's championship in Salt Lake July 9," teased Hack Miller in *The Deseret News*. "They've brought our Wilbur along pretty nicely in the mat business. He's a big and handsome feller with a fine figure. He's the handsome type — the best you could get for today's TV market."

It was almost as if someone were trying to convince Snyder to give up on the football dream, which he finally did after the 1953 season, but not without much notable effort.

Snyder, born September 15, 1929, in Santa Monica, was a football star and gymnast at Van Nuys High, who married his sweetheart Shirlee Ann Hanson right after graduation at the Little Church of Sherman Oaks. At the University of Utah, Snyder, like many players at the time, covered multiple positions on the gridiron. "Snyder weighs 210 and is canny at the catch," read a 1949 report, which also praised his placekicking. In April 1950, he dropped out of school.

"It was simply a case of needing money," Snyder said in a magazine profile years later. "I'd married Shirlee before my freshman year you see. So I went to work for my father in the trucking business. I also looked up Bob Waterfield, my old high school teammate and he got me a tryout with the Los Angeles Rams." When the Rams didn't bite at that 1952 training camp, he filled time working with his father until the Edmonton Eskimos of the Western Interprovincial Football Union called, and Snyder joined partway into the 1952 fall season, and played the next as well.

Before the 1953 season started, Snyder took to the mats, including a bout in Edmonton. "A new star hove onto the horizon at the Sales Pavilion Tuesday, in the person of a fellow named Wilbur Snyder. And before Wilbur is here much longer, he will be the toast of Edmonton's wrestling fraternity," praised the *Journal*. Notably, teammate Joe Blanchard was on the same card, heading down the same dual career road.

Blanchard said they never discussed their wrestling plans, and was not jealous of Snyder's quick success. "He got an instant break. He was a big, handsome guy, a good athlete. He was a good worker and did a good job." Gene Kiniski was a third tackle on those Eskimo teams that would turn pro wrestler.

The team tolerated the wrestling early in the season, but not when the playoffs approached, and rosters had to be set, including an eight-man American import quota. "There was no stipulation in our contracts that we quit on October 1," said Snyder in November 1953. "It was an unwritten gentlemen's agreement."

The six-foot-two-and-a-half inch Snyder threw his 230 pounds around in the ring much the same as he did on the field. "Wrestling helps you in football because there is no pre-season sweating into shape," said Snyder. "By wrestling in the off season, you're always in shape and the mat game sharpens your reflexes for football. I also use much of my football training in the ring."

After realizing there was far more money to be made in wrestling, Snyder told the Eskimos he was done in May 1954, and furthered his in-ring training with Warren Bockwinkel and Sandor Szabo — "They worked some of the rough edges off me" — and Tony Morelli in Hawaii.

"The guys around there, if you said, 'Come work out with Wilbur,' you worked out with him," Blanchard said of the Los Angeles scene. "Thesz was around then; Thesz worked out with him some. Wilbur, he was really a good athlete."

It took awhile, but eventually "The California Comet" assumed the mantle of "The World's Most Scientific Wrestler," and the move he most popularized was the abdominal stretch. The Milwaukee Journal dubbed Snyder "a veritable arsenal of virtue . . . armed with everything that is right and proper — including a crew cut, suntan and shell-like ears."

Snyder would also have a disciple in Nick Bockwinkel. "My dad did so much to train him that he was very kind and, of course, returned the favor and helped train me. So it wasn't so much that he was my idol, but everybody said, 'You almost look like Wilbur's duplicate.' I guess what I did was I mirrored him . . . his style and his movements, in the ring. I had a tendency to do that," Bockwinkel told Whatever Happened To . . .? Bockwinkel and Snyder would be an on-and-off team for a few years. Snyder would form other championship teams with Leo Nomellini, Dick the Bruiser, Moose Cholak, Luis Martinez, Pat O'Connor, Paul Christy, Pepper Gomez, Danny Hodge, Dominic Denucci, and Spike Huber.

If it wasn't for the break of working with Thesz early, perhaps Snyder wouldn't

DAVID MACIEJEWSKI

Wilbur Snyder ties up Nick Bockwinkel in an abdominal stretch.

have made much of a name for himself. "We made a lot of money together," remembered Thesz in the *Wrestling Observer Newsletter* following Snyder's death on Christmas Day 1991 in Pompano Beach, Florida, from heart failure while battling lymphatic leukemia. "He had the crew cut and was a football player and he really had it. He had good reflexes and learned to be a good performer quickly. We ran the feud all over the country, usually stretching it to three meetings (in each city) and sold out in a lot of cities that usually didn't do business."

Aside from Thesz, Snyder's early years are most intertwined with Verne Gagne, whom he knocked off for the U.S. title on April 7, 1956, at Chicago's Marigold Arena, after Gagne's five years as champ. Take their bout at Milwaukee Stadium in August 1956, with Jack Dempsey as the ref; it drew a record crowd of 16,069 for a gate of $33,689.90, bettering the previous attendance mark by almost 4,000 (Gagne versus Ric von Schacht in 1952).

In 1959, Snyder was a key cog in the attempts to get Detroit up and running again and there his career particularly started intertwining with Dick the Bruiser (Dick Afflis). Not only did they become great opponents, but they would become friends and business partners. In April 1965, the two started Championship Wrestling, Inc., with their wives as the figurehead directors of the corporation, and promoted around the Indianapolis area for decades under the World Wrestling Association name, and shared Chicago with Gagne.

While still a key part of the promotion, Snyder avoided the traditional trappings of a promoter and pushed himself at all costs, seemingly content to work the mid-cards, particularly tag team bouts. He was no slouch, though, and in the later '70s was still hitting flying head scissors and leapfrogging foes half his age. Snyder also resisted shoving his son, Mike, into the spotlight, when he debuted in 1974. "My father left the final decision to me, and I really seriously thought about it. I knew that I would have a lot of problems at first, because after all, a lot of people would expect me to be Wilbur Snyder all over again," Mike said in *Wrestling News*.

Lanny Poffo, whose father, Angelo, had some famed bouts with Snyder, got to know Snyder in the mid-'70s. "There was a guy who was a fantastic looking man, excellent babyface, everything you'd ever want for the most athletic looking guy. But he smoked and drank and did everything but he did it with discipline. He did it after the show. When he came to the matches, he was ready to wrestle," said Poffo. "He was like the handsomest man ever."

The promotion made both men rich, even with a failed attempt to invade

The Sheik's Detroit territory, and Snyder sold his share in 1983, and settled into retirement, having invested wisely, primarily in real estate.

SHAG THOMAS

Shag Thomas, hero to the Pacific Northwest.

It would not be an understatement to say "Shag" Thomas headbutted his way into fans' hearts. The year was 1960 and the place was the Pacific Northwest, where promoter Don Owen brought in the goateed Thomas as a villain, a role that would have been life-threatening for an African-American in some parts of the country. Tony Borne and Thomas terrorized the tag team scene for nearly a year until Thomas mistakenly flattened "Tough Tony" with his noggin one night, igniting one of the great feuds in the history of the region. In a series of slugfests that December, Thomas' cranial attacks sent Borne staggering to dressing rooms, leaving "Shag" as top man in town. That's using your head, and promoters were not shy about playing off it. "We used to say that he played football without a helmet, and that's why his head was so hard," chuckled Dean Silverstone, who promoted in Washington and ran Thomas' fan club at one point. "When he was a heel, no one was more hated, and when he was a good guy, there was no one more who was more popular."

James Thomas Sr. got into wrestling late in life; he was nearly thirty when he had his first professional match, and he was thirty-five before he set foot in the Northwest, where he'd become as familiar as wet weather. "The Destroyers and the Princes and the Madmen come and go — but jolly Shag (King Toby) Thomas goes on forever, or as close to forever as the indestructible members of the professional wrestling brigade can go," wrote Vincent O'Keefe of the *Seattle*

Times in 1964. And "Shag," built like a fireplug, adorned with a burgundy fez, still had another decade of wrestling in him after that.

Thomas was born August 11, 1924, in Bellaire, Ohio, part of a big family of five sisters and four brothers. The "Shag" handle goes back to his childhood days, said Shirley, his wife of thirty-two years. "He wasn't quite always neat. He was kind of a tough little guy, always carrying on with the other kids and they started calling him 'Shag.'" Thomas played football in high school and headed to Wilberforce, a historically black college, in 1942 as a trim 190-pounder unrecognizable to later generations of wrestling fans. He was drafted into the U.S. Army in 1943 and served as a corporal during World War II. Like a lot of vets, he headed back to college football after his service was up, hooking on with Ohio State as an offensive guard and defensive lineman in 1948 and 1949, and playing in the team's Rose Bowl win over California. Thomas went to camp with the Green Bay Packers, but at 225 pounds on a five-foot-seven frame, he was undersized even by the standards of the day. He headed to Canadian football, hooking on briefly with the Montreal Alouettes and the Toronto Balmy Beach, where his stocky build earned him the name of "the man without a neck." Thomas got into the wrestling business almost by accident. He worked out at promoter Al Haft's Columbus gym — a barn was more like it — to stay in shape, when some other wrestlers convinced him to try his hand as a pro. Haft always liked wrestlers with legitimate athletic credentials, so he put Thomas in the path of Luther Lindsay, another black footballer who went through training in Columbus a few years earlier. Shirley was on board with the decision. "He was an athlete and when he made his mind up that there was something he really wanted to do, he put his heart into it," she said. Thomas' first recorded match was in Columbus in March 1954, a draw with Jack Vansky.

Most black wrestlers of the era preferred racially hospitable territories, and Thomas was no exception, learning his craft in Ohio, the Utah–Idaho circuit, the Southwest, and western Canada. When he ventured south to Florida in 1956, it was as a footnote to history. Thomas wrestled down-and-out boxing great Joe Louis several times, including a bout in Fort Lauderdale, Florida, that spun into a media feeding frenzy for Louis because he didn't realize the arena barred black patrons. Thomas wore a lot of championship belts, to the extent he could get them around his bowling ball of a frame; he eventually got in the range of 260 to 270 pounds. Nicknamed "King Toby," another holdover from his Columbus days, he had a couple of turns with Haft's tag team championship, then, as a heel, claimed the International TV title and the International TV tag title in Los

Angeles in 1957. He and Borne won the Pacific Northwest tag team title in 1960. He'd hold it fifteen times in that decade with Rene Goulet, Pepper Martin, and Lindsay, among others. Tito Carreon wrestled Thomas as far back as the '50s in Oregon and western Canada and thought he was a good ring presence. "Shag Thomas was a great guy. He was just a heel with the rough stuff. He was a good villain, rugged that way, so he could get the people excited."

In the ring, Thomas didn't do much, and he didn't have to. "He had a different swagger about him. People believed in him," said John Buff, a wrestler and referee in the Northwest for twenty-six years. "He wasn't real active in the ring. His comebacks were short and to the point. He hit here at the right time. I do think working with Tony Borne had a lot to do with it." Sportswriter and wrestling historian J Michael Kenyon fell under Thomas' spell as a fan and started a club on his behalf that turned into a small business, with a whopping 800 dues-paying members at its peak. In 1961, Kenyon hooked up with Thomas at Eagles Auditorium in Seattle, Washington, and noticed he was walking a little slowly. Always outgoing, Thomas explained to the head of his fan club that he'd undergone a vasectomy just that day. "With a shrug, he went right into the ring and participated in a slam-bang, thirty-minute wrestling match," Kenyon recalled. "'Can't afford not to work,' he said, with the friendly smile he always seemed to have for me."

When Thomas landed in Portland, Oregon, he knew it was time to stop his travels and set down roots. "He said, 'One of these days, I'm going to run into a town where I think I want to raise the kids and when I do, that's why I'll bring you guys with me.' When he came to Portland to wrestle, why, he fell in love with Portland. He got familiar to a lot of people here and that's how he got into the public school system," his wife said. In fact, he stayed pretty much in and around Portland after 1961, though he made an all-black tour of Tennessee in 1965 with Art Thomas, Tiger Conway Jr., and Lindsay. Thomas left Ohio State a few credits short of graduation; he enrolled at the University of Oregon to finish his degree, graduating as a Duck not a Buckeye, as he wedged school between his wrestling appearances.

As he crossed into his forties, the physique became more rotund and he scaled back his wrestling, in part because high blood pressure prevented him from getting a license to wrestle in Washington. Owen kept him on as a referee, and Thomas wrestled in infrequent angles through 1976. Roger "Nature Boy" Kirby, who worked a lot in the Northwest, chuckled at one recollection: "Even when he was refereeing, at that point in time, he sometimes wouldn't even get down on the floor to count you out. He would stand beside you and stamp his foot on the floor for the one-two-three." Meanwhile, "Shag" had his finger in a lot of other civic activities. The degree turned into a teaching job at Jefferson High School, while Thomas ran a real-estate business that focused on rental properties. He ran unsuccessfully for Portland city council and the Multnomah County commission, and operated a tavern called "Shag's Arena." As third man in the ring, he often wore T-shirts touting his establishment, which gave bad guys something to shred when they disagreed with his calls. His health caught up to him on July 25, 1982, when he died in Portland at fifty-seven. "In this area, especially because they associated him with his children and several of them are still around," his wife said, "they still get called 'Shag' and 'Little Shag.'"

RUTH OMAN, PETE LEDERBERG COLLECTION

The beloved Johnny Weaver, as half of the Florida tag team champions.

JOHNNY WEAVER

Joe Hamilton just knew Johnny Weaver was going to be a star when he first met him in 1956 in St. Joseph, Missouri. Hamilton, younger brother of Larry "Missouri Mauler" Hamilton, was only eighteen at the time and helping Weaver, a wet-behind-the-ears rookie known as Johnny Ace, set up and haul rings from town to town for promoter Gust Karras on the trailer hitch of Weaver's '53 Ford.

"Johnny was a natural. He was a good worker right out of the box," said Hamilton, who would train with Weaver after setting up the ring. It wasn't long before Weaver was working for promoters Jim Barnett and Johnny Doyle in Indianapolis, teaming with veteran star and St. Joe native Sonny Myers as the Weaver Brothers. "Sonny Myers had a lot of influence on his style of work. He copied Sonny quite a bit, and Johnny turned out to be a premier performer," said Hamilton.

Just a few years later, both Weaver and Hamilton would be headliners, their paths crossing again in the Carolinas and Virginia. Hamilton, teaming up with veteran Tom Renesto as The Masked Bolos (a.k.a. The Assassins), would set attendance records throughout the territory for a grueling series of matches with Weaver and the 601-pound Haystacks Calhoun. The bouts would help establish Weaver as the top babyface in the territory — a title he never relinquished.

Weaver already had gained traction in the promotion, first venturing into the Carolinas in 1962 after successful runs teaming with Myers and Cowboy Bob Ellis. With good looks, athletic ability, and the innate ability to relate to his fan base, Weaver was a star in the making.

Rip Hawk, who had met Weaver while working on top in St. Louis for promoter Sam Muchnick, had been instrumental in bringing Weaver into the Carolinas to work for Crockett Promotions. Although Weaver was working on the bottom of the card, the savvy Hawk recognized star potential and knew he had the perfect candidate when Jim Crockett Sr. asked him where he could get a good babyface to pair with aging veteran George Becker.

"I know of a young guy who's out in St. Louis," Hawk told Crockett. "I'd be glad to give him a call." "Is he good?" Crockett asked. "Hell, yeah, and he's getting better every day," Hawk replied. And the rest was history.

Hamilton admits he still had to do a little prodding and pleading before promoter Jim Crockett Sr. would give Weaver the push Hamilton was sure the youngster would take advantage of. "Johnny had babyface written all over him. He was a handsome guy and he had the skill to go along with it," said Hamilton, whose lobbying worked and proved to be financially advantageous when the two teams sold out a big Fourth of July event at the Greensboro Coliseum. "It took thirty-six cops locked arm in arm forming a V wedge to get us out of the ring and into the dressing room. We were hemmed up in that dressing room until two o'clock in the morning," recalled Hamilton.

From Charleston to Norfolk and all points in between, the Carolinas and Virginia was a territory that thrived on unique characters who could make people believe and have them coming back each week for more. No name was bigger, and no wrestler was more beloved, than Weaver.

Kenneth Eugene "Johnny" Weaver, who passed away February 15, 2008, at the age of seventy-two at his home in Charlotte, was to wrestling fans in the Carolinas what Mickey Mantle was to baseball and Johnny Unitas was to football. He wasn't particularly flashy, but that was part of his appeal. He was a genuine everyman's hero who related to the predominantly blue-collar audience that followed the sport religiously.

Billed from Indianapolis, Indiana, but actually born in East St. Louis, Illinois, Weaver was the biggest fan favorite to ever come through the Carolinas. He arrived in Charlotte, headquarters of Crockett Promotions, in 1962 and made it his home. Occasionally appearing in other parts of the country, but only for limited amounts of time, Weaver always returned to the area that adopted him and the fans who made him their hero.

While Becker was the ringwise veteran and elder statesman of the territory, Weaver proved to be the ideal complement as his young babyface partner. It was a match made in wrestling heaven, especially since the Carolinas–Virginia circuit was a hotbed for tag teams during the '60s, and the majority of main events consisted of tag bouts featuring some of the top-rated combos in the business.

"At Becker's age, of course, Johnny carried the team," said Hamilton. "As a worker, Johnny was in the upper echelon. As far as his contribution to the business, he was always the ultimate professional. He had uncanny ring ability and was one of the elite performers in the business."

Becker and Weaver ruled the roost in the Carolinas and Virginia, holding the Southern and Atlantic Coast tag team belts and enjoying high-profile programs with a revolving group of formidable heel duos. "George was a great partner and a great man," said Weaver. "He was also a very good tutor. I was the 'young blood' so I did most of the wrestling, and I'd tag George when I'd get in trouble."

To veteran heel Rene Goulet, Weaver was everything a babyface should be. "I loved working against Johnny. He was over like a million dollars. He would sell, and when he came back, he was just so good. It was like a night off when you were in the ring with him."

There were other partners along the way with whom Weaver shared success and titles — such diverse stars as the popular Bob Ellis, mammoth country boy Haystacks Calhoun, strongman Sailor Art Thomas, rugged veteran Art Nelson (Neilson), and the acrobatic Argentina Apollo. His final tag team reigns would come years later, with Dewey Robertson and Jay Youngblood, in 1981.

But none would ever click the way Becker and Weaver did.

Weaver could only chuckle when thinking about the many tag matches they won with him using his signature sleeper hold and Becker — all five-foot-eight and 185 pounds of him, and jokingly referred to by his opponents as "skinny legs" — applying his vaunted abdominal stretch. "I can't count that high," Weaver would say.

A generation of Mid-Atlantic fans grew up watching Johnny Weaver battle the bad guys. To long-time pundits like Dick Bourne, Weaver was a sports star of the first order. He was a good-looking, smooth-working babyface with an All-American smile and an easy-going personality. He was, in wrestling parlance, "over.'"

"He was such a household name back then," said Bourne, who runs the Mid-Atlantic Gateway website. "As a kid in the '60s and early '70s, I could list on one hand who the real sports stars were. There was Johnny Unitas, Pete Rose, Wilt Chamberlain, and Johnny Weaver. That's how big he was to us."

Johnny Weaver helps a beaten and bloody Dick Slater from the ring.

Although Weaver's specialty was tag team wrestling, he also was an accomplished singles performer who held a slew of titles and was a top challenger to every NWA world champion from Lou Thesz to Gene Kiniski, Dory Funk Jr., and Jack Brisco. And when his in-ring days started winding down, Weaver parlayed his talent into other areas of the business.

A student of the game, Weaver was universally respected by those he worked with. To long-time star Blackjack Mulligan (Bob Windham), Weaver was the anchor for Mid-Atlantic Wrestling and was a steadying force who knew the territory better than anyone else. "Johnny had the greatest mind in the business," said Mulligan, who added that his friend had a book of finishes that covered every match he had ever worked. "One night I asked him if he would decode that thing. He was the best finish man in the business. He was a master at this business."

Les Thatcher, whose first real break came teaming with Weaver and Becker

Johnny Weaver and Rip Hawk in 2007.

in six-man tags, recognized Weaver's impeccable sense of timing and pacing in the ring, qualities he also applied to his resumé as a detailed booker. "He knew that a good babyface had to sell to have the platform for a fiery comeback. When Weaver slapped on the sleeper, all the fans in the house knew it was time to start putting your coats on for the trip home."

Weaver filled many roles in the wrestling business — as a main-event performer, a booker and office man, a color commentator in the announcing booth, and a mentor to many. Affectionately known as "the dean of professional wrestling," his storied career spanned more than four decades.

Weaver told the Mid-Atlantic Gateway site that he could tell when his in-ring days were numbered. "You know how I knew time was passing me by? I was always fan friendly, and I would get dressed and go out and talk to the people all the time during all of the matches up until it was time for me to go on. I did that for years and years and years. The girls would all run up and hug me. And then finally, they started running up to me, the girls, and they'd throw their arms around me, about a hundred of them, and they'd whisper in my ear, 'Go get Ricky Steamboat.' And then I knew I was over the hill."

Weaver continued to play a vital role in the success of Crockett Promotions long after his career inside the squared circle was over, serving as an elder statesman and mentor and putting over new stars such as Greg Valentine,

Roddy Piper, and Tully Blanchard. He even made a brief return in 1987 to teach "American Dream" Dusty Rhodes the sleeper hold, renamed the "Weaver Lock," in a program with Lex Luger.

"There's a lot of people who came through this territory and worked the towns, and it seemed like Johnny was here forever," said promoter Greg Price. "Johnny knew wrestling like the back of his hand. Not only the wrestling part, but the promotion part, too. You see a lot of guys who leave wrestling and try to promote shows and book, but it's like apples and oranges. It's two different things. But Johnny was so good at both. He was equally as good at promoting as he was wrestling. He knew every back road and every contact. He had relationships with everybody — every building, every town."

When his wrestling career officially ended in 1989, Weaver took a position with the Mecklenburg County (North Carolina) Sheriff's Department, a job he held until his death. In his fifties at the time, Weaver became one of the oldest candidates to take the basic law enforcement test, even though he was tougher, stronger, and in better shape than some officers half his age. He spent most of his nineteen-year second career transporting prisoners on the same back roads he'd traveled as a wrestler and promoter.

Like most heroes, though, Weaver wasn't perfect or infallible, nor did he hold himself up as a role model. His thirty-five-year relationship with beautiful women's wrestling star Penny Banner was far from the ideal marriage, and their image as the All-American couple was more fictional than fact, with the two eventually separating. Both would readily point out, though, that something wonderful came out of it, and that was daughter Wendi.

"Both of them came from broken homes," Wendi explained. "My father and mother, even though they had a feisty life together, they did love each other. They never did divorce."

And, she added, her dad never forgot his fans. "Every Christmas, we'd get Christmas cards and candy. My dad would get presents. He appreciated everything that he had and what the fans were doing for him, and I think that's the way he tried to give it back, to make sure he was there when they wanted to talk or they wanted to see him."

It was that intimate connection with fans that made Weaver more than just a hero in the ring. He was an inspiration to many who wanted to take up wrestling as their trade.

"We didn't have baseball or football in the Carolinas back then. But the wrestling came to your town or your high school gym every week and you could actually reach out and meet Johnny Weaver and talk to him," said Don Kernodle. "Johnny wasn't a character. He was a person."

Fifty years have passed since Johnny Weaver first captured the hearts of wrestling fans in the Mid-Atlantic area, but he remains a hero and an icon to those who will never forget the days when "that rising young star from Indianapolis" battled the bad guys each Saturday on a black-and-white television screen. "When he got here, he really found his home," said Rip Hawk.

Daughter Wendi Weaver put Weaver's impact on a generation of fans into perspective. Long after Weaver hung up his boots, his second career with the Mecklenburg County Sheriff's Department required him to pick up a singularly violent prisoner at a state prison. Weaver's superiors warned him: "This guy is really bad. He's lashing out at all the other sheriffs up there. Make sure he's secure."

Down the hall walked Weaver to take custody of the dangerous inmate. Suddenly, the prisoner stopped cussing and fighting his handlers. "You're Johnny Weaver! You're Johnny Weaver! Oh my God! Man I used to watch you with my grandma in front of the TV." As Wendi recounted, "That guy turned. It was a childhood memory. He wasn't mean any more; he wasn't lashing out. I think my dad said the guy wanted to know all the stories about wrestling as they drove back to Charlotte."

COWBOYS & INDIANS

DON EAGLE

Don Eagle, the lean, lithe, full-blooded Mohawk who popularized a haircut and who had a legitimate claim to one of the many world titles in 1950, knew the value of marketing and tried to capitalize on it throughout his all-too-brief career. He would sell homemade Native kewpie dolls at ringside, hold contests for Indian blankets in the arena, and peddle T-shirts, leather belts, girls' head scarves, vests, hankies, and pencils through the mail. His injury-plagued career winding down, he even briefly opened Don Eagle's Mohawk Village in Logan County, Ohio, in 1962.

Traveling coast to coast, rarely homesteading in any territory, his long Cadillac usually carried a twenty-foot canoe, and it was more than a prop, said Don Leo Jonathan. "We used that old canoe. He had an outrigger built for that old thing. I've been out with him. I used to go out to the reserve, and we used to go to the Lachine rapids, spear sturgeon, and shoot ducks and geese. He used it. He was quite a sportsman. Two things that he loved were Indian cornbread and roasted goose."

The journey was a big part of his success, said Frankie Cain, explaining that it meant Don Eagle didn't have to be beholden to one promoter. "His gimmick, of course, was the thing that got him over with the fans, his entrance and every-thing. Don wasn't a great worker, but he was pretty damned good. He had that solidness about him," said Cain. "He was a babyface that traveled around the country and they didn't do really anything with him; he traveled quite a bit all over and he was a hell of a worker, but you can't beat the office."

Carl Donald Bell was born August 25, 1925, on the Kahnawake reserve in Quebec, nine miles from Montreal, on the south shore of the St. Lawrence

A young Don Eagle captured the nation's attention.

River. His father, John Joseph Bell, was Chief War Eagle, a light-heavyweight wrestler in the '20s who wrestled the Montreal–Detroit corridor. "He was raised by his mom and dad, and War Eagle was not home much, and he divorced Emma. Emma was pretty much a single mother," said John Kim Bell, one of Don Eagle's six children through multiple relationships.

When Don Eagle turned sixteen, War Eagle returned to the reserve, and took his son to work on high steel, mostly in New York. "That's where they start training at the Y," said his son.

As Don Eagle's manager for many years, War Eagle enjoyed the spotlight and was quick with a quip.

"How long did you wrestle, War Eagle?" he was asked by the *Pittsburgh Post-Gazette* in 1949.

"Five feet, eight and one-half inches," he replied.

The chief was told the question pertained to time.

"Oh," he chuckled, "365 days a year. Leap years, 366."

Having spent some time on the road with his father, Don Eagle elected to give boxing a try, fighting as Carl Bell or Carl Donald Bell. In 1945, he went as far as winning a Novice Division Golden Gloves title in Cleveland, Ohio. As a professional, Bell was managed by Jack Kearns, who also handled Jack Dempsey. Bell's career ended after a couple of dozen fights, with seventeen knockouts. "He took it up, and did pretty well, but his hands were brittle," summed up Billy Two Rivers, his greatest protégé. His reason for quitting boxing is just one of the many mysteries around Don Eagle. Was he shot by poachers on his land in Vermont, as John Kim Bell heard growing up apart from his father, breaking his hand in seventeen places falling off his horse? Or did he accidentally shoot himself in the hand, as childhood friend Brad Reynolds asserts? "He got shot in the hand. He was trying to play quick draw. At least that's what I heard, and that's what I have in my scrapbook," said Reynolds, who as a teenager in rural Vermont hung around Don Eagle, going fishing and hunting, riding horses and taking care of the wrestler's dogs when he was on the road. "We did an awful lot of things together. He was quite the joker. He loved the younger kids. There was always a group of us down there."

At the same time as he was giving boxing a whirl, Bell had also started wrestling professionally, debuting as Chief Don Eagle in Indianapolis on March 6, 1945, and beating Red Dawson. By mid-1946, he had started to move up the card across the country, facing names such as Ray Steele and Bronko Nagurski (in St. Louis), Joe Savoldi (in Kansas City and Chicago), and Reginald Siki (in

Duluth, MN). But a June 7 bout with Dick Raines in St. Louis resulted in seventeen months on the sideline with shoulder and back injuries.

Coming back in late November 1947, it didn't take long for him to get in the world title picture, unsuccessfully challenging National Wrestling Association champion Orville Brown a half-dozen times in the Midwest, and, when the National Wrestling Alliance was formed in 1948, he took on titleholder Lou Thesz in locales as diverse as Des Moines, Iowa, and Montreal. Thesz remembered Don Eagle as a "very colorful" performer. "He did the little dance. The people were kind of Indian-oriented at that time, and everything was pro-Indian," said Thesz. "It was wonderful because he was a good attraction. But when we're speaking about an attraction, and we're speaking of wrestling, we're speaking of two different ballgames."

On May 23, 1950, Don Eagle beat Frank Sexton in Cleveland, Ohio, in a best-of-three-falls match for one of the versions of the American Wrestling Association world title. The newspaper accounts focus on a twenty-nine-year-old fan, William Jost, Jr., who had driven from Erie to see Eagle in the bout, and was apparently so into the bout at Public Hall that "he didn't know he'd shot himself in the leg until another spectator pointed to the blood."

Don Eagle would only hold the title for three days, falling victim to a double-cross in the ring against Gorgeous George in Chicago on TV, taped at the International Amphitheatre, the referee pulling a fast count on the third fall. "After Referee Earl Mollohan had counted three, signifying that Gorgeous George had pinned the Indian for the third and deciding fall, the Mohawk grappler attacked the referee and created terrific confusion," read a *Wrestling As You Like It* Chicago program from June 10, 1950, saying that the win was for the European and Eastern titles. The mystery continues to this day.

"Watching the tape, it really looks like Don Eagle was genuinely surprised and outraged, that there was indeed a double-cross. And from what we know of George, he would have gladly gone along with this, assuming it was the promoter Fred Kohler's idea, and not George's," said The Human Orchid's biographer, John Capouya. "It got him, briefly, another title. He might have seen it, or justified it to himself, as just an exaggerated practical joke or swerve."

Later that year, Eagle beat Gorgeous George on August 31 in Columbus for the AWA title. He continued to take bookings right across the country, sometimes with the belt, sometimes not. On May 1, 1952, when Bill Miller beat Eagle by DQ in Pittsburgh, promoter Al Haft chose to recognize Miller as his champion, while Boston's Paul Bowser stuck with Eagle, until November 1952, when Bowser dropped recognition of the title with Eagle off on injured reserve.

Eagle was often a source of promotional tug of war. In a December 9, 1950, letter to NWA President Sam Muchnick, Chicago promoter Fred Kohler slammed Columbus, Ohio's Haft for billing Eagle as a world champion over the recognized Thesz. "Al Haft has made claims that he has a just grievance with me. Ask him what his grievance is, and take the following things into consideration when he answers. He pleaded with me to advertise, publicize, and develop Don Eagle as an attraction in Chicago and on television. After doing this, he tied up Don Eagle in a managerial contract with [Boston promoter] Paul Bowser, making it necessary for me to consult Chief War Eagle, Paul Bowser, and Al Haft for any match that I might want Don Eagle to participate in."

A major show at Yankee Stadium in New York City in June 1950.

Needing time off to heal his aching back and collect himself after the trials of the road, Eagle went home to Kahnawake to recuperate. He and Two Rivers became great friends, and when he went back to wrestling, Eagle took the fifteen-year-old Two Rivers with him. The two Mohawks would tag team off and on from 1955 to 1959.

It was Don Eagle who suggested to Moose Cholak that he get into wrestling after he left the Navy. In Vermont, he had a unique ring, said Reynolds. "He had a wrestling ring up by his little cabin up on Eagle's Point. We'd all get a bunch of pine needles — the area was loaded with pine trees — and we brought pine needles up there, and covered them with a great, big canvas. They'd bring these guys in, like Ray Bentley and Jim Lewis, those guys, and he'd train them up there." Eagle also acted as the trainer for his nephew Little Chief Norman Kirby, a Golden Gloves boxer.

By the mid-'50s, Eagle's schedule became less hectic, as he settled into Florida or North Carolina for lengthy runs that would have been unheard of a decade before; yet he would still show up on cards from Montreal to Columbus to New York City.

Always aware of the power of his name, he tried to get a camp for boys set up in Vermont in the early 1950s, but ended up concentrating on his wrestling career. In May 1962, Don Eagle's Mohawk Village did open outside Lima, Ohio, but with a drive-in theater; the dream of Indian Curio shops, a long house night club, and a motel never materialized. "They were going to create a Don Eagle DisneyWorld theme park," said John Kim Bell, who is an Officer of the Order of Canada for his works as a composer. "I know we had drawings when I was a kid of the site, he brought them over to show my mother, from whom he was divorced at the time."

The 1960s were a time of less intense fame for a man whose 1951 marriage made the Associated Press wires, who had service clubs running Don Eagle Nights, and who golfed in charity tournaments with Perry Como, Ed Sullivan, and Dizzy Dean.

Reynolds said his old friend was different then, and recalled helping him move his furniture from the cabin in Vermont, the land having been sold to the state, back to the Kahnawake reserve. "Don was a different man then. I don't think he could take the comedown from being a wrestler and all of the fans and everything else. He had a hard time with that, I think," said Reynolds. "He was just a completely changed man."

For the last few years of his life, Don Eagle appears sporadically on wrestling cards, confined generally close to Montreal and New England.

That Don Eagle died on March 17, 1966, of a gunshot wound, in his home on the Kahnawake reserve, there is no question. By whose hand remains the mystery.

John Kim Bell, partly to leave a legacy for his own young son, teamed with his wife to make a documentary on the life of Don Eagle in 2010, which aired on Canada's Aboriginal Peoples Television Network. The last hour of the film focuses on what happened at the end of his father's life.

"The stories that broke were that it was a suicide, but according to the early police report, they concluded that it wasn't a suicide, something about where he was laying and where the gun was, the nature of gunpowder and wounds," said Bell.

"I never read the police report, and I heard conflicting stories," said Jonathan. "A lot of times when you know a person, there's just certain things that you figure they would never do. I heard that he had terminated his own life. I found that hard to believe."

"Don was alcoholic, and was desperate, and had his wife Jean and three kids, Hunter, Star, and Flint, and was living in the lake house on the lake that my grandfather owned," said Bell. "He kept asking my grandfather, War Eagle, for money, and they would get into fights about it, because Don was destitute. War Eagle had him shot and killed."

Following his death, writers across the continent took a moment to recall Don Eagle's legacy. "Many teenagers and small boys adopted Don Eagle's haircuts to the dismay of their parents. The Eagle haircut consisted of a narrow strip of short hair from the forehead to the back of the head," wrote John Kirker in the *Steubenville (Ohio) Herald Star*. "Wrestling was such a drawing card at the time that the late Jack Ganson of Cleveland seriously considered building a spacious arena, primarily for wrestling going on a regular schedule all winter. The plans never got off the ground."

Jonathan concluded that Don Eagle was a pioneer. "I think the main thing with him, besides the fact that he was a good wrestler, a scientific wrestler, I think he gave the white people, or the rest of Canada, a better look at what the Native people were like," he said. "You've got to understand . . . there was a time when the only Indian was a good Indian, and then a lot of people started thinking that the Indians got a raw deal, but they are still Indians. But then as things started to progress, the Indian status in the eyes, First Nations peoples, stand different in the eyes of their fellow Canadians than they did forty years ago. It was a slow process, but one that I think Don Eagle sped up."

"COWBOY" BOB KELLY

Cowboy Bob Kelly was a working man's hero from the time he first stepped foot into a Mobile, Alabama ring. "I was a referee and a handyman who did jobs, put out the window cards, swept the floor and did everything that was needed, and the people knew that," he said. Before long, his working man's journey

CHRIS SWISHER COLLECTION

Cowboy Bob Kelly had the common touch with Gulf Coast fans.

became part of a narrative that the fans gladly bought into. "They saw me come through the ranks. The relationship just bloomed."

Kelly was as loyal to the fans as they were to him. To that end he never turned heel. Truth be known, it's highly unlikely that Kelly would have ever been able to sell that role anyway. "I couldn't ever figure out why some guys wanted to be heels and take the chance on getting beat up or killed all the time. Most of them just loved it. I always figured they needed extra money for what they did."

Like many of the top babyfaces of his era, Kelly made himself accessible to his fan base, going into the towns, frequenting stores and restaurants, socializing with his followers. He was an "everyman" his fans could relate to.

"We had many good guys to root for, but far and away the most popular was Cowboy Bob Kelly," wrote Gulf Coast wrestling historian Michael Norris. "The man in the white hat was the combination of all things good in America. The slow-talking cowboy who played fair until his opponent carried his foul tactics too far, but was the roughest and toughest when it came to a fight. Cowboy Bob was John Wayne, Wyatt Earp, and Roy Rogers all rolled into one. He was the hero to thousands upon thousands of Gulf Coast Wrestling fans. He was my hero."

Just how beloved was Kelly? So much that fans would storm the ring to help their hero when heels got the upper hand. "I've had them come into the ring to help me and carry me on their shoulders. They would be completely beyond themselves. If I was hurt they'd be concerned. When I'd go on TV and tell them something, they'd believe it. We sold a lot of tickets."

During a tag team match one night in Mobile where Kelly teamed with The Medic against Rip and Randy Tyler, all hell broke loose when the three other participants turned on the Cowboy. Kelly was lying prone when he felt someone put his hand on him and whisper in his ear: "Just lay still, Cowboy, we'll take care of these sons of bitches." At first, said Kelly, he thought it was referee Burrhead Jones. But upon further review, Kelly discovered that it was a group of black fans who had come to his aid. "There were probably eight or ten who got into the ring. The only thing that saved everybody was a big fire extinguisher that Rip got a hold of and used like a whip to run everybody out of the ring."

Going up against Cowboy Bob Kelly in a Gulf Coast ring during the '60s and '70s was a risky proposition for heels. Curtis Smith got to experience what it was like on more than one occasion. "He was so scared one night that he couldn't even go to his motel. The heat was on him so bad that fans were circling the motel, and he couldn't get in there," recalled Kelly.

"To know Bob Kelly was to like him," added Smith, who first locked horns with the white-hat-wearing Cowboy as part of a team with Billy Spears known as The Blue Yankees. The masked duo was cutting a swath through the Gulf Coast in 1969, and Kelly was the man one had to go through to make main-event money. "We used to fight in the ring, out of the ring, under the ring, in the bleachers, outside the building. People went nuts. Nobody could touch Bob Kelly."

Cowboy Bob Kelly came as close to being in the heel camp as he ever would when he once agreed to team with bad guy Rocket Monroe against another heel team in the territory. It was part of an angle designed to turn Kelly at the climax of the storyline. But something happened that night that Kelly would never forget. "A little girl came up to me as I was walking down the aisle. She was crying and she grabbed me around the leg."

"What's the matter, honey?" he asked the young fan. "Cowboy, please don't turn on us," she pleaded. "Don't worry about nothing," Kelly assured her.

"I'll never forget that. She wasn't just talking about *her*. She was talking about *everybody*."

The office sentiment was that perennial good guy Kelly could have drawn some major houses as a heel. But that little girl changed everything. No amount of money, he said, would have been worth it. "When I got back to the office, I told [booker] Lee Fields, 'Just don't even think about that anymore.'"

It was Fields who had given Kelly his first big break in the business. Kelly needed a job, and Fields needed a right-hand man he could trust.

"I told Lee that I wasn't beyond sweeping the floors or cleaning up the rest rooms. He told me that was exactly what he was looking for." Kelly attributes a great deal of his success to Fields and doubts he could have ever established that rapport in any other territory.

Kelly enjoyed the added advantage of being a booker in the territory for part of his run. If a town experienced a lull or "if somebody left in the middle of the night," Kelly would fill the void and step back into the ring and bring the house back up. "I tried to keep myself in good shape so that if a babyface did get mad and leave or get hurt, that I could just go out and take his place, and the people wouldn't mind it."

A member of the wrestling team during his stint in the U.S. Marine Corps in the early 1950s, Kelly enjoyed his first main-event success in Louisiana while still working as a ref in the Mobile area. Fields, who also had owned the Baton Rouge–Lafayette area, worked with Kelly on a plan to elevate the referee to a star attraction on his shows.

A match with rugged Jack Dalton put Kelly on the wrestling map. The plan was for Kelly to lose his first few bouts but at the same time elicit sympathy from the crowd who'd view the rookie as a major underdog. Kelly kept getting beat, but he kept coming back. He eventually beat Frank Dalton and got a chance at the meaner "brother" Jack. Jack Dalton, who later changed his name to Don Fargo, was one of Kelly's favorite opponents and took part in what Kelly calls his most memorable match. It was a sentimental favorite, said Kelly, because his dad got to see him wrestle in person. Kelly's father saw only two of his son's matches — his first official pro bout in 1963, and one in 1972 against Fargo in Pensacola.

Kelly, who used the bulldog headlock as his coup de grâce, emerged victorious and recalled fans jumping into the ring at the sold-out arena following the match. "It was pandemonium. I looked for [Dad], but I didn't see him at first. When I jumped out of the ring, he was standing right outside, and he put his arm around me and put my arm in the air." The match would become even more special after his father died later that year due to heart problems. Kelly's mother never got to see her son wrestle in a live match.

Born Robert Raymond Kelley (he dropped the final "e" after a promoter misspelled his name) on June 28, 1936, on a farm in rural Kentucky, Kelly was

Bob Kelly and honoree Ronnie Garvin at the Cauliflower Alley Club reunion in 2008.

trained by Wee Willie Davis and Doug Kinslow and started his wrestling career in 1959 as a referee and ring announcer. He was in North Bay, Ontario, when wrestler Terry Garvin (Terry Joyal) called Fields and asked him if he could use a hand. Garvin gave Kelly a ringing endorsement and handed the phone to his friend.

"That was a long way from North Bay, Canada, to Mobile, Alabama. I told him I didn't have much experience, but I told him I'd do anything he wanted me to do. I already had four kids at the time, but I packed them all up. I loaded up everything I owned. It was like I knew him. Lee didn't treat me like a referee or a beginner." Fields, said Kelly, was looking for someone who wanted to do things differently. Fields eventually entrusted Kelly with some of the territory's top towns. They began doing so well in Louisiana that they were "kicked out" by politicos who saw an opportunity to pad their own coffers.

"The politicians considered Lee an outsider," said Kelly. "As long as we weren't making a whole lot of money, they weren't saying anything. But when we started selling out in Lafayette and Baton Rouge, they figured they could do that themselves and they took Lee's license." At the time, Fields was using the money out of Louisiana to help keep his struggling Mobile operation up. "He was about done in Mobile," said Kelly. Fields borrowed $25,000 on his house to keep the promotion afloat, and Kelly asked his boss for one year to promote

STEVEN JOHNSON

Mobile and Pensacola. If he didn't double up those towns, he promised Fields, he'd be gone.

Fields gave Kelly six months, about as long as the money would last, and the rest is history. Kelly secured bigger buildings, began weekly shows, changed nights, and doubled the houses in less than a month, virtually saving Fields' business. While the soft-spoken Kelly is reluctant to take credit for the turn-around, his arrival on the scene coincided with the territory's ascension.

With the exception of an occasional visit to another area while on vacation, where he would make a special appearance on another promoter's show, Cowboy spent most of his career wrestling in one territory.

Kelly had an ample supply of heels to work with in the Gulf Coast, a lengthy list including names such as Don Fargo, Rocket Monroe, Eddie Sullivan, Curtis Smith, Rip Tyler, The Wrestling Pro (Leon Baxter), Gorgeous George Jr., Bobby Shane, Jackie Fargo, Greg Valentine, Dr. Jerry Graham, and Ron Bass. He eventually vanquished them all, because that's what good guys are supposed to do.

But it would have never happened without his best friend. After more than a decade, Kelly still has a hard time talking about Fields without getting emotional. "Lee was my best friend. He always will be. I loved Lee like a brother. Meeting Lee Fields was a blessing in my life. How else could you explain an old country boy from the farm in Kentucky, with no wrestling experience, and no family member even smart to the wrestling business, staying in one territory and making it to the very top and staying there?"

Kelly has been happily married for over fifty-five years to the love of his life, Chris, with whom, he said, "it was love at first sight and every sight afterward. Chris and I have traveled up and down many roads over the years. I have dragged her from one end of the country to the other and have caused her to spend many months living with our four kids in motel rooms with nothing to cook on but a hot plate. Through it all she has never complained and cheerfully packed our bags when it was time to move to the next place. She has been the anchor that has kept me from slamming into the rocks."

Kelly, who remains active in his mid-'70s and owns a wrecker service in Mobile, goes in every day to make sure things are running properly. "I'm working every day. I might look it [age-wise], but I don't feel it," he laughed.

He serves as president of the Gulf Coast Wrestlers Reunion and is a member of the Cauliflower Alley Club Board of Directors. Kelly worked his last match in 1987, although his final full-time year was 1977 when he officially retired in Mobile. He said he's always amazed when fans ask him for an autograph or want to talk about a match that happened more than forty years ago.

"It's unbelievable that people still remember me. I can hardly go anywhere without being stopped by people who want to talk wrestling. The kids are all grown, but they remember."

It's hard for locals to forget a hometown hero.

CHIEF LITTLE WOLF

A few years ago, Barry York, a historian and researcher at the Museum of Australian Democracy, dipped his academic toe into the waters of pop culture by examining Chief Little Wolf, a wrestler familiar to U.S. and Aussie audiences from the 1930s to the 1950s. As part of his due diligence, York solicited fan recollections of Little Wolf through appearances on TV and letters to newspapers. He expected a trickle of responses. Instead, he got a wave. "I received several hundred letters and this is extraordinary in Australian terms. We have a tenth of the U.S.A. population, so think of it as several thousand," he said. "I was very surprised, mainly because it had been about four decades since the Chief had wrestled in Australia. Despite that period of absence and his return to U.S.A. in 1980, he was still important to many people."

That's as good a way as any to sum up the importance of Chief Little Wolf, née Ventura Tenario, a Navajo Indian from Colorado and a born entertainer. During a celebrated world title match with champion Danno O'Mahoney in 1935, the Chief kept complaining that ringside photographers in New York were taking his picture only when he was down and out. After a while, he steered the Irishman near the cameramen and barked, "All right, boys, go ahead but take your time. I'll hold him till you give the word." He was wrestling in Seattle, Washington, in 1940, when he was called as an expert witness to a coroner's inquest into the death of John Stevens, a referee who died following a rough match. Little Wolf wasn't even in the deadly bout, but he still managed to steal the show. Stripping to the waist and rising from his seat, Little Wolf woofed, "You don't think a man has to be tough to be in this business?" and directed a spectator to slug him in the stomach.

Compared with Little Wolf, the stylers and profilers who followed were mere pikers. A typical getup circa 1935, courtesy of Oakland, California sportswriter

Alan Ward: a felt sombrero, blue shirt and white tie, blue single-breasted coat with white piping, white gloves similar to those of a traffic cop, white riding trousers with black lacings, and Western boots "with an etched design reminiscent of a million Roman candles exploding in an attack of delirium tremens." Imagine how that flamboyance must have looked through the eyes of a child. David Little Wolf was living in the late 1940s with his biological father and stepmother in California when the Chief sidled up along with David's biological mother Dorothy in a snazzy, two-tone green Pontiac. "You want to come with us?" Little Wolf asked. "Yeah. Do I get to ride in that car?" David responded. At his sister's home in California's San Fernando Valley, the Chief told his new stepson to strip, piled the clothes in a heap, set them ablaze, and bought him a new wardrobe.

There were no fancy clothes and fancy cars when Little Wolf was born in abject

COURTESY OF SCOTT TEAL/CROWBAR PRESS

Chief Little Wolf makes his way through the crowd in Australia.

poverty on November 25, 1911, in Hoehne, Colorado, just north of the New Mexico border. His mother, who died when he was young, was Navajo, and his father Joe was part Navajo and part Spanish. He had only three or four years of formal education before heading out with his dad as a farmhand and learning to box on the side. Little Wolf started boxing on small carnivals and touring shows, and picked up wrestling in part by training with future world champion Everette Marshall from nearby La Junta. The dividing line between his carnival and pro career is blurred, but Little Wolf first wrestled for pay in the late 1920s and was working as an undernourished five-foot-nine, 155-pound middleweight in May 1932, when he lost in Albuquerque, New Mexico, to a junior middleweight title claimant named Yaqui Joe.

He continued as a middleweight for a couple of years, but the summer of 1934 found him in Hawaii, where he rode the waves, ate all day, and was reborn as a heavyweight, up to about 210 pounds. The added bulk did a world of good, as he won a surprise victory over Man Mountain Dean in San Diego that December. Wrestling boss Toots Mondt latched on to him and pushed him as a more alluring champ than blasé titleholders Dick Shikat or Jim Browning. When he was ready to put his opponent away, Little Wolf cut loose with a cry like a wild-eyed savage and slapped on his Indian deathlock, a standing leg grapevine submission. "The Indian's got world of color and, frankly, that's something Shikat and Jim lacked," Mondt told reporters. With Mondt behind him, Little Wolf was primed to be a major national attraction. He got a great buildup by beating Gus Sonnenberg and unmasking the Scorpion as Milo Steinborn in Los Angeles as a prelude to a February 1935 match with Jim Londos for the world title. But Londos refused the booking, earning a temporary ban in California and New York in one of the intra-industry squabbles that characterized '30s wrestling. "The game needs more 'color' and to be Navajo is the answer to the promoter's prayer. How far he goes depends on Jim Londos. His refusal to meet the chieftain is a good argument in the latter's favor," wrote Stubby Currence, a legendary West Virginia sportswriter.

If Little Wolf could cause that much ruckus in the States, imagine what he could do in Australia. He headed there for the first time as a bad guy in 1937 and took the nation by storm. "I'm sure we would have had many entertainers from overseas who were extroverted and charismatic — but none who were Native Americans. This really was exotic in Australia back then," York said. "We still had an official White Australia policy, just to show you where we were at as a society." He returned each year from 1939 to 1941, eventually turning into the fan's choice. In 1948, back in Colorado, he beat Danny Dusek for the Rocky Mountain championship, but he still visited Australia annually and laid down permanent roots in 1952, a welcome figure despite tossing Sydney promoter Harry Miller over the ropes and into the crowd during one match. "I made a name for myself here when I was all washed up in America. Suddenly, I went boom," he explained to *The Age* of Melbourne. Radio broadcasts of his bouts brought him even more acclaim. He loved Australia, its people, and the lack of discrimination, his son said. "The fact that he had a white wife and white children didn't mean a thing to anybody. Nobody ever questioned it," David said, pointing to the contrast he once witnessed when the family was in Georgia on its way to New York. "He couldn't go into a bar in a lot of places then."

Little Wolf's feud with Dick Raines ran forever, even toward the end of his career, when he'd ballooned up to 275 pounds. Reportedly sidelined by an illness, he was sitting ringside during a 1953 match in Melbourne when Raines was clobbering Don Beitelman (Curtis) with his lucky horseshoe. Suddenly, Little Wolf rose up, grabbed the horseshoe, clocked Raines and the referee and challenged his rival to a match with all the money going to charity. "Do I look sick?" he bellowed. On the side, he operated circus shows, where he'd ride in on a steed, give a talk, and demonstrate wrestling holds against a backdrop of animals and performers, including his family. He was not an ideal dad or husband; he booted David out of the house, eventually left Dorothy for wife number three, and drank to wicked excess. Still, his son looks back on the Chief with fondness, thinking about how he reached out to thousands of kids the way he first reached out to him. "We used to go to hospitals unannounced, veterans hospitals and children's hospitals, and I had to leave. I couldn't take it. But he'd get right among them and let them play with his skin. They were fascinated with that red skin and the feathers. And it was real. He'd come out crying, especially when visiting the children." Oh, and those stunning headdresses? Thank Gorgeous George for furnishing the material from his turkey ranch. "He would send us bagfuls of beautiful white turkey feathers and my mother would dye the tips and she would make the headdresses. Gorgeous George provided the feathers. Just watching my mother work on them was amazing," David said.

The Chief last wrestled in August 1958 in a tag team match. A series of strokes that started shortly thereafter left him in a nursing home, partially paralyzed, barely able to talk, an eyelid taped open so he could see. For nearly twenty years, his home was a care facility in Parkville, Australia. In 1980, an Australian newspaper found him before he made a final passage to the United States, where he died in Seattle in 1984. During the course of the interview, the Chief slowly reached over and playfully punched a friend, saying, "We climbed the high mountain, didn't we boy?"

WAR CHIEFS OF THE MAT

At the Pro Wrestling Hall of Fame in Amsterdam, NY, there's a shrine to the "War Chiefs of the Mat," who were some of the greatest Native wrestlers in history. A deer skin in the shape of a shell is embroidered with the most recognized "Warriors of the Mat"; a tomahawk, eagle feather, tobacco pouches, and ermine pelt further symbolize the battles they went through.

Some of the men, including Wahoo McDaniel, Don Eagle (and his father War Eagle), and Billy Two Rivers, are featured elsewhere in this book.

But others are deserving of mention in a section on Cowboys and Indians, including:

Bob Finnegan interviews Chief Big Heart.

CHIEF THUNDERBIRD: From his debut in 1933 until his retirement from wrestling in 1955 in Saanich, B.C.'s Chief Thunderbird was the first big name native wrestler from Canada.

He was born Jean Baptiste Paul in 1896, the hereditary chief of the Tsartlip Indians at Brentwood on Vancouver Island, son to Tommy Paul and grandson to Ben Paul, both of whom were noted chiefs with the tribe. "My people wanted to make a medicine man out of me," Thunderbird recalled in a 1965 interview with the Victoria *Daily Colonist*. "They kept putting me in cold water as part of the ritual. Finally, I ran away from home to attend a mission school at Kuper Island, near Duncan. I wanted to be an athlete more than anything else." At Indian college in Tacoma, "The Chief" was an active athlete, getting a remarkable eight sports letters in boxing, wrestling, baseball, basketball, track and field, football, soccer, and lacrosse. After thirty-two pro boxing fights, he turned to wrestling. In the 1950s, he took England by storm. "They treated me like a human being over there," Thunderbird once said, and joked to the British reporters upon his arrival, "You must have kept all your nice people here — and sent your mean whites to my country. Because they certainly wound up stealing it from us Indians." He retired from wrestling in 1955 when he broke a leg in two places; he had told people that he wanted to wrestle until he was sixty years old. Gardening was a passion in his retirement years. He died November 24, 1966, in Saanich, and a totem pole, done by Thunderbird's nephew Benjamin Paul, was unveiled to the public in August 1969.

CHIEF BIG HEART: With his best territories being Florida, the Carolinas, Georgia, and New York, Chief Big Heart won crowds over with his solid work on his solid 250-pound frame, and finished off his foes with the Bow and Arrow hold. Born an Osage on March 5, 1927, in Pawhuska, Okla., Richard Gilbert Vest got into wrestling in the mid-'50s and worked until the late '60s. He died April 22, 1993, in Palm Springs, Calif.

Chief Thunderbird.

SUNI WAR CLOUD: Joseph Vance Chorre Jr. was among the first of the big TV stars, wrestling out of California; in fact he wrestled throughout a film career. Jerry Christy, the nephew of Vic and Ted Christy, got to see War Cloud at his peak. "He was an Indian, he did the war dance and all that stuff," Christy said, adding that War Cloud's war dance was "the best out of all of them." Born of Wassak heritage on November 14, 1914, in Los Angeles, the six-foot-two, 237-pound Chorre turned pro about 1947, and wrestled through the mid-1960s, using the Indian deathlock as his finisher. Legend has it that Jim Thorpe, the incredible athlete from the first half of the twentieth century, discovered Chorre and suggested pro wrestling; Thorpe would often act as his manager, and "stroll up to the sports department of the morning paper and chat with the reporters" about his protégé. Like Thorpe, Chorre excelled at many sports. "You know, if I wasn't making the big money that I get for wrestling, I'd make a career out of softball," War Cloud said in 1950. While working in Europe in 1953–54, Chorre worked as Sitting Bull. His most noted acting role came in 1951, as Mr. Denny, the coach in *Jim Thorpe All-American*, (1951); Chorre, whose mother was character actress Gertrude Chorre, had more than twenty movie roles from 1935 to 1951. He died from a heart attack at his L.A. home on June 14, 1987, falling against the bathroom sink, causing a pipe to burst. "Unfortunately he kept his belongings on the floor and the water damaged most of his things," lamented his daughter Heather Chorre Garcia.

KIT FOX: A member of Oklahoma's Delaware Tribe, six-foot Fox was turned onto pro wrestling by promoter Leroy McGuirk. "Kit has a bag of tricks plus a powerful and agile body and his 229 lbs. glide all over that ring with ease," reads a 1957 story. Fox's career was ended when a car accident wrecked his back. One of his post-wrestling jobs was as a card dealer in Vegas. In 1994, he went in for a bypass surgery and didn't survive.

TATANKA: A friend set up the six-foot-two, 285-pound muscle-bound Chris Chavis with "Nature Boy" Buddy Rogers, who hooked him up with his old partner, Larry Sharpe, in a New Jersey wrestling gym. Originally from Pembroke, N.C., and of the Lumbee tribe, Chavis' career got rolling in 1990 with another old Rogers crony, George Scott, who was attempting to re-start the Carolinas as a promotion. The following year, Chavis debuted in the WWF as "The Native American" Chris Chavis, before he became just Tatanka. "I wanted an authentic Indian name because I'm a full-blooded native and this one was the best," he said in 1999. "It just had a ring to it." Tatanka learned quickly from the likes of Rick Martel and Bam Bam Bigelow. "The way you get taught like that is you get paired up with a veteran and you shut your mouth," he said. Regularly one of the top competitors in the WWF, both for the World and Intercontinental titles, Tatanka had a heel run with "The Million Dollar Man" Ted DiBiase as his manager. Tatanka left the WWF in 1996, and returned nine years later for a brief run.

TEX MCKENZIE

Everyone says the same thing about Tex McKenzie, and believe it or not, it's meant as a compliment: he was terrible in the ring, uncoordinated and clumsy, but man, could he draw. McKenzie admitted as much, saying he was "never much of a worker, but I sure got over."

Want further proof? Sandy Scott recalled one such incident in the Carolinas. "We were in a six-man tag match and the referee said, 'You can't throw anybody over the rope.' Tex turned with his finger and hit me right in the eye with it. He said, 'You mean, that rope there?'" Scott laughed. "I felt sorry for Nelson Royal; they were partners. Poor Nelson was banged around so much. He supplied the action and he knew his spot, and he would tag Big Tex and Tex would clean the ring up."

Leave it to Gene Kiniski to get to the point. "Fuck, he was a big, likeable person. He could draw, but his athleticism left a lot to be desired. He was a klutz."

"He was just a big, lovable old boy. The people liked him. He could never have been a heel," said Reggie Parks. "The cowboy types were always babyfaces. Everybody liked cowboys — the guy who always gets the girl."

McKenzie's widow, Betty Gerfen, agreed with Parks. "I don't think he could have been any other way because he had a fantastic personality. He talked with everybody, and he just made everybody feel good. He'd see this little old lady sitting there. He would stop and tell her how beautiful she was, what a nice outfit she had on. He just was so outgoing and had such a wonderful personality — and funny.

"He had charisma. People were just drawn to him. I don't know if it was size or what, but people could feel that he was a very, very nice guy."

The first time she met Tex, in Dallas, Betty thought the six-foot-eight, 285-pound behemoth was a lineman for the Cowboys, when in fact he was the son of a sheriff from Fargo, North Dakota, who went to art school before ending up a pro wrestler.

ROGER BAKER

Tex McKenzie relaxes in his hotel room.

Francis Hugh McKenzie — "Frankie" to his family — was born April 10, 1930, and lived on a farm until he was ten years old. The clan moved to the city since their father had been elected sheriff for an eight-year term. His size wasn't a huge surprise; his father was six-foot-three, his mother five-foot-nine, and there were seven-foot cousins on both sides of the family.

McKenzie headed for Minneapolis, and lived at the YMCA during his post-secondary schooling, where his main interest was photography. "He was really tall and skinny when he graduated from high school. I bet he gained fifty or eighty pounds in a year or two, because he started working out at the Y," recalled his sister, Joan Grothe. Two of the people he worked out with were future actors James Arness and Peter Graves.

On a return to Fargo, he opted to help a friend who had been paralyzed in a diving accident start a gym in Dallas. It was there that he began pro wrestling.

He would fall under the influence of notorious promoter Jack Pfefer, who used him as Goliath.

But it was starting in 1954 as Tex McKenzie that he achieved his greatest fame, stepping over the top rope, using his knee lifts with his long stride, turkey stomping an opponent or trapping them in a rocking chair body scissors. His finisher was a devastating bulldog headlock.

"He was all arms and legs," said Gerfen. "His embrace was so gentle, yet so firm also. He hugged everybody, men, women, he didn't care. He just put his arms around anybody and hugged them."

"I think he will be remembered as the cowboy that won the war," surmised manager Percival Al Friend. "He was on fire right from the word go. He'd get in there and battle with the best of them, it didn't matter." McKenzie's biggest main event run came around the Great Lakes in the early 1970s as a gangly challenger to The Sheik's U.S. title.

Away from the ring, however, things weren't always smooth. In 1955, his wife was killed and daughter, Debbie, seriously hurt, in an auto accident thirty miles east of Seattle in the Snoqualimie Pass. "The brakes on the house trailer failed. He was shooting down the mountain. They ran into another car, and those people were killed," said Grothe. "Connie was trying to protect Debbie, who was in the back seat in a bassinet, and she started to go over the back seat as they crashed, and she was killed outright. Hugh broke his back when he was thrown. It was snowy and very bad up there. He came to as the ambulance came, and he said, 'Well, what about the baby?' And they said, 'We didn't see a baby.' They looked in the ditch, and there was Debbie in the ditch. Had he not come to at that time, she would probably have been left to freeze to death." Connie's in-laws in San Antonio nursed Tex and his daughter back to health. During his time off, McKenzie was a publicist for Pearl Brewery. It was there he met his second wife, Martha, with whom he had two sons. Two more short marriages followed, until he wed Gerfen in 1976.

A year later, McKenzie retired. He and Betty spent oodles of time on his sailboat, and he returned to his artistic roots, designing and building high-end luxury homes, mainly around Seattle and Anacortes, Washington. He died May 31, 2001, in a Victoria, B.C. hospital.

Chief Jay Strongbow demonstrates his war dance.

DAVE BURZYNSKI

CHIEF JAY STRONGBOW

Nick Kozak was Joe Scarpa's tag team partner in Hawaii, and they were chatting one day about the increasing amount of "gimmicks guys" in professional wrestling. "I remember Joe saying, 'Yeah, you'll never catch me doing that. I'm not a gimmick man. I'm just Joe Scarpa,'" Kozak recalled. A few years later, Kozak turned on the TV and saw a new Native-American in action. "The guy was doing his comeback with an Indian war dance. 'God, that guy looks familiar.' I'm looking and looking . . . When Joe made a comeback, he used to pump his arms back like a broken chicken wing. I went, 'Oh, my God! Joe Scarpa! Joe Scarpa is Joe Strongbow? An Indian?' Shit, I couldn't believe it."

It's true, and yet it isn't.

Legend has it that Vincent J. McMahon once said to Scarpa, "You'll never make any money because you're just a *dago* from Jersey." McMahon's bank statements would prove otherwise.

"I'm not really a chief. It's a title they hung on me," said Chief Jay Strongbow in a 1977 newspaper interview, revealing a surprising amount in an era of strict kayfabe. He also lamented the rigors of the road. "The hassle of the traveling and being away from my family. People think it's a good life but they don't realize what a hassle it is."

Both comments reflect on Joe Scarpa, the son of an Italian-American construction worker from New Jersey, who managed to fool the masses in the biggest territory in North America with his Native-American act and later become a key behind-the-scenes agent in the World Wrestling Federation, choosing to stay on the road for years after his in-ring work was finished.

Uncomfortable in today's reveal-all world of professional wrestling, he held his cards close to his chest and was reluctant to talk about much at all about the past. "People put stuff on the internet, not half of what they say about me on there is true," Strongbow said, declining to clarify.

He was born Joseph Luke Scarpa on October 15, 1932, in Philadelphia, though if you were to ask him, it would be Pawhuska, Oklahoma, and his mother was Cherokee. Scarpa often said he started in 1947 in California, but it was closer to 1957 when "Joltin'" Joe Scarpa began his career, a decent athlete who decided to try pro wrestling, with his first bout against Al Galento.

"I had an opinion about pro wrestling, until I wrestled and they showed me that my opinion was wrong," Scarpa said in a December 2003 shoot interview with Highspots. "I learned that I wasn't as bad as I thought I was." Those early years were rough, with mat burns on the arms and chin. "They'd scoot you along like a vacuum cleaner," he complained.

The early days of the six-foot-two, 265-pound "Flying" Joe Scarpa are in marked difference to the style of the WWWF, a big man's territory where the moves were simple and power-based to convey the action to the large arenas on the East Coast. "Flying Joe caters to barefoot stylings, patterned after the famed offensive of Argentina Rocca, one of wrestling's biggest names," reads a 1958 preview in Chillicothe, Missouri. "Many wrestlers like to cavort around the ring barefooted. Scarpa claims it gives greater agility and so far no one has questioned that. His leaping style has proved the undoing of many foes, simply because he managed to get an advantage before they could get set."

Though he lacked color, Scarpa was a solid performer and used in prominent spots in Georgia and Florida especially, where he held numerous titles, and challenged NWA world champion Lou Thesz on a few occasions for the strap.

Scarpa said he was in California in 1970, working with Gorilla Monsoon, who told him that McMahon, the New York–based promoter, was looking for an Indian for his territory. Scarpa jumped at the chance and never looked back.

With his headdress, long hair, frilled boots, and colorful tights, Chief Jay Strongbow made an immediate impression, and with the reach of the Capitol Sports broadcast, he became a star from Washington up to Toronto and Detroit.

WWF ring announcer and unofficial historian Howard Finkel grew up watching The Chief at Witchsi's arena in Massachusetts every Friday night. "In my eyes, one of the greatest people ever to put a pair of tights on," said Finkel. "He was an instant success. He was a sensation. He had many a battle, many a score was settled."

Strongbow became the No. 2 babyface in the promotion for pretty well the next decade, playing second fiddle to WWWF champions Bruno Sammartino and Pedro Morales. As such, he never got a chance to have a run with anything but the WWWF tag titles (four times, with three different partners).

He had his gimmick down, and it translated into the other cultures. "Strongbow just goes into his high-stepping war dance. Audience war-whooping, and if you've never heard thousands of Puerto Ricans war-whooping, you haven't lived," wrote Joe Jares in 1974's *Whatever Happened To Gorgeous George?*

Finkel said Strongbow never needed the WWWF title. "The true people's champion in my eyes and we announced him that way, as the people's champion. He had magnetism, he had tremendous grit inside the squared circle, and he knew how to play on the emotions of many a fan."

Scarpa did have a way of playing on the feelings of his colleagues as well. Many deride him for his stinginess, for being a stooge for the office, or for his transformation into the Chief, forgetting much of where he came from.

In late December 1976, Strongbow and Billy White Wolf (Adnan Alkaissy) won the WWWF tag titles. Eight months later, a non-cancerous lump was found in Alkaissy's neck, and doctors had to operate, ending the team. "That split up the team between myself and Chief," said Alkaissy. "He was a very, very difficult person to get along with, in the ring, outside the ring, on the road. The man was just too much — I'm a straight-

Joe Scarpa.

shooter, I'm honest and I'm naive, but he was so difficult. So when I did the operation it was also to get away from him."

Frank Hill was asked by McMahon to assume the role of Jules, the younger brother of Jay, and the Strongbows would hold the WWF tag titles twice in 1982. Hill was diplomatic about his time with Scarpa. "We got along fair. We weren't kissing, hugging buddies. But we got along."

After the Strongbows came and went, Jay Strongbow became a bit player in the expanding WWF, enough of a name to still mean something, but too old and out of shape to compete realistically. He became a backstage agent, running towns and "babysitting" the youngsters. "They knew that I knew what I was doing, because I drew a lot of money. They respected me for that," he said.

Through his backstage power, he did influence a lot of careers, whether it was suggesting the coconut to Jimmy Snuka's head on Piper's Pit, or accompanying Tatanka to the ring for a brief time in 1994. Hulk Hogan's "Hulking up" comeback is a direct rip-off of Strongbow's firey war dance comeback. Mentoring was a role he had long played, and he takes pride in the accomplishments of men like Jack Brisco and Jimmy Garvin whom he affected directly.

"Joe was a great coach. He taught me how to fire up during a match, how to get the crowd involved, how to react when a heel does something dirty to you in the ring. I was totally green and I soaked it all in like a sponge. Joe used every available moment to teach me," wrote Brisco in his autobiography. "He was a master of psychology in the ring. He had it down to a science."

Besides the psychology of the business, Scarpa, a member of the Pro Wrestling Hall of Fame and WWE Hall of Fame, also mastered the economics of it. Just a couple of years into his career, he bought Buddy Fuller's farm in Loxley, Alabama. A few years later, he purchased a farm in Griffin, Georgia, where he and his wife Mary Lee raised their adopted son Mark (who wrestled a little as Mark Young). Medical issues forced him from the WWF in 1997 and he spent his retirement years on the golf course. He never recovered from a fall in December 2011, and he died April 3, 2012.

BILLY TWO RIVERS

Billy Two Rivers carried a great weight around with him, and took his role seriously. "I wasn't a hero, I was an ambassador," he explained. "Representing the Kahnawake specifically, the Mohawk people, and then the Native people of North America."

In a world filled with Italians who played Indians, Two Rivers was the real thing through and through. In fact, when he became one of the biggest stars in the history of British wrestling, the newspapers investigated.

"[The Mohawk people] had a long history of relationships with the British crown, since 1759 when we assisted the British in the siege of Quebec City. So there were a lot of historic things I was able to talk about over there, to the media, the papers, and whatnot. What was interesting was they checked to see if I was genuine," he said. "I had myself, my language, my culture, my home address, my passport. 'What's your real name?' 'Billy Two Rivers!'"

The Kahnawake territory, just outside Montreal, Quebec, has been home to Two Rivers ever since he entered the world in May 1935. He was raised on a small street in the community, surrounded by wisdom. "I grew up in a situation where the elders were all around me. As a child, I just wandered around, automatically heard things, and they just stuck with me. It's helping me today."

A hero to his people was Don Eagle (Carl Donald Bell), who had followed his father, Joseph War Eagle, into professional wrestling. In 1950, Eagle came home to Kahnawake to recuperate from the trials of the road. He befriended a young Two Rivers, and when he went back to wrestling, Eagle took the fifteen-year-old Two Rivers with him to Columbus, Ohio, in 1954. "He saw some potential in me becoming a wrestler. He invited me to go back with him when he went back to his training process after his back had healed properly," said Two Rivers.

It took two years of training with Eagle before Two Rivers would debut in February 1953 in Detroit as a junior heavyweight. Teaming with his mentor from 1955 to 1959 helped polish Two Rivers' ring and interview skills. "He always made it a point that it was Don Eagle from the Mohawk community of Kahnawake. A lot of times the wrestling announcers would say Don Eagle from Montreal or Don Eagle from Quebec, Canada. And if that was done, he'd correct it . . . I took that as an example too to my travels."

On his own, with his tomahawk chop to the throat and war dance, Two

A young Billy Two Rivers is ready for action.

Rivers was a success in Florida and the Carolinas, and at the tail end of his career, in Montreal for the Grand Prix Wrestling promotion.

In the Carolinas, Two Rivers befriended Tinker Todd, who would be his hookup for superstardom overseas, including England, France, Italy, and Spain. "It was a cowboy movie type of thing. I would be the cowboy, he would be the Indian," recalled Todd.

His success in England, however, was the result of a coin flip. Invited to head west to Calgary or overseas, he left it up to luck. Television-wise, England was behind North America at the time, and his exotic headdress, Mohawk haircut, and dancing stood out immediately. "It was unbelievable. I arrived there about three months after wrestling had come on ITV," he said. "So it was there and I could produce. It was a natural marriage between that type of media audience and myself."

Todd laughed at the memory of Two Rivers' arrival. Dale Martin Promotions had a small apartment for visiting wrestlers to crash in, and Two Rivers and Todd had bunked down for the night when a drunk announcer came in, and, mistaking the newcomer's head for a cat, bounced a shoe off his noggin. "He thinks it's the damn cat, but it was Billy's Mohawk haircut," howled Todd. "Billy hopped out of there screaming and yelling and jumping all over the place. I had forgotten all about that — that was many years ago! He was scared to death. The guy says, 'We're being attacked by Indians!'" The friends would travel the United Kingdom together, sharing a love for British history.

"Billy is a showman *par excellence*. He plays to the crowd, he becomes a fighting-machine hard to top and harder to stop," wrote British announcer Kent Walton in his memoir. "On the one hand, he has the exotic appeal of the unusual, on the other he has the skill, toughness and tenacity of the top-flight wrestler. Add the two together and you have something that fills wrestling-arenas and boosts TV viewing-figures."

After years on the road, his daughters begged him to return home, so Two Rivers did, in the early 1970s, and wound down his career. "I was more or less of a journeyman. I traveled and was more of an attraction. Like they say, 'Did you hold many belts, win many titles?' It only happened when I came back to Montreal in the latter part of my career that I stayed in one place long enough to, say, wrestle for a tag team championship or something like that. The rest of the time, I traveled more or less as a journeyman. People went to see the Indian."

He'd invested his money wisely, much of it around Kahnawake, and was content to stay grounded. In 1976, he was approached about running for council, but put it off for two years, thinking himself too young. Then for the next twenty years, Two Rivers was the elected Chief in Council, taking advantage of his travels and experiences as a de facto "external affairs minister" for the council. The Assembly of First Nations would continue to benefit from his wisdom for years to come as well.

Two Rivers is not one to brag, but he was a key figure in Canadian politics — though he is full of disdain for the word — for decades.

"I've always been front and center," Two Rivers concluded. "I've always figured out that whatever happened to me, there was a reason for it. When I had to draw upon whatever experience I'd gathered in my lifetime, it served its purpose when I had to do it at any particular time."

"COWBOY" BILL WATTS

Billy Red Lyons and Cowboy Bill Watts are ready for their opponents.

Being a babyface is a piece of cake compared to being a heel, says "Cowboy" Bill Watts. But the added complication comes when you own the territory and are one of the top heroes.

"Hell, the heel has to do it all! He calls the match, he sets the psychology. It's much easier to be a babyface, much easier. But the next thing is, you can't be what you're not. In other words, you can't be a great heel if you don't have some heel quality," he said. "The heel is the guy that was truly the ring general, in most cases. He was the one that ran and set the stage, set the match, and ran the flow of the match. So if I was working in the ring, and the guy was a quality heel, I would let him call my match, even if I owned the territory as long as he was calling the match in a manner that I thought fit the direction that we were going."

And that direction for Watts was mostly a straight line, going through people, whether it was in his early days as a tough, young ruffian who was establishing a name for himself, or as a promoter in the Mid-South territory, made up of Louisiana, Arkansas, Oklahoma, Mississippi, eastern Texas, and southern Missouri.

"I never considered myself a good worker, I considered myself that I knew how to get over," Watts said.

Watts' story begins in Oklahoma City, where he was christened William F. Watts Jr. on May 5, 1939. He grew into a big kid, 210 pounds by Grade 8, and naturally got into football, and, with some urging, wrestling at Putnam City High. Watts chose the University of Oklahoma, but was never a starter on the outstanding Sooner teams. In his sophomore season, in November 1959, Watts was in an accident, his car being hit by a train. During the recovery process, Watts started lifting weights, something the football establishment frowned upon, but which he loved. He shot up to 315 pounds, and had further difficulty fitting in, outweighing his wrestling opponents by upward of sixty pounds. Feeling that his days were numbered at OU, Watts signed a pro football contract with the Houston Oilers; when that didn't pan out, having punched a coach, he accepted the suggestion of fellow OU alum Wahoo McDaniel to try pro wrestling.

"Without a doubt, if I hadn't gotten into wrestling, I'd have ended up in the penitentiary or dead because of the environment I had created for myself," Watts wrote in his confessional autobiography.

In October 1962, he started as a pro wrestler in Indianapolis, playing semi-pro ball with the Warriors at the same time, initially taking on OU's marquee heavy-weight Dale Lewis, who had also turned pro. Within a year, he had beaten out a name for himself in Texas and in the Tri-State territory that he would later run.

But he wasn't a natural, said tag partner Jerry Kozak. "We were in Little Rock, Arkansas in a tag match. Me, I'd jumped over the ropes. He went to jump over the ropes, and he caught his leg on the top rope and fell. I couldn't stop laughing."

In an April 1963 letter to promoter Jack Pfefer, Watts made a pitch for work. "I am only interested in making money and becoming the best worker in order to do so. Lou Thesz, Bill Miller, Karl Gotch, Leroy McGuirk, Scott Brothers, and Mike Clancy are some of the boys you can check with about me," he listed; Clancy offered his reference in a separate letter: "Bill is a real good boy — big and strong and a good worker. You may be able to do something for him, and if you can he will really appreciate. We have been working tag teams together here and doing real well."

It was Wild Red Berry who saw something in Watts, and suggested him to New York promoters Vince J. McMahon and Toots Mondt. He bought his first cowboy hat to debut in the territory as "Cowboy" Bill Watts. He started as a babyface, and got a big break working with Killer Kowalski.

"I got over in New York doing twenty-minute broadways with Kowalski. That's what got me over in New York, not only with the people, but with Vince McMahon Sr. He watched me and Kowalski in Washington, D.C., sent us on twenty-minute broadways, and we tore the joint down and he booked that everywhere," said Watts. "I'm the kind of babyface that liked the heel to stay on me. It was so simple with Kowalski. He was going to attack me viciously. Whatever he decided to attack, he was kind of like a pit bull." Watts and Kowalski rode together and the veteran mentored the up-and-comer. "I used to fly his airplane before I had a license," admitted Watts.

Then he teamed with Gorilla Monsoon, winning the area's tag titles. "We didn't stay together too long because the office couldn't control us too well," he said. "When we got angry, which we did one night with [Chief] White Owl and [Argentine] Apollo in a little spot show, and guzzled both of them — Monsoon didn't like Apollo and I didn't care much for White Owl, and things just got out of hand. They were the babyfaces and the people were just sitting on their hands as we beat the shit out of them."

Watts would follow a long line of partners who turned on WWWF champion Bruno Sammartino, seeing no other way into the world title picture. The foes would meet at Madison Square Garden in "The Most Talked-About Match in Wrestling History" on February 22, 1965, followed by another sellout a month later, and a third, less successful bout, in May.

Out in San Francisco, Watts furthered his wrestling education, learning from the likes of Jim Hady, Joe Scarpa, and Ray Stevens. "That's how the business used to be. You learned on the road. The guys would talk to you or chew your ass the whole trip," Watts said. "You learned who to listen to and who not to listen to." In Minneapolis, he followed Verne Gagne around, learning the ins and outs of promoting. On stopovers to Japan to wrestle, Watts took in the groundbreaking Hawaiian TV program, where wrestlers did extended promos and skits. "That's when I realized that people cared more about what the guys were saying. Why was that? So the people were interested in the personalities, and there was so little that you could do that was new and different in the ring."

In Florida, Watts worshipped promoter Eddie Graham, and became his disciple as a booker. He really hooked with Dusty Rhodes there too, and they would battle in many cities across the country. "He was stiff, a big ol' guy, a man's man, stiff as hell. We laid them in, opening each other for real a couple of times," said The American Dream. "A broken ankle in Jackson, Mississippi, with him, and the match kept going. He broke a couple of ribs. He was tough, man."

"Bill didn't use a lot of technique, just a lot of thumping," summed up "Big" John Quinn.

From 1976 on, Watts concentrated his attention on the Tri-State territory, buying into the Leroy McGuirk–run promotion, and eventually taking over completely. As the hometown hero, secretly pulling the strings behind-the-scenes, he was a different Watts than the Cowboy who had been in New York or Florida. Portrayed as a no-nonsense tough guy, Watts conserved his energy for

COURTESY OF SCOTT TEAL/CROWBAR PRESS

Bill Watts rips at Ron Fuller's face.

management headaches, but booked himself strong, doing color commentary and coming out as the savior into the mid-'80s, beating down foes almost half his age.

"His territory made more money when he wasn't a wrestler, except the times when he would come back on special occasions. They'd have that great upswing of business because Cowboy had a cause, and he hadn't been seen, and he was fresh again, and people knew he wasn't going to be around for a long run, it's going to be in and out, it was destination-specific," said Watts' referee and announcer Jim Ross. "But I think one of the hardest things to do in the business is to be the top star and the booker. It's really hard to keep your eye on all the balls that are flying up in the air, and focusing on your own work, your own conditioning, and your own in-ring performance, being objective and spotting that one kid that's in the second match that is going to be a future star, all those things. It's just hard. It's just a hard, hard process."

Or, as Rhodes put it, "Bill was better as a friend than he was as a boss, for me," he said. "I left Florida and went there to work for him exclusively in his territory. I had been flying in and out. And when I did, after one week being there, I knew I'd made the biggest mistake of my life to that point. Luckily, I went back to Florida."

Watts' gruff, bombastic personality rubbed many the wrong way; he would fine wrestlers for infractions big and small, and fire someone who didn't obey his law. "Bill Watts was a good booker. He knows the business. He knows what it takes, but he cannot get along with his talent," said Tom Jones. "He had a way of walking in and talking to you that would really set you off."

Watts' reputation, good and bad, stayed with him after he sold his Universal Wrestling Federation (the re-named Mid-South territory) to Jim Crockett Promotions, as he moved into positions of power in World Championship

The 2005 WrestleReunion in Tampa, Florida, featured (back row) Mick Foley, Bill Watts, and Kevin Von Erich, as well as Jack Brisco and Harley Race.

Wrestling and, briefly, the World Wrestling Federation. He helped propel the careers of everyone from Rhodes to Ernie Ladd to Junkyard Dog to Ted DiBiase to Sting to Ron Simmons; it's hard to imagine the world of professional wrestling today without Bill Watts' contributions.

"A lot of the guys that knock Bill Watts are guys that probably never worked for Watts, because a lot of guys couldn't work for Watts," said Buddy Landel, who put 100,000 miles on his car in one year with Watts. "Let me tell you, if you ever worked for Bill Watts, you were two things: You were a good worker, or a great worker; and you were tough. Bill Watts didn't hire anybody who wasn't actually a tough guy."

And fans in his territory believed in that tough guy.

"Bill Watts, he had an ego bigger than himself, but he was still over," concluded Gene Petit, who worked as Cousin Luke and the Mongol. "You go into Louisiana now and stop to ask somebody, and they're going to tell you, 'I remember The Spoiler, I remember Bill Watts, I remember Danny Hodge, I remember Junkyard Dog, Hacksaw Jim Duggan.' Those are some of the big names that these people still remember."

NATIONAL ERA

JOHN CENA

Don't call John Cena a babyface.

"Babyface and heel. I hate those terms. As long as you have something that you can hold on to, people will attach themselves to that. It's really not even a clean-cut distinction anymore," he ranted.

Time and time again, Cena is brought up by his peers as the sole pure babyface in professional wrestling today.

"I'm lucky enough to kind of be myself, so if it was one of those things, let's say playing a superhero on TV, and I'm really not that way in real life," he said. "My work ethic, my value system, everything is pretty much as is that you see on TV, that happens off camera. It's pretty easy, it's not too much of a stretch for me. If you meet me outside of this, I'm pretty much the same way as I am on television."

What he preaches on the weekly WWE shows — hustle, respect, loyalty — is indeed him. "Word Life" means everything he says is true. When the WWE needs a public face that it can trust, Cena is there.

"You have to start with the quality of the human being," WWE CEO Vince McMahon told the *Boston Herald*. "John is an extraordinary human being; he's honest, he's loyal . . . But he's like a throwback to the type of individual it's difficult to find these days, someone with old-fashioned values."

"John Cena is a prime example of what it means to be champion," The Big Show said in the book *The WWE Championship*. "I don't think he even goes home. Whether you like him or not, you're not going to outwork him. The kid doesn't know surrender, and that's not just a slogan for his T-shirt. John Cena can run eight weeks in a row, not go home, and still outwork everyone around him,

John Cena locks his STF finishing hold on Cody Rhodes.

all with a smile on his face. That's a real credit to the kind of guy he is and the work ethic he has."

Cena was born April 23, 1977, and grew up in West Newbury, Massachusetts, the second of five boys, but he was so heavily into football that he never really understood his father's love of pro wrestling. His rebelliousness against the traditional white-picket-fence life, with his love of rap music, funky clothes, and his tricked-out Chevy Nova, forced him into the gym at age fourteen — and 125 pounds — just to be able to protect himself. By eighteen, he was entering small-time bodybuilding contests.

After graduating from Springfield College, a Division III NCAA school, where he studied exercise physiology and played on the offensive line, he wanted a change of scenery, and took off for Los Angeles. There, he landed a role in 2000's *Manhunt* TV show as "Big Tim Kingman," a reality show (which WWE co-produced) in which the contestants were dropped off on an island and challenged to survive against hunters with paint guns.

While he was employed at Gold's Gym in Venice, California, someone suggested wrestling and directed him to the L.A.-based Ultimate Pro Wrestling school. His sculpted look, complete with square jaw, blue eyes, and blond Mohawk on his six-foot-one, 240-pound frame, helped him stand out.

One of his best friends there was Samoa Joe (Joe Seanos), whom he credited as one of the grandfathers of Cena's Thuganomics. "Way back in the early days when we started, we would stay awake on road trips by freestyling. When we weren't on road trips we would be at his house and his mom would cook us Samoan BBQ and we would eat so much we would pass out. We would sit around outside and freestyle," Cena said.

His schooling in the WWE style of wrestling started in Ohio Valley Wrestling, where he was The Prototype. It was a remarkable class, featuring future stars such as Dave Batista, Randy Orton, and Brock Lesnar.

In 2002, he debuted in the WWE, initially as a clean-cut, small-town hero. That morphed through a combination of his desires and his skills into the gangsta Cena, with bling, throwback jerseys, and baggy pants. He admitted to *Men's Fitness* in 2005 that the transition took guts. "I'm not afraid to fail. A lot of the guys get shook up about doing things wrong. I get shook up about not trying enough shit. I'm not afraid to try something new and look stupid. As soon as they let me rap on Smackdown! I ran with it. That doesn't mean I'm any better or smarter than anyone else — just more likely to take chances." His rap album, *You Can't See Me*, dropped in May 2005.

But the respect didn't come his way from the look, or the at-times weak-looking, hokey in-ring shenanigans (the You Can't See Me wave springs to mind); it came from the muscle. The visual of Cena with the 500-pound Big Show on his shoulders probably did more for his career than anything else. "He is one of the strongest guys I've stepped in the ring with," Orton once said. "Pound for pound, I think he is the strongest. The way he trains, his discipline, he keeps getting better every year."

Cena swears it's an honest physique. "I never have tried steroids, but no matter how much I say that, nobody is gonna believe it, so I've given up," he said in *WWE Unscripted*. "I've been accused of taking anabolics since I was sixteen. As a matter of fact, I had a urinalysis in prep school because I went from about 150 pounds to 225 in a matter of like six months."

Having toyed with the U.S. title in 2004, Cena has been in the WWE main event picture ever since, winning the world titles on both brands on numerous occasions.

"When you win it for the first time, I think it's the satisfaction that you finally did it. But then the very next day you realize, okay, it's just starting," he said after his sixth title win. "Now, having success for a sixth time, I know what's in store, not only from a brand standpoint and what's going to happen on WWE, I certainly will be in for some new challenges, but for instances such as this, I know my schedule will be completely full, just because of the fact that everybody wants to be able to interview the champ."

What everyone *doesn't* want to do in this day and age of sports entertainment is cheer for the hero simply because he's the hero. When the bad guys try so hard to be popular — and move their own merchandise — it has a polarizing effect on the WWE fan base. The women and children adore Cena, shrieking and celebrating his every move; the men are more complex, and cannot bring themselves to wholeheartedly support him.

"Any reaction is a great reaction. That's what you're out there for — to get a reaction, whether it's positive, negative, or in between," said WWE scout Jerry Brisco. "He's doing his job. He's getting you involved in it, whether you boo him or cheer him."

Cena remains Cena.

"It's funny because Cena gets so much crap from people, and he stays true to it, like a true babyface," said Steve Corino. "Shawn Michaels was an awesome babyface, especially with his comeback. Whereas Cena has that smirk to the smart-marks, where he knows that they'll hate him, but 75% of the people are going to cheer for him."

MAGNUM T.A.

J.J. Dillon still finds it hard to talk about the October 1986 night when he snuck into the back of Charlotte Memorial Hospital with Ric Flair, Tully Blanchard, and Arn Anderson to see Magnum T.A., who was paralyzed in intensive care following a horrific single-car accident. "He was lying strapped on an apparatus face down with one of these halo things around his head and he was on a machine that went ch-ch-ch-ch-ch. Pause. Ch-ch-ch-ch-ch. It was rotating back and forth to keep him alive. We talked to him, and I don't know if he knew we were there. It's hard to talk about that kind of thing."

Five months later, Terry Wayne Allen walked out of a rehab hospital. Tentatively and uneasily, to be sure, but he did it. His wrestling career was over, and he'd never attain the world championship for which he was being groomed. But lying motionless in that hospital, he drew on the lessons that promoter Eddie Graham taught him in Florida about the babyface comeback. Fight from the bottom. Dig down deep. You're in a struggle of epic proportions against a formidable foe. Overcome insurmountable odds. "Inside, the impact it was having even further gave me drive. 'I don't know if I can completely overcome this or not, but I'll be darned if I'm going to just give up,'" Allen recalled thinking. "I wasn't giving up from the moment they wheeled me into the emergency room and the guy said, 'You've got a million-in-one shot of ever walking again. The best you can ever hope for is to sit up in a wheelchair and have somebody feed you.' All that did was make me more determined than ever to overcome those odds."

The twenty-seven-year-old Allen was about the hottest thing in wrestling when his red Porsche 911 skidded on a wet road just a few miles from his Charlotte, North Carolina, home around 2:30 a.m. on October 14, 1986. As he lost control, the car swerved and spun sideways into a utility pole. Allen never lost consciousness, but his fifth cervical vertebra had burst and he had no sensation below his chest. Emergency responders knew they had a crisis on their hands. At six-foot-three and 235 pounds, he was too big to pull from the tiny sports car, so they spent the next hour removing the car from him, opening the door with an air chisel, peeling away the top with a hydraulic cutter, and yanking the steering wheel, which trapped Allen, with a "jaws of life" hook. An eight-member surgical team spent three-and-a-half hours removing bone fragments, replacing discs, and refashioning a vertebra with bone from Allen's hip.

Allen wasn't impaired and though he might have been a few miles over the posted forty-five mph speed limit, the accident was a fluke. Another vehicle, unlike his rear engine-mounted Porsche, almost certainly would have handled differently and he would have been home in minutes. Instead, that single disastrous moment opened his eyes to the hold he had on wrestling in the Mid-Atlantic. Phone calls from fans clogged the hospital's switchboard; the staff fielded an estimated 10,000 calls in the four days following the crash. Fans deluged the hospital with flowers, balloons, and teddy bears, and security guards had to keep them from climbing fire escapes to get to Allen. "It was crazy. It was like John Wayne was in a real-life deal, got shot, and everyone wanted to find out what was going on. So it didn't hit me until then," Allen said. "It never ceases to amaze me, the impact of something I loved so much and would have done for free if I didn't need to eat. But it's touched everybody in a different way and I guess having a devastating, career-ending accident and them seeing how I handled that real-life challenge made everything very real for everyone."

It would be misleading to focus exclusively on the crash; Allen had a neat career before and he's worked hard since. He grew up in the Hampton Roads

At his peak, Magnum T.A. battles Nikita Koloff over the U.S. title.

area of Virginia and started wrestling as a 135-pound ninth-grader at Norfolk Collegiate High. By his own characterization, he stunk, losing all but his final match in his first year. By the time he was a senior, he pinned everyone in the state tournament and was Virginia private school champion at 167 pounds. More importantly, he became utterly convinced that hard work and unwavering persistence pays off. "You don't wake up and win the lottery and become successful. You've got to do everything in steps in a building block process to obtain goals. So you set short-term and long-term goals so you can feel like you're making progress throughout that process, no matter how painful and agonizing it might be. I really had no idea that I was going to have to put it in practice in the biggest challenge of my life."

Allen wrestled briefly at Old Dominion University, lettering in 1977–78 as a freshman for the Monarchs, and contemplated joining the Navy SEALs before taking a stab at wrestling. Buzz Sawyer befriended him, worked with him a little, and though Allen politely refuses to say it, took advantage of the kid. Allen wound up chasing down Sawyer in Portland, Oregon, during the winter of 1980–81, when he finally got a break. Princess Victoria was getting into wrestling at the same time, and Allen caught her eye as a greenhorn in promoter Sandy Barr's gym. "He'd open up the bay door when we were in there training

Magnum and Nikita reunite in 2008.

on a good day. It was about seventy-five degrees one day, and he had worked me and Magnum so hard that I looked over at Terry, and there was steam coming off the top of his head," she said. "I knew Magnum had talent before he ever started training." He spent time in Southwest Championship Wrestling before going to Florida, where Graham and Rhodes gave him his first real wrestling education. Allen was supposed to head to New York at that point, but Ernie Ladd, booking for Bill Watts' Mid-South office, instead wooed him to Louisiana as a fresh baby-face. Magnum T.A., a tag Andre the Giant gave him, saying he resembled the Tom Selleck TV character, started there in May 1983, as Watts was overhauling the direction of his promotion to attract a new generation of young fans. After a couple of fits and starts, he found a groove as a rough-hewn motorcycle rider, with enough good looks to attract the women and enough attitude to appeal to the men. The character matched his natural persona — he said he and Dusty Rhodes had kicked around a similar idea — and his career went into overdrive in 1984. "We repackaged Magnum T.A. We bought him clothes and outfits and stuff and had him start dressing to attract the young," Watts said. "We also made him the champion. We bought a new North American championship belt. It was twenty-seven pounds of silver and gold. I think he was the first one to carry the new belt, which he hated because it was so damned heavy."

In the waning days of 1984, after less than four years in the business, Allen joined Jim Crockett Promotions as booker Rhodes brought him to replace Barry Windham, who had bolted for the WWF. Superstation WTBS gave his belly-to-belly suplex national exposure and suddenly Allen's future was as souped up as his 1340-cc Sportglide Harley. "When he walked into a room, it was like a king had come," said his friend Dale Swaringen, who owned the Harley-Davidson operation in Charlotte at the time. "It was like Elvis Presley had walked in or maybe twice that much. I don't think there was a person in this place who wasn't in awe, and for Harley people to be in awe was something special." The "I Quit" match between Allen and Tully Blanchard for the U.S. title at Starrcade '85 was so brutal and compelling that it spawned a generation of imitators. Nickla "Baby Doll" Roberts was in Tully Blanchard's corner as Magnum and Blanchard pounded on each other, until Blanchard surrendered rather than being gashed with a broken chair leg. "I knew it was going to be bad. I knew that just from going in there and what was halfway planned that we were supposed to get across," she said. "He and Tully beat the crap out of each other for almost two years. There was solid heat there and the way they felt about each other came out."

"Intense" was the way Nikita Koloff described his Cold War battle with Allen that was the centerpiece of the 1986 Great American Bash tour, and Allen's last big hurrah. "I've heard many comments from fans over the years who said, 'We watched those matches. I don't know about any of the other matches, but that match between Magnum and Nikita was real,'" Koloff said. A month after the Bash, Allen's car hydroplaned on Sardis Road. "The new heir to the throne would have been him. He was the heir to what throne I had at that time in our organization. He was definitely groomed to be king. Then shit happens," Rhodes said. Baby Doll agreed, saying the sky was the limit. "I really think that Magnum could have been like another Hulk Hogan — even better, because he could do more things than Hulk Hogan, and not be like that cartoon character. Magnum could have done movies and anything else he wanted to."

After his rehabilitation, Allen worked for a while as a TV commentator, but found himself out of a job when Turner Broadcasting took over the Crockett business. He worked long hours to pay off six-figure medical bills; his insurance at the time of the crash only covered $25,000. In time, he found a nice niche around Charlotte in the cellular communications construction business. He and his wife Courtney, Blanchard's ex, had twins in 2007 and Allen said he "got really educated here at forty-eight years old about what all this baby stuff is about." He even has a loose connection to today's WWE — he is the godfather of Rhodes' son Cody. Still in pain a lot of the time, he scrawls autographs for fans with his one good arm, with absolutely no complaints. "I guess it is in a way, a life lesson, a life story. Everybody can say what they want. But you never know what anyone's going to do until you're faced with something that enormous, overwhelming. I'd like to think we've all got enough survival instinct in us that we're not going to give up in the face of adversity."

CHRIS SWISHER COLLECTION

Rick Martel, heartthrob and AWA world champion.

RICK MARTEL

For the first five years of his career, Rick Martel never made a move without consulting his older brother, Michel, twelve years his senior. Then, all of a sudden, Michel was gone, his heart giving out after a match in Puerto Rico on June 30, 1978. He died in the passenger seat as his partner, Pierre Martel (Frenchy Martin), drove to the hospital.

Just twenty-one years old, Rick was dispatched to get his brother's body.

"What a weekend it was for me," he recalled. "When I talked to Frenchy that Friday at 3 a.m., I didn't sleep all night. When I took that flight at seven o'clock that morning, I got onto the island real early, 8:30. When I got there, I called Frenchy's number and there was no answer." For the rest of the day and into the next, Martel frantically tried to reach his brother's partner. Eventually, he walked into a police station, where he was directed to an apartment building where the wrestlers were known to stay. A superintendent let Rick in, and he found Frenchy asleep under the table awaiting his call — with a phone that wasn't working.

Getting the body back to their native Quebec City was a nightmare. The flight was San Juan to Philadelphia, then Philly to Montreal, then Montreal to home. Only Eastern Airlines didn't get the coffin transferred in time for the flight to Montreal. The next day, Eastern switched Michel's body to Delta, which had no records of him.

"They lost him for a while. It took all afternoon before finally he arrived in Montreal. The guy called me from Montreal, four o'clock in the afternoon. 'Okay, he's finally here. He's going to be there at 7,'" said Rick, who then faced the challenge of convincing their mother that he wanted to keep wrestling — it's what Michel would have wanted.

Fortunately for wrestling fans, Evelyne Harvey, mother of six, allowed her remaining son, Richard Vigneault, born March 18, 1956, to keep going — and go he did. An early piece of advice, that a territory didn't need two young, good-looking babyfaces, meant that there was no point sticking around Quebec for $25 pay weeks, where Raymond Rougeau, the promoter's nephew, was setting hearts aflutter.

With two uncles who dabbled in wrestling around *la belle province*, and a love of powerlifting, Michel's entry into pro wrestling in 1968 was perhaps not a surprise. But with Rick, who started seriously working out when he was just thirteen years old, it was an obsession, something he needed and wanted to do.

"Michel was my idol, my teacher, my mentor. He was everything to me. He started me. In fact, he made a point of making me get in touch with the wrestling world. I remember when I was twelve years old, he would bring me with him to the wrestling, bring me into the dressing rooms," said Rick, who spent a few weeks with Michel in 1972 in Stampede Wrestling. "He'd say, 'You know one day, you're going to be in professional wrestling . . . we're going to team up.' He really gave me that fever, that passion." To achieve his goal, Rick boxed instead of playing hockey like his friends, a plan laid out by his brother. "If I became any good at all in this wrestling business, it's strictly because of Michel."

Fast forward to the summer of 1973, when Michel was working in Nova Scotia. Another wrestler got injured, and a replacement was needed immediately. Michel pitched his seventeen-year-old brother. "I had wrestled amateur, Olympic-style, Greco-Roman style, but I had never wrestled professional," recalled Rick. "So he called me up on a Friday night and said 'I'd like you to get on a plane tomorrow and start professional wrestling.'"

It was love at first match. Rick went back to high school for one day that fall, and never looked back.

Knowing things at home were bleak, Martel went abroad, learning English en route: he was a star in New Zealand as a three-time British Empire/Commonwealth champ; an undercard guy in Texas; a perfect complement to a young Tommy Rich in Georgia; a calm balance to the wild Roddy Piper in the

Pacific Northwest. All the while, he was studying his heroes, like Jack Brisco. From June until September 1979, Martel was part owner with Steve Rickard and Peter Miavia in the Hawaiian promotion, acting as the booker at just twenty-one years of age.

After Michel's untimely death, Martel seemed to find a new level and in 1980 was rewarded with the WWWF tag team titles on two occasions, alongside Tony Garea. "Tony had a big impact on my professional life and also personal life. He was like the brother that I lost," said Martel. "I got really close with him."

It was just a precursor for what was next — the AWA world title.

Martel was the champ in Hawaii, and worked against AWA world champ Nick Bockwinkel, with manager Bobby Heenan, on the island, to a one-hour draw. "I kind of took them by surprise. They had never heard of me before," said Martel. "I guess they kept that in the back of their minds and somebody mentioned my name to Verne Gagne. I guess that he called a couple of people in Hawaii and found out about me."

Bockwinkel, who dropped the AWA belt to Jumbo Tsuruta, felt that the Frenchman was an ideal standardbearer. "Why Martel? He had a hell of a body, good looking as hell, a thick head of hair and the woman wet their pants whenever he comes in the room. Plus he had that little bit of a French accent to add it to mix," Bockwinkel told MemphisWrestlingHistory.com. "Top that off with the fact he's one of the nicest guys you'll ever meet. I would have loved to have seen him stay champion for a longer time."

The May 13, 1984 title win over Tsuruta in Minneapolis was his crowning achievement, admitted Martel, even if he wasn't happy with the match. "They didn't know who the hell he was; he wasn't really a heel," he said. "That was hard to get that going, because emotion is an important part of wrestling."

In the ring, Martel showed fire like few others; jaw clenched, fists balled, chest hair matted with sweat, hair shaking, he made his comeback, putting villains back in their place.

He had dream title versus title matches with NWA world champion Ric Flair in the U.S. and in Japan. "Martel had a million-dollar look and could perform as smoothly as [Ricky] Steamboat when he wanted to," wrote Flair in his autobiography.

When his AWA world title run came to an end in December 1985, at the unlikely hands of Stan Hansen, who was a regular in Japan at the time, Martel took the chance to return home, and invested in the local promotion.

"Dino Bravo was here, and Gino Brito. And Montreal wrestling needed some new blood. And now that I was established overseas and internationally, I wanted to come back to Quebec and show my family, my friends, and also the Quebec fans, that, 'Hey, here I am, and I'm from Quebec, now I'd like for you to come see me, see what I've done, what I've accomplished, what I've become,'" he explained.

According to International Wrestling promoter Brito, it didn't work the way they all anticipated.

"I must say, and there's no prejudice here, but Rick Martel, as good as he did here, never did as well as Dino Bravo did as far as drawing power," said Brito. "Even when we put one against the other, we built it up in Quebec City, which was his hometown. We wanted to do something like the rivalry between the

Michel Martel raises the arm of his young, rookie brother, Rick.

Nordiques and the Montreal Canadiens in hockey. In Quebec City, you had over half the people cheering Bravo. People were saying to me, 'What's Martel doing against Bravo? He doesn't have a chance.' They didn't believe in him as much. He was hard to sell." Years later, the French Historia channel did a documentary on wrestling in Quebec and barely covered Martel. In part, that was because Martel's most famous days came in the WWF, and footage was too expensive.

Martel's return to the WWF in 1986 came alongside Tom Zenk in the Can-Am Connection. Zenk seemed like Martel from a decade past, a pretty boy on his way up. "When I saw him in the ring, I said wow, because it's so strange. He really was so similar to me. His style. And later on I found out that Tom had been watching me a lot and kind of copied my style and did a lot of the moves that I was doing," said Martel, who mentored the youngster the way his brother and Mark Lewin had looked out for him.

The partnership didn't last, however. Zenk has always claimed that Martel had a better deal with WWF promoter Vince McMahon; Martel cited jealousy. Regardless

Jerry Brisco, Rick Martel, and Nick Bockwinkel at the 2011 Cauliflower Alley Club reunion in Las Vegas.

of the conflict, Zenk was replaced with Tito Santana, and as Strike Force, Martel got the WWF tag belts back around his waist, sixteen years after his first run.

After years of begging for the chance, Martel got his wish to be a heel, walking out on Santana. A short while later, at J.J. Dillon's suggestion (who had known Martel in Nova Scotia back in 1973), he morphed into The Model, complete with his Arrogance cologne.

"It was a change that I needed at that time to motivate me," he said. "To keep me going, to keep reaching higher and higher. That was a big challenge for me because, of course, everyone was against it from the start. Nobody believed that it would work because I was so established as a babyface-type wrestler."

In interviews in particular, he was able to be someone different. "When I turned heel, that's the one thing that I enjoyed the most, was the interviews, because you could play with it so much, especially in those years, when it was black and white."

But in reality, Martel is indeed one of those nice guys. "I like people, and I enjoy people. It was never an effort for me to see the fans and shake their hands. I like nice people and when people are nice to me, it's a great exchange. I win too," he said.

If he wasn't a good guy, "Leaping" Lanny Poffo wouldn't have traveled to

Quebec City for Martel's fiftieth birthday party and written a poem — in French — for the occasion. "Rick is the kind of a guy that I wish I would emulate," said Poffo, citing Martel's thirty-plus-year marriage to Johanne, and the couple's adopted daughter, Coralie, from China. "But unfortunately, the best I can do is be his friend . . . When we do talk, we don't talk about events or people or gossip, we always talk about ideas. He's an ideas man, and so am I. Whenever I talk to a guy like that, it brings out the best in me. Plus, on the road, he was diligent. He's the most conscientious guy I've ever run across."

SHAWN MICHAELS

In 2010, World Wrestling Entertainment released a DVD that ranked Shawn Michaels as the top performer of all time. While debatable on many levels, in truth it is an acknowledgment of the in-ring skills of "The Heartbreak Kid" that convinced so many young fans to follow their "boyhood dream" and enter pro wrestling.

It's also a testament to his longevity; he was one of the few who worked for peanuts in the 1980s in the small territories, such as Kansas City, and made millions in the 2000s.

While his personal conduct has often been questioned, what with the partying, politicking, and losing his smile, no one ever doubted his love of the business.

"I am what I would consider to be an old-timer, and the one big difference between us and the newer guys is that the newer guys — and I don't mean this critically — don't have a genuine, genuine, genuine appreciation for the business, because I don't know that they would do it for nothing," he said in *WWE Unscripted*. "You get your Undertaker, you get your Steve Austin — none of us got into it for the money. We got into it because we wanted to do it, and then it exploded and it got so big, and we realized you could make a future, so it was even better. There was a time when I drove down the road in a beat-up car that my parents helped me get; there was a time I was eating out of tin cans; there was a time I was staying in hotels that were not pretty. You don't have that anymore. It's not the newer guys' fault, the business has just gotten better. But to say that they have the same appreciation for it that we do, I just think that would be inaccurate. Because of the circumstances, they can't have the same appreciation."

And it's fair to say that with his return to action in 2002 — after back surgery, starting a family, and turning his life over to God — Michaels really had two distinctly different personalities. There was the one who was young and headstrong, cocky in his abilities, and at times detested by fans and peers alike. The second Michaels wore a crucifix to the ring, honed and polished his image, and became a true icon, adored by those backstage as a leader and a mentor, and in the crowd, who saw his Second Coming as a blessing.

"I've watched Shawn grow from the Shawn that I met to the Shawn that I know now," said Kevin Nash in 2005. "What an incredible human being he is now. He is just, he is as good as it gets. It's nice to see guys, especially your closest friends on Earth, when I've got a couple of them falling off the face of the Earth; it's nice to see some of them go the opposite way."

From the age of twelve, Michael Shawn Hickenbottom, born July 22, 1965, at the Williams Air Force Base in Chandler, Arizona, always insisted that he would be a pro wrestler. With his father in the military, the family moved often — England, Texas, Washington, D.C. — and while the family patriarch served in the Vietnam War, Shawn lived in Iowa with his mother, brothers and sister. In 1982, Hickenbottom had his first wrestling match, a staged skit with a buddy during the Randolph High School Talent Show in Randolph, Texas. It was also in Randolph where he became serious about weightlifting to further propel his football talents, a game he'd played since the age of six.

After just two semesters at Southwest Texas State University, he talked to Southwest Championship Wrestling promoter Joe Blanchard about trying out, and was directed to Jose Lothario for training. "He listened so good to me and just followed what I told him," Lothario said in a radio interview. His first territory was as an enhancement talent in Bill Watts' Mid-South territory in 1984, where Watts fined him every day for the first two weeks for various offenses, including being late. Up next was Kansas City, where veteran Roger Kirby got to work with the athletic youngster who was "just willing to learn, and wanting to learn." He also spent time in Blanchard's San Antonio promotion.

In K.C. he first met Marty Jannetty, and the two would be paired as the Midnight Rockers in the AWA. "Young, handsome, and charismatic in the ring, they were clones of other tag teams created to attract young rock and rollers, especially women, to the matches," wrote AWA announcer Larry Nelson. "During the latter years of the AWA, they became the tag team champions and the league's top draw."

Naturally, the team wanted to get to the WWF, and did, briefly, in the summer of 1987, but they were fired for living a little too hard after midnight. Tails between their legs, Jannetty and Michaels returned to the AWA for a last

Nobody sold better than Shawn Michaels.

run and claimed the AWA tag titles for a second time. In 1988, they got back to the WWF as The Rockers, and their high-flying antics meshed nicely with more ground-based teams, such as the Nasty Boys and the Twin Towers of Akeem and Big Bossman. Being a small dog in the fight helped him, said WWF referee Jim Korderas. "Just watching him in those tag matches with Marty against guys like Haku and the Barbarian, and the way he sold for those guys, the guy was phenomenal, even back then."

In January 1992, Michaels threw Marty Jannetty through the plate glass window of Brutus Beefcake's Barber Shop set, signaling to the entire world that he was ready to be solely in the spotlight. Upping the sexy, with risqué outfits, posing in *Playgirl*, and bragging about being The Boy Toy and The Heartbreak Kid, Michaels quickly made main-event status, challenging the world champion Randy Savage and claiming the Intercontinental title. Backed by the Kliq, friends away from the ring who wielded tremendous stroke backstage, Michaels was on top, winning the WWE world title three times, most famously as a co-conspirator in the most famous screw job in modern wrestling history, when he beat WCW-bound Bret Hart for the WWE title at Survivor Series in November 1997 in Montreal thanks to a referee's fast count.

A career-ending injury in 1998, the result of falling on his back onto a casket during a match, set Michaels on a different path. He had his then final match at

"The Showstopper" Shawn Michaels battles his ex-bodyguard Diesel.

WrestleMania XIV against Stone Cold Steve Austin. "It was real difficult to work with Michaels," Austin told writer Kevin Sullivan. "He was like that cantankerous Ferrari: When he's ready to go, he can go like nobody else. But when he didn't want to go, there were a million reasons why he wouldn't. He did have some back problems, but he also had a lot of attitude problems and personal problems as well."

In January 1999 Michaels had two vertebrae fused, and later that year married former WCW Nitro Girl Whisper (Rebecca Curci), opened a wrestling school in San Antonio with Paul Diamond (Tom Boric) and Rudy Gonzalez, and promoted his Texas Wrestling Alliance. Three of his students made the big-time: Daniel Bryan (Bryan Danielson), Brian Kendrick, and Lance Cade (Lance McNaught). He became a father in 2000, but struggled with drug addiction, taking dozens of painkillers and muscle relaxants a day.

Michaels credits his wife, family, and becoming a born-again Christian in 2001 for helping him get straight.

"It was the genesis of what turned my life around," Michaels told a Texas newspaper. "I had my first encounter with God inside of a deer blind. Just sitting there waking up with the animals and looking at the stars. I was not in a great place in my life at that time. I started thinking there has to be more to life than this. Hunting was the start of that for me. It changed my life all for the better. My connection with the Lord grew immensely from that point on."

Moving from an on-air commissioner role in the WWE to an in-ring performer again after four years on the shelf was a big step. For the next eight years, he put any of those regrets he had about his career's premature ending aside, working as a professional, whether on top against Hulk Hogan in a dream match at SummerSlam or going on fifth against Chris Jericho to steal the show at WrestleMania XIX. With his new attitude, Michaels was helpful to young talent, and an inspiration to a whole new generation of wrestlers who had grown up watching him.

His battles against The Undertaker at WrestleMania XXV and XXVI, including his retirement match, will always be in consideration as a couple of the greatest matches of all time. Michaels is vehement that he is done as an in-ring performer. "I'm not going to wrestle again. The only way a 185-pound guy made it in that business is to do something nobody else ever did. The best thing I can do is to stay retired, because nobody ever stays retired. I'll still be part of the company. You never really get out of the WWE unless you're wearing concrete shoes at the bottom of the Hudson River — but no more active wrestling."

Pro Wrestling Illustrated's Dan Murphy said that The Heartbreak Kid's body of word stands on its own. "When looking at Shawn Michaels' legacy, I think you really have to look at his career pre–WrestleMania XIV and post-comeback in 2002. Before his 'Mania match against Steve Austin and his sabbatical, Michaels had the reputation of being a self-absorbed prima donna, and his complicity in the 'Montreal Screwjob' certainly didn't do much to change that perception," mused Murphy. "But after his comeback, Michaels did much more to cement his legacy. He wrestled a string of incredible matches (including a record seven consecutive *PWI* Match of the Year winners), and he also did what had always resisted doing before — he jobbed to opponents. He helped to create new stars. He showed concern about people other than himself, and that is the lasting legacy he leaves behind."

TOMMY RICH

In conversation, Tommy Rich might downplay his fame as the first true national babyface — "I was just a little country boy that come to Georgia and found a home," he'll claim, but facts are facts. There was a time, thanks to the reach of *Georgia Championship Wrestling* on WTBS, that perhaps Rich was the most famous wrestler on the planet.

As a boy in Philadelphia, Steve Corino worshipped Rich. "I flicked on WTBS, and the first thing I see is Tommy 'Wildfire' Rich talking to Gordon Solie. At that moment, I became a wrestling fan. To me, when I was a kid, Tommy Rich was the ultimate babyface," said the former NWA world champion. "Here's this Tennessee country boy on the *Georgia Championship Wrestling* program, telling me how he wants me to come to the Omni because (drops into the voice), 'My momma told me, she told me, you never let somebody beat you, Buzz Sawyer. When I get to the Omni . . .' I'd be like, 'Ahhhh! Mom! We've got to go to the Omni!' She'd go, 'Steve, it's fourteen hours away.'"

Not only was he a star on the Atlanta-based Superstation from 1977 to 1982, but the wrestling magazines fell in love with Wildfire, well before his four-day reign as NWA world heavyweight champion in 1981.

"Understand that the reason we put anyone on covers was, no matter how much the staff loved wrestling, the publisher, Stanley Weston, was in the business to make money," said former *Pro Wrestling Illustrated* editor Bill Apter. "He was a magazine publisher. It was my job, as well as the job of the other editors, to figure out who was really going to sell on the magazine, and Tommy Rich was one of the maybe dozen consistent sellers for many, many years." PWI was on the ball right from the start, naming Rich its Rookie of the Year in 1978, its Most Improved Wrestler of the Year the following year, and, in his triumphant 1981, Rich was named Most Popular Wrestler of the Year.

It isn't hard to assess what made Thomas Richardson a star. He was cute enough for the girls to fall for him, tough and volatile enough for the guys to respect him, unpolished enough on the microphone to be endearing, and polite enough for the grandparents watching to approve.

"I wouldn't say I was a pretty boy," said Rich. "There were some guys that didn't like me, that liked to see my ass whooped. At the same time, if you don't do nuthin' bad to nobody, it's kind of hard to have something against them. I did the best I could, and I'm sure I pissed off a couple of people around the country."

In 1974, Richardson was a standout football player at Hendersonville High School, a healthy six-foot-three and 240 pounds. His parents knew wrestler Eddie Marlin well, and through him, he met Jerry Jarrett, the co-promoter in Memphis. The initial training was at Jarrett's home, where it was a challenge.

"Tommy went through every possible thing I could do to discourage him — but he wouldn't give up," Jarrett told writer Scott Bowden. "So we started training him, and he was a good-looking kid who turned out to be a decent wrestler."

Other mentors included Tojo Yamamoto and Wahoo McDaniel, who once told Rich, "It doesn't matter if the other babyfaces like you or not. You make sure all the bad guys like you because they're the ones that can make you or break you."

And the wild-eyed Southern boy faced a real A-list of baddies during his era, shedding buckets of blood into his blond hair against the likes of "Mad Dog" Buzz Sawyer, Abdullah the Butcher, Ivan Koloff, the Fabulous Freebirds, and Harley Race.

One of his early triumphs came over Ox Baker in Atlanta for promoter Jim Barnett. "If you knew Barnett, if he liked some-body, he was on fire for them," explained Baker, who was booked to draw with Rich, lose by countout, and then lose outright. "I have to say, for a fellow starting out, he had more talent than

Gordon Solie interviews a fired-up Tommy Rich as Ray Candy listens in.

you can shake a stick at. He had a lot of charisma."

The titles Rich held are legion, from the Georgia heavyweight title, to the Southern and USWA titles in Memphis, to tag championships with the likes of Tony Atlas, Stan Hansen, Thunderbolt Patterson, Wahoo McDaniel, Bill Dundee, Eddie Gilbert, Dutch Mantel, and Tojo Yamamoto.

Wrestlers would come to Georgia to be on WTBS just to appear to be bigger stars when they returned to their home territories. Imagine what it was like for the focal point of the show, the charismatic youngster whom everyone rallied behind.

"I was something they hadn't ever seen in Georgia, and the rest hadn't seen around the country. I was the first blond-haired boy that had come to Georgia. I was on national TV. I could take an ass-whoopin' and never did give up — and people never did give up on me. It's kind of like a blue collar worker; they want to whip that bossman's ass," Rich theorized. "I think I was kind of that guy that they could sit and holler for me, and get rid of some of that anxiety, maybe. I thought about it many times, and it's just hard to say why. I was just very lucky. God blessed me, and I thank all the rasslin' fans around the world, because if it hadn't been for them, God, I wouldn't be here."

The Georgia promotion expanded its traditional house show territory to include West Virginia, Ohio, and more. It was "big" to head north, Rich said. "I mean, it was like a rock 'n' roll star when we went up there, carried the show up there. That's when you really knew you were somebody. It was something, because the people would just chase you like you was a rock 'n' roll star or sumthin'."

But any discussion of Rich has to include his NWA world title run, orchestrated behind the scenes by Barnett. At twenty-four years of age, Rich peaked.

"That was another milestone in my career, too, beating one of the greatest world heavyweight champions in the world, Harley Race, beating the best. I had the opportunity to be in that category," he said. "A lot of guys might be bitter about it, but it's all been good to me."

The last part is a matter of interpretation. Ego, partying, weight gain, and feuds with bookers derailed the Rich steamroller. He never came close to hitting the heights again, though he didn't stop trying — and still wrestles on occasion today.

Al Snow said Rich doesn't get his due as to how great a worker he was. "A testament to how over he was as a babyface, he would leave and go to another territory to be a heel and get that much more heat as a heel," said Snow. "Tommy Rich was a pretty boy, before Hogan he was really the first national babyface. That guy was red hot as a babyface. He'd go to Memphis and they'd turn him heel and he'd get a ton of it."

Memphis was indeed Rich's last truly great run. It was 1987, and Rich had been away from the spotlight. Austin Idol, with arrogant young manager Paul E. Dangerously (later ECW founder Paul Heyman) as his second, had been battling mainstay Jerry Lawler for almost a year. Their feud peaked with a hair versus hair match in a cage, where Rich emerged from under the ring to turn on Lawler. It was the *Wrestling Observer Newsletter*'s Feud of the Year in 1987.

The heel Rich saw his career briefly revitalized, and he would campaign again in the AWA and in the NWA, before fading from view again. His last national moment came when Heyman spotlighted his old friend in ECW from 1996–2000 as "Big Don" Tommy Rich in the Full Blooded Italians.

SGT. SLAUGHTER

U.S. champion Sgt. Slaughter.

Listen up, maggots! The Sarge was once beautiful, and that attracted enemy fire. In 1974, "Beautiful" Bobby Remus was preening around a ring in Vancouver, British Columbia, when he heard fans laughing. "I looked behind me and there was Bob Ramstead behind me blowing me kisses. He started to look at me like I was some kind of beauty queen or something," Remus said. That night, Slaughter told his wife that "Beautiful" Bobby was getting a dishonorable discharge. He cut his hair, returned it to its normal dark brown, and wrestled as "Bruiser" Bob Remus, one step in the transformation to Sgt. Slaughter, the first celebrity to become a G.I. Joe doll.

Ten-hut! Even if you don't know a boot stomp from a boot camp, you probably know Sgt. Slaughter, the jut-jawed, gravel-voiced Marine. In 1984, after Remus flipped from a decade as a brow-beating heel to a staunch defender of the flag, Hasbro inked him as part of its G.I. Joe product line. Remus voiced his own character in the animated G.I. Joe TV series and worked as a spokesman for Hasbro, which put out four Sgt. Slaughter action figures in less than five years. "Sgt. Slaughter is easily one of the most polarizing figures in G.I. Joe lore," said Josh Wigler, a pop culture writer for the Comics Alliance website. "On one side of the fence is a contingent of fans that don't believe a real-life wrestling icon should have been allowed on the Joe squad. On the other side of the fence is everybody with substance, taste, and a brain."

As befits a future soldier, Remus got hooked on wrestling through clandestine ops. He was born in August 1948 in Meeker County, Minnesota, and raised west of Minneapolis. Remus was four or five years old, sleeping on a pullout couch, when he heard what sounded like people being killed in an adjacent room. "Here was my father and bunch of his friends and my uncles yelling at the TV screen, watching professional wrestling," he said. "I started to fake like I was sleeping on Saturdays and I'd crawl out there and watch the show without them even knowing it."

After he graduated from high school, served in the Marines, and joined his dad's roofing company, Remus got a face-to-face with Verne Gagne, owner and champ of the American Wrestling Association. He tagged along with a sports-writer for a story on Gagne's training camp, accepted a challenge to get in the ring, and endured an agreed-upon beating. That done, the twenty-four-year-old Remus asked if he could defend himself and ended up on the mat with Ric Flair and Billy Robinson. According to Remus, Gagne pulled them apart when things got testy and asked him his name. "I said, 'Bob Remus.' 'Is your father Rudy Remus?' I said, 'Yes sir.'" Responded Gagne, "He put the roof on my house, for crying out loud."

COURTESY OF SCOTT TEAL/CROWBAR PRESS

"Beautiful" Bobby decided to tough it out as a Marine instead.

In December 1973, Remus debuted against Paul Perschmann, his training partner and the future "Playboy" Buddy Rose. His early days were spent as "Beautiful" and "Bruiser" in the Pacific Northwest and the AWA. The change in name and rank came from watching *The DI*, a 1957 movie starring Jack Webb about a Parris Island, South Carolina, drill instructor. "I dug out my old campaign cover and my fatigues," Slaughter said in a WWE interview. "Of course, nothing fit at that time, but the idea was there." Buck Robley was booking Kansas City, Missouri, and pushed him in 1976 and 1977 as Bob Slaughter, with an ex-drill instructor look and attitude. "Him and Paul Ellering, they all came about the same time. You could see in their work that they had something, charisma or something about them, that was willing to help you," Robley said. Extremely agile for a six-foot-five, 300-pounder, Slaughter held the Central States heavyweight championship three times.

Remus was back in Minneapolis, wrestling as the masked Super Destroyer Mark II, and doing home improvement work on the side, when he got to be friends with Pat Patterson. "He was just going through the motions, working here, working there, then we'd go play golf. He was just an easygoing guy; he didn't think he was going to get anywhere," Patterson said. When Patterson headed to New York, Remus showed him a picture of the Sgt. Slaughter character — he'd first used the name in Georgia in 1977 — and asked him to give it to WWWF owner Vincent J. McMahon, who loved the idea. "Bob was pretty deadpan at first," said Gagne's son Greg, a top AWA star. "He really found himself when he became Sgt. Slaughter. It was something he believed in and fans pick up on that. It fit him and he found himself." Starting in 1980, he became one of the federation's top meanies, offering $5,000 to anyone who could break his cobra clutch. His April 1981 alley fight with Patterson at Madison Square Garden remains the standard for early-WWE hardcore matches, winning Match of the Year honors from the *Wrestling Observer Newsletter*. "I imagine that the reason that we don't see that match as often as we should is there was too much blood," Patterson said. "It just happened."

Ole Anderson brought him to the Mid-Atlantic in the late summer of 1981, where Slaughter cracked the whip on a pair of underling privates, Don Kernodle and Boris Zhukov (Jim Nelson). Just to make sure his recruits had the same experience he did, Slaughter sent Zhukov to the video store to rent *The DI*. "We practiced and studied a lot off *The DI*. We'd react to him and we'd rehearse stuff. He was into the character and he got me into it too," Zhukov said. His colleagues have similar stories about his inventiveness. As DI Bob Slaughter in Central States, he coaxed his opponents into calling him "Gomer," after the *Gomer Pyle, U.S.M.C.* TV series, and then recoiled in mock horror when crowds picked up on the chant. He got a Cadillac and covered it in camouflage. With Kernodle, Slaughter laid out the entire program for a red-hot tag team feud with Ricky Steamboat and Jay Youngblood in 1982 and 1983, although Jim Crockett Promotions threw cold water on one vision. "We had an idea to have two young, beautiful girls come out in camouflage hot pants and they were going to be Sgt. Slaughter and his privates, beautiful girls like they do now," Kernodle said. "But they didn't want to spend the money."

Slaughter returned to the WWE in spring 1983, and started a feud with The Iron Sheik the following January that moved him from black hat to white hat in record time. It culminated in a boot camp match in Madison Square Garden, and fans lapped it up when Slaughter led the audience in the Pledge of Allegiance. "I drive around in a camouflage car and the fans used to tear it up because they hated me," he said at the time. "Now they tear it up for souvenirs." By December, though, he was out of the federation and back in the AWA after fighting with McMahon about licensing and endorsement rights. From a publicity standpoint, the split was for the best. "I couldn't be with G.I. Joe and WWE, so I tried something different and I was still wrestling for the AWA and Verne Gagne. He allowed me to promote G.I. Joe on his show, and it was a great time. The promotion was that you can't buy Sgt. Slaughter, you had to earn him. You had to call in a number and send in proofs of purchases."

Larry Zbyszko, an opponent in the AWA, said Slaughter came along at just the right moment, when bitter memories of Vietnam were fading and military service was less stigmatized. "By the mid-'80s, after all the *Rambo* movies, and the G.I. Joe, becoming a soldier became a popular thing," he said. "Sgt. Slaughter was over because of the way he looked, because of the way that America now saw its fighting guys. And he looked like a Marine with that big jaw sticking out. It was easy to get in the ring with Slaughter and have a great reaction because the people wanted it that way; they accepted him."

His return to the WWE in 1990 culminated in controversy, when Slaughter allied himself with Iraq at the time of Desert Storm as the buildup to an exploitative "Superstars and Stripes Forever" main event against Hulk Hogan at WrestleMania VII. Years later, he lamented, "We decided to bring Sgt. Slaughter back as an Iraqi sympathizer to get the American soldiers off their butts and start thinking about kicking butt. Then the war escalated. The only regret I have is if I had [offended] anyone who lost a loved one in that war. It was only meant to be good guy versus bad guy. It was all entertainment and business."

Sadly, the line between image and reality became blurred in August 2009, when Slaughter's nephew, Army Ranger Cpl. Benjamin S. Kopp, was killed by gunfire in Afghanistan. "Now," he said, following a funeral at Arlington National Cemetery, "Ben is my hero." In recent years, Sarge has been an ambassador for WWE, attending charity events and representing the company in public; he's met six U.S. presidents along the way. "It's a title that I think is better than being a world champion or whatever it is, to go out and promote the product, the television shows, and the WWE itself."

JIMMY "SUPERFLY" SNUKA

It all comes down to footwear. When Jimmy Snuka wore boots, he was a bad guy. When he was barefoot, he was a good guy. "I don't like to wear shoes anyway," he joked. Forget what he might be wearing; what people remember about "The Superfly" is the flying.

The word innovative gets thrown around way too much, but in Snuka's case, there is legitimacy to it. His athletic moves and superfly splash from the top turnbuckle every night in the '70s and '80s were a forerunner of the flippity-flop style that took over in the 1990s. "Well, I guess I created it all for them, brutha, you know and I love it," Snuka said. "I love it because I guess I'm a role model, you know, and everyone wants to follow you."

By the same token, a lot of things have been mythologized

COURTESY OF SCOTT TEAL/CROWBAR PRESS

The always personable Jimmy Snuka.

about the six-foot, 250-pound Snuka, including his dives from the top of the steel cage. But as much attention as the leap in Madison Square Garden in June 1983 on Don Muraco (after he'd lost the bout) might have got, in part from Mick Foley writing and always talking about it, Snuka did the same move around the horn in various cities.

Even his origin stories and wrestling beginnings have been told with so much hyperbole that a coconut is needed to smash away the bunk.

He was born James Reiher (since legally changed to Snuka) on May 18, 1943, on the island of Fiji. Though he has claimed to be a fire dancer and a cliff diver in Fiji, and that baseball got him to Hawaii, in reality his family migrated first to the Marshall Islands, then to Hawaii when he was eleven years old. Attending school for the first time, he struggled in his new home, entertaining tourists at the Polynesian Cultural Centre with his fire and knife dances and falling into the bodybuilding culture. While training for competitions, such as Mr. Hawaiian Island and Mr. Waikiki, and playing rugby, he met a lot of the wrestlers in Dean Higuchi's gym, known at various times as Dean's Gym, the Power House, and the Health Studio of Hawaii.

Cowboy Frankie Laine was one of the wrestlers who befriended Snuka in the gym. "I looked at him. Holy mackerel, what a body he had on him. He was always to himself. I got to know him a little bit. I started talking to him about it and convinced him to give it a try," said Laine. "So we had the ring set up always at the arena in Honolulu. We started going down there to teach him some moves."

It was Laine who called Don Owen in Portland, Oregon, and convinced the promoter to give a newcomer a try, sight unseen. Snuka, working as Big Snuka, was an instant success in April 1971. Recognizing that having the rookie in the ring too soon would be a negative, Snuka instead was captured doing feats of strength, Fijian dances, or tricks like opening pop bottles with his teeth or arm wrestling over a burning candle. His headbutt got over thanks to Laine smashing a cement block over Snuka's head with a sledgehammer.

He made a big impression on the Pacific Northwest, including future wrestler Princess Victoria (Vicki Otis). "I've still got the autograph Jimmy Snuka gave me when I was nine years old. I have an autographed picture of him in his tight blue trunks he used to wear, with the shell headdress," she said. "He was my hero. He was a flyer, he was exciting, and he was sweet to the kids. Jimmy never walked away from that ring without signing autographs. And, of course, he was a babyface."

"By the time I got to Portland I was really ready. Frankie told Don Owen about me — I started going in and out, coming back to Portland. He was very sweet to me," recalled Snuka. "It used to rain up there — and the snow, my goodness. Me, I'm not a snowman, you know. I like the summer. But it was okay. It was a lot of fun, brutha. It was nice to see different parts of the world. This business took me places I never even dreamed about."

Indeed, Snuka would return to Portland and Hawaii throughout his career, an odyssey that included the AWA, San Francisco, Texas, the Carolinas, Atlanta, New York, and Japan, before hitting the heights of stardom as the second-most over babyface after Hulk Hogan in the WWF at the first WrestleMania in 1985.

Fans only familiar with his WWF days missed Snuka in his prime. In Portland, Snuka was a rising star, said his veteran tag team partner Dutch Savage. "We would make the heels look like seven million dollars. That way, when we made our comebacks, they were wild and furious. Jimmy could sell rugs to an Egyptian."

In the Mid-Atlantic territory, Snuka's wild-eyed Islander look got over huge, whether a good guy or a bad one. In 1979, he took on "Nature Boy" Buddy Rogers as his manager, before Gene Anderson bought Snuka's contract; Rogers would return to Snuka's side in the WWWF. He held the U.S. singles title, feuding with Ric Flair and Ricky Steamboat, and the territory's tag titles with Paul Orndorff and then Ray Stevens.

At his peak in 1983, Snuka was one of the most popular wrestlers in the world, and that was before the WWF global juggernaut had really begun to get rolling. Much of the success can be attributed to the coconut.

Piper's Pit, hosted by Roddy Piper, was in its early stages, and Hot Rod was given a brown paper bag with bananas, pineapples, and coconuts in it before having Snuka on a segment. "I'm with Snuka, and 'Here's a banana for your Fijian climbing trees, here's a pineapple for you, so you eat at the luau,'" recalled Piper. "I get to the coconut. I drop it on the table. I look at Jimmy like, 'Are you sure about this?' I dropped another one. Then I asked myself the dumbest question I ever asked myself, 'Does Jimmy know how heavy a coconut is?' He's from Fiji, Rod! Brother, like Nolan Ryan, I wailed back and I just nailed him and it just exploded. Jimmy has never been the same."

The Snuka–Piper feud was a large part of the underlying excitement for the main event of the first WrestleMania, where Superfly was in the corner as Hulk Hogan and Mr. T battled Piper and Paul Orndorff, with Bob Orton Jr. in their corner.

In and out of the WWF/WWE throughout the decades, Snuka carved such a legacy that he was brought back, at age sixty-four, to team with Steamboat and Piper against Chris Jericho in a legends match at WrestleMania XXV.

As the years passed by, Snuka would wrestle fathers and sons, like the Ortons, and, at the shows, would be meeting the children — and grandchildren — of his fans. Two of his own children took to the ring as well, with his son, Sim, working in the WWE as Deuce, and his daughter as WWE Diva Tamina.

Though his Superfly Splash is a sad second-rope spectacle now, he doesn't see a time when he'll give up performing. "Anytime they call, and they want the Superfly to meet the people, meet the kids, whatever, that's my trademark, and that's what I do, brutha."

Yet for all the good words Snuka may say, there is still a dark side to him that has never been properly explored — and probably never will be. He struggled with a recreational drug problem for much of his career. Snuka has also had brushes with the law, including a February 1983 incident outside Syracuse, New York, where it took nine sheriff's deputies and two police dogs to drag Snuka — still in his underwear — from his hotel room, after a fight with his girlfriend, Nancy Argentino. On May 10 of that year, Argentino was found gasping for air hours after Snuka's matches in Allentown, Pennsylvania, and died that night; he was never charged with a wrongdoing, but an investigation by Irv Muchnick found that the Lehigh County Coroner Wayne Snyder "immediately suspected foul play" and notified the district attorney.

Still, there is no denying Snuka's iconic status. He entered the WWE Hall of Fame in 1996, and in 2012, was accepted into the Pro Wrestling Hall of Fame. Ankle surgery in early 2012 resulted in an campaign to get fans to kick in towards the cost.

STING

Do you remember the famed heel turn of Sting on Hulk Hogan? The one where Hogan was in the ring, wearing his traditional, heroic, red and yellow garb, and the bad guys had beaten him down. Then Sting came to the rescue with his baseball bat only to switch sides. Oh, you don't remember? Well, it happened. But it didn't go down as planned.

"I came in and chased off all the heels, helped him up to his feet, and then whacked him with my baseball bat. That was going to be the beginning of my switch to heel. They cheered me for doing it. Then on the TVs and every other town that we went to after that, they still cheered me. It just didn't work," Sting recalled. The storyline was quickly rewritten. "I remember Eric Bischoff saying one time, 'If we do something like that, we'll just shoot ourselves in the foot. We have no reason to do that. If the wheel's not broken, don't try to fix it.' I think that's actually a pretty good rule of thumb."

Whether it was in his flat-topped, neon-outfitted gimmick from 1986 to 1995, or in his black trenchcoat with dark, messy hair, Sting has always been on the right side of the fence. Or in the words of Father James Mitchell, "Sting comes on like he's the ultimate purveyor of grace and goodness in the world."

Born March 20, 1959, Steve Borden grew into a six-foot-two, 260-pound musclehead in Venice Beach, California. His physique caught the eye of Red Bastien, who was training wrestlers with Bill Anderson and Rick Bassman. Bastien envisioned a foursome of hulking behemoths — Powerteam U.S.A. — that would dominate pro wrestling. Of the quartet (Borden, Jim Hellwig, Mark Miller and Garland Donohoe), only Borden ("Rock") and Hellwig ("Flash") had the desire to stick with it, and were remodeled into a raw team known as the Blade Runners in the low-paying Memphis promotion.

"When I started my wrestling career, at the very beginning I was a babyface, and I didn't have a clue," Sting admitted. "We were so bad that [promoter] Jerry Jarrett had to switch us heel. We were bad even being heels, so he had to get rid of us." They went to Bill Watts' UWF promotion, where Hellwig bailed — eventually to become the Ultimate Warrior — and Borden became Sting. "I saw something good in Sting," wrote Watts in his autobiography. "He was very nervous and tentative."

When the UWF was bought up by Jim Crockett Promotions, the booker for the NWA, Dusty Rhodes, made sure the incoming talent put over his established boys. Sting

HOWARD BAUM

WCW world champion Sting makes the rounds at ringside.

was the one that stood out, and Rhodes started the build for a future world champ, winning a Lethal Lottery and the right to face Flair. "So Sting is really coming into his own right there," Rhodes said on the *Secrets of the Ring* DVD. "He was big, he was The Franchise, he was The Guy. I'd decided that before the Gary Justers, the Jim Herds, and those guys got into power. That was going to happen, they couldn't stop him . . . He got himself over, let's put it that way, to the point that you weren't going to keep him down."

The match that made Sting a true headliner in everyone's eyes came on March 27, 1988, at the first Clash of the Champions special on TBS, airing to compete with WrestleMania. Ric Flair, the NWA world champion, battled Sting to a forty-five-minute draw. Yet the chase had to continue, with storyline twist after storyline twist until July 7, 1990, when Sting finally beat Flair for the title.

He would only hold the prestigious belt until January 1991. "I think it was hard as a babyface. At that time, Vince McMahon was the only one that was

Another foe falls victim to Sting's Scorpion Deathlock.

able to push a babyface in that role, and it was Hulk Hogan, then the Ultimate Warrior," Sting mused. "In WCW for years, it was Ric Flair, and the babyfaces chasing the heel. That's just the way it was. I think that the WCW wrestling fan, that's just what they wanted."

There would be a lot more gold for Sting — six WCW world titles total, three with TNA, tag titles, the U.S. belt, and more. But he was always the big fish in the small pond, "The Franchise" for WCW, the sole survivor when so many were jumping for the promised land of the WWF. "We had a lot of guys leaving," he said. "I was the only one that stayed. I remember feeling at one time like I am literally the only guy left."

His heart was indeed with WCW. "He has tried so much to pull this WCW organization together. He wants so much for this company to succeed," said Madusa Miceli in 1993. "He is the needle that is sewing everything together, trying to keep the guys together. He spreads himself so thin . . . He's a real leader. I know the guys look up to him."

Part of the respect came from being such a team player. "I had some legendary matches with Sting. Just a pure athlete," Vader told the *Monday Night Mayhem* radio show. "He could do basically anything I asked him to do. The answer was always yes."

So when WCW started its upward trend in 1996, thanks to the invading New World Order of Kevin Nash and Scott Hall, and the heel turn of Hollywood Hogan, it was natural for the WCW fans and wrestlers to rally behind the one who had been loyal all those years.

But a change was in the wind. Sting had been growing his hair out, and not dyeing it blond. While doing his makeup in the locker room, Hall asked him if he'd seen a recent movie, *The Crow*, with Brandon Lee, son of Bruce Lee. Sting hadn't, and Hall said it would be a good look for him, and would create an Undertaker-like aura. "I was trying to change my image into a more edgy character," Sting confessed in 2000.

The metamorphosis worked, and even though he didn't work a match from September 1996 to December 1997, instead dropping in from the rafters or interfering in matches with his trusty black baseball bat, he was one of the hottest stars in wrestling. "That show was centered on him and his fight against the nWo," said Mitchell. "He's been a very important, influential character in the wrestling business." Sting's return to the ring to claim the WCW world title from Hogan at Starrcade '97 is still the best-selling non-WWE wrestling pay per view in history. After dropping the belt four months later to Randy Savage, Sting was a solid performer for WCW until the company was bought by the WWF in the spring of 2001.

Choosing to stay home rather than take a pay cut and go work for the WWF — with whom he had negotiated off and on over the years — Sting faded from view, resurfacing in 2004 with a book and movie about his life and how Jesus Christ saved him from an addiction to painkiller drugs.

Out of loyalty to the Jarretts, who hired him when no one else would, Sting agreed to join TNA on a part-time basis, working big events and select TV tapings, but not house shows.

He missed the life, if not the travel. "When I was sitting, not sitting at home doing nothing, believe me, because I've been ultra busy, but for five years, it never escapes you, the thoughts of being in the ring, the roar of the crowd, a good storyline, success, WCW becoming the number one wrestling organization in the world and you're a big part of it. I missed it. I did miss that part of it," Sting admitted.

"This is my last run, there's no question about that. I'm not going to try to fool anybody. I don't have all that much left in me, especially with some of these guys out there now and some of the stuff they're doing," he said. "I've had some of the younger guys come up and say, 'Yeah, you're the reason that I'm in wrestling.' Those are moments when you just think, 'Wow. That's intense.'"

When Sting finally does hang up the boots for good, his legacy is secure, said Kurt Angle.

"I will never say he's the greatest. I will never say he's the most popular. I will never say he was the best technician. But he was in the top five in all of those," said Angle. "He has been able to reinvent himself for twenty-five years. He is a great Christian man. Nice, humble, decent. Sting is a real man. He is like a brother, father and the kind of guy you wish your child would grow up to be like."

JIMMY VALIANT

His career was neatly bisected into two parts, and so was his life. There was the good Jimmy Valiant and the bad Jimmy Valiant in the ring, and there was the good Jimmy Valiant and the bad Jimmy Valiant outside of the ring. The bad Jimmy Valiant had booze, cocaine, and conceit on his side. The good Jimmy Valiant had legions of hysterical fans, plus an angel — his wife Angel, whom he credits with helping him shed his demons. Valiant met her at an autograph signing in southwest Virginia in April 1991 and proposed on the spot. She was a little harder to get than that, but not by much. They were married that August. "Brother, it's like one of those cowboy movies with Roy Rogers and Dale Evans riding off into the sunset," he said. "Couldn't have imagined it would turn out like this."

Seldom have two wrestling characters been such polar opposites. "Handsome"

Jimmy Valiant was one of wrestling's most bloodthirsty heels of the 1970s, teaming with wrestling brother Johnny in a mega-hot tag duo, and generally making life miserable for Jerry Lawler in Tennessee. When he became the "Boogie Woogie Man" in the Mid-Atlantic promotion in 1981, he was full of wondrous, over-the-top merriment, sporting the longest beard in the business, waving and dancing, kissing every girl in the arena — slim, heavyset, or otherwise — and smooching ringside announcers. The interesting thing is that Valiant said he stuck to his same arsenal and still told little white lies in the ring, but now the fans accepted it. "I never changed my style,"

COURTESY OF SCOTT TEAL/CROWBAR PRESS

Two of the most dominant personalities of the 1980s were "The American Dream" Dusty Rhodes and "The Boogie Woogie Man" Jimmy Valiant.

he said. "I'd grab someone — Bruiser could, Crusher could too, because we were character babyfaces. We could take a chair and hit the guy, pull his hair. The guy'd say, 'Hey, he pulled my hair.' The ref would ask if we pulled his hair and me and or Bruiser or Crusher, we wouldn't even say no. We'd say, 'Heck, ask the people.' And they'd say no; they'd lie for you."

In 1983, Gary Hart brought Kabuki to the Carolinas, and he knew exactly who he wanted to work with. Kabuki blew his famous mist — actually Kool-Aid — in Valiant's eyes, using a different color every night. "I looked like a rainbow, brother," Valiant laughed twenty-five years later. "You couldn't shampoo that junk out." For a year, they were off to the races. Reflecting on the feud before he died in 2008, Hart called it the easiest money he ever made. "Pandemonium from the time the match starts till it ended . . . A lot of guys like [Ric] Flair, he would say, 'Let's put something between Kabuki and the Boogie Woogie Boy before I go on,' because it was hard to follow Jimmy Valiant. I mean, he was really over in the Carolinas as well as anyone who had ever been there."

Boogie was not a master of a thousand and one holds; he was not the thinking man's wrestler, and he never pretended to be. He was a crowd pleaser, a character babyface who kept it light. In the middle of the feud with Kabuki, Valiant lost a loser-leaves-town match, only to re-emerge under a black bank robber's mask as Valiant's buddy Charlie Brown from "outta town," an idea cooked up by booker Dusty Rhodes. Corny? Of course. Effective? Woo, mercy daddy, was it ever! "What he would do is in the middle of the match, he would make a big strong comeback on Kabuki and I and put us both down, and then he would look to the people and pull up the mask and then he would wave and pull it back down. Every night he would do that, the building would just blow," Hart said.

ROSE DIAMOND

Jimmy Valiant with his Angel.

Valiant was born James Fanning on August 6, 1942, in Tullahoma, Tennessee, and raised in Hammond, Indiana. He was mostly into football and bodybuilding, and got into wrestling when he was working at a health club in Calumet City, Illinois, for old pro Frank Zela, a.k.a. Boris Volkoff. Former world champ Bobby Managoff was at the club as a masseur and served as a mentor. "Great guy. We'd just talk about wrestling, about tying up. Bobby was so easy and so laid back, so helpful not only to me but to other people that wanted that knowledge about wrestling," Valiant said.

For about five years, he was a good-looking, clean-cut fan favorite, best known as Big John Valen, a steroid creation; Valiant said daily doses of dianabol helped him load up to 290 pounds. Fritz Von Erich gave him the Valiant name in 1969 in Texas to differentiate him from Johnny Valentine. His big break came a year later when he headed to New York. Owner Vincent J. McMahon okayed a turn on tag team partner Chief Jay Strongbow that formalized Valiant's status as a heel. "I went from making five hundred to fifteen hundred a week, which was unreal money to me, overnight everything happened that fast," he said. As a singles competitor, Valiant was too entertaining to be a villain, even when he crashed a guitar over Lawler's head a few years later during an angle in Memphis. He ended up replacing Lawler as top babyface in the promotion when "The King" was out of action with a busted leg. Upon entering the Carolinas in 1981, "Handsome" tagged off to the "Boogie Woogie Man." Owner Jim Crockett and booker Ole Anderson wanted him to change his name because there was a surfeit of obnoxious bleached blonds in the neighborhood, with Ric Flair leading the pack. How about Boogie Woogie, Valiant blurted, for no particular reason. "Ole said, 'Can you grow a beard?' and I said, 'Yeah.' He said, 'Grow it away, man.' Together, we put that thing together honestly in like a twenty-minute meeting." Valiant wanted an entrance song; he'd done big business in Memphis with "Son of a Gypsy," produced by Gary Hart. He suggested "Boy From New York City" by Manhattan Transfer, and got a vacant stare from the un-hip Anderson, who ultimately went along with the music.

Boogie debuted at the city armory in Lynchburg, Virginia, against Ivan Koloff. In his new guise, he announced he was from Lynchburg, and told his admirers that, in fact, Grandma Valiant still lived there. When he arrived at about 6 p.m., he saw what he had wrought. "It exploded. [Office agent] Sandy Scott was there and he said, 'Oh my God, I've never seen this.' The line went all around the building and it sold out. Boom! It clicked right away." As it turned out, Grandma Valiant had enough homes in the territory to start her own real estate brokerage, and Boogie zealots were in all of them. True story: one night at a Fredericksburg, Virginia, area high school, Valiant had forgotten his "Old Lady," a two-by-four he used to guard his back when no one else would. The school's athletic director dug into the supply closet and lent him a girls' softball bat, which he used to great effect before returning it after the match. As the AD left the locker room, an overalls-clad fan studied him and finally asked, "Is that Jimmy Valiant's 'Old Lady?'" The athletic director thought for a few seconds and decided, "Why, yes it is." The fan's response was immediate: "I'll give you $100 for it." The bat and the C-note quickly exchanged hands.

Valiant said the character worked because he is more Boogie than Handsome. "As a heel, I never let people get that close to me so they never knew. But as Boogie Woogie, you can't act crazy, you can't be nuts, you can't be real loud. I'm really easy and laid back." Sir Oliver Humperdink called Valiant and Rhodes the best babyfaces he ever worked with, saying Boogie was so unique that he didn't have to abide by wrestling's norms. "Boogie would never sell to any extent, he would just dance slower and slower," Humperdink told the Mid-Atlantic Gateway in 2005. "You'd start working on him, and he'd go down on that one knee and he'd do that little shaking thing. You know, he'd never really sell . . . Then when it was time for him to come back, he'd do that crazy stuff and the people would be going absolutely nuts."

Rocky Johnson held the Southern tag team championship with Valiant in Tennessee in 1980. He wasn't high on Valiant's give and take in the ring, saying he took more than his share of a match. But he was one of the most unusual characters the "Soulman" met. "He's from Mars. Or he believes he is," Johnson said. "He's goofy, he's nice, he's for real." Dave Brown, who called Memphis wrestling with Lance Russell for more than two decades, still shakes his head at the way Valiant transformed right in front of his eyes. "I was always amazed to watch him in the back because Jimmy was so quiet and mild-mannered. But when he came through that dressing room door, he just exploded, 'Wooo, baby, Handsome Jimbo from Mempho!' He used to call Lance 'Lancer,' and at the time Jackson Browne was hot, so he called me 'Jack-son.'" At one point, desperate for Valiant to stay in Memphis, owners Jerry Jarrett and Lawler bought him a house. That lasted six weeks. One day, Jarrett found a handwritten note. "Love you, brother, gotta go." Jarrett said he and Lawler were fortunate to unload the house, which Valiant and then wife Big Mama had decorated in all black. "Jimmy is part aborigine and he had wanderlust," Jarrett joked.

The wandering part ended when he met Angel. Valiant still runs his Boogie Wrestling Camp every Sunday afternoon, a ritual at a little gym on his property tucked away in the foothills of the Blue Ridge Mountains south of Roanoke, Virginia. He'll ride with his workers to places as far away as Mississippi and Arkansas, and then travel all night to be back in time for camp. "I'll always be a goodwill ambassador. You never hear me say anything bad about it. I'm not bitter. I love the business. I love those young kids. I see a young kid and I try to help him. I'll always be involved because I've got BWC."

KERRY VON ERICH

Bill Colville can still hear the calls: "Do you want to go feel good?"

He'd parlayed his deep friendship with the family into a role as bodyguard/caretaker to the Von Erich boys at the height of their early '80s fame. As such, he saw all the drugs, the partying, and the blind adoration.

He saw things no one else did.

"Do you want to go feel good?" was Kerry Von Erich's codespeak for an unscheduled visit to the children's ward at a local hospital. No media, no agenda, just him and Colville using Kerry's fame to do a world of good. "We didn't tell anybody we were going . . . no cameras, no nothing," said Colville. "On more than one occasion, I saw Kerry stop in waiting rooms, where parents had children in surgery, and Kerry would actually get on his knees and pray with them — and sit there, through the surgery, until they came out. Just whatever moved him, where he felt like he could help somebody, he did it."

Kerry Von Erich receives some roses before his bout.

It's a rare positive story about the Von Erich Dynasty, one of wrestling's most infamous tales of fame, excess, and tragedy. Even family loyalists, such as "Cowboy" Johnny Mantell, a World Class Championship Wrestling mainstay, will admit the bad outweighs the good. "The family sort of put themselves in a position where there are probably more negatives now than there are positives."

With his long, curly hair, Adonis-like physique, and shy smile, Kerry Von Erich far outreached the fame of his brothers, David and Kevin, who were better athletes and in-ring workers, and Mike and Chris, who were put in the impossible position of trying to fill the shoes of their much older siblings. World Class was an early pioneer in syndication, reaching markets outside Texas with its first-class television production and popular music, and further — a 1985 tour of Israel required the Israeli army to escort the World Class crew everywhere.

Kerry's time on ESPN with the AWA, and his two-year run in the WWF as The Texas Tornado, which began in July 1990, brought him to a whole new audience, claiming the Intercontinental championship, and working on major events such as WrestleMania and SummerSlam and the *Saturday Night's Main Event* broadcasts on NBC.

Remarkably, little was ever made of his skills wrestling with just one foot, his right foot having been amputated as a result of a motorcycle accident in 1986, and kept secret for years until the summer of 1988, when in an AWA match with Colonel DeBeers, his boot came off. Laughable denials tried to keep kayfabe, and the WWF even took the USWA/AWA to court in Illinois in an attempt to keep Von Erich from wrestling Jerry Lawler on a pay per view, citing an antiquated law prohibiting boxers and wrestlers with only one limb from competing.

Kerry Gene Adkisson was born February 3, 1960, in Niagara Falls, New York, where his father, Fritz Von Erich (Jack Adkisson) was a star villain. When Fritz bought the Dallas-based wrestling promotion, the family settled outside of town. In high school, Kerry took to bodybuilding and football, and, like his father, excelled at the discus throw, taking both the state and junior national championships as a senior; in college, he managed a throw of 178 feet. Though the family mythologized his discus talents as Olympic-caliber, the fact is that it wasn't at that point, and there was never any doubt that he was going to follow into the family business. David and Kevin had started wrestling months apart in 1977, and the six-foot-three, 260-pound Kerry debuted on Thanksgiving weekend in 1978, taking advantage of a college break from the University of Houston, where he had a football and track scholarship, and would be working full-time by the summer of 1979, when he dropped out of school.

Though the Von Erich boys may have been pressured to get into wrestling by their forceful father, he was not booking their matches, protecting them and making them stars; instead he was concentrating more on the family's cattle business and real estate holdings. The job of making the Von Erichs stars fell to the likes of bookers Gary Hart or Ken Mantell, and office workers like Bronko Lubich.

In 2008, shortly before his death, Hart talked about the Von Erichs and the reasons for their success. "Number one, they were great athletes. Number two, they had fantastic physiques and, number three, not one time did they ever say my dad's the boss, you've got to do what I want to do. Never. They were first class kids who listened and paid attention. These were good kids. The rumors and the stories about them are not true. It was a combination of things, young good-looking kids that followed their father and became bigger than Fritz had ever been. They followed him big time and they're the ones that popped the territory. Fritz, you could get a house with him once every two or three weeks. With the boys, you could get a big house with them every week. They were

Kerry Von Erich winds up to punch NWA world champion Ric Flair during their famous May 1984 bout at Texas Stadium.

great kids, easy to work with, easy to develop, and do anything in the world to make the match work."

Hart was very careful to pick who would work with the Von Erichs, however. Bill Irwin was one of the chosen few. "They were all very good in the ring. You had to work with them. They were strong, they weren't going to back down, they weren't going to just die on you. They were going to fight," said Irwin. "You had a little bit of a fight with them to get them down and get them to sell because they were always coming back. But they were fine. They didn't have problems if you were calling a spot or something."

A babyface as well, Mantell only worked with Kerry on one occasion, in a tournament for the Texas heavyweight title vacated when Gino Hernandez died. "Kerry had a lot of charisma, there's no question about that. He had a lot of good points to him. But you've got to remember that the entire time that the Von Erichs were on top here in Dallas and hot, and I'm talking really '81, '82, '83, '84, a little bit '85, when they were on top and hot, it was because of the people they were with in the ring, because they had to be led," Mantell said.

That went for outside the ring, said World Class announcer Bill Mercer. "If we had to plan an interview with him, between bouts or something, we'd go over the questions and the answers. He'd come out to the ring and he and I would go over them again before we went on TV, before we taped it. It was just one of those things, he couldn't remember things very well."

The pinnacle of Kerry Von Erich's career came as a result of tragedy, when David died in Japan on February 10, 1984, at the age of twenty-five.

Stepping into his brother's spot, Kerry would defeat Ric Flair for the NWA world title on May 6, 1984, at the first David Von Erich Memorial Show at the Cotton Bowl in Dallas, with a gate of $402,000, which was the second-largest gate in pro wrestling history at the time. "Little did any of the 32,123 fans, wrestlers, Kerry, or Jack himself realize that single moment, at which point they were on top of the world and their future under the 100 degree Texas sun seemingly would burn bright forever as the premiere family and promotion in the world, that this was actually the beginning of the end," wrote Dave Meltzer in the *Wrestling Observer* following Kerry's gunshot suicide on the family's Denton ranch on February 18, 1993, as he faced jail time for prescription forgery.

"Kerry Von Erich was one of the most gifted athletes of all time and had a career that was second to none," said Flair. "But he was on drugs, and his father failed miserably to understand the problem. And that's why he's gone. His dad was in denial. I blame everything on his dad. It was a very sad case. But he was a gifted athlete." Flair concurred that Kerry had to be led. "Are you kidding? He showed up with his boots unlaced for an hour broadway. But I loved Kerry to death, and it is what it is. But he was a really nice kid."

For those who knew him best, like Colville, who was a pallbearer at Kerry's funeral, a frequent trigger to the past is the Rush epic "Tom Sawyer," with its line about "The Modern Day Warrior," which would become Kerry's nickname. "I can't even listen to it," confessed Colville. "I probably took Kerry to the ring 2,000 times to that song over the years."

ANTI-HEROES

BRUISER BRODY

"Not only do you have to know how to kick people around, you have to know how and when to put your name on the paper," said Frank Goodish in 1985, neatly summing up an anti-authoritarian career where his Bruiser Brody persona fought with promoters over each and every penny almost as often as it did the foes he dwarfed in the ring.

Wrestling's greatest anti-hero and independent contractor, there's something about Brody that still resonates with today's fans almost twenty-five years since his murder in a Puerto Rican dressing room in July 1988. He's been the subject of two books, retro figures have been released, and his name is constantly brought up in discussions about the greatest of all time — *Wrestling Observer Newsletter* Hall of Fame (Class of 1996); #14 on the *Pro Wrestling Illustrated* list of the 500 best singles wrestlers of the "PWI Years" in 2003; #18 in John Molinaro's *Top 100 Pro Wrestlers of All Time*.

Why does Brody still matter? "There's nobody like him today. There could be nobody like him today, it's a different world," said Dave Meltzer of the *Wrestling Observer*. Brody couldn't be Brody in the modern world of wrestling. "Making money doing indies, difficult. Japan isn't Japan anymore. You can't go back and forth, everyone's got a contract. With him, he was comforted by the idea that no matter what he did, there would always be a place for him — because there were so many places. Now, nobody has that luxury."

In a rare, candid States-side interview, circa 1986, Goodish justified all the trips to the little one-horse towns, bringing his wild, unpredictable act to those who otherwise would have just seen him on TV and read about him in the wrestling magazines. "I wrestled in Madison Square Garden; I know that feeling. I

Bruiser Brody, ready for winter weather or a brawl.

wrestled in the Boston Garden; I know that feeling. I wrestled in the Cow Palace in San Francisco; I know that feeling. I wrestled in the Forum in Los Angeles; I know that feeling," he said. "When people look at Bruiser Brody on TV they don't get near as emotional as they do sitting there at ringside. So all these people in all these rural communities, if they don't have a chance to go out there and touch Bruiser Brody and see him in person, he's really not at the top of his business. He can only be at the top of his business when he reaches those in New York City, those in Waxahachie, Texas, those in Newville, West Virginia, those in Unionville, Pennsylvania. You can only be at the top when all wrestling fans get to be in touch with you, and that can't be done on TV."

Goodish was born June 18, 1946, in Detroit, and grew into a six-foot-four beast of a man, weighing 263 pounds. A football and basketball star in high school, Goodish briefly attended the University of Iowa as an offensive tackle. "I got into some discipline problems there," said Goodish in 1971. "You don't have to emphasize that, but then I'm not going to attempt to hide it either." He transferred to West Texas State University in Canyon, Texas, near Amarillo, an outlaw, small-college football factory that produced such future wrestling stars as Dory Funk Jr., Terry Funk, Dusty Rhodes, Tito Santana, Tully Blanchard, Bobby Duncum, Scott Casey, Ted DiBiase, and Stan Hansen, who would later become Brody's most successful tag team partner. Brody, however, eventually was kicked out of school for disciplinary reasons. "One thing I like about West Texas State is that they've given a lot of athletes a chance. And I'm very grateful for that."

His pro football career, from 1968 to 1973, was equally tumultuous; he played for the Continental Football League's San Antonio Toros and Fort Worth Braves, serving stints as linebacker on the Washington Redskins' taxi squad, and briefly trying out for the Edmonton Eskimos of the Canadian Football League. "I wanted to stay active so when another club decided to give me a shot in the future, I'd be in shape physically," he summed up in 1971.

In the subsequent years, his football feats grew, both through promotional ballyhoo and his own tellings. The vagabond football life justified the leap to pro wrestling, his part-time gig as a small-time Texas sportswriter never gaining much traction. "When I signed my first contract with the Redskins in 1968, it was for the minimum base salary of $14,500," he said. "A beginning wrestler, by comparison, could make from twenty to fifty thousand dollars in his first year. A guy who's been in the business say for ten years could make from twenty to one hundred thousand dollars and a guy who's been around for fifteen to twenty years could make from twenty to two hundred thousand dollars. Potentially, a guy could make a lot of money depending on what kind of businessman he is."

Having been pushed by Ivan Putski to seek out San Antonio's promoter Joe Blanchard for wrestling work, Goodish would debut under his real name in late

1973. In the Mid-South territory, he was teamed with another refugee of the Continental Football League, Stan Hansen. The heel team was too good to last, said promoter Bill Watts. "I broke them up as a team. They got so mad, they gave me their notice. They were holding each other back. I said, 'You guys are going to be phenomenal singles, but you're different, and you guys are a bad influence on each other as a team. I'm breaking you up.'"

Hansen went his way and Goodish his, as the newly renamed Bruiser Brody, his dark hair untamed and unkempt, eyes wide and fearsome, often carrying a chair, chain, or board to the ring to mangle an opponent.

"He wasn't the classic wrestler. What can you say? Kind of a human monster. He was so big and so awesome. His motions when he was angry — feigned anger anyway — were just overpowering the way he scared everybody, going crazy in the ring," recalled announcer Bill Mercer of Dallas, which Brody called home off and on for his whole career. "It's a different appreciation for somebody who was enormous, could handle himself, and probably could never be beaten, except illegally."

Brody quickly gained a reputation for saying what he thought, and was unafraid to walk out on a show if he thought the business end of things wasn't on the up and up.

He had formed his impression of promoters early, said Johnny Mantell, who rode with Brody through Louisiana early in his career. "He said, 'Man, you're a real wrestler, you're real in the ring. What you do is good. Everything you do is the right thing to do. Don't ever let a promoter embarrass you or do something that does not fit your person. Respect yourself and respect this business, and it'll always respect you,'" recalled Mantell.

Whether he was fighting Bruno Sammartino in the WWWF, the Funks in Texas, or Abdullah the Butcher across the globe, Brody was a box office draw, always working the same violent style, no matter if he was clocking a heel with a chair or carving open the forehead of a hero.

"He had an air about him that got him over almost everywhere he went. On the other hand, he took advantage of that attitude, too. If you were in the ring with him, if you didn't have the guts to cut him off, he'd just eat you alive," said former NWA world champion Harley Race, who had a piece of the promotion in Kansas City.

"He was so intimidating he just scared me to death," said Ric Flair. "I probably wrestled him in twenty-five or thirty-hour broadways. He was always in phenomenal shape. He let me hit him as hard as I could. He never complained

Brody replaces Abdullah the Butcher's head with a trash can.

at all." Yet Flair knew that Brody was always looking out for Brody as well. "I always said that if he ever had a problem, talk to the promoter," Flair added. "Talk to Bob Geigel or talk to Harley. 'I'm just here to wrestle you and do whatever you want to do.' But he was great to work with. I thought he was a wonderful guy. I wrestled him at Budokan for an hour. We had a great match, but he was so over over there, that when I held him down, I said, 'Just trust me, let me hold you down.' Where I respected him the most was that he trusted my decisions."

In Japan, Brody was revered. "Brody made a living working in Japan," noted Emerson Murray, author of *Bruiser Brody*, a book comprised of interviews with people who knew Goodish. "He made enough money for his family to live comfortably. The work he did in the United States was extra. He drove promoters insane because they were so used to wrestlers that needed their work no matter how paltry. Brody would come along and his name would ensure big money at the gate, but that promoter had to pay Brody what he promised him or Brody was gone. Brody would also go and tear the house down. If a card was lagging or if Brody was wrestling someone he respected, or even if the mood struck him, Brody would hit the ring, put on a show, take it to the floor, and just tear the place apart. The blood would flow, the chairs would all get thrown and knocked over, the fans would be running, screaming."

Meltzer saw first-hand what Brody meant in Japan and came away with a new appreciation. "I thought when it came to Japan, he was a really brilliant worker. He knew his character, he played his character, he was absolutely sensational at his character. I was at many, many live shows with him, and he was Bruiser Brody," said Meltzer. "I was there live, and I talked to the guys he was in the ring with, and everyone would say the same thing — that he was actually sensational. He knew exactly what to do, when to do it, how to do it, when to work stiff, when to work not so stiff." Brody was an expert at knowing when to throw a stiff kick, catching the audience off-guard and making believers of his act.

His feuds with promoters were no show, though. Watts never used him again, having heard stories of his colleagues getting burned. "His word was no good. Frank became a liar. The only thing that you have basically in this business is your word, and if you give your word to somebody that you're going to show up and work a match, then you should." Brody would arrive at the arena, walk around, checking out the attendance and letting the fans see that he was there, and then hold up the promoter for a different deal. Should he wrestle but not be happy, he would hold a headlock for excruciatingly long periods or, conversely, be in and out in a flash.

With wrestling companies folding up in the mid-'80s, Brody would head to Puerto Rico on a regular basis. Larry Sharpe was his manager in Puerto Rico, though he was fired about a week before Brody was knifed. "When he first came to Puerto Rico, I saw him and I said, 'That man's going to get stabbed and killed here,' but I always thought it would be by a fan," said Sharpe. During the final swing of a four-day Puerto Rican tour, the forty-two-year-old Brody was slain on July 17, 1988, in a hot, steamy locker room, at Juan Ramon Loubriel Stadium in the suburb of Bayamon, nine miles from San Juan. Several stab wounds to the stomach punctured his lung and liver, and Jose Gonzales, a.k.a. The Masked Invader, a ring opponent, sometimes partner and booker of the World Wrestling Council promotion, was charged with murder. The alleged murder weapon, a knife, was never recovered by police as it had disappeared from the scene of the crime. Gonzales was acquitted after pleading self-defense, with many of the American wrestlers who were there that evening uninvited or unable to testify at the trial.

Goodish left behind a wife and young son, and one of the most memorable, if rocky, wrestling careers in history.

Yes, he was difficult to deal with, but Murray encourages people to look at it from Brody's side, and his efforts to protect his reputation. "He could have lost a match, but he couldn't let people beat him up. It would have just been ridiculous, and he would have lost all credibility," he said, justifying the battles with promoters. "Nobody else was going to look out for him, so he had to look out for himself."

HOWARD LAPES COLLECTION

Milwaukee's most popular son, The Crusher.

THE CRUSHER

In December 2005, Milwaukee promoter David Herro put on a tribute to The Crusher, who had died of a brain tumor on October 22. Herro said he ran the show to make sure no one forgot The Crusher — as if that was actually possible. "The Crusher is more than just a wrestling icon here in Milwaukee, he is like the father, the grandfather, the pillar of Milwaukee and Milwaukee wrestling," said Herro.

"I'll do this for The Crush," said former AWA world champion Nick Bockwinkel, when previewing his appearance. "I think it's just my respect for one of the legends. Even though he was a gigantic pain in the ass at times, and one of the more difficult people to work with, he still was business and he epitomized the corner saloon and all those good ol' boys in the local neighborhood drinking their beer and telling their stories. With that in mind, he filled arenas, especially in the part of the country where he was most popular."

Herro had a recent story of Reggie Lisowski — The Crusher — in one such bar. It was 2004, shortly before Crusher went in for surgery. "We went out for dinner and to a corner pub for a few drinks," said Herro. "The bar was packed and there were a few obnoxious guys talking stupid and looking even more stupid. Crusher just stood there and watched and watched and watched like he was waiting for someone to act silly toward him. After a few more minutes Crusher looked at [fellow organizer] Jack [Koshick] and myself and told us: 'You know, I ain't never lost a bar fight before.' We quickly decided it was time to go."

In 1977, Crusher, in his gravelly voice, talked about those bar fights during a TV interview on *Wisconsin Sports World*. "There's always gonna be some jerk that had a couple beers, thinks he's a tough guy. Once in a while you've got to whack 'em and knock 'em down. But not really, not too much trouble. Just like you go in a bar sometime, you maybe had it happen to you 'cuz you're a celebrity, and some drunk is sitting there having two or three beers, afraid to go home, he knows his wife's gonna beat him up. Or some punk kid has a couple of beers. So these are the kind of guys you gotta straighten out once in a while. But usually you beat them with one slap in the mouth."

George Lentz, the world's leading authority on all things Crusher, said that his celebrity still lives on in Milwaukee. "The Crusher is still remembered around town. I'd say anyone over the age of thirty definitely remembers him," said Lentz. "You don't hear much about him by happenstance anymore, though. I did hear him mentioned on radio station WKLH a few months back when they were talking about famous Wisconsin feuds. They had people call and email in and I remember one of the morning show hosts saying, 'Here's a good one: The Crusher versus Mad Dog Vachon.' That feud goes back thirty-five to fifty years, so obviously people still recall it."

As for Vachon, he has more than a few scars to remember The Crusher by. "It was unbelievable, the big blow-up between him and I. He almost killed me one time. It was on TV. He banged my head on the metal table," recalled Vachon. "He was not even involved in that match, it was a tag match. [Edouard] Carpentier was one of my opponents, and I forget who the other one was. Anyway, he banged my head. You know those folding banquet tables? They have tin on the side. He banged my head on that, and I had twenty-two stitches. People tell you it's all ketchup. Well, I sprinkled everybody at ringside! When you're wrestling, your heart beats so fast, and it was such a narrow cut. Everybody was full of blood. By the time I got to the hospital, I was almost out of blood." One of the security guards at the studio that day was an off-duty policeman, and he took Mad Dog and his brother Paul "Butcher" Vachon to the hospital, fighting traffic on the way without his cruiser. "I had two hands on the cut, and Paul had two hands on the cut, and the blood was seeping through our fingers." The doctor said that he was lucky to be alive.

This being wrestling, the blood and brush with death only meant good things for business. "We had return match after return match in Minneapolis, Twin Cities, everywhere in the AWA," said Vachon, estimating that together they drew at least $3 million in the various return matches. "We got some of it, but [AWA promoter Verne Gagne] took most of it!" (Vachon attributed part of the success of the matches to the fact that Gagne was on a month-long vacation in Hawaii. Every day, he'd call his assistant Wally Karbo to find out how everything was going. Wally would say that everything was fine, not overselling the success. "He wanted to come back to screw everything up!" said Mad Dog.)

Lisowski was born in 1926 in South Milwaukee. A fullback on the South Milwaukee football team, he got into wrestling overseas. "I started wrestling in Germany where I was stationed with the 1st Infantry in 1944–45," Lisowski told the *Chicago Tribune* 1956. "I had been a weightlifter and had done a little amateur wrestling at the Milwaukee CYO as a kid." In November 1949, he debuted in Milwaukee — "Rettie Lifowski" reads the ad — and initially struggled to balance work and wrestling. "I came up through the saloons. I started wrestling for two dollars a night," he said on *The Making Of* . . . TV program in 1974. "I wrestled in skid row in Denver, where they took up collections. I took on anybody in the saloon in the middle '50s to make myself enough money to eat."

The working man image was no gimmick. "I think working people identify with me because years ago I worked when I wrestled, too," Lisowski told the *Milwaukee Journal* in 1985. "I worked at Ladish, Drop Forge, Cudahy Packing House. I was a bricklayer. But finally, I got away from punching the clock."

"In all my research on The Crusher, the most surprising thing I would say is finding out bits and pieces of his personal life — the death of his infant son, the fact that he played for South Milwaukee in the first Parks League before going into the service," said Lentz. "Once he became The Crusher though, he kept his Reggie Lisowski days very guarded and concentrated on the image he had as Crusher."

The break came in Chicago, where Fred Kohler ruled the roost and had nationwide exposure for his wrestlers through the DuMont Network. Soon, Lisowski was on the road. Knocking out a sportscaster in Albuquerque, New Mexico, with a full nelson, Lisowski made the wires; he had told the crowd, "I can't let go!" during the demonstration, and fans had to pry his fingers apart. "It always happens when I apply that hold," he said. "My fingers just swell up."

Lisowski had great success with Art Neilsen as a partner, and a "brother" was soon to follow. Journeyman Stan Holek knew he'd gotten his own break with the

A young Reggie Lisowski.

pairing. "Well, I knew I was going to make more money than I was making!" he laughed of their three-year pairing, which began in early 1956. "He was pretty knowledgeable about everything. He was sharp. He was a businessman. He knew if he had to speak up, he certainly would. I had a lot of respect for him."

After splitting from Holek in the summer of the 1959, Lisowski made his transformation. He perfected his persona, chomping cigars and drinking beers in publicity shots, changing his name from Crusher Lisowski or Killer Lisowski (supposedly a cousin of Killer Kowalski), to Da Crusher. His training regimen was unorthodox. "I usually find a saloon on one end of town, have a couple of beers, then I run on the other end, have a couple of beers, then I go on the other end, have a couple of beers, so by the time they close I'm in pretty good shape — one way or the other," he said in 1974. At those bars, he'd be dancing the polka with the "dollies" — "I never say a woman is fat. I call 'em the big dollies. Any woman who weighs under 200 pounds is small to me."

No one would ever call The Crusher small. Though just six-foot, he packed 260 or so pounds around his beer belly. His heel days of the 1960s had him with short, cropped hair, and a wide-eyed, menacing growl, leading *Wrestling World* to name him the "Most Feared Wrestler Today" in an April 1964 issue. His epic feuds with Gagne and Vachon resulted in three short AWA world title runs between 1963 and 1966.

While he had formed memorable teams with Neilsen and Holek, and would later win tag titles with Red Bastien, Billy Robinson, Baron Von Raschke, and Tommy Rich, it is with Dick the Bruiser, one William Afflis, that Crusher is most associated. Claiming to be cousins, the look-a-likes won the AWA world tag titles five times and a number of other tag titles as well. "He was a great tag team partner," Bruiser said in *Wrestling Revue* in 1974. "He knew exactly what I was going to do in the ring and I felt the same way about him."

The transition to hero had happened unexpectedly — how 'bout dat? The future Masked Superstar, Bill Eadie, was a Pittsburgh lad who had been conditioned to love Bruno Sammartino but found something else in The Crusher. "He'd come out and do an interview with Iron City [beer] on his shoulder and talk about going to the Polish and the Croatian clubs and dancing with all the ladies. I didn't know he was a bad guy. I just liked him . . . Bruno was the hero but Crusher was over."

With Bruiser settling into promoting the Indianapolis territory, The Crusher entered the 1970s on his own. He'd simplified his wrestling style, dropping the full nelson for stomach claws and the wacky bolo punch, winding up his right hand to deliver an uppercut to his foe, knocking them out. Soon, more comedy spots followed, included eye pokes, his interviews became all about "dem bums" and "turkeynecks," and he coined memorable nicknames for colleagues, like "Jerkwinkel" for Bockwinkel or "Irene" for Bobby Heenan. Pat Patterson laughed at the memories of working with The Crusher in the 1970s. "The people loved him," he said. "He didn't have to do much, they bought him, hey, that's all there is to it."

Though he is best known for his time in the "Crusher Country" of the AWA, The Crusher would still venture out to help Bruiser in the WWA. In late 1979, he even made a brief championship run in Georgia alongside Tommy Rich.

In August 1981, Crusher abruptly stopped wrestling, perhaps due to a dispute over money with Gagne or because he legitimately suffered nerve damage in his right arm during a match with 450-pound Jerry Blackwell. "I was laid up for two years; I just came back," he said in 1985. "All the nerves in my right arm were damaged, I had no strength in it at all. The doctors said I'd never wrestle again. But I started my own therapy, and now, it's pretty much back."

Regardless, when Hulk Hogan jumped to the WWF in December 1983, Gagne mended the fence and The Crusher was called upon to fill Hogan's headlining status in the territory. When Crusher and Baron Von Raschke dropped the AWA world tag titles to the Road Warriors on August 25, 1984, it signaled a transition to a younger, hungrier promotion, and Crusher appeared on AWA shows less and less frequently.

In September 1986, The Crusher took his act to the WWF when they were nearby his Milwaukee home, whether guest ring announcing, managing — usually to counteract Heenan — participating in battle royals, or filling in for the injured Dynamite Kid in the British Bulldogs, or under a mask as Crusher Machine. He even teamed with Hogan to beat King Kong Bundy and Big John Studd in Milwaukee in October 1986. When the WWF *Over the Edge* pay per view came to town in May 1998, The Crusher and Vachon were honored in the ring, leading to Crusher bopping a verbally abusive Jerry Lawler with his plaque.

His fame never left him. There was a Crusher Day on July 31, 1994, in Milwaukee; World Championship Wrestling honored him in 1993; the Cauliflower Alley Club paid tribute in 2000. When he was hospitalized for hip replacement surgery, St. Francis Hospital in Milwaukee had to put a guard on his door to deter admirers. Upon his death, there was a resolution in the Wisconsin Senate paying tribute to what he meant to the state: "Lisowski may have been a villain in the ring but he was a true friend to the people," it read.

DICK THE BRUISER

Ox Baker succinctly summed up the lengthy career of Dick the Bruiser, one of the most memorably violent characters in pro wrestling history. "The Bruiser was the best heel in the business for twenty years, but then he decided to become a babyface, and for the next twenty years, he was the best babyface."

But in no way, shape, or form did William Frederick Afflis, born June 27, 1929, in Delphi, Indiana, ever alter his style. "The world's most dangerous wrestler" was always the same straight-ahead, intense, growling, scowling thug with a mug only a mother could love. And even then, he must have tested the patience of his widowed mother, Margaret, in their Lafayette, Indiana home, as she rose to prominence in the Democratic Party, bailing him out of trouble again and again.

"His style never changed. He didn't sell anything when he was a babyface and he didn't sell anything when he was a heel," explained J.J. Dillon. "So if you were working with Dick the Bruiser, you were going to earn your money that night because if you poked him in the eye or hit him with a low blow, it didn't matter because he'd just turn around and do the same thing back to you."

Dick the Bruiser, a face only a mother could love.

"I've always wrestled the same way. I didn't change," Dick the Bruiser, never one to shy away from a writer or a camera, told the *St. Louis Post-Dispatch* in 1991. "I think the fans changed in the mid-'60s. They started to follow me and like me. I don't know if they were tired of the way the country was going or what."

Dick the Bruiser, with his barrel chest and constant scowl, not only *looked* like a madman who would rip your arms off just for fun, but he *sounded* threatening too. While playing for the Green Bay Packers on both sides of the line (1951–54), Bruiser was struck in the throat and silenced for six months, leaving him with his familiar gravelly voice. "Most guys don't think it's for real, but it is," he told *SPORT Magazine* in 1964. "A lot of them bums, wrestlers, that is, try to copy me. They think I got a perfect voice for a wrestler."

But it was more than the voice. "When you got in there, it was like a cage full of lions or tigers. He was ripping and snorting and everything else," recalled Freddie Blassie in 2003. "Not much wrestling, just the superior man emerged victorious."

It would seem that Afflis was born for the gridiron, but he didn't have the discipline to listen. In Indianapolis, he was constantly getting into trouble, and found some direction working out at Hoffmeister's Bodybuilding Studio, and loved to show off. "Even in mid-winter, he covered his ample chest with no more than a T-shirt two sizes too small," wrote high school friend Bill Libby in the SPORT profile. "When the girls would gather round, Bill would take a deep breath and split the shirt down the middle."

Afflis began football in Indianapolis, but finished his run at Lafayette High, where he made All-State as a guard in his senior year; in wrestling, he dislocated a shoulder. At nearby Purdue, Afflis had been working out with the team as a high school student, but in 1948, he was sent packing when he clobbered the line coach with his helmet. Blink-and-you-miss-it stints followed at Notre Dame ("the midnight curfew beat me in two weeks"), Alabama, and Miami. It turned out that the University of Nevada-Reno was the place for him. Now going by Dick he worked as a casino bouncer at Harold's Club where he vented his frustrations on unruly patrons. "I liked bouncing," Afflis said. "I lasted until I hurt too many stiffs."

A 16th round draft choice, 186th overall, of the pre-Lombardi Green Bay Packers in 1951, the five-foot-eleven, 252-pound Afflis was on the weak squad until 1954, playing offence or defense for forty-eight games, wherever his bruising style of blocking was most needed. "I like football," said Afflis in 1964. "I liked knocking heads. In pro, a lot of guys were as big as me, so it took some technique, too. But wrestling was a better buck."

While still at Reno, he took part in two half-time wrestling exhibitions, fought under professional rules, with Buddy Brooks, who had represented the Reno YMCA in a Pacific AAU tournament. In June 1954, Bill Afflis made his true pro wrestling debut, winning two falls from Ramon Cernandes in Reno. In early 1955, he was going by Bruiser Afflis in the Midwest, which evolved to Dick the Bruiser by mid-year. After less than a year and a half in the business, he was challenging Lou Thesz for the NWA world title.

On June 1, 1957, Bruiser beat Wilbur Snyder to win the United States heavyweight title in Chicago's Marigold Gardens. The national exposure on promoter Fred Kohler's TV show helped his standing considerably, and he was soon an in-demand villain across the nation. "Right away, he had it," Lou Thesz told the Wrestling Observer in its obit for Bruiser. "He had the image and he lived the part. He believed he really was Dick the Bruiser."

That image carried over to newspaper interviews, where Afflis would brag about lawsuits, knifings, and his 300-plus stitches, and show off where a bicep muscle had popped out, which he'd never gotten fixed. The press ate up his April 1963 real-life barroom fight with football star Alex Karras, who had been suspended for the season for gambling and had turned to pro wrestling to make a few bucks. Bruiser was arrested for assault and battery, and later got off with a donation to the Detroit police pension fund. Two cops were injured and filed damage suits in federal court, which garnished his wages in Detroit, where Bruiser later fought a bitter promotional war with The Sheik (Ed Farhat).

In 1964, he described his style. "I use anything that comes to me. All I want to do is get the job done, give the fans some action and get out and drink some beer." Johnny Powers warned not to sell Bruiser short. "His style was punch, kick, forearm, smash, drive in on you. And he didn't sell a lot. He didn't give a lot, but what he gave made sense."

"You know a lot of guys said he was a masochist," said frequent opponent "Cowboy" Bob Ellis, whose birthday cake Bruiser once memorably destroyed on air. "You get with it and feel all of the crowd. Then you know you've got you a match and don't mind those potatoes." Sometimes it was the fans getting the worst of it. "I was banned in Cincinnati one time," Bruiser once recalled. "I threw a lady in a wheelchair up in the ring and broke her leg. Really, I just threw the wheelchair at the guy. But she was in it."

In Reggie Lisowski — The Crusher — he found a doppelganger and frequent tag team partner; they were two gnarly-looking fire hydrants who loved to boast and brawl. They would team off and on for much of their latter careers, and were inducted into the Pro Wrestling Hall of Fame as a tag team in 2005.

Studying the results in St. Louis, one of the key cities in wrestling history, as NWA president Sam Muchnick ran things, it is fascinating to see how Dick the Bruiser went from a wild mad man who would run across the tables in the elegant Khorassan Room, grabbing a patron's beer and washing himself down, to an iconic figure who could draw 19,027 for a losing battle against NWA world champion Ric Flair in 1982 at Kiel Auditorium.

Unconventional at its best, he would turn on his fellow villains one night, but be back smashing in the skulls of the gallant fan favorites a month later. By 1969, he was an out-and-out babyface, but not one that kissed babies and waved the flag.

Larry Matysik, who was a fan before getting involved in Muchnick's office, points to a January 9, 1970 bout where Dick the Bruiser challenged NWA champion Dory Funk Jr. at Kiel as being quintessential Bruiser. After taking the first fall, Bruiser appeared to have won the second, but referee Joe Schoenberger saw Bruiser using the ropes for leverage, and disqualified the challenger for the fall, prompting Bruiser to clobber the ref and then Funk with a chair to have the match tossed out. "Dory is the hugest babyface in the world. Dory's at his peak, he's got the title less than a year, he's at his peak," said Matysik. "It was incredible noise, incredible electricity in the audience, but at best they were 50/50; half were for Bruiser, half were for Dory."

Later, running his own Championship Wrestling promotion in Indianapolis until 1985, with Wilbur Snyder as his partner (until 1982), Bruiser would credit Muchnick for lessons learned — though Muchnick, a non-wrestler, never kept talent down, promoting himself at the top of cards at the expense of everyone else. "I never got along with Sam Muchnick when he was a promoter and I was on his wrestling cards," Bruiser told the St. Louis Post-Dispatch in November 1989. "He was always chastising me — for hitting referees or spectators, or maybe fighting after the match was over. Sam suspended me a lot. But I understood him, even then. I've matured now, and Sam and I are the best of friends. I phone him in St. Louis every week."

"A lot of people didn't understand Dick," Muchnick said upon hearing of Afflis' death. "If I had to walk down a dark alley with a lot of money, Dick is the guy I would have wanted as my bodyguard. I went to his daughter's wedding and saw him cry when he walked her down the aisle. This guy had a big heart."

Wrestling was a major part of Afflis' family as well. Married four times, he had two children, Michelle, who married wrestler Spike Huber (twice), photographer/manager Scott Romer, and wrestler "Golden Lion" Tim Replogle; and Karl, who wrestled as Leroy Redbone and The Masked Strangler. He invested his money wisely in real estate, and knew the value of his visage and voice, doing promos for radio stations, a steel company in Ohio, and car dealerships.

His death on November 10, 1991, in Largo, Florida, was uniquely Bruiser. Having returned from a trip to Japan, where his 1967 Tokyo match with Shohei "Giant" Baba is still talked about, Afflis was suffering from flu-like symptoms. Ever the fitness fanatic, he was working out with the weights in his home gym when a blood vessel burst in his esophagus, killing him almost instantly.

The world had lost one of its most memorable real-life characters, but he still lives on through the tales of his colleagues.

Announcer Lance Russell had never met Bruiser until one day at ringside in Memphis. "He started intimidating anybody, including me, who would look him in the eye. He comes down there, and I'm sitting at this table at ringside in the Coliseum. Here's a nail sticking out, about an inch and a quarter, something like that, from this old, rickety table that was down there. That Bruiser puts his hands on his hips and takes his forehead and drives that nail right back into that table. I'm telling you, he did it! If I hadn't have known better, I would have sworn that they gimmicked the nail on his instructions. But they didn't do that."

"He had bravado, and I think for him that's a perfect word. He had a bravado about him that was kind of unique," said Powers, describing Bruiser at the doorway to the dressing room, his chiseled, naked body tanned, leaving a really white derriere. Bruiser would switch his cowboy hat from his head to his privates. "I still can see it. He was flaunting his malehood to one of the willing female fans."

When Dick the Bruiser was inducted as a solo act into the TV Era category of the Pro Wrestling Hall of Fame in 2011, "The Destroyer" Dick Beyer handled the tribute and relayed an anecdote. One time, Bruiser knocked on his hotel room door in Chicago. "We went over to the Marigold Arena to work out. We worked out for about two hours, a little bit in the ring and a lot on the weights. On the way back, about 11 a.m., he said, 'We need to stop to get some beer.' So we stopped and got some beer, but we mixed it with V8 juice. That was our breakfast."

JACKIE FARGO

"Often imitated, never duplicated." Jackie Fargo is an octogenarian now, but the slow, syrupy delivery of his catchphrase still beckons to anyone within earshot, and his humor and mock outrage come across just as though you were sitting with him on his front stoop in China Grove, North Carolina, sipping iced tea, or — even better — something stronger, listening to tales of bygone days.

Like his start, for example. It happened back around 1949, not long after Henry L. Faggart got out of high school, and after he'd wrestled successfully in the North Carolina state championship tournament. Old-timer Johnny Long spotted him at a meet in Goldsboro and asked if he'd like to be a professional wrestler. A trip to Columbia, South Carolina, where the Fabulous Moolah lived, and Fargo, a better name for wrestling, was on his way.

> JACKIE FARGO: Johnny Long and Moolah was running a little territory right around where I live here and that's how I got started working for Johnny Long, little small towns, making $10 a night. From there I went to Cuba, even got to Cuba before Castro. I really enjoyed that. Pedro Godoy got me in there. Had me under a mask. When I was over there I got $250 a week. Well, that was a lot of money for me back then. And all my expenses paid and lived in the best hotel over there, three meals a day. Well, 'bout my fourth week, here comes a letter. Dear Jackie Fargo, Your uncle wants you. Had to leave there and go in the damned Army.

Jackie Fargo leans on Andre the Giant as excited fans surround them.

Having kept the country safe from foreign intervention, Fargo went to New York in 1953 for the first time for Toots Mondt, only he did it as Dick Bishop. He wrestled for about six weeks under the nom de combat in January and February against the likes of Al Kashey and Roland Meeker.

> FARGO: Dick Bishop, that was a no-good, low-down, fourteen-carat son of a sapsucker in New York. I was Dick Bishop. They wanted to make a Jewish boy out of me.

His career took off in late 1956 when, back under the Fargo banner, he tagged with Don Fargo, who wrestled as "Wildman" Stevens. They fit in perfectly with the colorful, brawling style that Vincent J. McMahon was pushing in the Northeast and held the first tag team championship in the old Capitol Sports promotion, feuding with Antonino Rocca and Miguel Perez. In the South, as the Fargos, they held the world tag team title in the Tennessee–Alabama territory nine times in three years.

> FARGO: I was the person people loved to hate but they loved me. In other words, when I would go up there and I'd be beating the hell out of somebody, and more than once, they'd

try to crawl in the ring on you. I loved that because boy, I'd catch 'em coming right under that bottom rope, and I'd catch 'em in the teeth with my foot. As much as they hated me, they loved that Fargo strut. Boy, they'd boo the hell out of me, but they loved that.

Fargo was working in Nashville when talent scout and promoter Jack Pfefer walked into his life. He hadn't solicited him as a manager, and it was a wild mix — Fargo, a son of the South, and Pfefer, a Jewish-Russian with idiosyncrasies right out of a Woody Allen short story. But the relationship lasted for about a decade and Fargo credits Pfefer with giving him a boost in the billfold.

> FARGO: He come in and said, "I'm your manager now, you know." I said, "What?" He said, "I'm your manager." I said, "Okay." But listen, he booked us in New York and he didn't ask them what to do. He told 'em what they was going to do. He'd say, "Mine Fargos will go over this in so-and-so." He booked us in Chicago and New York, just everywhere. Charlotte, we got big money, too. He made me work with Ricki Starr in Madison Square Garden and I really didn't want to go, but there was so much money, I couldn't turn it down. Pfefer had a lot of pull, but people didn't know. But I knew, I was around him a lot, and I knew he had pull. These damned promoters were scared to death of him.

Fargo dutifully provided Pfefer every week with a report on the houses; an update on "Elmer," his pet name for Don; and a cut of the check. "All the boys call me Pfefer Jr. They say I am learning your tricks. I told them that would take many years to learn your tricks," he said in a letter tucked away in the library at the University of Notre Dame. In 1961, Fargo would become world champion in Boston for Tony Santos and Pfefer, fully understanding his manager's insecurities.

> FARGO: Listen, if we're in Nashville and going to Huntsville, Alabama, a hundred miles away, we're halfway to Huntsville and a black cat runs across, it's "Take me back, Jay-kee, Take me back!" Oh, he was that bad. He wouldn't walk under a ladder for any amount of money. You got time for a quick story? He and I and Donnie are going from Jackson, Tennessee, to Nashville and Donnie and I were always pulling shit on him, you know? I had a flat tire. "Vot the hell are you doing, Jay-kee, you son of a beech! You should have had the tire fixed before we left, you son of a beech, you!" He's screaming and hollering and I'm looking around and I'm changing the tire with Donnie and laughing, and I hear somebody. "Jay-kee! Hey, Jay-kee!" I could barely hear it. I say, "What the hell is that?" And I look down about forty feet down there, he'd fell off a cliff. Oh, that was funny as hell.

There is no official record of the first wrestler to switch from the wicked to the righteous, but if Fargo wasn't the very first, he was certainly in the lead pack. His "turn" came in fall 1961 on TV, and was repeated in different versions throughout Tennessee. Len Rossi was suffering a serious whipping in a tag match with Mephisto and Dante, while his partner Tex Riley was out of commission. Fargo was walking out of the studio with his gym bag when promoter Nick Gulas rushed at him to persuade him to intervene. Tennessean Randal Brown, later a wrestler, promoter, and ring builder, said the image is still as sharp as it was to him as a fan half a century ago.

> *RANDAL BROWN: Jackie's laughing at him, flipping his hand at him, telling him to go away, whatever. Nick pulls out a stack of money and starts counting out the money, trying to just pay him to go up and stop it. He kind of ignores him and as he's walking by the ring, he sets his bag down and steps up on the apron because they're inviting him to join the party. He just casually steps through the ropes and kind of grins "yeah." He rears back, and Jackie had the prettiest punch I'd ever seen because it was real, and for the next four or five minutes kicked the crap out of all of them except Len Rossi.*

Suddenly, Fargo was the good guy, tagging with Rossi and then Lester Welch — that duo would trade the Southern tag team title with Mephisto and Dante eight times in the next six months in Tennessee and Alabama. But the stylistic change between Jackie the Angel and Jackie the Devil was nowhere to be found.

> *FARGO: I just stayed the same. I'd go in there and still pull hair and get something out of my tights to hit them with and they'd still just cheer me. No, I didn't change my style at all. Kept strutting, the long blond hair and the people just accepted me. I don't know why; they just couldn't understand why people came to me. I understand because my nature is just a fun-loving guy. I always, instead of slipping out of the back door, sit down at the ringside and sign autographs for a while. I'm one of the very few that would ever do that. I remember when I first started I'd go in to wrestle and get beat in two or three minutes in a preliminary match and I'd go out and stand and just hope somebody asked me for an autograph. Nobody ever did. And that stuck with me all these years, that's why I take an extra few minutes to sign autographs.*

In the late 1960s, The Fabulous One scaled way back on wrestling; he had too many other fingers in various pots. He and a buddy named Eddie Bond peddled Fargo Burgers at their Southern Frontier restaurant in Memphis, and Jackie

DAVE BURZYNSKI

Jackie Fargo threatens the referee and manager Dr. Ken Ramey.

had a fling as a country-and-western singer. When Jerry Jarrett started booking Memphis in the early 1970s, he headed to the Southern Frontier in a bid to lure Fargo back to the ring full-time. On August 8, 1972, Memphis hosted the ultimate stipulation match when Al Greene put up $5,000, his brother's Southern junior heavyweight belt, and a pledge to skip town for a year, against Fargo's hair. Three thousand fans were turned away, and they missed the shearing. Fargo started wearing a mask around town and during a wild, six-man, forty-four-fall match in Memphis, because he wanted fans to remember him the way he was. "It's stringy and even ugly but it's my trademark," he said.

> BUCK PATTON, Memphis sportswriter: One week from that humiliating defeat, Fargo came back to wrestle, bearing still red scars on his nose and lip. They were for real no matter how much the purists doubt the sport. Two weeks later . . . Fargo had himself locked in a fourteen-foot square cage with Greene and before the doors were unlocked, Greene had apologized to the world for questioning Fargo's heritage. All contrived? Hardly, but I'm sure the most was made of the situation. It's been a good show no matter how or why it was carried out.

Working in the Tennessee territory would test the patience of a long-haul trucker. Trips stretched from Memphis to Chattanooga to the east, Birmingham, Alabama, to the south, and Louisville, Kentucky, to the north. There was nothing like a road trip with Jackie Fargo.

EDDIE MARLIN: *We had to go to Lexington, Kentucky. He called me and he said, "I'm gonna go to the horse races; how about going with me?" I said, "All right," and he picked me up and we were going through the Blue Grass Parkway. He was running a hundred miles an hour and I looked over and he was shaving! We got to the horse track and he jumped out of the car and told the boys, "That red Cadillac back there — park it." I started to get my money out and he said, "Put your money up. At the race track, your money won't spend." He'd bet the high-priced money and I'd bet the two-dollar tickets. I never will forget it, going through that Blue Grass Parkway a hundred miles an hour and him over there with an electric razor.*

Jackie's brother Sonny — whose real name was Jack Lewis Faggart — wrestled a little and refereed a lot for Jim Crockett Promotions in the Carolinas. Two or three times a year, he'd travel to Tennessee to rescue his brother from some despicable evil-doers as "Roughhouse" Fargo, an otherwise unimposing inpatient with buggy-whip arms at the state mental hospital in Morganton, North Carolina.

BROWN: *It was like clockwork. They'd beat Jackie up on TV, they'd bust him up real bad, and they'd drag him up to the microphone — Gil Greene was the guy in Nashville — and Gil Greene would be holding him up. "Aww, Gil, they ought not do a man like this. But that's all right. That's all right. Listen . . . do you hear it? Can you hear it, Gil? Can you hear it? Do you know what's happenin'? The gate is swingin' open. It's swingin' open. They haven't oiled it and it's rusty. That's right. That's right. I ain't gonna tell you who's on the way. But they're letting him out. He'll be here next week." It just kind of made cold chills go up my spine every time I heard him do that interview because you knew there was fixin' to be two weeks of the most hilarious stuff you'd ever seen in your life and the houses were going to be packed.*

Oh, yes, hilarity. A Fargo calling card. If anyone ever had more utter delight in being a wrestler, he ought to report to Fargo home base in China Grove pronto.

DON KERNODLE: *He had a 1976 burgundy Cadillac and his handle — that's back when CBs were hot — his handle was Santa Claus. I'm not kidding you, this is the* truth — I've been with him a million times. He'd hear the highway patrols on the radio and he'd say, "Hey so and so, this here is Santa Claus. I'm going to be coming up through. I'm going to put my cruise control on about ninety; I want you to check and see if my speedometer is right." He was an icon over there in Tennessee.

JERRY JARRETT: In the dressing room he was the most entertaining person I've ever seen. Jackie would come out of the john with toilet paper trailing behind him and walk out into the arena, and I'd have to run and catch it before he went out in the people. Here was our superstar with toilet paper hanging out of his pants. He was relentless on the new guys, the greenhorns in the business. Jackie would get stark naked, stick the end of his toothbrush in his butt, and walk around these kids and turn around and say, "Has anybody seen my toothbrush?"

Fargo was the Southern junior heavyweight champ six times at various times between 1959 and 1979. Even more important was the fact he got Jerry Lawler going in the business. In 1974, he officially passed the torch to Lawler in a King of Memphis feud. The feud was still going in July 1999, when Lawler, approaching fifty, pitted the hair of then love interest Stacy Carter against the hair of Fargo, nearing seventy. It was perhaps the first instance in wrestling history of grandchildren watching their grandfather's hair shaved off in the ring. Lawler wrote about his mentor in his autobiography, It's Good to be the King . . . Sometimes.

JERRY LAWLER: Looking back, I think he sold for me more than he did the other guys he wrestled and I think it was because he felt partially responsible for me being in the business, and he wanted me to be a success. Nobody could sell like him. You'd hit him, and his head would reel back with that long blond hair of his flying. And, oh man, if he would get blood . . . his blond hair would turn completely red.

For years, Fargo operated what he euphemistically called "my place of business," a little gambling parlor in China Grove where the numbers were played and the guys hung out. Just like his trip with Marlin to the horse track, wagering, his friends say, is as much a part of him as the strut.

LANCE RUSSELL: Every time I think about Fargo, I remember we went together or maybe we met over at the dog track in West Memphis, Arkansas, one time. I loved the dogs . . . they flew so much faster, the whole course, there wasn't that length of time between the races. I go over there and I'm seeing Fargo at the end of this particular race and he said, "How'd you do, pally?" Everyone was "pally" to him. I said, "Well, I came close; that was about all. How about you?" He said, "Take a look," and he's holding a stack of tickets about two inches high. I said, "Holy mackerel! Did you have that quinella on that thing?" As it turned out, he shows me his other stack of tickets which was about eight inches high. He had bought every combination on every dog in the race. He couldn't miss. He couldn't win, but he couldn't miss. And Jackie Fargo, if you had a pari-mutuel window, he wouldn't have cared if it was chickens, dogs or horses.

Often imitated, never duplicated.

CM PUNK

There are so many aspects of CM Punk that are completely foreign to the wrestlers who laid the path for him. He doesn't smoke, he doesn't drink, he doesn't do drugs, he's covered in tattoos, he's against promiscuous sex. Outspoken well before 2011's "Summer of Punk," Phil Brooks has long been a media darling, able to talk to fanboy websites or Sports Illustrated. It's more than the media though; he understands his followers far better than his predecessors ever did, with their condescending jokes about the number of teeth in the first row of ringside and constant need to validate the legitimacy of the wrestling business. "I'm just happy people are emotionally invested enough to tweet to me 6,000 times a day that I suck," he told ESPN.com, summing up the direction of the pro wrestling business — instant reaction, instant gratification.

"If something sucks, I've always been completely vocal about it, and I've been punished many, many times because of that. But I don't think I'd be in the spot I'm in right now if I wasn't me," Punk told GQ.

There was nothing instant about the route the six-foot-one, 220-pound Brooks took to the upper echelon of the WWE, however. He began backyard wrestling in the mid-'90s, using his CM Punk name, before being trained in a more conventional manner. "I wanted to be a wrestler ever since I was very, very small. It was all I ever wanted to do," said Punk, who was born October 26, 1978, in Chicago. "My dad was an electrician, so I guess I was supposed to go to trade school and do that, but I never wanted to. I thought it made a lot more sense to try something I loved, or at least give it a shot. I didn't know how to do it, so me and my friends would jump around in the backyard after pay per views and beat each other up."

The "straight edge" clean-living lifestyle is a result of a father who "had a little problem with the alcohol," a mother who needed a glass of wine before bed, and both parents smoking like chimneys. Punk says he knew there was a better life ahead. He just had to want it badly enough. "I grew up poor. I didn't have a lot of money. I never got a car. I had hand-me-down clothes. Christmas always pretty much [stank]. But I saw the amount of money they would spend on cases of Old Style and cigarettes. As a kid, I remember wanting Megatron for Christmas and they'd tell me they couldn't afford it, yet I watched them smoke four packs of Marlboros a day. It didn't make any sense to me."

In wrestling training, Punk found focus, and a best friend. "I showed up at Steel Domain in Chicago and he had already been training there for a couple of months. He hadn't had many

BRUNO SILVEIRA

CM Punk, always dangerous with a microphone, or a megaphone.

matches at the time, so we basically showed up together. We were the only ones really capable of much there and formed a bond almost immediately," said Colt Cabana (Scott Colton). "We loved wrestling and had a huge passion for it. We picked it up the quickest. We both had that natural ability for it and formed a strong friendship." The two traveled the highways and byways together for four years.

With Ring of Honor, Punk and Cabana — The Second City Saints — were tag champs on two occasions, and Punk was really put on the map with a series of vicious bouts against Samoa Joe. "My year was topped off by telling that story with Joe, the two one-hour draws and then the finale," Punk said in early 2005. "I'm just glad everybody enjoyed it. I'm very proud when you have guys comparing our trilogy in 2004 to the likes of Steamboat and Flair. You'll never hear that from me." He ascended to become ROH world champion, and threatened to take the title with him to the WWE, where he signed in 2005, before ultimately dropping the belt.

Agreeing to the WWE deal finished one chapter of his career. "It was bittersweet, but I knew that I had to move on. That was totally my choice. I had done everything that I could possibly do there, and I needed more challenges. I like to be challenged on a daily basis. I wanted to see if I could make it here in WWE. I got in the best shape I possibly could, and I got a bunch of bookings for extra work in dark matches. I just tried to give them no excuse why they shouldn't hire me." Assigned to the developmental Ohio Valley Wrestling territory, Punk won the OVW heavyweight title, the OVW TV title, and a share of the OVW tag team title.

In June 2006, he was called up to the ECW roster, and claimed that title. Up next, on Smackdown, he feuded with the likes of Edge, Rey Mysterio, and The Undertaker, leading his Straight Edge Society as a Koresh-like cult leader. The heel espousing the healthy lifestyle was as ironic as it was entertainingly patronizing to the audience. Drew Hankinson was Luke Gallows, one of Punk's disciples, and saw first-hand the reactions he drew, the batteries and coins being tossed, the verbal maligning. "It was insane. He translates, and people have an emotional attachment to him, that's for sure, whether it's positive or negative."

After three short runs with the world heavyweight title, Punk was reassigned to the Raw roster, and was again asked to be a leader, helming the New Nexus and making Randy Orton and John Cena's lives miserable; it was only the beginning.

In July 2011, with his contract up for renewal, Punk began making noises about leaving the company, and in one memorable rant at the end of Monday Night Raw, he listed everything he thought was wrong with the wrestling industry, slamming everyone up to and including his bosses, before the microphone was cut off midstream. "I'd like to think that maybe this company will be better after Vince McMahon is dead. But the fact is, it's going to be taken over by his idiotic daughter and his doofus son-in-law and the rest of his stupid family," Punk spat about Stephanie McMahon and her husband Triple H. Then he did as he vowed, taking the WWE title at the Money in the Bank pay per view on July 17 from John Cena. He made a number of non-wrestling appearances, including at a Cubs game at Wrigley Field, before WWE's entreaties brought him back, now an outspoken babyface, appealing to the anti-authoritarians and insiders in the crowd tired of Cena and his hustle, respect, and loyalty mantra. Punk has said that by the time he left the stage and picked up his phone, he had more than 200 text messages.

"Punk is Punk, and that's what has made him so amazing over the years. He had a live mic, and he was able to do it," said Cabana, to whom Punk has given regular shoutouts in interviews, even wearing a Cabana T-shirt on *Raw*.

"The person that CM Punk sort of portrays, it really is him. In a business where a lot of times sticking to a format is congratulated and complimented, CM Punk has sort of stayed out of that form and stayed out of the mold," Christopher Daniels told the *Miami Herald*. "He has finally been rewarded for the fact that he is different. I think there was never a question about his talent, whether it was in the ring or on the microphone."

Punk has never wavered from his message, never changed his style, never been anything else but himself, whether working as a purported babyface or heel. And he's pretty confident about those abilities. "From bell to bell I don't think there's anyone in the world that can touch me at what I do."

THE ROCK

Like many veterans, Pat Patterson's first memories of Dwayne Johnson are of a youngster in the dressing room, bouncing on the knee of his dad, Rocky Johnson, or holding the hand of his mom, Ata, daughter of High Chief Peter Maivia. It's his *next* memory of Johnson that really matters, though.

One day in early in 1996, Patterson got a call from a young man who identified himself as the son of Rocky Johnson. Patterson knew enough of Dwayne to enquire about his football career, which had taken him from being a defensive tackle for the Miami Hurricanes to the taxi squad of the Calgary Stampeders. But Johnson didn't want to talk about that; his bad back had derailed any football dreams. He had returned to Tampa, Florida, and wanted to meet with Patterson, who was a key behind-the-scenes player in the WWE.

"Goddamn, when I saw him get out of the car, he looked like a fucking city block he was so built. And handsome," recalled Patterson, awe still in his voice. After some small talk, where Patterson made sure that the six-foot-five, 260-pound Johnson had a backup plan if the wrestling life didn't work out — he had studied exercise physiology and criminology at the University of Miami, aspiring to be an FBI agent or the Secret Service, lessons perhaps learned while being arrested a few times for fighting in public and theft — Patterson made a fateful call to his boss, Vince McMahon. "I said, 'Vince, you don't want him tomorrow, you want him yesterday.' He said, 'Send him over.'"

The Rock and John Cena topped Wrestle Mania XXVIII in Miami.

Johnson had only been training for a few weeks with his father, learning the art of falling and bumping in an unforgiving boxing ring, but in reality, his education had been going on since his birth on May 2, 1972, in Hayward, California. The only time he got to spend time with his dad was in the arenas, soaking up the antics of Patterson and Ray Stevens in San Francisco's Cow Palace, or the fans' worship of Dusty Rhodes in Florida. It was in Hawaii, when he was eight years old, that Johnson first gave serious thought to being a pro wrestler — despite witnessing the struggles that his family was going through trying to keep the Hawaiian promotion afloat. During his junior year of high school, living in Bethlehem, Pennsylvania, as his father plied his trade for the WWF, the college football recruiters came sniffing around, and his dream of wrestling was put on hold for an education and some time on the gridiron.

Aside from being a part of the Hurricanes' 1991 national championship as a role-playing freshman wearing number 94, Johnson's injury-plagued football career ended up being pretty non-eventful. His contributions to the University of Miami have been more substantial; he donated $2 million with then wife Dany Garcia (a rower at Miami) toward the construction of an on-campus alumni center, and, in 2007, $1-million for the football facilities renovation fund, resulting in the Hurricanes' locker room being renamed in his honor.

Released by the Stampeders in October 1995, he moved back to Tampa. With Rocky insisting that he listen if he wanted to be trained, Dwayne took his lumps and bumps, until he was hooked up with the WWE. From there, it was the fast-track, with a rave-inducing tryout in Corpus Christi, Texas, against Steve Lombardi, that had all the boys in the back asking where he'd been working previously; it was his first match.

The rookie was dispatched to the company's developmental territory in Memphis, where he earned a guaranteed $150 a week (only $100 less than he had been making in Calgary), and where he was dubbed Flex Kavana. "It turned out that he knew more than the guys down there so he couldn't learn anything," Rocky Johnson told Alex Marvez. Six weeks later, having made almost daily calls to the front office, a meek Rocky Maivia debuted on WWE TV, wearing his "hokey babyface trunks."

Rocky's humility, which has been credited to his mother, was rare in the wrestling business. Rocky knew his role and was afraid to rock the boat. "I don't know where I could be. Anything could happen. I would just like to be considered in a couple of years one of the best young talents around. One of the guys that the older guys pass the torch on to," he imagined in January 1997. Getting booed was a surprise, and he was on the phone constantly with his father, trying to figure out what to do.

Placed in the heel faction, the Nation of Domination, he got to play the cocky heel for the first time. Or not. In a lengthy *Rolling Stone* profile, his wife said those skills were always evident. "He had an extreme amount of confidence, this eighteen-year-old, punky football player," she recalled. In the Nation, he emerged from his shell, and from behind the imposing shadow of group leader Ron Simmons, who was known as Faarooq, he stole the last word — and the spotlight. "I'm glad that I had a good part in getting him where he got," said Simmons in a Highspots.com interview. "He had it, but what he didn't have was the right send-off, the right character."

That character became The Rock, a third-person referencing, catchphrase spouting, cocky, over-the-top tattooed showman who could bring it — with his raised eyebrow and body language — as well as say it: "Layeth the smackdown . . . Roody-poo candyass . . . It doesn't matter what your name is! . . . Do you smell what The Rock is cookin'?"

It was the start of "a once-in-a-lifetime performer for our industry," said Paul Heyman.

"Dwayne Johnson turned it into a million dollars. From that day forward, he ate, drank, and pooped The Rock. In front of that camera he became larger than life — and he worked at it every day," wrote Vince Russo in *Forgiven*. "There never has been, and there never will be, a bigger star in the world of sports entertainment than Dwayne Johnson. And I'll tell you why. Yeah, he's got the looks, the physique, and the rap — but so did a lot of others before him. What puts Rock heads and tails above the rest is his *brain*."

To that end, The Rock wasn't doing the high-risk maneuvers that his colleagues seemed to insist on. Instead, he used the People's Elbow, a jazzed-up elbow drop, originated on house shows to make the boys in the back laugh; or his Rock Bottom finisher, where his opponent's back takes all the brunt of the move. "I'm not all busted up like a lot of the guys are because I've never really put myself in a lot of danger and taken a lot of risk in the ring. I've never ventured to the top rope, that's for sure," The Rock said in *World Wrestling Entertainment Unscripted*. "I would always rather concentrate on charisma and energy when I perform. If I can emit energy that nobody else has — truthful, powerful energy — and mix that with a little bit of charisma and with the right antagonist or protagonist, I can usually get the right connection with the crowd, and I don't have to be jumping off ladders."

He sure found the right antagonists in the likes of Mick Foley, Triple H, and "Stone Cold" Steve Austin, who was perhaps the greatest moneymaker in the history of wrestling.

"If Rock was wrestling somebody else, I wanted to have a better match than him and he wanted to have a better match than me. So when we were together, we wanted to have the best match we could, and we wrestled so much that we both knew what each other's strengths were and we played to those strengths to put on some great matches," Triple H told IGN Sports.

Austin also praised The Rock in an ESPN.com interview. "We brought out the best in each other and every time we got in the ring, magical things happened. We always wanted to be the best on the card and make people glad they came out to the show."

The merchandise at the height of the Austin/Rock era, from 1997 to 2003, flew off the shelves. They moved magazines too, said Stu Saks, the publisher of *Pro Wrestling Illustrated*. "We had The Rock on several covers, beginning in 1999. Those issues did well, but they didn't spike sales to the degree that Hulk Hogan's image did during the mid- to late-1980s. We'd have Hogan on the cover as often as we could. At the peak of The Rock's popularity, there were several other wrestlers whose appearance on the cover would produce similar results, including Steve Austin, Kurt Angle, and even Bill Goldberg," said Saks. "Now, if we could have had polybagged a CD-ROM of Rock doing his best promos, I think we would have had something. But somehow I think the folks at Titan Tower would have frowned on that."

But the wrestling ring couldn't contain The Rock. Moviemakers came calling, and soon he was well beyond guest roles on *That '70s Show* (playing his father) and *Star Trek:Voyager* (as a Pendari champion), and starring in huge movies, like *The Game Plan*, *Fast Five*, and *The Scorpion King*.

In short, life has been good for Dwayne "Dewey" Johnson. According to his father, each year for his birthday, his son deposits a million dollars into his bank account.

"I was able to take things to another level that I didn't anticipate and I don't think the industry anticipated," concluded The Rock in *Unscripted*. "The people who show up to watch this stuff want to see good versus evil, and they want to let their hair down, and they want to have a good time. Those of us that do this should never forget that, or have illusions that we're anything but what we are, which are entertainers. I could go on forever about this. I love this shit."

Paul Bearer, the mysterious urn, and the Undertaker in 1992.

THE UNDERTAKER

Respect is a word that comes up again and again with The Undertaker. On the surface, the gimmick of an undertaker straight out of the westerns of the 1950s, dressed in a long, black trenchcoat and wide-brimmed hat and heading to the ring is a bit goofy. But it has stood the test of time when thousands of other more promising ideas have come and gone.

The key to the success of The Undertaker is that respect.

"Undertaker really is a phenom. The name fits. The longest-running successful gimmick performer in history, few have more respect in

The Undertaker clamps down on The Rock.

GEORGE NAPOLITANO

the ring, in the dressing room, or among the marks," wrote Mark Madden, former WCW announcer. "Class act, too."

The old-timers often praised him as well. "I think I'd like to take the Undertaker back to my time," said former NWA world champion Jack Brisco in 2001. "The Undertaker could have worked in any era of professional wrestling and been top dog," Dutch Savage concurred. "He reminds me of an old-fashioned worker, in a certain way. He's probably really the only true worker there . . . he could get heat with a rope."

He commands respect in the dressing room. In the unofficial role of judge and executioner for the company, he presides backstage, ruling over the Wrestler's Court, settling grudges big and little. "It just sort of happened through time," Undertaker told James Cybulski of The Score TV station in 2002. "First, I think the guys respect the fact that I've been here, it'll be thirteen years this year. For most of those thirteen years, I've been on top. But I think they all know that they can trust me, they trust me to give them the right advice and help them do what's right for our industry. They know that I put our business first and foremost before anything else within our industry."

The word that doesn't get bandied around — but should — is consistency. Setting aside the mistaken motorcycle-riding, outlaw "Biker-taker," circa 2002, The Undertaker persona has been remarkably unchanged. His in-ring talents have evolved, notably to include mixed-martial arts moves, but from his funereal march to the ring to his throat slash warning that the end is near, the skills remain the same. "The Undertaker is a guy the fans like," said Steve Austin in 1999. "You keep guys like that the way they are."

As well, the WWE has been consistent keeping the man behind The Undertaker, Mark Callaway, from speaking out of character.

In a rare interview with Cody Monk of the *Dallas Morning News* in 1999, Callaway, a native of Houston born in 1962, talked about being a fan of the World Class Championship Wrestling program growing up and his decision to opt out of basketball at Texas Wesleyan University in Fort Worth to pursue his dream.

While in his junior year, Callaway started training to be a pro wrestler. The six-foot-nine center sought his coach's approval to continue training while in his senior year. "I had every intention of coming back and playing that last year," Callaway said. "The coach asked me about wrestling and I said it was something that I was interested in doing. We had some words, so I quit the team. He ran me down in the papers, saying that I was the first player he had ever lost to pro wrestling."

Roundball's loss was the squared circle's gain, and Callaway dished out pain on the side as a bouncer.

Callaway debuted in 1989, and given his size, was pushed quickly — under a mask. First, in Memphis, he was The Master of Pain, and then in Texas, he worked as Texas Red and The Punisher. Finally, in WCW, he was allowed to be himself, as "Mean" Mark Callous. Initially, he floundered in the bigger company, but an opportunity to be a partner of Dan Spivey in the Skyscrapers tag team got him some much-needed attention. When his WCW contract was up in 1990, he took a leap of faith, left the company, and met with Vince McMahon about joining the WWF.

After a meeting at McMahon's home Callaway wasn't hired. "They didn't have much going on for me," he told TSN's *Off The Record* program. McMahon called a while later, asking, "Hello, is this The Undertaker?" Callaway thought it was a joke, but eventually clued in; "Hell yeah, I'm your Undertaker."

His initial opponent, Hulk Hogan, wasn't a believer. "When The Undertaker came on, I went, 'Wait a minute, we're training, we're saying our prayers, we're eating our vitamins, and the place is going crazy. The Undertaker? Bodybags and dead people? That'll never work.' Man, I was wrong."

Cain the Undertaker debuted at the Survivor Series, led to the ring by Brother Love. "I remember that virtually no one at the live event booed the entrance of The Undertaker that night," recalled ring announcer Howard Finkel on WWE.com. "It was more of an 'oooh and aaah' type reaction, because of his uniqueness that he projected on that Thanksgiving night in 1990."

Next, he was an associate of "The Million Dollar Man" Ted DiBiase before he was paired with Paul Bearer (William Moody), who, in real life, was a licensed mortician who had known Callaway in Dallas when he was manager Percy Pringle III. The managers kept The Undertaker away from the microphone for years, other than the prophetic "Rest In Peace."

The plot twists between Paul Bearer and 'Taker's "brother" Kane (Glen Jacobs) are far too complex to ever explain in a few words. To have lasted more than a decade as foes and family is a remarkable accomplishment. Like Undertaker, Kane has stayed fairly consistent with his character since his debut in 1995.

"It's always great to be out there with him because he is a great performer and I think if you were to ask any professional wrestler anywhere in the industry who they would want to have a program with it would be The Undertaker," Kane told Brian Fritz of *Between the Ropes*.

Through all the compelling storylines — WrestleMania epics against Shawn

Michaels, an undefeated mark at 'Mania, the hardcore battles with Mankind (Mick Foley) — and the lame ones — stolen urns, Undertaker versus Undertaker, the Ministry of Darkness — The Undertaker has survived. His need for time off to heal has proven to be a boon, both lengthening his career and allowing for memorable, creative finishes to a program (he's gone from the casket!) that only enhanced the mystique of the character.

There is no mystique over Mark Callaway.

"In the ring, The Undertaker is just a god," said Matt Morgan. "I've watched tapes and tapes and tapes of him and Kane when they were younger, and I've seen the evolution of their careers. He is the best big man in the history of our business. He's flawless. There's no hole in his game."

The Undertaker has left the building.

ACKNOWLEDGMENTS

By now, we have a pretty good idea that writing a book like *Heroes and Icons* is not something that happens in isolation. Outside of our thankfully very understanding families and friends, we have come to rely on a large, supportive group of historians, writers, and researchers. In fact, we dedicated this book to the historians who delve deep into this fascinating, mostly undocumented world of professional wrestling.

It used to mean sitting in front of old newspapers or a microfilm machine, writing out results by hand. While the technology has changed, with newspaper archives online and PDFs instantly available with the click of a mouse, the time and dedication has not. If anything, it has increased for the legends of the wrestling historian world, like J Michael Kenyon, Steve Yohe and Don Luce; since more is readily available, and time ticks away for all of us, many feel compelled to work harder and faster on these little vanity projects. It might be the results for Bakersfield, California, in 1952, or finding the debut match of Johnny Barend, or establishing that it should be Vanka Zelesniak over Zelezniak.

Time and time again, these historians have been there when we needed them, readily sharing of their finds, and helping point us in the right direction. Maybe we should write a book called *The Pro Wrestling Hall of Fame: The Historians*. Words cannot do justice to what they have meant, but still, we will try to list some here in deep appreciation: Fred Hornby, Scott Teal, Tim Hornbaker, Dan Anderson, Dave Cameron, Tom Burke, Matt Farmer, Mark Hewitt, Lib Ayoub, Jim Zordani, Vance Nevada, Ed Garea, Joe Svinth, Mike Lano, Mike Rodgers, George Schire, George Lentz, Bill Murdock, Will Morrisey, Hisaharu Tanabe, and Glenn Stout.

Writing-wise, we continue to benefit from the wonderful world of SLAM! Wrestling and the Sun Media newspapers. Many of the secondary quotes in this tome are the result of the work of Tim Baines at the *Ottawa Sun* and the likes of Colin Hunter, Jon Waldman, Bob Kapur, Marshall Ward, Matt Bishop, Dave Hillhouse, Corey David Lacroix, Jason Clevett, Richard Kamchen, Brian Elliott, Blaine van der Griend, and others at SLAM! Wrestling, all of whom threw in an extra question or two during interviews they had lined up already. Other writers have shared contacts or stories, or allowed us to quote from their works; case in point is Mike Mooneyham, who was so much help with *The Tag Teams* and *The Heels* that he was invited to work on *Heroes and Icons*. A special mention goes out to Bill Apter, who has been a friend for many years, for his help. The proliferation of wrestling books over the last decade has sure made life a lot easier as well.

The internet has allowed passionate collectors to show off their prizes, whether it is programs from Maple Leaf Gardens or the Greensboro Coliseum, posters from England or Florida. To the men and women who take the time to scan and post their goodies, a hearty thank you.

We owe thank yous to the public relations staff at WWE, TNA, Ring of Honor, both past and present, and to the librarians at collections both big (the Library of Congress) and small (Logan County Historical Society in Bellefontaine, Ohio; Linda Sousa, Russell Library, Middletown, Ct.; DeKalb County Public Library, Decatur, Ga.; Lisa Worley, Williamson, Texas, County Museum; Bryan Dawson of the American Hungarian Federation; La Junta, Colorado Library).

At ECW Press, editor Michael Holmes and publisher Jack David have been unwavering supporters for a decade now, patiently waiting for this book, knowing that quality takes time. The rest of the staff there has dealt with everything from tax issues to publicity crises. Thanks for putting up with us through six books now.

On a personal level, Greg wouldn't have been able to do much work without the grandparents and friends in the neighborhood who watched Quinn; now six, Quinn's met everyone from Tiger Jeet Singh to Rick Martel to Butcher and Mad Dog Vachon. The kids of Mike and Steve are at a much different stage, what with the weddings and providing grandkids and all.

Finally, there are the Heroes and Icons themselves, who put their bodies on the line night after night simply to entertain. Our society has always needed heroes, and professional wrestling has always been there to provide them.

Softball anyone? A team of wrestlers, organized by Nelson Royal, takes to the field in Mooresville, NC, in the early 1970s. The squad is made up of, left to right, back row: Mike Stallings, Paul Jones, Danny Miller, Bill Crouch, referee Angelo Martinelli, Ed Wiskoski, Johnny Weaver, Sonny King, and front row: Bob Bruggers, Nelson Royal, Tiger Conway Jr., and Les Thatcher.

NOTES ON SOURCES

With each year, this job gets easier, because so much more is available electronically, whether it is a photo emailed from Australia or a newspaper from 1934. The flipside, though, is that, in a way, this job of researcher/writer/historian feels a little less special. No longer is it necessary to spend days and days in the library handcranking through microfilm; a so-called amateur historian can dig up gems now just as easily as a professional archivist. Even the interview is no longer solely the realm of trained journalists; anyone can set up a podcast and ask an old wrestler to be on the show.

Yet there will never be many books like *Heroes and Icons*. It's too much work, too many interviews, too many late nights combing through online archives. The headache of balancing fact against fiction in a tome like this is counter to the wrestler autobiography, where one person's recollection and opinion is all that matters.

PHOTOGRAPHERS

Roger Baker was a writer and photographer for magazines like *The Wrestler*, *Inside Wrestling*, *Wrestling Revue*, and *Boxing Illustrated* from 1958 to 1973.

Howard Baum, whose work has appeared in countless magazines since the early '80s, has both his original photography and his wrestling-based pop art available at his website, www.HardWayArt.com.

Dave Burzynski was a regular photographer around the Detroit territory until getting to live out his dream as manager "Supermouth" Dave Drason.

Bill Cubitt has photographed Stampede Wrestling and WWF events in Calgary since 1981. His favorite memory is looking at his hundreds of photographs with Stu Hart at the Hart mansion. BillCubitt.smugmug.com

Andrea Kellaway is a Toronto-based photographer, who captures witty and powerful portraits. www.AndreaKellaway.com

Mike Lano's photographed and reported on wrestling, boxing, MMA and TV/movie celebs globally since 1973. wrealano@aol.com

Pete Lederberg lives in Fort Lauderdale, Florida; owns negatives from other photographers dating back to about 1970 and has been shooting wrestling himself since 1987. home.bellsouth.net/p/PWP-flwrestlingpix

Bob Leonard of Regina, Saskatchewan, shot images of Calgary's Stampede Wrestling from 1963 to 1989, and he is an executive board member with the Cauliflower Alley Club. bob.leonard41@hotmail.com

Mike Mastrandrea is a Toronto-based photographer and has been shooting wrestling for over 20 years. His work has been seen in publications across North America, Europe and Asia. He took the cover photo of CM Punk winning the WWE championship at Survivor Series 2011. "I knew it was what they were looking for the moment I shot it," he said. slam.canoe.ca/Slam/Wrestling/Gallery/mastrandrea.html

David Maciejewski was a regular at ringside from 1996 to 1974 in Milwaukee, and even took some photos on the road in Tampa Bay. www.DavesClassicWrestlingPhotos.com

George Napolitano is widely known as one of the world's premiere wrestling photographers. He lives in New York.

PHOTO COLLECTIONS

Chris Swisher Collection — Includes the Lil Al Vavasseur collection of negatives and photos, negatives from part of the Earle Yetter collection, the Detroit

The ever-smiling Mighty Igor.

area from the '60s and '70s, negatives taken by Scott Teal from the '70s, the collection of photos and items from promoter Fred Ward of Columbus, Ga., all encompassing the 1930s to the 1980s. www.CSClassicWrPhotos.com

Courtesy Wrestling Revue Archives — Brian Bukantis is the publisher of *Wrestling Revue* and curator of the *Wrestling Revue* Archives. www.WrestlePrints.com

Department of Special Collections, University Libraries of Notre Dame — The photos in this book come from the Jack Pfefer Wrestling Collection, housed at Notre Dame. www.nd.edu

Scott Teal Collection — A deserving recipient of the James C. Melby Award by both the Cauliflower Alley Club (in 2008) and the Tragos/Thesz Hall of Fame (in 2011) for his contributions to professional wrestling journalism, Scott Teal has written and published books and newsletters, produced DVDs, and hosts a reunion for the wrestling legends. CrowBarPress.com

Yukon Eric and Billy Red Lyons check out the muscles of fellow babyface Sailor Art Thomas backstage in Hamilton, Ontario, in 1964.